AF590993

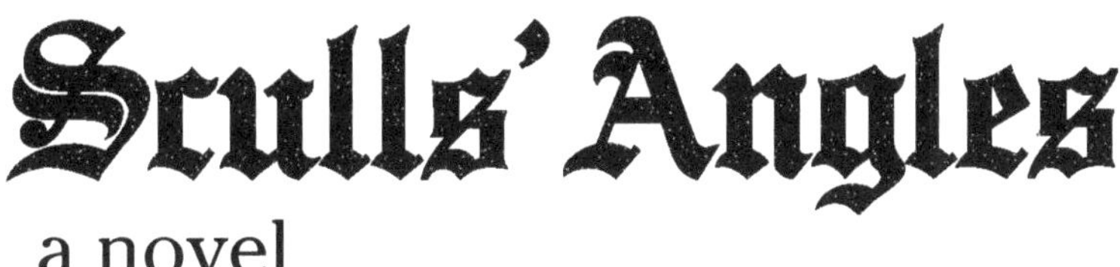

a novel

PARASITIC VENTURES PRESS

The New York Times

AUGUST 8, 1943.

Marriages

SCULL—REDNER—Mr. and Mrs. Benjamin Redner announce the engagement of their daughter, Ethel, to Robert C. Scull, son of Mr. and Mrs. Meyer Skulnik.

JANUARY 9, 1944.

Marriages

SCULL—REDNER—Mr. and Mrs. Benjamin Redner announce the marriage of their daughter, Ethel, to Mr. Robert C. Scull, son of Mr. and Mrs. Meyer Scull, taking place today at Sherry's, 300 Park Ave.

JANUARY 10, 1944.

Notes

NEW YORK

Ethel Redner Bride Here

Miss Ethel Redner, daughter of Mr. and Mrs. Benjamin Redner of New York, was married to Robert Cooper Scull, son of Mr. and Mrs. Meyer Scull, also of this city, yesterday afternoon at Sherry's by the Rev. Dr. Israel Goldstein.

FEBRUARY 8, 1948.

CAMERA NOTES

Metropolitan Club Show —Movie Gala Night

THE third annual "Tops in Photography" show will be held on March 4, at the Hotel Pennsylvania. The program will include a panel of speakers, an international exhibition of prints, two of the year's finest amateur motion pictures, and the showing of outstanding color slides. The show is sponsored by the Metropolitan Camera Club Council, which represents a hundred camera clubs in the metropolitan area.

In addition to the international print exhibition, which will include scientific, documentary and pictorial subjects, there will also be a display of prints entered by the camera clubs. Tickets at $2, tax included, may be obtained from Mrs. Mildred Scales, secretary, Metropolitan Camera Club Council, Inc., 106 West Thirteenth Street.

MOVIE GALA NIGHT

The annual Gala Night of the Metropolitan Motion Picture Club will be held Friday, April 9, in Hunter College Theatre, Sixty-eighth Street. Tickets at $1.35 may be obtained from Joseph J. Harley, 27 Overlook Road, Summit, N. J.

ANNUAL AWARDS

A silver cup has been awarded by the Manhattan Camera Club to Harvey A. Falk for achieving the highest score in the salon class monthly print competitions held during 1947. Arnold Summers and Robert Scull tied for high score in class A. David Teich won a medal for print-of-the-year, and Howard Foote for slide-of-the-year.

CONTEST EXTENDED

The deadline for submitting entries in the "Naked City" Photography Contest sponsored by Willoughby's has been extended to Feb. 15. Send prints to Willoughby's, 110 West Thirty-second Street.

EVENING COURSE

An evening course in photography for beginners is being given by Mary Anderson at the Brooklyn Y. W. C. A., 30 Third Avenue. Classes are held Monday evenings from 7:30 to 9:30.

EXHIBITIONS

Photographs taken by Paul Perez in Mexico, Central America and Europe will be exhibited through Feb. 18 at Dowling's, Inc., 570 Fifth Avenue.

OCTOBER 24, 1948.

Births

SCULL—Mr. and Mrs. Robert C. Scull (nee [illegible] Redner) of 24 Parkside Drive, Great [illegible] joyously announce the arrival of Jona[illegible] David on Oct. 16, 1948, at the Woman's [illegible]tal.

JULY 29, 1951.

Births

SCULL—Mr. and Mrs. Robert C. (nee Ethel Redner), are happy to announce the birth of Jonathan David's brother, Stephan Paul, July 24, 1951, at Woman's Hospital.

OCTOBER 5, 1952.

Births

SCULL—Mr. and Mrs. Robert C. Scull (nee Ethel Redner), 24 Parkside Drive, Great Neck, happily announce the birth of Laurence Jay, brother of Jonathan and Stephan, on Sept. 26, 1952, at Woman's Hospital.

MARCH 22, 1960.

Deaths

SKULNIK—Meyer, beloved husband of Rose, dear father of Sophie Horowitz and Robert C. Scull. Services Tuesday, 2:30 P. M., at "The Riverside," 76th St. and Amsterdam Ave. Please omit flowers.

MARCH 5, 1961.

CON: In Defense Of His Critics

"PERSONAL OUTBURSTS"

TO THE EDITOR:

On numerous occasions Mr. Canaday has overstepped the bounds of art criticism and has used the pages of The New York Times for personal outbursts beyond the limits of decent criticism. I am constantly astonished that the pages of your newspaper can be used for this type of journalism.

ROBERT C. SCULL.
Great Neck, N. Y.

NOVEMBER 11, 1963.

11th Annual Tour Of Radcliffe Club Scheduled Here

Trips to Art Collections on Dec. 7 and 14 will Help Scholarships

The Radcliffe Club of New York's 11th annual tour of distinguished art colleceions will be held on two consecutive Saturday afternoons, Dec. 7 and 14.

Mrs. Cranston Jones is chairman for the event, which will benefit the Radcliffe College Scholarship Fund of New York. Co-chairmen are Mrs. August Heckscher, Mrs. Lawrence Munson and Mrs. Frederick Steinway. Mrs. Sidney Solomon is honorary chairman.

Collectors who will open their homes on Dec. 7 are Roger Seydoux, France's chief delegate to the United Nations, and Mrs. Seydoux; Mr. and Mrs. Vladimir Golschmann, Mr. and Mrs. Charles V. Hickox, Mrs. Albert D. Lasker, Mr. and Mrs. Robert Scull and Mrs. Vanderbilt Webb.

The next Saturday those holding sponsor tickets will be able to see the collections of John Hay Whitney, former Ambassador to Great Britain, and Mrs. Whitney; Mr. and Mrs. Armand P. Bartos and Mr. and Mrs. Artur Rubinstein.

Members of the benefit committee include Mrs. James H. Beckman, Mrs. Erwin R. Beit, Mrs. Edgar P. Berry, Mrs. Bronson Binger, Mrs. John Libby, Miss Nanette Rodney, Mrs. Robert Rosenman, Mrs. Gray H. Twombley, Mrs. Sidney Freidberg, president of the club; Mrs. Roy Goodman, Mrs. Justin Colin and Mrs. Peter Buttenwieser.

More than 100 junior members of the club will act as hostesses for the tour.

Tickets and further information may be obtained from club headquarters at the Berkshire Hotel, Madison Avenue at 52d Street.

MARCH 18, 1964.

TV Review

'Eye on New York' Views Pop Art

PAUL GARDNER.

COLLECTORS of pressed butterflies probably watched "Eye On New York" last night with indignant horror. Forgetting the socially insignificant ills that dominate most dreary documentaries, the WCBS-TV series explored with sophisticated amusement the strange, mad, awful, wonderful world of pop art.

The school of painting, sculpture and construction, thing in the American scene including the kitchen sink, is the liveliest topic of cultural conversation. It also made a lively TV show—one that should have upset casual observers, mystified impatient philosophers and pleased the anything but lonely crowd of pop artists.

•

In a half hour, Gordon Hyatt, the producer, took viewers on a brisk trip to the chicken farm-studio of George Segal, sculptor; the opening of a new pop art show, where the guests seemed part of the paintings; and into the home of Robert Scull, an influential pop art patron.

When asked if he could live and eat with his incredible collection so close, Mr. Scull showed how simple artistic adjustment is. His family dined in a room overshadowed by James Rosenquist's "Silver Skies," an arrangement of Coke bottles and tires.

Ethel Scull, his pretty wife, smiled while the camera absorbed Andy Warhol's 35 smiling Ethel Scull portraits. As for the two Scull children, they obviously loved their parents and enjoyed full-course meals.

The American home is still safe.

APRIL 23, 1964.

Tenant on 5th Ave. Wins $890 Rent Cut For Loss of Room

Court-ordered rent reductions, usually applied to slum tenements, were applied yesterday to a 10-room apartment on Fifth Avenue. The rent there was cut from $890 a month to zero.

Three judges of the Appellate Terms of the State Supreme Court ruled that a tenant, Robert C. Scull, did not have to pay any of the rent for a fifth-floor apartment at 1010 Fifth Avenue, near the Metropolitan Museum of Art. The building's owner, Fifth Avenue Estates, Inc., had brought the suit to compel payment.

Mr. Scull maintained that the three-year contract he had signed with the landlords on April 17, 1962, called for 11 rooms, not 10. The landlord maintained that one bedroom in the apartment was actually two rooms, but the court ruled that a servant's room adjacent to a service hallway outside the apartment should be considered part of the apartment and turned over to Mr. Scull.

The court said, "Superficially, it may appear harsh to deprive landlord of the entire rent for loss of one room out of 11."

"However, the tenant is entitled to all the space for which he agreed to pay and he need not accept less," the judges ruled.

OCTOBER 8, 1964.

GALLERY MARKET HAWKS ART ON RYE

Store Display Is Set Up for Pop Food Creations

By GRACE GLUECK

"The American Supermarket" opened Tuesday night at 16 East 78th Street with recorded music, free blintzes and a bustling crowd, but without any competitive threat to the city's food shops.

The prices were horrendous the supplies were scant and the place is closing within a month. In fact, even the food displays were fake.

The truth is, "The American Supermarket" is a show of Pop art, staged by the Bianchini Gallery, on the same premises where it normally exhibits more conventional works. But for this display, the gallery got itself up as a real-life store, with counters, aisle signs and a turnstile. Its stock was a collection of Pop art food items, created (or sometimes simply embellished), by such artists as Andy Warhol, Claes Oldenburg, Mary Inman and Bob Watts.

Customers entering the store are confronted with a freezer case featuring wax meats and cheeses by Mary Inman. For $33 one can buy a sirloin steak or a hard salami, while a succulent cold roast beef sandwich goes for $27. Marked as "Specials," 3 for $18, are genuine cans of Campbell's soup, with labels autographed by Andy Warhol.

Chromo Canteloupes

And at the rear of the store a fruit and vegetable stand is filled with tempting inedibles such as Bob Watts' chrome canteloupes ($125) and wax tomatoes in gray, white and blue (3 for $15).

A steady stream of customers poured in on Tuesday. They were greeted by the proprietor, Paul Bianchini, who took orders on a grocer's pad. "Pick me out a fresh one, Paul," Robert Fischer, an advertising man, said, pointing to a box of $12 chrome eggs by Bob Watts. Sheldon Pollock, a young executive, paid $17 for a package of four wax doughnuts. But the fastest-moving item was a $12 paper shopping bag, designed by Andy Warhol—plain white with a red Campbell's soup can.

Most of the customers were just looking. They poked at plaster pumpernickels, squeezed wax peppers and fingered flock-covered Rome Delicious apples. Someone left a couple of real chocolate cookies on the bread counter. They looked fake. The gifts—boxes of genuine frozen blintzes donated by an advertising agency—caused some confusion. "I'd rather have make - believe blintzes," one woman said.

One minor incident marred the festivities. At the height of the crush, Mr. and Mrs. Robert Scull, well-known pop art collectors, decided to withdraw a pair of real looking beer cans, wrought in bronze by artist Jasper Johns, that they had lent to the show. "I don't want people touching them," Mr. Scull said, as he upicked them off a pyramid of genuine Ballantine cans. "When the gallery makes a protective covering for them, I'll bring them back."

"That's right," Mrs. Scull added. "We can't be too careful. After all, we did lose that sausage at the Venice Biennale."

NOVEMBER 29, 1964.

Supper at Pierre Dec. 8 to Follow Israeli Art Show

Cultural Foundation to Benefit—Opening at Jewish Museum

The premiere of "Art Israel: 26 Painters and Sculptors" at the Jewish Museum on Dec. 8 will be followed by a supper dance in the Pierre's Cotillion Room.

The Women's Division of the America-Israel Cultural Foundation, which has arranged the party, will provide special buses to take guests from the museum to the hotel. The art show will open at 9 P. M., and the supper dance will begin at 10:30 P. M.

Walworth Barbour, Ambassador to Israel, and Abraham Harman, Israeli Ambassador to the United States, are patrons of the premiere. The art show will continue at the museum through Jan. 24 and then tour leading museums in this country and Canada.

The tour has been arranged by the foundation and the International Council of the Museum of Modern Art. The works were selected by Dr. William C. Seitz, associate curator of the department of painting and sculpture exhibitions at the Modern Art, from museums, studios and private collections in Israel and Paris.

Mrs. Sidney L. Solomon, is chairman of the supper dance. Proceeds will help support the foundation's cultural exchange programs with Israel. Mrs. Oscar Kolin is chairman of the foundation's fine arts committee, and Mrs. Jesse Zizmor is vice chairman.

Committee members are Mrs. Jacques Schupf, Mrs. Matthias L. Spiegel, Mrs. Jack Wexler, Mrs. Isidore M. Cohen, Mrs. Nathan Goldman, Mrs. Doris Hakim, Mrs. Ben Heller, Mrs. Philip J. Levin, Miss Mala Rubinstein, Mrs. Robert Scull, Mrs. Theodore H. Silbert, Mrs. Pierre Simon, Mrs. Harriet Mnuchin, Mrs. Seymour Pristin and Mrs. Bernard K. Marcus.

The foundation's office is at 2 West 45th Street.

JANUARY 12, 1965.

Television

(C) Color (R) Repeat (P) Premiere

WCBS-TV	2	WOR-TV	9
WNBC-TV	4	WPIX	11
WNEW-TV	5	WNDT	13
WABC-TV	7	WNYC-TV	31

7:30 (2) Eye on New York: Avant-garde art. George Segal, sculptor; Robert C. Scull, collector; others (R)

(4) ● **MR. NOVAK:** "An Elephant Is Like a Tree," James Franciscus; Celeste Holm, guests

(5) Tales of Wells Fargo (R)

(7) ● **COMBAT:** "The Cassock," World War II story; James Whitmore, guest star

(9) ● **MILLION DOLLAR MOVIE:** "The Colditz Story," John Mills. British P.O.W.'s intriguing plans for escape

(11) Lloyd Thaxton Show

(13) ● **PREVIEW: 89 CONGRESS:** "Congress and the Nation's Children." Neil MacNeil is commentator

(31) Teen Age Book Talk: "We Are Not Alone," by Walter Sullivan, science editor, The New York Times

JANUARY 24, 1965.

Art Notes

To Lend Or Not To Lend

By GRACE GLUECK

"MY paintings are like my children—never home," complained a well-known collector the other day, wistfully seeing three of his Rauschenbergs off on an extended museum tour. "I'd like to stop lending, but I don't think I should." His comment was fairly typical. With U.S. art museums in a fever of exhibition activity demands on collectors these days are almost incessant. "It's getting more and more difficult to borrow items for exhibit," Mrs. Adelyn Breeskin, special consultant to the National Collection of Fine Arts, at the Smithsonian Institution was recently quoted as saying. "One reason is because the same collectors are called on so many times to lend their works."

Collectors themselves admit they're getting cagier. "We don't object to a show that has real substance," say the Arnold Maremonts of Chicago. "But we are more watchful of where our paintings go."

A major collector complaint is the increased circulation time of exhibits. The high cost of staging big shows nowadays often lures 3 or more museums to pool funds—with the show circulating to each contributor. A 3-month run in New York can thus stretch into a year on the road. Lenders to the Max Beckmann show, for example, which closes next Sunday at the Museum of Modern Art, won't get their paintings back until the end of 1965.

An even bigger headache is the increasing incidence of damage. "I wouldn't mind how long my paintings were away if they'd only come back in good condition," says Whitney Museum Trustee David M. Solinger, who's had paintings returned with pigment flaked off and frames split. Works owned by collector Robert Scull, who lends heavily and often, have been stolen, scribbled on and smeared with fingerprints. What's more, collectors often get short shrift from insurance companies. "They sometimes seem to think that any extraneous mark on a painting is an improvement," grumbled one lender.

Museum men reluctantly agree that, despite their own extensive precautions, lenders face risks. They cite such factors as lack of properly trained personnel, the difficulties of close supervision, the shortage of guards and the fragility of materials. "And you never can tell," said one official glumly, "when a cleaning lady will poke her broom handle through a canvas."

To some collectors, though, the joys of lending will always outstrip the hazards. "There's such a hunger for art," says Mrs. Burton Tremaine, who with her husband has recenty lent some 50 works for placement in U.S. embassies, "that most lenders want to do as much as they can. It's especially important that pictures should go where they're not often seen. Who knows how a painting may bring a change in outlook—or freshen the views of another artist."

MARCH 15, 1965.

$350 Lunch on Wall, Not Menu, Attracts 750 to Four Seasons

Donors to Mental Health Funds Pay $25 to View Latest Items in Pop Art —and Wonder What They Are

By RICHARD F. SHEPARD

An inedible sandwich, costing $350, which is steep even by Four Seasons standards, greeted visitors to that Park Avenue restaurant yesterday as they paid a $25 cover in behalf of mental health, the nation's if not their own.

The sandwich was the downstairs appetizer of an ambitious pop art exhibition that pushed the tables out of the plush upstairs and turned it into a one-day gallery.

More than 100 works by 44 artists, some on loan from private colections and some-price-tagged from $50 to $4,500—from nine established galleries. The canvases, hanks of hair, wooden soup cartons, pictures that talk back and a gimmicky HO model railroad layout were insured for more than $2 million and drew 750 visitors.

View Is Divided

The art was either eye-repelling or eye-catching depending upon the beholder. The comment seemed to be divided between the hang - the - expense school of admiration and the hang - the - artist school of scorn.

There were some hopes that this display would cause a wave of shock reminiscent of the landmark Armory show of 1913, when modern art came to America. But, as one observer, looking around at the lavish restaurant setting, said, "In this setting, it looks tame."

The crowd ranged from trade (dealers and artists), through connoisseurs and society (Mr. and Mrs. Robert C. Scull). There were many names—Walter Wanger, Marisol, and Mrs. Constance Baker Motley, Borough President of Manhattan, to drop just a few.

$1,500 Baseball Player

The objets d'art included Leo Jensen's "Champion's Choice," a metal baseball player with a box of Wheaties in his torso ($1,-500), a prosaic empty laundry bag hanging from a green background by Aaron Kuriloff ($500), a real refrigerator with a cartoon on the door by William Reddig, called "Draw One" ($450), and a circle of track carrying a white engine that shoved a blue-painted table-tennis ball over a column of air that bounced the ball high enough to pass through a loop of wire on the engine when it came through on the next round.

The occasion benefited the National Association for Mental Health, the New York State Association for Mental Health and the Mental Health Associations in New York City. It also lightened the day for the staff of Stuart Levin, director and president of the Four Seasons.

JUNE 12, 1965.

ROSENQUIST'S 'F-111' AT JEWISH MUSEUM

The biggest pop art painting in the world, James Rosenquist's 85-foot "F-111," is on display at the Jewish Museum, Fifth Avenue and 92d Street.

The 51-panel extravaganza on billboard scale illustrates products of our industrial civilization ranging from light bulbs and tires to an atomic explosion cloud, all superimposed on the fuselage of an F-111B jet fighter-bomber.

The work, which recently occupied the four walls of a room at the Leo Castelli Gallery, takes up only two in a second-floor gallery of the museum. The walls measure 69 feet 4 inches by 41 feet 8 inches. "F-111" was lent to the museum by Robert Scull, who bought it for a reported $60,000 last month.

The work will remain at the museum through Sept. 8 and then will be shown in Sweden and other European countries. Mr. Scull, who is not prepared to house it himself, is pleased with its accommodation at the museum. "I'm glad it's not in a warehouse," he said yesterday. "I want people to see it everywhere." The New York University Art Collection, he noted, has offered the painting a home between its travels.

JULY 15, 1965.

Books of The Times

Behind the Maid, a Tire and a Toothpaste Grin

By ELIOT FREMONT-SMITH

POP ART. By John Rublowsky. Photographs by Ken Heyman. 212 pages. Basic Books. $12.50.

POP ART, which Harold Rosenberg once described as "advertising art advertising itself as art that hates advertising," may deserve this book. Like pop art, "Pop Art" is chic, banal, unanalytical, anti-critical, historically vague, repetitive, fatuous, possibly a "put-on" (meaning possibly leg-pulling, but whose leg?), up-to-the-minute (give or take a few years) and high-priced. And like pop art, it seems interested less in art than in the promotion of certain artists and their sponsors.

Prominent among the artists here are Roy Lichtenstein (comic strip blow-ups), Claes Oldenburg (plaster hamburgers, giant rag-filled cakes), James Rosenquist (painted billboard collages), Andy Warhol (Campbell soup cans, Brillo boxes, Liz Taylor) and Tom Wesselman (nudes and toilet seats). Each of these is given a separate chapter.

Prominent among their sponsors are Richard Brown-Baker (private income), Leon Kraushar (insurance), Leon Manuchin (corporation law), Robert C. Scull (taxicabs) and the proprietors of the Manhattan galleries, Castelli, Green and Stable. And notable by omission is Lawrence Alloway, curator of the Guggenheim museum, coiner of the phrase "pop art" and—too bad for him!—reportedly author of the forthcoming rival book on the movement.

Praise and Inanity

To each of these (excepting Alloway) John Rublowsky, the free-lance author of "Pop Art," gives chirping, incoherent praise in a text that must be one of the most inane in all art writing. His favorite words are "esthetic," "multileveled" and "sensitivity:" none is defined, and they appear to be interchangeable—perhaps intentionally so, pop art being the glorification of cliché.

Nevertheless, one can make out some of the genesis and ideology of the pop art movement through Rublowsky's dazzled gaze. The movement grew out of, and was an antithesis to, abstract expressionism, with Jasper Johns and Robert Rauschenberg, employing commonplace symbols and "found objects," the major catalysts. But it also sprang independently into the heads of artists who were unknown and unknown to each other. At the same time, "the school was and is a collectors' movement . . . the collectors led the way."

"It is ironic," Rublowsky adds, "that an art based directly on the most common images of our world should appeal to the most sophisticated tastes. Irony is, however, very much a part of our world—a world that pop art expresses so eloquently."

Nor is this all. Rublowsky dismisses the notion that pop art owes anything to Dada, and asserts that by taking "its esthetic from the commonplace and [seeking] those terrible beauties concealed in the vulgar and banal," pop art "reflects a democratic ideal."

Thus all can be equalized, both principles and people—except, of course, the pop-ular artist. By successfully communicating the "essence" of certain "truths" about today, he "becomes a cultural force—an ornament in the crown of men." In this Elysia, efficiency is hailed as equality's twin: "if gra-gracious service is rapidly disappearing from the world, so are the servers and the servile," Rublowsky hymns. "With the pop movement, American art becomes truly American for the first time and thus becomes universal. . . . [deriving] its unique vision and inspiration from the mythogenic forces generated by a new social and economic reality."

Well, it gives an idea of Rublowsky's pattern of thought and style. As a writer he is certainly unique if not downright mythogenic, and every reader will have his favorite passage.

No book can be all bad. Ken Heyman's photographs of the artists and their sponsors at work and play are plentiful and superb. Perhaps the most revealing is a picture captioned "Dining room, Robert C. Scull home."

It shows the collector and his family at dinner, seated on antique chairs that are protected from contamination by transparent plastic covers. A maid, perhaps not servile but in uniform, stands ready with a silver tray of lamb chops. Behind her on the wall, dominating all, is a huge Rosenquist advertising billboard mural depicting a squawking turkey's head, a tire, a smiling toothpaste face, an auto windshield and a soft-drink bottle. Thus through pop—*plus ça change*—the Sculls can picnic in the countryside at home.

What of the Future?

Pop art is today's big art business—but what of tomorrow? Rublowsky blandly doesn't say. (Nor does he give any facts or figures about the business, or indeed much else.) But if Andy Warhol is the philosophical leader of the movement, and Rublowsky implies he is—"All Warhol's work is multileveled and can be interpreted in many ways"—then perhaps we have a clue.

Warhol's aim has been to totally depersonalize and mechanize art, to express the machine by completely mechanical techniques. ("What an audacious solution!" Rublowsky writes. "What depths of the man are revealed in this gesture!") If he succeeds, then a curious situation may arise. People may begin to wonder about Warhol's fees. If he—or any of the *others*—aren't creating art, if it all is truly mechanized, then why should they be paid? Why not, in fact, get one's Brillo boxes from the Brillo factory, one's Campbell cans from the A & P? Why not (the Sculls may ask) picnic in the countryside for free?

Audacious questions, but the logic of the movement and of this book propels them out. The future of pop art? The lesson should be clear: unless direction is changed at once, the future of pop art may be—poverty. An ironic lesson, but then, as Rublowsky says, irony is a part of the world pop art so eloquently expresses.

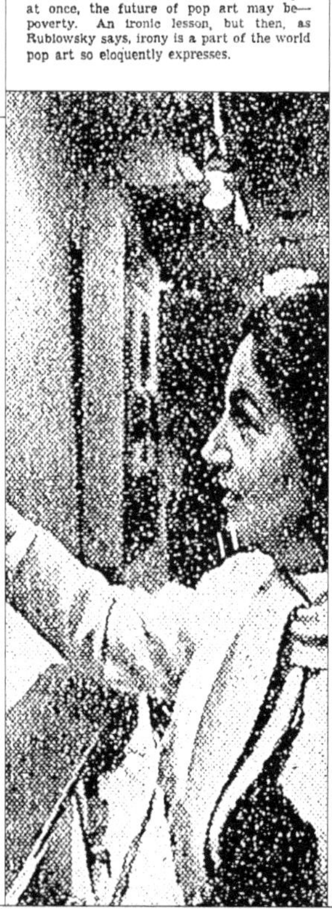

JULY 22, 1965.

Tiffany presents an Exhibition of Table Settings by the following Distinguished Collectors with paintings and works of art from their collections

MR. LARRY ALDRICH

MR. AND MRS. JOHN DE MENIL

MR. AND MRS. JOHN JAKOBSON

MR. PATRICK LANNAN

MR. AND MRS. ALBERT A. LIST

MRS. GERTRUD A. MELLON

MR. AND MRS. ROY R. NEUBERGER

MR. AND MRS. BERNARD J. REIS

MR. AND MRS. ROBERT SCULL

Through August 21, 1965

TIFFANY & CO.

FIFTH AVE. & 57th ST. • NEW YORK

San Francisco • Beverly Hills • Houston

OCTOBER 13, 1965.

The Rubinstein Jewels: $371,715 and Memories

By MARYLIN BENDER

THE flamboyant jewelry of Helena Rubinstein, the tiny cosmetics tycoon who died last spring at the age of 94, was sold at auction yesterday at Parke-Bernet Galleries.

The collection of 187 pieces brought $371,715 in a 2 hour and 45 minute bidding marathon conducted by John L. Marion. The proceeds of the sale will be divided between Miss Rubinstein's estate and the charitable foundation she established a dozen years ago.

Considering the enormous amount of publicity that preceded the auction, it turned out to be a rather disappointing event. The crowd of 1,500 who jammed the main auction gallery and spilled slightly into two adjoining rooms equipped with television monitor sets contained a mere sprinkling of celebrities. Those private clients who had left their bids ahead of time and stayed away from the sale were swept away by the professionals.

Dealers carried the day. Immediately after the sale, a diamond dealer who identified himself as David R. Balogh of Miami Beach announced that he represented a syndicate of five jewelers for whom he had spent close to $200,000.

In a Paper Parcel

Louis Daoud, a jeweler of Fort Lauderdale who paid almost $100,000 for 35 pieces including a sapphire and diamond starfish hand ornament that Miss Rubinstein said had been given to her by Sarah Bernhardt, carried his acquisitions away in a brown paper parcel wrapped with splinter cord.

The largest single purchase was made by a Boston wholesaler, S. Sydney De Young, who paid $33,000 for a 70-carat sapphire ring set in gold. The total of his purchases came to $60,000. Van Cleef & Arpels bought a 51-carat yellow diamond for $18,000 and an emerald and diamond pendant necklace for $10,750.

A La Vieille Russie, a Fifth Avenue shop specializing in antique jewelry, and S. J. Phillips of London, two of Miss Rubinstein's favorite emporiums, bought back several pieces they had originally sold to her.

Among the few private customers who managed to satisfy their yearnings for some of Miss Rubinstein's possessions were Mrs. William Woodward Jr., who secured a pair of emerald, pearl and diamond pendant earrings for $1,350, and Amy Greene, beauty editor of Glamour magazine and wife of Milton Greene, the photographer. Mrs. Greene paid $600 for a necklace of graduated ruby beads and $85 for a gold and enamel compact by Verdura.

Although published reports prior to the auction quoted experts as estimating the sale would fetch close to a million dollars, Harold Weill, the beauty queen's attorney and one of her executors, pronounced the proceeds "a fair price." Mr. Weill said that the auction of her vast art collection, which will probably take place next spring, would undoubtedly rack up more impressive totals.

Ward Landrigan, head of the auction gallery's jewelry department, pointed out that the value of the collection as jewelry per se was not the determining factor in this sale. "The primary thing was Madame Rubinstein and the second was the rarity of the pieces," he said.

None of Miss Rubinstein's relatives were present. "The family felt they couldn't attend," Mr. Weill said. "They were too emotional about it." She had willed several pieces of jewelry to relatives.

Several friends and employes like Patrick O'Higgins, who usually traveled with her, and Nancy Levey, her executive secretary for 13 years, were on hand.

"She gave me a ruby and pearl pendant, a small diamond ring and some carved coral beads," recalled Mrs. Levey, who looked wistfully chic in a gray flannel costume with a rabbit chinchilla hat. "She just reached into a box."

Mrs. Levey said she was surprised that a wide blue enamel bracelet set with rose diamonds given to Miss Rubinstein by her grandmother when she was a girl in Poland was put up for sale rather than having been handed down to a relative. It went for $300.

'I Was Just Curious'

In the audience were a few fashionable women like Mrs. Robin Butler, the blonde socialite who works for Christian Dior-New York, and Mrs. Robert Scull, the pop art collector who is auctioning 20 of her paintings tomorrow at Parke-Bernet. Mrs. Scull came in a beige tweed Chanel costume and left early. "I was just curious and besides I'm not really interested in antique things," she said.

Wyatt Cooper, the writer who is married to Gloria Vanderbilt, said he was interested in No. 103, the emerald and diamond necklace that Van Cleef bought.

"But I'm not bidding because my wife is ill and hasn't seen the things," he said. "I'm afraid to buy it and get it home and find she thinks it looks like Coca-Cola drops."

Most of the observers, though, were the stone-faced professionals and a blend of college students, aged matrons and idle housewives who had ambled in from the street. Mrs. Betty Culp was accompanied by six children ranging in age from 11 to 5. Three were hers, the others belonged to a friend.

"We came in from the Columbus Day Parade," she explained as Mr. Marion coaxed the bidding on a jade necklace up to $1,050, paused for a fraction of a second to gulp from a red tumbler and went on his breathless way.

OCTOBER 13, 1965.

French Have a Fur Show And End It With the Frug

By ANGELA TAYLOR

FURS, feathers and the frug were all whipped together in a Gallic froth Monday night at the French Consulate. The furs—and some of the feathers—were supplied by Saks Fifth Avenue's Revillon salon for a fashion show paraded in the drawing room of the consulate at 934 Fifth Avenue. The dancing came later, when French Consul General and Mrs. Michel Legendre, both experts at the frug, whisked their guests and the music upstairs to a room cleared for action.

If Revillon has its way, women will be wrapped in furs around the clock. Sleeping pajamas had white rabbit jackets, nightgowns were covered with Mongolian lamb peignoirs, and a monkey fur poncho topped other pajamas.

If mink is for football, chinchilla, this year, is for a country stroll, particularly if one has chinchilla boots to match. On the other hand, lynx has left its sports habitat for the bright lights of the city, in a floor-length coat in the grand manner.

Paris Represented

The fashion show in the audience drew as many eyes as the professional one—women who owned French couture originals (or copies) wore theirs loyally. Mrs. Legendre was in short white brocade by Nina Ricci and Mrs. Jacques Revillon wore Saint Laurent's pale green smock dress yoked and sleeved in silver fish net.

Mrs. Frederick Eberstadt, Odgen Nash's daughter, watched the show in Cardin's camel-colored hooded suit, and Mrs. Robert Scull, wife of the art collector, danced in Ohrbach's copy of Chanel's puffy white silk suit.

"She saved $600 on it. I wish I'd been in town to shop here," said Mrs. Raymond Loewy, wife of the industrial designer. Her gold brocade Chanel was the real thing.

If the Duchess of Windsor had come to the party, she would have found herself in good company. The gray and black checked Dior suit in which she disembarked here last week was worn by white-haired Mrs. William Wasserman, whose late father was publisher of an English language newspaper in Japan, and young Mrs. Michael Aquino, wife of a Saks branch store manager.

No gathering is complete these days without one of Saint Laurent's Mondrian shifts—Mrs. René Bouché wore hers with a diamond pin. One of America's famous diamonds, a 55-carat solitaire worn by Mrs. Ernest Byfield Jr., was kept company by a big diamond bracelet and simple black chiffon from Dior.

Although most of the women in the audience had left their furs at home, Mrs. Raymond Johnson arrived in the sleeveless black mink dress she had worn earlier to Bonwit's reception for Crown Prince Harald of Norway. Mrs. Johnson wore her feathers on her head, in the form of an enormous hat of black plumage.

OCTOBER 14, 1965.

Abstract Paintings By Expressionists Sold for $284,000

By SANKA KNOX

The first auction sale in New York to offer only abstract expressionist paintings was held last night at the Parke-Bernet Gallery, 980 Madison Avenue. Twenty pictures were sold for $284,000.

Twelve of the paintings were consigned by Robert C. Scull, owner of a fleet of taxicabs. Most of the proceeds from the paintings, Mr. Scull said, would go to a foundation he and his wife had formed to help artists.

An auction of only sculpture —the first at Parke-Bernet— followed the sale of paintings. Today a sale of impressionist paintings will be held that gallery officials said will bring some of the most important pictures to be offered in many years.

Some of the artists represented last night were apparently having their first appearance at auction.

Clyfford Still's dramatic "Painting—1951" brought $29,000, and Barnett Newman's "Tundra," a large orangey oblong divided by a thin line, was hold for $26,000.

The star of the show was William de Kooning who brought the highest price — $37,000 for "Police Gazette," painted in 1955.

"Wild Field" by Mark Tobey was bought for $14,000 by the Sidney Janis Gallery of New York.

Franz Kline's "Shenandoah" brought $19,000 and his "Initial" $18,000.

A typical Mark Rothko, "Reds Number 22," went for $15,500.

The total sale of paintings and sculpture was $471,000. The auction was conducted by Peter C. Wilson, chairman of Sotheby's, the London auction house that now owns Parke-Bernet.

OCTOBER 22, 1965.

A Classicist Scores With a Contemporary Audience

By BERNADINE MORRIS

ALIX GRES, the Paris fashion designer whose shyness is legendary, was the star of a luncheon at the St. Regis Roof yesterday when high society met haute couture under the aegis of the Musicians Emergency Fund.

Three hundred women and a handful of men dressed up to do homage to the couturier who is widely admired but rarely seen. The last time she was in this country, two years ago, Mme. Grès showed part of her collection at the April in Paris Ball. This time she brought almost all of it, ranging from poncho-topped pants suits to wear in the country to tentlike evening dresses that had women longing for a palace to wear them in.

Women who had never owned a Grès dress before, like Mrs. Joseph A. Meehan, co-chairman of the committee that arranged the luncheon, left the hotel yearning for one. Mrs. William B. Jaffe, the other co-chairman, who wore a beige suit by Guy Laroche, and Mrs. Pierre Simon, in a white Courrèges coat, recalled buying a Grès evening dress some years ago. They both said they were eager to get another right away.

Although she is known for her classically draped jersey dresses — the fabric was known as Alix jersey in the nineteen-thirties — Mme. Grès showed a contemporary feeling in loose dresses that juxtaposed two or three screaming colors.

She sat quietly at the head table wearing a white side-closing coat and the tightly wrapped turban that has been her trademark for 30 years. On one side of her was Mrs. Hervé Alphand, wife of the retiring French Ambassador, who quickly removed her mink-collared Guy Laroche tweed coat to show her simple beige wool Grès dress. On her other side was Mrs. Michel Legendre, wife of the French Consul General who took off her belted Revillon leopard coat. Her Grès dress was white.

The three costumes set the color scheme for the room, except for the women wearing Chanel suits and those whose pink suits complemented the décor.

Among the audience, Chanel was the reigning Paris couturier. There were tables of women in her fluffy, soft tweed suits.

Mrs. Ira Guilden, whose husband is a financier, wore a red Chanel with blue ribbons threaded through the neckline while Mrs. Robert C. Scull, who collects paintings, wore a belted green suit.

As she scanned the audience, Mrs. Stephane Groueff, whose beige and white outfit was by Venet, remarked, "We'll have to save our Chanels for the country."

It wasn't all Chanel, however. Mrs. Lewis Iselin Jr. and Mrs. Frederick Eberstadt both chose St. Laurent's Mondrian dresses. Mr. Eberstadt, the photographer, wore a Cardin suit.

Both Bill Blass, the designer who was recently made a partner at Maurice Rentner, and Adele Simpson, whose clothes are worn by Mrs. Lyndon B. Johnson, said they liked the collection even better than when they saw it in Paris last summer.

"She is coming to see me Monday," Mr. Blass said.

Mme. Grès has a busy social schedule before she returns to Paris Tuesday. Last night she attended a dinner honoring the Alphands. This afternoon she will go to a reception at the Plaza Hotel given by Bonwit Teller and the Allied Chemical Company where her nightgowns of Caprolan nylon for Cira Creations will be shown. This will be followed by another presentation of her collection at the French Consulate.

She hopes also to get to Lincoln Center, the Metropolitan Opera, the Frick Museum and the costume departments of the Brooklyn Museum and the Metropolitan Museum of Art.

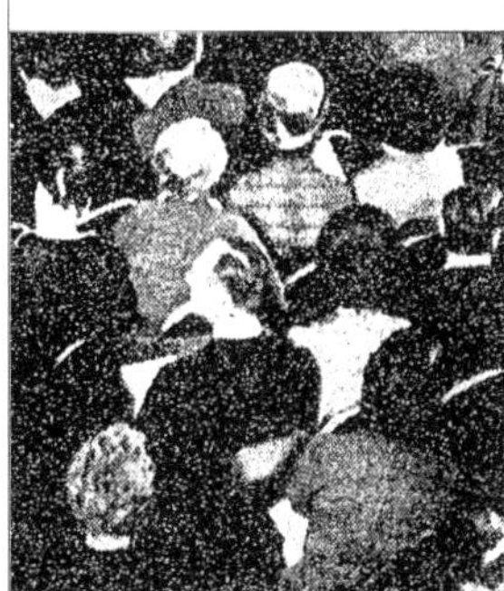

OCTOBER 24, 1965.

Art Notes

'No!' Says Yes Art

By GRACE GLUECK

MANIFESTOES flying, a new aesthetic expression known as Yes Art opened last week at the Fitzgerald Gallery. It might be described as a kind of counter-Pop, that puts Andy Warhol square in the enemy camp.

"Yes Art is a sensual, uninhibited, beautiful and above all affirmative expression of the times we live in or don't live in," says the manifesto. "A Yes Artist doesn't necessarily have to see anything or paint anything to create a painting. A work of art can be made merely by coming across an object that strikes an artist's fancy, and by signing it, he can make it into art."

True to its manifesto, the gallery shows a single Brillo carton signed by Dillon Dillon for $1,000, plus fold-your-own cartons for $4.95. Further variations on the Brillo theme are a stippled, Seurat-type painting called "Brillo Pointilliste," a cubist work called "Brillo Descending a Staircase," and a Brillo trademark done in needlepoint by the wife of the Brillo Company treasurer, Mrs. John Loeb. Other Yes Art: an all-black painting by computer No. 741-193, "Affluent 8-Pack," a group of gilded Coke bottles topped by nipples, a portrait of Rembrandt with a Met-sized price tag of $2.3 million. There is also a work of living sculpture, a girl named Sophia Blickman, at the same price as the Rembrandt. The gallery will give S&H Green Stamps (known as "the camp stamp") with every purchase, including Miss Blickman.

"It's kind of a humorous protest against the promotional aspect of art today," said Ed Fitzgerald, the gallery's director. "The promotion, not the painting, is what counts. Some galleries today are simply circuses. So ours is a Yes circus. There's no reason to scratch eyes and pull hair. If we can get back at them in their own way, OK."

SEGAL & CO.

The friends and relatives of sculptor George Segal, cast from life in lumpish white plaster, have taken up informal residence at the suave Sidney Janis Gallery. A plaster couple relaxes on a bed, a young girl lies on a mattress listening to hi-fi, an old woman broods before a dummy tenement window. "Yes, she's my mother-in-law," acknowledged Segal, small as life and twice as natural among his plaster "presences." "It's true that the people and their settings all have some association for me. But I want to suggest or evoke an experience, rather than represent it realistically. The sculptures are general, as well as specific. They're not posed and they're not candid. If the composition is successful, it should provide an insight, a revelation."

Segal casts his famous plaster people in parts, applying wet mix to the live models in small squares. The process takes three hours and is ruinous to clothes (as a pair of well-known pop art collectors found when they posed for their tintype in plaster, titled "Robert and Ethel Scull"). Then he assembles the results. He may work on a figure for a month, highlighting certain features, blurring others.

"The whole thing becomes a process of selection. I have to be sure I like the basic posture. Then I work on minute gestures of hands, heads or extremities. The gestures have to be psychologically true to the subjects. I also consider them in relation to the space of the whole composition," said Segal, who started out as a painter. "I find that very exciting—to take a piece of real space and compose it just as severely as a painting."

Segal takes equal pains with props and settings. He frequents lumber yards, neon sign shops and store fixture houses. "I assemble lots of things, then start eliminating them. I rearrange those whose shapes I like until their relationship seems to work for me. I build things, then tear them apart. It takes forever."

For one tableau, which evokes his late father's butcher shop in the Bronx, he found steel meat racks and a chopping block at a butcher supply house. He ordered a sheet of clear plastic for the show window. But he looked in vain for a suitable set of Hebrew letters—the kind that identify butcher shops as kosher. "All the ones I saw were somehow too fat and gross. So I finally made them myself—longer and thinner, the way my memory saw them."

MET'S MAILLOL

Putting its faith in the committee system, the Metropolitan Opera has just acquired the first piece of sculpture for its new home at Lincoln Center. As might be expected, the choice is a high-minded one: a nude "Standing Figure" by the French sculptor Aristide Maillol. ("Anyone who'd quarrel with *that* would knock Truth and Beauty," was one trade comment.)

The sculpture was acquired through the local Marlborough-Gerson Galleries. It is actually a gift from New York's Henry L. and Grace Doherty Foundation, which is also footing the bill for a pair of murals commissioned for the Met last April from Marc Chagall. The selection was mulled for some time by the Met's Art Committee, headed by the noted collector Robert Lehman, and by the Art Committee for Lincoln Center, whose chairman is C.B.S. president Frank Stanton.

"Everyone looked at a lot of things before the committees and the donors agreed on this," noted Herman E. Krawitz, assistant manager of the Opera. "We'll put it in the front lobby." Several more art purchases are in the works, but the Met isn't talking about them yet.

PERSONAL APPEARANCE

By what could only be a handy coincidence, the U.S. visit next month of Princess Margaret and her husband, Lord Snowdon (photographer Antony Armstrong-Jones) will occur around the time his new book about the London art scene is released here. "Private View," with A-J photos plus text by art critics John Russell and Bryan Robertson, is now selling in England for a strapping 7 guineas (about $20). It weighs a robust 5 pounds, and small wonder. It touches not only on English artists from Turner to Bridget Riley, but such meaty topics as art schools, government arts policy, collectors, critics, dealers, museums, auctions and art parties. "This superbly illustrated book takes you behind the scenes ...reveals exactly what happened to make LONDON—THE ART CAPITAL OF WORLD," touts a flyer from its London publishers. Time-Life Books will launch it here Nov. 19, through the International Book Society.

The royal pair is expected, incidentally, to attend the opening of "The English Eye," a 30-year survey of British art at the Marlborough - Gerson Galleries here, opening mid-November. The book, its sponsors say, will not beplugged at the party.

COLLAGE

Works donated by artists from all over the world (Ben Shahn, Picasso, Henry Moore, Alberto Giacometti, Victor Vasarely) have so far raised over $14,000 for the World Campaign for the Relief of South African Political Prisoners at London's Savage and Cassel Galleries. The money will help toward prisoners' release and aid their families . . . Sir John Rothenstein, retired director of London's Tate Gallery, has published Vol. I of his autobiography, "Summer's Lease," will also edit "The Masters," a weekly art magazine of great painters and their works . . . Upcoming shows on the new Israel Museum's exhibition agenda: Picasso, Paul Klee and, next summer, the Henry Pearlman collection of New York.

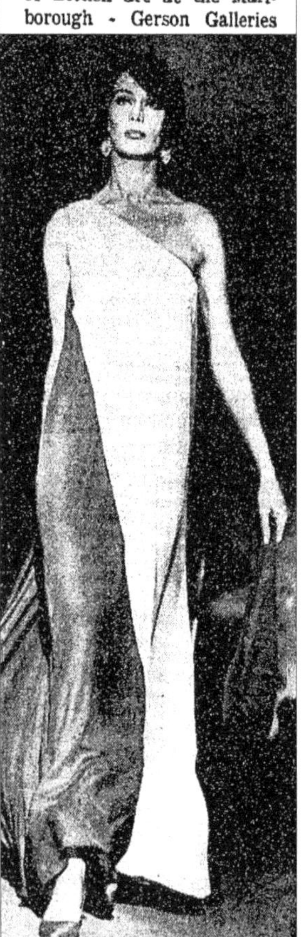

NOVEMBER 18, 1965.

Over the Rainbow Room: Modness

By ANGELA TAYLOR

IN the staged hush of the Rainbow *Grill*, 65 stories above Radio City, tourists in little mink stoles and little beaded bags sat at tables lighted by shaded pink lamps and pointed out the Empire State Building in the drifts of fog outside.

Past soundproof walls, in the Rainbow *Room* next door, a rock 'n' roll singer who calls himself Monti Rock 3d (to the cognoscenti, he is still known as Monti the Hairdresser), stomped around on the polished floor in a head-to-toe outfit of silver brocade to cries of "More! more!"

The dignified Rainbow Room, which still thinks of itself as a glamorous setting for nineteen-thirties debutantes in white chiffon and elbow-length gloves, had a firecracker on its hands: The management had rented the premises Tuesday night for a Mod Ball, a supposedly private party given by a group called Le Cercle d'Or.

Posters Appear

The private party began to go public when posters appeared around town urging anybody who had $25 and a fancy getup to join the fun. There were also rumors that a flock of celebrities would appear, maybe even some royalty.

Jerome Brody, Inc., the company that runs the Rainbow Room, says this approach led it to attempt to cancel what it feared might be a brawl. It was too late. The Rainbow Room then took protective measures.

Burly uniformed guards were posted to keep out gatecrashers. All but two official photographers, hired by the management, were supposed to be barred even if it disappointed the Mods, who had obviously been working for weeks on their getups.

Flying Feathers

The dance floor was a whirl of bell-bottom pants, midthigh skirts and old-fashioned high-laced shoes, plus velvet knee breeches, "granny" dresses and flying feathers.

Kay King, who works for a magazine, wore silver pants and a huge hair-bow made of aluminum foil. Mrs. Ruth Lachman, ex-wife of Charles Lachman, a founder of Revlon, came in a striped union suit—"I found it at Gimbels" —under a sandwich-board arrangement of black and white vinyl.

Her long-haired escort, Crawford Greenleaf, wore an exaggerated Beatle suit with a visored cap and gold kid shoes.

The so-called Mods—many of them overaged and too prosperous to qualify as the real thing—had gone on the silver standard.

Mrs. Robert C. Scull, wife of the taxicab fleet operator and Pop art collector, came in the same silver pants outfit she had worn to another party last week and found herself at the bar with Terry Karutz, a fashion coordinator, dressed in an identical rig.

The undoubted queen of the ball was Edie Sedgwick, the superstar of Andy Warhol's underground movies. Miss Sedgwick shone in a pants suit of cloth-of-silver and wore huge silver earrings. As the music and the temperature got hotter, she divested herself of the jacket and stood in a tiny silver bra and bare white skin to the hips, where her pants started.

"You don't think it's a bit much?" she asked anxiously.

There might have been an answer from the Rainbow *Grill*, but they turned out the lights over there at 2 A.M. and went home.

In the Rainbow *Room*, there was another rock 'n' roll combo on the stage and nobody cared to respond—except perhaps the landlord.

DECEMBER 24, 1965.

SHOW AT MUSEUM STARS MACHINES

People Also Appear in Cast of Exotic Spectacle

By GRACE GLUECK

Was it an operetta? A Japanese Noh drama? Amateur night? Or, as one member of the audience asked, the Jewish Museum's version of a Hanukkah party?

The puzzlement was caused by "The Tinguely Machine Mystery, or the Love Suicide at Kaluka," a mystery play by Kenneth Koch, that opened and closed Wednesday night at the Jewish Museum. In its cast were artists (Larry Rivers, Syd Solomon, Niki de Saint-Phalle), poets (Kenward Elmslie and Arnold Weinstein) and three machine sculptures (by Jean Tinguely).

Such was the advance demand for tickets that the museum had to schedule two performances, one at 9 and one at 11. Ticket pickets outside the museum greeted early arrivals with signs asking for spare admission cards.

"It really has everything going for it," a bearded young photographer, one of the first to arrive, said hopefully. He was followed by such "in" art luminaries as Harold Rosenberg, the critic; Rosalyn Drexler, artist, playwright and novelist; Mr. and Mrs. Robert Scull, collectors, and Jacques Kaplan, furrier to the art world.

Plenty to Watch

To reach the scene of action, viewers filed past Torah crowns, Sabbath candelabra, prayer shawls and other ritual objects in the museum's second-floor galleries. In the impromptu auditorium they were greeted by a whirring, clacking chorus of Tinguely machines.

The play, which began after a fitful, lengthy overture by the machines, was a ragout of Gilbert and Sullivan, 18th-century opera, Keystone cops and charades. Its crosscurrents had crosscurrents and its subplots had subplots.

Larry Rivers, playing a corpse that sprang to life as a police chief, stomped raucously around in a cop's tunic and leather boots. His wife, Clarice, dressed as a Princess in a red velvet gown of Elizabethan cut, fluttered cloyingly between him and a white-garbed detective, played by Sol Solomon.

Jane Freilicher, a painter cast as the City of Odessa, spent most of the time hunched in a monkey-fur coat next to the Tinguely machine named for the same city. Occasionally she bestirred herself to take stage center and deliver such lines as, "I often think of my waterfront, and sometimes weep."

One-Night Stand

And there were Niki de Saint-Phalle in black leotard, waving what looked like a rubber plunger, Arnold Weinstein in an admiral's suit, and Alexander Iolas, an art dealer, and Kiki Kogelnik, an artist, as the pair of suicidal Japanese lovers.

"Thank God this is only a one-night stand," murmured one viewer after the first few minutes. But most of the audience, like parents watching their children in a school play, preserved a respectful silence and tittered encouragingly when the script seemed to call for it.

Machines clacking, characters dying, audience wilting, the one-acter ground finally to its end with a burst of music by Morton Feldman. The cast of 13 bowed. The spectators rushed up to shake their hands.

"*I still think it had everything going for it,*" the bearded young photographer was saying as he packed up his equipment.

But as the crowd made its way down the narrow staircases to the museum's first floor, a theater producer observed to a friend, "The best performers in that cast were the machines."

MARCH 13, 1966.

Multiple Display Of Art to Assist Education Unit

Works of 7 Decades to Be at 10 Galleries—Preview April 26

A collection of art since 1895 —arranged in 10 galleries here —will form an exhibition benefiting the Public Education Association. The multiple show will have a champagne preview April 26, and will be open to the public April 27 through May 21.

There will be 370 paintings and sculptures on loan from collectors, museums and galleries here and abroad. The show, "Seven Decades, 1895-1965, Cross-Currents in Modern Art," will mark the 70th anniversary of the beneficiary.

Works from 1895 to 1904 will be at Paul Rosenberg & Co., 20 East 79th Street. Other groupings by period will be at M. Knoedler & Co., the Perls Galleries, E. V. Thaw & Co., Sal-

denberg Gallery, Stephen Hahn Gallery, Pierre Matisse Gallery, the André Emmerich Gallery and the Galleria Odyssia. The most recent works, from 1955 to 1965, will be at Cordier & Ekström, Inc., 978 Madison Avenue.

Private buses will be available for the preview.

W. Averell Harriman, Ambassador at Large, and Mrs. Harriman, at whose home a planning session was held recently, are among those lending works to the show.

Others are Mr. and Mrs. Carter Burden, Mr. and Mrs. Robert C. Scull, Mr. and Mrs. Arthur G. Altschul, Mr. and Mrs. Lee A. Ault, Mr. and Mrs. John de Menil, Mr. and Mrs. Henry J. Heinz 2d, Mr. and Mrs. Ralph F. Colin, Miss Adelaide Milton de Groot, Mrs. Marcel Duchamp, Philip Johnson, Mrs. Albert D. Lasker, Mr. and Mrs. Albert A. List, Mrs. H. Gates Lloyd, Mrs. Bliss Parkinson, Mr. and Mrs. Richard Rodgers, Mr. and Mrs. Robert W. Sarnoff and Mr. and Mrs. Burton Tremaine.

Chairmen of the benefit committee are Mrs. Frederick E. Donaldson, Mrs. Victor W. Ganz, Mrs. John H. Loeb, Mrs. Matthew A. Meyer and Mrs. Stanley G. Mortimer Jr.

Governor and Mrs. Rockefeller head the honorary committee. Others serving are Arthur A. Goldberg, United States delegate to the United Nations, and Mrs. Goldberg, Mayor and Mrs. Lindsay, Senator and Mrs. Jacob K. Javits, Dr. James B. Conant, president emeritus of Harvard University, and Mrs. Conant and Francis Keppel, Commissioner of Education.

The education association, whose offices are at 20 West 40th Street, is a volunteer organization that seeks to improve public schools and colleges.

APRIL 20, 1966.

'Where to?' Asked the Cab Drivers—and So Did Riders

6 Major Events Keep Partygoers on Run During Evening

By CHARLOTTE CURTIS

Except for Mrs. James Biddle, a du Pont Copeland whose new baby gave her a legitimate reason for staying home, nearly everybody who is anybody socially was out on the town last night—whooping it up in what was widely held to be the most hopelessly overscheduled evenings since the World's Fair opened two years ago.

The thousands of partygoers, including every sort of representative of what passes for Society in New York, were faced with an agenda involving six major gatherings and countless minor ones—most of which seemed to overlap.

The Bolshoi Ballet's 7:30 P. M opening-night curtain cut into black-tie dinner parties organized to promote the new Banque Continentale, and the dinner parties cut into the Bolshoi, whose performance benefited the United Nations International School, and into the New York City Ballet, which was raising money for its production fund.

That was merely the first round. The deluge came later.

Champagne by the Fragonards

The bank's dinner parties, held in such diverse places as Le Pavillon, the Plaza and the home of Mrs. Preston Long, the decorator, ended around 9:30 so guests could regroup for their after-dinner coffee, champagne and liqueurs beside the Fragonard paintings Mrs. Long had installed above the Aubusson rugs in the bank's 18th-century French interior.

By this time, a bewildered ballgoer had been admitted to the Kips Bay Dinner Dance, which was rolling along merrily at the St. Regis, by handing over tickets for a dinner concert at the Pierre next Wednesday.

The Whitney Museum of American Art, which is moving into new quarters next September, had flung its doors open in preparation for what was termed "the final social gala—sort of a farewell" with champagne and dancing. And John R. Drexel 3d was still hoping to get to the champagne supper at the United Nations.

"It's a perfect horror," Mr. Drexel said before he and Mrs. Drexel began their party rounds. "I'm not sure how we're going to do it."

Just in From Hobe Sound

Mr. Drexel, a Philadelphia banking heir who votes in Newport, R. I., and frequents New York, had just flown in from Hobe Sound, Fla. Neither he nor Mrs. Drexel, the former Noreen Stonor, felt they were up to the onslaught. But they were willing to try.

Their schedule, with Mrs. Drexel first in a green Molyneux suit and then a brown Oscar de la Renta evening gown, started at the Visiting Nurse Service's cocktail-hour preview of portraits of friends and ancestors drawn by celebrated artists. This event, the only big one without significant competition, was held in the late afternoon at Portraits, Inc.

Col. Serge Obolensky's bank dinner (the affable White Russian's public-relations concern is helping to publicize what is actually a sumptuous branch of the Franklin National Bank) came next, with Mrs. Jacob K. Javits, wife of the Senator, trotting around in Rudi Gernreich's brown and beige shift.

"I have another Rudi," Mrs. Javits said. "It's all lightning and thunder."

Mrs. Javits also said that her husband was at a different dinner (for advertising writers), but that she expected to see him later so they could go dancing. After dinner, the Drexels went scooting off to inspect the Banque Continentale itself at 785 Fifth Avenue.

They had given their $100 Bolshoi tickets away, Mr. Drexel said, "because we can't do every thing." But they did want to attend the postballet party in the United Nations delegates dining room."

"I'm sure it will go on long enough," Mr. Drexel said hopefully.

Mrs. Lytle Hull, Mrs. Ogden Phipps and Mr. and Mrs. Roy Neuberger were among others on the horns of an equally imposing dilemma. Mrs. Hull, a grande dame who doubles as den mother of the Musicians Emergency Fund, said the heck with the Bolshoi ("I'll go tomorrow night for our own benefit") and stuck by the New York City Ballet until after the performance.

She was not around the Promenade of the New York State Theater for the discothèque party after the ballet, however, and she had never intended to be.

"I've been to discothèques, unfortunately," Mrs. Hull said, "but my eardrums were so injured I doubt if I ever go again."

Mrs. Hull's decision cost her an encounter with the New Order—six musical types from Trude Heller's downtown nightspot who rocked 'n' rolled around in shirts designed for them by Emilio Pucci.

Alfred Gwynne Vanderbilt, the sportsman who rarely appears at charity balls, and his elegant wife, done up in an orange and black evening suit by Normal Norell ("I look a little Halloweenish"), were among those who took note of this musical phenomenon. They also went to Portraits, Inc., where tickets were only $7.50 apiece and their friend, Mrs. Pipps, was chairman.

"I do like the Brockhurst picture of me," said Mrs. Phipps, whose benefit raised more than $4,000. "I don't mean because it's of me but because of the art work itself. It is a magnificent pencil drawing."

Mrs. Rodman A. de Heeren, wife of the Palm Beach devotee, was just as pleased with the drawing Augustus Johns had done of her.

"He did two of them—the other one I have in Biarritz," she said. "He was telling me about his great friend Mondigliani, and I think this portrait has a Modigliani look about it."

Mrs. Phipps's schedule, like the Neubergers, also included the New York City Ballet—which meant she did not see U Thant, Secretary General of the United Nations, who presided over the Bolshoi opening. And although Mr. Neuberger is a member of the Whitney Museum's board of directors, they did not go to the gala farewell.

If they had, they would have run into Mrs. G. Macculloch Miller, the former **Flora Payne** Whitney, and her daughter, Mrs. Michael Irving. They were there to watch the dancers whiz by such economy-size contemporary art works as Roy Lichtenstein's "The Little Big Painting" (68 by 80 inches) and John Day's "I Lie Alone" (43 by 59 inches).

Besides the Secretary General, who was accompanied by Mr. and Mrs. Tin Myint, his son-in-law and daughter, box holders at the Bolshoi Ballet premiere included Mrs. Albert D. Lasker, the philanthropist; Mrs. Vincent Astor, author and philanthropist; Lawrence Wien, whose holdings include the Empire State Building, and David Rockefeller, president of the Chase Manhattan Bank.

Mrs. Robert Scull, the taxi tycoon's wife and pop art collector, was with Fernando Sanchez, who designs lingerie for Warner Brothers. Lord Caradon, Britain's delegate to the United Nations, was with his wife.

Harry Belafonte was at the Bolshoi, too, along with Mrs. Murray Fuhrman, the physician's wife who was chairman of the benefit; Chief S. O. Adebo, United Nations delegate from Nigeria; Nikolai T. Federenko, United Nations delegate from the Soviet Union; Robert S. Benjamin, board chairman of United Artists and president of the United Nations Association for the U. S. A., and Mrs. Barry Feinstein, who is the Mary of the Peter, Paul and Mary singing trio. None of them went to the Kips Bay dinner dance.

"I'm exhausted and I'm not really trying to do very much," said Mrs. S. George Zauderer, who was recovering at Kips Bay from a dinner she herself had given on the previous night. "If anybody asks me to anything more, I don't know what I'll do."

Mrs. Zauderer, whose husband is in the investment business, was with Anthony M. Del Balso and his wife, chairman of the ball.

"Everybody gives parties in April," Mrs. Del Balso moaned. "Everyone comes back from Florida bursting with energy and ready to go."

Charles J. Hollerith Jr., the stage producer, and his wife had apparently not been in Florida. But they were there, too.

"It's enough to get my husband out for one event," said Mrs. Hollerith, who was gowned in emerald green by Arnold Scaasi and wore emeralds and diamonds. "But we did go to a cocktail party."

Meanwhile, back at the Biddle home, where two-week-old James Copeland Biddle was the central attraction, his mother was doing more than reading and watching television. While her husband was at the New York City Ballet, she was planning her own benefit.

"I'm on a committee to save Olana, the Frederick Church house in the Hudson River Valley," she said. "Our benefit's going to be held at Knoedler's in May. I hope there's no conflict."

JUNE 19, 1966.

Le Parc Takes Painting Prize For Kinetic Works at Venice

By HILTON KRAMER

Special to The New York Times

VENICE, Italy, June 18—The first prize for painting at the Venice Biennale was awarded today to an Argentine artist, Julio Le Parc, who is not in any conventional sense a painter. The first prize for sculpture was shared by the Frenchman Etienne Martin and a Danish sculptor, Robert Jacobsen.

In the category of prizes specifically designated for Italian artists, Lucio Fontana was given the top award for painting and Alberto Viani for sculpture.

Each of these four awards, one of them to be shared in this case, brings two million Italian lire ($3,200). But the real benefits of the prizes are the exhibitions and sales that inevitably follow in their wake.

No American artist received any award this year. Two years ago the first prize in painting went to the American Robert Rauschenberg, an award that caused a scandal whose repercussions could still be felt at this year's Biennale. Among the other prizes, the David E. Bright Foundation of Los Angeles gave three awards of 500,000 lire each to the German sculptor Günter Haese, the French pop painter Martial Raysse and the English sculptor Anthony Caro. The Bright Foundation also awarded a smaller prize, 100,000 lire, to Arthur Luis Piza of Brazil.

The $1,000 prize awarded by the American collectors Mr. and Mrs. Robert C. Scull went to the young English painter Richard Smith. The Scull award specifically excludes American artists. Other minor awards went to Masuo Ikeda, Ezio Gribaudo, Enrico Castellani, Mario Ceroli, Constant, Milan Laluha and Vasso Katraki.

Mr. Le Parc is a kinetic constructionist whose exhibition at the Howard Wise Gallery in New York last fall attracted some attention. Though he is not especially well known, it is widely assumed that the prize went to Mr. Le Parc as the result of a deadlock in the jury. This year's deliberations are said to have been the fiercest in many years. In awarding the painting prize to an artist who is not a painter, the jury is reported to have recommended that the conventional division of the prizes into painting and sculpture categories be abandoned in the future.

Altogether, this year's Biennale seems to have been concerned from the beginning to discredit painting as an independent art. Only the Scull award to Richard Smith and an award by the United Nations Educational Scientific and Cultural Organization (given by a separate jury) to the German painter Horst Antes have granted painting any official recognition.

The emphasis in this year's Biennale has been on theatrical installations, Kinetic "environments" and pop art sideshows. In this sense, Mr. Le Parc is indeed representative of the spirit that has prevailed in the exhibition as a whole.

SEPTEMBER 12, 1966.

Bergdorf Imports Long Coats --- Some Short Ones, Too

By BERNADINE MORRIS

ANDREW GOODMAN, the president of Bergdorf Goodman, said he liked the two calf-length outfits that opened the store's import collection Friday, but Mrs. Stavros Niarchos, wife of the shipping magnate, and Mrs. Robert Scull, wife of the taxi tycoon, weren't so sure.

"I guess they're great for Paris and Zhivago country where it's so cold," said Mrs. Scull, who was among the private customers viewing the first formal showing of European haute couture fashions. Mrs. Scull was wearing a pink and purple checked Chanel coat and skirt with a pink blouse, and noticed that there weren't any Chanels in the collection. She wasn't very concerned because she admitted she had closets full at home.

Mrs. Niarchos, who is the former Charlotte Ford, commented that the long styles "don't fit in with things today." Her sleeveless brown wool dress was by Princess Irene Galitzine, who also was not represented in the Bergdorf collection. It reversed to white and gray dots and cleared her knees with room to spare.

Mr. Goodman said he didn't expect the long skirts to catch on this year, but he thought they might exercise a restraining influence on the young.

"I'm a little alarmed with the skirts I see in the street," he said. "Some of the young crowd seem to be going around in loin cloths."

One of the long styles that elicited these comments was Dior's green and black coat with a high leather belt. The second was a beige tweed suit by Fabiani with a long skirt that buttoned over a matching short one.

While the long clothes almost stopped the show, it managed to go on, and about 60 other styles appeared, roaming freely over the Paris haute couture. Givenchy and Dior were represented by eight styles each, Balenciaga by six.

There were a few styles by Laroche, Patou, Castillo, Ricci, Saint Laurent and Grès. Even Balmain and Dessès, who rarely appear in import collections here, were represented.

The collection as a whole was strong on big coats, including Givenchy's white one with a brown leather belt pulled through slits at the sides and tied at front, and a pale blue coat reversing to white by Fabiani.

It was accompanied by a narrow blue wool dress, which provided an excellent background for the hats that Bergdorf's custom milliner, Halston, brought back from Paris. They included Balenciaga's small white visored cap, Saint Laurent's nailhead-studded helmet, and Lanvin's puffy chartreuse beret, all snappy enough to be worn with above-the-knee skirts.

Prices for the clothes start at $800 in the store's custom salon on the second floor.

SEPTEMBER 27, 1966.

Ohrbach's and Alexander's Battle to Hectic Draw in High-Fashion Clash

34TH ST. TEAM IS SALES VICTOR

But Uptowners Have Edge in Attracting Society—Fans Crowd Arenas

By ENID NEMY

THE two giants in the line-for-line copying of European couture fashions met head-on yesterday. Both emerged clutching laurels.

Alexander's may have rated a slight edge in attracting society figures; Ohrbach's leaned heavily on show-business celebrities, but when it came to the jingle of the cash register, the 34th Street store won hands down.

The day was astounding, confusing and, for someone like Mrs. John V. Lindsay, who goes to few fashion shows, it was "amusing."

For Ohrbach's, the store that began the whole thing by integrating fashion and society at its special showings, and Alexander's, the Bronx-born store that branched out to 58th Street for its finishing school course, had scheduled their customers' shows for the same day.

Ohrbach's had reserved its date last March. The store informed Ruth Finley, publisher of Fashion Calendar, a listing of industry events, that its showings would be on Sept. 26 at 12:45 P.M. (A second show was held at 5:45 P.M.)

Alexander's decision to hold its shows on the same date was announced in May. A spokesman said that George Farkas, chairman of the board, wanted to have the show on Monday and the choice of the same date was a "coincidence." He added that when Mr. Farkas learned that Ohrbach's would be showing the same day, "He considered it a challenge."

It was touch and go the whole day as members of the Social Register, actresses, diplomats' spouses and just plain housewives scurried between the two stores by whatever means available, from chauffeur-driven limousines to subway.

At Ohrbach's, the password was chaos, but it was the kind of chaos appreciated by the accounting department. Even before daylight dawned, members of the affluent society who enjoy bargains had slipped in the back (35th Street) entrance of the store for their pre-show fittings and purchases. By the time the store officially opened (10:15 A.M.) and the red carpet was laid at the front entrance, the scene inside was bedlam.

The Search Is On

"Where's somebody to take my money?" Where's the gold Chanel?" "Where's the brown Balenciaga?" The voices had lost their well-bred tones.

"Moddom, everything is on the floor," replied the harried sales clerks.

On 58th Street, all was serene. Young girls decorated with tri-color rubbons (red, white and blue and greens, red and white) stood at each escalator and on the third floor, 1,500 wooden chairs surrounded the runway, awaiting the first of four scheduled shows. Two of them—at 11 A.M. and 3 P.M.—were for the benefit of the Soldiers, Sailors' and Airmen's Club (at $5 a seat) and the remaining shows—at 1 PM. and 6 P.M.—were for the general public on a first-come, first-served basis.

There were several customers in the fitting rooms, but as at Ohrbach's, others had been in last week to look over the dresses and place their orders (Mrs. Searle Whitney for a pink Patou gown and Mrs. Thomas Hitchock for a Fabiani brocade ensemble). Still others left their final decisions until after the show.

At 10:15 A.M. the first of the women with $5 reserved seats arrived.

Backstage, the titled women who had been imported to model the collection ("The shows for the general public won't have the royalty," said a store spokesman) were putting finishing touches on their make-up. Lady James Crichton-Stuart from England, who had finished her own, was brushing eye-liner on Princess Sophie Troubetzkoy of Paris.

"I don't know why they had to have it on a Monday. There is no time to get hair done," moaned the Princess as a young man from Charles of the Ritz-Vidal Sassoon brushed out a long fall (the same hairdresser was credited with the coiffures in Ohrbach's show).

Reseating Mrs. Lindsay

Shortly before show time, Mrs. John V. Lindsay and friend, Mrs. Evan Thomas, wife of the executive vice president of Harper & Row, were escorted to seats in the fourth row. They were spotted by a news photographer, who informed Mrs. James H. Van Alen, a co-chairman of the benefit, who quickly ushered them to places of honor in the front row.

Mrs. Lindsay, in a purple sleeveless dress by Kaspar of Joan Leslie, said she rarely gets to fashion shows and felt "slightly depraved" at the idea of seeing two in one morning.

(Later, at Ohrbach's, she added "I am amused at the number of ladies who have come from Alexander's.")

(There was a small exodus before the end of the show, since Alexander's got off to a late start at 11:30 A.M. Many women were worried about missing Ohrbach's 12:45 P.M. curtain time).

Susan Schein, a 22-year-old redhead who accompanied Lynda Bird Johnson on her recent trip to Spain, was there on her "lunch break." Miss Schein, who is now a "girl Friday" with an architectural concern, penciled her own comments on the program but disappeared immediately after.

Mrs. Raymond Johnson didn't plan to go on to Ohrbach's. She had made her mark for the day in a pants suit of black and white pony by Jacques Kaplan set off with a white leather beret by Adolfo.

A more restrained group, who left only to go to the Colony for lunch, was Mrs. Van Alen, Mrs. John H. G. Pell, Mrs. Lauris Norstad and Mrs. Vincent Astor.

Orhbach's not to be outdone, also had a pants suit in the audience. Mrs. Henry Berger (the former Anita Louise) wore her Ginala design with a ruffled blouse.

Back to Home Base

Mrs. Berger, listed as a patroness for the Alexander show, planned to hop over there for the afternoon showing, as did Mrs. T. Suffern Tailer, another Alexander patroness who was wearing an Ohrbach Chanel copy she had just bought.

Mrs. William Wrightson, whose husband is a cousin of Huntington Hartford ("We're the quiet part of the family") got up before dawn for her drive in from Rumson, N. J.

"The chauffeur drove me out of Jersey when it was still dark," she said. "My husband thinks I'm crazy."

Mrs. Wrightson bought Balenciaga's feather dress for $450 even before it appeared on the runway. She had hoped to wear it to a ball on Oct. 19, but was told there would be a four-week delivery date. She ordered it anyway.

But Mrs. Robert Scull, wife of the taxi tycoon, had more foresight. She got to Ohrbach's last week, as did many of the other knowledgeable women, and reserved the feathered dress and Saint Laurent's brocade ($195), one of the best-sellers. She planned to wear the brocade to a private party last night and the feathered gown to the Whitney Museum opening tonight. She hadn't given much thought to when she would wear her other two purchases—Givenchy's stretch dress at $85 and Balenciaga's madras coat at $295.

Mrs. Henry Fonda had ticked off four numbers during her sortie to Ohrbach's last week (Saint Laurent's velvet cocktail dress, his long long medieval gown, his silvery brocade and Jean Marie Armand's wool gabardine dress).

She brought along her husband yesterday "to approve."

"I don't have a thing to say about it," said Mr. Fonda. "I'm just here."

Mrs. William Paley and her daughter, Mrs. S. Carter Burden Jr., were not present, but were reported to have made their selections last week. Mrs. Burden, who was a major attraction at Ohrbach's spring showing, was replaced this season by Greta Thyssen, an actress who thinks she might be in a new version of "Hellzapoppin." She was the cynosure of all eyes as she was escorted to her front-row seat. She swayed along in a brilliant print jersey by Ken Scott that was either several sizes too small or an indication that the figure has indeed returned.

Miss Thyssen shared her front-row billing with such luminaries as Joan Fontaine; Lisa Kirk, the nightclub singer; Mrs. Gower Champion, the dancer and wife of the director, and Peggy Cass, the television panelist. Also ensconced in the front row was Hope Hamilton, swathed in blue fox and the blondest hair this side of platinum.

OCTOBER 4, 1966.

JANIS ART SHOW VISITED BY POLICE

Unhurried View of Erotica Prevented by Crowd's Size

A much-heralded show of erotic art mildly titillated nearly 1,000 viewers at the Sidney Janis Gallery last evening, but for the moment at least failed to arouse the police.

A uniformed police captain and a sergeant called at the gallery early yesterday morning and left with a copy of the show's catalogue. They were, said Sidney Janis, the gallery's owner, "civil and a little bit reticent."

At 5:45 P.M., when the crush in the gallery had all but smothered the art, two more policemen appeared. They told Mr. Janis that the gallery was "getting too crowded" and left without taking in the art.

The gallery had limited its cards of admission to adults only, and stationed a Pinkerton man at the door to pick up invitations. The crowd included a highly vocal segment of the New York art and literary scene, including some of the artists represented in the show.

"It's really brought out all the voyeurs," said an art dealer, noting he had come only to escort a young lady friend. "It's a vast deception, fantastically watered down," said Herb Brown, a painter of erotic art whose work had not been chosen for the show.

But Mrs. Robert Scull, a well-known collector, thought well of it. "It's very beautiful, very exciting," she said. "Why does everyone get so hysterical?" Sidney Kingsley, the playwright said, "I think it's all very sweet and innocent."

The biggest attraction was an exhibition by Bob Watts called "4-Film Cinema for Environment." A flickering melange of anatomical sections thrown on the walls of a darkened room, it broke down early in the evening.

Another temperamental work was Larry Rivers's electrifying "Lamp Man Loves It," a giant piece that vied with Mr. Watts's work in viewer popularity. One of its bulbs began to flicker, and the artist had to dash out for a replacement.

By 6:30, a queue had formed in the lobby of the building at 15 East 57th Street, waiting for elevator space. Mr. Janis said he expected the crowd would "continue to build until the show is over." He also noted that he did not expect police action.

"People who expected a sizzling show were bound to be disappointed," he said. "I told the police we've been doing serious shows for 18 years and were not out for publicity."

OCTOBER 24, 1966.

But Will Paper Dresses Pass the Test of Time?

By JUDY KLEMESRUD

Special to The New York Times

HARTFORD, CONN., Oct. 23—Paper dresses passed the acid test here last night as 150 women danced everything from the frug to the fox trot in them at the Wadsworth Atheneum's Paper Dress Ball.

The only near-disaster—a torn shoulder strap on a gown designed by Jon Haggins for his model, Myrna—was quickly mended with a roll of cellophane tape that Haggins carried in his pocket "just for emergencies."

The art museum ball, the traditional opener of the Insurance City's social season, was sponsored this year by the museum's women's committee for the benefit of the building fund. It netted $5,000, said the chairman, Mrs. B. Rush Field, who described the ball as "the most glamorous we've ever had."

Mrs. Field, whose husband is an investment banker, wore a short A-line dress covered with multicolored paper flowers that was designed for her by Bill Blass.

"It's lovely," she said, "but frankly I think I'm a little old to be wearing my dresses two inches above my knees." Mrs. Field is 54.

Other costumes at the ball included a paper pants suit covered with paillettes, a dress that was "whipped up in 45 minutes" out of white bathroom tissue by T. M. Prentice, a Manhattan architect, for his wife, and Rudi Gernreich's transparent plastic dress with paper decals pasted on in strategic places.

The Gernreich dress was modeled at midnight by his mannequin, Peggy Moffitt, who introduced the California designer's topless bathing suit two years ago. Miss Moffitt wore the bottom half of a red bikini under the plastic dress, and a paper headdress that looked like a cross between something Cleopatra and Chief Sitting Bull might have worn.

"I guess you might call it peep art," Mr. Gernreich said as some of the 700 guests, who had paid $35 a couple for tickets, stopped in the middle of a vigorous Charleston to crowd around Miss Moffitt for a closer look at the garment.

"I'm predicting it will replace the basic black dress," the designer said, trying hard to suppress a smile.

When a photographer asked Roger L. Stevens, chairman of the National Council for the Arts, to pose with Miss Moffitt, he refused but said he thought paper dresses were "marvelous ideas."

"But I really can't give them my approval," he added, "because every time the Government approves of something, it tends to kill the idea."

James Elliott, who was named director of the 124-year-old museum last May, was wearing an orange and gold paper cummerbund that matched his wife's gown. He said the paper ball theme was chosen because of the current interest in paper dresses and because the museum's first charity ball in 1936 had a paper theme at which the decorations were made of newsprint.

"We like to combine tradition with innovation here," Mr. Elliott said. "We were the first museum in America to have a Picasso exhibition, and he seems to have done quite well."

Mrs. Rebekah Harkness, philanthropist and art patron, wore a red, white and blue paper gown designed by Tzaims Luksus. The pattern matched a huge octopus-shaped pin by Salvador Dali that she wore on her left shoulder. In the center of the pin is a pearl known as the Star of the Sea.

"I guess it's one of the largest pearls in the world," Mrs. Harkness said, adding that she had never counted the number of rubies, diamonds and emeralds the pin contained.

Wearing a black, gray and white Luksus gown was Mrs. Robert Scull, a former model who asked that her husband be called "a well-known art collector" and not "a taxi-cab tycoon."

Mrs. Scull said she wore her paper dress all the way from New York instead of changing into it at the museum as many women did "because I felt if it's a dress, I shouldn't worry."

At the museum's request, Mr. Luksus designed six dresses for the ball, and said he tried to match the dresses to the women's personalities. He was quick to point out that the colors in Mrs. Scull's dress didn't mean she had a drab personality.

"My wife's is black and white, and I certainly don't think she's dull," he said.

Other designers asked by the museum to create paper ballgowns were Elisa Daggs, Judith Brewer, Margot West and Gene Neil. Many of the dresses they designed will be donated to the museum's costume collection.

Fabric designers who donated their services included Julian Tomchin, Tom Isbell, Peter Max and Gene Silbert.

"It's still hard for me to believe that people will do things for free," said Samuel J. Wagstaff, curator of paintings. "The only thing we had to pay for was a $14 charge for shipping the paper here for the women who wanted to make their own dresses."

Mr. Wagstaff said that 750 yards of Kaycel, the official paper fabric of the ball, was donated by Kimberly-Stevens. He said the fact that a daughter of one of the company's executives worked for the museum probably had something to do with it.

The museum's Avery Court, a main floor area that is three stories high, was decorated with a neon ceiling sculpture resembling the aurora borealis by James Rosenquist, the pop artist. Hanging from the sculpture were strips of silver paper resembling icicles.

A large, 17th-century Flemish statue called Venus Attended by Nymph and Satyr, by Pietro Francavilla, was draped in the same silver paper.

There was only one paper moon, and it was pinned to the head of Mrs. Monty Purdy, who came dressed as Diana the Huntress. The white and gold paper costume that she made included a golden bow and arrow and golden sandals.

Her husband, who is vice president of New Medical Techniques, Inc., a medical supply company in Stamford, Conn., said he was wearing disposable paper underwear so he could feel in the spirit of things.

About 2:10 this morning, after Paul Landerman's band had played "Good Night Ladies" and the last guests were trickling out of the museum, one blonde matron, who refused to identify herself, said:

"I can't believe what's happened to sedate Hartford. It's like being in an Italian movie."

NOVEMBER 8, 1966.

Patterns and Colors Steal the Show

By BERNADINE MORRIS

PANTS, at least the daytime variety, received short shrift as New York spring fashion shows entered their second week yesterday.

"You're not going to see any pants suits, bloomers or lace underpants," Vincent Monte-Sano promised before the Monte-Sano & Pruzan coat and suit collection was shown. He kept his promise.

Three-quarters of the Maurice Rentner collection was over before Bill Blass, the designer, showed his first pants outfit. It was in black lace and, like the printed silk ones that followed, was meant to be worn late in the evening when pants have long been socially acceptable. Other evening pants were only glimpsed through the side-slits of the long dresses they accompanied.

With the pants issue out of the way, designers were free to concentrate on what seems to be the major spring fashion development: the use of colors so strong they seem to vibrate, and patterns that accent the shock.

"Women who never wore a bizarre print before will do so next spring," Mr. Blass said confidently.

With his jagged lightning stripes, brilliantly colored abstractions and patterns admittedly inspired by a kaleidoscope, he seems to have gone as far as it is possible to go in this direction.

But the shapes are simple, like the tent dress that shows no signs of vanishing. In addition to the wild prints, it shows up in cotton brocade, heavy silk crepe (stark except for a stripe or two of beading) and fragile-looking laces that shine with a metallic glitter.

The laces brought a swift reaction from the corner of the room where Mr. Blass's private admirers sat in their winter costumes calculating their spring wardrobes.

A number of them wore touches of fur—Mrs. Michel Legendre's peach-colored coat by Jacques Heim and Mrs. Robert C. Scull's gray checked tweed by Chanel both had white mink collars. Mrs. Legendre is the wife of the French Consul General in New York, and Mr. Scull collects pop art. Mrs. Frederick Eberstadt, whose husband is a photographer, wore Saint Laurent's white vinyl coat horizontally striped in black mink.

The applause from their corner indicated that Mr. Blass was on the right track with his metallic laces—and his flounced black lace dresses too.

The response to Mr. Blass's jumper outfits was less spontaneous. There were narrow skirts that rose under the bosom and had suspender straps that made them look even longer than the tent dresses. They were worn with white blouses and short jackets — some sleeveless — that kept the straps under cover.

Belted waistlines also appeared in some of the spring daytime costumes, but these also were concealed by the jacket or coat that topped the tuck-in blouse and skirt. Prices start at $150.

Mr. Monte-Sano, who is convinced that women are confused by some of the oddments offered them in the name of fashion, held up a chart diagraming succinctly his three basic spring silhouettes.

Women who pay $300 or more for his spring outfits should have no trouble identifying the tube as the relaxed, straight silhouette they have felt comfortable in for years; the winged T-shape as the sleeveless or short-sleeved coat that shelters a bare-shouldered dress or a suit, and the cone as the gently flared coat or suit that enables them to kick up their heels.

In vivid plaids, vibrant geometric patterns or sharp greens, yellows or pinks, these shapes express the way women want to look today, according to Mr. Monte-Sano.

This season he is carrying on alone the concern started 42 years ago by his father and Max Pruzan. Mr. Pruzan retired last March and Jacques Tiffeau, the designer who had been with the concern for more than a decade, left a few months later to concentrate on his own business, Tiffeau & Busch, Ltd.

Mr. Monte-Sano is determined to dress women "as women — not children or freaks," he said.

NOVEMBER 11, 1966.

The Painting on the Dress Said 'Fragile'

"I DON'T like his work," said a skinny young man clutching some textbooks covered in wrappers marked St. Francis College. "But I came anyway to see Andy Warhol because he's a phenomenon."

Of the 80 or so people crowded around a silver tinsel - wrapped platform Wednesday afternoon on the street floor of Abraham & Straus, about three-quarters of them were young people, apparently from Brooklyn schools, who seemed to have come for the same reason.

At 2:30 P.M., the phenomenon settled into the back of a limousine the store had sent for him and other members of the Velvet Underground.

The Underground, Mr. Warhol explained, is "our rock 'n' roll group. We travel around the country to all sorts of different places, museums and big dance halls. It's sort of funny, we haven't gotten the young kids. It's sort of the other group—the smart people."

On the trip to Abraham & Straus, where Mr. Warhol was to paint some plain white do-it-yourself paper dresses that are sold for $2 with their own paintbox, the artist fingered the rhinestone scarf Tiger Morse, the fashion designer, had just given him, and complained softly that he couldn't find any "classic tacky leather jackets"—like the one he was wearing — in the stores anymore.

Nico, who was to wear the dresses while they were being painted, sat near him in the back of the car, fingering her long blond hair, a little longer and a bit darker than Mr. Warhol's silver blond tresses, which matched the pale, luminescent make-up on his face.

A Psychedelic Pioneer

"She's the first psychedelic singer," said Mr. Warhol, nodding toward Nico, who sings with the Velvet Underground. "They do like two-hour-long songs, with only buzzing from a burglar alarm in between."

In the front of the car was Gerard Malanga, a dancer with the group, who was going to do the actual work on stage while Mr. Warhol supervised. Next to him was Paul Morrissey ("He's our mama, so we don't get lost on the road," Nico said, laughing), who was holding Ari, Nico's 4-year-old son.

"I have to make Ethel Scull a dress because she's going to a fancy dress party," said Mr. Warhol, smoothing down several large painted-paper bananas that were lying across his lap. "I thought I might paste some paper bananas on a dress at the store," he said.

There was a densely packed crowd standing in the narrow corner around the paper dress boutique when they arrived.

"I wonder if paper dresses are better than vinyl," Mr. Warhol murmured uncertainly as he moved toward the platform. "What do you think? Vinyl ones are so beautiful, but they're uncomfortable, hot."

Nico came back from a dressing room where she had changed from her camel-colored wool slacks into the plain white paper shift, little-girl white lace stockings and T-strap shoes. She stretched out full-length on a bleached oak desk covered with paper towels that had been hastily brought up on stage for the show.

Mr. Malanga held a metal silk-screen frame over the supine Nico while Mr. Warhol poured magenta paint through it. Little Ari, crouched under the desk, sprayed phosphorescent green paint on his mother's stockings.

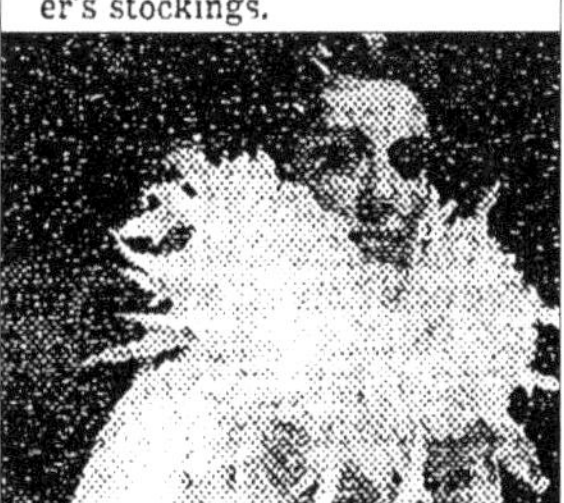

A Gregorian chant-like monotony of amplified guitars and male voices drummed through a loudspeaker. Then Nico's voice on a recording came on singing "All Tomorrow's Parties."

Nico adjusted her position on the table and the silk-screening was continued on her hip. Down the front of the dress, in bright magenta, over and over, was the word: FRAGILE.

"It's just scraps from around the house," Mr. Warhol had explained earlier, pointing to the silk screen frame. "I never really worked with them."

The audience watched quietly, looking more dazed than interested.

"How can you say he's painting it," said a round-faced teen-ager who was carrying a book entitled "Art In the Early Church." "All he did was design the stencil."

"It's no different than Rodin," her companion rejoined, uncertainly. "He made the clay model and somebody else sculpted."

"I came by purposely all the way from the Bronx," said a small, motherly looking woman with glasses. "I saw his pictures of Marilyn Monroe in that new museum the day it opened."

A stout woman standing nearby sniffed loudly. "That's a good painter? I could do it better myself. I thought he was going to handpaint, not just spill the paint all over."

"What is the purpose of this?" a woman called out from the back of the crowd as Mr. Warhol glued the paper bananas on another white paper dress Nico had changed into.

A woman from the store's feature events department took the microphone. "This is to show you what you could do yourself with the white paper dresses and the paint kit," she explained. "These dresses Mr. Warhol is doing now are going to be donated to the Brooklyn Museum," she announced.

The audience tittered. Applause broke out in several quarters.

A recess was called as Mr. Warhol attached the last banana.

"The whole thing is like a dime store," Mr. Warhol said, looking around happily as he walked off the platform. "You know how you used to go to a dime store when you were a kid. Oh, that's it. They ought to sell paper dresses in the dime store."

Ingrid Superstar Arrives

He paused, looking thoughtful. "If Reagan can win, we can do paper dresses," he said, as Ingrid Superstar suddenly appeared on the platform.

"Yes, that's her name, Ingrid Superstar," said Mr. Warhol. "She's with the Velvet Underground too."

"She's always late for these things," Mr. Malanga said bitterly, casting a sidelong glance at the fluttering Ingrid, who wore a chain of heavy metal hearts around her neck.

In the seventh floor executive conference room to which the Warhol party adjourned for a half-time press conference, Ari wandered around sleepily, clutching a pack of chocolate Chesterfield cigarettes to his narrow chest.

A spruce-looking young man in a business suit stepped up and introduced himself.

"I'm Ronald Bard," he said, "vice president of the Mars Manufacturing Company. We make the dresses."

"We made a movie last night," Mr. Warhol was saying in the corner, as he sat back in a fake Gothic chair. "It was about being paranoid in a dress shop. It's called 'Paranoia.'"

Mr. Morrissey leaned forward. "He made a movie yesterday afternoon, too," he said.

"Yes," said Mr. Warhol. "It starred my mother, who played an aging peroxide movie star with a lot of husbands. We're trying to bring back old people," he said, a little sadly, and he got ready to go back downstairs, where he thought he might stamp his name all over one of the paper dresses.

NOVEMBER 12, 1966.

Society Wears Its Dreams to Go to a Party

By JUDY KLEMESRUD

ABOUT 250 people displayed the stuff their dreams are made of Thursday night at the Watson Keep Blairs' "Come as Your Favorite Dream" party. Judging from the costumes, nightmares are quite prevalent among the affluent these days.

Charles Addams, the cartoonist, looked like a monk, but said he was a "defrocked ghoul."

Mrs. C. Suydam Cutting, Mrs. Blair's aunt and wife of the retired art collector, wore a 50-year-old silver wig and a black eye patch because she wanted to be "a bad dream."

Valerian Rybar, the interior designer, said he was a "switched-on dream" in his black leather motorcycle suit with a white crash helmet that had a revolving red light on top.

Susan Stein, daughter of the president of the Music Corporation of America, wore a silver motorcycle suit with a baby blue crash helmet, "because I don't want to get hurt if I have another accident." (Last winter she suffered head injuries when she fell off a motorcycle in Bermuda and wasn't wearing a helmet.)

The party, in honor of Mrs. Blair's daughter, Mrs. Philip Harari (the former Mary McFadden), of Johannesburg, South Africa, was held in the Blairs' five-story town house at 109 East 64th Street. It marked Mrs. Harari's first visit to New York since she married the de Beers diamond executive two years ago.

Girl of the Future

Mrs. Harari was dressed as "a girl from the year 2200." Her costume, designed by Halston, the custom milliner at Bergdorf Goodman, included shocking pink tights and a shocking pink turtleneck pullover. Sewn to her shoulders were strips of pink, silver and green metallic foil that billowed to the floor.

"I wish I could be reincarnated in the 23d century," she said. "We could be in Mars, and jet around the world, and nobody would look old, because estrogen and silicon would be perfected by then."

Originally, Mrs. Harari was to have worn a see-through body stocking under the strips of foil, with shocking pink pasties to keep her from being arrested.

"My husband didn't think it was appropriate," she said.

Mrs. Blair, whose husband is a vice president of Morgan Guaranty Trust Company of New York, came to her own party dressed as a concert pianist. ("I *can* play, you know.")

About 20 spectators, who stood in a drizzle to watch the guests arrive, appeared to be having as much fun as the merrymakers inside. A chauffeur who said he was rented for the evening, "just like most of the other guys here," performed magic tricks for them.

The onlookers included Thomas Cordray, an employe of the Jamaica Tent Company, who installed a canopy over the entrance of the town house at 8:30 P.M. He sat in his car parked in front of the town house until the party was over, then took the dripping canopy down.

Paper dresses were everywhere, and one of the most unusual was made of huge yellow and black paper bananas by Andy Warhol, the pop artist, for Mrs. Robert C. Scull, whose husband owns taxicabs and collects pop art.

Although state law makes it illegal to wear a mask on the streets of Manhattan, several guests arrived in them. Halston, who came as a cheetah ("This is the year for cheetahs"), said he planned to wear his mask all evening if he could stand it. His date, Minnie Cushing, daughter of Mr. and Mrs. Howard G. Cushing of Newport, was also a cheetah.

James D. Robinson 3d, an investment officer for the Morgan Guaranty Trust Company of New York, wore a huge bull's mask and a sign that said: "I'm dreaming of the time to jump back into the market." His wife, representing the stock market, wore a gold lamé dress and a headdress of flowing ticker tapes.

Lesley (Topsy) Taylor, who divides her time between Newport and New York, where she is a beauty editor for Vogue magazine, said she wore a plunging black brassiere and a long skirt made of African fabric because she dreamed she went to Africa in her Maidenform bra.

Mrs. William S. Paley, wife of the board chairman of CBS, wore Norman Norell's silver sequined evening pajamas. "I'm a fish," she said.

Mrs. Anne McDonnell Ford, representing "a plain dream," wore Irene Galitzine's long, pale green silk coat trimmed with gold, gold lamé pajamas, and a gold lamé ribbon in her hair.

Dreams of Green Hornet

William M. Fine, publisher of Harper's Bazaar and Town and Country magazines, wore the costume the Green Hornet wears on the television series. He said it wasn't too difficult obtaining it, because he is a director of the company that produces the show.

"It's Marilyn Monroe," a bystander exclaimed as Mrs. Jaquelin T. Robertson slinked by in a silver wig, a silver fox stole, and a tight blue silk dress. "No, I'm Marlene Dietrich, the blue angel," she replied with a heavy German accent. Mr. Robertson, an architect, came as Gen. Jeb Stuart of the Confederate Army.

Mrs. Thomas Kempner, wife of the investment banker, wore a white leotard covered with white ostrich plumes and a headdress of white ostrich plumes. "I started off as a white ostrich," she said, "but my children told me I should be the white rabbit from Alice in Wonderland."

Her husband wore a black velvet smoking jacket because he said he dreamed he could spend an evening at home once in a while.

Mr. and Mrs. Alfred Gwynne Vanderbilt, both in gold brocaded jackets and black pants, came jointly as Camelot.

Looking like a Spanish flamenco dancer, Oscar de la Renta, the dress designer, escorted Anita Colby, the beauty writer and former model, who wore a bright pink caftan that he designed.

"I dreamed I was a Harper's Bazaar model," she said.

At one point late in the

party, while records played by Slim Hyatt, disk jockey at Shepheard's, were going full blast, Andrew Murphy, a television salesman who lives a block away, strolled over to see what was going on.

"Oh, a party," he said, obviously revieved. "For a minute I thought a discothèque had opened in the neighborhood."

JANUARY 1, 1967.

Art Notes

. . . And an Arty New Year

By GRACE GLUECK

IF only a Happening would happen in the Great Hall of the Metropolitan Museum. If Henry Geldzahler could find the campy furniture he seeks. If the Government would just increase its financial support of the arts!

As the 1967 New Year's bells ring out, these and other vital wishes are being wished by people who, in one way or another, made news on the 1966 Art Front.

Thomas P. Hoving, Parks Commissioner and newly appointed director of New York's Metropolitan Museum:

"I wish that at the Metropolitan I could help to make as many people as possible have the same kinetic thrill as I do when I look at a great work of art—to communicate to them something of the excitement of the time in which it was made, the excitement that impelled its creator to fashion it."

Lawrence Alloway, ex-curator of the Guggenheim Museum, now writer-in-residence at the University of Southern Illinois:

"I wish they'd round the corners of the Whitney Museum so we'd have two Guggenheims."

Harold Rosenberg, author, critic, now a member of the Committee for Social Thought at the University of Chicago:

"I want people to think more. That's my wish for the art world of 1967."

Stephen Weil, manager, Marlborough-Gerson Gallery:

"I wish that other galleries would get out of show biz and back into art dealings."

Jim Dine, now artist-in-residence at Cornell University:

"I wish I could stay away from New York City forever."

Robert Scull, collector:

"I hope for a year of worthy creations by newer and older artists. I also pray for an end of the Vietnamese war, so that we can all enjoy these beautiful things so much more."

Howard Lipman, collector of contemporary sculpture:

"I'm running out of space, so I wish for a breed of sculptor who makes things the size I can use — preferably miniatures."

Sidney Janis, 57th St. dealer whose gallery staged last fall's Erotic Art show:

"I wish Tom Hoving would put on a Hapening at the Metropolitan Museum and invite artists who really create Happenings. I wish also for a larger and larger audience of exhibition visitors of the younger generation, who really dig the new."

Andy Warhol, pop artist turned cinematographer, creator of the current "The Chelsea Girls":

"I wish the city would stay like it is right now—everything's so great. Lindsay has made it all so marvelous. I wish for a President like Lindsay."

Henry Geldzahler, associate curator of American paintings at the Metropolitan Museum, now program director in the visual arts for the National Council on the Arts:

"I, wish there was more Federal money to give to artists in 1967. And I wish for some 1930's furniture for my apartment."

Leo Castelli, dealer:

"I would like it to be a great season for everyone on the scene. More activities and more circuses—why not?"

Barnett Newman, controversial artist and senior exhibitor at the 1965 São Paulo Bienal:

"I would like to see stopped those artists and their art-politics writer-friends who are always polluting the air by praising their own "integrity" and each other's, while constantly raising a stink about their betters. And Happy New Year to everybody!"

JANUARY 11, 1967.

Halston: A Balance of Fact and Fancy

By ENID NEMY

THE star of yesterday's show at Bergdorf Goodman was too busy backstage to appear, but his hats and his ready-to-wear spoke for him.

Halston, the milliner-in-residence for custom-made hats and latter-day designer of boutique clothes, had his stiffest competition from the illustrious audience assembled for his spring collection.

There were names from the Social Register (Mrs. Frank Ellis Pierce 3d, Mrs. Joseph A. Thomas, Mrs. Boyd P. de Brossard) and literary names (Anita Loos, Jacqueline Susann). There were representatives of the art collecting world (Mrs. Robert Scull) and the cosmetics industry (Mrs. Charles Revson).

There were the flamboyant in fashion and the restrained, herded together in long rows of chairs that virtually preempted the fourth floor. Boots of every length and material nudged alligator pumps; Galanos and Norell coats rubbed shoulders with leopard and mink; chin-tied sombreros vied with little beanie caps.

Fashionable Shepherds

And shepherding the flock were Jo Hughes, the super-saleswoman who refused a title when she slid over to Bergdorf's last year from De Pinna, and Elieth Roux who, just about the same time, exchanged her title as assistant manager of the House of Dior in Paris for the position of co-directrice of the store's custom department.

Eventually, the cheek-kissing ran its course and the hum of gossip dimmed to allow recorded sound effects and music to reverberate throughout the room.

Halston was prepared to offer further proof of why his name is synonymous with well-dressed women.

The brief, swiftly paced show was a delicate balance of fact and fancy. The fact was manipulation of shape that relied on design alone; the fancy emerged in the touches of humor and flashes of bravado that announced a secret delight in fun rather than reason.

Thundering Sound Effects

The sound of a thunderstorm introduced his suggestion on how to look in the rain. A pale blue pants suit had a long safari jacket and matching visored cap; a beige suit, with an eased skirt, was worn with a stitched hat with a rolled brim.

And then the sunshaders came out, with a good number of the hats large enough to be parasols. Gigantic cartwheels, bretons and off-the-face designs were done in solid and striped lacquered straws and straws combined with prints to match a dress.

The biggest, for a summer garden wedding (but not for town house gardens unless the guest list is small), was a multilayered white organdy that undulated gently with every movement.

For less formal garden occasions, the designer provided a sunshade cap in green linen, with vinyl inserts, to be worn with his green coveralls and white shirt. For the beach, he suggested a bright orange bikini and billowing robe in terry cloth with a turban in the same fabric.

Classical Millinery Shapes

Halston always excels in his classic shapes in millinery, as he does with his clothes (this season shown with loose belts). His current collection is no exception.

Manipulated berets in felt or multicolored straw; caps that are a cross between a polo cap and a policeman's helmet; pale and softened fedoras and cowboy or sombrero hats, at times tilted up and at others down, all had their turn. The colors went from muted pastels to the vivid, with no middle approach. Often, they were combined in an outfit, as with a clear purple hat that was teamed with a dress and jacket in apricot.

The designer retained his fondness for chin straps, some of which were in the same fabric as the hat and others in gold chains. For his casual designs the straps were fashioned from scarves.

Transparent but discreet was his shirtwaist dress of black synthetic organza, with oversize bow, worn with a halo beret in the same fabric.

His evening ideas are both large and small in scope. A token hat of shocking pink satin was shaped into a stiffened letter X to sit at the back of the head; a chignon hat of curled yellow feathers matched the yoke of a coordinated dress.

Another coordinated evening costume came in the form of a garden of violets planted on a jacket and shown with a cluster of violets covering the back of the head. One of the larger designs was an adaptation of the coolie hat massed with curled green feathers.

JANUARY 20, 1967.

Eating This Jewelry Is Not in Good Taste

By JUDY KLEMESRUD

THOSE long-time favorites at cocktail parties—Ritz crackers and pretzels—are now hanging from women's necks and dangling from their ears.

The pieces are called "bread jewelry" by their creator, John Fischer, a 36-year-old Manhattan painter and sculptor who signs each piece "J. Fischer" in black paint.

"I consider them more valuable than diamonds," Mr. Fischer said, almost gravely. "Bread is the staff of life, and when a person gives such a symbolic gift, it is warmer and must have love in it."

Despite Mr. Fischer's appraisal of his jewelry, so far it hasn't posed any serious economic threat to the girl's best friend. Earrings made of Ritz crackers or pretzels are $2 a pair, and are available in both pierced and screw-back styles. Necklaces are $2.50 ("I'm working on one that will combine both crackers and pretzels—very complex") and bagel paper-weights "bagels are too heavy to wear") cost $3.

The cheapest item, a Ritz cracker pin ($1), can be worn as a protest button without having a slogan painted on it, the bushy-haired artist said. "It stands for 'Make Bread, Not War,'" he said.

To eat or not to eat? "Well, they're covered with epoxy resin, which makes them obnoxious-tasting," he replied. "I could make them without it, but then they might crumble or attract roaches."

Mr. Fischer, who also plays piano with a jazz trio bearing his name, dropped one of the epoxied Ritz cracker earrings on the floor to demonstrate its durability. It remained intact. However, when one of the pretzel earrings was later dropped accidentally, it split in two. Apparently it's all in how you drop them.

The Belgian-born artist's preoccupation with bread began during the occupation of France, where he had fled after Hitler's armies invaded Belgium.

"I had gone through the War without bread," he said, "and then one day we received a shipment of white bread. From then on it took on a mystical quality for me."

In December 1964, Mr. Fischer exhibited several bread sculptures at a show at the Allan Stone Gallery, 48 East 86th Street. Among the works were a loaf of Russian black bread skewered with bolts ("Wounded Bread"), which sold for $150, and three bagels joined by a padlock ("Padlock with Bagels"), which sold for $125.

The bagel sculpture was bought by Robert Scull, the pop art collector and taxicab fleet owner, along with a $175 loaf of bread that had a file baked inside.

Mr. Fischer's bread jewelry is distributed by Mass Art Inc., and is available at Fandango, 141 East 52d Street, where Kenneth Kneitel, an owner, said the items had to be re-ordered several times during Christmas ("People really flipped over the bagel paperweight"), and at The Gift Arbor, 319 Bleecker Street, where the Ritz cracker pin is the number one seller.

At present Mr. Fischer is busy preparing his spring line, which he says will include "many surprises."

"All I can say now is that women will soon be wearing melba toast and matzohs," he said.

JANUARY 22, 1967.

Fashions Lunch Feb. 2 to Benefit Cancer Patients

Society of the Memorial Sloan-Kettering Will Meet at Waldorf

The Society of the Memorial Sloan-Kettering Cancer Center will hold its annual luncheon and fashion show on Feb. 2 in the Grand Ballroom of the Waldorf-Astoria.

Mrs. René Bouché is chairman. Guests will bring rummage that will be sold at the society's Thrift Shop, 1410 Third Avenue to raise funds for free patient care at the Memorial Hospital for Cancer and Allied Diseases.

The luncheon chairmen are Mrs. Zachary Scott, chairman, patronesses; Miss Minnie Cushing, arrangements, and Mrs. William G. Cahan, hostesses.

Mrs. John N. Lindeke is Thrift Shop chairman, and Mrs. Randolph B. Marston is president of the society.

On the luncheon committee are Mrs. Clarence A. Barnes Jr., Mrs. John R. Drexel 3d, Miss Isabel Marting, Mrs. Charles B. Finch, Mrs. Henry T. Mortimer, Mrs. Henry J. Heintz 2d, Mrs. Armin St. George, Mrs. Paul L. Hughes, Mrs. Theodore Weicker, Mrs. Harold L. Behlke, Mrs. Arthur A. Houghton Jr. and Mrs. Gardner Cowles.

Also, Mrs. William Leonard, Mrs. Osborn Elliott, Mrs. Ernest H. Martin, Mrs. Roswell L. Gilpatric, Mrs. Donald Perkins, Mrs. Jacob Javits, Mrs. Donald M. Halsted and Mrs. James Werblow.

Among the patronesses are Mrs. Duncan MacGuigan, Mrs. Jean Mauze, Mrs. Bevan Holliday, Mrs. H. Lawrence Bogert Jr., Mrs. George Hyam, Mrs. Robert C. Scull, Mrs. Thaddeus F. Walkowicz, Mrs. Lauris Norstad, Mrs. Leon A. Radler and Mrs. Bigelow Watts.

Tickets may be obtained from Mrs. Harry Rafter at the society, 444 East 68th Street.

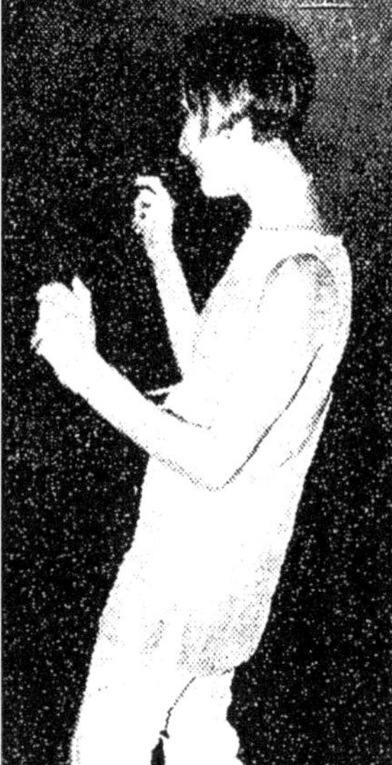

FEBRUARY 7, 1967.

Summer Opens a One-Week Stand on Seventh Avenue

By BERNADINE MORRIS

SEVENTH AVENUE was a street for three seasons yesterday. In the air was the snow of winter; crowding the streets were hand-trucks laden with the clothes of spring; in the showrooms were the first presentations of the styles of summer.

Jacques Tiffeau opened a week of summer fashion shows on the avenue by slashing the sides of bodices, tilting hemlines and having fun with play-clothes, a new area for this coat-and-suit designer.

Traditionally, summer has been a mild little season for fashion, designed to keep the sewing machines going between Easter Sunday, the apotheosis of spring, and July 4, the signal for fall clothes to start arriving in stores.

Not so now at Tiffeau & Busch, at Chester Weinberg, who opened later in the day, or at other designers who will show later in the week. They're using the time to test out ideas for their most serious collection, which is fall.

Two of the ideas being tested are belts, which are making a comeback, and hemlines, which have been so short so long many people feel they have to go down.

Tiffeau, who started his belt-testing with his spring collection a few months ago, seems to have mastered the technique. He manages to wrap sashes around the midriff and waist without losing his easy, relaxed look.

To catch passing glances as well as breezes, his newest décolletage is bare at the sides instead of at the conventional middle. It appears on linen daytime dresses as well as playsuits, which everybody thought were swimsuits.

Some had pointed little overskirts that didn't interfere with his side exposures but did perhaps indicate that Tiffeau, one of the first designers to raise hems well above the knees, was now contemplating lowering them.

As the models in their snappy little dresses dashed across his showroom, a camera crew from the United States Information Agency recorded their movements for a television show to be beamed to many parts of the world.

Lucite jewelry, which Mary Carmen, the designer, calls her "space stuff," dangled from the models' ears and arms.

Miss Carmen, an actress who began making her own earrings six months ago, said Saks Fifth Avenue had bought her designs and Accessocraft, a jewelry manufacturer, would mass-produce some of them.

One mannequin wore three large globes of clear Lucite suspended on a chain from one ear; others had giant Lucite circles on wrist or thigh. Golo's plastic shoes completed the other-wordly effects.

Tiffeau contributed to the today-going-on-tomorrow look with abstract prints, short chiffon dresses gathered from a high waistline and loose shifts draped subtly to one shoulder. Prices start at $125.

Chester Weinberg, whose mood is usually less playful than Tiffeau's, touched some of the same fashion bases. He, too, belted dresses and tinkered with hems.

When belts were at the waist, he balanced the skirt fullness with elbow-length capes or jackets. Many dresses were belted high or shaped high without belts.

"It's fun to start working on a new silhouette—how much can you do with a chemise?" asked the designer, who has headed his own concern for less than a year but has already acquired such fans as Dinah Shore and Mrs. Robert Scull, wife of the pop art collector.

They look to him for "wearable clothes, not too expensive." And with the possible exception of silk jersey bloomers, that is what he provides for summer, with prices starting at $100.

The experimentation takes place at the hem of a couple of side-wrapped shifts. The hem is higher in front than at the sides and back.

FEBRUARY 12, 1967.

A Fashion Show And Party Listed To Aid Italian Art

Rescue Group to Gain at Feb. 22 Event at St. Regis-Sheraton

A gala cocktail party and fashion show will be held at the St. Regis-Sheraton Roof on Feb. 22 for the benefit of the Committee to Rescue Italian Art.

Mrs. Arthur A. Houghton is general chairman for the benefit, which will be underwritten by Martha of Park Avenue. Valentino of Rome will present a preview of his spring collection and will receive the "Martha Award" for outstanding achievement in the world of fashion.

Vice chairmen for the event are Mrs. William G. Cahan and Mrs. Robert C. Scull.

Committee members include Mrs. Vincent Astor, Mrs. William S. Paley, Mrs. Agnew Bahnson, Mrs. Walter C. Baker, Mrs. Philip Bastedo, Mrs. Richard G. Bernhard, Mrs. Roswell Gilpatric, Mrs. Robert Graff, Mrs. Robert L. Hoguet Jr., Mrs. Edward F. Hutton, Mrs. Leonard Bernstein, Mrs. James Biddle and Mrs. George A. Braga.

Others are Mrs. James B. Conant, Mrs. Osborne Elliot, Mrs. Charles W. Engelhard, Mrs. James Fosburgh, Mrs. Edgar W. Garbisch, Mrs. Donald Hyde, Mrs. Mario Pansa, Mrs. E. Bliss Parkinson, Mrs. Paul G. Pennoyer, Mrs. John Barry Ryan, Mrs. Samuel P. Reed, Mrs. John Pierrepont, Mrs. Alfred W. Jones and Mrs. Gilbert Miller.

Also, Mrs. Edward J. Mathews, Mrs. Earl McGarth, Mrs. Paul Moore, Miss Susan Stein, Mrs. Theodore Weicker, Mrs. Arnold Whitridge, Mrs. Edward M. M. Warburg, Ilka Chase, Miss Alice Tully, Mrs. Frank Schiff, Mrs. Maurice Silverstein, Mrs. Charles M. Spofford, Mrs. Kempner Throne, Mrs. Alfred Gwynne Vanderbilt, Mrs. Lowell Weicker, Mrs. Donald B. Straus and Mrs. Walter N. Thayer.

The beneficiary, formed after the floods in northern Italy last fall, is a nationwide volunteer organization sending professional help and materials to Italy.

Further information may be obtained from the group, Room 235, 717 Fifth Avenue.

FEBRUARY 17, 1967.

Pop Fashion: Don't Count It Out

By MARYLIN BENDER

THE fashion diviners, those magazine editors and merchants whose job it is to stimulate obsolescence, say it's dead. Those designers and customers who wished it would go away and stop bothering them, say it's finished, passé.

It's pop fashion, that rebellious explosion detonated simultaneously in 1962 in London's Chelsea and Carnaby Street, in the studios of the ready-to-wear designers of Paris, and in the fertile imagination of American designers such as Rudi Gernreich. The chain reaction reverberated into the haute couture.

Pop fashion, by that or any other name, is here to stay. Crazy stockings and hairdos, grossly synthetic fabrics, comic messages printed on dresses—these can be the ingredients of pop fashion. But, essentially, pop fashion is an irreverent attitude that bridles at solemnity about clothes.

Pop in Paris Haute Couture

The spring haute couture showings in Paris last month and the recent spate of summer collections on Seventh Avenue made it clear that pop has not gone away. Yves Saint Laurent, who only got around to putting pop art symbols like ruby lips and pink torsos on jersey dresses last fall, used African sculptures and a flowered bridal bikini for gags.

Plastic, the one material that comes to mind when pop is mentioned, was utilized by Pauline Trigère, the Seventh Avenue elegante. Oscar de la Renta, pet designer of the pedigreed, used it too.

Even James Galanos, who practices haute couture on a ready-made basis, strewed daisies on the kind of vinyl that looks like a kitchen tablecloth. He combined it with white piqué for patio pajamas for industrialists' wives.

By contrast, Rudi Gernreich (whose topless bathing suit of 1964 cast aside all doubts that the pop era had dawned) and Jacques Tiffeau (like Gernreich, a pioneer of the hiked hemline and the cutout) behaved rather tranquilly.

Their once radical ideas are now accepted fashion currency. Gernreich thinks that fashion is in a state of transition anyway. Tiffeau delivered his witty remarks with zany jewelry. The message of his clothes, however, was real fabric (no plastic needed), beautifully cut and draped for girls with real bosoms. Avant-garde designers like Tiffeau are thinking in terms of sexy femininity.

"Everybody wants to look pretty," said Jean Rosenberg, vice president of Henri Bendel, the specialty shop that foresaw the boutique movement, as well as the yé-yé and mod developments. "Pop fashion in the sense of being ugly and tough is finished.

"Flashing lights and obviously blatant, shiny, hard things are over, but all the giddiness and playfulness remains. The word pop is terribly dead. We're saying pretty and fun rather than pop."

"Of course, our notions of what is pretty and what is pop have changed," Miss Rosenberg added. "What was pop two years ago is acceptable now, particularly if it's functional and youthful and isn't done purely for shock value.

"Vinyl, for example. For a raincoat it can't be beat. With holes for an evening dress, it doesn't make sense. All of the stretch things, the opaque leg, the leotard with short skirts and showing lots of body will continue. I love legs and showing lots of body."

"Pop as a word is finished but pure modern fashion is here forever," said Ida Sciolino, friend and patron of the movement in her capacity as manager of the junior dress department at Bloomingdale's.

"What was pop is pace-setting now. People over 40 who are not in the fashion business or who were involved in the truly elegant end wouldn't acknowledge it or sneered at it. But it's not evil. It's an imaginative, wonderful thing.

"Like any fashion, the attention-getters take the vulgarity from it instead of the delicious part," she said.

"Gentle, that's the word. Gentle but modern." She held up two mini-dresses — one a zip-front knit, the other in clashing patterns of print and stripes—made by the Youthquake Division of the Puritan Fashion Corporation. A few weeks before, buyers and fashion editors had seen them at a fashion show put on by the manufacturer in its factory. On that occasion, the dresses had looked anything but gentle.

The mannequins emerged to the ear-piercing strains of the Gurus, a long-haired pop music group. Up and down the runway, they performed the jerk and other exercises of free-associating dance in order to display designs by Emmanuelle Khanh, Tuffin & Foale of London, Betsey Johnson, the least inhibited of the younger American designers, and other pop fashion disciples.

There was lots of transparent plastic, paper dresses and bikini evening dresses. One mannequin's bosom fell out of the bikini dress while she was convulsively modeling it. There were outfits made of graphic negative fabric on which designs can be inscribed with a high intensity lamp so that they glow in the dark for hours after. It was terribly psychedelic, which is the word they are using instead of pop in the mass end of the fashion business.

Happening in Health Club

The evening before the Puritan show, a happening was staged for buyers and the press in a basement health club in the Henry Hudson Hotel. "Dig it Man! It's going to be a Trip," promised the invitation to the collection of sleepwear designed by Tiger Morse for Weldon Inc.

And it was a trip, of sorts. Lewd movements were enacted on the diving board before the gaze of such stalwarts of pop society as Andy Warhol and Mrs. Robert Scull, the pop art collector.

Tiger Morse, the hostess, appeared in silver jeans and shirt, the giant sunglasses that are her trademark and a dead butterfly painted on her cheek. She tumbled into the pool at one point, as did a male guest clad in a transparent plastic shirt and mink chaps.

Seymour Marrow, president of Weldon, Inc., left the party before it got rolling and shortly after a Washington newspaper reporter called his attention to the fact that the aroma in the health club wasn't sweat. It was pot.

A few days later, Mr. Marrow conceded that the party might have been a mistake but he defended the merchandise.

"We were trying to spark something unusual and different, to break into new directions," he said. "We have been identified with the classic type of sleepwear which has a declining share of the market. We couldn't break out of that just by being a little less classic. We had to blast the buyers.

Only about 30 or 40 buyers attended the nighttime Weldon showing. The rest went into the company's showroom in broad daylight, saw that the Morse-designed culotte pajamas and printed tent nightgowns were harmless and pretty. Bloomingdale's will have them in stock around April 1.

Eight months before, Tiger Morse had been used by Bergdorf Goodman to prove that a bastion of elegance could be a swinging store.

Bergdorf's put a collection of Tiger Morse dresses in vinyl and printed cotton (priced from about $150 almost to $500) in the windows with motorcycles as props. Passers-by were fascinated not only by the Hondas but by the rear décolletage of one of the dresses.

Sense of Humor Necessary

"We believe this is a period where you have to have a bit of humor about fashion," said Leonard Hankin, executive vice-president of Bergdorf's, which has assigned its custom designers, Halston, the milliner, and Emeric Partos, who works in furs, to think up expensive fun.

"The theater of fashions seems to be taking a more strident form. The role that fashion plays today is a social experience as much as a clothing of your body," he said, enunciating a basic tenet of pop fashion philosophy. "Important personalities have developed on the American scene via fashion."

"I love pop fashion," asserted one of those personalities, Susan Stein, daughter of Jules Stein, chairman of the Music Coporation of America. A multilingual Vassar graduate and one of the most energetic party givers on the pop society circuit, she was one of the first purchaser's of Yves Saint Laurent's transparent dress last year.

"I love my holey dress so much that I bought it in four different colors," said Miss Stein, alluding to an English crochet mini-number that reveals lots of Miss Stein in a peek-a-boo manner. "But I don't wear it every night. I wear what suits my mood and my occasion. I can't tie myself down to one look.

"Pop fashion is marvelous for buying a little inexpensive dress," she said.

Mrs. Scull, another extrovert who has made a social ascent via pop art and pop fashion, said, "Sometimes I feel like something cute, funny and amusing, as long as it's not too tricky, not too silly. It has to be elegant." She cited Paco Rabanne, Emmanuel Ungaro, Saint Laurent and Courrèges as designers who can manage the impossible.

"I still wear Givenchy sometimes, though. Other times I want something gayer. But the point is you can't go back anymore. The age of elegance isn't there. Nobody wants it."

Being a lady is no longer a primary ambition in fashion terms. If pop fashion is evolving, it is in the direction of erotica on a broad spectrum from vulgarity to relaxed sexiness.

A photograph in the Jan. 27 issue of Life magazine showing a nylon knit bathing suit that set new records in rear décolletage brought the ambivalent feelings of merchants to light. At least one buyer of a Fifth Avenue store was called to account for ordering it by her superiors. She explained that the version from which she ordered had been four inches higher.

The designer of the suit, Miss Rikki of Sport Trio, had diminished it at the request of the magazine.

"To make a point, you sometimes have to exaggerate the effect," Miss Rikki said. "I like it, though. It's very clean and nice. We've seen cleavage in front, why not in back?"

MARCH 9, 1967

Bergdorf's Pursues Its Foreign Policy

By BERNADINE MORRIS

BERGDORF GOODMAN fired an international fashion salute yesterday and everybody seemed pleased. The store presented its 52-piece spring import collection to an audience that included a Parisian and an Italian designer represented in the show and the chairman of the Incorporated Society of London Fashion Designers, Edward Rayne.

The designers perused the clothes as avidly as the customers who were about to pay $900 or more for the custom copies from Bergdorf's workroom.

Michel Goma, who designs for Patou in Paris and said he was in New York "for the fashions and the pleasure," enjoyed seeing his swinging tent dresses, which gave a lilt to the showing. But he admitted to Andrew Goodman, the store's president, that they were indeed "un tout petit peu plus long." One of 14 Paris designers whose clothes were in the show, he was represented by four styles.

Alberto Fabiani, who had five styles in the show, more than the four other Italian designers represented, looked tense as his specialty, coats in double-faced fabrics, were shown, but relaxed visibly as his pleated crepe tennis dress with a crystal beaded top stirred up a storm of applause.

Fabiani arrived here last week "to work on a fur collection for Fishbein on Seventh Avenue," he said. He was referring to Herbert Fishbein, who heads the Herbert Milton manufacturing concern, for whom Fabiani has designed for a decade.

Other official visitors included Mrs. Roger Seydoux, wife of the French Ambassador to the United Nations, in a snappy brown and white plaid suit by Pierre Cardin (who was not represented in the show) and Michel Legendre, the French consul general, who was sitting in for his wife.

"She's in France, but I'm glad I came," he said. "It was a good show and I'll come next time."

Expensive Stockings

Also pleased with the sampling of European fashions, plus one by a Canadian, was Mrs. Robert Scull, wife of the pop art collector, who was wearing brown and white checked stockings by Valentino with her white Givenchy coat (he and Dior were the high scorers with six styles each) and a white Chanel dress (she didn't show).

"I just got the bill for the stockings and I nearly died, but I love them," she said.

Mr. Goodman explained that the clothes proved that "despite the wacky things, there are clothes for ladies in Paris." He added that they were selected "for private ladies of elegance," whereas manufacturers went "looking for headlines."

"We always do marvelously well with Balmain, and the manufacturers don't even go there," he said.

The four Balmain styles, especially the tiny-waisted long gown with pink ribbon decorations, received their share of applause. Other less publicized names such as Madeleine de Rauch, with a beige front-zippered suit, Jean Dessès, with a black and white checked evening dress, and Madame Grès, with a dotted silk organdy float, also fared well.

Olivia, Canada's sole and unexpected entry, also met Mr. Goodman's standards of elegance with a navy plaid wool day dress.

Yves Saint Laurent provided fireworks with a dress in a swirling purple, green and yellow print with a sash swathed around the hips. The interest was not in the gypsy print as much as in the ankle length.

Halston, the store's custom milliner, made an impact in his own way with hats he selected from Paris couturiers. They ranged from Saint Laurent's sensible fedora to Balenciaga's black organdy witch's cap, and included a white chignon cap by Givenchy that suggested a child's weird sand castle.

MARCH 16, 1967

Champagne and Kisses for a Young Designer

By JUDY KLEMESRUD

FERNANDO SANCHEZ, who first gained fame designing women's underwear, yesterday showed an audience of 200 at Bergdorf Goodman some of his designs that women can wear in public.

After his 18-piece ready-to-wear collection ("I whipped it up in a month") was paraded, he was greeted with loud applause, champagne toasts, back-slaps and kisses.

As far as Bergdorf's customers were concerned, 30-year-old Fernando, a former assistant to Yves Saint Laurent, had arrived.

"C'est une très bonne collection," commented Pierre Bergé, director of the Saint Laurent salon in Paris. He led the applause for several of Mr. Sanchez's dresses, and he seemed to favor the three that had large ruffles on the bodice.

"Oh, they are my closest friends," the Spanish-born Mr. Sanchez said, pointing at Mr. Bergé and Mrs. Yvonne de Peyerhimoff, directrice of the Saint Laurent salon. "We have known each other forever."

"That is true," interjected Mrs. de Peyerhimoff, who was wearing a yellow and navy plaid Saint Laurent suit. "But we applauded him not because we are friends, but because it [the collection] was good."

The whole morning was heady stuff for the young designer, who was displaying his first ready-to-wear collection in the United States. Before the show, Mrs. Robert Scull, whose husband owns a taxicab fleet and collects pop art, came backstage and presented him with a red rose.

"Angel, oh my sweet," she said, bussing him on the left cheek. After the show Mrs. Scull admitted she didn't yet have any clothes by Mr. Sanchez, but added that she adored him, and that he was "a great personal friend."

Mr. Sanchez's clothes were shown in the second half of a back-to-back show with Gigliola Curiel, the Milanese designer who elected to stay in her home on Lake Como for this one.

Zippers From Top to Bottom

Many of Mr. Sanchez's daytime dresses were zippered from top to bottom, and most had some sort of belt—sometimes at the waist, sometimes a few inches above.

The audience "oohed" when the models unbuttoned the jackets of several costumes in light check patterns to reveal bodices in a solid contrasting color, decorated with a scroll motif.

Mrs. Curiel, who is known for her use of flamboyant colors, did not disappoint her fans. Especially colorful were her evening gowns, including two in rainbow stripes, another in shocking pink, and a fourth with giant zig-zags of turquoise, plum and purple.

Both designers' clothes will be sold as part of the Plaza Collections on the fourth floor. Mr. Sanchez's range from $200 to $500, and Signora Curiel's from $250 to $1,000.

Mr. Sanchez said he would continue to do ready-to-wear collections for Bergdorf's, as well as boutique fur collections for Revillon and lingerie collections for Warner's. The green-eyed, bushy-haired designer described himself as "a Parisian who is the son of a Belgian mother and a Spanish father." He said he spends about five months a year in Paris, five in New York, and two in Morocco ("It's my resort country").

As a young man of 17, he was a classmate of Yves Saint Laurent at the Ecole Syndicale de la Haute Couture in Paris. A few years later he became an assistant to Saint Laurent at Christian Dior in Paris. "I did all the crazy things that nobody ever bought," he said.

APRIL 28, 1967

Safari Clothes for Trip to Africa, Sportswear for Just About Any Locale

By NAN ICKERINGILL

"I DON'T want to look like a great white hunter," Col. John H. Glenn Jr. said firmly yesterday to a salesman at Abercrombie & Fitch. The first American to orbit the earth was there to be fitted for further explorations —earthbound this time. Colonel Glenn will narrate a documentary for Wolper Productions (who picked up the tab for his safari clothes) on the explorations of Stanley and Livingstone in Central Africa. The documentary, scheduled to be shown on television next January, will take him to an area he has passed over twice but never seen. It will be the first in a series on explorers that Colonel Glenn will narrate.

The ex-Marine knew exactly what clothes he wanted—and what he did not want.

"I'd feel I had to come on singing in that," he said, rejecting a sports coat in safari cloth. Apparently other people had felt the same way because the jacket was marked down from $68.50 to $30.

A classic belted bush jacket was eliminated as being too much like a military uniform.

Some Norwegian openweave shirts were also turned down. The store was planning to let him have the $9.50 shirt free to test it for them, but he wasn't willing. "I can't see looping down the trail in 120 degrees in a knit shirt," he said.

He decided he would look a "damn fool" in an Australian bush hat and settled for the type of fisherman's hat that looks battered even when new. He battered it considerably more before trying it on.

Whenever he could, he shifted the conversation from safari clothes to the space program ("I still work for NASA part-time as a consultant."). He compared the old-time explorations to modern space probes and commented that "one of the themes that runs through exploration is that you don't know the value while you're doing it."

He said that the Stanley-Livingstone explorations had helped open up Africa and that the space program had already given such side benefits as aid in treating hypertension ("We're tense all the time in space," he admitted) and Teflon skillets (Teflon was developed as a heat shield in the space program).

As he talked, the 46-year-old, 5-foot 10-inch former astronaut gradually accumulated a pile of clothes in a size he described as "big." They included a very casual safari jacket ($29.50), matching khaki pants ($18.50) and shirt ($9.50)—all destined to spend three days in a washing machine so they will look used. He also bought the fishing hat and a light poncho, cushion-soled socks and hiking boots. He steadfastly refused to model anything.

"He's a man," his wife apologized, with an accent on the last word. "He doesn't like to seem artificial."

Mrs. Glenn thought he looked good in the clothes, but confessed she thought he "looks good in anything—even his old slacks."

She added that she and their two children—David, 21 years old, and Lyn, 20—would accompany him to Africa but were not buying any new clothes for the trip.

"We'll make do with what we already have in our wardrobes," she said, without a trace of resentment.

•

Sylvia de Gay, who retired from designing last June but became "terribly bored," returned to the fold yesterday with a collection for Bergdorf Goodman that was dominated by silver sportswear, and lacy dresses.

"My life just wasn't geared to sitting around and being social," the ebullient, 40-year-old blonde said before the show. "I have to have a place to go in the morning or I vegetate."

Miss de Gay, who gave the world the silver dress, obviously believes that American women are not about to go off the silver standard. Her 50-piece collection, which she described as "not kooky or mod — just simple," included a silver vinyl trench coat, white pique dresses and slacks shot with silver slashes, and white voile blouses sprinkled with silver dots.

Mrs. Robert Scull, wife of the pop art collector and taxi executive, wasn't too happy with all the glitter.

"I had hoped that silver had had it — I'm so sick of it," she said, although she fairly shone herself in a bright yellow vinyl raincoat by Saint Laurent that she wore over a purple, yellow and red striped jersey dress also by Saint Laurent.

The audience of 300 people also included Patrick de Barentzen, who is here from Rome with his ready-to-wear collection. He said he thought the show was very nice.

Many of the clothes and scarves had question marks on them, which Miss de Gay said had become her trademark. Her husband, Robert Sloan, the former sportswear manufacturer who also "retired" last June, wore a gold question mark pin on his necktie.

"They [the question marks] stand for 'What is sportswear?'" Mr. Sloan explained. "To us, the answer is that there is no limitation where sportswear is concerned."

Miss de Gay, who won the Coty Award in 1965, described one of her dresses as having "the look for summer." It was a $55 orange silk jersey shirtwaist, worn with purple tights.

One of the designs—a pair of bright yellow overalls — failed to appear in the show because the model could not squirm her way into them. It was explained that there had not been enough time for fittings.

All of Miss de Gay's clothes cost under $100. They will be sold in the Miss Bergdorf department on the fifth floor, and will bear the label, "Sylvia de Gay for Miss Bergdorf."

The Sloans shut up shop suddenly last summer, stunning the industry. At the time they said they couldn't take the "terrible pace" they had maintained since starting the highly successful Robert Sloan Sportswear Inc., seven years ago.

Miss de Gay said her husband would handle all the business arrangements for her new line. "This way he won't have any of the headaches of manufacturing," said the Brooklyn-born designer whose real name is Sylvia de Ghuee.

•

The Young Elite Shop at Saks Fifth Avenue has a new décor and a new designer.

The designer is Frank Smith, who has contributed a collection of spring-summer sports and casual wear. Mr. Smith has been creating classic styles at Evan-Picone, for which he will continue to work.

The collection, which will be available at all Saks stores, is dominated by linens and dotted Swiss fabrics in bright prints or in color combinations such as lemon yellow, black and white; navy, marigold-orange and white; and lemon, turquoise and orange.

The styles are simple, and include blazer jackets with an Edwardian cut; kilts, pleated skirts and slip dresses, and combinations of separates.

One outfit had a double-breasted, lemon yellow blazer, with a white cotton, tucked shirt and cuffed black linen Jamaica shorts. Another had a waist-length navy jacket piped with marigold orange that was shown with a floor-length white skirt with side closing.

Prices range from $19 for a classic linen shirt to $60 for a two-piece, double-breasted, gray linen dress.

The Young Elite Shop's new décor, by Ernest Bonnoma, includes a floor of blue and white tiles in the wide aisle that leads to a series of departments for shoes, sportswear and evening dress. Each of the rooms housing the departments has also been redecorated.

MAY 2, 1967

To Hear the Fashion Crowd Tell It, It's Written in the Stars

By JUDY KLEMESRUD

NOWADAYS, when the rich and their pet designers get together, the conversation is as likely to be about "my astrologer" as it used to be about "my psychiatrist."

For many members of the fashion crowd — and a host of others in less rarefied circles — the stars are doing much more these days than just twinkling.

Victor Joris, designer for Cuddlecoat, refuses to fly unless his horoscope indicates that travel conditions are favorable. Mrs. Robert Scull, whose husband owns taxicabs and collects pop art, follows astrology "like mad" because it helps keep her mind off the Vietnam war and the fact that her son is of draft age. Bill Blass, the designer, has the British magazine Queen airmailed to him so its astrology column won't be out of date. And Mrs. Francis du Pont, widow of the financier, has been known to conclude business deals at 3:30 A.M. because her astrologer deemed that time propitious.

"I'm like Mr. Dior—I wouldn't dream of opening a collection without consulting my astrologer," said Adele Simpson, who was a student of astrology long before its current revival.

Born under the sign of Capricorn ("I'm a goat"), Miss Simpson said she planned all her showings for the 28th of the month because she and her five sisters were all born on that day. So was her daughter and her grandchild.

Mainbocher said he had planned to be an opera singer until Evangeline Adams, the astrologer who is alleged to have advised J. P. Morgan on financial matters, told him in the early nineteen-twenties that he would become famous instead in a field involving "color and moving figures."

"I was terribly upset at first," the designer said. "But eventually I became editor of Paris Vogue and eventually I became a designer. It kind of makes one wonder."

Vibrations Forecast the Day

Diana Dew, probably best known for the electric dresses she created for Paraphernalia, reads her horoscope every morning before going to work. She said she had learned how to interpret it from her sister, who is an astrologer in Cambridge, Mass.

"The reading helps me pick up vibrations so I know what to expect during the day," she said. "Today I'm supposed to be cautious in my dealings with strangers."

The attractive 23-year-old blonde said people who take psychedelic drugs — as she has—gained a better understanding of astrology and its vibrations.

"The whole scene is just a groove," said Miss Dew, whose fall line will include jersey knit dresses with signs of the zodiac on them.

Another designer, Tiger Morse, is doing a line of sweatshirts that will have the zodiac signs where the name of a college would ordinarily appear.

"I've always wanted to live in a planetarium," said Miss Morse, who has had her horoscope cast (set up on a chart) by several astrologers and who lives in a very earthbound pad on East 58th Street. "I just go screwy over anything involving the stars."

Miss Morse believes that she, too, has a few talents in the occult. "A lot of people have called me a witch because I can read their coffee grounds," she said.

Halston, custom hat designer at Bergdorf Goodman, said he was a charter member of the Taurus Club, a three-year-old organization that meets once a year for lunch around April 25 to celebrate members' birthdays. He said the fact that Taurus was a bull may have had something to do with his decision to fill his East 55th Street apartment with objects made of horns.

Donald Brooks, who is on the West Coast designing costumes for his first major movie, "The Star" (with Julie Andrews as Gertrude Lawrence), said one of the reasons he had decided to try Hollywood was because an astrologer told him he would be successful in two areas of his career.

"I was thrilled right down to the tips of my brand-new Guci loafers," he said.

A permanent, prominent Californian —Mrs. Sven Lokrantz of old-guard Los Angeles society—said she never gave a party unless the date was approved by Carroll Righter, an astrologer who often reads the stars for the movie stars.

"The only party I didn't check with Carroll turned out to be a disaster," Mrs. Lokrantz said. "The Swedish glogg caught fire and burned the dining hall."

But not all of astrology's disciples plot their lives in harmony with the heavens.

"One of my astrologers told me with tears in her eyes that I should run out and divorce my husband," said Mrs. Leonard Holzer, a model and actress who is sometimes called Baby Jane. "With the same amount of tears in my eyes, I laughed in her face."

Belief Started With Babylonians

Astrology is believed to have started 5,000 years ago with the Babylonians, who erected great stone ziggurats from which to chart the planets. Nebuchadnezzar, a king of Babylon, was said to have had astrologers who predicted the future not only by the position of the planets but also by examining the liver of a newly killed boar.

Astrology has since enjoyed periodic revivals, one of which occurred during the nineteen-thirties, when people spoke as casually of their astrologers as they did of their bootleggers.

Today, approximately 18 million Americans are interested in astrology, according to Paul R. Grell, executive secretary of the American Federation of Astrologers. The federation's membership includes 1,200 of the nation's 5,000 full-time astrologers. They charge from $5 to $500 to cast a horoscope.

"Most people won't admit they believe in it," said Sydney Omarr, a Los Angeles astrologer whose column appears in 200 newspapers, "but 10 out of 10 people know the sun sign they were born under."

In essence, the theory of astrology is that the character of every human being is determined by the position of the stars, planets, sun and moon at the moment of his birth. Therefore he is affected, for better or worse, by the changing position of the heavenly bodies all through his life.

When an astronomer — a scientist who studies celestial phenomena—hears theories like these, he is likely to shudder, or swear, or both. Dr. Gibson Reaves, professor of astronomy at the University of Southern California, who has done research on astrology ("it's even crazier when you study it"), said:

"As a science, astrology died in the middle of the 17th century. It remains dead as a science because it simply does not work."

Dr. Milton A. Kline of Manhattan, echoing the viewpoint of many psychiatrists, said: "The only way astrology can be accepted is if it is regarded as a source of amusement."

Many reasons are given for the current revival. Mollie Parnis, who returned to designing at the advice of her astrologer after the death of her husband, views it as an outgrowth of a decline in organized religion. But Dr. Cyril C. Richardson, dean of graduate studies at Union Theological Seminary, disputes this theory.

"Astrology is the sort of thing that is sought after in a period of crisis," he said. "It has much more to do with the Vietnam war and general unrest than with either a decline or advance in religion." He added that it was not uncommon for religious people to go into astrology.

Magazines Get Into the Act

Zoltan S. Mason of Manhattan, an astrologer who has forecast that Mrs. John F. Kennedy will never remarry ("she belongs to her country"), believes much of the new interest can be traced to the astrology columns now appearing in such magazines as Elle, Queen, Harper's Bazaar, Cosmopolitan and Town and Country.

"Everyone is mad about it," said Nancy White, editor of Harper's Bazaar, discussing that magazine's new column. "We haven't had a single complaint, and that surprised me. Astrology seems to have become a status topic these days."

SEPTEMBER 21, 1967

Richard Smith, British, Wins Grand Prize at 9th Sao Paulo Bienal

By HILTON KRAMER

Special to The New York Times

SAO PAULO, Brazil, Sept. 20—Richard Smith, the 35-year-old British painter, who divides his time between London and New York, has been awarded the $10,000 grand prize by the jury of the ninth Bienal de São Paulo.

Jasper Johns, the American painter, who is represented in the "Environment U.S.A.: 1957-1967" show in the American section of the bienal, was one of 10 artists awarded equal prizes worth $2,500.

The other winners in this category were the sculptor Baldacini Cesar of France, the painter Flavio Carvalho of Brazil, the painter Carlos Cruz-Diez of Venezuela, the graphic artist Fumiaki Fukita of Japan, the painter Tadeuz Kantor of Poland, the sculptor David Lamelas of Argentina, the painter Michelangelo Pistoletto of Italy, the graphic artist Josua Reichert of Germany and the constructivist Ian Schoonhoven of the Netherlands.

The jury refused to make a special award for the Brazilian artist who gave evidence of the most original artistic research. Opinion was unanimous that there was no artist in the vast Brazilian section of the bienal original enough to merit the prize. This is certain to cause something of a scandal in Brazilian art circles.

It is the custom of the bieneal prize system not to grant more than one award to a single country. While conforming to this unwritten law this year, the jury issued a statement condemning this system and urging that it be changed. Had this system been suspended this year, it is a virtual certainty that several more artists from the United States would have figured among the awards. Robert Rauschenberg, Claes Oldenberg and Andy Warhol were names prominent in the discussion.

Frenchman Draws Attention

There were several surprising omissions on the award list. The Canadian abstract painter Jack Bush, whose exhibition is much admired here and who is practically the only representative of color-field painting in the bienal, is reported to have figured in debate over the top prize.

A young French artist, Jean-Pierre Raynaud, whose room of pure white neo-Dada objects and constructions has attracted a great deal of attention, was also expected to take a prize. Mr. Raynaud is clearly going to be an important figure on the international art scene in the next few years. His show at the bienal is already scheduled for exhibition in museums in Amsterdam and Stockholm, and at least one American museum director has arranged to purchase his work. But the award to Mr. Cesar precluded an award to Mr. Raynaud.

In the same way, the award to Mr. Smith prevented consideration of the British sculptor William Turnbull.

When first word of the awards got out last night, it was reported that Mr. Cesar would decline his prize. Clearly expecting the top award himself, he is reported to have said that he would have accepted the lesser award only if Mr. Johns had been voted grand prize. The French seem particularly sensitive to losing out to the British.

At the same time, the minor award to Mr. Johns is widely regarded here as a kind of joke. In international circles, Mr. Johns is already established as a classic, and the feeling is that he should have been voted the grand prize or considered above the competition.

Mr. Smith is a well-known figure in New York, where he has lived off and on for several years. The most important of his works in the bienal, large shaped canvases painted in acrylic, were exhibited last season at the Richard Feigen Gallery. His recent work combines the impulses of both hard-edge abstraction and minimal sculpture. It remains painting, but painting constructed in three dimensions.

When he showed in the British pavilion of the Venice Biennale last year, he won the prize offered by Mr. and Mrs. Robert C. Scull for the best young painter who was not an American.

The bienal prize jury is made up of representatives from the United States, Britain, Germany, Argentina, Belgium, Japan, Mexico, Poland and Brazil. Andrew C. Ritchie, director of the Yale Art Gallery, is the American member.

It is more or less assumed that jury members will lobby for the artists of their respective countries; in the past, commissioners of the national sections have actually served as jury members. It is not surprising, therefore, that seven of the nine countries represented on the jury also figure in the awards. The British member of the jury, Alan Bowness, served on the committee that selected Mr. Smith's pictures for the bienal.

Smith 'Absolutely Delighted'

Mr. Smith, who was reached here yesterday at his studio, said, "I'm absolutely delighted to win the prize. I'm sorry I'm not there."

"I think the prizes are, in a way, anathema," he continued, "because it's impossible to grade on a purely art scale. The critics' choice is partly dependent on such factors as depth of representation, nationality and worth. I think I'm very young to win such a major prize."

Mr. Smith will be 36 years old next month. He was born in Letchworth, a town 40 miles north of London. He has been painting professionally since 1957, when he got out of school, he said. He plans to use the prize money for the purchase of a house in London. "It's something we've been thinking about for a year," he explained. Mr. Smith and his wife, Betsy, are the parents of 1½-year-old son, Edward.

"We've been doing a lot of traveling these past several years and we're tired of it," he said. But, he plans to keep his New York studio. The artist's family left for England on Tuesday. However, Mr. Smith will remain here until Christmas to help prepare a display of his work at the Feigen Gallery, 24 East 81st Street.

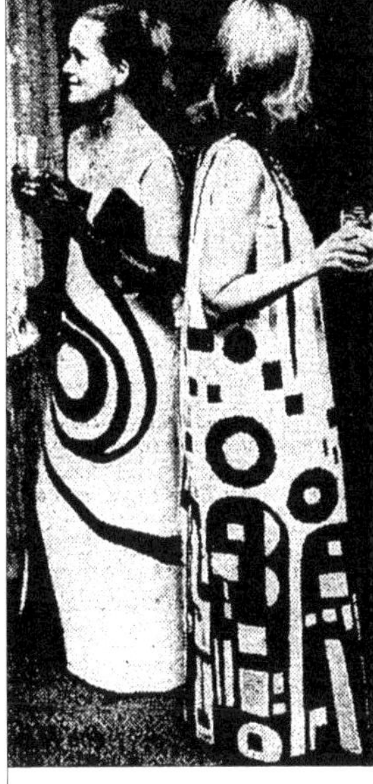

SEPTEMBER 21, 1967

Now It's Alexander's Turn

By BERNADINE MORRIS

A LOT of women drove up to Alexander's yesterday in limousines and Southampton tans.

They came to see the store's collection of copies of imports and to aid The Society of Sloan-Kettering Cancer Center. The blend of high fashion and good cause was a happy one, appeasing the consciences of those women who may have felt fashion was frivolous.

"We have a big building program and must raise millions," said Mrs. Gardner Cowles, wife of the publisher, who arrived with Mrs. Nelson A. Rockefeller. They were cochairmen of the charity event. The Duchess of Windsor, the honorary chairman, sent her regrets.

Mrs. Rockefeller, who wore a navy and white wool costume by Pertegaz, from Chez Ninon, which was made to order, said she was eager to see Alexander's ready-to-wear original fabric copies.

Mrs. Richard L. Harris, whose husband is vice president of the United States Line and who was one of the 250 patronesses, said she would have come even if she hadn't been a patroness. Her daughter, Laurie, works for Alexander's.

Mrs. Harris, who came to the first showing in a sleeveless black knit dress she bought at Bloomingdale's, left in a belted gold Antonelli ($99) that fit without any alterations. "Except it might be a trifle too long," she said. The hem grazed the top of her knees.

The presentation of 45 styles by 15 European designers was repeated four times during the day on the store's third floor, where 1,200 seats had been set up.

"Two of my friends came early and brought their breakfast in paper cups," said Mrs. John R. Fell, who is a member of the charity group's administrative board and was busily seating her friends during the two benefit performances, at 11 A.M. and at 3 P.M. She was delighted that all the seats, which cost $5 or $10, were sold for both shows. The 1 P.M. and 6 P.M. shows were open to the public.

One of the breakfast-bringers was Mrs. Lloyd Hilton Smith, whose husband is a Houston oil man. She was taken with the gray Balenciaga coat ($175) but planned to come back later to try it on "when it was less frantic."

Likes Casual Look

Her neighbor in Southampton, Mrs. George C. Sherman, whose husband is an insurance broker, was attracted by the "evening dress with the sweater, because it looks so casual." The sweater is jeweled and the outfit, by Lancetti, costs $795.

Mrs. Serge Semenko, wife of the Boston financier, bought one of them, along with Saint Laurent's blue and silver brocade evening dress with a mink-edged matching cape. The most expensive dress in the collection, it costs $1,500 and the store only had enough fabric for three outfits. Mrs. W. Palmer Dixon, whose husband is with Loeb Rhoades, stockbrokers, settled for Givenchy's striped fleece coat at $310.

It wasn't only the showstoppers that were selling. The little nothing wool day dresses by Antonelli, in pretty colors like peach and gold, were checking out at $99 and $129— there were five of them — faster than anyone could count.

So were the Chanel suits (a white one at $325 and a black evening suit with fringe at $295), a Saint Laurent leather coat with sable collar and cuffs at $450 (there were 24 special orders before the day was over) and a Heinz Riva coat with a belt that looked like giant paper clips ($210).

The store was particularly pleased with the reception of its five Riva styles because they regard the designer, who recently opened his own couture house in Rome and who used to work for Galitzine, as a protégé.

"After shopping at the Paris couture for 15 years, I can't tell the copies from the originals," said Mrs. Robert J. Leder, wife of a theatrical producer. "Except for the prices," she added.

Mrs. Robert C. Scull, who turned up in a yellow Courrèges dress (she was at the Ohrbach's import show the day before in a lime green Courrèges, both from his new collection), put her name down for Saint Laurent's black velvet knicker suit ($250). Her husband collects pop art and owns a taxi company.

Other interested visitors were John and Derek Brenninkmeyer of the family that owns Ohrbach's, Alexander's big competitor in the import fashion show business. They were invited to see the collection.

OCTOBER 1, 1967

. . . and One of Its Generators

By GRACE GLUECK

"MAYBE," Richard Smith suggested wryly the other day, "I won the Bienal prize on *merit*."

Pause. At the arty little bar, heads swivelled his way. A startled waiter let a Martini glass crash. The interviewer put down her BIC ball point. "You're suggesting," she said incredulously, "that you won the grand prize of $10,000 at the São Paulo Bienal last week solely on recognition of your *talent*? Without dealer machinations? Without jury rigging? *Sans* politicking by certain art magazines?"

"Sure," said Smith, imperturbably.

Well, after all, why not? Smith, a young Englishman who orbits between London and New York, is not exactly a stranger to kudos. Fellowships and grants have fallen his way. His work is snapped up by big-league acquisitors. Last year he was honored by a major retrospective at London's Whitechapel Gallery and, at the Venice Biennale, he took the Robert C. Scull prize for the best exhibit by a non-American.

But, in the downtown uniform of Levi jacket and jeans the other day, his head seemed fairly unturned. "I still feel like an unknown painter," he said. "I hope the prize nudges through a few big commissions for me, but I don't regard it as the climax of my career." A small shrug. "Don't misunderstand me. I wouldn't at all mind being a household word. My ambition once was to make the visual taste of an era, as the Adam brothers did in the 18th century. But things move too quickly today. You're lucky to have an impact for a month or two."

Now 36, Smith belongs to the first generation of British artists whose style of art—and life—was deeply affected by doings across the Atlantic. "Not only were we dazzled by the postwar U.S. painting shows that came to London in the '50's, we were fascinated by *things* American—jazz, architecture, the movies. We read certain magazines and saw certain films and played certain records. We sort of consciously chose America."

Smith's seven years in art schools ("one stayed that long in order to keep qualifying for grants") included a stint at London's pop-conscious Royal College of Art, where he contributed articles on mass culture to the school magazine. (One, entitled "Sitting in the Middle of Today," dealt with furniture as a form of symbolism in the movies.) There he also imbibed the McLuhan mass media message via "The Mechanical Bride," an early MM work. Possibly it helped crystalize his current oeuvre —giant shaped canvases (arrived at through pop out of abstract expressionism) whose increasingly abstract forms continue to reflect his interest in mass packaging.

"I think my generation founded the taste that the whole London swinging scene is based on," he says. "I can remember girl students dressing like Toulouse-Lautrec models—dark eyes, no lips. We were making attitudes outside of Bohemia. We broke clean with our elders—we didn't have to come on with their arty point of view. We looked with favor on everyday culture and began to think of our paintings as non-fine-art objects. For a certain time, we had a community."

With his prize money, Smith hopes to buy a house in London ("things are so expensive in New York") where he'll live with his American-born wife Betsy and their infant son, Edward. But he intends to maintain a studio here. "I consider myself a citizen of two worlds. Though England has the corner on the decorative arts, there's very little in the way of substantial painting. Even though English artists no longer look to the States for taste, New York is still more radical, and they come here for the art. Besides, with the hippies, America's come up with a new ambiance. I'm sure if I were 21 today, I'd be in San Francisco."

FUN & GAMES

Speaking of hippies, heard about the one on display in artist Paul Thek's new show at the Stable Gallery? It's not a real live hippie, of course, but a life-size wax effigy (molded by Thek in his own image) serenely stretched out in a pink ziggurat "tomb." So realistic is the effect that gallery visitors tend to tiptoe reverentially up to the glass door of the "tomb" and speak in whispers.

The "corpse" has had not only visitors, but a number of tributes. A troupe of live flower children paid their respects and left on the floor near the tomb (a) a pot of asters; (b) a single filter tip cigarette; (c) a cluster of wilted daisies; (d) a dried apricot and a half-slice of buttered whole wheat / bread, minus a bite and (e) a note that read, "Oh, if Jesus was in New York I would say hello to him, I would be nice to him. Jesus is marvelous and he has pretty hair."

A slightly tarter tribute was sent to the artist himself by dealer John Bernard Myers, of the Tibor de Nagy Gallery: "Dear Paul Thek—If you get a wire saying, 'Come, come immediately,' from Madame Tussaud,

Do so."

OCTOBER 18, 1967

Benefit Party to Open City Museum Show on Nov. 8

The expansion fund of the Museum of the City of New York will benefit from a party on Nov. 8 opening the exhibition "New York—The Scene—'67/'17."

Mrs. Winthrop W. Aldrich and Mrs. William G. Cahan are co-chairmen. The party, in the museum's Alman Gallery, will echo the exhibition theme—the contrast of life in New York in 1917 and 1967—by transforming the gallery into a Palm Court and the auditorium into a discothèque.

Committee members are Mrs. Alfred Gwynne Vanderbilt, Mrs. Maurice Silverstein, Mrs. Robert Scull, Mrs. Duncan McGregor, Mrs. Randolph Marston, Mrs. Moss Hart (Kitty Carlisle), Mrs. Osborn Elliott, Mrs. John R. Fell, Mrs. Roswell Gilpatric, Mrs. Peter Lind Hayes, Mrs. Edgar Bronfman, Mrs. Ernest Martin and Mrs. Gardner Cowles.

Among the patrons are Mrs. August Belmont, Sylvan Oestreicher, Mrs. Mellon Bruce, Mrs. Edgar Leonard, Edward Laroque Tinker, Mr. and Mrs. Thor Thors Jr., Mr. and Mrs. John Pierrepont, Mr. and Mrs. Amory Houghton, Mrs. Reginald B. Lanier, Miss Dorothy Lossinsky, Mrs. Flagler Matthews, Mr. and Mrs. Peter Frelinghuysen Carleton, Mrs. Louis S. Auchincloss and Duncan Harris.

Also, Mr. and Mrs. Clarence G. Michalis, Mr. and Mrs. Bruce Gimbel, Mr. and Mrs. Elisha Dyer, Mr. and Mrs. Daniel Rose, Dr. Herbert Willis Schein, Mrs. David A. Schulte, O. Dryson Pappay, Mr. and Mrs. Theodore Weicker, Mr. and Mrs. A. Phillippe von Hemert, Herbert R. Silverman, Thomas Leffingwell Pulling and Mr. and Mrs. Jacob M. Kaplan.

Tickets for the benefit are $50 each. The committee has arranged bus service after the party with stops from the museum at 103d Street along Fifth Avenue to 57th Street.

JANUARY 2, 1968

The Subject of the Hemline Comes Up: Will It Go Down?

By BERNADINE MORRIS

THE big fashion cliff-hanger for 1968 is whether hemlines, officially poised above the knees for several seasons, are ready to take a plunge of a foot or so to calf level.

There are bulls, bears and hedgers among designers, fashion merchants and the clothes-wearing public, all of whom have a vested interest in hemline stability.

The bulls have their eyes on London, where the mini-skirt was born in the early nineteen-sixties and the young avant-gardists today find they can turn more heads by covering their knees than by showing them.

The bears, many of whom were relatively late converts to the short skirt cause, are satisfied with the status quo. While they do not necessarily advocate thighs in full view, they do insist on a show of knees. Each inch of skirt below them adds 10 years to a woman's age, they maintain.

The vast majority of fashion analysts, however, occupy a fence-riding position. They see the calf-length skirt (called "maxi" in Europe) worn for special occasions—blistering cold days, evening parties where a floor-length dress seems too staid, and as a beach cover-up next summer.

Adolfo, the custom milliner, has no conflicts. A calf-length felt skirt of his design has covered some of the most fashionable knees in town. He had created the skirt last July as a background for his fall hat collection.

"First Isabel Eberstadt [the daughter of Ogden Nash] came in for one," the milliner recalled. "Then everybody came."

"Everybody" includes such Adolfo regulars as Mrs. Ahmet Ertegun, wife of the president of the Atlantic Recording Corporation; Mrs. William P. Rayner, whose husband is assistant to the president of Condé Nast publications, and Mrs. Samuel P. Reed, whose husband is with Engelhard Industries, the precious metals concern.

Longer Skirts at Parties

They've been wearing them to parties this fall. So have Mrs. Robert C. Scull, wife of the pop art collector; Penelope Tree, the 17-year-old daughter of Mr. and Mrs. Ronald Tree, whose mother was a member of the United Nations Human Rights Committee, and Mrs. Wyatt Cooper (Gloria Vanderbilt).

"First they want it in black, and then I do it in colors," said Adolfo, who charges $85 for his wraparound skirts. Mrs. Cooper, with six, may have the record, but he doesn't remember how many Mrs. Scull owns.

The two women were enchanted with their long skirts, which they wore with frilly blouses at night. So they each asked him to make a wrap for daytime, and Adolfo came up with a felt cape.

He has sold only 100 capes, for which he charges $125, "because they got a late start." But a new version will serve as a backdrop for his spring millinery show tomorrow.

Not all the women who are wearing Adolfo's sable hats this winter are interested in his long skirts.

"My children's great-grandmother in Sparta is wearing her skirts that length," said Mrs. Harilaos Theodoracopoulos. "She's 85 years old."

The former Betsy Pickering was a fashion mannequin before her marriage to the Greek shipping executive. She thinks that short skirts not only make women look younger but also are "right for our time." Mrs. Theodoracopoulos dismisses calf-length skirts as "nothing but a flash fad."

"I've just come back from London and I've never seen so many short skirts," said Adele Simpson, the designer.

"American women have the most beautiful legs," she added, "and there is more girl-watching today than there ever was. Lots of girls who never had any attention at all are getting stared at in their short skirts." She calls the long ones "ugly and cumbersome" and thinks they're getting more attention than they deserve.

"We've shortened 1,080 coats this fall and if hems go down I'll kill myself," said David Dix, a partner in Ben Kahn, the fur house.

But the majority of designers are trying to see how the wind blows.

"I don't see any demise of the short dress," said Norman Norell, who has contributed to the ups and downs of hemlines for close to 50 years.

"I'm trying some longer ones, I'm experimenting," said the designer, who will show his spring collection in nine days. "It's a very tricky thing. They have to be terribly young looking, but I am trying them for day and afternoon."

"I'm not sure I want to see women wearing calf-length dresses on the street," said Gayle Kirkpatrick.

But he did make a group of calf-length styles in terry cloth. He calls them barefoot beach dresses and hopes women will slip them on over bikinis next summer.

"I'd been fighting the idea," said Geoffrey Beene, "but I made up one in crepe, as part of my Mafia group for spring, sort of tongue-in-cheek. I liked it so much I made a couple more."

The first dress in "the length Sicilian women wear to funerals" was in black; the others are in white and yellow. When Mrs. Jacob K. Javits insisted he make her a calf-length dress to wear to her husband's testimonial dinner in December, Mr. Beene began to think that by next fall "we may be ready for the length."

Jacques Tiffeau, who first lowered the boom on hemlines in coats for fall, 1966, thinks that by next winter both short and long skirts can co-exist.

For Special Occasions

Chester Weinberg, who made one of the most popular of the calf-length dresses this fall in gray velvet banded with chinchilla, followed it with some printed taffetas for spring. He sees them for "very special occasions." Among the 200 women who bought his gray velvet for $265 are Mrs. S. Carter Burden Jr., the daughter of Mrs. William S. Paley; and Mrs. William G. Cahan, the wife of a surgeon, who wore it to a party at the Museum of the City of New York.

Sandy Smith of Modelia is delighted that he sold a couple of hundred of the mid-calf-length coats his designer, Don Simonelli, made this fall, and that action is even brisker for spring.

"If everything goes down next fall, nobody's wardrobe will be worth a nickel," he said happily.

Stores don't think such devaluation is likely, but they are playing with longer skirts. Saks Fifth Avenue thinks the skirts have a special place for after-ski and at-home wear. Bonwit Teller and Bloomingdale's are among those planning dress promotions in February.

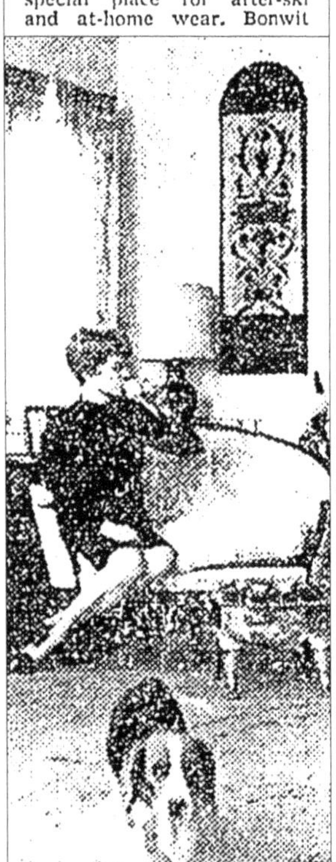

Collegiate Enthusiasm

Lord & Taylor picked Christmas week for its presentation of black crepe dresses with white ruffles and calf-length skirts because the college girls would be in town. It soon found the "floor jumping with college girls trying them on."

"Any young girl who wore a mini found this right for a party," a spokesman said.

"We see it as an additional length," said Charles Glueck, fashion director of Jonathan Logan. His company made the dresses, which sold for $30.

"It's not going to change everything," Mr. Glueck said. "Only Paris has the authority to do that."

But Geoffrey Beene is not willing to give Paris the last word.

"We're strong enough to do it here," he said. "If five or six of us got together, as they used to in Paris before World War II, we could put it across. Long skirts—or something else."

JANUARY 4, 1968

Look of Spring: Berets, Brims

By BERNADINE MORRIS

QUESTION: What have "Gone With the Wind" and "Bonnie and Clyde" to do with the hats women will be wearing in the next few months?

Answer: Apart from the death and destruction, both films exploit the romantic past. As far as milliners are concerned, anything that's romantic is good for their business.

So the fluttery, flower-laden, big-brimmed hats of the old plantation days in the South and the austere berets of the Depression were revived in three spring millinery collections introduced yesterday.

Adolfo's version of Bonnie's beret comes in gray, blue, green or red felt and is accompanied by a matching cape in the mid-calf length that he popularized in black among his customers this fall. An alternate topping for the cape is a larger beret set on a ribbon band and derived, according to Adolfo, from the one the artists wear in "La Bohème."

Only the ushers who guided the customers to their seats and one client, Mrs. Robert C. Scull, wife of the pop art collector, donned the longer skirt for the noon-hour show. Mrs. Scull covered hers on the snowy day with a calf-length coat bordered in Persian lamb by Victor Joris.

But the miniskirted clients, such as Mrs. Ahmet Ertegun, whose husband is president of the Atlantic Recording Company, and whose short red calf coat and skirt was by Lawrence Kaye, applauded Adolfo's newest calf-length skirts each time they appeared.

Covered With Flowers

They were in white organdy, with the ribbon sashing the waist picking up the color of the flowers that circled the brims of the hats. Some were completely covered with field flowers.

"The flowers are great," said Mrs. Ertegun who, like the other women in above-the-knee boots and towering Adolfo toques of sable, mink or snow leopard, thought wistfully of garden parties next summer.

Adolfo's flowering romantic costumes will undoubtedly replace Pucci's blatant prints at some of those parties.

Mr. John covered his program with a photograph from "Gone With the Wind" and opened his show with some reminiscences of his first meeting "30 years ago with a green-eyed girl who was going to play Scarlett."

Vivien Leigh pleaded with him to let the people see her face before they looked at the hats he made for her, he recalled, and he couldn't agree with her more.

With the film revived, he calls his show the "Romantic Plantation Collection," but he holds himself in check. The hats stop this side of being costumes because, he reluctantly admits, "We have a different way of living today."

Though the brims are a trifle wider, the crowns larger and the hats "a bit on the feminine side," Mr. John avoids a profusion of flowers and other symptoms of an attic look. His favorite trimming is a pretty ribbon circling the crown and sometimes streaming down the back. His favorite shape is a crisp, alert-looking sailor, but he does very well with a clean-line cloche.

Archie Eason, who made hats in Jacksonville, Fla., until he came to New York four years ago, has updated Bonnie's beret by dotting it with two dozen small bells. He also attaches bells to a chain around the crown of a derby, to lanyard-like chin straps and to the top of a fez as his acknowledgment of the hippie movement.

Softening the Fedora

He likes flowers, too, especially "wild flowers that look as if they had just been picked." He places them at the side of gangster-like fedoras to soften the severe air.

Adolfo has his calf-length skirts; Eason has his overskirts. They are net affairs decorated with patent leather cut-outs or flowers to match the headdresses. Since hats stopped being the focal point of a costume, milliners are determined to spread their influence to other parts.

Prices for custom-made hats start at $65 at Adolfo, $50 at Mr. John and Eason. The three also design ready-to-wear hats that are considerably less expensive.

JANUARY 28, 1968

Art Notes

Not One Boring Picture

By GRACE GLUECK

BIG PICTURE

"My God, it's a billboard to end all billboards," gulped a collector when he first saw James Rosenquist's Pop spectacular, "F-111," completed in 1965. And so it was. Hung at the Leo Castelli Gallery, "F-111's" 51 panels stretched a length of 85 feet, depicting the fuselage of the controversial F-111 fighter-bomber. On *that* were superimposed such contemporary images as a Spam sandwich, a Firestone tire, an angel food cake, a nuclear blast, and a smiling tyke crowned by a hair dryer.

The giant Popscape was soon purveyed to Castelli buff Robert C. Scull who, declaring it "the most important statement made in art in the last 50 years," reportedly plunked down a superprice of $60,000. Since then, according to Scull, like a real airplane the work has kept going, touching down in the U. S. and Europe "wherever a large enough wall space was available." (Last fall, about 37 feet of it appeared at Brazil's Sao Paulo Bienal.)

Now, come Feb. 6, the giant oeuvre will zoom back home, to put in a 90-day appearance at a prestigious hangar indeed, the Metropolitan Museum of Art. Why? "It's an important series of pictures, ergo we show it," explained Met director Thomas P. F. Hoving tersely. The painting, flanked by smaller 19th- and 20th-century French and American "machines" (such as Leutze's "George Washington Crossing the Delaware") will hang in a ground-floor hall between the Met's armor collection and Medieval Art.

The F-111's Met debut has been solemnly hailed by Scull and Henry Geldzahler, Curator of Contemporary Arts, in a forthcoming issue of the museum's Bulletin. Says Geldzahler: "Rosenquist's F-111 is not only the largest Pop work, it is the grandest. (It) stands as the symbol of the industrial-military complex of our time, a paranoic landscape worthy of Dali. The question of quality seems irrelevant when one is confronted with the F-111. In its own terms the painting is so powerful and consistent that the viewer's total attention is given to absorbing it."

Will the F-111 have a permanent berth at the Met? "Well," says Scull warily, "I'm always thinking of its final resting place, but I haven't really decided. It's a big commitment for a museum to make, and it's wanted for viewing by many." From the Met itself: no comment.

FEBRUARY 17, 1968

Art: New Hangar for Rosenquist's Jet-Pop 'F-111'

By HILTON KRAMER

JAMES ROSENQUIST'S immense pop painting entitled "F-111," which dominated the American exhibition at the 1967 São Paulo Bienal and has been widely exhibited in European museums since it was first shown here at the Leo Castelli Gallery in 1965, went on view yesterday at the Metropolitan Museum of Art.

The painting is executed as a series of panels, and measures 86 feet long and 10 feet high when completely assembled. At the Metropolitan, it occupies three walls of a large gallery. Accompanying the Rosenquist work, which is on loan from the collection of Mr. and Mrs. Robert C. Scull, are three paintings from the Metropolitan's permanent collection: "The Rape of the Sabine Women" by Nicholas Poussin, "The Death of Socrates" by Jacques Louis David and "Washington Crossing the Delaware" by Emanuel Gottlieb Lieutze. The museum has mounted this motley assemblage under the rubric of "History Painting—Various Aspects."

•

"F-111" takes its title, of course, from the fighter-bomber of that name, and juxtaposes images of this military aircraft with a variety of commonplace motifs from the realm of consumer advertising and photojournalism. These motifs include, among other disparate images, an angel food cake, an oversize Firestone tire, a child's head under a hair-dryer and a mushroom cloud from a nuclear explosion under an umbrella. The picture is organized as a giant montage, with each section designed to be "read" separately and, at the same time, as part of the over-all image. Pictorially, the style might best be described as buckeye cubism.

A museum spokesman has described "F-111" as a "painted comment on the industrial-military aspect of the American scene." The director of the Metropolitan, Thomas P. F. Hoving, has declared that, in his opinion, the work "makes an important and timely statement," not only because of its form and expression "but sociologically as well." Mr. Scull, the present owner of the painting, has contributed an article to the March number of the museum's Bulletin in which he offers the view that the work is "a milestone in the visual literature of what is perhaps art's greatest theme: the struggle between life and death."

To descend from these dizzying altitudes of rhetoric, where the wish is father to every thought, to the humbler, more terrestial realm where Mr. Rosenquest's creation actually exists, is to find oneself confronting a slick, cheerful, overblown piece of work that is, expressively, on a level with the commercial art from which its visual materials are drawn. Far from prompting any deep emotions about the fate of civilization, this is the kind of visual spectacle—gay, extrovert, technically adept, but irredeemably superficial—that leaves the spectator feeling as if he ought to be sucking on a popsicle.

If there is an important sociological phenomenon here, it will be found in the way the Metropolitan has mounted the painting, not in the painting itself. The notion of employing Poussin and David as some sort of support for the Rosenquist work is itself an idea of stunning vulgarity and insensitivity, and thus not without significance in the realm of museum standards and responsibilities. Indeed, it betrays a total indifference to esthetic standards to include the Lieutze painting in a class—no matter how defined—with Poussin and David, but I suppose it was necessary to come up with a work of high kitsch that would provide a transition from the high art of these French masters to the high camp of "F-111."

●

All in all, this showing of Mr. Rosenquist's painting is a lamentable event. True, the picture is famous, and Mr. Rosenquist enjoys an international renown because of it. But no one at the Metropolitan is willing to claim greatness for the work—even Henry Geldzahler, the curator of contemporary arts, avows that the "question of quality seems irrelevant"—and only greatness could justify still another mounting of the painting under these prestigious auspicies.

Still, there are aspects of the occasion that one will long remember. Mr. Scull's contribution to the museum's Bulletin, for example is a classic of its kind.. After recounting his personal adventures in and out of the artist's studio, Mr. Scull offers us his personal response to the picture in question: "For me, the F-111 is tremendous. I am not referring to its size, although it is certainly a tour de force in this respect, with some 850 square feet of real excitement. . . . It presents the essence of the United States' relationship to the world, displaying the equation of the good life of peace, with its luxuries and aspirations, and our involvement with the potential for instant war and final annihilation.... It speaks to all mankind, employing the plain language of everyday men, not the secret signs of the specalist."

I wonder if it was art historical contributions of this quality that Mr. Hoving had in mind when he announced some months ago his ambition to make the Metropolitan "the Harvard of museums?"

FEBRUARY 18, 1968

February's Prospects Brightened by a Formal Dinner-Dance

By CHARLOTTE CURTIS

IT looked for a while as if February's social activities were going to be nothing more than zany parties. Then Mrs. Albert D. Lasker came to the rescue.

The philanthropist, who periodically fills the spacious white interiors of her Beekman Place town house with friends, gave a formal dinner Thursday night followed by a dance.

According to Mrs. Lasker, the gathering was "a little party for Chuck and Lynda Bird," which is to say Capt. Charles S. Robb, U.S.M.C., and his bride, the former Lynda Bird Johnson, and they turned up hand in hand.

Mrs. Lyndon B. Johnson, done up in a gold dress with dangling earrings, was there, too. And both Mrs. Johnson and Mrs. Robb had pulled-back hairdos with wispy little curls, which may or may not mean that everybody else will run right out for similar coiffures.

"All I want is for Chuck and Lynda Bird to have a good time," Mrs. Lasker said before her party began. "It's all for them."

The Robbs, who were married at the White House on Dec. 9, responded by shaking hands with as many of the 126 other guests as they could and by dancing cheek to cheek. Captain Robb kissed his wife on the forehead every now and then. And Mrs. Robb kept slipping her right arm around her husband's waist.

While all this was going on, Mrs. Johnson was standing next to a big white sofa, talking with such people as Paul Hoffman, head of the United Nations Special Fund Committee for International Development, or Mrs. Robert Sarnoff, whose husband is president of the Radio Corporation of America.

The Duchess of Buccleuch, who has something like three stately homes (two in Scotland and one in England). was complimenting Kenneth J. Lane, who designed her frankly fake earrings. And Miss Warrie Lynn Smith, a bridesmaid at the Robb wedding, was describing life as she lives it in Washington.

"I'm definitely not with the C.I.A.," Miss Smith told Giancarlo Uzielli, the stockbroker. "I'm with the Foreign Service."

"Oh no you're not," Mr. Uzielli said laughingly. "You're Agent Double-O Smith."

Besides cocktails and dinner, there were waiters with silver trays of champagne, waitresses with little sandwiches for the dancers and music throughout the house. And, as usual, Mrs. Lasker had indulged her passion for masses of fresh, casually arranged anemones, carnations, tulips and roses.

Such parties, while typical of what New York's elegant social establishment is about, are really not what's happening in New York these days.

Out along the fringes of what is generally accepted as society, there are "new" kinds of gatherings—a black-tie cocktail party that started at 10 A.M., a formal dance at a Horn & Hardart, and charity doings at which the chairman wore a full-length chinchilla wrap with shocking pink lounging pajamas and two wigs.

Then there was the dinner and dance Robert C. Scull, the taxicab tycoon, and his wife gave for James Rosenquist, the artist. They had their dinner at their Fifth Avenue apartment. The dance was in a loft on Lafayette Street not far from the Bowery.

Mrs. Scull, like Mrs. Lasker, had what she called "a very, very small party." There were nearly 200 guests. And she, too, had music (the Scarecrows dress to match their names and play amplified electronic guitars) and flowers (brightly colored little paper ones that were sprinkled over neon-pink, green or yellow satin tablecloths).

"I tried for something vulgar, something haphazard on purpose," said Joel Schumacher, who did the decorations. "I wanted it more sleazy than vulgar. When you're dealing with a dance, it has to be elegant or like a discothèque. I hope it's nightclubby."

It was, and Miss Susan Stein, whose father heads the Music Corporation of America (and who also goes to Mrs. Lasker's), adored it. So did Mrs. Betty Friedan, author of "The Feminine Mystique."

"But you have to grow up knowing this sort of thing to appreciate it," Mrs. Friedan shouted over the boom boom of the music.

Nathan Cummings, chairman of Consolidated Foods Corporation, grew up before the invention of whatever form of rock 'n' roll the Scarecrows were playing and long before the era of so-called psychedelic environments.

But even he was out on the dance floor for a few minutes, gamely hopping around beneath the yards of kitchen aluminum foil that had been suspended in panels from what apparently was yet another of Mr. Rosenquist's neon sculptures.

Aside from what onlookers diagnosed as a great talent for the African twist, Miss Stein's chief contribution to the evening was the remarkable way in which she hitched up her full-length black and white zebra-striped evening dress.

"It goes like this," she said, doubling the long skirt up under a belt. "It's a miniskirt. I can wear it either way."

Guests were impressed, too, with Mr. Scull's sideburns ("My son told me to get with it") and his floppy black velvet tie; with Larry Poons, the artist, who identified himself as Jack Daniels; with Robert Rauschenberg, the artist, who managed to dance with two women at once, and with Mrs. Scull.

The hostess was in ruffled white organdy with a daisy-trimmed bolero. She had a Pinkerton man and two men from her husband's taxi company at the door to keep out crashers. And when a man she didn't want got through, she herself publicly told him to get out.

"We had a party like this," said Mrs. Henry Berger, who is Anita Louise, the actress. "I don't know what you'd call it, but it was black-tie with hot dogs and chili."

"And Eskimo pies," Mr. Berger said. "It was loads of fun."

Everybody at Mrs. Lasker's thought her party was fun, too.

FEBRUARY 25, 1968

It Would Be Awfully Nice If We Were All Wrong About the Whole Thing

By JOHN CANADAY

"F-ONE-ELEVEN" is a series of 51 panels adding up to a length of more than 85 feet, painted by James Rosenquist, that appears to be an effort to bring pop art of age. The Metropolitan Museum is an institution nearly a hundred years old, directed by Thomas P. F. Hoving, that to date has been dedicated to the exhibition and preservation of works of fine art. Currently "F-111" is on exhibition in the Metropolitan. I am of two minds about the whole thing. Sometimes I think "F-111" comes off worse than the museum does. At other times, I think the museum comes off worse than "F-111" does.

As an ex-painter of the kind of gigantic signs that urge us to see this or that movie on Times Square, Mr. Rosenquist, a charter member of the American pop art group, has held from the beginning an indisputable claim to legitimacy. Where his less fortunately trained colleagues had to synthesize styles reflecting the vulgarities of the American scene upon which pop art capitalizes, Mr. Rosenquist's sign painting was triumphantly vulgar to begin with. His bumptious awfulness has been his strength.

*

The weakness of "F-111" is that Mr. Rosenquist, or somebody acting as his mentor, decided that bumptiousness was not enough, that it was time Mr. Rosenquist turned out a Social Document with a Program. "F-111" is it. Named after the fighter-bomber of the same initial and number, "F-111" is an assemblage of billboard size, billboard style illustrations of industrial-military aspects of our society, from lightbulbs to the hydrogen bomb. A visual double entendre, included at the far right in the illustration above, shows a mess of spaghetti with tomato sauce that might be human entrails—this, at least, is my interpretation of the passage. The climactic panel, also visible here, shows a little girl under a hair dryer that could be the nose cone of a space missile, a double comment (as I see it) first on the cultural perversion that takes little girls into beauty shops and then on the misalliance of science and barbarism by which the same little girls may be atomized.

This one panel shows that "F-111" could have been a good thing over-all; standing alone, it is at least a wry if not powerful comment—a sick epigram of sorts. But it cannot carry the rest of the panels, where the point is not extended but only belabored, and belabored feebly at that.

A fundamental trouble with "F-111" as a social comment is that it negates its reason for being: although it is full of sinister prophecies of the end of our world, it says at the same time that our world is so hideous that we might as well blow it up and be done with it. But to worry about whether or not "F-111" has a reason for being is to take it too seriously. Pretentious and juvenile in conception, Mr. Rosenquist's great big pseudo-editorial is not too bad when it is taken as an entry in the vaudeville sweepstakes of the international exhibitions where it has been prominently exhibited. At the Metropolitan, on the other hand, where our standards are lifted the minute we enter the doors, "F-111" becomes an embarrassing exposure How weary its photomontage approach to composition; how stale its pretensions to literacy; how flat its declamation; how unprofitable its effort to invest the agreeable highjinks of pop art with sober meaning. Pop art in "F-111" takes up where Salon art died a well-deserved death almost a hundred years ago. It is an outsize picture aspiring to eloquence but ending in fustian, successful in one ambition alone, the ambition to occupy a large amount of wall space in a prestigious institution. The Metropolitan has been stirred to take Poussin's "Rape of the Sabine Women," David's "Death of Socrates," and a variation of Leutze's "Washington Crossing the Delaware" from their places in other galleries and has hung them with "F-111" under the title "History Painting—Various Aspects." Even "Washington Crossing the Delaware" deserves better than this, and the other two paintings are simply sold into prostitution. A coherent exhibition of aspects of history painting could very well conclude with "F-111," but the Metropolitan's slapdash, last minute effort to justify a lapse from policy is difficult to stomach.

*

Or perhaps it is not a lapse from policy. Perhaps it is symptomatic of new policy, which would make things even worse. We are assured that Mr. Hoving is engaged in the admirable program that he outlined when he assumed the directorship, and in that promise we must put our faith. But while great projects are gestating, we are being treated to rather trying evidence of a taste for stuntsmanship that seems to have been acquired while he was doing a good job as Park Commissioner. He made a beautiful transition from the cloistered Metropolitan to the limelight of that job, but now that he is back, he seems to miss the excitement.

The museum's announcement of its discovery that its famous Greek horse was a fake, was made in the museum's auditorium with flourishes unequaled by anything since the first time a woman was sawed in half on a public stage, and one almost feels, upon entering the Great Hall nowadays, that one must check to see whether a bicycle rental stand has been installed by the sales counter and whether the Grand Staircase has been turned into a ski slope. Either innovation would be more welcome than a departure made in connection with the exhibition of "F-111," when Robert C. Scull, who with Mrs. Scull owns the painting, was invited to expound his ideas in a fireside chat for the museum's Bulletin, supplanting the curators and other scholars who normally contribute to that publication.

These comments, of course, are made from this writer's judgment that "F-111" is not a painting up to the Metropolitan's standards, and his feeling that surely Mr. Hoving knows it isn't. That is not fair to Mr. Hoving, since he has stated that he finds "F-111" to be of timely sociological importance—but such a conviction on his part is in itself distressing. There seems to be no way out.

Except, of course, that there is always the rest of that wonderful place, the Metropolitan Museum of Art, to wander around in. Just forget that we made any objections.

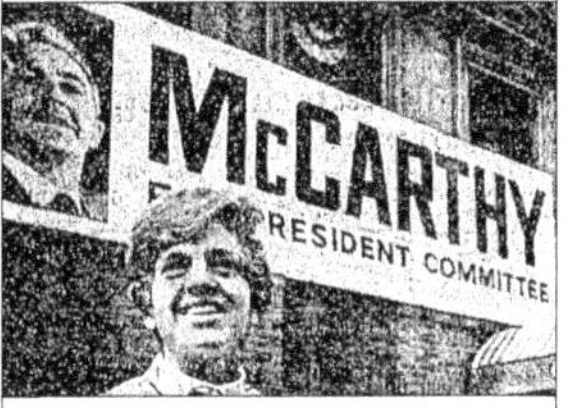

APRIL 12, 1968

McCarthy's Women Charm Voters on Campaign Trail

By MARTIN ARNOLD

"In the beginning it was this existentialist thing, but I'm beginning to believe this fantastic thing could happen and we could just elect a President," Betty Friedan, the author, happily told a room full of people in her West Side apartment yesterday.

They were awaiting the arrival of Mrs. Eugene J. McCarthy, wife of the candidate for the Democratic Presidential nomination, and Mrs. Robert C. Scull, wife of the pop art collector, was saying, "she must have a chance to rest, *poor thing.*"

"She has a wonderful face," chimed in Myrna Loy, the actress.

For, Mrs. Abigail Quigley McCarthy, a handsome woman who was a Phi Beta Kappa student, holds a master's degree in English and has taught English literature in college, the cocktail party was the end of a low-keyed but busy day of campaigning here for her husband. Last night, she was scheduled to attend a reception in Scarsdale.

Mrs. McCarthy started her day campaigning with her daughter, Mary, 18, at Columbia University, where they spoke to several hundred students in the McMillin Theater.

"I feel that many people support Gene as a candidate because he was the man who stepped forward this year without thought of personal loss," she said. "They may not know his 20-year history in politics as I do."

"Some of you are too young to remember the terror of the other McCarthy era," she told the students, referring to the late Wisconsin Senator, Joseph W. McCarthy. "Such a terror, such a freezing, that many men of great honor and great name weren't there. But Gene went on the air to debate him because he always fought the scapegoat theory of history.

"I was terrified. I was dragging my feet. I felt that someone should do this, just as last November I felt the same thing, but that it shouldn't be him. I was dragging my feet all the way."

"That's the kind of thing a wife remembers," Mrs. McCarthy said. "It's all of the same with Gene. The whole style of his campaign. The thoughtful approach and the move to action when action must be taken." The students cheered.

Mrs. McCarthy was wearing a yellow silk dress with a black-and-white polkadot bow at her neck. She described her hairdo as a "french twist."

"Womens Wear Daily called it a 'school teacher's hairdo,'" she said, "but I don't feel that way."

Pointing to the hemline of her daughter, Mary, which was several inches shorter than her own, she said, "That's the generation gap everybody's been talking about."

After Senator Robert F. Kennedy entered the campaign, Senator McCarthy had said that he wasn't worried because he had "a secret weapon." He added: "I'm going to bring her on at the right time. She's been thinking and not saying very much."

Not an Issue

The "secret weapon" was his 12-year-old daughter, Mary, a seventh-grade student who is home in Maryland. The Columbia students who heard Mary yesterday seemed to believe she was "secret weapon" enough for any candidate.

Slender with black bangs and alert eyes, she fielded questions for more than 30 minutes with the poise of a political professional.

One Columbia student stood up and said that the Federal Government had a policy of persecuting homosexuals, and where did Senator McCarthy stand on the question?

"That hasn't been an issue in this campaign," she said quickly to loud laughter and applause. "But I assume he would be against persecuting anyone, including homosexuals."

Another student asked if her father would remove J. Edgar Hoover as chief of the Federal Bureau of Investigation. She drew friendly laughter again from the students when she replied: "I don't know if he will, but I'll certainly suggest it."

Mary McCarthy has taken a leave of absence from her sophomore year at Radcliffe to campaign for her father. The two other McCarthy children, are Ellen, 20, who graduates next year from Georgetown University's School of Foreign Service, and Michael, 16, who attends Georgetown Prep.

Following the appearance at Columbia, Mrs. McCarthy went to Frank's restaurant, 315 West 125th Street, in Harlem, for a luncheon with 27 women civic leaders, most of whom were Negroes.

They were impressed with her intelligence and charm, one said, but all noted that of the four McCarthy staff members in attendance, none was a Negro.

Mrs. McCarthy told the women that her husband had a strong civil rights voting record and that during her trip with him to the funeral of the Rev. Dr. Martin Luther King Jr., they got the feeling "that good will eventually triumph."

At the party later at Miss Friedan's house, blank checks were passed out for the guests to make campaign contributions.

JUNE 1, 1968

JUNE 4, 1968

A Boutique That's All Wrapped Up in Politics

By VIRGINIA LEE WARREN

"IT COSTS $100," said Mrs. Bernard Aisenberg of a McCarthy button pinned on her watermelon pink dress, "but we expect anyone to get four years' wear out of it." She thought a minute and then said, "I mean, eight."

That was the spirit rampant yesterday at the formal opening of what its backers fondly believe to be the first political boutique: McCarthy's Mart, on the ground floor of Citizens for McCarthy headquarters, 64 West 56th Street.

Mrs. Aisenberg, a painter who lives in New Rochelle (her husband, a civil engineer, is president of Independent Democrats there) is the designer of the $100 button. It is actually a pin of 14-karat gold set with a tiny diamond, a ruby and a sapphire (to represent red, white and blue) and with the name "McCarthy" lettered in gold. It is the most expensive item at the boutique.

"I designed it so someone who wanted to show she was for McCarthy when she was dressed up could pin it on a cocktail dress or something like that," said Mrs. Aisenberg.

It is too early to tell how many women want to put campaign insignia on their dress-up clothes—the $100 item was introduced just yesterday. But the boutique, which has been having a trial run for the last 10 days, has found that a lot of women want to wear scarves and kerchiefs with their candidate's name printed liberally all over them. Of white rayon twill with lettering in blue, the scarves bring in $2 apiece, the kerchiefs $1.50.

Also on sale are buttons, including some that say "Republicans for McCarthy," for 25 cents; blue earrings with "Eugene" in white for $2; floppy-brimmed hats of the white rayon, McCarthy-lettered twill for $3, and the same twill by the yard for $2.

To show what can be done with the material, Mrs. Howard Cook, a volunteer saleswoman, wore a dress that she had made from it.

"It took about three yards," she said.

Hedda Hendrix (Mrs. Sol Edelbaum), who is more or less in charge of the boutique, had on a scalloped apron, also made by Mrs. Cook. And Mrs. Robert C. Scull, who, with Hedda Hendrix, cut the ribbon at yesterday's opening, wore a midiskirt of the same over-all design; it had been whipped up for her by Adolfo.

Posters and Records

McCarthy's Mart is to be open every day except Sundays from 10 A.M. to 9 P.M. Other articles on sale include Ben Shahn peace posters ($4 unless signed by the artist, then $75); men's cuff links and McCarthy-banded boaters for $2; a long-playing record, "The Wit of Senator McCarthy," for $5; and a 45-rpm record by Peter, Paul and Mary, "If You Love Your Country," for $1.

There are also ceramic coffeepots, guest towels and pre-Columbian figures that seem to have nothing to do with any political campaign. They have been donated and the pre-Columbian figures, priced from $25 to $50, have been selling surprisingly well.

Among those on hand for yesterday's ceremony was Robert H. Gimbel, son of Bruce Gimbel, president of Gimbels. Young Mr. Gimbel was more than welcome—he gave $50,000 to the McCarthy campaign when a fund-raising rally was held at Madison Square Garden a couple of weeks ago.

JUNE 18, 1968

Deaths

REDNER—Anna, beloved wife of Benjamin, devoted mother of Florence Naren, Lillian Kaplan and Ethel Scull, cherished grandmother and great-grandmother. Services and interment private.

AUGUST 18, 1968

The SAME Day: heeeeeewack!!!

THE PUMP HOUSE GANG. By Tom Wolfe. 309 pp. New York: Farrar, Straus & Giroux. $5.95.

THE ELECTRIC KOOL-AID ACID TEST. By Tom Wolfe. 416 pp. New York: Farrar, Straus & Giroux. $5.95.

By C. D. B. BRYAN

TOM WOLFE's first book, "The Kandy-Kolored Tangerine-Flake Streamline Baby" was a success when it was published in 1965, not so much because of *what* he said about publicity-seeking social climbers, stock-car racing drivers, teen-recording entrepreneurs and lonely divorcee mothers intimidated by the "Nanny Mafia," but *how* he said it. Wolfe's style of journalism was something new, entirely his own, as young and exuberant and frenzied as the period he was depicting.

He intimately knew and wrote about what was happening—not just now, but *NOW!*, with an explosion of asterisks, exclamation points, italics and puppyish enthusiasm. So what if occasionally he seemed almost to parody himself? When Wolfe was good, he was very, very good . . . but when he was bad he took on The New Yorker in a two-part article for Clay Felker's New York Sunday magazine supplement of The Herald-Tribune. And, oh God, the arteriosclerotic old boys, as Wolfe would call them, slapped his wrists right up to his epiglottis—not so much because his New Yorker article was filled with gross inaccuracies (which it was), but because he had been *rude* (which he had been).

Now, Tom Wolfe has published two books the same day. *Two books*:::::

————heeeeeewack————

The same day!!!!! Too-o-o-o-o-o-o *freaking* MUCH!

"The Pump House Gang," like "The Kandy-Kolored etcetera," is a collection of short, intimately subjective pieces about publicity-seeking social climbers, California surfing entrepreneurs, motorcycle racers, lonely London socialites and Eastern businessmen intimidated by the Not Our Class, Dear, Mafia. Wolfe's style is a little more subdued. He is a little older, and a lot more compassionate. There is still a lingering rhetorical "so what?" that one asks oneself after reading some of the pieces, simply because, no matter how fresh a treatment an unrefreshing subject is given, one still remains bored. Teen-age California surfers are bores, really. Playboy's Hugh Hefner is a bore, really. The New York Hilton is a bore, really. Actress Natalie Wood is a——well, her taste in art is a bore, really. And yet, Tom Wolfe manages somehow to imbue them all with a semblance of life, no matter how depressing they may seem.

The best piece in this collection is "Bob and Spike," Wolfe's portrait of Robert and Ethel Scull. Superficially, it is a devastating caricature of New York society and its art world; actually, Wolfe has written a perceptive (and, at times, quite moving) story about two people in love with each other and Society. Wolfe, in his introduction, compared Hefner to Fitzgerald's Gatsby. Scull (a taxicab fleet owner *cum* Pop Art taste and Aristotelian ambitions) would have seemed the more striking comparison. Although Wolfe points out that others might snigger at the Sculls' social aspirations, he does not. With a great deal of compassion he has skillfully drawn the portrait of an absolutely contemporary New York couple. So what if they're not entirely *likable*? They have *moxie* and style—and one ultimately feels the same sort of affection for them that one feels, say, for the New York *Mets*.

Unfortunately, however, "The Pump House Gang" isn't really much more than a remake, a "Son of Kandy-Kolored." It's good enough, but not in the same league as "The Electric Kool-Aid Acid Test," which is why I suppose he had it published on the same day, almost as if he, himself, looked upon it as a throwaway.

"The Electric Kool-Aid Acid Test" is an astonishing book. It is to the hippie movement what Norman Mailer's "The Armies of the Night" was to the Vietnam protest movement. Mailer was precisely the right author to capture the essence of those two days last October, when students, academic liberals, the intellectual New Left, the militants and nonmilitants and the marching mothers confronted the American Nazis, the Federal marshals and the United States Army on the steps of the Pentagon. Wolfe is precisely the right author to chronicle the transformation of Ken Kesey from respected author of "And One Flew Over the Cuckoo's Nest" to an LSD enthusiast, to the messianic leader of a mystical band of Merry Pranksters, to a fugitive from the F.B.I., California police and Mexican Federales.

"The Electric Kool-Aid Acid Test" is a celebration of psychedelia, of all its sounds and costumes, colors and fantasies. Wolfe, like Mailer, participates instead of merely reporting. Wolfe, like Mailer, makes no pretense of being objective. And it is Wolfe's involvement, as it was Mailer's involvement, that makes his book so successful, just as (inexorably) such involvement created some flaws. At times, Wolfe seems to be as indiscriminate an observer as a wide-angle camera panning back and forth across crowded rooms. At times, he dollies in for closeups of characters or incidents whose significance is never determined. And at other times he piles elaboration upon elaboration until reality is buried under illusions of evaluation.

It is Wolfe's enthusiasm and literary fireworks that make it difficult for the reader to remain detached. He does not hesitate to tell us what to think, how to react, even what to wear as he wings us along with Ken Kesey and his band of Merry Pranksters in a brightly painted, Ampex-loaded cross-country bus. Or on a weekend romp with the Hell's Angels. Or at a successful taking-over and turning-on of a Unitarian church convention. Or into the unintended debacle Kesey's Pranksters made of a protest rally, before they went into hiding in Mexico. Wolfe has written a marvelous book about a man I suspect is not so marvelous; and my reservations about this book stem from my feeling that some of Kesey's dazzle-dust still lingers in Wolfe's eyes.

Kesey's Commandment was that one must go beyond LSD, "graduate from acid," as he proclaimed over and over again. But Kesey never seemed able to, and never will be able to until he can graduate from his awesome sense of self-importance. Kesey never was advanced as far as another and younger apprentice mystic, Franny Glass, who 11 years ago was "sick of ego, ego, ego. My own and everybody else's." Kesey comes across in this book as a man inordinately aware of his own heroic potential. (So did Mailer, in "Armies of the Night," but he had a sense of humor about himself which one sorely misses in Kesey.)

Wolfe wrote in his Author's Note, "For all the Pranksters, as I have attempted to show, the events described in this book were both a group adventure and a personal exploration. Many achieved great insight on both levels." We-e-e-e-ll, I'm not so convinced about that. I would have liked to find in the book some evidence of their attempts to articulate those great insights, the new knowledge they gained of themselves which they didn't have before. I accept that they achieved more self-confidence, but insights . . . ? What happens often with LSD (and what, I suspect, happened with Kesey and the Merry Pranksters) is that one dominant member of the group provides or insinuates or directs all of the insights and, of course, they are *his*. The others accept them, absorb them as if by osmosis, digest them, but these insights don't-really-have-any-meaning. One must go beyond acid. God is Love. Yes, well . . .

Throughout "The Electric Kool-Aid Acid Test," Wolfe refers to dropping acid as "the *experience*"; and no matter what one says pro or con LSD, it is a profound experience. And this, I think, is why Wolfe's book is so significant: it accurately and absolutely depicts the change that has occurred in the ethics of the American young, whose contemporary morality is based upon esthetic rather than social values. If it's *beautiful*, do it. The Protestant Ethic (work is the way to salvation and worldly achievement a sign of God's favor, to which one adds a pinch of forsake pleasure now for deeper and greater satisfaction later) is being replaced by the fundamental value of the immediate, direct experience, the Pleasure Now principle.

Drugs do provide the immediate, direct experience, the Instant Profundity, witness Kesey and his Merry Pranksters; *but* one finds it difficult to accept Kesey as a leader, mystic or otherwise, after he permitted the Electric Kool-Aid to be served at the Watts Acid Test, where many people drank it unaware the Kool-Aid was heavily laced with LSD. That's playing God with people's minds and nobody, *nobody* has the right to do that. If there ever was an opportunity for Wolfe to draw some objective conclusions about Kesey, that was the moment. Wolfe chose not to. He never looked back, but instead continued to describe the activities of the band of Merry Pranksters as if to suggest it was all in good fun. A lot of the book *is* good fun. It is an astonishing, enlightening, at times baffling, and explosively funny book.

"The Pump House Gang" is illustrated adequately by the author; "The Electric Kool-Aid Acid Test" is not illustrated. Instead, Wolfe has slipped in some of his poetry. *Slipped in.* Which reveals how his style has been influenced by

Influenced by.

Edgar Allan Poe and Rudyard Kipling and a host of anonymous limerick authors.

Poe. Kipling:::::

Huhhhhhhhhhnnnnnhhh

Ulalume. Gunga Din. The Tomb.

BRANGGGGGGGGGGGG . . . .

E-e-e-e-e-eEE!

About that poetry: Nevermore.

OCTOBER 6, 1968

Art Notes

Moving Mother Earth

By GRACE GLUECK

A BACK - TO - THE - LANDSCAPE show is burgeoning at — of all places! — the Dwan Gallery, though you can't exactly call it a revival of the Barbizon School. The medium (and message) is Mother Earth herself—furrowed and burrowed, heaped and piled, mounded and rounded and trenched. Called "Earthworks," the show boasts projects by nine artists who reveal their geophilia in photos, models and actual chunks of ground.

Robert Morris, for instance, has contributed a 6x6-foot pile of unsculptured terra firma. One of Claes Oldenburg's entries is a case of loam fraught with active earthworms. And Walter de Maria has sent from Germany a blown-up photo of a Munich gallery, whose floor he has carpeted wall-to-wall with dirt.

"We hope to get away from the formalism of studio art," says Robert Smithson, one of the show's prime movers, "to give the viewer more of a confrontation with the physicality of things outside. It's diametrically opposed to the idea of art as decoration and design."

*

Smithson, whose previous work has run to "perspective systems," has come up with a complex contribution that he calls a "non-site." It's a 5-part series of wooden bins, arranged in a perspective scheme and filled with limestone fragments from a mineral dump in Franklin Furnace, N. J. (a famous haunt for rock hounds). Shown with it is a blown-up aerial photo, pinpointing the actual sites from which the limestone was taken. The viewer can heighten his "participation" by touring them.

"This brings an abstract, rather than natural awareness of the landscape," says Smithson, who rejoices in the "dualism" between the rock (raw material) and its bins (an artificial, gallery-type scheme). "The earth to me isn't nature, but a museum. My idea is not anthropomorphic. It relates to man and matter rather than man and nature."

Even deeper into the ground thing is Mike Heizer, a 23-year-old ex-painter who comes from a family of geologists and mining engineers (his father is a digging anthropologist). Accompanying Smithson and his wife Nancy on a rock-hunt last summer in the West, Heizer put down a series of "earth liners" along a 520-mile string of dry lake beds running from Las Vegas to Oregon. His "conglomerate project" consists of eight 5-part clusters of light-catching trenches—12" deep, 12" wide, 12' long—positioned according to the sun's East-West trail.

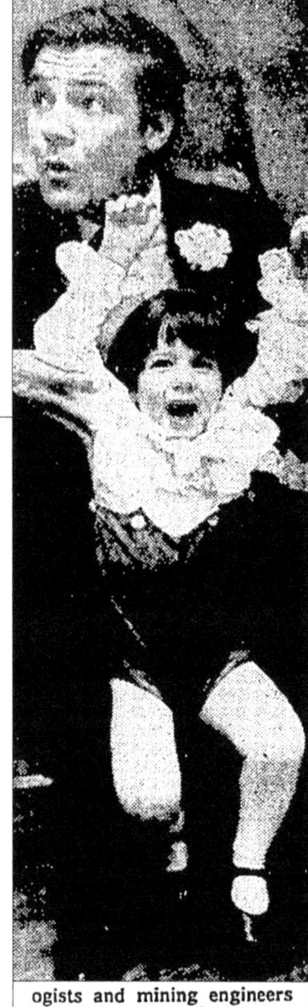

"I refuse to draw limits because a work isn't practical," Heizer says. "In fact, my earth liners can be collected, if someone wants to put them in his yard. I did them in the desert because no one wanted them." (Actually, Heizer's desert works are "owned" by collector Robert Scull, who has already made a proprietary tour of them by helicopter.)

The "historical" work in the show is a grass-wall sculpture of 1955, done in Aspen, Colo., by 68-year-old Herbert Bayer, a versatile ex-Bauhaus man. A giant ring of turfy earth (shown in a blown-up photo) it might have been turned out by a cosmic Jello mold. "If we were a museum, of course," muses Virginia Dwan, the Minnesota Mining (hmm!) and Mfg. heiress who owns the gallery, "we could have started with the Mayans and Egyptians."

The notion for the show goes back two years, when Smithson was hired as an art consultant by Tippetts - Abbett - McCarthy - Stratton, an architectural - engineering firm working up proposals for a Dallas-Fort Worth airport. His ideas for "aerial art" — sculptured mounds of earth and gridworks viewable from low-flying aircraft—are under consideration. But so far, the airport has not got off the drawing board.

OCTOBER 30, 1968

NOVEMBER 24, 1968

Art Notes

An Erotic Auto, A Roomful Of Fog

By GRACE GLUECK

COLLAGE

The "anonymous" Los Angeles art disposal service, described in this column last week, was really hatched by John Manno, an L.A. artist-teacher, according to the L.A. Free Press. Why? "The things in the galleries don't represent real works of art—they're mostly the dealer's choices of what they think will sell," Manno told the newspaper. On its initial run, in a labeled dump truck, the A.D.S., alas, collected nothing . . . For his temporary quarters in the new Executive Office Building, Pres.-Elect Nixon has borrowed from the National Collection of Fine Arts ten 20th-century American paintings. The catholic selection (chosen by the NCFA) includes John Twachtman, William Zorach, Fritz Glarner, John Marin, Abbott T. Thayer . . . Yale University has transformed the one-time United Restaurant, a former student haunt on Chapel St., into the United Restaurant Gallery, a showcase for student work, organized and operated by students in its school of Arts and Architecture . . . Two more collectors On Collecting Art: Roy S. Neuberger, whose book, "An American Collection," has been published by Harry Abrams; Robert Scull, who is working up something for Macmillan.

JANUARY 7, 1969

Mr. John and Adolfo: Hats and Whatnot

By BERNADINE MORRIS

SHOEMAKERS can stick to their lasts, but milliners better not cling to their hat blocks. They wouldn't survive in a day when hats mean fur warmers in the winter and head scarves in the summer.

It's the twilight of the great milliners, but Mr. John and Adolfo aren't sobbing into their egrets. They've simply managed to retool.

"What does it matter if I sell a hat or a belt or a pair of pants?" Mr. John asked before his spring "millinery" show yesterday morning.

"There's no such thing as a hat maker any more," he added without a trace of bitterness. Actually, there was a feeling of exhilaration as he boasted of "carrying on the revolution started by the kids with their attic clothes." His mission is "to give the movement refinement with a beautiful piece of linen or a silver belt," he explained.

As for Adolfo, who got a lot of his fans up in midi-length skirts last year, he has plenty of new fantasies in mind for them this spring.

White organdy pinafores, for example, which some of the faithful are likely to wear over nothing but skin. The models wore them over basic black jump suits. Then there are totally flowered overalls worn over totally sheer blouses. They're as defiantly picturesque as Marie Antoinette at Le Trianon or anybody's favorite romantic. Who cares if the suspenders have a tendency to slip down one arm? Mrs. Robert C. Scull, for one, couldn't wait for hers to arrive. The taxi magnate's wife plans to wear the one made of anemones to a party she's giving tomorrow.

Oh yes, the hats. There were hats, of course. With the pinafores, deep-brimmed straws, shading the face, with crowns rimmed in flowers. Or smooth white straws covered with coarse black veiling. With the blooming overalls, a bunch of the same flowers—poppies, tulips, geraniums or anemones—tucked in the hair.

His and Her Hats

With practically everything else, including city clothes, white felt snap brim or creased crown hats, not unlike the ones men wear. Why not, with women wearing pants? Adolfo makes them for men, too, and cites Mr. and Mrs. Wyatt Cooper as one of the couples who are enthusiastic about his and her hats.

Mrs. Cooper, who is the former Gloria Vanderbilt, admitted that she and her husband each have "those Cossack-looking things in curly fur," but she wasn't wearing hers to the show. She arrived bare-headed in Adolfo's new daytime coat in fireman red; it reached to her shoe tops.

With his enormous coolie hats in lacquered red, green and black, Adolfo may have come up with an answer to the nagging question of what to wear with pants. After all, Chinese peasants wear trousers too.

Though Mr. John's invitations still warn that "guests will not be admitted without hats," he admits this is an anachronism.

"To wear a hat at the wrong moment is dangerous," he says.

What the right moment is must be decided by the wearer, but Mr. John makes plenty of interesting suggestions, down to a pink terry cloth hat and skirt to wear to the beach.

Mr. John is still responsible for some of the best-looking hats in town, but he obviously isn't taking them too seriously. A scarf edged in beads or feathers and tied under the chin qualifies as a hat. So does a sliver of chiffon wrapped around the forehead.

His outstanding design has a stitched brim and a belt slipped through loops on the crown and looks like the trench coat with which it should be worn. Other styles are like paper bags, and they're made of the same cotton knit as the T shirts they accompany. Dirty hair hats, girls used to call them long ago. Now the hair can be tucked into them even when it doesn't need a shampoo.

He has hats made of caning, like chairs, and hats of bright prints to match handbags and scarves. Both kind are worn with handkerchief linen dresses ("the more you wash them, the better they get, like a stew," says the designer), with denim shifts dotted with grommets and with cotton pants made of an elastic so they fit anybody.

But the silver belts, the chains, the beaded necklaces and the cotton lace stoles are given equal billing.

The golden age of the milliners may have ended, but a visit to their custom salons, where hat prices start at $65 and pants may cost $300, is a lot more fun now.

JANUARY 31, 1969

Pamela Zauderer Wed to Robert T. Sakowitz, Houston Merchant

By JUDY KLEMESRUD

Miss Pamela Georgea Zauderer, one of the more glamorous rich girls about town, was married yesterday to Robert T. Sakowitz of Houston in what was probably one of the most spectacular nuptial events in Manhattan in some time.

The wedding's highlights included:

¶A string quartet from the New York Philharmonic playing the traditional wedding music.

¶A medieval theme, which was carried out in the bride's and bridesmaids' gowns, and later in the decorations at the reception for 700 persons at the St. Regis-Sheraton Hotel.

¶10,000 yellow roses flown in from Texas at a cost of $8,000, for use as centerpieces at the reception.

¶A six-tier wedding cake with a cowboy and cowgirl on top.

"This is the wedding of the year—so far, anyway," said Ralph Aquino, floral designer for the hotel, who came from a vacation in Aruba a week early to tend to the elaborate floral arrangements.

The ceremony was performed at 4 P.M. in the home of the bride's parents at 911 Park Avenue by Rabbi H. J. Schachtel of Houston. It was attended only by members of the couple's families.

Miss Zauderer is the daughter of Mr. and Mrs. George Zauderer of New York and Apple Blossom Farm in Mount Kisco, N. Y. Mr. Sakowitz is the son of Mr. and Mrs. Bernard Sakowitz, of Houston and Thunderbird Ranch, Woodlake, Tex.

The slender, dark-haired bride, who was given in marriage by her father, wore a medieval-styled gown of white wool designed by Donald Brooks. The gown was crisscrossed in front with white moiré cording, and its matching belt gave it a monk's robe effect. She wore a white braided tiara decorated with silk tassels and carried calla lilies.

Mrs. Peter O. Duchin, sister of the bride, was matron of honor. The attendants were Mrs. Oscar S. Wyatt Jr., sister of the groom; Miss Lammy O. Johnstone, Miss Marcia Meehan, Mrs. Manuel de Miranda, Mrs. Sherwood Schearer and Mrs. Paul S. Young. They were dressed similarly to the bride, except their gowns were of deep amber velvet with white tassels dangling from the sleeves.

Jason E. Duchin, nephew of the bride, was the ring bearer. He wore a white ruffled blouse and gold velvet breeches.

The bridegroom's father served as best man. Ushers included Oscar S. Wyatt Jr., brother-in-law of the bridegromm; Steven B. Wyatt and Douglas B. Wyatt, nephews of the bridegroom, and Peter O. Duchin, brother-in-law of the bride.

Shortly before the ceremony, Mrs. Zauderer said that she had at first been a little hesitant about her daughter's wedding plans.

"I didn't approve of her ideas on the gowns," she said. "They certainly weren't like the ones in Julie Nixon's wedding. But then I decided this is how young people are expressing themselves today. And now I'm with it."

The bride comes by her avant-garde fashion ideas quite naturally. She has been director of publicity for Paraphernalia, the far-out boutique chain, where dresses generally sell for less than $100.

The bridegroom, on the other hand, is executive vice president of Sakowitz, Inc., of Houston, the specialty store chain that is presided over by his father. Sakowitz dresses often run a bit higher than those at Paraphernalia; a bejeweled gown by George Halley in the store's Christmas catalogue was offered for $125,000.

"We sold one," the bridegroom said, "but I can't reveal his name. All I can tell you is that he's from Brazil."

In addition to the 10,000 yellow roses, the St. Regis Roof and Penthouse were festooned with orange and gold medieval banners that were draped tentlike from the ceiling. The bride had requested them because she wanted to block out the pink ceiling, which she considered "too wedding-ish."

"I wanted the reception to look like a party or a dance," she said. "I think it should really be fun, and not just to pay respects to the couple. This kind of shocked my mother."

Music for dancing was played by brother-in-law Peter Duchin and two of his orchestras. Mr. Duchin said this was one gig he was doing "pretty close to free."

"The musicians will be paid, naturally," he said, "but I'm not taking a thing."

A few minutes later, Mr. Duchin had to join the receiving line to retrieve his son, Jason, 2, who was rolling around on the floor in front of the bridal party because he wanted to be with his mother.

"Jason, stop that foolishness!" Mr. Duchin said, in a tone that was much stricter than the smile on his face.

The guests included Mr. and Mrs. Charles Revson, Mrs. Robert Scull, Mr. and Mrs. Joseph S. Lauder, Margaret, Duchess of Argyll, and Mr. and Mrs. Giancarlo Uzielli.

When Mr. Uzielli went through the receiving line, he startled the bridegroom by kissing him on both cheeks, Italian style.

Mrs. Sakowitz, a graduate of Brearley School and Briarcliff College, attended the Institute of Fine Arts and the National Academy of Art. She was presented in 1962 at a dinner dance given by her parents at their home in Mount Kisco, and was on the committee of the Debutante Cotillion and Christmas Ball.

Her father is president of George Zauderer & Sons, a real estate and investment firm.

The bridegroom is an alumnus of St. John's School in Houston and Harvard College, where he received a degree cum laude in 1960. At Harvard he was a member of the Fly Club and Hasty Pudding-Institute of 1770.

The couple, who will have residences in both New York and Houston, plan to spend their honeymoon camping out at the Sakowitz ranch in Woodlake, Tex. Then they plan to fly to Europe on a six-week buying trip.

"That's when Pam will find out what it means to be married to a retailer," the bridegroom said.

MARCH 12, 1969

Jockey Club, an Elegant 'Barn' for Dining, Opens in Glitter

By CHARLOTTE CURTIS

Yet another spiffy Jockey Club opened here last night with the usual party and an appropriately glittering array of reasonably young guests, and, like a lot of establishments of the same name, the club at 123 East 54th Street isn't a club at all but a reasonably charming restaurant.

"It's not Pavilion," a publicity agent for the restaurant explained. "We didn't want that. It's good American cooking with man-size portions."

The explanations also included predictable paeans for the fashion artist Joe Eula's racing murals—the pièce de résistance being 31 feet of what looks like flat racing across open country in Maryland or Virginia. Mr. Eula said it was the view from a barn.

"You're in this barn, see, looking outside," he said happily. "The inside is all soft pink lights with big heavy white soup tureens for the white tulips—fresh tulips. Over your head are the beams."

Besides pink lights, soup tureens and fresh tulips, this particular barn has wire screening separating the bar from the main dining room, drawings of jockeys leading horses and nude women across the bar and—as a reminder of what in authentically horsey circles are known as racing or jockey silks—a Silk Room for private parties with nary a silk in sight.

Mr. Eula covered the walls in this room with a green, brown and yellow Ken Scott print of prancing horses. The fabric is Ban-Lon.

"It's stunning," said Mrs. Diana L. (Didi) Auchincloss, who saw the room at various stages of the decorating. "I love it."

Mrs. Auchincloss, the former Diana Lippert, is a member of the American Cancer Society's board of directors, and it was she who organized the $75-a-couple black-tie benefit opening for nearly 300 of her friends. Thomas Auchincloss, the stockbroker and her former husband, was among them.

"We're sometimes at the same parties," she conceded, and she didn't look the slightest bit upset.

Mrs. Auchincloss's dress was of long white cotton lace appliquéd with blue flowers. It was a ladylike gown at a party dominated by undernourished girls in flamboyant gypsy costumes, pants suits with deep, deep V's down the front, or skirts just short enough to be dismaying. These are the girls with all the hair, the little evening bags slung over their shoulders and the beige-to-brown eye make-up.

The invitations said 8 P.M., which is when the bar opened, but few of the guests arrived until 8:30 and dinner wasn't served until after 9:30. In the meantime, Mrs. Auchincloss and her chief assistants, Mrs. John I. Brokaw and Mrs. Thomas G. Cushing, showed their friends around.

Mrs. Brokaw, the former Nannette Cavanagh, is the wife of the lawyer and is Mrs. Robert F. Wagner's niece. She wore Oscar de La Renta's long red, white and blue flower-printed skirt with a white organdy blouse, a navy blue vest trimmed in red, a wide blue sash, masses of gilded chains and gold ram's head earrings.

"I have four sets of chains," she said, "but one chain is three tiers. I guess that makes six strands all together."

She also had her long blond hair streaming down her back.

"You have to, with this gypsy look," she confided. "It looks leaner."

Mrs. Cushing, whose husband is in Bankers Trust's international department, wore a tent of big blue paillettes. She said there was no point in her trying to look like a gypsy.

"I'm about to have a baby," she explained. "I just hope I won't have to go to the hospital in the middle of the party."

During the cocktail hour, when nearly everybody was around the bar, Mrs. Robert Scull, wife of the art collector, said she'd never seen so many men in plain old black dinner jackets.

"Stockbrokers I'll bet," she observed correctly. "It's a shame. They should look so sensational."

At about the same time, Miss Toinette Rousseau, daughter of the Howard Johnson executive who lives in Palm Beach, was arriving with John L. Loeb Jr., the banker. And Maria Livanos, daughter of the late George Livanos of the Greek shipping family, was off in a corner with Stephane Cattaui of Paris pretending they weren't engaged.

"It's a secret," Miss Livanos said, although half the guests had come over to deliver the usual best wishes.

Then there was the cloud of white feathers with the Princess Grace face and the terribly neat hairdo. She turned out to be Mrs. Stephen H. Spahn, who was neither a model nor an actress.

"My husband's headmaster of the Dwight School," she said. "The kids love it that we're young."

After drinks came a dinner that began with crabmeat au gratin and went on to steak, a green salad and a plate of strawberries mixed with whipped cream in a meringue. Herb Gruder, who owns the Jockey Club as well as Ad Lib, used to call the dessert Boccone Dolce.

"But nobody understood it," he said. "I changed it to La Dolce Vita."

During and after dinner, there was dancing to Peter Duchin's orchestra—the only dancing on the restaurant's agenda. Mr. Gruder thinks people usually like peace and quiet while they eat, and he intends to give them that on regular nights.

John R. Drexel 4th of the Philadelphia banking family was there with his fiancée, Miss Pamela Braga, and the list of invited guests included Clifford V. Brokaw 3d, the young investment banker who's been weekending in Palm Beach; Charles Addams, the cartoonist; Mrs. Edward F. Hutton, widow of the investment banker; Wendy and Heidi Vanderbilt, and lots of people who aren't either skiing or sitting in the sun.

Nobody from The Jockey Club, whose members guard the records and interests of thoroughbred racing in the United States and Canada, was there, although Miss Cynthia Phipps, a daughter of Ogden Phipps, was on the benefit committee.

The Other Jockey Clubs

Nor were there guests representing the Paris or London Jockey Clubs, which run racing abroad, the Madrid Jockey Club, a restaurant, the Washington Jockey Club, still another restaurant, the Maryland Jockey Club, one of the nation's oldest sporting associations, the Royal Hong Kong Jockey Club, a racing club with trackside boxes the size of living rooms, or the Miami Jockey Club, which is a first-class apartment-hotel development with 2,500 paid-up members.

And if anybody was up from Atlantic City's Jockey Club, a night spot that once had its liquor license suspended for what was alleged to have been a "lewd" strip tease, he didn't identify himself.

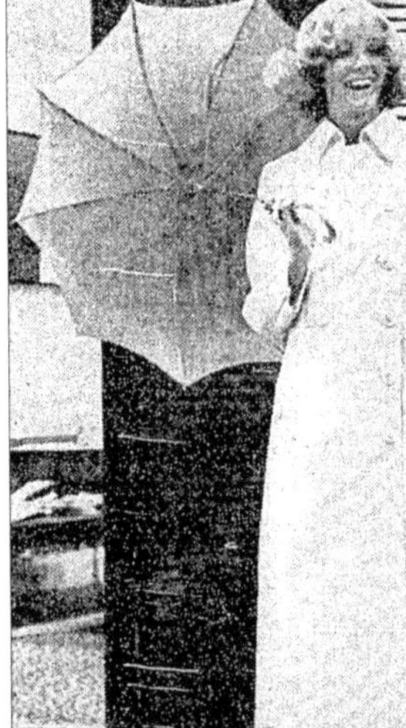

APRIL 7, 1969

For Girls Who Want to Be Noticed, It's the Floor-Sweeping Coat

By BERNADINE MORRIS

CAUTION: The next girl you see running around in broad daylight in a coat long enough to sweep the floor is not necessarily left over from the night before. She may merely be wearing the new daytime length for coats.

When everybody is wearing skirts above the knees, a girl has to do something different to get people to look. There are two things she can do: Take off some clothes or put on some clothes. These days she can attract more attention by putting them on.

How long has this long coat thing been going on? Well, not counting the Victorians, for about six years. That's when Rudi Gernreich showed a long tweed coat to wear to football games and Christian Dior showed a Ninotchka kind of thing to wear on sleighs. Nobody paid much attention.

Wasn't there some talk about long coats a year ago? There was, but nothing much came of it because they weren't long enough. They were about mid-calf length.

A lot of women didn't like the length because, if they were out of their teens, they said it made them look older, and if they were short, they said it made them look dumpy.

The floor sweepers give them a long, clean line from top to bottom. Make them look taller.

Who says so? Norman Norell, for one. Last year he tried calf lengths. He went right back to short skirts in his next collection. Now he says calf lengths were dowdy, but he's happy about the ones that go down to the floor. "I'm glad they've gone all the way," he says.

Who's wearing these long coats? Women such as Mrs. Wyatt Cooper (Gloria Vanderbilt) and Mrs. Robert C. Scull, the art collector's wife. They wore calf lengths last year and graduated to the longer ones without any trouble. Also, youngsters like Penelope Tree who were among the first to take up miniskirts. And lots of secretaries, fashion editors and girls around Bloomingdale's.

Why girls around Bloomingdale's? Because the store's on the East Side where the swingers live. And because it's been selling long coats since last August when it opened its Mic Mac shop.

The store sold "every one we could get our hands on," according to Dick Hauser, a Bloomingdale's executive. That included about 300 Mic Mac styles, which came from Europe, at $150, 40 leather coats lined in curly white lamb at $350, and hundreds of canvas coats from La Flaque de Paris (a New York concern) at $75.

A Nationwide Style

The canvas coats were designed by Victor Joris, who's been making long coats for at least five years but says "this is the first year they've been selling." They've been selling in such places as Beverly Hills, Chicago, Youngstown, Boston and Philadelphia as well as in Bloomingdale's

Fired by success, Mr. Joris has done a long coat in linen for summer.

Who needs a long coat for summer? Anybody who wants to be looked at. Gayle Kirkpatrick designed one in poplin with matching shorts. He thinks it's a great idea for the beach.

Maybe for the beach, but is it practical for the city, with puddles and buses and grime and all that? Practical has nothing to do with it. Next thing you'll be saying women are wearing long coats to keep warm.

Don't they keep them warm? Sure they do, but so do woolen stockings. Adolfo — he's the one who made the coats for Mrs. Cooper and Mrs. Scull — thinks they make women look romantic.

With Long Pants, Too

Besides short, what do they wear them with? Mostly with long pants. Ilie Wacs did a batch of long coats for Originala for fall and they all have pants to go with them. Lavino Verna of Laurence Gross likes them with a long sweater and a short skirt.

Are women really going to wear them? If they want to be noticed.

"Nobody wants to look ordinary any more," said Don Simonelli, another designer who's been pushing long coats for at least five years. "Everybody wants to dress up."

If the style is going to catch on, it's going to be this year, he added. Like most designers, he can't think of a better reason for a woman to buy a new coat than to get one that descends to the floor. If she wants to, she can even wear it at night — though that isn't really the point.

APRIL 11, 1969

Museum Gives a Party For the Robert C. Sculls

Special to The New York Times

WASHINGTON, April 10—Robert C. Scull, looking sideways at one of the Corcoran Art Gallery's marble angels said, "I thought it was a joke—I thought someone was putting me on when they said the Corcoran wanted to honor me as a collector of art.

"You know, we've always thought of the Corcoran as such a traditional gallery. And me, well, I've just commissioned earthworks in the Nevada desert."

The occasion was a "Salute to Mr. and Mrs. Robert Scull," given tonight by the Friends of Corcoran Gallery.

Asked why the group was saluting the Sculls, who live in New York and who are well known for their Pop-and-Beyond art collection, one Corcoranite said, "Why, for the publicity, of course."

Then she added quickly, "We wanted to encourage collecting in Washington. So we thought that the Sculls—after all he started collecting with Renoir—would be the ones to begin with. You hear so much about the Sculls."

Class With a Capital C

Mark Sandground, president of the Friends of the Corcoran, explained the salute this way:

"We thought the Sculls were the most colorful collectors today. Their collection of op and pop is so well known, we thought they would add class with a capital C to the Corcoran."

Mr. and Mrs. Scull gave themselves a dinner beforehand in the wood-paneled Georgetown Club with its pewter plates and fake Federal décor.

Mrs. Scull wore an Adolfo pants suit trimmed all over with yellow, white and blue cornflowers. She topped the pants with a full-sleeved organdy sash.

Mr. Scull, who owns a fleet of taxicabs, wore a big black velvet tie with his Edwardian-cut formal clothes.

"My wife a few months ago threw away all my clothes and bought me this sort of thing," he said. "I never noticed what I wore before. A gray suit is a gray suit. But I really like these new men's fashions. I even wore flowered trousers last week in Barbados, and my son said, 'great Dad.'"

A Beard Like That

At the dinner, Joseph Hirschhorn, who is giving Washington his great collection of modern sculpture, teased Henry Geldzahler, curator of American art at the Metropolitan Museum, about Mr. Geldzahler's beard.

"If I had a beard like that," said Mr. Hirschhorn, "I could go to the bank and ask them for $2-million and the bank president would sign it just like that" as he pretended to write on his napkin.

Mrs. Scull said she planned to give a party in October in Mr. Geldzahler's honor when a show of 20 works of the Sculls' collection will be open at the Metropolitan.

During the toast Mr. Geldzahler said of the Scull's art collection: "They were early and they were right."

Every woman seemed to be trying to wear her most modish outfit to balance Mrs. Scull's well-known reputation as one who wears the newest first.

Mrs. James Haritas, the wife of the Corcoran's director, had on a black lace pants suit. Mrs. Gilbert Hahn Jr., wife of the City Council chairman and Washington's own pop art collector, wore a black miniskirt with a bare midriff.

Among other guests were Mrs. René Bouché, widow of the artist; Richard Bellamy, former owner of the Green Gallery; James Rosenquist, the pop artist, and his wife.

MAY 12, 1969

It's Soul Food for Show Folk at Southern Free Theater's Fete at Waldorf

By JUDY KLEMESRUD

The aroma of Southern fried chicken wafted through the Grand Ballroom of the Waldorf-Astoria Hotel last night where 800 persons—many of them connected with showbusiness and most of dressed as if they were—paid $100 each to dine on "soul food."

The dinner benefited the Free Southern Theater, a six-year-old group formed to make theater available without charge to people in the poor black communities of the rural South.

The co-chairmen of the dinner were Bill Cosby, the comedian, and Ava Gardner, the actress, who said her southern upbringing was one of the reasons she volunteered for the job.

"There wasn't much theater of any kind when I was living in the South," said Miss Gardner, who was born in North Carolina and now lives in London. "And what little there was was not always available to blacks."

It was the 45-year-old actress's first experience as an organizer. She showed up an hour late, looking like a gypsy in a gold beaded vest and striped chiffon skirt.

"I've never been on a committee before, much less a chairman of one," she said. "But I've ended up being a regular committee lady — I even put two tables together!"

The invitations to last night's party said "dress informal," and most guests took the directive literally. The men showed up in Edwardian suits with ruffled shirts or turtlenecks with bell-bottom trousers and beads, beads, beads. For the women, it seemed to be either pants or the gypsy look.

Perhaps the most eye-catching person at the dinner was Cynthia Mitchell, whose head was shaved entirely bald except for a few tufts of hair on top that were caught with a strand of pearls.

"It's just a hairstyle, that's all," said Miss Mitchell, who described herself as "an actress and model."

The benefit set several "firsts" at the Waldorf, which is not usually known for the informality of its banquets.

"We've never fixed soul food before," said Eugene R. Scanlan, the hotel's director of food and beverage, "and we've never served 'family style' [pass-around servings on each table] before. In the past, waiters have served each and every course at the Waldorf."

The menu included fried chicken, beer, cornbread, collard greens, black-eyed peas and rice, sweet potato pie and pecan pie. There was also one very non-soul food item: consommé Madrilène.

Mr. Cosby apparently did not find the dishes tasty.

"That's not soul food!" he said, at the start of the entertainment program. "Even if you do have a grease ring around your mouths, that's not how soul food tastes. We should have had pizza."

At that point, many of the guests cheered and applauded in agreement with him.

The entertainment was almost as star-studded as the audience. Among those who performed were Lena Horne, Jack Lemmon, Ed McMahon, Duke Ellington and his orchestra, Liza Minnelli, Jerry Orbach, and members of the Free Southern Theater. Mayor Lindsay also sang a song about his political problems that was off the record to the press.

The audience included Gregory Peck, who said he had eaten soul food "many times," Lauren Bacall, Sidney Poitier, Rosalind Russell, Neal Simon, Diana Sands, Godfrey Cambridge, David Janssen, Myrna Loy, Harry Belafonte, Ann-Margret, Soupy Sales, Arlene Francis, and Kenneth Battelle, the hairdresser.

There were so many celebrities, in fact, that members of the dinner committee had problems with the seating lists. It seemed everybody wanted to be close to Gregory Peck.

"Our biggest problems occurred when a person asked to be seated near a celebrity and the celebrity didn't want to be seated near him," Mr. Peters said. "Finally, we decided to spread our celebrities out as best we could."

One guest who showed up unexpectedly was Muhammad Ali, the boxer once known as Cassius Clay, who spent most of the evening looking disgusted and complaining about the fact that so many white people had turned out for the dinner.

Pauline Trigere, the designer, said she made a special trip from her country home in Connecticut to attend the dinner.

"I should be watching my tulips instead," said the designer, who wore a pair of black and white evening pajamas by Pauline Trigere. "That means if I do anything on Sunday, I should stay home and rest."

Mrs. Robert Scull, wife of the taxicab fleet owner, said she came to the dinner because she believed in doing anything she could to "further integration."

"I'm trying to raise money to get Gian Carlo Menotti's new opera put on and I'm having trouble," she said. "So I can imagine what kind of trouble these people have when they try to raise money."

Mr. Peters said the benefit would help realize the Free Southern Theater's goal of matching a Ford Foundation grant of $50,000. The money will enable the group to continue its free performances in cornfields, barns and tents throughout the South.

"The theater brings beauty to poor black Southerners who might not travel more than 20 miles from home in their lifetime," Mr. Peters said. He paused for a moment, then added:

"But then there are a lot of people in the Bronx who don't, either."

MAY 13, 1969

Hugh Shannon Show Will Aid Strang Clinic

Hugh Shannon has created a one-man show for the May 22 dinner dance at the Rainbow Room that will benefit the Preventive Medicine Institute-Strang Clinic. The singer-pianist is donating his services for the evening.

Mrs. H. Spencer Martin, Mrs. Charles B. Tranum and Mrs. Henry S. White are co-chairmen of the event. Members of the executive committee include Mrs. Jane Brandt, Mrs. Randall M. Dubois, Mrs. William Husten, Mrs. Lawrence Lowenstein and Miss Josephine Lyons.

Among the members of the general committee are William A. Bartle 3d, Mrs. Ruth Dubonnet, Mr. and Mrs. Robert D. L. Gardiner, Mr. and Mrs. Robert Scull, Mrs. James Reeves, Mr. and Mrs. Walter F. Pape Jr., Mr. and Mrs. Walter Shirley Jr., Mr. and Mrs. Thomas F. Madigan and Mr. and Mrs. Robert Bragarnick.

The Strang Clinic is a nonprofit diagnostic and research center for the detection and prevention of cancer and causes of other serious illnesses. Its building is at 55 East 34th Street, where tickets to the dinner dance are available at $50 each.

MAY 23, 1969

If You Want to Keep One Step Ahead

By BERNADINE MORRIS

SAY this for Jon Haggins. He isn't one for drifting down the musty corridors of the past. He's more likely to visit a discothèque for ideas than museums and his clothes look it. They cling, flutter and sometimes expose. Sexy, of course, but not salacious. At 25, Mr. Haggins is on the right side of the generation gap.

Giogio di Sant' Angelo is of the moment, too. Boy, is he! Tasseled curtain sashes, brilliant scarves and nailhead-studded leather belts. Priestly vestments, Renaissance brocades and fringed Indian buckskins. All wrapped up in one heady package. What could be more contemporary?

When it comes to dresses, both designers think of slithery jerseys that lie limp as a rag until somebody puts them on. With the right person, they crackle.

When it comes to fashion shows, both think of gardens.

Mr. Haggins had his mannequins descend from the parlor-floor balcony of the East 49th Street town house of Mrs. Walter Reade Jr. into the rear patio.

Decorates Theaters

The former Dolly Martin, an interior designer, said she and Mr. Haggins "have been friends for a long time—I used to meet him at parties before I was married." Now she decorates her husband's theaters. ("He owns about 15 in New York, 90 all together," she said.)

"I didn't know what to expect when Jon asked if he could have his show here," said Mrs. Reade. "But now I'd like to do some shows for charity—if the neighbors will accept it."

She was wearing a gray and white pants suit by Princess Galitzine, with enamel chain suspenders at Wednesday's show, but she also wears some of Mr. Haggins's clothes "when they're a little covered."

Some are covered by scarves or poncho arrangements carrying a yard or so of fringe. Most wrap and tie, without any buttons or zippers to stiffen them up. There's a fringe-bearing leotard that is Mr. Haggins's idea of basic black.

Sant'Angelo isn't adverse to basic shapes either, but he doesn't stop at fringe. To a little cashmere pullover sweater (it serves as a dress, but let's not worry about that) he adds, say, a scarf around the waist and a couple more around the head, a leather garter around the thigh and a couple of leather belts around the hips, a medallion around the neck and a plastic handbag on the shoulder. It matches the plastic boots.

Mannequins dressed like that danced yesterday through the bar and into the garden of the Timothy Restaurant and Winery on Lexington Avenue, run by Timothy Remy, a former model. They showed what a simple, with-it, daytime costume was all about today.

Sometimes they were entwined in lariats of scarves knotted together as if to facilitate a second-story elopement. Sometimes they carried a pushcart load of mesh handbags. Or wore rhinestone vests like jackets of mail.

They were done up for evening in patchwork dresses, long fur coats, medieval chasubles, Venetian doge brocade robes or black suède dresses with fringed edges and rhinestones around the neck.

"When you put anything of his on, you zing," said Mrs. Robert C. Scull, whose husband owns taxicabs and collects pop art.

She feels that with Sant'Angelo on one hand and Adolfo on the other, a woman can have all the fashion support she needs. Like Adolfo, he makes clothes for women whose mission in life is to stay one step ahead of fashion.

JUNE 11, 1969

$15-Million Art Sale Falls Short

By CHARLOTTE CURTIS

The "Fifteen Million Dollar Art Auction for Youth" at the Hartman Galleries last night wasn't a $15-million event at all—merely a rather special $270,000 party that got just slightly out of hand.

"We hope to sell several million dollars worth of art and things here tonight," said Joey Adams, the comedian turned assistant auctioneer in behalf of the Police Athletic League and the Actors Youth Fund. "We want the money for the kids."

It was the last time a million anything was mentioned. The Hope Vase, a lavish urn ornamented with solid gold and said to have been made for the Lord Hope who owned the Hope Diamond, sold for a mere $20,000. And it went this way all night.

"I've never been so bored in my life," said Mrs. Robert Scull, wife of the art collector and taxi cab tycoon. "I'm leaving."

Big Spenders Leave

And at 9:30 P.M., just 45 minutes after the auction had begun, Mrs. Scull did leave, followed by such other potentially big spenders as Mrs. Samuel Newhouse, the publisher's wife; Joshua Logan, the director, and Miss Wendy Vanderbilt.

But before she tiptoed out of the blue tent over the gallery terrace where the auction was held, Alfred Gywnne Vanderbilt's dark-haired daughter did her turn on the platform. She helped the auctioneer sell Willem de Kooning's "Torso."

"No, no," cried the crowd when the de Kooning oil painting went up for display. "It's upside down."

This information didn't help much. In a minute there were more protests, particularly from a seemingly anguished Joseph E. Levine, art collector and film producer whom Mr. Adams described as "the greatest showman since Cecil B. DeMille, Barnum and Mike Todd."

"It's on its side now," Mr. Levine complained.

Goes for $4,000

The painting was finally righted, and Miss Vanderbilt went on about her business. Her chief contribution consisted of a well modulated but inaudible sentence or two and a dazzling smile. She looked remarkably like the plastic store mannekins for which she modeled. The painting, with an asking price of $3,500, went for $4,000.

Mr. Levine was back later, a volunteer auctioneer with a Pierre Pouvis de Chavannes charcoal sketch on his hands. He studied it admiringly.

"Let's start the bidding at $50,000," he said jovially.

He was offered $5,000, bid $10,000 himself, was interrupted for a bid or two by voices from somewhere across the crowded room, and ended up having auctioned, bid and bought the sketch for $12,000.

"Very nice," he said.

"Now that," Mr. Adams announced, "is my idea of a big man."

Poliakoff Abstract Given

Nathan Cummings, chairman of the Chicago-based Consolidated Food Corporation, and his wife were useful, too. They donated a Serge Poliakoff abstract expressionist painting, and Mrs. Cummings auctioned it for $4,000. Then Mr. Cummings took to the platform.

"This," he said, eyeing a red and green painting, "is a good work. I'm going to ask for a substantial bid."

The bidding started and ended with Mrs. Cummings's $5,000. Mrs. Charlotte Ford Niarchos, one of the four chairmen, seemed pleased.

"We're getting there," she said in her big, bass Middle Western voice.

Mrs. Niarchos, in a little minidress of black paillettes that resembled monkey hair, lifted paintings, praised the jewels ("Now this is divine"), auctioned a Meissen soup tureen ("I guess I'm supposed to say, 'How much am I bid' "), and nearly lost one of her own enormous diamond earrings.

"That will never do," she said, retrieving the jewel. "If they find it, they'll auction it."

The gathering, like all such tax-deductible auctions, began and ended with quantities of champagne. Mr. Adams said that was because champagne warms people up.

"This is a new thing for me," he added. "Suddenly I'm mixing in Society. They're charming, lovely people. I never knew what a Charlotte Ford Niarchos was like before. I'd met them before but I never knew them as people. Why this darling little Charlotte and Janet [Mrs. Donald Chipman, another chairman], they're just delicious. It's not like what's happening in the colleges, is it?"

No, and it wasn't like the elegant action associated with Mrs. Niarchos's previous benefits, but the auction (named for the dollar value on all the merchandise available throughout the gallery) raised more money in a single night than the better charity balls.

JULY 20, 1969

Movies

Will 'Easy' Do It for Dennis Hopper?

By TOM BURKE

DENNIS HOPPER? Oh, yes, the intense, forthright, pale-eyed boy in "Rebel Without a Cause" and "Giant" and those ponderous late-fifties television dramas. What ever happened to Dennis Hopper?

What happened was that Hopper told Hollywood where to put its antediluvian system, was industry-blackballed, ate peyote, smoked pot, dressed like Billy the Kid, let his milk-chocolate hair grow untended, met Peter Fonda, dropped acid with him off-screen and on ("The Trip"), kept insisting that he could direct a significant film, proved he was right with "Easy Rider," a moving account of young misfits crossing the Southwest on motorcycles (he wrote it with Fonda and Terry Southern, and co-starred, but directed it by himself, and promptly won the 1969 Cannes Festival award for the best movie by a new director), and came to New York to promote its local premiere.

And now he sits in a midtown actors' bar, empty this afternoon, except for a few aging chorus boys who have trailed in, dragging their airlines bags, for a beer between auditions. Some of them glance at him curiously. For one thing, he is wearing his felt outlaw's hat, Mexican shirt and Navaho talismans. For another, he is younger than almost anyone in the room. Actually, he is 33, but there is something distinctly untainted about him, something untouched, dedicated, committed. He is, in fact, utterly committed to moviemaking. This year, he dissolved his 1961 marriage to Brooke Heyward, Leland Heyward's daughter, because "the day I started 'Easy Rider,' Brooke said, 'You are going after fool's gold,' and that didn't read too well with me. Brooke is groovy, we even have a beautiful little girl, but you don't say that to me, man, about something I've waited 15 years—no, all my life—to do."

He laughs his quick, oddly apologetic laugh, doodles invisibly with his finger on the side of his Irish coffee glass, says that he had thought all interviewers were old and square ("It's not what they ask, man, it's who they *are*"), and that he hadn't expected somebody young. "It's groovy, man. Beautiful. I feel very comfortable." For this reason, perhaps, he does not wait for questions. Instead, he says, "Dodge City. I come from Dodge City, Kansas. In movies about Dodge City, they always put in big mountains but there aren't any. Just endless wheat fields, this fantastic flat horizon line, incredible electric storms, sunsets like the northern lights. Every Saturday, I'd walk from the farm into town with my grandmother, who had her apron full of fresh eggs. We'd sell them and use the money to see whatever picture was playing: Roy Rogers, Gene Autry, Smiley Burnette. Then all the next week, I'd live that picture. If it was a war picture, I'd dig foxholes; if it was sword-fighting, I'd poke the cows with a stick. Those dark little Kansas theaters, Saturday afternoons, man, that was big news to me. The old cliché, dig? Like Thomas Wolfe wanting to see where the trains were going to. I wanted to see where those movies were coming from."

Eventually he saw. When he was 14, the family moved to San Diego. "I'm creative, man," he says, straight-faced, eyes smiling, "because of my big disappointment: seeing real mountains and real ocean for the first time. Wow, what a bring-down! The mountains in my head were much bigger than the Rockies. The Pacific was the horizon line in my wheat field. Anyway, I was terrible in school, because I didn't like reading. I've read maybe eight novels in my life. I'd rather live it, man, get out in the street, get it *on*. But I did win debating contests, and apprenticed, summers, at the La Jolla Playhouse, and did Shakespeare at the Old Globe Theater. When I went to Hollywood, though, I was going to be either a matador, a race-car driver or a boxer. In Spain, if you're broke and lousy in school, you become a matador. In Italy, you race cars. Here, you box, or act. I boxed and got beat up, so acting was the only thing left."

The bar's jukebox vibrates as The Fifth Dimension segues from "Aquarius" to "Let the Sunshine In." He smiles toward the music, gently asks the tired waiter for another drink, and recites the would-be movie actor's litany: impenetrable studios, disinterested agents, starvation ("I stole milk from porches, occasionally I'd hit an orange juice"), a tiny television role, a big one, and sudden offers from five movie companies. "Columbia called first, and I was brought into Harry Cohn's huge office, with about a hundred Oscars stacked behind his desk in an arc, like a rainbow. I'd never seen an Oscar before." Laughing, he mimics the legendary Cohn. " 'I seen your TV show, kid, you got *it*, you're a natural, like Monty Clift! What else you done?' I told him about the Shakespeare, and he yelled to an assistant, 'Give this kid some numbers'—money—'and put him under contract! But we'll have to send him to a coach for a year, to take that Shakespeare out of him.' At that point, I said to Harry Cohn, 'Go ——— yourself.' Whereupon I was barred from Columbia. I didn't go back there for 15 years, until they agreed to release 'Easy Rider,' and I walked through those gates to start the editing. Freaky."

At Warners, things were happier, partly because he never had to talk to Jack Warner, mostly because of the two pictures he made with James Dean—"Rebel Without a Cause," in 1955, and "Giant," in 1956. "There'll never be anybody like Jimmy again, man. It was, in a strange way, a closer friendship than most people have, but it wasn't the kind of thing where he said, 'Let's go out and tear up the town.' Sometimes we'd have dinner. Also, we were into peyote and grass before anybody else. This is my 17th grass-smoking year. Sure, print it, why not? You can also say that that was real pot we smoked in 'Easy Rider.' I've already been busted once for possession, in L.A., but that's another story.

"Anyway, about Jimmy: what we really had was a student-teacher relationship, the only one he ever had, as far as I know. When we were making 'Rebel,' I just grabbed him one day and said, 'Look, man, I gotta know how you act, because you're the greatest!' So he asked me, very quietly, why I acted, and I told him what a nightmare my home life had been, everybody neurotic because they weren't doing what they wanted to do, and yelling at me when I wanted to be creative, because creative people ended up in bars." He looks around solemnly. "Which I later found out to be true. Anyway, Jimmy and I found we'd had the same experience at home, and that we were both neurotic and had to justify our neuroses by creating, getting the pain out and sharing it. He started watching my takes after that. I wouldn't even know he was there. Two days later, he'd come up and mumble, 'Why don't you try the scene *this* way.' And he was always right. His death blew my mind. I couldn't get it together, man, for a long time afterward. Because I really believed in predestination—that something protected gifted people until they could realize their potential. Jimmy was going to direct, and he would have been great. What's wrong with most movie directors is that they understand one aspect of a film, like photography, editing, or acting, but not all the aspects together. Jimmy did. He'd started to refuse to take direction, because all he got was *bad* direction . . ."

*

After Dean's death, Dennis started refusing direction, too, from Henry Hathaway, among others. He and Hathaway clashed while making "From Hell to Texas" in 1958, and it got around that he was unemployable. Years passed before Hathaway rehired him, for a small role in "True Grit," but Dennis doesn't regret the lean period. "I had to live out that rebellion," he asserts, his pace quickening as it always does when he speaks with conviction, "or I wouldn't have learned. If you don't refuse, at one point, to do what you don't believe in, you're never gonna grow, or get bigger than the guy who's telling you wrong. I got stronger. This time, when Henry started shooting, and said, 'No trouble from you, kid, this is a Big Duke picture, and Big Duke don't understand that Method ———,' I just nodded. I knew I was now technically proficient enough, and personally strong enough, to do Henry's number, and also do mine. There are advantages in working for the big studios once in a while. Like bread, for one. I consider it the same as, say, working for the Catholic Church in the Renaissance. If you want to paint the big ceiling, man, you gotta deal."

*

But for "Easy Rider," no deals. When Dennis and Peter Fonda acted together in "The Trip" in 1967, they ended up going out into the desert and shooting the acid-trip sequences by themselves, with their own funds, because no one else, including director Roger Corman, wanted to take the time or spend the money. Dennis directed, and though he had been a professional photographer for some time, this was his first attempt at moviemaking. He 'was instantly hooked, but no one was willing to back Hopper and Fonda in their own venture. They both got involved in other people's motorcycle pictures: Peter's "The Wild Angels" made millions, and Dennis's "The Glory Stompers" at least showed a profit, "and Peter and I decided the only way we'd get backing was another bike film. But a *different* one. Then Peter called me at, like 3 A.M., and said he'd been sitting around getting stoned and playing his guitar and he'd had this idea. It was 'Easy Rider.' Our real luck came when Bert Schneider and Bob Rafelson said they'd produce it. They gave us complete control. They just said, 'Go and do your thing and come back and show us.' And we did, man. Except for the Mardi Gras scenes, we just started out on our bikes across the West and shot entirely in sequence, as things happened to us."

Then a scenario wasn't used? Wrong; a script was carefully completed before shooting, "but it was left flexible enough that we could add to it or change it as we traveled. Some things never changed. For instance, I knew that I wanted to use songs that were already popular, rather than a new score. I knew that Peter and I and the girls we meet would never be seen totally nude in the nude swimming scene, because I wanted to show the over-40 crowd that it is possible to play like innocent children in the nude without getting into sex. Even simple nudity would have killed the point.

"And I wanted to use actual residents of the towns we went into, and let them say pretty much what they would actually say when they saw our long hair and so on. I'd outline what I wanted in a scene, give them a few specific lines, and let them improvise from there. As for our characters, Peter's and mine, they were thoroughly set in advance. I've never seen a movie in which the director acted that he didn't come out the star, and it was important to me that Peter be the star, not because he's Peter Fonda, but because his character in the movie, Captain America, is the leader, the good guy. You can't have a John Wayne without a Ward Bond, though, so I took upon my character all the burden of explanation, the cynicism. Together, we're symbols of this country today—Captain America, man, is *today's* leader—and when the small-town lawyer joins up with us, you have a real American cross-section. As we watch them, we think of them as nice kids, but they're actually in their early thirties, an age when the Establishment says they should be working, contributing. Instead, they're peddling dope. Because that seems no worse to them than the Wall Street tycoon spending 80 per cent of his time cheating the government.

"Everybody seems confused about the end of the picture, and all I'm saying there is that we aren't very different from the two guys in the truck who shoot us. That all of us, man, are herd-instincted animals, that we all need each other. And *why* can't the different herds mingle? I was in the freedom march, man, Selma to Montgomery, and there was this guy at the side of the road who was urinating on us as we passed, and yelling 'White trash,' and I thought, 'Wow! Can't he see, can't he get it together? We only look different, we're all part of the same herd.' He kept shouting at me, 'Hippy, Commie, longhair!' Wow. I mean, *I* don't care if *he* has short hair!"

Guru hair vs. crewcuts, beads vs. golf shirts, motorcycles vs. Toyota Coronas; in rural America, the dichotomy proved more appalling than Dennis and Peter had dreamed. "Every restaurant, man, every roadhouse we went in, there was a Marine sergeant, or a football coach who started with, 'Look at the Commies, the queers, is it a boy or a girl?' We expected that. But the stories we heard along the way, man, true stories, of kids getting their heads broken with clubs or slashed with rusty razor blades—*rusty* blades, man — just because they passed through towns with long hair. And not just in the South. In Montrose, Colorado, where we made 'True Grit,' I walked into a bar and immediately a guy swung at me, screaming, 'Get outta here, my son's in Vietnam,' and the local sheriff was right behind him, screaming that *his* son was in Vietnam, and I said, 'Now wait a minute,' that I was an actor and there with the movie, whereupon the boys' high school counselor started screaming to get out, that *his* son was in Vietnam. And I thought, 'What if I wasn't an actor, what if I was just traveling through and was thirsty?' So I said, 'Okay, I'm hitchhiking to the peace march,' whereupon eight guys jumped me. Incredible, but true, I swear.

"With 'Easy Rider,' in Baton Rouge, the Vanilla Fudge was playing next door to our hotel, and when we went over, these beautiful local kids came up and said, 'Oh, wow, your hair's so long, man, we want to grow our hair like that.' They were so groovy. And in the hotel dining room, there's this table of senators, and one of them is screaming that Rockefeller is going to put a nigger in Bobby Kennedy's position—this was like three days after the assassination—and that if he does, they'll take care of the nigger, because they know how to deal, down here, with niggers in politics. At that point, I told *him* to get out. But, man, how do you get it together? Those beautiful kids next door, full of love, grooving on the Vanilla Fudge, and that guy? At what point do they turn into *him*? Maybe he was once a groovy kid too . . ."

He shakes his head. As if on cue, the Fifth Dimension sings again. He smiles a moment at the irony, then says, "I dunno, it's a nightmare. What I want to say with 'Easy Rider' is, 'Don't be scared, go and try to change America, but if you're gonna wear a badge, whether it's long hair, or black skin, learn to protect yourselves. Go in groups, but go. When people understand that they can't tromp you down, maybe they'll start accepting you. Accepting *all* the herds.'"

It is time for him to go, and we start out of the bar, but he does not seem to want to stop talking, about films, the one he has made, the ones he's going to make. In the process of his divorce settlement, he explains, he relinquished to his wife the house, the car, his motorcycle, and his art collection — he had bought Warhol, Rauschenberg and Jasper Johns when Robert Scull was still collecting taxis—so that he would be allowed to keep his share of the "Easy Rider" profits, whatever they may be. "I took a chance, man, but I believe in the picture, and it's going to give me my freedom—to make more like it, and to get out of cities. I've noticed that a film I'm directing is affected by the place I'm making it in, and in cities, I get sick. You don't have to sit in the L.A. smog the whole year to make a movie. I've got to get back to the country, to an earth *feeling*, like when I was a kid. You know: touch a leaf, see if it has bugs under it." He laughs. "I've gotta see if I really am this sensitive loner, or if that's just an image I made up for myself."

Outside, the daylight turns the Simonized surface of his hired limousine to silver, and he shields his eyes. "Taos, man," he says, getting in. "Taos, New Mexico. There's freedom there. They don't mind long hair. The herds mingle."

As the car edges into Eighth Avenue, he glances out once at the filthy street, then closes his eyes, preferring his vision of Taos.

AUGUST 3, 1969

MOONGLOW

By GRACE GLUECK

"Shocking," a collector said the other day, lamenting the omission of an artist from man's first moon landing.

"Know one in good enough shape to send?" a listener piped up.

Nevertheless, artists have been mulling over the moon as a medium. Take Claes Oldenburg, for instance. He believes that the man-in-the-moon legend could now be nicely realized, by creating a giant lunar face. So huge would its features be, that on the moon they'd lose their facial identity. But they might also serve other functions. What looked on the earth like eyes, for example, could actually be a pair of widely-separated lunar observatory domes. "By taking a consensus, you might arrive at a face that would be ethnically attractive to all peoples of the world," Oldenburg muses. "Think of it beaming down benevolently, a giant omnipresence. You could take your kids out in the yard at night and say, 'There's God.'"

*

Geophile Robert Smithson, on the other hand, views the moon as an Earthwork. He is tickled with the astronauts' transport of rocks from luna to terra (a recent photo of the boxed moon rocks is curiously reminiscent of a Smithson "site-non-site" exhibition last fall at the Dwan Gallery, in which he took stones from a specific "site" in New Jersey and displayed them in the gallery "non-site" with maps and photos of this habitat). "It's fascinating how the astronauts jettisoned all that technological equipment just to bring back rocks," Smithson observes. "I think it's a vindication of the site-non-site dialectic, going from a central point out to the fringe and making the fringe known back at the central point."

How would other artists play with the moon? Here are some speculations, recently received from selenophile readers:

Christo—Wrap it in Pliofilm and twine.

Lucas Samaras—Stick it with pins like a giant pincushion; spike it with glass shards.

Bob Whitman—Cover it with Mylar for use as a space mirror.

Noguchi—Design a lampshade for it.

Andy Warhol—Project an endless movie on it (to be titled, "Blue Moon").

Jasper Johns—Paint it as a target.

Donald Judd—Cube it.

Roy Lichtenstein—Throw a Ben Day screen on its surface, program it to play '30's songs—"Moon Over Miami," "Harvest Moon," "The Moon Belongs to Everyone."

Jules Olitski—Spray it with acrylics.

Michael Heizer (earthworks artist)—Dig a string of trenches connecting the Sea of Tranquility with the crater Aristarchus; sell them to collector Robert Scull.

September 21, 1969

New, Newer, Newest

By JOHN SIMON

"SPEED KILLS!" is the drug-traffic signal displayed on many walls with which Kilroy tries to head us away from methedrine. But an even more dangerous killer is our living speed itself, the speed with which we embrace and drop fashions, tastes, beliefs: the tempo of our race through esthetic and spiritual environments for the sake of being contemporary, mod, now—with it, ahead of the game, out of sight. But there is just as little sense in outrunning the Joneses as in keeping up with them; in either case, we are living our lives to impress others, instead of to express ourselves.

Most of us would resent being called cultists, yet we are sectarians and victims of the Cult of the New. We want the latest models of cars and clothes, this year's hit songs and school of painting. In automobiles and other technological commodities the new model may indeed introduce significant improvements, though more often than not it is just a new line here, an additional gadget there. The master-car, the Rolls-Royce, changes minimally, if at all, from year to year. Clothes, particularly women's, change radically but pointlessly every year. Just when we get used to the miniskirt, we must learn to love the maxi, both of which may coexist while anathemas are hurled at the midi. That, of course, will be next year's fashion. At least these changes are insignificant and seldom irreversible; indeed, reversibility is what they depend on.

But when we come to art—and I don't mean pseudo-art, like pop music—this greed for the new becomes disastrous. And it cannot all be blamed on the producers and middlemen; a large part of the guilt is the consumers'. For in the arts, as elsewhere, the obsolescence is built not so much into the product as into the consumer's mind. It is there that, thanks to various overt and covert forms of advertising, the "new" has been implanted as an end in itself. And a very convenient criterion it is for minds that neither know nor care much about the arts; for whereas it is extremely hard to determine what is good and what is bad, anyone can distinguish the new from the old. The Theater of Cruelty succeeds the Theater of the Absurd, and is itself closely followed by the theater of improvisation whose heels are trampled by theater of mixed media, which is jostled by the theater of total participation and theater in the streets, which is tailed by theater in the nude. In art, merely to enumerate all the movements that have cropped up since the still-surviving abstract expressionism would easily use up the rest of this column.

There are three main causes of this unappeasable itch for novelty. First, **there is the snob value of the new, the one-upmanship in having already bought, read, seen, heard, smelled (there was a short-lived cinematic gimmick — smellies) the latest thing. There is even** something vaguely endearing about this: next to being creative and innovative, being a pioneer in recognizing and promoting significant innovations is held to be best. But there, alas, is the catch: the innovation has to be significant.

Secondly, there is the misunderstanding of the nature of art. Some confuse art with technology (this category, by the way, includes a good many so-called artists). Thus the new painting, which uses a shaped canvas, is seen as an improvement; the new sculpture is better because it moves — as if sculptures were supposed to race one another (some day, no doubt, this too will come); the new stage production is better because it uses mixed media—you get several genres for the price of one. This derives from equating an art form with a contraption, say, a television set, which may indeed be more useful for incorporating ultra high frequency; it is also the ultimate offshoot of that debased and debasing doctrine, "the medium is the message."

Art is also mistaken for news. In our news-oriented culture (which at all levels, tends to confuse information with gossip), it seems only natural that Clive Barnes should be a more important critic than Walter Kerr because you read Barnes the next morning, Kerr only next Sunday. By the same token, your television reviewers are becoming more important yet: you can have them the same night as the dramatic event. Least noteworthy is the serious, speculative critic, whom you might have to wait for as long as a month or more. What good is he, when the movie or play under discussion everywhere is the one that just opened?

The third, most crucial and disturbing, reason for the Cult of the New is boredom. The same boredom that lies behind far more distressing social ills: divorce, suicide, certain types of crime. One is tired of looking at the same kind of paintings, listening to the same kind of music, going to the same sort of shows. This, regrettably, is tantamount to being tired of the same partner in love, tired of the same *modus vivendi* within the law, tired of life itself. It is, ultimately, a failure of understanding and love; in our case, understanding and love of the arts.

In a recent interview in Book World, the novelist Doris Lessing remarked, "I tend to like slow-moving books, books that take their time and contemplate all the way through." Of course, such books also take the reader's time, but the choice is painfully simple: either we create time, or our lack of time destroys us, turning us into automata or addicts, time-servers or good-time chasers. The test of a true work of art is that it does not tarnish: an opera like "Wozzeck" is good for any number of hearings; a painting by Rauschenberg or a sculpture by Oldenburg *should* bore us from the moment after we've looked at it, for it is a facade over a void. If within a short time we get bored with a work of art, either it is not a work of art or we are not art lovers. It is understandable that one of the creators of the most boring pseudo-art, Andy Warhol, should have praised the dullness of Albee's "Tiny Alice" in order to elevate boredom to a positive artistic value.

*

One of the big problems here is overabundance of money in hands short on culture and taste. This is particularly noticeable in the fine arts, where collectors like Robert and Ethel Scull have been leaping (to adapt a phrase of Harold Rosenberg's) from vanguard to vanguard, without showing the slightest resistance to any new movement. Such people turn art into a vulgar market place. There, as Hans Magnus Enzensberger has written, "the future of the work of art is sold before it has even occurred. What is steadily being offered for sale is, as in other industries, next year's model. But this future has not only always begun; it is also, when tossed out into the market, always already past. Tomorrow's esthetic product offered for sale today proves, the day after tomorrow, a white elephant, and, no longer sellable, wanders into the archives in the hope of the possibility that, 10 years later, it might still be palmed off as the object of a sentimental revival." And that is how camp is born—but that is another story and does not concern us here. (Enzensberger's important essay, from which I quote, is entitled "The Aporias of the Avant-Garde," and is reprinted in "Modern Occasions," edited by Philip Rahv.)

Observing that "the forcing of creation by promoters of novelty is perhaps the most serious issue in art today," Harold Rosenberg goes on to note, "Novelties in painting and sculpture receive notice in the press as new *facts* long before they have qualified as new *art*. . . . To deny the significance of the new product begins to seem futile, since whatever is much seen and talked about is already on its way to becoming a *fait accompli* of taste. By the mere quantity of interest aroused by its novelty, the painting is nudged into art history."

That is the art-as-news fallacy I spoke of before, at work with a vengeance. **It is the dishonesty and suspect friendships of art dealers, the vainglorious inanity or sheeplike conformity of museum directors and curators, and the ignorance, gullibility, moneyed mindlessness of the collectors that bring about ultimate chaos. The buyers are not even able to recognize that most of their novelties are really old hat.** As Erich Kahler says in his important but little-known book, "The Disintegration of Form in the Arts," "Dada, this exuberantly inventive movement, uncommitted, flexible, humorous as it was, using all imaginable means of provocation, anticipated everything that today is carried out by pedantic bores." The same absurd, anachronistic state of affairs is noted in poetry by the British critic A. Alvarez, who comments on "the odd phenomenon of the latest avant garde being largely a rewrite of that of 50 years ago." No one, he says, exaggerating only slightly, is **"bothered that Pound looms behind Charles Olson's shoulder and William Carlos Williams towers over Robert Creeley's. The stuff is felt to be modern simply because it *looks* modern. The avant garde is acceptable because it is essentially reactionary, harmless."**

*

The line of defense against these abuses should be drawn, at the very least, in the reviews and critiques. The public is often just as willing not to be duped, but, untrustful of itself, it looks

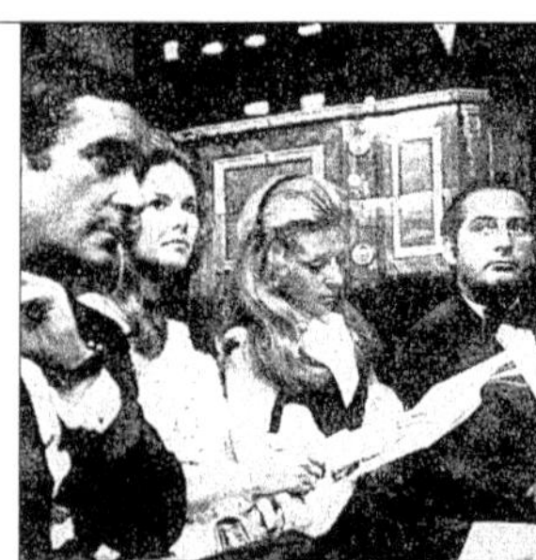

for critical spokesmen to bolster its conservative impulses. The critics, however, tend to fail it. The most insidious reason for this is what has aptly been named the Hanslick Syndrome. Eduard Hanslick (1825-1904) was a powerful Viennese music critic, now remembered mostly for his attacks on Wagner, which posterity has proved wrong. The majority of our critics — excepting the obvious lowbrows, and not even all of them —are afflicted with the Hanslick Syndrome. Turn to The New York Times, and you will see the wildest fatuities of a Ronald Tavel or Julie Bovasso hailed as delightful contributions to our drama.

Perhaps you will pardon me, therefore, if I reproduce here from memory (there is no written text) some of the words I improvised last March, upon receiving the George Polk Award for my film criticism. The audience included many reviewers for various mass media.

"In 1934, after a visit with the philosopher Henri Bergson, the great poet and critic Paul Valéry jotted down in his notebook: 'He too thinks of sensibility as a kind of resistance. I was surprised.' This aperçu is even more needed in 1969. We live in a time when critics are only too eager to jump on any avant-garde bandwagon that pulls up before their front doors. They are so afraid of becoming the laughing stocks of the future that they are perfectly willing to reduce the present to a bad joke. Although most reviews are written on wood pulp, they should be as carefully thought out as if they were committed to paper with 100 per cent rag content. This will not ensure the critic's rise from rags to riches, but at least the mind he'll save may be his own."

To be sure, this critical "resistance" must not be overdone. It would be just as deleterious to reject all new art out of hand as it would be to throw the old overboard as if it were so much ballast. Back in 1918, one of the idols of today's American youth, Hermann Hesse, pointed out the absurdity of the categorical rejection of either the old or the new. The critic who nowadays wants to be fair to both, Hesse observed, has "a bitterly hard time of it. But why shouldn't critics have a hard time? That's what they are there for." What precepts can one give critics, even assuming that they wanted them? The basic critical method—perhaps the only one—is still, as T. S. Eliot put it, "to be very intelligent." But what about the public? Are there any practical hints for the audience?

Here, again, the solution is to think more about art, or not to think about it at all. If one's interests do not truly lie in the arts, there is no point in force-feeding oneself or allowing others to do it to one. In that case, though, one should abstain from pontificating, vociferating, and trying to dictate tastes. One should content oneself with the old, much-maligned formula of "knowing what one likes," in whose name much less damage has been done than in that of liking what one thinks one ought to like. But if one is going to get seriously involved with the arts, even as an appreciator, one simply has to drink more deeply from the Pierian spring. And this, **inevitably, means reading up on the arts, not just consuming them. Nothing is more meaningless than the ever increasing figures of concert, theater and museum attendance that the foundations are so fond of recording and crowing about. Exposure *alone* guarantees** nothing; it is apt to be just another form of rubbing against, gaping at, and reaching out for the new, without absorbing anything.

*

The most probably useful thing the layman can do is to find two or three very different critics or writers on the art he is interested in, and, like any jury, decide on the basis of hearing out at least two sides of the argument. The only difficulty here is in finding a *decent* conservative critic of the art in question. Things have changed in a most remarkable way. The wholesale obsession with the new in the arts—as well as a generally much greater, though often merely neurotic, concern with the arts — has as its consequence that far-out avant-garde movements are no longer consigned (as until now, often unjustly, they were) to the lunatic fringes of art; rather, they have become the dead center, the very Establishment. **When Thomas Hoving exhibits a huge monstrosity by Rosenquist in the Metropolitan Museum — where even genuine artists, if they were still living, have not been accorded such testimonials; when paintings by true masters such as Poussin and David are dragged down from their usual place to come and lend prestige to Rosenquist's mural, a piece of ill-painted poster art, as the most casual inspection of the sloppy application of pigment revealed; when Robert Scull, the owner of the picture, is, again unprecedentedly, invited to fill** up the pages of the Met's Bulletin with uncritical praise of the modern masterpiece he owns — a radical change is upon us.

As recently as half a century ago, as large and important a group as the Surrealists still passed for artistic buccaneers and outlaws; now, however, any miniature movement, say, the light-show makers or the minimalists, is exhibited, sold, written about and extolled wherever you turn. The periphery and dark corners—where one is barely noticed, exhibited, subsidized, published, heard from—are reserved today for the conservatives: artists, critics, and scholars. I am not arguing that the conservatives in art are better than the radicals. But I am saying that until they too are heard from, the serious danger exists that our arts will become ever more frantic, psychotic, solipsistic and, above all, divorced from any relevance to humanity.

OCTOBER 15, 1969

To Complement Today's Fashions—a Hairdo From the Past

By BERNADINE MORRIS

GUESS what everybody's talking about in fashion these days? Hair. Hair piled up on the top of the head and knotted into a bun. They're calling it Gibson Girl, French concierge, La Belle Epoque and pompadour but any way you describe it, it's the hottest hairdo in town.

Mrs. William P. Rayner, her own hair properly twisted yesterday afternoon twisting high, spent a few moments her mother's suddenly antiquated George Washington ponytail into a contemporary bun as they waited for Oscar de la Renta's spring collection to begin. Her mother, Mrs. I. S. V. Patcévitch, whose husband is chairman of Vogue magazine, submitted silently.

Meanwhile, Mrs. T. Suffern Tailer, wife of the sportsman, was impatiently waiting for the show to start. "I came to see what I'm going to do with my hair next season," she said, patting her properly upswept pompadour.

Mrs. Tailer was among the women converted after Oscar's last collection, presented May 15, which has become kind of a landmark in the revival of the pompadour. The designer and his wife, Françoise de Langlade, fashion and beauty consultant to the president of Elizabeth Arden, had concocted the idea together with Suga, a Japanese hairdresser, who piled all the mannequins' hair on top of their heads.

Coiffure for Star

Oscar had seen the hairdo on Brigitte Bardot in Paris last winter. "She was wearing a black top and black pants and I thought it was very modern," he explained.

As a result, a lot of women who've been wearing their hair like that for years have suddenly found themselves at the head of fashion.

"I've been doing it up before I went to bed like this for 30 years," said Mrs. Ben Shaw, whose husband is the Seventh Avenue financial backer.

"I gave up hair rollers and hairdressers when my second child was born and he's 19 now," said Mrs Margay Lindsey, who has her own fashion merchandising office.

Of course, some women are not so handy and have to rely on hairdressers. Kenneth, who calls the coiffure "pillow hair" because you take out the essential hairpin and the hair spills over the pillow, says it's the most popular hairdo he's doing.

By Popular Demand

"All my clients are asking for it," said Marc Sinclaire of Charles of the Ritz, who, in addition to piling up Mrs. Rayners' hair, has pulled the same trick for Mrs. Charlotte Ford Niarchos, Mrs. Giancarlo Uzielli (the daughters of Henry Ford 2d), Mrs. Harilaos Theodoracopulos, whose husband is in shipping, and Mrs. Robert C. Scull, whose husband owns taxicabs.

"I started about two years ago on Mrs. Scull when she wore Adolfo's pinafores for parties," Mr. Sinclaire recalled. "It didn't catch on so well until this summer."

He is pretty enthusiastic about the hairdo. "Those women at the turn of the century knew what they were doing," he said. "It stays so well and it doesn't matter if the hair is thick or thin. All you need is a rat."

The newest versions on Oscar de la Renta's mannequins don't even need a rat. At yesterday's showing of spring clothes, the hair was skinned back closely and then knotted on the top of the head. With the evening clothes, a few tendrills were pulled loose to straggle intriguingly.

It wasn't just hair that attracted attention at the show. Eyes did, too. The mannequins all had green, blue or violet masks painted on their faces painstakingly by Pablo. That's something to watch for on the street.

And the clothes? Contemporary, of course. Black taffeta dresses with white ruffles around the neck. Long coats over short dresses or rompers. Trimly tailored blazers over shirtdresses. Abstract-printed sheer dresses in hot colors, pants and dresses over pants to float around parties. All that's in his regular collection ($250 to $3,000).

In the boutique line ($90 to $235), there are pants suits, low - flounced dresses and checked taffeta party dresses with lacy pantaloons under them. Contemporary, in fashion, is a many-splendored thing.

Not all the upswept hairdos are in Oscar's showroom. They're spreading all over Seventh Avenue. Mollie Parnis was enchanted with her new mannequin, Elizabeth Palacio, whose hairdo was Victorian, the puffy kind. She adopted it about two weeks ago because she wanted a softer look, Miss Palacio explained. It served with Miss Parnis's short, swirly day dresses, her tweed coatdresses and her party sheers in Persian - patterned silks by Julian Tomchin and abstract prints by Tzaims Luksus. The prices are $165 to $500.

OCTOBER 17, 1969

Metropolitan Museum Opens Big Centennial Show

By GRACE GLUECK

"New York Painting and Sculpture: 1940-1970," the first of the Metropolitan Museum's five big centennial shows, made its belated bow last evening with all the standard features of a major museum opening today: a glittering crowd, music, refreshments and a picket line.

The 1,500 formally clad guests at the invitational opening, which was postponed one day because of the Vietnam Moratorium, were greeted by members of the Art Workers' Coalition, who paraded in front of the Fifth Avenue facade. They were protesting the lack of Negro and—a new note—the scant female representation in the show.

The exhibition, which the museum says is the largest showing of contemporary United States art ever brought together, has more than 400 paintings, sculptures and drawings by 43 artists, whose work has helped establish New York's precedence over Paris as the art world capital. It opens to the public tomorrow.

Organized by Henry Geldzahler, curator of the Department of Contemporary Arts, the show includes such artists as Milton Avery, Alexander Calder, Stuart Davis, Helen Frankenthaler (the lone woman), Arshile Gorsky, Hans Hofmann, Edward Hopper, Robert Motherwell, Claes Oldenburg, Jackson Pollock, David Smith, Frank Stella and Andy Warhol.

Even before its opening, the show, described by Mr. Geldzahler as "not a general inventory of the past three decades but an evaluation, a sorting out of major themes and figures," has caused a buzz in the art world because of its controversial omissions. Among the artists not included are such well-known figures as Louise Nevelson, Seymour Lipton, Larry Rivers, Marisol and Reuben Nakian.

But the proto-pop artist Jasper Johns, who has a room of drawings and another of paintings in the show, defended the choices last night. "The artists represented here and those who aren't are not that far apart," he said. "What's here gives a certain idea of work done over a period of time that's valuable to young people. They hadn't had a chance to see a grouping of this sort."

Last evening guests strolled through the spacious second floor galleries, sipping drinks and nibbling tiny sandwiches to the strains of several kinds of music. There was a festive fanfare by Virgil Thomson, one of five specially commissioned compositions for the centennial show. Then there was hard rock, frugged to in the Frank Stella room by some of the swinging guests. And in a nearby roomful of pop art, the collector Ethel Scull watched mournfully as a smaller, staider combo played decorously in front of her portrait by Andy Warhol, partially concealing it.

The guests, who ranged from dinner-jacketed Met trustees to artists in leather pants and aviation helmets, included a contingent led by the sculptor Mark di Suvero who grouped themselves on the floor before a Larry Poons painting and picnicked on champagne and sandwiches.

Mr. Geldzahler, clad in a blue velvet dinner jacket, wandered from room to room accepting congratulations. "There's nothing in the show I don't like," he said, pausing in front of "White Velvet," a sculpture of crushed auto parts by John Chamberlain.

The Xerox Corporation, responding to a new Metropolitan policy of soliciting corporate sponsorship for special shows, contributed $150,000 toward the exhibition's cost. The museum will charge the general public $1 for admission to the show, with students paying 50 cents. On Mondays, admission will be free.

A rumor that the museum would institute a general $1.50 admission charge after Jan. 1 sparked one of the "protest items" on leaflets handed out by the pickets. "$1.50 for cultural deprivation," the leaflet read. "Should the emerging cultural explosion be limited only to those with $1.50 in their hands?"

Thomas P. F. Hoving, the museum's director, branded the rumor of a general admission charge as "nonsense."

"We have no plans to charge admission after Jan. 1," he said, "although we've said many times before that if we're cut further by the city we'll have to go to measures like that. But at the moment the situation looks pretty good."

OCTOBER 23, 1969

Ballet's Friends Rejoice And Raise Money, Too

By ENID NEMY

Representatives of the theatrical, artistic, social and diplomatic worlds got together last night to celebrate the appointment of the American Ballet Theater as the official ballet company of the John F. Kennedy Center for the Performing Arts in Washington, and, incidentally, to raise money for special ballet performances for disadvantaged children across the country.

The 800 guests—500 who had paid $75 a ticket and several hundred who were members of the ballet and film companies — saw the world premiere of the film "Giselle" at Alice Tully Hall in Lincoln Center. Many stayed on for the postperformance champagne reception.

Bust most of the action had taken place earlier in the evening at 15 cocktail buffet parties given for any ticket holder who cared to attend. Almost all of them did.

One of the more notable exceptions was Mrs. Aristotle Onassis, who dined privately and arrived at the hall exactly two minutes before the scheduled 9 P.M. curtain and 19 minutes before the actual start of the film.

A Preference of Parties

Mrs. Onassis, wrapped in a huge chenille-fringed black stole, worn over a fringed black above-the-knee dress, was accompanied by Oliver Smith, a co-director of the Ballet Theater. She smiled as the hundreds of guests still in the foyer parted like the Red Sea to allow her passage.

Guests who were interested in the cocktail parties had been asked to list, in order of preference (one through four), the party they would like to attend.

"We tried as best we could to fulfill a person's first choice," said Mrs. William Zeckendorf Jr., chairman of the event that was expected to raise between $30,000 and $40,000.

Hosts included Charles Addams, who gave his party in the East Side apartment of Mrs. Winthrop Rockefeller, wife of the Arkansas Governor; Agnes de Mille, Licia Albanese (among those in greatest demand), Mrs. Beverly Kellogg Weicker, Andy Warhol and Ultra Violet, Consuelo Russell, granddaughter of the Duke of Marlborough; Sverker Astrom, Swedish Ambassador to the United States, and Hermione Gingold.

In most cases, the parties worked out as a blend of friends and strangers; some consisted solely of guests unknown to the hosts and a few ended up as gatherings of friends only.

Erik Bruhn, one of the stars of the film, was a guest of Mr. Astrom. The Ambassador, who acquired his taste for ballet during a previous posting to Moscow, entertained 30 friends and strangers with such delicacies as sautéed salmon and kidneys and sponge cake garnished with green marzipan.

"Mr. Bruhn is a colleague of mine," Mr. Astrom said. "He is a Swedish Government employe." (Mr. Bruhn is head of the ballet component of the Royal Swedish Opera.)

Licia Albanese, the opera star and wife of Joseph Gimma, partner in the Wall Street firm of Hornblower & Weeks-Hemphill, Noyes, spent the day in the kitchen before donning a green and gold sari dress and greeting her 40 guests.

"I cooked, myself. I am very proud," she said, surrounded by a buffet of small rigatoni, lemon scallopine, salad and cassata. "To make things the way I like, I must do it myself."

Miss Albanese, who said her first love was ballet "and then I found out I had a voice," was delighted with her unknown guests.

"It's nice to know other people," she said.

Mrs. Robert Scull, wife of the taxi-fleet owner and art collector, didn't agree. She wanted to be with friends—"strangers frighten the living daylights out of me and, heavens, I know enough people already"—and went to the party given by Mrs. Weicker.

Mrs. Scull, who appeared in a black felt midiskirt and yellow and black bolero by Adolfo, said she wasn't going to many parties these days because she was "bored with the whole running-around bit." She attended this one, she said, because "ballet is one of the beautiful artistic forms."

"I am matured," she announced. "I was missing too many good things in life, like reading. My husband said 'You're finally growing up.'"

Mrs. Weicker, who pooled her guests (22 in all) with those of Mrs. Albert Lasker, said she had a "very congenial party because we all know each other."

At the home of Agnes de Mille, the choreographer, everyone was a stranger, but Miss de Mille had no doubts about their caliber.

"I am sure they are nice because they are interested in dancing," she said.

Miss de Mille, whose first choreography (for "Obeah," a black ballet) was done for the American Ballet Theater, was willing to do anything she could to help the ballet, other than invite the guests to her party.

"I told them they would have to do the inviting," she said. "I have never in my life asked a friend to pay to come into my home. I don't mix these things."

The Entire Spectrum

One of the unusual gatherings was that co-hosted by Andy Warhol and Ultra Violet at the ApoGEE Gallery in Greenwich Village. A mélange of guests munched on hot dogs, hamburgers and pretzels.

Ultra Violet, who was born in France with the name of Isabelle Collin du Fresne, said she was terribly interested in the dance and that, as a matter of fact, she had been thinking that the present system of social dancing was all wrong.

"After working all day, people are too tired to stand up and dance," said the young woman who was an underground star and has now reached, she said, "middle to upper ground" level.

The woman who originated the preperformance parties didn't show up at any of them, although she did get to the performance.

"I'm a little embarrassed that I thought of it and left it in the hands of others to do the work," said Mrs. Samuel Beard, whose husband worked on special projects with Senator Robert F. Kennedy.

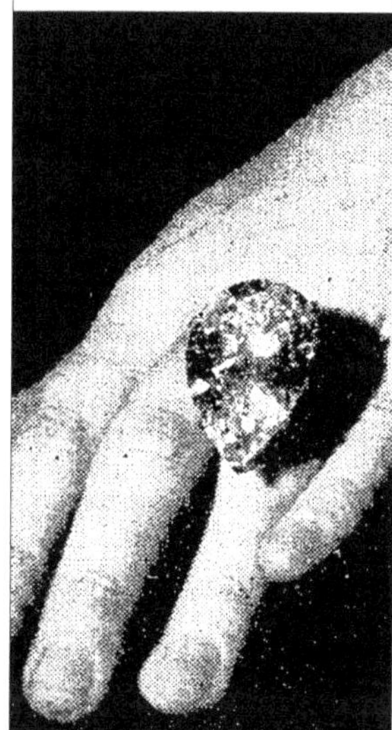

OCTOBER 24, 1969

Cartier Pays a Record $1,050,000 for Somebody's Diamond

By CHARLOTTE CURTIS

A DIAMOND the size of a peach pit went for a record $1,050,000 at Parke-Bernet yesterday. The auctioneers wouldn't say who was selling it, and Cartier, which bought it, wouldn't say what they were going to do with it, but everyone agreed it was the costliest gem stone ever auctioned.

The exceptional, unnamed stone, which experts pronounced flawless, weighs 69.42 carats. It may be called the Cartier Diamond unless the Fifth Avenue jewelry store was acting for a private customer, and a Cartier spokesman wasn't saying.

If there is such a customer, Elizabeth Taylor Burton, apparently isn't it. Al Yugler of Frank Pollack & Sons, who said he was representing the actress, withdrew from the contest when the price reached $1 million.

For Mrs. Onassis?

There was also serious talk among the diamond men that the real buyer was Aristotle S. Onassis, who planned to give the jewel to his wife, the former Jacqueline Kennedy. But Cartier refused to comment.

"The diamond is the Cartier Diamond now for the moment," said Robert H. Kenmore, chairman of the Kenton Corporation, which owns Cartier and such things as discount stores, Georges Kaplan furs and Valentino couture. "If someone should want to change the name, they can. But it is the Cartier Diamond while it is in our possession."

Mr. Kenmore added that he was "not a free agent," which seemed to indicate a private customer. But it was he who did the bidding, and it went quickly indeed.

The first bid was $200,000, and from there, with nine people bidding, it rushed to $500,000, then bogged down among the bidders who raised each other by $25,000 each. At $600,000, the bids dropped to $10,000 apiece, then sped ahead to $850,000, on to $1-million, when the underbidder dropped out, and finally to the $1,050,000. Perhaps a minute had elapsed.

Men and women leaped out of their chairs as the bids climbed, turned to watch Mr. Kenmore in a back row, and cheered and applauded at the point of sale. Mrs. Robert Scull, wife of the art collector, said she'd never seen anything like it.

"Wowee," she said. "That was something, wasn't it?"

Difficult to See

The diamond was displayed in its platinum setting with two side diamonds, but the ring was so far from the front-row spectators that hardly anyone could see why it was considered so important.

The stone has been described as being like the Krupp Diamond, the 33.10-carat, emerald-cut stone worn by Vera Krupp von Bohlen and sold in May, 1968, to Mrs. Burton for $305,000. Both diamonds were cut and mounted by Harry Winston, the New York jeweler, who also was one of the bidders.

Previous High Price

The previous world auction record was $385,000 paid for a diamond necklace from the estate of May Hayward Rovensky, a New Yorker, in 1957. The 83-carat Jahangir Diamond was sold in London in 1957 for $40,000 and the 70.20-carat Idol's Eye sold at Parke-Bernet in 1962 for $375,000. Neither was of the quality of the Cartier Diamond.

The 44.5-carat Hope Diamond, by comparison, cost Mr. Winston $700,000. But it was appraised for between $1- and $2-million when he gave it to the Smithsonian Institution in 1958. So yesterday's auction record does not mean that the Cartier Diamond is the most expensive in the world—only that it brought more at auction.

The sale, open to the public, began at 1:45 P.M., after Parke-Bernet's quiet uniformed guards released a silk cord that had held perhaps a dozen anxious ladies back from the big velvet-curtained auction room.

By 2:30, the room was jammed with 800 dealers, agents and a few social figures who bid a grand total of $2,686,145 (a record for an American jewel auction) on 162 lots, mostly from the estate of Florence Bacon Gould Sturgeon, a thoroughbred racehorse owner.

As usual, the bids came in a variety of ways. Some men raised and shook their hands. Others gave vigorous forward nods. But most were invisible except to the auctioneer's trained assistants. Only two extra police guards stood by to protect the jewels.

A Seahorse Clip

Edward J. Hand, the trucking tycoon, bought a diamond seahorse clip ($375) for the lady who accompanied him to the sale and helped send a ruby and diamond necklace up to $70,000. It went for $76,000. And Mrs. Philip Levin, wife of the financier, looked wistfully at a wide ruby bracelet studded with enormous marquise diamonds.

"But I never buy jewelry without my husband," she said.

Mrs. Robert Gurney, wife of the industrialist, waved and waved from the balcony above the black leather seats and finally caught the auctioneer's attention. She wanted a ruby and diamond flower brooch, and got it at $4,750.

Mrs. William B. Jaffee was in the balcony, too, but purely as an onlooker. Her brother, Walter Annenberg, is Ambassador to the Court of St. James's, and she has an extensive jewel collection.

Jewel auctions are serious business, but when the auctioneer got to something called a ¾-inch platinum drill bit, he sounded just a little nonplussed.

"I guess it's for the man who has everything," he said to a ripple of snickers. "Could we start at $100?" he asked. There were no bidders. "Well, how about $75?" he said hopefully. Still no bidders. So the bids started at $50, ended at $75 and the room rocked with laughter.

Sold to Dealers

The best of the jewels went to dealers. Sidney de Young of Boston paid $142,500, the second highest price at the sale, for an emerald and diamond brooch scores of women had admired before the show.

Members of New York's diamond brigade were not out in force either, mostly because they weren't interested.

"I don't need any more diamonds," said Mrs. Charlotte Ford Niarchos, Henry Ford 2d's daughter. "Why would I bother?"

Mrs. Peter I. B. Lavan, wife of the attorney; Mrs. Joseph Lauder, the cosmetics manufacturer, and Mrs. Archie Preissman, wife of the Beverly Hills real estate man didn't bother either.

Lack of Cash

"Diamonds aren't much of an investment these days," Mrs. Lavan said. "And with the market the way it is, there isn't much cash around."

"Nobody I know wants a diamond," said Mrs. Preissman, who has plenty. "The prices have skyrocketed in the last few years. The insurance is up too high. We're all afraid of robbery. I'm putting everything away."

Mrs. Lauder agreed with Mrs. Lavan and Mrs. Preissman and said she didn't think diamonds were very fashionable either.

"They don't look right with the beading on dresses and the jeweled necklines," she said flatly. "I'm not wearing mine."

NOVEMBER 2, 1969

Film Premiere and Supper Will Aid Actors Studio

Some 500 society and theater personalities are expected at the Trans-Lux West Theater and the Pierre on Nov. 18 for a double-feature benefit to raise money for the Actors Studio.

The world premiere of Elia Kazan's Warner Brothers movie "The Arrangement" will be the first attraction, which will be followed by a champagne supper at the hotel.

Mr. Kazan wrote the novel, adapted it, produced the movie and directed it. Kirk Douglas, Faye Dunaway, Deborah Kerr, Richard Boone and Hume Cronyn have the starring roles.

Spyros P. Skouras is chairman of the benefit. His committee includes Countess Josephine Annesley, Mrs. Charles W. Engelhard, Irving Mitchell Felt, Robert D. L. Gardiner, Mrs. Oscar Hammerstein 2d, Mrs. Joshua Logan, Mr. and Mrs. Charles Revson and Robert C. Scull.

The vice chairmen include Harry Adler, Ted Ashley, Harry Brandt, Leo Jaffe, Alan King, Laurence Tisch and Jack Valenti.

Tickets to the benefit, at $100 a person, may be ordered from Frank Berend Associates, 29 West 56th Street.

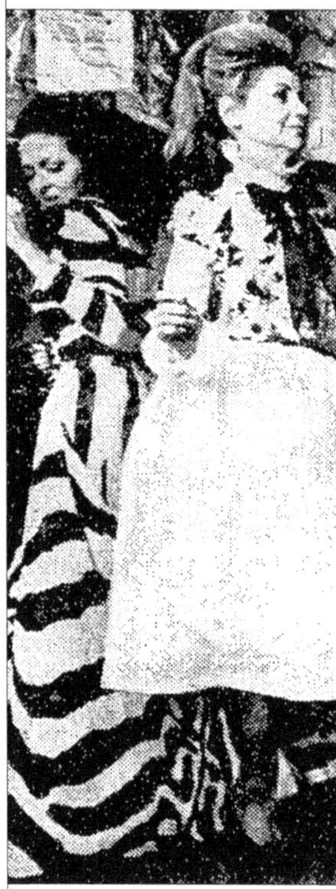

DECEMBER 2, 1969

Turn of Century Is Toasted, Late But in Style

By CHARLOTTE CURTIS

The Nine O'Clocks dance club had its highly publicized "Turn of the Century Party" complete with tiaras, upswept hairdos, enormous hats and extravagant costumes at the Plaza last night, and as Sam LeTulle observed somewhat wryly. "It's clothes, clothes and more clothes—more for the women than the men."

Mr. LeTulle, the Texas-born architect, was absolutely right. He designed the decorations, which involved adding potted palms and candles to the Plaza's already palm-fringed Palm Court and palms, gilded candelabra and giant hanging baskets of red and pink roses to the Terrace Room beyond.

Courtesans and Lionesses

Then, after double-checking to make sure the Terrace Room's fountain was working ("It's so very Edwardian"), he went out and rented a flashy antique military uniform with lots of gold braid.

Several other men rented similar costumes, and the men in white tie and tails looked perfectly marvelous, too. But it was still very much ladies night.

What mattered was who was impersonating which elegant courtesan, dance hall queen or social lioness of th eyears between 1890 and 1910, and the time, effort and money that had gone into these preparations was not inconsiderable.

Mrs. Wyatt Cooper set out to look like her cousin the late Consuelo Vanderbilt, and in her ruffled, corseted way she succeeded. Consuelo married the ninth Duke of Marlborough, immediately became the toast of America's robber baron society and starred as a beauty at Ascot in the days of King Edward VII.

It took Adolfo and his staff of three two days to put Mrs. Cooper's bouffant costume and giant hat together, and when they (and the hairdresser who came to her house at the last minute) had finished, she was mauve from head to toe, and Adolfo, ordinarily a talkative man, was virtually speechless.

"She is too beautiful," he moaned.

Mrs. Cooper was by no means the only beauty among the 275 club members and guests. Margaret, Duchess of Argyll wore a fitted black velvet dress with a low neckline, a pearl and diamond choker and a diamond tiara, and although she insisted she wasn't dressed to represent anybody ("I'm nobody, that's who"), she could have been the Duchess of Marlborough in the Boldini portrait.

"I crossed the Atlantic for this party," the Duchess said. "I like this sort of thing."

Mrs. John R. Drexel 3d, whose mother and father became engaged under one of the Plaza's palms, wore a white ruffled lace dress, a Victorian wig and the diamonds her father gave her mother in 1911 when they were married.

"But the pearls are from Bonwit's," she said. "I didn't really go to a lot of trouble. I wore this dress last summer in Newport."

Mrs. Ernest L. Byfield Jr., wife of the advertising executive, settled for black velvet and taffeta, a hat with ostrich feathers and masses of diamonds.

"I am Cleo de Merode," she explained. "She was an actress or an opera singer—one of those great French beauties."

Then there was Mrs. Giancarlo Uzielli (Anne Ford), who didn't get around to consulting with her designer (Chester Weinberg) until yesterday morning; Mrs. Lawrence Copley Thaw in white lace re-embroidered with pink and pink ostrich feathers in her hair ("I'm Lady Windermere's fan without the fan"), and Mrs. Robert C. Scull, wife of the taxicab tycoon.

Mrs. Joshua Logan had problems, too. Her black feathered hat was so high she couldn't get herself into her car sitting up.

"So I stretched out in the back of the station wagon," she said. "On one elbow."

Mr. Logan was rather pleased with the way he looked, particularly with his bushy auburn eyebrows, his bushy mustache and his bushy bangs.

"I've got hair for the first time in my life," he said happily. "I've got eyebrows just like other people."

"He looks just like Howard Lindsay in 'Life With Father,'" Mrs. Logan said, and there were those who agreed—mostly because they hadn't the vaguest idea what Howard Lindsay looked like.

"I said to Adolfo, "What-ve you got?' and he said, 'Something very romantic.' It's like one of the Wyndham sisters out of a Sargent portrait with my hair up à la belle époque with tendrils. I certainly hope it stays up."

Neither Mr. and Mrs. Gil Shiva (Susan Stein) nor Mrs. Cornelius Vanderbilt Whitney were inelegant either. Mr. Shiva glued on a lavish 19th-century mustache and sideburns for the night, and his dinner jacket resembled those worn in earlier times. Mrs. Shiva's costume was flown in from Universal Studios, her father's film company.

"I'm a green-velvet red head with a parasol," she said, and indeed she was—her naturally dark brown hair tucked up under an ornate wig. Mrs. Whitney wore Oscar de la Renta's gold-lace gown with the high ruffled gold lace collar and long sleeves, a gold veil like one shown with the dress in a recent Vogue magazine and her very own, very old diamond tiara.

"Trying to look like someone else is a little silly," she said. "It's all so pseudo-looking. I could say that I'm my own great-grandmother having tea at the Plaza in 1899, but my great-grandmother didn't have tea there. I think I'll just be me—Mary Lou Whitney."

Mrs. Charles Revson had pretty much the same idea. She was herself in a Pierre Balmain gown of apricot satin with a multicolored sequin top, butterfly sleeves and a rather spectacular ruby and diamond tiara.

"Harry Winston wired four necklaces together," Mrs. Revson said, "and that's my bodyguard over there."

She pointed to a man in street clothes who stood a discreet 10 feet away from her, and when she moved off to talk with other guests, he followed her.

The party began with a long list of multi-course dinner parties at people's homes and didn't actually get around to the Plaza until nearly 10:30 P.M. At that point, there was a champagne reception (in case anyone was thirsty) in the Palm Court around a tiered table decorated with palms, grapes, ferns and stemmed glasses.

It was during this interval that Mme. Elsa Schiaparelli, one of Paris's most successful couturiers, explained that her dress was a 1969 brocade from St. Laurent, that she really didn't want anything to drink and that she never wore costumes.

While she was talking, Col. Serge Obolensky made his entrance. He wore a Cossack uniform with a red tunic, blue pantaloons in boots, and all manner of military paraphernalia, including a jeweled dagger set with coral. The ladies were ecstatic, and there were little shrieks of "Serge, darling" all over the room.

"I didn't know it would be that successful," Colonel Obolensky said when he wasn't kissing and being kissed by his admirers. "It was made for me for a 1911 party in London. I wasn't sure I could get into it."

By 11 P.M. everyone was beginning to wonder when the dancing was going to begin, and it finally did—after the mirrored doors to the Terrace Room had become stuck and then forced open and Meyer Davis and his orchestra had played "Frankie and Johnny" at least twice to an empty room.

Mrs. Revson, her husband and her bodyguard were among the first to cross the threshold, and after them came such other guests as Ray Stark, the producer, and his wife; Earl Blackwell, the club's founder and party organizer; Donald Brooks, the dress designer; Iva S. V. Patcévitch, the publisher and Mrs. Patcévitch, and scores of others.

Before long, the guests were dancing to such typically bouncy turn-of-the-century music as "In the Good Old Summertime," "Sweet Adeline," "My Gal Sal" and "Let Me Call You Sweetheart," and by 12:30 this morning, it was time for crepes and creamed chicken (in case anyone was still hungry), and yet another chorus of "Shine on Harvest Moon."

DECEMBER 9, 1969

The Fashion Decade: As Hems Rose, Barriers Fell

By MARYLIN BENDER

IT WAS the decade of fashion and now it is ending. In the 1960's, fashion spilled out of the closet and into politics, the arts and big business. Politicians' wives and social climbers learned to drop designer names. The proper answer to the formerly impertinent question, "Whose dress are you wearing?" was not, as Lady Bird Johnson, Mary Lindsay and Happy Rockefeller discovered, "My own."

Neither they nor any other female public figure ever attained the influence of Jacqueline Kennedy. The brunette queen of the New Frontier became the Pied Piper of fashion for the masses as well as the darling of Seventh Avenue, the Avenue George Cinq and the Via Gregoriana.

The first White House chatelaine to think like a Vogue editor, she acted as a model of superconsumption.

Jacqueline Kennedy and Middle America

Trends may have been set early in the decade by couturiers, later on by the anonymous young and the alienated, but Jacqueline Kennedy disseminated them to middle America. Because of her, women grew bouffant hairdos and crowned them with barren pillboxes, hid their curves in little nothing dresses, their eyes behind mammoth sunglasses.

It was a decade in which the center of fashion gravity shifted from the garment to the accessorized body beautiful, from the Paris haute couture to the boutiques everywhere. Youth was sovereign. Camp dethroned good taste. The rich stole their fads from hippies who rejected materialism. Black beauty emerged.

The 1960's also witnessed the marriage of fashion and society. Bill Blass, Oscar de la Renta and Chester Weinberg, the dress designers; Halston, the milliner; Kenneth Jay Lane, the fake-jewelry maker; Kenneth, the hairdresser, and Pablo, the make-up man, catered to society women who, in turn, invited them to dinner and dances.

Women like Mrs. Robert Scull, wife of the pop art collecting taxi magnate; Susan Stein, daughter of the entertainment mogul, and Mrs. Carter Burden, born and wed into Establishment wealth and power, became household names purely through the clothes they wore and the parties they gave.

And eyes would invariably turn toward Jacqueline Kennedy. In the fall of 1966, when she hiked her skirts above her knees, so did cautious housewives over 30.

Later, she let her hair go wild in a childish mane, dieted to a razor thinness, which she vaunted with sausage skin pants and poor boy sweaters. But these styles had been set by such younger, blond film idols, pop socialites and mannequins as Brigitte Bardot, Baby Jane Holzer and Twiggy. By then, Jackie had slipped off her pedestal with her marriage to Aristotle S. Onassis.

Fashion meant more than clothes in the sixties. It was life style, image, social prestige, an index of contemporaneity, a sales ploy.

Yves Saint Laurent Shower Curtains

Those white Courrèges boots were injected into advertising campaigns for refrigerators. Mods in lacy stockings promoted banks. Dressmakers lent their names to unrelated products (Yves Saint Laurent shower curtains, the Cardin interior of a Simca car) or became design empire builders like Emilio Pucci, whose 4-ounce, printed jersey dress was an international status symbol.

Led by Pierre Cardin, many of them wandered into men's wear and found it more lucrative. For women's clothes had begun to disappear during the 1960's either in fact (millinery, gloves except in winter, stockings in summertime, girdles and bras for the young or emancipated anytime) or by erosion (the miniskirt and the bikini, topless or micro) or replacement (pants suits by day or night, for the office or a ball).

The sixties began without waists, bosoms and knees. At the end, nearly everything was showing. But change and reaction have set in. Fashion socialites are turning to social activism. The chic of the approaching seventies is a sweater and skirt (or pants). The new look is the nonclothes look, the no-make-up, the noncoiffure.

Sic transit fashion.

DECEMBER 22, 1969

Bejeweled 'Eggs' For Evenings Out

By ENID NEMY

THERE'S a fine line between the fashion shepherds and most of the time it's drawn in intangibles.

One of the intangibles is discovering new fashions; another is being sufficiently astute to spot the fashions that will likely start a trend. Sometimes it's done by women who make a career of these things—the shoppers of the world who buy in such quantity that they literally can't miss. Other times, the discovery comes almost by accident. Whatever the case, being the first is apparently a heartwarming, if pocketbook chilling, experience.

First With Ideas

The newest fashion accessory for evening has already been snapped up by several women who have frequently managed to be among the first with other ideas. It has also been bought by some fashion conservatives who merely "fell in love" with it.

The latest "it" is an enameled evening bag that is apparently destined to be clutched in a lot of palms this season. Clutched is about the only way it can be carried; this product of India is shaped like a fairly healthy ostrich egg. The top has a little flower, outlined in silver and precious stones; precious stones also girdle the approximately 10-inch circumference.

It is, if educated forecasts mean anything, about to displace last season's favorite—the silver and gilded Cambodian animals that made every major social event look like a miniature zoo.

"The animals are finished," said Miriam Marshall, who discovered them in the first place. "They have had their evenings out; now they can just sit on tables."

Miss Marshall, the imagination behind Port of Call at Henri Bendel, hesitates not at all at predicting the demise of one of her major items. She is also importing the Indian bags.

The bags, about 3½ inches high and 5 inches long, are sufficiently capacious to hold half a package of cigarettes, lipstick, a small compact, a folding comb, keys and any money left over after laying out $550 for the bag itself.

Among those who have bought the bag or who have placed orders, are Mrs. Stephen Howard Spahn, Mrs. Robert Scull, Mrs. Edwin Hilson and Mrs. Samuel Newhouse.

Mrs. Spahn received her ruby-decorated, sapphire blue bag as a birthday gift earlier this month. She had seen it, "fallen in love with it," and told her husband about it.

Husband Inspected It

Mr. Spahn, the headmaster of the Dwight School and a trustee of the Thomas Dooley Foundation, made a personal inspection trip.

Mrs. Spahn, who has a menagerie of silver Cambodian animals on her living room tables ("we bought them in Cambodia and I used one or two as evening bags"), also plans to use the egg bag as a decorative household accessory when it isn't in evening use.

"I haven't seen anything as beautiful, even in India," she said. "This is the kind of little touch I like, different but elegant."

DECEMBER 29, 1969

People Who Used to Buy Clothes Regardless of Cost Asking Price Now

By MARYLIN BENDER

EVERYONE'S talking about fashion prices these days, and they're saying different things. But all of the signs and the conflicting statements point to a bursting of the fashion bubble of the mid-to-late sixties.

"We're entering a totally new era, a new society, a new social structure. All values are changing. It affects the attitude toward clothes," says Rudi Gernreich, who has retired from some of his fashion designing enterprises and is moving in new directions, such as costume design.

Gernreich on Money

"Money no longer has value as a status symbol," says Gernreich. "It's tacky to flaunt it. And modern, thinking people are not putting it on their backs."

Some of the highest priced clothes have been selling better than ever and winning new converts. Some of the awfully high, but not the highest priced, designer clothes didn't move out of Seventh Avenue showrooms last fall—and those that did have been marked down in stores.

Some of the sovereigns of Seventh Avenue—Oscar de la Renta, Geoffrey Beene, Donald Brooks and Jacques Tiffeau—are turning out boutique lines to sell in stores at one-third to one-half the prices that their major collections fetch in the designer salons.

Some merchants blame the tumbling stock market and a recessive economy for sluggish sales. Others deny the connection or even the fact of price resistance among fashion-conscious women.

Nevertheless, most agree that the era of reckless spending and fashion obsession has ended for the time being. The fashion consumer, whether she is the wife of a millionaire or a middle-income American, is thinking about value again.

"They all ask the price," says Halston, whose boutique clothes sell in stores like Bloomingdale's with price tags from $35 for a blouse to $300 for a tie-dye-print pants suit.

"They" are women like Mrs. William S. Paley, Mrs. Charles Engelhard Jr. and Mrs. Aristotle S. Onassis, who first met Halston when he was Bergdorf Goodman's custom milliner. Now they pay from $250 to $650 for the custom boutique clothes that he runs up only for friends and clients of long standing.

"The rich are feeling a little bit guilty about being rich," Halston said.

"Besides, they were abused by the French and Italian couturiers with bills that ran to $15,000 or $25,000 from one couture house," he continued. "That's big money, and most of those ladies would rather give the money away to charity now."

Feeling Guilty

"Prices are so expensive that you feel guilty spending that kind of money, especially with what's happening in the world today," said Mrs. Robert C. Scull, whose pop art collection and passion for fashion made her a sixties celebrity.

Mrs. Scull said she would not "go above $400 for anything. I wouldn't allow myself."

"Ten years ago, you could get something custom-made for $400, but now those prices have doubled and tripled so everyone's backing away."

She said that boutiques had opened "a whole new trend of thought in clothing. You don't feel guilty about shopping in boutiques." She often shops at Adolfo, another custom milliner who has ventured into boutique design.

"We don't care any more. We want to look nice, but we don't have time for fittings," said Mrs. Frank McMahon, wife of the Canadian utilities magnate.

"I used to go to Mainbocher, and I've kept everything I ever got from him, but I just can't go for the fittings," she said. "And there are other ways I'd rather spend money."

"I think Bill Blass is still great, and so is Oscar de la Renta, but I'm getting Oscar's cute boutique things," she said. "You still have to spend a lot on a ball gown to really look sensational, but you don't wear them much, and I just don't think about clothes any more. We women are just getting sense."

When Bergdorf Goodman closed its custom salon last May, Andrew Goodman said, "Everyone is much more conscious of worldwide problems, and being overly extravagant is in poor taste and not of the moment." The average made-to-order dress costs $1,100.

"When a husband has just been to a meeting of the Urban League Coalition, he is not enchanted to have his wife recite at the dinner table about the $4,000 beaded dress she has just bought," Leonard Hankin, Bergdorf's executive vice president, declared the other day.

"Sense of Timeliness"

He also attributed the new mood to "a sense of timeliness, of a person not being interested in museum-like quality in clothes."

Mr. Hankin described the Christmas selling season at Bergdorf's as "very good in money in units, but the pattern is different." Where the custom fur salon would have sold 55 or 60 sable pieces in recent Christmases, this year half that number was sold, and "many took the forms of linings or combinations on the outside."

The couture boutique which carries Givenchy ready-to-wear ($75 to $1,500) is thriving, he said, and a new, synthetic diamond called the Carnegiegem, which sells for $60 a carat, was being snapped up at the rate of five stones a day.

"Why bother to have a $100,000 diamond sitting in the Manufacturers Trust vault when a $600 stone makes walking around less hazardous. There's a new sense of let's spend money sensibly," Mr. Hankin went on.

"Besides, I think women would rather have more things that seem exactly right when the need manifests itself than a limited wardrobe of great things."

Diagonally across Fifth Avenue at Bonwit Teller, Mildred Custin, the retiring chairman of the board, said that the Designer Salon was gaining "more devotees for Galanos and George Halley than ever." The two designers are considered to be at the pinnacle of fashion in price and workmanship.

"Women who are accustomed to wearing expensive clothes are still buying them, but instead of buying five, they may buy four. They're not buying cheaper clothes, though," Miss Custin maintained.

Mr. Galanos commented that he felt "you can go just so far, and I've been willing to take less markup rather than raise prices when my labor rises."

The least expensive Galanos dress currently sells for around $600.

"At least we are giving quality and the best workmanship," he said. "But there is a tendency for women to be a little hesitant these days. When they bring home bills for $2,000 dresses, it sounds rather unrealistic. Why, you can get a small automobile for that."

Sees No Resistance

Danny Zarem, who directs the merchandising of Bonwit's boutique, couture and European collections, as well as the men's departments, doesn't see resistance to price among wealthy women, "but there is a slight breakdown in the status barrier of the haute couture."

"The really chic women is now cutting back and forth between Courrèges and Galanos and the $65 Beene jersey dress," he said. "The woman who, years ago, would have had Givenchy whip up her cruise clothes is now buying $30 pants and body sweaters without labels. There's a new status in buying inexpensive clothes."

Pauline Trigère says that she is constantly trying to resist the inflationary force of rising costs of labor and materials. "Women want to buy a Trigère at $200 retail, and it's a problem for me," she said. Over 600 Trigère black jersey dresses from her fall collection sold in stores at $250 each. But a whipcord trouser suit with a sweater and seven-eighths coat for $600 didn't fare as well.

"Everybody wanted it, but they didn't buy it so well. I think they're not sure yet in the provinces that pants will stay," she said.

A silver fox-bordered suit for $975 also sold well, Miss Trigère said, "because women were sure they'll wear it for four years," but embroidered evening dresses are posing a problem.

"Women are not willing to pay $1,000 as frequently as they used to," she added.

"I don't believe boutiques are going to solve the problem for Seventh Avenue," Miss Trigère concluded. "I'm just going to keep trying to make attractive, smashing clothes that don't cost a million."

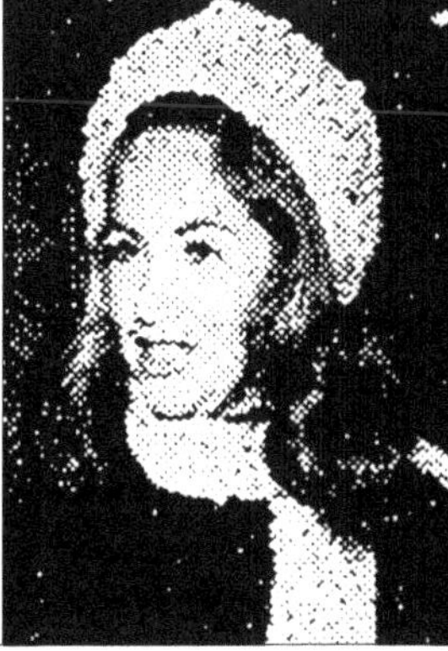

JANUARY 6, 1970

Sometimes at Hat Shows They Get to Showing Hats

By BERNADINE MORRIS

NOBODY goes to a hat show any more just to look at the hats. Sometimes there aren't any—a headband, a flower, a scarf tied under the chin is enough to keep the millinery franchise.

People go to see where hemlines are plummeting or what's new about pants. And at Adolfo, they go to see what each other is wearing.

Everybody admired Mrs. Wyatt Cooper in her black and white patterned Adolfo coat with fringe at the bottom at his spring show yesterday. It nearly reached the floor and she wore it with a red knitted newsboy cap and scarf. The former Gloria Vanderbilt was bubbling about her new job as design director for the Riegel Textile Corporation, which starts this week.

"I want to design marvelous fabrics that are inexpensive—fabrics for baby clothes, auto coverings, everything," Mrs. Cooper said.

Mrs. Robert C. Scull, wife of the pop art collector, was concerned that the zipper wasn't working properly on the black ribbed sweater and thick crocheted skirt—the skirt was only calf length—that Adolfo had just delivered. But the outfit was cozy enough so that she didn't need a coat, she said.

Mrs. Richard Feigen, whose husband runs an art gallery, was perfectly happy with her Adolfo outfit, which she called "the most practical thing I've ever had from him." It was a long wine coat over a striped tunic and pants.

Viveca Lindfors, Model

At Mr. John's show, the leading attraction was Viveca Lindfors, the actress, who first modeled for him as a gag but has been at it for nearly 10 years. This time she brought along her daughter, Lena, who works for Harry N. Abrams, the art book publisher, and who was married New Year's Eve to Martin Fried, the stage director.

"Mr. John is the house designer," said Miss Lindfors, who often gave her daughter's dress a motherly tug before the two of them stepped out on the runway.

When they got around to hats, both designers showed styles that were so integrated with the rest of the clothes, hardly anybody noticed.

Adolfo only goofed once, with a group of big, elaborately flowered hats he attributed to Manet and which prompted one spectator to remark, "That's what killed the millinery business."

The rest of the time, he stuck to felt, straw, silk or crocheted hats that blended in well with the business at hand.

The business at hand was divided into two rather schizophrenic parts. On the one hand, there were the free-wheeling, easy-moving jersey pants suits, generally in white, which are today's answer to the little black dress of yesteryear, and a lot more swinging.

Like the little black dress, it could be varied from day to day, with crocheted or striped jersey vests substituting for its matching cardigan coat.

Tight-Waisted Blouses

But for women who get nervous with all this freedom, there are ballooning-sleeve, tight-waisted blouses and skirts that the designer also attributes to Manet. Their counterparts were also seen on the riverboats of the Mississippi in the late 19th century, and the women who were wearing their clothes long today à la Adolfo found them enchanting.

Mr. John declared that he, too, was romantic, but he favored coarse cottons, such as denim and the stripes trainmen wear. His dresses were loose shirtwaists, caught in with belts of linked metal plates or jeweled leather and hung with lacy shawls or scarves.

They alternated with denim shirts and pants, which looked fine with denim bags and hats. But Mr. John sent one pants outfit out with a flower-laden hat.

"You may not believe it," he said. "I do." One wonders.

JANUARY 11, 1970

Displaying Wife: Style Changes

By MARYLIN BENDER

Styles in showing off have a tendency to keep up with basic economics. So it is that the inflated sixties ended with some recessive symptoms even in the way the tycoons of the seventies will be displaying their most precious possessions, namely their wives.

As the Women's Liberation Movement leaders, like David Rockefeller's daughter, Abby, know too well, no one clings more adamantly to the reactionary notion of regarding woman as a male appendage, than a venture capitalist.

The affluent 1960's were the most ostentatious decade since the Gay Nineties, and the reckless twenties, when Vanderbilts, Lorillards and Millses settled their brides in Newport chateaux, steam yachts and private railroad cars. The sixties have had more and bigger millionaries as well as tax laws not specifically designed for but certainly conducive to making an exhibition of oneself and one's spouse or steady companion.

Diamonds and Rubies

Aristotle S. Onassis, the Greek shipowner blessed by international tax laws, uses his yacht Christina as an office. It was there that he presented his new wife, Jacqueline, with a million dollars worth of diamonds and rubies as a wedding present.

The Christina is a converted Canadian frigate but the Ultima II, named after a line of cosmetics by Charles Revson, chairman of Revlon, was originally designed as a yacht. It's one of the world's largest.

Mr. Revson bought it from Daniel K. Ludwig, the shipbuilder and operator whose financing formula Onassis and others have emulated. The rangy Mr. Ludwig, whose life style may also be copied by magnates in the seventies, detests ostentation and publicity to the same degree that the bantam Mr. Onassis has cultivated it. The only Ludwig less known to the public and press than Mr. Ludwig is Mrs. Ludwig.

The third Mrs. Revson, on the other hand, has not only acquired since her marriage in 1964 the Ultima II, a Westchester estate and a Park Avenue triplex formerly owned by the late Helena Rubinstein, Mr. Revson has also given her a fashion image, including dressed by Norell, jewels by Van Cleef & Arpels and a place on the International Best Dressed List of 1968.

Here she was enshrined with Mrs. Alfred Bloomingdale (retailing and the Diners Club), Mrs. Harilaos Theodoracopulos (shipping again) and Mrs. Charles Engelhard Jr., wife of the precious-metals industrialist who rotates on three continents among four houses, three apartments and the inevitable Canadian salmon camp.

Current moneymakers and their wives are rated not only by their far-flung dwellings (separated by an ocean or at least half a continent) but the private or company plane to shuttle among them with their interior decorators.

When it comes to surface transportation, the Rolls Royce shows signs of becoming the fashion-industry vehicle. A distinctive capitalist prefers the Mercedes 600 Grand Salon and if he is Monroe Meyerson, president of the Central Rigging and Contract Corporation, he has the name of his wife, Leila, inscribed on the door.

Mobility, then, is one gift that the 1970's tycoons will continue to offer their wives. Mobility includes partying on an international scale — like the balls given at their respective estates in Portugal by the Antenor Patinos (Bovian tin) and the Pierre Schlumbergers (Texas petroleum equipment)

International society and its attendant couturiers, hairdressers and decorators were kept in a frenzy for months preparing for those galas, which were, after all, anachronistic, comes-the-revolution affairs.

A Museum Piece

More in the mood of the seventies was the weekend of festivities allied to the opening of the Sonja Henie-Nils Onstad Museum in Oslo that summer. Mr. Onstad, a Norwegian shipowner, engaged Earl Blackwell, president of Celebrity Service, and "a special international events director" to organize the event down to luring a well-mixed gaggle of newsworthy personalities and amusing them with dinner parties and boat rides around the fjords.

Mr. Blackwell is currently occupied with the organization of Raffles, a private dinner club in Manhattan, and Tamboo, a private resort club in the Bahamas. Both are designed for people with money who want to be alone with other congenial people with money.

Tying a wife's name to the arts never goes out of style. In the case of a wholly secure, super-rich art patron like Nelson Rockefeller, it may man festooning his wife, Happy, with enormous Brazilian aquamarine jewelry sculptured in gold by a Brazilian artist. Mrs. Rockefeller has confessed to feeling "inhibited" about wearing the massive collection, but she does, cheerfully.

No Reservations

Mrs. Owen Cheatham, wife of the chairman of the Georgia-Pacific Corporation, has no such reservations about her Salvador Dali-designed jewelry. One of the pieces is a gold and diamond cotton boll.

Robert C. Scull, the taxi fleet owner and pop art patron, has had his wife, Ethel, sculpted in plaster by George Segal. Charles B. Wrightsman, the oil producer, arranged for the education of his wife, Jayne, in French furniture and fine arts. The hobby involved collecting in a rising market but culminated in the contribution of a suite of 18th century rooms bearing their names to the Metropolitan Museum of Art. Mr. Wrightsman is a museum trustee.

"Status is getting to the point where it's more to do with doing good like giving a museum a painting for the world to see, or sponsoring an artist or the humanitarian things like buying beans for Biafra," expalined Halston, who used to be Bergdorf Goodman's custom milliner. He now runs a super-duper boutique in an East Side brownstone where the wives of centimillionaires repair to be outfitted.

Easy for Thieves

They have discovered that showing off in public, as they did in the Sixties, has its disadvantages. "The ladies with jewelry have all been robbed. They don't want their homes photographed for the magazines because every thief finds out where the doors are," says Halston, who not only makes their clothes but is invited to dinner, too.

Playing poor has been a recurring vogue among the wealthy ever since Marie Antoinette. Now it's back again in the form of couturier-boycotting and buying bargains in boutiques.

"The dress that costs astronomically is in bad taste now. It's not the time for it," says Mrs. Frank McMahon, wife of the Canadian utilities man. "Even if your husband can afford it, you can't let those bills go to his secretary at the office," she added.

JANUARY 17, 1970

COLLECTORS and DEALERS

SOUND OFF

Conversations on Art Collecting

February 3 ... ROBERT SCULL
10 ... BETTY PARSONS
17 ... LEO CASTELLI, SAM GREEN
24 ... DONALD KARSHAN
March 3 ... TIBOR DE NAGY
10 ... EUGENE M. SCHWARTZ

Subscriptions to series: $40. Members: $30. Individual admission: $7. Benefit Youth Programs—tax deductible. Checks payable to:

THE NEW YORK CULTURAL CENTER · 2 Columbus Circle, New York, N.Y. 10019

JANUARY 20, 1970

in the museums

THE METROPOLITAN MUSEUM OF ART 1870/1970

Exhibitions:
NEW YORK PAINTING AND SCULPTURE: 1940-1970 through 2/8
PRINTS BY FOUR NEW YORK PAINTERS through 2/1
THE ART OF THE MEDIEVAL BLACKSMITH (The Cloisters)

Concerts and Lectures:
Jan. 20—Lecture: **A Collector's Involvement** by Robert C. Scull. 8:00 p.m. Grace Rainey Rodgers Auditorium (GRR) $3
Jan. 21—Adult Film Program: **Jasper Johns; Robert Rauschenberg.** 2:30 p.m. Junior Museum Auditorium (JMA)
Jan. 22—Poetry/Music/Dance: **An Evening of Dance with Twyla Tharp.** 8:00 p.m. GGR $4
Jan. 24—Adult Film Program: **Claes Oldenburg; Colossal Keepsake Number One.** 2:30 p.m. JMA
Centennial Concert: **Sviatoslav Richter.** 8:30 p.m. GRR $15
Jan. 25—Lecture: **5000 Years of Art: Two Madonnas by Giovanni Bellini** by Allen Rosenbaum. 3:30 p.m. GRR
Fifth Avenue at 82 Street, 736-2211. Mon.-Sat. 10-5; Tues. to 10 p.m.; Sun. & Hol. 1-5.

FEBRUARY 1, 1970

It's Called Earth Art —And Boulderdash

By ROY BONGARTZ

MODERN art has escaped into the wilderness, and a search party may have to be sent out to find it. The new Earth Art is hoping to skip out on the insiders who have made the avant-garde into a kind of currency, an admission ticket to a rarified international social scene, a badge of in-ness, far-outness, somewhere-elseness and too-muchness. Succeeding waves of action painting, abstract expressionism, pop and op and minimal arts have been captured and sequestered by hip art patrons vying to sponsor the most scandalous artists in town. In this procedure, certain of the artists turned into prima donnas who could autograph a shoe and sell it for a fortune, while the patrons became famed far and wide for cranking up the momentum of art history to a breakneck speed.

But now what has happened is that the new art has slipped its rails altogether. Many artists, in what is probably a futile revolt against the socialite, show-biz art scene, have simply taken their work from the theatricality of gallery, museum, and penthouse wall, and have made off into the mountains, rivers, deserts and oceans with it. Hardly anybody sees it out there in the wilds, but that is O.K., because the viewer—the former museumgoer or gallery customer—does not matter any more. Get with it, please: the new Earth Art can be as invisible as a buried length of pipe, as ephemeral as a sled track on the snow, as slightly existent as dots on a road map, as unfindable as pieces of chalk on the ocean floor. Earth Art—the term is used along with others, such as Earth Works, Ecologic Art, Impossible Art, Conceptual Art or Microemotivism—can be a hole dug and then filled up, footprints made into plaster casts, a room carpeted with dirt, a wheat field scored by a harvester. It can be a salt crystal growing in a glass tube, a cliff wrapped in plastic sheets, a mountain peak shrouded in felt.

Earth Art can, in fact, be anything the artist says it is. Iain Baxter, a Vancouver practitioner who used to paint on the shadows of trees on snow, now merely ennobles certain objects that strike his eye, such as a bridge, a gas storage tank, or a billboard, by snapping pictures of them, so that they thus become what he calls Aesthetically Claimed Things. Each of his A.C.T.'s is carefully numbered.

"BOULDERDASH!" cried one critic; in fact, a large part of the traditional art world, and most of the public, are convinced that the whole act can be nothing but a weird, elaborate put-on, a faddish stunt like flagpole-sitting or hula-hooping. But artists have always outraged right-thinking citizenry by claiming new fields for art. What is new here is this stopper: ordinarily you cannot *see* this art. Nobody is going to trek out into the boondocks or swim around under water in the hope of catching a glimpse of a masterpiece before it gets blown over with sand or washed away—with the rare exception of such patrons as New Yorker Robert Scull, who chartered a plane to fly over a series of holes linking dry lakes in Smoke Creek Desert, Nev. Scull had commissioned Michael Heizer, 25 years old, to dig the holes out there as a 520-mile-long stretch of what the artist calls "negative objects." Says Heizer, "In the desert I can find that kind of unraped, peaceful, religious space that artists have always tried to put in their work." Scull, who has commissioned a dozen such works, says he does not need to actually see them. "It's enough for me that Heizer is out there," he says.

This very private, almost religious meditation of the artist before his work does give the new art a mystical quality that is part of the general effort to escape the commercial gallery-museum world. In this, artists probably can never succeed, since some sort of patronage is obviously needed to pay, for example, $1,000 a day for the hire of earth-moving equipment in the desert. (A new concern of art patrons thus becomes the bills from contractors and real estate taxes on the land the piece is built on or dug out of.) And there is no question that as far as the patrons are concerned, there is as much prestige involved in paying for a desert excavation as there used to be in sponsoring a Happening or buying a signed soup can. But the current resurgence of interest in world ecology does find a serious echo here, where artists try their best to return directly to the primordial earth—to see it, feel it, sense it in some pure and straightforward way, untrammeled by society's cliques and dollars.

Oddly, Earth Art has a number of early predecessors that in their own times could not be seen whole, except from some unreachable vantage point in the sky: the vast intaglio outlines of humans and animals on rock in Peru, the Ohio mound builders' 1,254-foot-long Great Serpent, the 350-foot-long figure outlined in the natural chalk below the turf on White Horse Hill in Berkshire, England, to celebrate an 871 A.D. victory of Alfred the Great—all of these can be viewed only from the air. The question they raise is exactly the same as the one concerning modern earth artists; if nobody can own it or even see it, what is the point? Whether the current explanation could apply to those ancient works is a teaser, but most of our young earth artists today agree that what sustains them is not the finished work, not its artistic values, its worth in money, its effect on viewers—not even its real existence; rather it is the idea of the work and the doing of it that counts, and that is all. Puerto Rican sculptor Rafael Ferrer, who dumped tons of leaves in various piles around Manhattan, commented on this act: "You get rid of the finished-product thing. You stop fiddling around with composition."

ANOTHER forerunner was a plan by an Italian astronomer, Giovanni Schiaparelli, who a century ago discovered canals on Mars through his telescope. To establish contact with the Martians, he wanted to dig desert trenches in "universal" triangles and squares, fill them with gasoline and set them afire at night. But his aim was to communicate, unlike these moderns, who take more after the late French Dadaist Marcel Duchamp; half a century ago the famous Dada spirit had already invented "Ready-Mades," which were simply objects selected as works of art—a snow shovel, for example—just like Baxter's Claimed Things. And now, Robert Morris brings Dada to the deeper ecological concerns of our own day by taking ordinarily despised materials, such as a pile of dirt and grease, into the gallery.

But Earth Art seems to be more at home in the countryside; one of the first to envision this was California sculptor Walter De Maria, who 10 years ago reported: "I have been thinking about an art yard I would like to build. It would be sort of a big hole in the ground. The digging of the hole would be part of the art."

Even earlier, in 1935, the American architectural sculptor Isamu Noguchi proposed an earth work to be visible only from planes at Newark Airport, but it was turned down. Of course, the stoic Presidents on Mt. Rushmore and the 69-foot-tall Confederates on Stone Mountain in Georgia are Earth Art, too, but it is not the same, because the new aims are so different. The new art was first recognized in an "Earthworks" show at Manhattan's Dwan Gallery in October, 1968. Says Virginia Dwan, "Our original idea was just to show earth as a medium, but it's difficult to know where to draw the line." It was further consecrated by Willoughby Sharp's Earth Art show at Cornell a year ago, and by later exhibitions at the Whitney and the Museum of Modern Art in New York.

DETAILS of recent works give some insight into the elusive imagination of these young artists. Digger Michael Heizer, who has a current "show" — mainly blown-up photographs—at the Dwan (to Feb. 5) has been provided by the gallery with two square miles of Nevada desert to build "the world's largest sculpture." He is out there now with machines, removing 40,000 tons of sand and rock. One of his earlier works, entitled "Circular Surface Drawing," consisted of an excavation in the Nevada desert with the freshly dug dirt piled by the edge so that it was gradually washed back into the hole by rain. Such physical change caused by natural forces — fast, as ice melting, or slow, as the erosion of rock—is a central element in many works. Heizer likes digging because, he says, the art world is already full of objects, and this way he can "create without creating a thing." The latent dislike of galleries and museums comes out frequently; last year, as part of a show, Heizer smashed up the asphalt outside the Kunsthalle museum in Berne with a house-wrecking machine; at the Whitney show, one exhibit consisted of part of the building's foundation that had been somewhat malevolently dug away and ground into dust by a guest artist.

Another hefty piece by Heizer is made up of three granite blocks, weighing 30, 52 and 70 tons, that he moved 60 miles across the Great Basin desert and dropped into cement-lined holes dug for the purpose. Afterwards, he noted: "The rental system allows the artist practically any application he desires." And, in a bit of hyperbole to suggest the boundless possibilities of his medium, he added: "It is now possible to rent a nuclear explosion." Patron Scull says Heizer's works "ennobled me and my surroundings. The vast open spaces have become my gallery." (Other patrons of Earth Art include New York businessman Ray Kaufman, New York manufacturing executive Horace Solomon, John Powers of the Aspen Center of Contemporary Arts, Houston oil millionaire John de Menil, Detroit Art Institute curator Sam Wagstaff, Milan industrialist Teppino Agrati, as well as private galleries here and abroad.)

Also an originator of the form is Richard Long, 25, whose works reflect the relative mildness of his native English landscape. Last spring he fashioned a gentle stretch of undulating turf in New York's Battery Park and he has climbed three times to a 19,000-foot peak of Mt. Kilimanjaro, in Africa, in order to swaddle it in felt. He has plucked daisies to form a daisyless X-form in a field; what may be his purest piece was untitled, and consisted of seven rocks "carefully" placed along a suburban street. His most disembodied work—a kind of cerebral, memory art without any physical bits and pieces needed seems to be the aim of a lot of Earth Art—is, or was, entitled, "Walking a Straight Line for Ten Miles, SW England, Shooting Every Half Mile. Out. Back." The shooting was done point-blank at the ground, in front of the walking artist with a movie camera, for six seconds at each half-mile pause; the resulting film is what there is of this one, just as photos are the only proof that many of these project ideas were ever carried out at all.

In fact, some artists believe that the mere thought is quite sufficient. Edward Kienholz, a West Coast sculptor, now contents himself with framing and displaying neatly typed accounts of proposed works, which is a good deal easier, certainly, than actually making them would be. His "Cement Store," for example, calls for a hole to be made in the roof of a real grocery store, through which cement would be poured until the inside was entirely filled, right up to the walls, doors and windows. Another artist, Robert Barry, went Kienholz one better. In the Kunsthalle, he displayed an idea that he had not yet had at all, in the form of a card reading: "Something which is very near in place and time, but not yet known to me."

The surprise is that these descriptions, in place of reality, bring us circuitously back to old-fashioned, castoff, linear *words* again. What a fine moment for the poor little devils to return, unexpected, in the service of art. As art gets more abstract—clear off the canvas and into the secret regions of the mind—what but words can help us? Will the artists become finally poets, or even composers of music, or mathematicians? New York sculptor Bob Smithson, who rented an air-conditioned Dodge to drive around Yucatan and place a large number of mirrors in the ground, described the artistic effect this way: "One couldn't help feeling that this was a ride on a knife covered with solar blood." That this sort of solipsistic art is hard to parody was proved in a recent takeoff by Art News, in which the total *oeuvre* of a fictitious enfant terrible was said to be five sketchbooks: the first had its drawings erased, the second was blank, the third had its pages torn out, the fourth was burned up and—the masterpiece—"the fifth sketchbook simply was never purchased." The trouble with such kidding is that the notebooks would clearly be considered substantial enough nowadays for somebody to commission as a project.

YET most of the artists are dead serious, not only about their work as personal experience, but also as a way to break free of the stultifying gallery scene and marketplace commercialism, in a *mise en valeur* of the vast, amazing, unlooked-at countryside all around. Says another founder of the genre, Californian Dennis Oppenheim, 31: "Things like the Grand Canyon have always frightened artists. They've always seemed like forms impossible to duplicate or rival. Now artists have to be willing to meet these objects in their own ball park."

Like Iain Baxter, Oppenheim started out by marking certain sites that pleased him with aluminum plaques—a basic tenet in the new art is that craftsmanship is altogether beside the point and that the artist's role may be simply to point out the esthetic order in nature. Oppenheim next stretched out snow fence in patterns in a wheat field in Hamburg, Pa., until the farmer who owned the land called the police to stop him. The artist finally convinced the farmer that the field had artistic possibilities. He got permission to direct the harvesting in certain patterns, but only the fact that he intended to photograph the results seemed to make the project acceptable to the farmer. "My feeling," says Oppenheim, "was that the experience of directing the harvest was the main work, not the pictures." In another work, he managed to place several hundred pairs of boards, nailed together at right angles, along a thousand-foot expanse of Long Island Expressway embankment; he photographed his creation, titled it "Landslide" and got away before the police noticed what he was doing.

Last spring a hip farmer of Finsterwolde, the Netherlands, let Oppenheim direct the seeding of his wheat field in wide curves (title: "Directed Seeding—Wheat"). The trouble was that at the crucial moment of harvesting, Oppenheim was back in New York City. He got on the phone to the farmer and carefully instructed him to harvest only two swatches in the field, in the form of an X, and to save the wheat, not have it refined for bread (title: "Canceled Crop"). The grain was sent to a gallery in Düsseldorf in 500 sacks, where it was displayed, along with photos of the field before and after harvest, to considerable interest. "We're forcing an esthetic onto the raw materials," Oppenheim explains. "The grain, not being made into bread, was withdrawn from its normal usage—it's like not using the fields to make money out of them. I think it's the best thing I've done." Another he likes was a series of concentric circles marked in snow upon the ice of the St. John River, which forms the U.S.-Canadian border at Fort Kent, Me. Suspicious customs men watched worriedly as he shoveled his way around and around, apparently afraid he was in some way damaging their frontier. What Oppenheim liked about the work was that it not only cut through two political units, but into two time zones as well. He likes fooling with time; another project of his is to realign the North American time zones according to the flight paths of migratory birds.

GEOGRAPHICAL paradoxes please Oppenheim; one of his plans is to build a full-sized replica of Ecuador's Cotopaxi volcano in Smith Center, Kan., which is the geographical center of the continental U.S. ("This kind of courage is rarely seen in art," commented Artforum critic Jean-Louis Bourgeois.) Oppenheim has already drawn a rough approximation of the cross-country path of U.S. Highway 20 by sprinkling red dye on a calm sea just off a beach in Tobago. He then poured gasoline onto the dye, set it afire and titled the blazing red ocean "Route 20 Transfer."

He has also transplanted an essence of the New York Stock Exchange to the roof of a building at 27th Street and Park Avenue. For this exercise, commissioned by Horace Solomon, Oppenheim hired trash men to move a day's worth of ticker tape and stock orders from the floor of the New York Stock Exchange to the roof of the building where he has a studio. The debris was scattered around, just as it had been downtown. Oppenheim took the usual before and after photos, which are what Solomon got as his commissioned work. "I am not quite comfortable with it," Solomon admits. The idea interested him, he says, "because the Exchange is a basic American idea, a great American institution. We thought we could re-create the Exchange by moving all the papers to another location, and the roof did look just like the Exchange. Since I could not buy the Exchange, or the building with the papers on the roof, I had to settle for the documentation of the event. What earth works are, is a documentation for monuments. The Stock Exchange is a monument, the debris is a monument in itself. Very few of my friends understand what I am doing. To buy uncollectable art is a different intellectual idea."

Perhaps a bit easier to exhibit is Oppenheim's rendering of a 220-yard dash in a muddy field last fall. He made plaster casts of each footprint and stacked them up for a gallery show. "Condensation, forcing out space between a series of steps," he explains, "is like eradicating time intervals between musical notes. The result is a single sound, unbroken by silence." A more ephemeral piece was a blanket dropped into the sea and photographed until it sank out of sight.

A friend who has worked with Oppenheim in the Caribbean, Peter Hutchinson, guarantees that nobody will see his own creations; wearing scuba diving equipment, Hutchinson works at the bottom of the sea. "It's more fun than being in the studio," he says. He dammed up an underwater canyon with a dozen 150-pound sandbags. "I made a change in the pattern of water flow, and fish now have to swim over the top," he says. Hutchinson likes the slow growth of algae, fungus, and crystals, as well as the gradual rotting of vegetable matter; all these go inside plastic or glass containers in various works of his. In one piece, plastic bags of rotting bread, held under water by anchors, were kept buoyant by the oxygen released in fermentation. His most famous underwater piece was a string of calabashes, attached to moorings, that undulated in the current while being photographed. The artist admits that no one can own underwater art, but emphasizes that the pictures prove the works are not fakes, that they really were made.

When not in the water, Hutchinson dreams up projects for mountaintops; he wants to set up a 20-foot-high glass tube full of algae on the brim of a volcano in Martinique, the action here coming when the volcano's heat speeds up growth inside the tube; the same fires would, of course, keep art lovers from getting anywhere near the piece. Hutchinson imagines a future with a stable population in which machines would do all the work and people would be free to devote themselves to Earth Art: "Each individual would be allotted a part of a planetary surface to landscape. This would be his life's work, and his success or failure as a person would depend on how he manipulated this environment as a work of art."

BOB SMITHSON, another founder of the school, is most known for his "non-sites," piles of rock or dirt that represent real, findable, mapped ground. "What the artist does, the way he thinks, is valuable, whether or not there is any tangible result," he says. Smithson is fascinated by the live quality of color caught in the mirrors he planted in Yucatan: "Acrylic and Day-Glo are nothing to these raw states of color," he says. "Real color is risky, not like the tame stuff that comes out of tubes. Such mirror surfaces cannot be understood by reason. Who can divulge from what part of the sky the blue color came?" Smithson, who had a January show at the Douglas Gallery in Vancouver, has received a gift from the British Crown—a small British Columbia island that he is currently covering over with laminated glass.

Somewhat in a bag of his own is an ebullient Bulgarian named Christo Javacheff, who last year won the plaudits of fellow artists by wrapping up in plastic sheets a mile of Australian coastal cliffs near Sydney; commercial firms picked up the $130,000 tab just for the publicity. Many earth workers agree that the purest piece was done recently by Claes Oldenburg when he hired gravediggers to dig a grave in Manhattan's Central Park and then fill it in. In Providence, R. I., Richard Fleischner makes three-dimensional models of crypts out of taut string spaced out in his studio. He sees no need to go out and actually dig the underground vault, since his stringed space already expresses perfectly the idea that he has in mind.

Walter De Maria, 35, is one veteran of the school who does seek a minimum of communication with the public; next to a gallery display of a picture of a half-mile-long chalk line that he made in the Nevada desert, De Maria installed a live telephone with the notice: "If this telephone rings, you may answer it. Walter De Maria is on the line and would like to talk to you." De Maria, who favors desert work, was once jailed as an oil spy while bulldozing a mile-long trench in Algeria. An Earth Art milestone of his consisted of a foot of dirt spread over the floor of a Munich gallery.

Many of the two dozen or so professionally recognized American earth artists live in New York City, avidly follow one another's work and occasionally meet to talk shop at a couple of bars, the St. Adrian's Company or Max's Kansas City. In spite of their retreat into the wilds, their escape from the market place is far from a fact. A number of American and foreign galleries have had money-making shows. According to "idea broker" John Gibson, a dealer who is opening another show on March 10 at his display room in New York, earth pieces—some costing as much as $50,000—are priced on the basis of Rodin's traditional distribution: a third for materials, a third for the artist, a third for the dealer. Collectors may also content themselves with paying $500 to $1,000 for documentation — maps, photos, and sometimes scale models—of works they do not actually commission themselves. These standard dealings may some day change in the present art turmoil. Predicts Harald Szeeman, director of the Berne Kunsthalle, "The traditional triangle of studio, gallery and collector will be destroyed."

IT is the esthetic questions, not the finances, that keep this new art stew boiling. Young artists want to replace a false, dollar-rated art worshipfulness with some truer sense of the plain beauties of the land around them. Most art critics have not been very responsive, although William Johnson, in Art News, wrote: "These pieces will probably never be seen in the original, but by now this shouldn't upset any but the most paranoid of observers." James Monte of the Whitney says the work "seriously calls into question how art should be seen, what should be done with it, and, finally, what is an art experience." Less readily impressed is New York Times critic Hilton Kramer, who wrote, "I consider it out of order for a critic to pass judgment on work he has never seen." A London critic, Norbert Lynton, avers that "there is not enough thought content in most of these things to satisfy a donkey."

Critic Lucy Lippard writes, "A profound dematerialization of art may lead to the object's becoming wholly obsolete." Again and again, what bothers everybody is the absence of the object. Writes Jean-Louis Bourgeois, "Going to a gallery and finding only photos is a little like going to a whorehouse and finding only pornography. You feel gypped." Amy Goldin in Art News calls it "de-fanged Dada"—"It is the toughness of art that is lacking." The Nation's man, Max Kozloff, calls it "muzzy strewings . . . left to bemuse a society entangled in the debris of its own incoherence." Another, more optimistic observer suggests that since we cannot exhibit the work, we should just circulate the artist. In any case, it is agreed that art is getting up there in the realms of abstract thought. Says New Yorker critic Harold Rosenberg, "Much of contemporary painting and sculpture is art only through having sidled, leaped, or been smuggled into the universe of art works." The works are so much *idea* now that Rosenberg thinks artists ought to price them at the same rates that an advertising agency charges its customers—15 per cent—since all that the sponsor gets, in most cases, is publicity. But he nevertheless believes Earth Art to be a legitimate development.

"Again the issue is: What is art?" Rosenberg says. "Art exists only through this question. If anybody ever answered it, that would be the end of art." Thus it seems likely that whatever gifts Earth Art may have in store for us, its young diggers and drillers are not quite going to resolve that old problem, and art will probably survive its flight into the wilds in nearly perfect health. ■

FEBRUARY 1, 1970

What's New in Art

Lectures

NEW YORK CULTURAL CENTER, 2 Columbus Circle. "Sound Off," Robert Scull, Tuesday, February 3, 8:00.

FEBRUARY 2, 1970

Partisans Here Hold Strong Opinions in Battle Over Lengths

By JUDY KLEMESRUD

WE are about to enter upon The Great Midi Crisis of 1970. In certain quarters, it is sure to rival pollution as the No. 1 issue of the year. Not to mention Vietnam.

What it boils down to is this: Should a woman keep wearing her miniskirts? Or should she accede to the whims of certain fashion designers and drop her skirts to mid-calf?

Already, Seventh Avenue is quaking. Enemies are being made, and friends are being lost. Designers such as Mollie Parnis, Pauline Trigère and Sarmi are so concerned that they gave anti-midi speeches before their recent fashion shows. And designers rarely give speeches.

Will they, and other friends of the miniskirt, be able to hold the dike against such powerful fashion forces as Valentino, Saint Laurent, Dior, Oscar de la Renta, Donald Brooke, Women's Wear Daily, Vogue and Harper's Bazaar?

In a recent random survey around the city, eight women were opposed to the longer skirts, eight were in favor, and four were noncommital—but seemed resigned to the fact that the midis were coming. With few exceptions, the women who tended to like the midis were either over 40, fat—or sometimes both.

Of the 15 men who were interviewed, 14 were violently opposed to the midis. The other, Joseph P. Washington, a Manhattan cab driver, said a women's skirt length didn't make any difference to him, "as long as the dress looks decent."

Whether Men Like It or Not

"Women are gonna do what they want to anyway, whether we men like it or not, right?" he added, as his cab sped through Central Park.

"I won't take this sitting down!" said Mrs. Alan Siegel, a tall blonde in her 20's, as she wheeled her 5-month-old daughter, Stacey, near 75th Street and Third Avenue. "I don't think women can be pushed around like this anymore. I have no intention of wearing anything long for summer, and I will be very sad if the short skirts disappear."

Paul Newman, the actor, became red-faced when the midi subject was mentioned. "I think it's absolutely shameful that designers are able to get away with something like this," he said at Sardi's.

Would he like his wife, Joanne Woodward, to wear one? "My wife's got great legs," he retorted. "Why should she hide 'em?"

Sheila Turner, a slender brunette who is an editor at Scholastic Magazines, said she loved the midi length so much that she had just ordered a fur coat (muskrat trimmed with raccoon) in that length.

"I feel it coming," she said. "Right now it's strange enough looking that it's fashionable. And I always feel fashionable if I'm one step ahead."

"I think they're awful," said Harry Dawson, 28, of Manhattan, an English teacher at Seton Hall Preparatory School in South Orange, N. J.

"They look like the 1950 vintage Deborah Kerr movies," he added, over a beer in the Sixth Avenue Delicatessen, "and there's nothing more dated than that particular vintage."

Mrs. Robert Scull, wife of the taxicab tycoon and pop art collector, has been wearing midiskirts for almost two years now. And she plans to keep wearing them—even if everybody else does.

"It's such a graceful length," she said. "I know I have nice legs—and my husband feels that I do, too—but one should not be concerned only about showing one's legs."

Husband Favors More Minis

Her husband, she added, would be happier if she wore short skirts more often than she does.

The divergent opinions of teen-age girls, who are often the real fashion trend-setters, were typified by two girls who were shopping in Gimbel's.

"Midis look terrible," insisted Marie Valdez, 14, of Manhattan, a student at Cathedral High School. "Legs are supposed to show, you know, and the midi hides them."

"I love them," said Gloria Howard, 15, of Manhattan, a student at Newark Preparatory School, who was shopping for a midi. "I've always liked the movies of the 40's when the dresses were that length."

Mrs. Mildred Nadel, 45, a well-dressed Brooklyn housewife with blond-streaked hair, said she could remember the longer length "very well."

"I don't like the feeling of the hem hitting the back of the leg," she added, "but I guess I'll be wearing them in two years when everybody else is."

"They infuriate me!" said Howard Papush, 29, the red-bearded producer of the "For Women Only" show at WNBC-TV. "They make women look so foolish, so old. The designers are trying to create planned obsolescence, like the car-makers do in Detroit to make people think they have to run out and buy a new car every year."

Mr. Papush added that he had refused to let his wife buy a maxicoat this year because he thought they would be out of style next year.

"I think they [the midis] are beautiful, and very feminine," said Miss Sara Karlsen, 62, a Manhattan housekeeper. "And they don't give a man such lust, like a mini does."

"I look at them as a homosexual concept for a woman," said Mrs. Kenneth Slater, 30, of Manhattan, who works for the Scientology Foundation. "It covers the best part of her body."

"The mini," she added, "is where it's at for chicks like me with good legs."

Problem of Fat Knees

"I have fat knees," moaned Marcy Donovan, an 18-year-old secretary from Queens, as she wrote out a check for $96 at Macy's for two midiskirted suits.

"The minis exposed my bad points to the world, and now I'm going to cover them up again in the name of fashion."

Mayor Lindsay's opinion of the midis was probably the most succinct of all.

"I think they're a big letdown," he said. And that shouldn't make the Seventh Avenue dress manufacturers too angry.

FEBRUARY 27, 1970

When Ethel Scull Redecorates, It Is Art News

By CHARLOTTE CURTIS

ETHEL SCULL by Andy Warhol is on the road. In Plexiglas cases to protect the multiple enlarged snapshots from deterioration during museum exhibitions. Ethel Scull by George Segal is at home. Sitting plaster-cast immobile on the love seat in the marble hallway. Not far from two of Jasper Johns's American flags and Claes Oldenberg's stove with the papier-mâché sausages and rare roast beef.

And the real Ethel Scull? She's at home, too, unless she's at the warehouse sorting out the art collection. Or Kenneth's for her hair wash. Or Marc Sinclaire for her hair set. Or Bloomingdale's, where she buys socks for her boys. Or Adolfo or Giorgio di Sant'Angelo, where the midi skirts come from.

Rubbing Smudges Off

Lately, however, she's been at home rubbing smudges off what seems like miles and miles of white walls in the 11-room apartment and redecorating in her fashion. Things just don't look the way they did in 1969. Or any other year for that matter.

The walls are still white, of course, thanks not just to the painters who come in every summer to brighten them but to the bottles of Fantastik Mrs. Scull is forever spraying at even the slightest suggestion of a shadow. But the art works are different, and they have transformed the rooms.

"If we owned instead of renting," Mrs. Scull said frankly, "I suppose we'd knock out a wall or two now and then. But we don't."

As a result, the Sculls are locked into the shape of the rooms as they are and the generally gigantic paintings as they are, and, as Mrs. Scull says (adding that every major change involves "four Miltowns a day"), "It's not that easy to get everything to work."

In the seven years since Robert Scull, the taxicab tycoon, and his wife moved into what Mrs. Scull persists in calling "our tenement on Fifth Avenue" (because the elevator service is erratic and there are days when there's no heat or hot water), they have amassed one of the world's bigger and better collections of contemporary American art. And the apartment décor naturally enough, changes to suit the acquisitions.

"I've been hanging a lot of the newer boys," Mrs. Scull explained. "The younger ones who've been in storage."

The living room, which was an array of bright, chaotic streaks of abstract expressionist works in the mid-sixties, gradually became a veritable comic strip of pop art toward the end of the decade. Since the first of the year, however, it has become what Mrs. Scull calls "a mixed bag of early works," with the younger artists hanging side by side with some of the more established ones.

Dan Christensen, who sprinkles small bars over pastel clouds, is one of the new boys. His rainbow work hangs where Warhol's Ethel Scull hung until it went on the road.

"Christensen is marvelous," Mrs. Scull said. "Some of his paintings are 26 feet long. We had to put them in storage. He paints smaller now, thank God."

Robert Morris is new to the living room, too. Mrs. Scull had no qualms about putting his metallic, but lifelike, human brain on a massive antique wood coffee table not far from two antique French vermeil and crystal boxes and Lucas Samaras's box made mostly of millions of straight pins. The coffee table has been the center of a conversational grouping of sofas for a long time.

"We can't do the room any other way," Mrs. Scull said. "You can't push anything up against the walls. It doesn't look right."

Peter Young, who goes in for brightly colored staphylococcic curls of dots on enormous canvases, is the new boy in the dining room. Two of his paintings dominate a wall that in recent years has gone from abstract to pop to Larry Poons, who also is big on dots against solid backgrounds.

That nothing in the room, which also contains a Louis XV table with Louis XV chairs, several other big paintings and a harsh John Chamberlain metalworks on a pedestal, has not so much as a hint of dust or soot about it is not just a tribute to the efficiency of the Sculls' house staff but to their ingenuity.

"We put Scotch tape around all the windows in the apartment," Mrs. Scull said. "A little soot gets as far as the window sills but never on the paintings."

What musses things up, of course, are the human beings who either live in the apartment or come to visit. One crisis involved Mr. Warhol, who accidentally knocked over Mr. Oldenberg's bulky, overblown papier-mâché man's shirt and tie. But cigarette smokers distress Mrs. Scull the most.

"Twenty people here and you wouldn't *believe* the ashes on the floor and couches," she said. "I stopped using flowers in pots because that's where the cigarette butts went."

The real trauma of living with a periodic desire to change the surrounding behemoth paintings is the work needed to get them into and out of the apartment and onto and off the walls. Besides the Miltown, Mrs. Scull never faces this task without James LeBrun ("the only man I know who hangs paintings with reverence") and his helpers.

Mr. LeBrun untacks canvases that are to come down or manipulates their collapsible frames. He loops or rolls the paintings to get them through doorways, into elevators and out to the trucks. He reverses the procedure to get the new boys onto the walls.

"Anguish, sheer anguish," said Mrs. Scull, who goes through this process several times a year. "By the end of the day I'm a wreck."

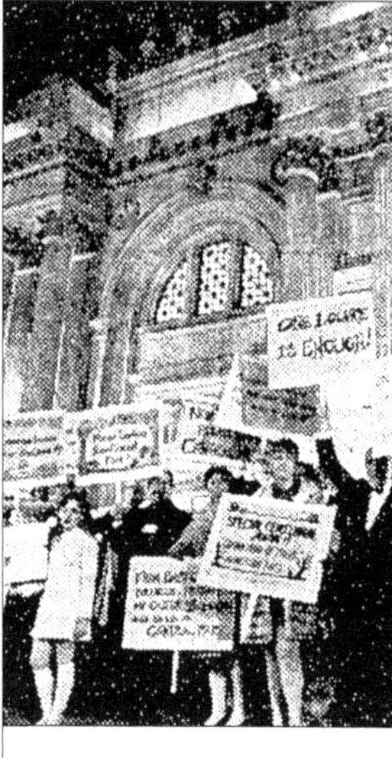

APRIL 14, 1970

Museum's Ball Draws Arty Pickets Too

By ENID NEMY

It was black tie inside and out at the Metropolitan Museum of Art last night. As the 3,000 formally clad guests prepared to ascend the granite stairway into the building for a Centennial Ball, a smaller group, many of them also in black tie, picketed along Fifth Avenue in what they termed a "quiet, non-action, dignified" demonstration.

The group of about 60, members of the East Side Conservation Committee, was protesting the institution's planned expansion into Central Park.

"We also feel very strongly about cultural decentralization," said Mrs. John G. Heimann, the chairman, who put on a broadtail coat and white kid gloves for her marching chores.

"We are not a bunch of precious people or little old ladies and bird watchers in space shoes. We are deeply committed to what's going on in the city."

Mrs. Heimann, whose husband is a partner in E. M. Warburg & Co., an investment firm, said:

"Picketing is not my thing, but there comes a time when one must put some quiet action where one's mouth is."

The quiet action was just that. The pickets contented themselves with placards reading, "The Met Could Enrich the City With More Branches Like the Cloisters," "Decentralize or Die," "Happiness Is a Park Tree," "Once Upon a Time There Was a Central Park." The protest was carried on in almost complete silence.

One of the most carefully coordinated demonstrators was Sheba, a black and white Dalmatian who trotted along in a white raincoat (her own) and a borrowed black tie.

"We walk in the park every morning, so she has a stake in this," said Esther Bubley, her owner.

The protest was greeted with cheerful indulgence by centennial celebrants.

"It's a tempest in a teapot," said Mrs. W. Vincent Astor, a member of the museum's anniversary committee and ball chairman.

Mrs. Astor, who showed up in a fringed turquoise silk gown, an American-made copy of a French couturier original, said, "We are not planning to encroach on the park at all, just the parking space. I think when they realize this, they will calm down."

Earlier Mrs. Astor had entertained 60 guests at dinner in her Park Avenue apartment. Among them were Gov. and Mrs. Rockefeller; C. Douglas Dillon, president of the Metropolitan, and Mrs. Dillon; William S. Paley, president of the Museum of Modern Art, and Mrs. Paley, and George Seybolt, president of the Boston Museum of Fine Arts.

Thomas P. F. Hoving, director of the museum, and Mrs. Hoving held their dinner party at the home of Mr. and Mrs. A. Ronald Tree. Mrs. Tree, a member of the committee, was in Europe.

Other hosts included Mr. and Mrs. Gardner Cowles, Mr. and Mrs. Arthur A. Houghton Jr. (he's chairman of the Museum's board of trustees), and Mr. and Mrs. Robert Scull.

The ball, believed to be the first sponsored by the museum, was expensive, with tickets at $125 each.

Four of the principal areas on the main floor recreated the more colorful eras of the last century. The Arms and Armor Court became an 1870 ballroom, designed by Parish-Hadley, Inc. A 25-piece string orchestra, led by Emery Davis, played a continuous series of waltzes.

In the Blumenthal Patio, reconverted into a room of La Belle Epoque by McMillen, Inc., Jack Harris of the Meyer Davis organization led a 10-piece tango orchestra.

Hot and cold canapes and Meyer Davis's playing such tunes as "Whispering," "Avalon" and "Body and Soul" were features of the Egyptian Sculpture Court, transformed by Burge-Donghia, Inc., into a roof garden supper club of the 1930's.

Baldwin & Martin, Inc., converted the U-shaped Fountain restaurant into a discothèque. Music was supplied by Watson and the Sherlocks, a rock band.

APRIL 18, 1970

Sharon Rockefeller's Fashion Mission

By JUDY KLEMESRUD

THERE were two big attractions in the ballroom of 1 Beekman Place the other day: Colorful patchwork fashions, and Mrs. John D. (Jay) Rockefeller 4th. Both are from West Virginia.

The fashions were handmade by 300 mountain women who are known collectively as Mountain Artisans. They practice their ancient Appalachian art in rural towns with such names as Sod and Dog Bone and Lost Creek and Warrior Mines.

"I don't have any sewing skills or anything like that," said Sharon Rockefeller, the ebullient, 25-year-old daughter of Senator Charles Percy of Illinois. "I work in the organization end of it."

Mrs. Rockefeller, whose husband is Secretary of State of West Virginia, is co-chairman of the board of directors of Mountain Artisans. She was dressed for the part, in a black and brown floor-length patchwork calico dress that she said her husband "just loves."

The fashion show and exhibit were held at the Beekman Place address, one of the most fashionable in town, because the ballroom had been made available to the group. There was a reason: Mrs. Rockefeller's parents-in-law, Mr. and Mrs. John D. Rockefeller 3d, live in the building.

'Long Ways From West Virginia'

"It's quite a long ways from West Virginia," Sharon Rockefeller joked, as she opened the fashion show.

The patchwork clothes were first modeled in the ballroom, and then the models walked out into an adjoining garden overlooking the East River. The spectators, who munched on corn muffins from West Virginia, were especially fond of a 10-year-old girl model who refused to smile because she had lost her brace.

Several officers of Mountain Artisans were in Manhattan a year ago, with just a few fashions and a lot of determination. Like Lew Alcindor, they just growed.

The current collection, which can be viewed Monday through May 1 in the Gotham Hotel, includes patchwork midiskirts, dresses, hostess gowns, gaucho pants, granny gowns, children's clothes, purses, quilts, pillows, scarves, tablecloths—and even patchwork boots.

Among the biggest hits of the show were the leather and suède skirts with unusual patchwork designs. One white leather mini is embellished with futuristic silver and gold patchwork figures.

"Last year we started out with zero, and by the end of the year we had grossed $100,000," said Mrs. Florette Angel, an ethereal blonde who is general director of Mountain Artisans.

One of the reasons for the success is that patchwork and quilted fashions caught on with such fashion leaders as Mrs. Wyatt (Gloria Vanderbilt) Cooper, Mrs. Robert Scull, and Mrs. Richard Feigen.

Patchwork Quilts to $2,000

The patchwork fashions and accessories are available at Lord & Taylor, B. Altman & Co., Saks Fifth Avenue, Bonwit Teller and Splendiferous. Prices range from $22 for a patchwork miniskirt to $800 for a silk patchwork evening coat and matching skirt. Quilts run all the way up to $2,000.

Mountain Artisans is funded with a grant from the United States Office of Economic Opportunity. It is a nonprofit organization.

Many of the Mountain Artisans were on welfare before they began sewing for money. They follow patterns sent to them from the group's headquarters in Charleston, W. Va. The women are paid $2 an hour for their work on the fashions, which are mailed to headquarters when completed.

"My house is full of patchwork things," Mrs. Rockefeller said after the show. "I have clothes and quilts and chair pads—they're very bright and fun to live with."

Even her 9½-month-old son, Jamie (he will decide at the age of 21 whether he wants to be called John D. Rockefeller 5th), has gotten into the act. His baby blanket is a tiny patchwork quilt.

MAY 10, 1970

Now Even in May, There's Just No Rest for the Partygoer

By CHARLOTTE CURTIS

AND so fall and winter got so socially over-scheduled that benefit chairmen began to think about the spring, and now look what's happened. Spring is the social season that matters and May is just plain chaotic.

Art gallery and museum extravaganzas have proliferated. Benefits have been hitched to ballet and baseball as well as Broadway. And the jewel auction has emerged as a newer way to raise money.

Then there are the charity balls. Despite constant complaints against them (usually by the very people who support them), they are flourishing. Yet competition for big names and benefit dollars is fearful. And two and three galas a night are not unusual.

Last week was typically frenzied, but Thursday night set some sort of record, even by May standards. It started with the Wally F Galleries, where Mrs. Frank T. Ryan (Marsha Gayle) was having a one-woman show, moved on to private dinners or the Animal Kingdom Ball and ended, for those willing to carry on until well after midnight, at the Museum of the City of New York's costume exhibition.

Party After Party

"What a week," Mrs. William B. Jaffe moaned at the museum as she and her husband, the lawyer, greeted and were greeted by friends they hadn't seen since the Wally F cocktail reception.

"Last night it was the Wildenstein. Tuesday we went to the Feather Ball. I think I'm going to drop in my tracks."

If the elegant Mrs. Jaffe should drop in her tracks some evening, she'll go down in the last word in midi lengths. She won the Feather Ball's grand prize — a mink coat.

"A magnificent midi mink," she exclaimed. "Like sable. Not that miserable brown mink."

Like others at the museum, the Jaffes started the evening with Mrs. Ryan, her ropes of enormous black and white pearls, her diamonds, her paintings, her friends from Europe and Palm Beach and her international financier husband.

Mrs. Ryan had persuaded Halston to run her up a pajama outfit of yellow, white, black and red chiffon like the colorings in some of her paintings, and she was in a very good mood.

"Of course I'm excited," she said as pals congratulated her. "And nervous."

Fashion Exhibition, Too

While Mrs. Ryan roamed the gallery, her friends sipped drinks and nibbled pretzels and nuts. They were as interested in each other as the paintings, and the women stared at each other's clothes.

"I don't care who wears the midi," Mrs. Joseph King, wife of the investment banker, said as dozens of women in midiskirts wandered by. "I'm wearing my French clothes short. But I hear that even some of my best friends are traitors."

At that point, the Count and Countess de Romanones appeared. He owns something like a fourth of Spain and she shows up regularly on the better-dressed lists. They actually wanted to see the paintings.

"Lovely," the American-born countess said upon confronting "Jockey's Loot," one of Mrs. Ryan's vast racing canvases. "Marsha paints very well."

The Count seemed to agree, but he was distracted by Richard Pistell, the international conglomerateur, and his wife, the former Carroll de Portago. Mrs. Pistell wore a black mididress with a black neckband. She looked more like Toulouse-Lautrec's "La Goulue" at the Wildenstein than Mrs. Ryan's highly colored works.

Long Cocktail Reception

After perhaps two hours, the Ryan party began to disband. But at the St. Regis Roof, the American Society for the Prevention of Cruelty to Animals party was just getting under way.

The A.S.P.C.A.'s Animal Kingdom Ball, which at 20 is one of the older of the big-time benefits, purposely has one of the longest pre-dinner cocktail receptions in New York. This is to give all the guests time to gamble with scrip money.

"People like to gamble for charity," said John Welsh 3d, vice president of Gartley & Mathieu, Inc. (financial advisers). "They come back year after year."

Games of Chance

Aside from vingt-et-un, dealt by middle-aged stockbrokers recruited for the occasion, the games of chance ran to the country fair with ring tosses, bird cages and something involving a Ping-Pong ball that's supposed to drop into a small-mouthed glass jar.

"It's hard," Carel van Meukelom, an investment banker, conceded as he attempted to toss hoops over a miniature poodle. "I'm not very good at it."

While some guests gambled, the others were at little tables fortifying themselves with drinks and cheese. Mrs. Edward N. Cole, wife of the president of General Motors, was among the nongamblers.

"I've given my money to the cause," Mrs. Cole said, without indicating how much. "I don't have any left to gamble."

Mrs. Cole, who'd come from Detroit for the party, wore turquoise and diamond earrings, a turquoise ring and what may be the most spectacular turquoise, diamond and sapphire necklace on the East Coast.

"I didn't have a thing to wear with it," she said, admitting the necklace was new, "so I took an earring to Orchard and Delancey Streets. I always buy my fabric there. I found what I needed and had my dressmaker make it."

The dress was a long-sleeved cloud of turquoise synthetic fabric with a scooped neckline. What's more, Mrs. Cole reported with some relish, "It's washable. I could just toss it in the washing machine."

Mrs. Cole was honorary chairman of the ball, but as much as she loves the A.S.P.C.A., it is not her favorite charity. She thinks retarded adults need more help.

"But I have dogs, horses, llamas and things," she added brightly, "and I do like animals."

The Coleses' llama lives at their farm in Atlanta, Mich., north of their home in Bloomfield Hills. And the llama's name is Mama Llama.

"I know that's not very original," she said. "But it sounded right."

Museum Filling Up

By the time the ballgoers were finally going into dinner, the museum was filling with the likes of Mr. and Mrs. Wyatt Cooper (Gloria Vanderbilt), Shirley Booth, the Joshua Logans, Mr. and Mrs. Robert Scull and Myrna Loy.

They had come to see the new theatrical costume collection, talk about the Seventh Avenue fashion showings and deplore the state of the world.

"Maybe the young people are right," Dr. Milton Berliner, the opthamologist, said, shaking his head. "I don't understand what's happening. But when you consider all the dishonesty . . . I don't know."

Dr. Berliner was with Mrs. Samuel Newhouse, wife of the newspaper tycoon. Their spouses, exhausted by the week's activities, were at home playing cards. Gen. John Coulter, the retired Air Force officer who may be counted upon to brighten up the better parties, took the night off, too. He went to the movies.

MAY 12, 1970

Shouts of 'Bravo' for Bill Blass's Long Look

By BERNADINE MORRIS

BILL BLASS finally did it. He made the long look palatable to a lot of women who were clinging defiantly to short clothes. Women such as Mrs. William F. Buckley, who said before his fall showing of Maurice Renter clothes at the Hotel Plaza yesterday afternoon, "I look like the Prime of Miss Jean Brodie in long skirts—I'm going to wear mine very short—or stick to pants."

Women such as Mrs. John Hammond, wife of the recording executive, who was wearing last year's Mainbocher silk dress "comfortably and happily." Or Mrs. Charles Revson, who said she hadn't gotten around to long clothes for day yet even though her husband, the head of Revlon, thoroughly approved.

In less than an hour, a lot of minds had changed.

"Where are you off to?" Mrs. T. Suffern Tailer, wife of the sportsman, asked Mrs. Buckley amid the shouts of "bravo," rare at any manufacturer's showing.

Summer Shopping

Mrs. Buckley collected her page and a half of notes, slipped on the plaid jacket of her Bill Blass suit murmuring, "I just got it this spring, and now it's outdated," and answered, "I'm off to the racks at Bloomingdale's to get something for summer."

"I'll come along and help," said Mrs. Tailer, who had, with foresight, provided herself with a long denim skirt from Bonwit's for the show. She thereby qualified as an expert.

Even women who have been running around in long skirts for a while thought Bill Blass had made a good job of it.

"I don't have to go to Europe—it's all here," said Mrs. Alfred S. Bloomingdale Jr., wife of the Diner's Club executive. Her blue and white Galanos suit was modishly long.

And the Saint Laurent Boutique fan club, which included Mrs. William P. Rayner, wife of the Vogue magazine executive, Mrs. Ahmet Ertegun, whose husband heads Atlantic Records, and Mrs. Robert C. Scull, whose husband is in the taxicab business, were all glad to have another place to shop.

What did Blass do to deserve all the huzzahs? After all, Seventh Avenue has been showing nothing but long skirts for two weeks now and a lot of the women have seen other shows.

"They're wearable," explained Mrs. Joshua Logan, wife of the producer. They're like the things I used to get from her," she added, pointing to her companion, Valentina, who once designed clothes for the theater and social sets. Valentina was captivated by the "black girl in black," who was, she thought, "beyond belief."

The black girl was Naomi Sims, who was also effective when she was wearing panne velvet prints rimmed in feathers around the ankle or brocade dresses aglow with gold.

When Show Goes On

These dresses would have been show stoppers anyway. But the Blass strength was that he also made clothes that women could think of wearing when they weren't interested in stopping shows.

Take the tweed jumpers or the gray flannel dress, for example. Look at them one way and they're cop-outs, for though they're the proper below-the-knee length, they're split to show an above-the-knee dress underneath. But, the designer isn't really begging the issue—he's easing women into long skirts and eliminating the squeals.

Nobody overlooks boots these days, and when brocade boots come out with brocade dresses, you can hardly overlook them.

Just to make sure he overlooked nothing, Blass ended his show with all-black fashions. Sheer socko, from the handkerchief - pointed chiffon to the hooded cape.

Seventh Avenue should be happy to have a hit on its hands.

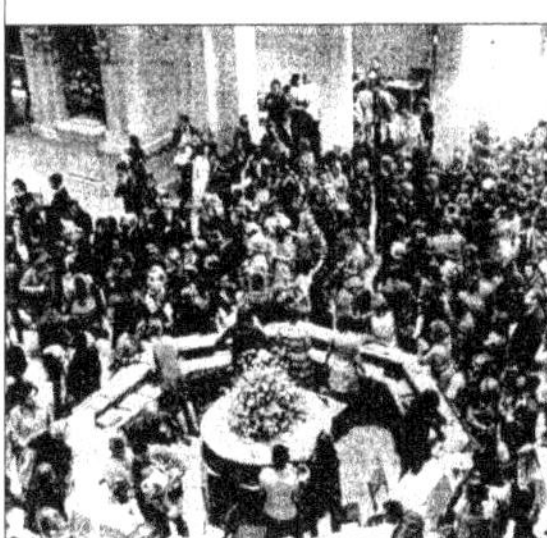

JUNE 28, 1970

Captivated Capital Rallies Round the Nathan Cummings Art Collection

Special to The New York Times

WASHINGTON, June 27—"Selections from the Nathan Cummings Collection" opened at the National Gallery of Art, here with all the trappings of a potentate's state visit—lacking only flags on the street.

Like a state visit, there was the dinner for 180 by the resident president, the return dinner for 500 by the visiting power, the exclusive luncheon for 80, the reception for 800 to include people not invited to sit down, and a larger reception for the gallery's mailing list, invited to look, not to eat.

Like a state visit, planning had begun more than a year ago with the National Gallery's David Rust and the Metropolitan Museum of Art's Claus Virch visiting Nathan Cumming's nine-room Waldorf Towers apartment, his Seagram Building office (he is honorary chairman of the Consolidated Foods Corporation) and to his estate, The Anchorage, in Charlevoix, Mich. They picked the House. It was not Mrs. Cummings's first visit. "I helped pay for the antique wallpaper in the diplomatic entrance," she said, "when Jacqueline Kennedy was there. We don't go as often now."

Mrs. Cummings did not buy a new dress for the occasion. "I've had this one for about a year. It's a Dior," she said. It was a dark blue with a faint purple hue—a long lace tunic over chiffon pants with a long scarf flying.

Just before dinner, she slipped away from the receiving line to give two Senators' wives, Mrs. Charles H. Percy and Mrs. Jacob K. Javits, a peek preview of the show.

"It's a very nice collection for that period of art," Mrs. Javits said later. "Mr. Cummings collects art from his generation. I like art from mine."

Going into dinner on the arm of Mr. Cummings was Mrs. John W. (Cathy) Warner Jr., Mr. Mellon's daughter, whose husband is Under Secretary of the Navy. Mrs. Warner was elegant in black with an over-the-shoulder fringe bag.

In the toast, Paul Mellon, who you'd think would have enough pictures of his own to keep him happy, confessed to larcenous thoughts about the Edouard Manet "Tangerines" painting. "I have exactly the right place for it," he said, and added he thought the collection showed "the discerning eye of a real and loving collector."

Mr. Cummings replied "I'm still a country boy. To find that Mr. Mellon thinks it is a good collection is wonderful for me. I'm just a humble guy who likes pictures."

Then everybody went in to see the selections from the collection themselves.

At the luncheon yesterday, the speeches were concerned with the Business Committee for the Arts' efforts to bridge the gap between the people who have the art to make money and the people who need money to make art.

When Gavin MacBain, head of Bristol-Myers, was almost through with his speech, the gallery's bell call system chimed on and on. Amid laughter, Carter Brown said, "It's calling the plumber. Maybe there'll be a deluge." Afterward he said privately with a grin, "Now Paul Mellon won't complain about the money for our new pocket buzzer call system coming in Monday. I hate the bells. It sounds like a department store."

At the luncheon Mrs. Cummings wore a white Adolpho hat, balancing her Sibley and Coffee midi.

Mr. Cummings, who has long white hair and sideburns, favors vicuña suits with red paisley linings and hand-made cuff links of precious stones. He decided, though, against wearing gold collar stays his grandchildren gave him. "They might slip out" he said.

At the reception last night, one guest looked at the other pictures from about 800 and selected the sculpture from about 60 pieces in the Cummings's collection. The show opens tomorrow to the public in the National Gallery to run through Sept. 11. It opens July 1, 1971 at the Metropolitan to stay through Sept. 7. In between it goes back on the Cummings's walls.

The selections began to arrive this month by plane, boat and truck at the National Gallery. One small varicolored onyx sculpture came down in Mr. Cummings's suitcase from New York the day before the exhibition. The 98-inch bronze Henry Moore sculpture, which had been sitting in a crate at the Metropolitan, had to be placed at the gallery with a crane.

Mr. Cummings had to learn to do without the Georges Rouault "The Theatrical Producer," which he usually hangs in his bathroom because "it makes me think."

Mrs. Cummings had to hang other pictures from their collection in their apartment and ask her expert in to adjust the lighting.

Meanwhile at the National Gallery, Carol Cutler was not only writing notes for the catalog, but also sitting down to two complete-with-wine rehearsal dinners with Ridgewell Caterers to ensure the gallery's evening would be a masterpiece.

The National Gallery's dinner was Thursday night. Paul Mellon, president of the gallery, stood with Carter Brown, director of the gallery, and Mr. and Mrs. Cummings in a line in the foyer to the Seventh Street entrance, which is only open on ceremonial occasions. Mrs. Mellon didn't attend her own dinner because she was visiting her daughter in Paris.

"We just got back from tea at the White House in time to change," said Mrs. Cummings. She and other wives and members of the Business Committee for the Arts — meeting concurrently here — had been welcomed by Mrs. Spiro T. Agnew at the White guests and said, "They'd look pretty good hanging on the gallery walls." She was talking about the red-and-white Givenchy silk of Mrs. Cummings, the exotic Indian embroidered dress of New York designer Adarsh Kavr Gill; the elaborate scrolled gold necklace of the sculptor Esther (Mrs. Leo) Weinrott of Philadelphia; the hand-printed Chloe of Paris blue-and-white silk of Barbara Levinson; the black-and-white printed tuxedo jacket of Herbert Cummings, Nathan's son; the Victor Jorges black crepe, with a deep split, worn by Mrs. Robert Scull, and the 200-year-old Indian sari that the wife of the sculptor Jacques Lipchitz made into a dress to wear with her emerald necklace.

Mr. Lipchitz, with flowing white hair curling at his shoulder, looked through the exhibit and said to Mr. Cummings: "It is a good collection. But I do not like not to see a Lipchitz."

Later last night at the dinner at the Washington Hilton given by Mr. Cummings, guests danced between the consommé Madrilene Romanoff, the paupietes of sole Kennebec ("I made them add some shrimp on top," said Mr. Cummings, whose company includes Sarah Lee Bakeries), a Cornish game hen, farci, boned to the order of Mr. Cummings, and the vacherine glacé with fresh raspberries ("put some candied violets on the top. Use fresh raspberries — a sauce looks as though it were frozen," directed Mr. Cummings).

The 1,800 chocolate mints and salted nuts came into town in Mr. Cummings's luggage from two of his Consolidated Food Companies.

Just before midnight, seven of the Nathan Cummings grandchildren, nieces and nephews, all of whom will be going on the European trip with their 73-year-old patriarch in a week, made speeches of appreciation to Mr. Cummings and sang "Joanne." (A song composed by Meyer Davis's orchestra for the Cummings wedding) to Mrs. Cummings. Mr. Cummings cried.

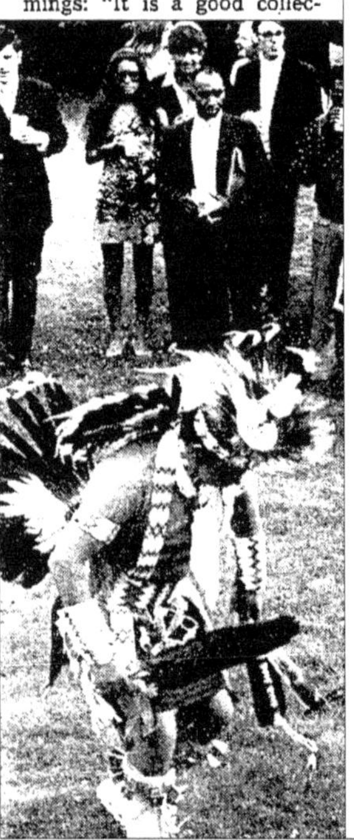

JULY 13, 1970

Andrew Stein Gives a Lavish Party on L.I. With Indians as Honor Guests

Comanche, Kiowa, Potawatomi and Social Tribes Attend

By CHARLOTTE CURTIS

Special to The New York Times

SOUTHAMPTON, L. I., July 12—For a while there, it looked as if parties for minority underdogs of one sort or another would come to a screeching halt.

Mr. and Mrs. Leonard Bernstein were severely criticized for entertaining Black Panthers in their Park Avenue apartment. Mrs. Randolph Guggenheimer got it for her spaghetti dinner for the Puerto Rican Young Lords. And Andrew Stein was denounced for inviting Cesar Chavez's Mexican-American grape pickers to his family's palatial Southampton mansion.

Mr. Stein, however, has refused to be intimidated. The young Assemblyman from Manhattan's Upper East Side was at it again last night—this time at a huge cocktail party in honor of the American Indian.

Nearly Everyone Is There

"The American Indian got the biggest screwing in American history," he said flatly. "This was their country and we took it away from them. We've ignored them for years. I think we should be doing what we can to correct this situation."

What Mr. Stein did, of course, was to invite scores of Indians and hundreds of frankly rich Southampton residents to his family's house, and, predictably, nearly everybody accepted.

Senator Fred R. Harris, Democrat of Oklahoma, and his wife, the Comanche who founded Americans for Indian Opportunity, were cohosts.

So were Mrs. Winthrop Rockefeller, wife of the Governor of Arkansas—she couldn't make it at the last minute because her plane forgot to pick her up—and Mrs. Eleanor Searle Whitney, former wife of Cornelius Vanderbilt Whitney and herself something of an evangelist. Mrs. Whitney was among the first guests to arrive.

"I've loved Indians all my life," she said, introducing herself to Perry Horse, a Kiowa from the Bureau of Indian Affairs, and John Shopteese, a Potawatomi who works for the Department of Health, Education and Welfare. "We must take action."

Mr. Horse and Mr. Shopteese nodded politely, stared at her floppy red and white pajamas with the Navajo turquoise and silver jewelry, and indicated that they, too, had loved Indians all their lives.

"There are still lots of myths that have to be changed," Mr. Shopteese said as Mrs. Whitney strolled off across the spacious lawn. "Why, people still think we originated scalping. We didn't. The French did—when they were in New England. They offered bounties for Indian scalps."

By this time, dozens of other guests had appeared. The Steins' black and white maids in gray uniforms with white aprons were passing trays of hors d'oeuvres. The bar was busy. And lots of people were gathering around Mrs. Harris.

"Awareness is really the most important thing we'd like to project," she said. "No more of this, 'Lo, the poor Indian.' That's out. We want to be more positive."

Crossing Tribal Lines

Mrs. Harris came to the party from an Iroquois Confederacy meeting in Geneva, N. Y. She wore a white pants suit printed with the Cherokee alphabet and a black, brown and white Cherokee alphabet scarf.

"I'm a Comanche," she explained to guests who didn't know. "I can't read Cherokee."

Then why the Cherokee alphabet?

"It's the only Indian language that's written," she said.

Senator and Mrs. Harris were accompanied by their daughter, Laura, who passed out brochures explaining Americans for Indian Opportunity. When the program began, Laura got to sit up on the big stone terrace with the honored guests, the performers and the pots of red geraniums.

Floyd Westerman, a Sioux singer, got things started with folk songs criticizing anthropologists, missionaires, Christianity, the Bureau of Indian Affairs and virtually every white man who'd ever had anything to do with the Indians.

He said some of the songs were from his new album, "Custer Died for Your Sins," which is to be introduced during a Crow fair at the Little Big Horn. Below him on the lawn, the guests went right on drinking and talking.

Plains Indian Fancy

Then came Mr. Horse, who'd changed his street clothes for what he called "a Plains-type traditional fancy dance costume of no particular tribe"—an outfit combining brightly feathered back and neck bustles, a feathered crown, masses of beads, a feathered wand, a short skirt and moccasins. Everybody watched as he danced across the lawn and applauded when he finished.

Mr. Stein, speaking into a microphone that still couldn't drown out the party talk, introduced Mrs. Harris.

She thanked her co-chairmen and introduced Senator Jacob K. Javits ("He's always been a great friend of the Indian"), Harry Williams, governor of Southampton's own Shinnecocks; William Seneca, governor of the Seneca Nation; Junie Langhorn, senior trustee of Long Island's Poospatuck Reservation, and several other Indian leaders.

It was then Jose Torres's turn to speak. Mr. Torres, the former champion fighter who's been called "Everybody's pet primitive," said: "Indians are human beings and must be helped."

He said there were girls out along the Steins' driveway, waiting for contributions.

It Makes a Great Show

That concluded the formal entertainment. But as far as Mrs. Robert Scull was concerned, the whole party was "a great show."

"They aren't to be believed," the taxicab tycoon's wife said as she looked at the motley fashions out across the lawn. "Did you ever see such get-ups? I haven't put my glasses on for fear I'll see something else. I mean, where are the real Indians?"

What Mrs. Scull was seeing was Indians in coats and ties and paleface Southampton women in beads, feathers, fringed leather and all the other bits and pieces of what passes for Indian fashion. William J. Goode, professor of sociology as Columbia University, was even more surprised.

"I'm absolutely staggered by the fashion," he said. "My God, the colors the men allow themselves. It's one thing for the women, but the men!"

Mr. Goode was hardly understated himself. He wore casual pants, a fish net see-through navy shirt, a necklace of big metal rings and sandals. Mrs. Betty Friedan, author of "The Feminine Mystique," said he was part of her "commune." What she meant was that they were guests in the same house.

"I know people are going to criticize this thing," Mrs. Friedan said, "but I don't care. It's better to be radical chic than chic effete."

Mr. Goode agreed with her. "This party's good," he said. "When there's an important issue I'm not concerned about motivations. You get people to work for whatever reason you can. It doesn't matter. If they come to see a Whitney or a Rockefeller or to pick up girls, I don't care, as long as the work gets done."

Mrs. Friedan and Mr. Goode were with Joseph Weinstein, the retired real estate man, and his wife. The Weinsteins said it was time for another Black Panther party. Red Wing, an 87-year-old Winnebago princess, said she'd never heard of the Panthers.

"All I know is Indians and how to make costumes for TV," she said. "I was in 'The Squaw Man' with Dustin Farnum. That was Cecil B. DeMille's first movie, you know."

AUGUST 10, 1970

Women's Liberation Gets Into the Long Island Swim

By CHARLOTTE CURTIS

Special to The New York Times

EAST HAMPTON, L. I., Aug. 9—Everything at the women's liberation party had gone pretty much according to plan. Then Representative Patsy Mink, Democrat of Hawaii, disappeared when she was supposed to speak, and a woman shed her blue jeans and dived into the swimming pool. After that, things were never quite the same.

The cocktail reception was a Women's Strike for Equality benefit. It was held yesterday in the sculpture-filled gardens around Mr. and Mrs. Robert Scull's starkly rectangular summer compound. By 6:30 P.M. perhaps 100 gaily clad guests had arrived.

"All I see are the committed, their husbands and the press," Mrs. Betty Friedan, author of "The Feminine Mystique," said as she surveyed the crowd. "I hope at least some of them are paying guests."

One Husband a Winner

Mrs. Friedan, founder of the National Organization of Women, was co-hostess along with Mrs. Wyatt Cooper (Gloria Vanderbilt), Mrs. Richard S. Coulson (Edith De Rham), Mrs. Scull and the writer Gloria Steinem. Mrs. Cooper failed to show, reportedly at the insistence of her husband.

"We had flak from some of the husbands," Mrs. Friedan said. "One man tore up his wife's invitation. I must say Bob Scull's been very nice."

Aside from a man she described as "our missing mathematician—he looks like Hemingway or Poseidon," Mrs. Friedan was accompanied by nine guests from her summer house—a group she persists in calling "my commune."

She is serious about such issues as abortion on demand, child care centers and equal pay for women. Yet it was her attire, a long red baby dress with teeny white polka dots, puffed sleeves and deep, deep decolletage, that caused the comment.

"You've liberated your dress," said Mrs. Coulson, author of "How Could She Do That," a crime book. "You are really liberated."

Mrs. Coulson, like some of the other "sisters" sipping drinks and eating little sandwiches there on the lawn, was fashionably liberated, too. She wore a flesh-colored body stocking, a long white see-through caftan and no bra.

"I chucked bras six months ago," she explained.

Real Heroine From Capital

By this time, Mrs. Mink, whom Mrs. Friedan enthusiastically called "a real heroine of the movement," had arrived. The diminutive heroine won that accolade by taking on no less a personage than Dr. Edgar F. Berman, former Vice President Hubert H. Humphrey's physician and a member of the Democratic Committee on National Priorities.

Dr. Berman had insisted that such factors as the menstrual cycle and menopause (or what he called "the raging hormonal imbalance") make women emotionally unfit for top executive jobs. Mrs. Mink, backed by scores of practicing physicians and psychiatrists, said he didn't seem to know what he was talking about. The fight was on.

The upshot was Dr. Berman's resignation from the committee and between 500 and 600 "overwhelmingly" supportive feminist letters on Mrs. Mink's desk. Yet Mrs. Mink, flown up from Washington especially for the party, denied she was a women's liberationist.

"I don't like to fit myself into any particular stereotype," she said.

For Individual Crusades

Mrs. Mink also opposed bra-burning as a way of calling attention to women's rights ("I don't see that anything can be accomplished by that"), wasn't sure why guests considered Aug. 26 such an important date (NOW and other women's lib groups expect to spend the day — the 50th anniversary of women's suffrage — in nationwide demonstrations in support of their cause), and said that although there was discrimination against women, each woman must work to eliminate it in her own way.

"Just because I'm interested in women doesn't mean I'm for women's liberation," she said as her little daughter, Wendy, looked on nonplussed. "I support all groups when what they do coincides with what I believe in."

When Mrs. Mink appeared

on the lawn with Mrs. Scull, both women were besieged with guests who wanted to meet Mrs. Mink and congratulate her. At the edges of the crowd, other partygoers were getting a little restless.

"I paid $25 for liberation and $25 to see the Sculls' house," said Dr. Robert Gould, a psychiatrist, "and the house is locked up."

"This is my first feminist party," said Mrs. Lilian Rixey, a grandmotherly Bridgehampton summer resident in a white pants suit. "I'm waiting for something to happen."

Tammy Grimes on Scene

Tammy Grimes arrived while Mrs. Rixey was talking. The actress, who guessed she was liberated, ("You're freer in the theater. There isn't as much discrimination against an actress"), was braless. But she wore a voluminous green caftan shirtwaist dress, so virtually nobody noticed.

At about the same time, Mrs. Timothy Cooney (Joan Ganz), was admitting that it had been her husband who interested her in the cause.

"He's the feminist in the family," said Mrs. Cooney, the president of the Children's Television Theater, which produces "Sesame Street."

"I was the Uncle Tom. I'm late in the movement. I see it differently now. This strike zeroes in on good issues. It's important and serious . . . If I'd been an ugly woman with brains I wonder how far I'd have gotten?"

At this point, Mrs. Friedan went to the microphone beside the Sculls' swimming pool and called the party to order. She thanked the Sculls for the use of their yard and said it was "time to finish the unfinished revolution of American women."

Housework Must Go

"They must be liberated from menial housework," she cried, hitching up her plunging décolletage. "In the churches, we must get them out of giving church suppers and to preaching the sermons. In politics, they shouldn't be looking up zip codes but be the powers. No more of this obscenity of one woman in the Senate.

"Nor the obscenity of women in industry," she said. "Their average wage is little more than half what men get. They are the last hired and the first fired. We've got to break this up."

Mrs. Friedan went on this way for perhaps 10 minutes, noting that "it's fine to be a mommy, but you have to be a person first," demanding "*her*story not just *his*tory," calling for participating in the Aug. 26 strike, and explaining that the party was "a great event—a political event and not just a fashionable event to get women into the paper."

Sociologist Sees Gains

William J. Goode, professor of sociology at Columbia University and president of the American Sociological Association, was next. He talked about what could be the new spread of power.

"Men won't be quite the center of attention they were in the past," he said. "It might be a great gain for men if women had power and weren't so full of rage."

His remarks, delivered in a blue velvet suit with a multi-striped shirt, were greeted with male and female "bravos." Then it was Mrs. Mink's turn. Mrs. Friedan introduced her, the crowd applauded and she failed to materialize.

"She's gone," somebody shouted.

"You're not serious," said Mrs. Friedan, looking pained. But Mrs. Mink had gone, apparently without a word to either Mrs. Scull or Mrs. Friedan. Miss Steinem was summoned to take her place.

She was discussing Dr. Berman's resignation when Jill Johnston, dance writer for The Village Voice, stripped to her denim shirt and black panties, and dived into the pool.

"It's hot," Miss Johnston said as she surfaced and removed her shirt.

"You're proving nothing," cried a voice in the crowd.

Miss Johnston, who was braless, went right on swimming. "It's really nice," she said, reaching the deep end. "I didn't even pay $25."

Enemy Within Surfaces

Mrs. Friedan muttered something about "One of the biggest enemies of this movement. . ." The rest was drowned out by the crowd. Miss Steinem tried to speak, too, but without success.

"It's a great pool," Miss Johnston yelled as she reached for a plastic surfboard, rolled over on her back and floated for a few seconds.

"We *are* going to be a big political issue," Mrs. Friedan shrieked into the microphone. "And now some of us will sing for you."

The sounds of "Liberation Now" came over the loudspeaker amid shouts of "Right on!" Mis Johnston, who'd finished four laps, climbed out of the pool, accepted a towel Mr. Scull held for her and tripped off into a zinnia bed. Everybody was talking all at once.

"I always say if you have a pool, you have a pool," Mrs. Scull said, shaking her head.

OCTOBER 13, 1970

A Party Opening Valentino's Boutique Is a Crowd-Pleaser

By BERNADINE MORRIS

The main attractions were the architecture and the people last night at the opening for Valentino's porcelain and glass boutique at 801 Madison Avenue, near 67th Street, and both could be admired from the outside. Because of the heat and the crowds, a lot of people brought their champagne out on the sidewalk.

"It's like a Hollywood premiere," said Geoffrey Beene, the American designer, who had been inside but didn't get a chance to see much. "It could only happen in America," he said, surveying the people behind the barricades. "Nobody else has that much curiosity."

Two young girls in midiskirts who had an excellent vantage point on the sidewalk helped prove the point.

"It's such fun to see the people going in and coming out," said Alice Saland, an aspiring actress, while her friend Margie Adelman nodded vigorous approval.

They didn't actually recognize anyone, but they thought everyone looked very exciting.

They saw Mr. and Mrs. Robert D. L. Gardiner—he owns Gardiner's Island—arrive in his-and-her jumpsuits. His was navy blue jersey, hers brown velvet.

They saw Mr. and Mrs. Howard Reed—he owns an art gallery, she is the director of Arnold Scaasi's custom salon—turn up in purple tweed outfits. Hers was a cape and a midiskirt, his suit was by Carlo Palazzi, the Rome tailor, he pointed out, not Scaasi.

They saw the tall mannequin known as Cheyenne arrive wearing a big cowboy hat and a jumpsuit open to her waist, and if the crowds let up for a moment, they could always watch Naomi Sims and Marina Schiano, models who were posing in the big glass cylinder that is the shop's show window.

Nobody seemed to notice that Aldo Jacober, the Italian architect, who had been working on minor installations right up to the 7 P.M. opening, was wearing just half a suit. He put his black jacket over his brown workpants because he couldn't find the other half.

Valentino and his director, Giancarlo, had found both parts of their black suits even though they were puttering around the place all day. Valentino, who had a purple handkerchief in his pocket and wore a flowered shirt, said he was pleased enough with how things looked even though the shop wasn't finished.

Postponed a Month

The opening had been postponed a month because of a fire in the elevator shaft and he was glad to see things finally get underway. The stock was all in palce, but everybody seemed to be paying more attention to the transparent plastic fixtures and the curved walls that made the place look like a chic womb.

The designer flew in from Rome over the weekend with his new boutique coordinator, Pilar Crespi, the 19-year-old daughter of Count Rudi Crespi, a Rome public relations man. Among the boutiques she will coordinate are those in Rome, Paris and Milan. She was wearing a white satin cape, which distinguished her from the salesgirls, who weren't selling anything, but just being sociable.

They were also trying out their new uniform: brown satin shirts, with V's woven into the design, and brown wool midiskirts. Part-time employes wear white shirts.

They'll all be working when the shop opens for business at around 4 P.M. today. The plan is for it to stay open Tuesday nights until 9 P.M., when Madison Avenue is closed to traffic. This has helped make the shop popular with its neighbors, who have formed an organization called MAGIC (Madison Avenue General Ideas Committee) with aspirations of making Madison Avenue a serious rival to Fifth Avenue as the city's main shopping street.

'European Looking'

"Very European looking," commented one partygoer after a tour of the five-story, converted brownstone building.

Among retailers who came to view the competition were Ohrbach's Sydney Gittler and Bonwit's J. Danny Zarem. Bill Blass and Halston were among the designers who took the champagne tour. But Mrs. Robert C. Scull, whose husband collects art and runs a taxicab company, came to do business.

"I told Valentino this belt didn't fit," she said, tugging on her white coat, which had just been sent from his Rome salon. "He told me how to fix it," she added.

NOVEMBER 1, 1970

Contemporary Paintings and Sculpture

Including important works by Dine, Johns, Kelly Kline, Lichtenstein, Louis, Noland, Oldenburg Pollock, Rauschenberg, Rosenquist, Rothko Smith, Stella, Still and Warhol. From the Donald and Lynn Factor Collection, Six Works from the Collection of Mr. and Mrs. Robert C. Scull Estate of the Late Alan R. Solomon and Other Owners Illustrated Catalogue $7. By Mail $8.50

On View from November 13

Sale November 18 at 8 p.m.

Cards of Admission Required for Main Salesroom

Parke-Bernet
GALLERIES • 980 MADISON AVE., NEW YORK 10021
(Affiliated with Sotheby & Co., London)

Closed Sunday and Monday
For Catalogues by Mail Address Dept. 20

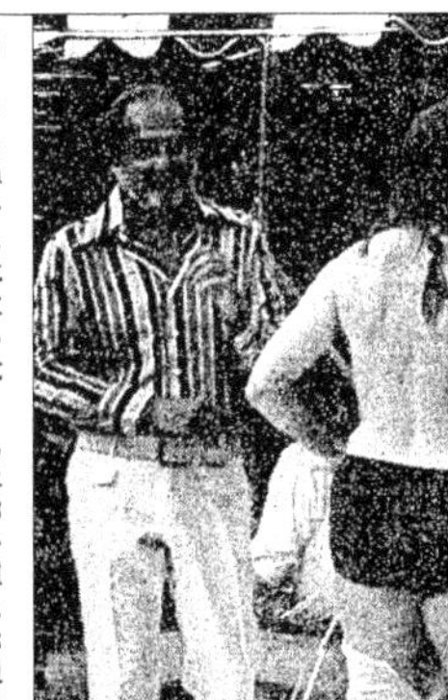

NOVEMBER 13, 1970

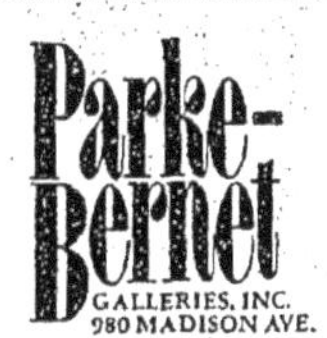

GALLERIES, INC.
980 MADISON AVE.

Affiliated with Sotheby & Co., London

Auctioneers and Appraisers

Sale Today at 2
Oriental Art
Various Owners

Now on View

10 to 5 • Closed Sunday and Monday
Jewelry Exhibition Closes Daily at 4:45

Valuable Jewelry

Including a diamond ring set with emerald-cut diamond weighing about 11.65 carats; a pair of diamond brooches set with 152 baguette diamonds weighing about 22.50 carats and two pear-shaped diamonds about 6.70 carats; Estate of the Late Mary Eleanor King and Other Owners Illustrated Catalog $3 Mail $4

Sale November 18 at 2

Contemporary Paintings and Sculpture

From the Donald and Lynn Factor Collection six works from the Collection of Mr and Mrs Robert C. Scull; Estate of the Late Alan R. Solomon and Other Owners Illustrated Catalog $7 Mail $8.50

Sale November 18 at 8

Admission to Main Salesroom by Card Only

To check further on current Exhibitions and Auctions, dial 535-8444

Sales Conducted by
Peter Wilson
J. L. Marion • Marcus Linell
E. L. Cave • E. J. Landrigan III
Kirk Igler • R. Woolley

NOVEMBER 14, 1970

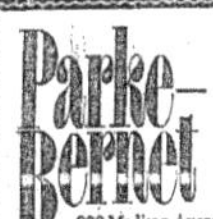

Affiliated with Sotheby & Co., London

Auctioneers and Appraisers

980 Madison Avenue, New York 10021

Sale Today at 2 p. m.
Fine French Furniture
Tapestries, rugs; musical boxes, pictures instruments and clockwork toys. Various Owners

Now on View

Tuesday through Saturday 10 to 5
Closed Sunday and Monday
Jewelry Exhibition Closes Daily at 4:45

Valuable Jewelry

Including a diamond ring set with emerald-cut diamond weighing about 11:65 carats; a pair of diamond brooches set with 152 baguette diamonds weighing about 22.50 carats and two pear-shaped diamonds about 6.70 carats Estate of the Late Mary Eleanor King and Other Owners. Illustrated Catalogue $3. Mail $4
Sale November 18 at 2

Contemporary Paintings and Sculpture

From the Donald and Lynn Factor Collection six works from the Collection of Mr and Mrs Robert C. Scull, Estate of the Late Alan R. Solomon and Other Owners Illustrated Catalogue $7. Mail $8.50
Sale November 18 at 8
Cards of Admission Required for Main Salesroom

Watches. Objets de Vertu and Miniatures

Estate of the Late Consuelo U. Ford and Other Owners. Illustrated Catalogue $2. Mail $2.50
Sale November 19 at 10:15 and 2

Important Gold Boxes

An exceptional collection of XVIII-XIX century gold and enameled boxes, many set with jewels and miniatures. Including a superb architectural snuff box, *Paris,* 1755 an oval box with miniatures of ports of France signed "de Lioux de Savignac", *Paris,* 1766-7 two Russian enameled boxes by Jean Ador *St. Petersburg,* 1780; and many diamond-mounted presentation boxes; a cigarette case and cane handle by Fabergé, *circa* 1900. Property of Miss Mary A. Boyle and of Covington/ReQua Family Trust
Illustrated Catalogue $4. Mail $5
Sale November 20 at 2

French•Italian and Other Furniture

Oriental rugs; decorative objects. Various Owners
Illustrated Catalogue $1.50. Mail $2
Sale November 21 at 2

For Catalogues by Mail Address Dept. 20
To check further on Current Exhibitions and Auctions Dial 535-8444
and for other Sales at

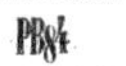

See Sunday's Times Classified Auction Page

Sales Conducted by
Peter Wilson • J. L. Marion • Marcus Linell
E. L. Cave • E. J. Landrigan • Kirk Igler • R. Woolley

NOVEMBER 15, 1970

Art Notes

Auction Where The Action Is

By GRACE GLUECK

STEP right up, folks. Lots 14 and 29 are "two of the most important Jasper Johnses ever to be sold at auction." Lot 33, a sleeper to watch, is James Rosenquist's "Silver Skies;" Lot 19 is the original version of Robert Indiana's rubric, "LOVE"; Lot 8 is the late Mark Rothko's red-on-red "No. 16-1960"; Lot 21 is a 17½-foot canvas by Kenneth Noland, and Lot 50 is a Campbell's Tomato Juice carton of painted wood by—guess who?

The heavy auction action will occur this Wednesday evening, when Parke-Bernet stages the biggest contemporary art sale in its history. Besides the above, other works on the block by stars of the '50's and '60's will bear the signatures of Franz Kline, Willem de Kooning, Jackson Pollock, Robert Motherwell, Robert Rauschenberg, Frank Stella and Claes Oldenburg. The auction is the first in which so many hot contemporary talents will be price-tested with major works at one fell swoop. What's more, the 50 items not only come from some well-known art-holders — Donald and Lynn Factor of Los Angeles, Mr. and Mrs. Arthur A. Cohen and Mr. and Mrs. Robert C. Scull of New York —they involve such top contemporary dealers as Marlborough, Pace, Knoedler, Janis, Emmerich, Rubin and Castelli, who represent most of the artists.

The auction, P-B promises, will topple the $60,000 "record price" *said* to have been paid at an auction last May for Warhol's "Campbell's Soup Can with Peeling Label." James Mayor, P-B's contemporary man, pooh-poohs the notion that the current recession will cause a buyer shortage. He estimates the take at over $1-million, with the two Jasper Johnses and the Rothko each fetching more than $100,000 apiece. A possible $90,000 will be plunked down for the Lichtenstein, a huge take-off on Abstract Expressionist brushstrokes, and maybe $50,000 for an Oldenburg assemblage called "Stove" and a Franz Kline painting, "Sabro IV."

*

Dealers and artists, not so sure as Mayor, are said to have given their teeth hard exercise on fingernails lately. "Since the dealers are represented by major works, they'll be forced to put their money where their mouths are," says an observer—meaning that if paintings don't "move" at the prices Mad. Ave.'s been asking, dealers will be forced to support them by bidding up and possibly buying them. "It's certainly the most important contemporary auction that's ever taken place," says Leo Castelli, whose Pop stable, along with Marlborough's Ab Ex one, has the highest numerical representation in the show. "But buying has lately been very selective. There'll be very high prices for the masterpieces, but the rest we don't know."

And why are the collectors selling? For a mixed bag of reasons. In the case of the Factors, it's a divorce settlement. The Cohens, who never could fit that 17½-foot Noland into their living room, say frankly that they want to convert some of their large collection into cash. But Robert Scull, whose six works (including one of the Johnses, the Rosenquist and the Lichtenstein) could bring as much as $400,000, puts it that he wants to "rearrange things in the house, bring in a lot of young people."

"After careful thought we've decided to let these few things go out into the world," he says, "because they're history, darling—and I'm not involved with history."

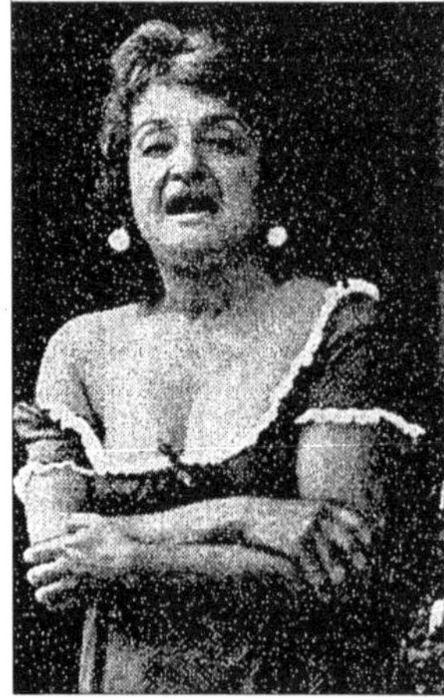

NOVEMBER 17, 1970

NOVEMBER 19, 1970

Painting by Lichtenstein Brings A Record $75,000 at Auction

By SANKA KNOX

Fifty works of modern American art brought $1-million, more or less, at an auction last night that was as remarkable for the audience reaction as for the prices for pop art and minor pieces.

The sale, at the Parke-Bernet Galleries, 980 Madison Avenue, was the first major event of its kind there, and nearly all the offerings found new owners. Applause a rarity at an auction, pattered through the salesroom time and again with the appearance or sale of a work, as spectators intently followed the fortunes of the various pieces.

Roy Lichtenstein's "Big Painting No. 6," a 1965 work in great waves of red, green and black washes, was the star of the sale, bringing $75,000. That equaled the previous record auction price paid for an American painting while its creator was still alive. The distinction is shared by the 19th-century's William Harnett. The Lichtenstein piece went to Galerie Rudolf Swirner of Munich, West Germany, and The Hague.

Even better things were expected at the auction. Of six works consigned by Mr. and Mrs. Robert C. Scull, two were bought back by the New York collectors. They were the late Mark Rothko's "No. 16—1960" at $85,000 and "Two Flags" by Jasper Johns, a double image of the American flag, for $105,000.

Other works with great expectations that were bought back were a quiet monochrome "Tennyson" by Jasper Johns at $70,000 and "Pink Disaster" by Andy Warhol at $19,000. Both are owned by Mr. and Mrs. Donald Factor of Beverly Hills, Calif., whose collection was on the block.

Buyers came from many states and from several foreign countries. Vincent Metzak of Arlington, Va., paid $60,000 for Clyfford Still's composition, "Indian Red and Black 1946-H," setting an auction record for that artist.

A realistic, three-dimensional construction of a stove with roasts, pots and vegetables by Claes Oldenburg, all in life size, also made an auction record for that artist. It went to Galerie Swirner for $45,000.

Other records were posted by "Faces," Morris Louis, which went to Mr. Metzak for $47,500; Ellsworth Kelly's "Gate" in red-painted steel, $18,000, to Dayton's Gallery, Minneapolis; Robert Indiana's "Love," a 60-inch square with letters of the word in red against blue and green, $19,000, to Nannette Woelffer of Munich.

Jackson Pollock's "Painting No. 23 (Frogman)" was bought back for $70,000 by its unnamed owner, one of about 10 paintings that failed to attain minimums established by consignors. But, pop art, apparently, did very well, from Mr. Lichtenstein's $75,000 piece to James Rosenquist's mélange, "Silver Skies," which went for $27,000, a record for the artist, to a New York dealer.

NOVEMBER 22, 1970

Who's a 'Somebody'? Depends on Who's Doing the Choosing

By CHARLOTTE CURTIS

Ward McAllister certainly wasn't the first American to make a list of those he considered better than everybody else, but since his invention of "The Four Hundred," an awful lot of people have made an awful lot of lists.

Inevitably, such lists raise the momentous (in some circles) question of who's important and who isn't, and the old question came up again not long ago at the New York City Cultural Council's black-tie theater benefit.

Crowds of New Yorkers lined up behind wooden police barriers to watch the rich, the celebrated, the elegant and the powerful stream into the Imperial Theater.

The sidewalk audience cheered for Gina Lollobrigida. But when Mrs. John F. C. Bryce (the A&P), Mr. and Mrs. Robert Scull (pop art), Mrs. Oscar Hammerstein 2d (widow of the lyricist), Mr. and Mrs. Joseph A. Meehan (stockbroker), Pierre Arpels (jewels), and Mrs. Charles Shipman Payson (horses and the Mets) arrived, the crowd merely stared or commented on the clothes and jewels.

It took Mayor Lindsay's appearance to get the crowd cheering again and clapping their hands. And as the last of perhaps 750 theatergoers moved across the sidewalk and into the lobby, a man who had been watching the proceedings delivered what to him was the final appraisal of the guests.

"Nobody's here," he bellowed from somewhere under the marquee. "Mayor Lindsay's the only big name."

The booming voice belonged to none other than David Lefkowitz. And although his ruddy face, brown corduroy jacket and baggy blue pants probably aren't familiar to Mrs. Bryce, Miss Lollobrigida, Mr. Arpels or Mrs. Payson, he has been looking at them for nearly 20 years.

Mr. Lefkowitz is a professional autograph seeker. Between April and the first of October, he doubles as a Good Humor man. In the winters, he may be found at virtually every highly publicized movie and theater opening or benefit in the Broadway area.

He disdains the French restaurants ("Nobody ever goes there") and the United Nations ("You can never get close enough to get an autograph"). Yet he's often at Sardi's, issuing a passing verbal commentary on the wide variety of persons who go into that theatrical district restaurant for dinner, supper and first-night parties.

He has been known to stand outside the New York Hilton, the Waldorf or the Plaza when what he calls "something big" is happening. And although his contact with what passes for Society is somewhat peripheral, he did "attend" Truman Capote's famous masked ball — a gathering he remembers as "only so-so."

In Mr. Lefkowitz's view, some people are better than other people, but — like most social arbiters — he's at something of a loss to explain why.

"It's up to me who's more important than another," he said. "Certain people I like. Certain people I don't like. I can't tell you why. It's a good question. Could be that some are more glamorous than others."

He didn't define glamorous (though it may be synonymous with his use of the phrase "big star"). But he did try to indicate how he rates the 3,000 or 4,000 people whose autographs he has collected either for himself or for sale — at prices ranging from $2 for Joseph E. Levine, the producer, to $15 for a President.

"I like big people," he said. "I like mayors, governors, Presidents. Those are big people. Or famous stars. Or Secretary of States. I don't go for business men. I wouldn't bother with Henry Ford or the president of General Motors."

Alfred Gwynne Vanderbilt, the sportsman and newly elected chairman of the New York Racing Association, is among those at the top of Mr. Lefkowitz's list at the moment.

Why?

"Because he's a millionaire," Mr. Lefkowitz said, "and he's a gentleman. I mean he's loaded; I can tell you that."

Governor Rockefeller is up there, too — not just because he's the Governor but because he, too, is a millionaire "and money counts." Yet Aristotle Onassis, who has as much or more money than either Mr. Vanderbilt or Governor Rockefeller, is considerably lower down on the list because, as Mr. Lefkowitz put it, "I don't care for him. Now, Mrs. Onassis, she's all right."

But Mrs. Onassis "isn't as good" as Ingrid Bergman ("a big star") or Mrs. Richard M. Nixon "because the President's wife is always more important" if they're in office rather than out—"no matter what party."

And Presidents, in a male chauvinist contention that won't sit well with women's liberationists, are "always better than their wives."

"Wives don't matter unless they're *famous*," Mr. Lefkowitz said, speaking of wives in general. "Sometimes I have to take their autographs to get their husbands'. But I wouldn't otherwise."

Now about William S. Paley, president of the Columbia Broadcasting System: Mr. Lefkowitz says "that's a good name" — hardly the highest accolade but better than some. Robert W. Sarnoff, president of the RCA Corporation, is "a good name" too.

Yet John Hay Whitney, former Ambassador to the Court of St. James's racing enthusiast, member of an old and distinguished family, and former owner of The New York Herald Tribune, doesn't even appear on the list.

"I don't know him," Mr. Lefkowitz explained.

Mr. Lefkowitz has never heard of Mr. Whitney's sister, Mrs. Payson, nor of Charles Revson, chairman of Revlon, Inc. And despite a recent Gallup poll showing that Martha Mitchell's name was familiar to 74 per cent of the population, Mr. Lefkowitz hadn't heard of her either.

"Who's that?" he asked.

Yet Mrs. Cornelius Vanderbilt Whitney, wife of the sportsman-industrialist, got what amounted to a rave notice ("She's important"). Richard Ottinger, the Democrat's unsuccessful candidate for the United States Senate, rated "a big man" label — only slightly lower on the list than the "very important" Duke and Duchess of Windsor.

Mr. Capote seems to be somewhere to the south of such lofties as Mr. Vanderbilt, Mayor Lindsay, Raquel Welch, President Nixon, Governor Rockefeller and Gregory Peck. But he's above Joe Namath (who has refused to give Mr. Lefkowitz an autograph on four successive occasions), and Mr. Namath is well above Mr. Onassis.

"Now Bennett Cerf, he's around all the time," Mr. Lefkowitz said. "All he does is write books. And Leonard Bernstein. He's *always* around. It's the ones you never see who you want."

One of the loftiest of the lofty whom Mr. Lefkowitz actually yearned to meet, observe and ask for autographs was the late Charles de Gaulle ("I don't think he ever came to New York"). Two others are "Queen what's her name—the one from England," and Lee Van Cleef.

Lee Van Cleef?

Good gracious, yes. Mr. Van Cleef has played the bad guy in dozens of Western movies.

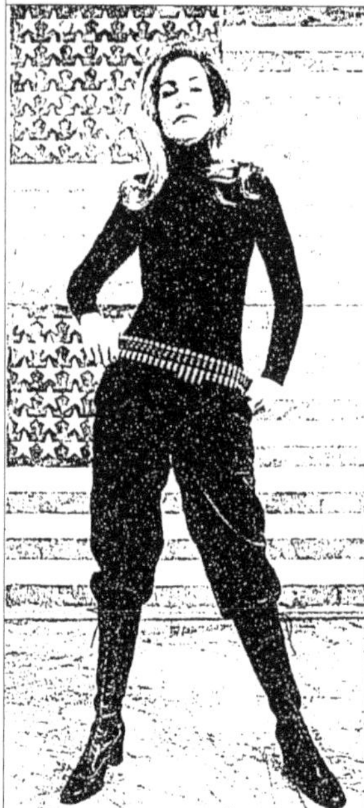

DECEMBER 9, 1970

Cartridge Belt Cute? Well, It's a Fashion

By ANGELA TAYLOR

Why would a woman who professes to be peace loving want to walk around with a belt of bullets slung around her hips or chest?

"My husband says it's militaristic, not militant," says Mrs. Charles B. Benenson, wife of the real estate tycoon. "I think I'm feminine enough to wear it, I don't look tough."

"I thought it was cute and amusing, I couldn't resist it," explains Mrs. Robert C. Scull, the art collector whose husband is a taxi fleet operator. Mrs. Scull wore her belt to a black-tie party the other evening, with her "Barbarella" black jersey jumpsuit—"It was a sensation."

Anita Tiburzi, a publicist, wore her belt across her chest to a party last week and Carole Mallory, a mannequin with the Stewart agency, wears hers with pants when she goes out on her modeling chores.

If a fad can be said to have gone over with a bang, it's the belt made of brass cartridge casing that fastens via several dummy bullets at the front. Stores in New York that have stocked the belt are amazed at the clamor, some have sold them out and have orders for the next shipment as soon as it comes in.

'Stopping Traffic'

"I'm stopping traffic," explained Mrs. Benenson, who has a cloud of red hair and the narrow hips that go with a size 4 figure. Mrs. Benenson first spotted the belt on an acquaintance of Le Drugstore, the restaurant-cum-general store at 1085 Third Avenue (64th Street). When he told her it was carried in the store's gift shop, she promptly bought one for $29—"It was too big, they had to remove eight or 10 bullets."

Mrs. Scull got her belt at Bloomingdale's for $25. "When I told the salesgirl I wanted to try it, she gave me such a look," she said. Bloomingdale's has sold its first shipment of 14 belts and is expecting more.

Tony Anton, president of the Veneziano boutique at 819 Madison Avenue (between 68th and 69th Streets), reports that he sold eight dozen belts in 10 days. His version is $35, but the bullets are silvered. Veneziano is also sold out, but expecting another order.

Manny Walker, at 498 Seventh Avenue (37th Street) has the $25 belt currently. Alexander's English-made version, also $25, is back in stock.

Two women are taking the credit for the fad. One is Francine Farkas, wife of Alexander Farkas, president of Alexander's. Mrs. Farkas spotted the belt in London and promptly arranged to import it for the store.

But it's a toss-up whether the belt was discovered by Mrs. Farkas, or Karen Ross, a Philadelphia housewife.

Saw It In London

Mrs. Ross said she saw the belt in a men's shop in London's Mayfair, thought it was fun and bought one for herself.

"When I got home, all my friends wanted it," she recalled. "One friend offered me $100 for mine."

Mrs. Ross's husband, Milton, is a manufacturer of electronic parts. She asked him if his factory might not be able to turn out a few belts for Christmas presents. By then the clamor was on—"Everywhere I went, people offered to buy the belt off my hips."

Mrs. Ross thought stores might want to carry it and approached a few. Currently, her husband's factory is as much in the belt business as it is in electronics.

"Only one hippie shop in Philadelphia turned me down," Mrs. Ross says. "They were afraid it would attract militants."

Militant or militaristic, the fad is booming. As Mrs. Scull explains, "I feel like Butch Cassidy and that's fun." She also said she hadn't heard any criticism so far, "but I'm sure there will be some."

JANUARY 5, 1971

The Way Adolfo Dresses Up Shorts, Women Needn't Be All That Daring

By BERNADINE MORRIS

"I used to wear sequined shorts when I lived in Hollywood — it was a scandal," Paulette Goddard remarked happily at Adolfo's fashion show at the St. Regis yesterday. "Hattie Carnegie made them for me in colors like bright yellow, and I wore them under a long mink coat, just like today. Nobody else had them."

That was more than 20 years ago, according to Miss Goddard, who now lives in Switzerland. She didn't exactly come to the show to see shorts, sequined or otherwise. She was looking for "some good American classics, you know—comfort and high style" to take back to Europe.

Well, Adolfo had them, too. Shirtwaist dresses (with a detour through Paris to become properly slithery). Blazer jackets (all crisp and linen-y, even when they're the topping for shorts). Good old workmanlike denim (sometimes embroidered within an inch of its life, but at the bottom, denim).

But, let's face it, shorts are what everybody's talking about, and Adolfo provides them. Like the Gibson Girl ginghams he did last year, the felt midiskirts a few years back, or the hats before that. (Before he went on to become the dressmaker to the beautiful people, Adolfo was a milliner. In fact, he still makes hats.)

He showed more hats this time than he has in a long while. Classic shapes like cloches, sombreros, fedoras and his old favorite, the planter. Things are apparently looking up for the hat people, even though shorts are what everybody's looking at.

Mrs. Robert C. Scull, the taxi tycoon's wife, who managed to be the first on anybody's block with the Gibson Girl, the felt skirt, and possibly the planter's hat, didn't miss a trick. She wore shorts to Adolfo's showing, green velour ones. She wore them with her bullet belt, a "Work for Peace" button, tights and boots. The shorts were by Halston, the other milliner-turned-designer.

"He does pretty good bottoms," Mrs. Scull said approvingly of Halston.

At least she knew where she stood. Practically every other woman, with the exception of Miss Goddard, wondered whether she'd dare to go out in public in shorts. Of course, a lot of them will.

Easy Decision

Adolfo made it relatively easy to decide. He wrapped some shorts in Spanish shawls. He put others under shirts and jackets. Some were in denim, some in clingy silk. One even was pleated, for the woman who worries about her hips. And to clinch it, he usually provides a skirt or a pair of gaucho pants in the same fabric. So a woman could reason, "I'll put on the skirt when I go into town; I'll wear the shorts when I'm home with a few friends." She knows what's going to happen to that resolution, but it gives her an excuse.

If there's anything that hits you in the eye after shorts, it's fringe. All those embroidered Spanish shawls, which decorated pianos through the nineteen-thirties, haven't been restricted to cloaking shorts. Some wrap up shirtwaist dresses. Some are turned into dresses. They all float fringe as if it were going out of style.

Fascinated With Burlap

Now, Adolfo isn't the only designer who's into denim, even though he's into it in a big way. He spatters it with silver stars or butterflies; he embroiders it in zingy plaids so it's dressed up enough to go out at night.

But he's about the only designer fascinated at the moment with burlap. He shows it in its natural potato-sack hue with a pocket stuffed with posies and a deep ruffle at the hem. It is, ostensibly, for gardening, and there's a big rough straw hat to reinforce the point. It's likely to be worn when there's not even a window box to water.

Of course, some women will prefer the sheer organdy dresses in their candy-box colors with delicate pale flowers embroidered all over them. But for the individualists, the ones who wore felt midiskirts when the length was too strange to be controversial, chances are the watchword for spring is burlap. And, naturally, shorts.

JANUARY 31, 1971

Is That a Way to Save Face? Sell Hot Pants?

JUDY KLEMESRUD

Hot Pants . . . Les Shorts . . . Shortootsies . . . Happy Legs. Suddenly the fashion industry, badly burned by its effort to foist the midi on resisting womankind, has counter-attacked. Its chief weapon: shorts.

At the Rome and Paris fashion showings this month, shorts were all the rage. Already last week New York fashionplates were braving the icy weather to be the first on the block to wear shorts to lunch, to fashion shows — even to black tie parties.

The midi, of course, was rejected by a thumping majority of American women, many of whom joined midi protest groups with catchy acronyms like GAMS (Girls Against More Skirt) and FADD (Fight Against Dictating Designers). So far, nobody's fighting hot pants.

William M. Fine, president of Bonwit Teller, who suggested that his employes wear midiskirts last fall so customers would feel more comfortable, believes the shorts are a reaction "to all the seriousness that invaded the fashion business last fall. We got into so many damn debates and it turned out to be the most publicized fashion election in history. This is the reaction. It's a game."

And who won the length debate? "Everybody won," he said. "Women can now wear the length they're in the mood to wear."

Phyllis Tweel, the 27-year-old publicist who founded GAMS, said she thought the hot pants were a way for designers to save face because the midi flopped. "They won't admit the failure of the midi," she said. "They just couldn't bring back short skirts. So short pants are their answer."

Hot Skirts, Too

Women's Wear Daily, the fashion industry trade paper, had pushed the midi, or the "Longuette," as they called it, last fall. Demonstrating its resilience, Women's Wear has now espoused shorts, coining the term, "hot pants," and last week it showed another new fashion that it said could be worn interchangeably with the shorts. To most observers it looked like the old mini, but to Women's Wear it was a "hot skirt."

Most Manhattan stores that sell hot pants reported last week that they were sold out almost as soon as new shipments came in. "They just go," said a spokesman at Roses are Red, Violets are Blue, a boutique at 308 East 53rd Street that had nothing but shorts in its window last week.

They come in all colors and fabrics — even mink. Jacques Kaplan, the furrier, reported selling "several" pairs of ranch mink hot pants at $195 a pair. But so far no one has bought any of Kaplan's green monkey fur shorts.

There is a wide variation in length, as well. As one fashion writer put it, "some barely [sic] cover the backside, others come as far as mid thigh." The most popular thus far seem to be on the short side.

Why shorts?

"They are an expression of the female's new freedom," said Dr. Jason Miller, a Manhattan psychiatrist, "and they mean she's no longer willing to be submissive to convention. They also show that she is on a serious mission to relate to other people — especially men. She may not be wearing them just to be sexually provocative, but because she desires to get attention as a prelude to a genuine relationship."

Mrs. Robert Scull, who is usually among the first in town to don the latest fashions, said she enjoyed wearing her hot pants "because it's so nice to show legs again. When I wore my first pair, my husband [he owns a taxi fleet] and boys were so ecstatic. It's 1971, and shorts are contemporary, and I think people are depressed by old-looking midiskirts."

But some fashion historians think the shorts fad is firmly rooted in nostalgia. "It's the look of the 30's and 40's," said Dorothy Tricarico, fashion and textile coordinator at the Design Laboratory of the Brooklyn Museum. "That's when Ruby Keeler and Deanna Durbin and Betty Grable were always seen in short shorts. And some of our other fashions now come directly from that period, too — hair ornaments, chokers, deep red lipstick, soft fluid fabrics, and a wide shoulder look.

"But hot pants are a first in one sense," she added. "In no other time in history have shorts been accepted for street wear and business as they are right now."

MARCH 2, 1971

Buffalo Bill Rides Again in Fashion and Memory at Party

By ANGELA TAYLOR

The wild, wild West came to the East Side last night. Dance hall girls and rodeo riders, chic Indians and just plain blue-jeaned cowpokes rode through the night in taxis rather than broncos, although one group went through the trouble of hiring a stagecoach.

Chalk up another hero for the crowd whose favorite word is "camp." He's Buffalo Bill Cody of the American Wild West, hunter of buffaloes and Indians and showman of the era when men who were men wore long hair and fringe.

"He was really an awful man," said a spokesman for the new restaurant called Buffalo Bill's, at 314 East 70th Street. "He killed a lot of Indians and helped destroy the buffalo. The whole idea is a put-down, camp."

To nail down the camp, the restaurant asked Giorgio di Sant'Angelo, the Italian-born, South American-reared designer, to be host at a party for its opening last night. Mr. di Sant'Angelo was a natural choice. He is famous for the rash of fringed, beaded and feathered dresses that well-heeled New York women have been whooping it up in at local parties.

Besides, he is the Pied Piper of a new wing of fashion society, a breakaway movement from the older, more conservative Seventh Avenue crowd whose leaders have been designers such as Norman Norell and Mollie Parnis.

The off-Seventh Avenue fashion branch includes Halston and Stephen Burrows, the designers; young models such as Berry Berenson and Loulou de la Falaise; photographers and artists such as Francesco Scavullo, Joe Eula and Andy Warhol, the artist and filmmaker, and his entourage. It also wraps up former models Carmen (Mrs. Richard Kaplan, wife of an architect) and Betsy Pickering (Mrs. Harilaos Theodoracopulos, married to a Greek shipping executive), who are devoted Sant'Angelo customers.

Mr. di Sant'Angelo asked 500 of his pals to come to the party, dressed in the manner of the world of Buffalo Bill. It was not, he made clear, a society party.

"I'm democratic," he pronounced. "I'm not interested in old social people. My friends are the young, interesting people who make up New York today."

Probably the only one of the party guests who knew Buffalo Bill personally is Diana Vreeland, editor of Vogue magazine. Mrs. Vreeland had accepted the invitation because, she said, "Giorgio is a helluva divine fellow and I have a bit of orange suède I can wear."

Mrs. Vreeland Remembers

Equally divine, in Mrs. Vreeland's memory, is Buffalo Bill himself.

"We used to stay at the Irma Hotel in Cody, Wyo., when we were kids during World War I," Mrs. Vreeland recalled. "Irma was his daughter. We used to come in from pack trips and stay there. He was divine to my sister and me. He gave us divine pinto ponies to ride. The hotel used to have a billiard room full of those marvelous chairs made of horn. Cody was only a block long, and there wasn't anything for the ranchmen to spend their money on, so they'd shoot pool for high stakes."

"I saw him last in 1917," she went on "That marvelous man standing at the railroad station — there was something elegant and Edwardian about him. We were crying because we had to leave our ponies. Then 10 days later, he and just about everybody in Cody were dead — Spanish influenza."

Although Mr. di Sant'Angelo emphasized that the party was not meant to publicize his designs, his showroom was picked clean. So clean that Carmen Kaplan never got the Sant'Angelo dress she ordered way back in October and came in a black sweater and pants and a beige cape ("They're Halston's, it serves Giorgio right").

Donna Jordan, Andy Warhol's newest superstar came with The Factory head himself and Jane Forth, the next-to-the-last superstar. Mr. Warhol settled for a drooping mustache and goatee to match his beige-colored hair and Miss Forth wore the stiff pigtails and Raggedy Ann hat she digs out for all parties— "I've worn it on Halloween since I was a kid." Even in the free-and-easy days of the rough West, Miss Jordan might have raised an eyebrow. She had poured herself into a pink-sequined bathing suit affair and poked a gun through the garter she wore on one thigh.

They hadn't invented hot pants in the last century, but Kimberly Harclероad, who is going to be married on Sunday to Jonathan Farkas of the department store clan, made hers look Wild West by adding a fringed chamois jacket. Mrs. Robert Scull, who drops a fad as soon as everyone else picks it up, substituted a suede miniskirt for the shorts she's been wearing lately.

"I'm a cowardly Buffalo Bill," Joe Eula explained. "My mustache is the wrong color, but it's real."

Halston, who said, "I'm very cowboy-looking naturally," spent most of yesterday running up fur chaps for himself and helping Pat Ast, his buxom assistant, to put together patched leather chaps and a fur vest.

The host had threatened to come as the first Savoy king of unified Italy ("It was the same period, the 1870's), but settled instead for being a rodeo star in a nail-studded navy outfit.

Saloon girls, Annie Oakleys, Indian scouts and cattle rustlers jammed the restaurant's long wooden bar, lapping up beer and wine ("Giorgio didn't want hard liquor") and wandering among the Indian-print-covered tables with their chairs draped in hides. They consumed chili and barbecued chickens and meat-and-potato pies.

MARCH 5, 1971

After a Quiet Spell for Parties, 'Suddenly Everybody Picked the Same Day'

By BERNADINE MORRIS

A popular British diplomat was returning to London. A former French journalist was celebrating his 50th birthday. A Moroccan ambassador was leaving New York. Not earth-shattering events, any of them, but sufficient to spark a spontaneous eruption of parties, the likes of which had not been seen since the heyday of the charity ball.

There was even a charity ball, the annual fund-raising event of the Sheltering Arms Children's Service, held at the Plaza. But that wasn't what stirred things up. It was the rash of private parties that constituted the social uprising that mystified hosts and guests alike.

The invited often had to juggle two or more parties; the inviters had imagined the evening was clear.

"In the middle of nothing happening for weeks on end, suddenly everybody picked the same day," lamented Mrs. Richard Feigen, who planned the biggest bash of all.

It was a dance for 150 friends to send Ambassador Frederick A. Warner, Britain's deputy permanent representative to the United Nations, off to his new assignment "with something he can remember."

'Absolute Blank'

The Feigens picked the date around Christmas when Ambassador Warner learned that he would be receiving a new assignment. (What his new post will be is still top secret, but it's supposedly a sensitive one.)

"The pages of my date book were absolutely blank, Mrs. Feigen recalled. "We didn't imagine there would be any conflicts."

The Feigens like to give a dance from time to time in their townhouse on East 79th Street, the lower floors of which serve as an art gallery. The marble floors, you see, are so convenient. Still, they hadn't had one for about a year and a half. Part of the city's social torpor, from which everyone seemed to awake at the same time.

After concentrating on more serious things—economics and ecology, politics and protests — everyone seemed ready for "just one night of gaiety," Mrs. Feigen observed.

Countess Susanna Rattazzi, whom everybody calls Suni, wasn't aware she was contributing to any social awakening. She simply wanted to cheer her old friend, Paul Mathias, on his 50th birthday. Nothing elaborate. Just a spaghetti dinner for a few friends.

Mr. Mathias, who for 18 years was the New York correspondent for Paris Match, looks 10 years younger, but Countess Rattazzi thought he needed cheering anyway. He retired a year and a half ago to start a new life, and is devoting himself these days to studying 16th to 18th-century art, especially drawings.

Well, she asked a few friends, he asked a few friends, the Italians began calling and you know how it is. The guest list began to grow. 24. 60. Who knows?

Known for Small Dinners

Certainly not the Countess, a gentle, serene woman whom her friends commend for her elegance and intelligence. She's known for small, agreeable dinners, never big parties.

A slender Italian woman with crisp, graying hair, she furnished a small apartment here this winter, where she plans to live quietly a few months a year, and write.

She wasn't quite sure how many people would be dropping by between 8 P.M. and 11 P.M. to partake of the small buffet and give the birthday boy a kiss.

Her brother, Gianni Agnelli, the maker of Fiats, had arrived from Italy on Saturday for a five-day visit.

"When Gianni comes here, he insists on going to all the museums and seeing all the people he knows and I do dedicate myself to him," she explained. She was so busy that she had little time for elaborate party preparations. Besides, she had luncheon guests in the afternoon.

"I'm not really a social person," she said seriously.

For the Richard C. Pistells, both of whom are big-game hunters by avocation, the dinner party they gave for Ahmed Taiba Benhima and his wife, both very social persons, was inherently a sad occasion.

'We Shall Miss Them'

"It's very sad because the Benhimas are going home and we shall miss them," Mrs. Pistell explained. Ambassador Benhima, Morocco's permanent representative to the United Nations for the last four years, was replaced by Ambassador Mehdi Mrani Zentar last week and returns to Morocco tomorrow.

To wish the Benhimas well, Mrs. Pistell, the former Marquesa de Portago, called together 26 friends for a black-tie dinner involving smoked trout, squab stuffed with wild rice, string beans amandine and glacé Marocaine (lime and pineapple ice with fresh strawberries).

Ambassador Jaime de Pinies, Spain's permanent representative to the United Nations; Billy Baldwin, the decorator; Jack Howard, the publisher, and Mr. and Mrs. Robert Scull (he's the taxi tycoon who collects modern art) were among those invited to toast the departing couple in three wines. It was, incidentally, the first party the Pistells gave in their new 11-room apartment on Fifth Avenue, to which they moved two weeks ago.

The Gardner Cowleses have a new apartment, too, a supermodern place to which they invited 14 good friends "for an informal evening at home."

It was, Mrs. Cowles explained, "just a small dinner I put together before I went to Europe." She had no idea, back in January, that she was adding to New York's burgeoning social life on the first Thursday in March.

Her good friends include the William S. Paleys (he's chairman of the Columbia Broadcasting System), Gov. and Mrs. Nelson A. Rockefeller, Truman Capote, the Oscar de la Rentas and Mrs. T. Reed Vreeland, editor in chief of Vogue magazine.

"I'm afraid some of my pals who were committed to me might wish they were going to one of the more elaborate parties," said Mrs. Cowles, who planned such a simple evening that she didn't even have a guest of honor.

Quiet Dinner at Whitneys'

The John Hay Whitneys also had a quiet dinner, but they managed an honored guest. She was Mrs. Milton Gandel, "a very close friend who is here from England," explained Mrs. Whitney, who denied that her party had anything to do with the social whirl.

Actually, more than one invitation for the evening was no handicap for the really industrious guest.

Mrs. Vreeland had three commitments (to the Countess Rattazzi, the Feigens and the Cowleses) and fully intended to fulfill them all.

It was only the problem of dress that daunted some of the guests. Françoise de la Renta, the designer's wife, who was invited to the same three events, was troubled because the dance was black tie. It was her husband's outfit that worried her—she planned to wear a long black dress that would be appropriate at any event.

"We simply don't have time for Oscar to go home and change," she said.

She chose the black dress basically "because it doesn't wrinkle" and also because, she added, "I'm always so underdressed I drive Oscar mad."

Mrs. Ahmet Ertegun, whose husband heads Atlantic Records, also chose a black dress. Hers was by Mme. Grès. Because her husband was out of town, she hoped to find an unattached man at Countess Rattazzi's party who was also invited to the Feigen dance.

"If Paul Mathias wasn't such a good friend, I'd have stayed in Southampton painting," she said.

Painting a House

She meant painting the old Stanford White house that Mac II, the decorating business she runs with Mrs. William P. Rayner, was refurbishing for sale or rental next summer. They hoped to have it ready by Memorial Day.

Everybody who could wrangle an invitation tried to drop by the Countess's apartment for any number of reasons. They included the desire to see her new apartment ("Modern in conception, without any modern furniture—totally unpretentious, only a few valuable paintings," according to a friend who had already seen it), and the wish to give the birthday honor guest a kiss or a gift.

Mrs. Leonard Holzer, who was known as Baby Jane in her modeling days and now divides her time between caring for her baby and working for the prevention of heroin addiction, took him a purple body shirt.

But what made a lot of people stop by twice was the rumor that Mrs. Aristotle S. Onassis, an old friend of the guest of honor, had said she would come. You don't run into the former Jacqueline Kennedy every place you go.

The guest list included City Councilman Carter Burden and his wife; Mrs. Vincent Astor, who lives in the same building as the Countess; Alexander Romanoff, whose grandmother was the sister of Nicholas II of Russia, and his bride, Mimi di Niscemi, who designs costume jewelry.

Mrs. Jacob K. Javits, who was going on to the Feigen dance, wore a black dress by Jean Muir with a long metal vest she bought in Rome last summer. Her husband, meanwhile, was giving a dinner for George F. Kennan, the former ambassador, in Washington, which she tried to organize long distance. "He does this all the time," she observed. "He's having 20 men, Senators mostly."

Praise From Decorator

Mark Hampton of McMillen, who decorated part of the Countess's apartment (the library, hall and dining room; Denning & Fourcade did the bedroom and living room) was there with his wife. The Countess was a heroine to her decorator.

"It was so easy to work with her — she had great, strong feelings about what she wanted," he said.

The Italian contingent included two fashion designers, Valentino and Princess Irene Galitzine, who stopped in after dinner with the Roger Millikens of the fabric mills ("I spent my first Christmas with them in New York 20 years ago"). Ambassador Pietro Vinci, Italy's representative to the United Nations, went there too.

Then he attended the Feigen dance, where he ran into Carter Brown, director of the National Gallery in Washington; Herbert P. Patterson, president of the Chase Manhattan Bank; Robert Motherwell, the artist; Alan Pryce-Jones, the writer; Orin Lehman, the politician who's been producing plays, and Lady Jeanne Campbell, daughter of the Duke of Argyll.

That's the kind of night it was. Everybody was out somewhere. Tomorrow, perhaps, they'll all be serious again.

"A strange thing to happen on a Thursday night," said a woman who hadn't been invited to any of the parties. "They must have had the servants switch their days off—or else everything was catered."

APRIL 14, 1971

In Israeli Manner, Caftans and Shorts

By BERNADINE MORRIS

You don't have to be Jewish to model Israeli fashions.

"Besides, you never know in New York who is or who isn't," remarked Wyatt Cooper, the writer, who is married to Gloria Vanderbilt. He was parading around the Central Park West apartment of the Yosef Tekoahs yesterday afternoon in a leather coat by Beged-Or, one of Israel's leading ready-to-wear manufacturers.

Last year, Mr. Cooper was the commentator at the annual showing of Israeli fashions, which is used to boost that country's bond drive here, as well as the clothes. The collection will be shown April 22 at a luncheon at the Hotel Americana, after which it will tour 63 cities in the United States and Canada.

For some of the models, yesterday's showing was a warm-up.

"The clothes are so beautiful," said Fawne Harriman, a 24-year-old actress whose last modeling stint was in her native Chico, Calif., when she was a basketball queen.

Her outfits included an ancient embroidered caftan and a quilted skirt, and she loved them all.

Yearly Event

But for some, such as Mrs. Skitch Henderson, the showing is an annual event.

"The clothes are getting more amusing," she said as she slipped into another Beged-Or outfit, bib-to-suède shorts.

"That's not new for Israel," observed Mrs. Tekoah, whose husband is the country's permanent representative to the United Nations. "They were wearing shorts in the cities 50 years ago, before it was Israel."

"I'm here every year," said Mrs. Herbert Rounick," a dazzling blonde who was Miss Israel in 1962 and whose husband is an American textile executive. "I always find things I want to own."

Mrs. Nissan Engel, whose husband is an Israeli artist, said the afternoon reminded her of her days in Paris before her marriage when she modeled for Givenchy, Dior and Cardin.

"My children are Jewish," she explained. "I was Catholic, but I converted."

Met Dayan's Son

Mrs. Howard Bellin, the former Christina Paolozzi, was enthusiastic about her modeling stint because, she said, "I met a young man who was Moshe Dayan's son, and he turned me on for Israel."

She wore a broadtail coat rimmed in white mink by Stefan Braun and a hand-painted batik skirt and top by Shelly Boutique.

"My mother is in Israel now and having a great time," Mrs. Bellin volunteered.

The other models included Mrs. Robert C. Scull, wife of the taxi tycoon, who wore an eggplant-colored coat over what she insisted were her own hot pants, and Monsieur Marc, who not only arranged the other mannequins' hair, but stepped out himself in a beige suède coat.

The clothes ran from caftans with ancient and modern embroidery, including one made from a prayer shawl, through beach clothes to evening dresses. The caftans attracted the most attention.

"Fashion is so bad, I would rather wear Israeli costumes," said Mrs. Bellin.

APRIL 16, 1971

Top Art Auctions Boom, Though Economy Sags

By GRACE GLUECK

"Haven't they heard of the recession?" asked a non-bidding viewer at Parke-Bernet last month, after a snappy auction in which 53 buyers paid $2.5-million for 66 impressionist and modern paintings.

Apparently not. First-class airplane seats go begging and co-op apartments don't sell. There's been a let-up in yacht buying, and sables have fallen off. But, despite a dip in the general art market, the best-quality works of art continue to topple records at the major auction houses.

Some of the prices have been set under sale conditions that have created controversy in the trade over whether the auction system is indeed a free market. But buyers are still willing to spend freely. This year at the three top houses, for instance, a silver inkstand fetched $187,000, a Chinese porcelain vase brought $226,680, a pear-shaped diamond was knocked down for $1,050,000 and a painting by Velasquez went for a world auction record of $5,544,000.

True, there's been a considerable slackening in sales of middle-quality works of art, running in price between $20,000 and $60,000 — the area in which the auction houses make bread-and-butter commissions. But officials of the top houses insist that the recession has not deterred their big-league customers.

"In recent months," points out Peter Wilson, the urbane chairman of Sotheby's Inc., the London-based auction house that is the world's largest, "when stocks were down, the very finest works of art in all categories fetched record prices."

His contention is echoed by I. O. Chance, chairman of Christie's, the world's second largest auction house, also in London.

"Works of top quality are now in global demand," maintains Mr. Chance, in whose salesroom last November the $5.5-million Velasquez was sold, "and therefore, even if there may be a temporary recession in one country, there are enough people in the world competing for comparatively few works to insure continuing high prices."

Over a five-year period, the trend of business has been decidedly up at auction houses here and abroad, though the deflated buying power of money has undoubtedly been a factor. At the top three—Sotheby's and Christie's in London and Parke-Bernet in New York, which was acquired by Sotheby in 1964 — sales figures have zoomed: from $31.3 million in 1965-66 to $59.9-million in 1969-70 for Sotheby's; from $20.3-million to $48-million for Christie's; from $23.5-million to $38.5-million for Parke-Bernet.

Smaller Concerns Gain

Even smaller concerns—the Hotel Drouot and the Palais Galliera in Paris, Phillips Son & Neale in London, Kornfeld and Klipstein in Berne, the Finarte Gallery in Milan—report increases of up to 300 per cent in their sales figures over the last half decade.

This year the effect of the recession on middle-range works of art will undoubtedly put a dip in the upward curve. So far, through the first quarter of this season, Sotheby's turnover (the gross value of goods passed through the sale room) has been $20.7-million, a drop of nearly $2.5-million from last season.

Parke-Bernet's figure is $14.8, a slump of nearly $1.3-million from last year. Christie's total, swelled by the November sale of the Velasquez, is, at $21.9-million, the only one up (by nearly $4.5-million) over last season.

And last summer Sotheby's, formerly owned entirely by its 33 partners, obtained an infusion of capital by selling 20 per cent of its stock to the Rothschild Investment Trust, the first outside investment in Sotheby's.

Auction Expanded

But business slump or no, the houses are expanding. In an effort to increase the popularity of their lively indoor sport, they are, for one, stepping into more specialized markets to reach new categories of collectors.

They are holding special sales of Russian art, Chinese art, Art Nouveau, Art Deco, Chinese snuff bottles, French paperweights and such offbeat items as wine, antique cars, old photographs, musical instruments, antique buttons, minerals and shells.

They are also attempting to broaden their clientele by branching out physically. Two years ago, for example, Parke-Bernet opened P.B. 84, a junior salesroom on East 84th Street, not far from the concern's elegant Madison Avenue headquarters, which specializes in weekly sales of furniture and decorations for budget collectors.

Growth Outside England

Its success — $1.7-million last season, up a half million over the season before—has encouraged other Sotheby, Parke-Bernet ventures—exhibition galleries in Houston, a branch office in Denver, the recent opening in Los Angeles of Sotheby's first all-season auction house outside of London and New York. For the last few years, Sotheby's has also held fall and spring sales in Toronto and in Florence, Italy.

And Christie's, while still viewing London as "the most important art market" has, in the last two years, "significantly expanded" its sales outside of England.

The reasons for the current strength of the auction market have much to do with widespread uneasiness about the value of money. In periods of inflation, experts have noted, people of wealth tend to put their money into commodities least affected by the economic weather. Over the long haul, the uniqueness of art objects has made them a durable investment, the more so as the number of competing collectors increases.

One factor in the increasing importance of the auction market — though auction sales still represent only an estimated 5 to 10 per cent of total art dealings throughout the world—is the high visibility of the transaction.

"The auction market is one area in which values are publicly exhibited and tested," explains Eugene V. Thaw, a private dealer whose own sales are said to run into seven figures, "whereas dealers' transactions are hearsay."

Advantages to Auctions

At auction, the advantage to the seller is a quick cash settlement without the months, even years, he might wait for a dealer to find buyers. And for the buyer it often—by no means always—results in a wholesale price without a dealer's mark-up.

Dealers, on the other hand, contend that their prices are very often lower than some artificially driven up at auction. Some modern "old masters," such as Picasso and Matisse, have never brought at auction prices that were as high as those of dealers. And dealers note that they also guarantee the authenticity of the works they sell, where auction houses do not.

Authenticity Not Guaranteed

The "disclaimer" — disavowing all house liability for authenticity—that forms part of the printed "conditions of sale" in auction catalogues is a controversial feature of the sales.

Nevertheless the top houses allow a 21-day period during which items can be returned, if proved counterfeit or of gross difference from the catalogue description. In addition, because of a 1968 law passed by the New York State Legislature at the urging of Attorney General Louis J. Lefkowitz, nonprofessional buyers get further protection.

The law extends the return period to a year, and it gives legal recourse to buyers whenever the catalogue or bill of sale unqualifiedly describes a work of art as being by a named author or of a named period, culture, source or origin.

'Research' Before the Sale

"We don't hold ourselves out as experts in authenticity," says Peregrine Pollen, president of Sotheby, Parke-Bernet. "We're experts in value. We do as much research as possible within a deadline period. We also consult outside experts when necessary. If they say no, we don't include it in the sale."

But despite the best efforts of reputable auctioneers to weed out fakes and to describe each item offered for sale, dubious works still exist in the market and occasionally creep into an auction. Even if they do not, their very existence can affect a sale—as for example, the March 11 event at Parke-Bernet billed as "Important 19th and 20th Century Sculpture."

At that sale, a bronze head of Sir Winston Churchill by the late Jacob Epstein, consigned by Huntington Hartford, the A.&P. heir, failed to find a buyer, though other casts of the head had previously sold at auction for as high as $21,000.

Although Parke-Bernet officials are reluctant to comment on the reason, some in the trade note that a series of stories in The London Sunday Times showed that an unknown number over and above the 10 limited-edition castings of the work had been made.

Boom Traced to 1958

The beginning of the present auction boom, say auction followers, goes back to 1958, the year of the landmark Goldschmidt sale in London. At that sale, Sotheby's sold seven impressionist and post-impressionist pictures for a total of more than $2-million. Mr. Wilson, serving his first year as chairman of the concern, wielded the gavel and reports that the fast action gave him a forecast of the auction market's potential.

"Until that time it was held that no one would spend more than $100,000 on a spur-of-the-moment purchase," he says. "The day after, a fanstastic number of pictures were sold in London and New York, because suddenly prices were hitched up."

Auctioneers speak of sales in show biz terms. And the theatricality of the plush-walled saleroom is heightened sometimes by big-name bidders, the brisk pace of the auctioneer, closed-circuit TV at important sales and last-minute telephoned bids from London, Zurich, Houston.

"There's no question that the charged atmosphere drives prices up, "Mr. Wilson acknowledges. "You create a climate—a crescendo, a diminuendo, a crescendo, a diminuendo, the end. Nothing should interfere with that tension."

The 'Mystery' of Auctions

Despite the auction's public nature, however, many people regard them as a glamorous mystery. What is meant by a "reserve?" What is a "buy-in"? And, most important, is the auction really a free market, or is it subject to controls and manipulations?"

The auction process begins with the seller, known as the "consignor" in the trade. When he decides to sell his goods at auction, the house places an estimate on his items.

Whether the judgment proves correct at the sale depends upon a number of variables, but mainly the number of potential purchasers. "No work of art has an absolute, clear-cut value," Mr. Wilson points out. "The price simply represents what one person at a certain time was willing to pay for a certain object."

Take, for example, the rare Velasquez sold by Christie's last fall. Though the house would not release an estimate on the work, a "guess-timate" by trade and museum sources hovered around $3-million. But because of the interest of three "hot" bidders—one of whom stopped at $3.6-million, leaving the two others to fight it out—the picture brought a figure nearly twice that.

'Reserve' Price Set

Once the estimate has been established, there is usually the delicate business of fixing a "reserve," the minimum price that an owner will take for his property. The reserve, known only to the consignor and the auction house is, according to Mr. Pollen, as a matter of policy no more than two-thirds of the median of the lowest and highest estimate. (In actual practice, this formula varies considerably.)

If, for example, the low estimate on a painting is $80,000 and the high $100,000, the reserve would theoretically be set at $60,000. If bidding does not reach the latter sum, the auctioneer, acting for the consignor, can then "buy back" or "buy in" the work, levying a service charge of 5 per cent, as opposed to the standard fees on successful sales that range between 12.5 and 20 per cent.

There has been much controversy between dealers and Parke-Bernet over the policy of reserves. A major charge is that the reserve violates the concept of a "free market" theoretically represented by the auction.

"The reserve puts an artificial floor under a painting which may or may not represent its true market value," says Klaus Perls, a prominent dealer. "If a work is for sale at auction, it should go to the legitimate highest bidder, whether the last price he bids meets the owner's reserve or not."

Reserve Policy Defended

But the auction houses argue that a reserve is necessary to protect the consignor. "The reserve is a fail-safe device," says Mr. Pollen. "Suppose, for instance, you have a scant, rainy-day audience and bidding is lethargic. Without a reserve, a work could go for less than it's worth."

A reserve also protects sellers against a "ring"—a group of collusive buyers (usually dealers) who agree to withhold bidding, allowing one of them to buy at a low price. Once the ring acquires its prize, it auctions it privately at a "knockdown" sale among ring members, for a price closer to its real value. The difference between that and the lower price is shared.

But while a reserve can save a seller from grief, it can also hurt the buyers. The reserve is secret, and the auctioneer is empowered to raise bids to the reserve point even against only one "live" bidder. Thus situations inevitably arise where a lone bidder is contending not in free competition but against the secret reserve itself.

Price Manipulation Used

Occasionally more indirect methods are used. A dealer or a collector may attempt to "run up" a painting at auction, choosing a representative work by a certain artist and putting on it as high a reserve as the house will allow. (Auctioneers prefer low reserves, since the lower the reserve, the less the chance of a low-commission buy-in.)

At the sale, several "bidders" will raise the work to just under its reserve and then—unless a "live" bidder becomes interested—the work is bought in at a price that tends to establish a market level. Sometimes dealers are so anxious to raise prices that they will bid over its reserve and pay a full commission.

The dealer, or other consignor, can use the raised price as a negotiating base for future sale of the picture, as well as for others by the same painter.

David Nash, director of the 19th and 20th-century paintings department at Sotheby, Parke-Bernet, says such price manipulations occur rarely.

"We try to prevent them," he adds, "and can refuse to take bids or consignments from people suspected of them."

He acknowledges that beyond those steps, there was nothing much the house could do to eliminate the "run-up" practice, though in the case of deliberate buy-ins a recently established system whereby the house does not report buy-in prices on its post-auction lists should prove and effective deterrent.

Warhol Painting Stirs Talk

A recent article in the German magazine "Capital," which has been circulating among dealers here, questions whether a "run-up" occurred in the sale last May at Sotheby, Parke-Bernet of a painting by Andy Warhol, which set a record price of $60,000.

Entitled "Soup Can With Peeling Label," the work was consigned by Peter Brandt, a young businessman and Warhol collector, and was estimated at between $40,000 and $50,000 by the auctioneer.

It was knocked down to Bruno Bischofberger, a Swiss dealer and friend of Brandt's, for $60,000. No major Warhol painting had been sold at auction before, and the highest dealer's price here was $50,000.

Mr. Brandt denies the magazine's observation—and trade talk here—that even though there were people willing to pay at least $50,000 for the work, it was bid up to establish a higher market level. The painting is now for sale at Mr. Bischofberger's gallery in Zurich for $75,000.

"The talk is completely entered the picture to sell it for more. In fact, the day after the sale, I was offered $120,000 for it, though I still wouldn't sell it for less than the reserve." (The picture is still for sale.)

Under normal auction practice, such buy-in prices would be included with the prices false," Mr. Brandt says. "Bruno tried to buy the painting from me many times, but I never wanted to sell. Finally I bought another and better 'Soup Can' painting. Bruno offered me $50,000 for the first one, but I decided to see how much it would bring at auction. I didn't know he'd go to $60,000."

Mr. Bischofberger says that before the sale, at which he was not present, he had offered to leave a bid of $50,000 with Parke-Bernet, but that the concern had told him it had bids for more.

"So I went up to $60,000," he says. "I can't blame dealers for saying, since they know Mr. Brandt and I are friends, that we made a deal to shoot up Warhol's prices, but it's absolutely not true."

There has also been discussion about the Nov. 18 sale of contemporary American paintings at Parke-Bernet at which buy-ins accounted for over $400,000 of the evening's $1,179,450 gross. Some of the buy-ins occurred at spectacular prices —for example, "Two Flags," a work by Jasper Johns, consigned by Robert Scull, a prominent collector in the contemporary field.

The much-heralded sale, one of the few to test prices in the relatively untried contemporary field, had many dealers and collectors jittery. Would the works, by stars of pop, abstract expressionist and color-field painting go below dealer price levels?

Buy-In Influences Market

Mr. Scull's painting, one of six he entered, had been estimated by Parke-Bernet at $140,000 to $160,000, although no major Johns work had been tested before at auction. A small oil on paper had brought $15,000 at an earlier sale. And the highest "official" price for a major Johns, according to the artist's dealer Leo Castelli, was $100,000.

Not finding a buyer above that at the sale, the Johns was bought in at $105,000, somewhat short of its $125,000 reserve. However, the buy-in established a market level for the picture, a fact with which Mr. Scull concurs.

"There's no question that the buy-in established a price," he says, "although I of successful sales in the post-auction price list, thus establishing them as prices of record.

Reserve Policy Debated

But, after extended discussions with the Art Dealers Association of America, an organization of prominent dealers that attempts to set ethical standards for the trade, Parke-Bernet recently began to eliminate from its post-sale price lists all items withdrawn, bought in or passed—that is, not bid on.

The house's action was taken with some reluctance, however. "I feel that the buy-in price of a picture is so close to what someone was actually prepared to pay for it," says Mr. Pollen, "that it's a bona-fide market reflection and should be included."

Ralph Colin, lawyer, collector and administrative vice president of the association, said he welcomed the amended price lists but would like to go further in dealing with the reserve problem.

One suggested measure is to make reserve figures public prior to the sale. But such a notion is vehemently vetoed by the auctioneers.

"A published reserve would kill the auction business," contends Mr. Pollen. "If they knew the price an owner would take for his goods, people simply wouldn't bid. We'd no longer be running an auction house but a retail business."

Some dealers say the reserve price makes the auction a retail business anyway. Despite their complaints, however, dealers stress that the auction houses are essential to them, because over the long run they have helped to lift prices generally, and because they have brought many new buyers into the art market.

"The successful auctions have paced and prepared the way for most dealers," says Eugene V. Thaw, president of the Art Dealers Association. "Without the auction establishment of prices, we couldn't sustain the public faith and interest in them."

Echoing these sentiments Klaus Perls, a former president of the dealers' association, points out: "No dealer would dare ask $5.5-million for that Velasquez. And if he asked and got it, who'd know about it?"

MAY 26, 1971

Boat Basin Decked In Splendor for Gala

By ENID NEMY

Everyone said "Christina, don't do it!" So, of course, Christina, who was the Countess Christina Paolozzi, is now Mrs. Howard Bellin, and has never been known to listen to advice under either name, went ahead and did it. A charity benefit.

"It's an exciting event," she said of the Spring Fever Gala held last night to aid the National Tay-Sachs and Allied Diseases Association. "Naturally, we're doing it to raise money, but it's not one of those dumb things held behind closed doors."

As a matter of fact, there were no doors, closed or otherwise. The event was held at the West 79th Street boat basin, which was temporarily transformed into a scene of ersatz medieval splendor.

The Hot Pants Gimmick

Peter Di Paola, who together with Mrs. Barry Hornig (Mrs. Bellin's sister) and Mrs. Bruce Bandaleone, spent several hundred hours cutting gold, silver, maroon and turquoise Mylar into strips, streamers, shields and banners, didn't quite know how he got involved, but he did know why.

"Cri is a friend of mine," he said, in a slightly resigned voice. Cri, pronounced Cree, is one of the diminutives of Christina used by those near and dear to Mrs. Bellin.

Mr. Di Paola, who is in the Unit Managers Department of the American Broadcasting Company, said he had minored in theater at college and had observed soap operas and studio shows being put together, so he had some idea how to go about things. He did not attempt to reconcile medieval décor with an evening of "Dance, Gambol, Picnic and Rock" and "revolutionary or establishment" dress.

Mrs. Bellin, whose husband is a plastic surgeon and who is herself a practitioner of stream of consciousness conversation, said she had originally decided "to hell with social people, important names and so on—unless they work." She was, however, forced to change her concept slightly after meeting rebuffs from some of the designers from whom she had requested contributions of hot pants. The pants were to be, and indeed were, worn by committee members "as a gimmick. You know, you've got to have a gimmick."

"Well, the first thing some of them asked me was who was on the committee list," reported Mrs. Bellin in a state of some indignation. "When I read the names to them, they said, 'Maybe we'll pass it up this year.' So naturally, we immediately started a superstar list."

The superstar list included Barbra Streisand, Jacqueline Susann, Camilla Sparv and Monique Van Vooren. Miss Streisand was filming, Miss Susann was at the Cannes Film Festival and Miss Van Vooren was in Leningrad; Miss Sparv's whereabouts were unknown.

Mrs. Bellin Wore Dress

But Mrs. Orson Bean, the co-chairman, was on hand, fresh off a plane from Australia. Her hot pants were kangaroo fur. Other committee members, a group that included Mrs. Robert Scull, Princess Egon von Furstenberg, Mrs. Howard Samuels and Mrs. Philip Isles, settled for designers like Adolfo, Halston, Bill Blass, Donald Brooks, Scott Barrie, Ann Klein and Geoffrey Beene.

Mrs. Bellin, who wasn't always so modest (she once posed in the nude for Harper's Bazaar) and is prone to exaggeration, said she was wearing a dress by Teal Traina because "I'd look ridiculous in hot pants." As she is young, slim, blond and attractive, no one knew what she meant, but they often don't.

Mrs. Marco Buitoni, whose husband donated 800 pizzas for the party ("No one will gain weight; they're very small pizzas"), put on a pair of rust satin hot pants and, for one evening, submerged her dislike of charity events.

To Set Up Centers

"This is the first time I've been active in something like this, because when I do something, I must do it seriously," said Mrs. Buitoni, who moved here from Rome five years ago. "I'd rather talk to people and have them look you straight in the eye than play social games. Saying 'hello' and 'how beautiful you look' is so boring. And what does it mean?"

Last night it meant, Mrs. Bellin hoped, more than $30,000 toward the establishment of Tay-Sachs centers to determine, before birth, whether a baby carries the disease. Tay-Sachs is an inherited disorder causing destruction of the nervous system. It usually strikes a baby at about six months of age and death often occurs by the fourth year. It is always fatal.

The money was raised through the sale of more than 800 tickets at $20 a person or $35 a couple (last year, fewer than 300 tickets were sold at $75 a couple) and from games of chance. Winners were paid off with articles from various boutiques. Merchandise from boutiques, including Cartier, Ben Kahn Furs, Valentino and Kenneth J. Lane, was also sold to guests, with 20 per cent of the proceeds returned to charity.

Almost all the expenses of the evening were underwritten, including Life, U.S.A., a rock band, contributed by RCA Recording Artists. Kentucky fried chicken was sent over by the Cosgrove-Kinney Corporation, wine by Allen's Restaurants, candy by Ferrara Foods, pastries by Patisserie Dumas and frankfurters, rolls and candy bars by Ward Foods. The Good Humor man was also present.

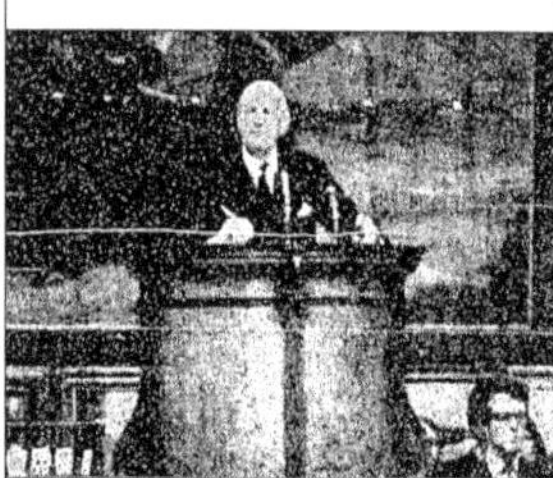

SEPTEMBER 27, 1971

4 Uptown Art Dealers Set Up in SoHo

By GRACE GLUECK

The invasion of SoHo, the grubby artists' neighborhood downtown, by a group of elegant uptown galleries was rousingly celebrated Saturday afternoon in a refurbished loft building at 420 West Broadway. Three established dealers—Leo Castelli, André Emmerich and Ileana Sonnabend—and John Weber, former director of the defunct Dwan Gallery on West 57th Street, officially opened quarters in the building, firmly establishing the presence of Madison Avenue in SoHo, the area south of Houston Street, and giving it its first multigallery complex.

The occasion also marked, more or less, the unofficial opening of the art season, and hundreds of art lovers were on hand exchanging gossipy greetings as they toasted the new art mart in wine and champagne.

"I'm overwhelmed by the space, the vitality, the people," declared the sculptor George Segal. "When you walk in, it looks like any artists' loft building. I'm glad there are a few dealers sensitive enough to show works in space of the same character as that in which they were made." And Roy Lichtenstein, the painter, mentioned "one positive thing, its larger space."

"It seems to allow for the kind of art that isn't just pictures."

The Opposite View

Others didn't quite agree. "So what's new?," asked the painter Lee Krasner after a four-floor inspection tour of the sumptuous galleries, each named after its owner. And Robert Scull, the collector, insisted, "They've just changed their uptown addresses. I thought in a loft building I'd at least see some bricks falling down."

The five-story building, a 19th-century architectural gem with cast-iron pillars, is flanked by a flooring company and a hardware concern. Once a warehouse for the A. G. Nelson Paper Company, it was remodeled at a cost of nearly $500,000 by its joint owners, Mr. Castelli, Mr. Emmerich and Hague Art Deliveries, an art transportation company that occupies the ground floor.

The dealers, each of whom will retain his uptown gallery (except for Mr. Weber, who is starting out new), originally saw the grimy colossus as a solution to the problem of storage space, virtually unobtainable in the Midtown area. "Then we thought why can't the space also be used to show art?," said Mr. Castelli. "It would be in the nature of a supplementary gallery, and it could also be more lively, less rigid than uptown."

Each occupant has 8,000 square feet of floor space, vast by uptown standards. "We built our dream galleries," remarked Mr. Emmerich, who boldly blocked out windows in his top-floor quarters and punched skylights in the roof for better lighting. Mr. Castelli divided his premises into three handsome exhibition areas and installed a projection room for films.

Mr. Weber also put in a projection room, painted his floors black and left the ceiling beams exposed, but Mrs. Sonnabend, afraid of "spoiling the beautiful space," left partitioning at a minimum to achieve a wide open arena.

For at least two of the dealers, the thrust into SoHo reflects a shift in exhibition emphasis. Mr. Castelli, who helped launch a number of pop and minimal reputations, views his downtown operation as "a more open situation, a shot in the arm for us."

Planning to focus a good deal more on films and videotape, he suited action to words at his opening exhibition with a wall of four simultaneous films, made by gallery artists Robert Morris, Bruce Nauman, Richard Serra and Keith Sonnier.

"Films will become increasingly important as an artists' medium," he predicted. "When the cassette is perfected, there are great hopes for a new kind of movement."

Mrs. Sonnabend, a Paris dealer who brought pop and minimal names to Europe, opened her Madison Avenue quarters last year and will now turn it into a showcase for Art Deco, the stylized objects of the nineteen-twenties and thirties currently in vogue. Convinced that the downtown area "offers a lot more possibilities for showing new people," she will concentrate her SoHo gallery on "interesting things that haven't been seen here yet."

And indeed her opening exhibition was easily the day's star attraction. Billed as "The Singing Sculpture," it consisted of two young English artists known as Gilbert and George, who stood atop a table in bronze make-up and with the gestures of mechanical figures repeatedly sang a music-hall version of "Underneath the Arches." The pair, who describe themselves as "living sculptures," drew a fascinated crowd and the comment from one viewer that "someone has finally dared to show what the art world is—vaudeville without pay." But the crowd stayed on.

The opening of the building on West Broadway comes after a "down" year for many in the art world, a year of, among other discouragements, declining sales caused by the recession. Even so, the four occupants of "420" view their own and SoHo's futures as fairly rosy.

"Historically there are two places to sell art—where rich people are and where artists turn it out," said Mr. Emmerich, whose uptown stable of "color field" painters—Helen Frankenthaler, Morris Louis, Kenneth Noland and others—will get additional exposure in his downtown gallery.

"The people who make reputations will certainly see SoHo—in fact they live there. And the real collectors would rather go to SoHo than uptown—it's more fun and close to the source. So we'll get the people who matter most."

FEBRUARY 22, 1972

Exhibition Pays Tribute to Art Gallery of the 1960's

By DAVID L. SHIREY

During its brief but spectacular existence in the 1960's, the Green Gallery became one of New York's most important art galleries. By the time it closed its doors at 15 West 57th Street in 1965, after five years in operation, it had acquired an international reputation as one of the major showcases of the avant-garde.

At a time when abstract expressionism was still riding the crest of critical acclaim, the Green Gallery managed to play a significant role in the development and establishment of both pop and minimal art. It helped secure the reputation of artists such as Claes Oldenberg, George Segal, Tom Wesselmann, James Rosenquist, Donald Judd, Dan Flavin and Robert Morris.

Because of its historic contribution to the art world and because of the esteem and affection that many in the art community feel for it, it was inevitable that someone would want to pay a major tribute to the Green Gallery. Robert Littman has now assembled at the Emily Lowe Gallery of Hofstra University, Hempstead, L. I., where he is director, a commemorative exhibition called "The Green Gallery Revisited."

The artists here are represented by fine examples in familiar styles, as they were originally shown at the gallery. More examples would have been welcome to indicate the esthetic range of these artists. But limited exhibition space has made this impossible. It also prevented inclusion of other distinguished artists who showed at the Green, such as the minimalist Ron Bladen, who works on a physical scale the Lowe Gallery could not accommodate.

Notwithstanding its emphasis on pop and minimal, the Green also showed, as the exhibition makes clear, the abstract expressionist paintings of Robert Beauchamp, the op canvases of Larry Poons, the surrealistic objects of Lucas Samaras and the expressionist sculpture of Mark di Suvero.

The Green Gallery represented a collaboration between the dealer Richard Bellamy and the collector Robert Scull. Funded by Mr. Scull, it was the brainchild and creation of Mr. Bellamy, who was 30 when the Green opened in 1960.

As an adjunct to the exhibition, several of the Green artists recorded on tape their impressions of Mr. Bellamy as a gallery director. Most of them agreed that he was endowed with extraordinary powers of judgment and perceptivity and possessed special talents for handling artistic personalities. "He sensed a totality larger than each artist's work," George Segal noted.

The exhibition, which opens today, runs through March 29. The Lowe Gallery is open free, Monday through Friday from 10 A.M. to 5 P.M., Saturday and Sunday from 1 to 5 P.M., and Wednesday and Thursday evenings from 6 to 9.

FEBRUARY 27, 1972

Art: Former Avant-Garde Gallery Remembered in Hofstra Show

By DAVID L. SHIREY

HEMPSTEAD, L. I. — Art Galleries come and go, but very few leave behind an image big or important enough to stir the memory. But the Emily Lowe Gallery of Hofstra University here is now paying tribute to one gallery worth remembering with its commemorative exhibition, appropriately named "The Green Gallery Revisited."

The Green suddenly emerged on the New York art scene in 1960 and disappeared just as suddenly in 1965. Within those five succinct years, the time it takes most galleries to get a foothold in the art community, the Green on West 57th Street had established itself as one of the most exciting and historically significant avant-garde showcases in New York.

At a time when abstract expressionism was still in the ascendancy as an art form, the Green was one of the first New York galleries to champion Pop art. It also was one of the first to pioneer in the austere statements of Minimal art.

Through its convictions and unflagging espousal of the new and the fresh, it showed unknown artists who are today part of the American pantheon of art, including James Rosenquist, George Segal, Tom Wesselmann, Claes Oldenburg, Don Judd, Dan Flavin and Robert Morris.

•

With good reason, the Hofstra exhibition, following the esthetic persuasions of the gallery, has featured these artists. Robert Littman, director of the gallery, has made a point of choosing, whenever possible, representative works of the artists and works that would have originally been exhibited at the Green.

Thus there are Mr. Flavin's industrial neon tubings, Mr. Segal's plaster figures, Mr. Oldenburg's pastries and Mr. Judd's unadorned construction. Although Mr. Littman was unable to display some of Mr. Morris's later primary structures, he was able to show some of the artist's earlier Duchampian pieces. The Rosenquist painting he chose is especially interesting as a transition work whose esthetic reveals a change from an abstract expressionist style to a Pop one.

It would be misleading, however, to say that the Green showed Pop and Minimal to the exclusion of everything else. If the gallery believed in the sensibility of an artist, it would show his work, no matter what his form of expression. Thus it gave exhibition space to the Op Art of Larry Poons, to the surrealistic pin boxes of Lucas Samaras and the expressionist sculpture of Mark di Suvero. There are two extraordinary examples of Mr. di Suvero's constructions in this exhibition, "Mother and Child" and "The Hand."

The success of the Green Gallery was due to the sharp eye and subtle intelligence of one man: Richard Bellamy. Mr. Bellamy had been co-director of the Hansa Gallery, another highly respectable gallery which closed its doors in 1958. In collaboration with Robert Scull, the collector, who funded the Green Gallery, Mr. Bellamy exhibited the work of artists he believed in, whether they were appreciated elsewhere or not. Most artists who were associated with Mr. Bellamy still praise him for his unusually sensitive talents. They feel that his dedication not only gave them a public audience, but also inspiration.

The Emily Love Gallery, where the exhibition runs until March 29, is open to the public, free of charge, Monday through Friday, 10 A.M. to 5 P.M., Saturday and Sunday 1 P.M. to 5 P.M., and Wednesday and Thursday evenings, 6 P.M. to 9 P.M.

AUGUST 21, 1972

Party on L.I. Assists Attica Defense

By ENID NEMY
Special to The New York Times

AMAGANSETT, L. I., Aug. 20 — "You've really got to believe in something to go to a fund-raising party these days," said one woman standing near a platter of steak tartare. "That radical chic business hurt us a lot."

There wasn't much radical chi at the George Plimptons' house here yesterday, perhaps because there weren't many people. Those who did show up, about 75 in all, were serious enough to pay $25 each for admission, give up several hours of a sunny afternoon and take in stride celebrity bartenders and guests like Gwen Verdon, Eli Wallach, Tom Paxton and the Rev. Daniel J. Berrigan.

The event, organized by Mrs. Victor Rabinowitz, who writes under the name of Joanne Grant, was to raise funds for the Attica Defense Committee. One lawyer present estimated that "millions of dollars" would be needed to defend the inmates—possibly as many as 105—who face indictment because of last year's uprising in the prison.

Two men who were in Attica during the rebellion and have since been released thoroughly approved of the party. They both realized, they said, that donations could be sent in without a social gathering, but that wasn't the entire point.

Hearing for Themselves

"It's better that they should be here, so they can personally hear what is going on," said Harold Walker, a vice president of the Attica Survivors' Committee. He was released from Attica in June after serving 44 months for armed robbery.

"I don't believe in jails like the Holiday Inn, where you go in to have a good time," said Joseph Little, who was in Attica on a manslaughter charge. "But the people inside should be treated like humans, not animals . . . this party is a good idea because it makes people aware."

Little, now a counselor at the Bronx Court Employment Project, is also a member of the Survivors' Committee.

Most of the men and women, wandering around in everything from terry-cloth turbans and long skirts to denims and chinos, agreed.

"Sure, I could have sent in a check, but this is the kind of thing where everyone should stand up and be counted," said Mrs. Robert Scull, wife of the taxi-company owner and art collector. Mrs. Scull was making one of her few social appearances since injuring her back on a Barbados beach last year. "What happened at Attica was shocking," she added.

Mrs. Scull, almost dwarfed by her two sons, one carrying a folding chair and the other a special cushion for her, said her accident had allowed her a lot of time to think.

"During the sixties, it was a gas running around everywhere, but now I want to do something," she said. "I don't know what yet."

Women Still Serve Food

Mr. Plimpton, who was keeping one eye on Medora, his 16-month-old daughter, and another on the guests, said he had agreed to having the party in the house he has rented for the last three years because he thought the cause was worthy.

"But I'm not really doing anything," he said as his wife and other women ran between the kitchen, the central deck and the silo-roofed living rom with platters of crisp, raw vegetables, stuffed mushrooms, ham and cheese.

"We've been involved in the civil-rights movement since 1963," said Mrs. Tom Paxton, as her husband, the folk singer, poured diet drinks and stronger spirits into the plastic glasses heaped on the bar.

"We see all this as a part of life, and we work at it," she continued. "The least pleasurable part is the fund-raising . . . it's more fun out in the field."

Shortly before 7 P.M., most of the guests ("a lot of people have to leave soon to go out to dinner," explained one woman) moved onto the sofas, chairs and zebra rugs in the living room to listen to Eli Wallach, Father Berrigan and Harold Walker. A few, like Andrew J. Stein, the Assemblyman from Manhattan's Upper East side, who perhaps had earlier dinner engagements, moved toward their cars.

No Place for Politics

The liveliest part of the gathering came after envelopes had been passed around for additional contributions (a total of $2,500 was raised), and the audience was invited to ask questions.

A debate ensued on whether the committee should make an attempt to recruit and include the guards at Attica, who were also, according to one, "victims of the system." It was decided that this could be another project.

A supporter of Senator George McGovern asked why the name of her candidate had not been mentioned. There were murmurs of agreement.

Mr. Wallach replied that the afternoon was for Attica and was not a political arena.

"I don't know anyone who is supporting Nixon, anyway," he added. Only a few people looked surprised.

OCTOBER 7, 1972

Quiet Return to Elegance in the Afternoon

By ANNE-MARIE SCHIRO

Mrs. Mortimer Solomon, wearing a green suit by Guy Laroche with red fox boa and hat from Revillon, waited patiently for the fashion show to begin at Saks Fifth Avenue. "I do hope the elegant look is coming back," she said.

Well, Mrs. Solomon, worry not. The other 349 women at the showing, plus some 400 who turned up two days later for Jo Hughes's luncheon show at the St. Regis, are on your wave length.

They're wearing suits, knee-length dresses or pants suits with tailored jackets as they combine shopping for their winter wardrobes with contributing to their favorite charities. The Saks show was for the benefit of the Kips Bay Boys' Club. Miss Hughes, Bergdorf Goodman's super saleswoman, held her show for Just One Break (JOB).

Name Around the Middle

On the runways were clothes from each store's pet designers, and many of them were represented in the audiences as well. Adolfo made a strong showing at Saks, where several women sported his knitted outfits, including Mrs. Paulette B. Harrison, a Kips Bay patroness. Her blue dress had her nickname, Polly, running around the middle of it.

Mrs. Robert Scull, carrying her own pillow to ease an injured back, wore a three-piece Adolfo to the Bergdorf luncheon.

"It's brand new," she said of the multicolor outfit. "I love these patterns, the way they're mixed. I'm getting more of them."

Other favorites were pretty much what one would expect: Donald Brooks, Chester Weinberg, Dior, Saint Laurent, Bill Blass and Halston.

Norman Norell hit the daily double at the St. Regis when Mrs. Charles Revson arrived moments after Mrs. Martin Revson. They wore identical beige-checked Norell shirtdresses. Providence worked overtime by placing the women at separate tables.

Mrs. Prentis Cobb Hale, in from San Francisco, held court at a ringside table while friends admired her gold lion pendant.

Husband Is a Leo

"It's my husband," Denise Hale said. "He's a Leo. See, the lion's feet are tied." She laughed. "It was a present for our first anniversary last month. David Webb made it. Isn't it amusing?"

Yes, and in a season of beautiful but sane clothes, women evidently appreciate the touches of humor. Witness: Two of the best-selling numbers after the Saks show turned out to be Adolfo's "name" dress and a Rudi Gernreich long black knit covered-up-front dress with a sheer back.

Sales were brisk after the Bergdorf's luncheon, too. Miss Hughes reported that her customers were ordering five and six numbers each, and that one woman bought 12. It should be a fashionable winter.

OCTOBER 29, 1972

Artist Redefines Black-Tie Dinner for a Princess

By CHARLOTTE CURTIS

Robert Rauschenberg's formal dinner for Her Royal Highness Princess Christina of Sweden was perhaps the most unusual interpretation of a black-tie party since somebody dressed a monkey in a dinner jacket and seated it next the hostess.

The host, an artist who once created a celebrated oeuvre by merely stencilling a box with the words "Art Work," had obviously risen to the occasion. He rejected the idea of wearing a suit made entirely of neckties.

"No," he said thoughtfully. "I think I have something more suitable."

After first settling his wavy shoulder-length coiffure with a bobby pin over each ear, he did indeed put on a white shirt and a black tie. But his jacket was an American Indian fringed suède relic embroidered with porcupine quills.

The Princess, apparently aware that an evening in the SoHo artists district in 1972 was not the same as a ball at the St. Regis she attended in 1965, dressed differently, too.

She wore ruffled tiers of green, black and red chiffon all right. But her neckline plunged daringly and there was no sign of white gloves, her diamond necklace or her tiara.

Before she arrived, Mr. Rauschenberg, whose friends had spent days preparing his house-around-a-chapel for the 309 dinner guests, explained the protocol.

"I've granted everybody immunity," he said. "You don't have to curtsey or bow. Sweden is a very liberated country."

The Princess, who'd studied art history at Radcliffe, seemed to agree. At an earlier reception, the unveiling of the New York art collection destined for Sweden's Moderna Museet, she said, "Nobody in Sweden calls me Princess anymore."

The host and guest of honor finally met on the fourth floor of Mr. Rauschenberg's house. The Princess and such other upper echelon types as the Swedish Ambassador got there by climbing up 80 steep steps.

"If you don't get your leg muscles developed tonight, you never will," said Mrs. Harold Reed, the art dealer's wife.

•

Once there, the visiting Swedes were surrounded by artists—including Roy Lichtenstein, Larry Rivers, Alex Hay, James Rosenquist, Oyvind Fahlstrom and Andy Warhol—Mr. Rauschenberg's SoHo friends and a sprinkling of refugees from the Upper East Side.

"I'm Penelope," said a young woman in a mint-green satin nightgown with a lace bodice and train. "I never use my last name."

Penelope was accompanied by her baby daughter, Hummingbird, who sat in the middle of the floor. Then there was a young woman who professed to be Moki or Moki Cherry. She said she hadn't decided whether she had one or two first names.

Moki, or Moki Cherry as the case may be, wore a beaded headdress with a peacock feather and bright red eye shadow. She said she'd spent the afternoon running up her pink and green satin tunic.

"The fabric?" she asked, looking a little puzzled. "Why that was easy. Some of it was in the garbage or draped over trees. The birds flew some of it in my window."

The Princess, who said she was having "a nice time," also met Kevin McCarthy, who had a "Men for Women for McGovern" button on his dinner jacket, and August Heckshen, the Park Administrator. Mr. Heckshen said he might be just a little out of date.

"Someone asked me which paintings I liked best and I said the abstract expressionists," he said. "That makes me the fifties, not even the sixties."

While Mr. Heckshen studied newer paintings stored behind the improvised bar (one was all gray with white chalk squiggles), Jeffrey Potter, the writer, sat on a filing cabinet, sipping his drink.

He said his name began J-E-F rather than G-E-O-F "because G-E-O went out with the American Revolution." But he was in black tie.

Mr. Potter was with Mrs. Armand G. Erpf, who has worked long and hard for Experiments in Art and Technology, which assembled the art collection and is raising funds to send it to Sweden. She is the widow of the financier.

"I love parties like this," she explained. "I really believe in supporting the arts."

Eventually, the important guests on the fourth floor went down to join the others for dinner. Tables centered with roses and daisies and mobs of people were jammed over three floors. Mr. Rauschenberg and the Princess sat in the chapel.

•

The meal began with fresh salmon flown from Sweden and served on paper plates. The wine, a Muscadet, was poured into plastic cups. When the entree was slow in arriving, Mrs. Jacob K. Javits left the Princess's table to help.

"It's impossible," she said. "There isn't enough space, but I did my best."

La Petite Ferme, the Greenwich Village restaurant, prepared the chicken with dill according to Mr. Rauschenberg's own recipe. Eventually it arrived with carrots in butter. By the time the fruit and cheeses were passed, there were no more paper plates or silver.

"It's great," said Robert Scull, the taxi tycoon, reaching across Mrs. Scull for the bread. "Just think of it as a picnic al fresco."

The Marquis Bernard-Alexis Poisson de Ménars, Chancellor of the Order of the Grand Occident, thought it was marvelous, too.

"I haven't had fruit in a basket since I left France," he said, helping himself to seven grapes, four strawberries and a banana.

Brief speeches, mostly inaudible tributes to art, the artists, the fund-raisers and the friendship between Sweden and the United States, were delivered on all three floors. Outside the chapel, one exchange turned into something of a debate.

"Women are just as responsible for this collection as men," Jill Johnston shouted during one speech. "Larry Poons drew his elipses and his wife painted them in and Patty Oldenburg [the former Mrs. Claes Oldenburg] sewed every stitch of those soft typewriters and things herself."

Miss Johnston, the self-styled "lesbian nationalist" who rarely goes anywhere these days without a purple and white "Dyke" button pinned to her United States Marine Corps jacket, was rewarded with applause, mostly from the women.

Back in the chapel, Billy Kluver, an E.A.T. impresario, was busily presenting the Princess with what he called a medal, and she dropped it. Shortly thereafter, Miss Ellen Johnson, an art historian from Oberlin, read Mrs. Lichtenstein's palm. By this time, it was nearly midnight. Most guests didn't stay for coffee.

NOVEMBER 2, 1972

Burden Plays Host to a Fund-Raising 'Bash for Bella'

By JUDY KLEMESRUD

Although Carter Burden didn't really like the name of the party, he was the host last night of what was billed as a 'Carter Burden Bash for Bella" in his palatial duplex apartment overlooking the East River.

"I may bash somebody before the night is over," the 31-year-old City Councilman said, after hearing how press releases from Citizens for Bella (Abzug) headquarters had described the fund-raising event.

After all, the millionaire politician had already banned photographers, perhaps recalling pre-political days when he had a "silly rich boy" image after pictures of him and his former wife, Amanda, were published in the glossy fashion magazines, showing them amidst their River House (435 East 52d Street) splendor.

But like most politicians, he soon regained his composure, and went about the business of raising money for the campaign chest of his "friend and ally," Congresswoman Bella Abzug.

It was a somewhat different party as fund-raisers go. The guest list was limited to 100. The tab was $50 per head. The guests had been promised a peek at Mr. Burden's "stunning showplace on East 52d Street," but then found they were restricted to the first floor. (Larry Bilello, an aide of Mr. Burden's, made sure they didn't make their way up the curving staircase.)

But there was plenty on the first floor to satisfy all those partygoers who might have come to see how the other half decorates—or at least what a $250,000 decorating job can buy. For starters, there was a cabinet full of colorful glass bells, a collection of tin soldiers, a room full of camel and monkey statues, and modern art by the likes of de Kooning, Stella, Rothko and Warhol.

"Oh, I just saw one of my old Jasper Johns in the other room," said Mrs. Robert Scull, wife of the taxicab tycoon and pop art collector, as she inspected the premises. "We sold it at an auction a few years ago."

At around 7 P.M., Mr. Burden, looking lean as a cowboy in a brown velvet blazer, very faded blue jeans and brown moccasins, climbed up to the fourth step of the curving staircase, directly under a glittering crystal chandelier, and introduced Congresswoman Abzug, who was in burgundy.

"I like to call my style vigor," she said, to a chorus of adoring laughs. "Others call it style, but whatever it is, it's out of place here in all of this majesty."

"That's not what I'd call it, Bella," Mr Burden interjected, smiling but puffing intently on his pipe.

Earlier, when asked whether she thought the guests had paid $50 each to see her or the Burden duplex, Mrs. Abzug laughed and replied:

"I had a big event at Katz's delicatessen on the Lower East Side, and people came for that, too. Last Friday, I had a $3 event and on Saturday I had a $5 event. Upcoming is a $12 event. I have events for every price range."

And then it was Assemblyman Albert Blumenthal's turn on the staircase—to do some fund-raising. But first he chided Mr. Burden on his WASPy pronunciation of the word, "chutzpah," in introducing Mrs. Abzug.

"If you're going to be ethnic, Carter," the Assemblyman said, "you've got to learn to clear your throat as you say that word."

Mr. Blumenthal raised almost $5,000 in auctioneer style for Mrs. Abzug, who by this time had left to attend four other campaign events.

"I'll give $50 if Rex Reed matches it with $50," shouted Gloria Steinem, the feminist leader. "Where is he?"

"In the bar," someone answered.

"Actually, he earns more than I do so he should give more," Miss Steinem added.

Mr. Reed appeared out of the smoky recesses of the bar, and scribbled out a check for $100.

"I hope this means that I'm never accused of being a male chauvinist," the entertainment writer commented.

Other guests at the party included Mayor Lindsay, Marlo Thomas, the actress; Jerome Kretchmer, the city's Environmental Commissioner; Joe Bologna and his wife, Renee Taylor, the actors; Paul Simon, the singer, and Alan King, the comedian.

"I saw George McGovern today," said Ruth Gordon, the actress, after the speeches were over. "I was right up close to him in a parade, and I said 'Hurray' and then I burst into tears. Maybe I'm too emotional for politics."

Toward the end of the party, several guests were complaining about not being allowed to climb the curving staircase lined with charcoal drawings, many of them nudes.

"My wife and children are still in the process of moving out," Mr. Burden explained, "and there are a lot of packing boxes up there. Besides, I don't want people in my bedroom."

Then why open up his apartment for a fund-raising party?

"Because if you're gonna try to raise money," he replied, "you need Paul Newman or Robert Redford or Barbra Streisand or an apartment. I guess I have an apartment."

Or at least, a first floor.

NOVEMBER 21, 1972

Fireman's Ball: At First It Was Considered Just a Little Party

By BERNADINE MORRIS

Everybody was asked to wear red, black or white to the Fireman's Ball, a quiet little fund-raising party at the Museum of the City of New York. So guess what happened? Most everybody seemed to have a quiet little fireman red dress hanging in her closet, or managed to acquire one.

Mrs. John V. Lindsay's version had a red satin shirt top and a beaded skirt, and it had been hanging for four or five years. "It's been black every night for me for a week, and I couldn't face it again," Mary Lindsay said. Her husband stuffed a red bandana in his dinner jacket pocket to keep the faith.

Mrs. Lawrence Copley Thaw and Mrs. Alfred Bloomingdale chose red gazar dresses by Christian Dior. Mrs. Edwin Hilson's cape-collared red dress was by Givenchy, and Basha Szymanska, the fashion model who arrived with her fiancé, Lue Rudin, wore a slithery shirtwaist dress that she had picked up at Holly's Harp in Beverly Hills.

Stays With Norell

There were some exceptions, of course.

Mrs. Charles Revson, who owns at least one sizzling red sequin dress by Norman Norell, turned up in a simple little black wool—by Norell. And Mrs. Robert Scull wore an unadorned white knitted dress by Adolfo while her husband was resplendent in a red ruffled shirt under his dinner jacket. "I buy my shirts in Times Square shops now," he said.

But everyone made an effort, said Mrs. Bennett Cerf, one of the organizers of the party. She wore a fireman red dress made in India by Saz (her escort, former Mayor Robert F. Wagner, had a fireman hat in a paper bag that he threatened to put on "later").

Mrs. Cerf's co-chairman, Mrs. Charlotte Ford, settled the clothing situation easily. She simply kept on the white Mollie Parnis dress she wore in the fashion show early in the evening.

"This saves me the problem of making a decision," she explained. Not all of the volunteer fashion mannequins took the easy way out. Mrs. Thomas Kempner exchanged the striped bathrobe dress by Chuck Howard that she modeled for a one-shoulder black jersey by Mme. Grès.

From the Fifties

Maizie Cox, whose brother is married to the former Tricia Nixon, exchanged her Chester Weinberg pants suit for a red and black dress that belonged to her mother.

"It really fits as if it were made for me," said the tall, blond Miss Cox. "But it's very old. It's from the 1950's."

The party, which was conceived as an intimate affair, the kind you would give in your own home if your home was a mansion, was subscribed to quickly. The organizers simply told their friends.

"We were sold out before we even started," said Mrs. David Evins, another co-chairman whose special province was selecting the food: clear mushroom soup, chicken pot pies, popovers, vanilla ice cream and brownies.

"My idea was to do something American for a change," Mrs. Evins said. "And to operate without any kitchen space, we had to have something prepared ahead."

The party was also billed as "A Century of New York Fashion," with the museum providing some styles from its costume collection, going back to 1872, to carry it out. But most of the volunteer mannequins were wearing contemporary clothes made of Qiana, a synthetic material put out by DuPont, because the company had underwritten the evening.

Hot Dogs and Chili

There were other contributions too.

"Frank Sinatra gave us the hot dogs—he owns stock in the company that owns Nathan's. And he got us the Michelob beer, too," Mrs. Cerf said. "P. J. Clarke's gave us the chili."

These refinements were for the Fireman's Picnic, an adjunct to the ball, held for 150 younger members of the museum and their guests, who paid $25 a couple for the evening. The tariff for the ball proper was $100.

Not all the mannequin-patrons were wildly enthusiastic about the dresses assigned to them.

"I don't think it does anything special for me," said Mrs. Gardner Cowles of the printed button-front dress by Jerry Silverman she had on. "But then, it doesn't hurt either," she added.

"It's not the real me," observed Mary Sykes Cahan of the Teal Traina printed shirtdress she had on. "But it's for a good cause."

When complimented on her off-white dress, Barbara Walters said smugly, "The designer made it for me."

When she told the designer, Kasper, that she always worries about what to do with her hands, he said he'd make a cape for her. So the television personality looked quite composed and regal as she swept down the museum's marble staircase in her new role as fashion model.

Since it was a little family party and everybody knew each other, the mannequins all got a big hand from their 220 friends sitting on little gold chairs in front of the staircase. They were the ball's regular subscribers. The younger members, who went to the picnic, weren't invited to the fashion show—there wasn't enough room.

Arlene Francis drew the biggest response as she sashayed down the stairs in her striped dress by Dominic Rompollo, waving to the audience in old movie star fashion, but most of the mannequins engaged in a bit of mugging.

After the show, everyone filed up the staircase to the second floor, where tables had been set with red cloths and candles.

The fire engines and fire-fighting equipment contributed almost as much to the festivities as the food and fashions. Joseph Veach Noble, the museum's director, said that the old engines are one of the most popular attractions at the museum. Henry Callahan of Saks Fifth Avenue, who took care of the decorations, agreed.

He moved some of the equipment upstairs, draped a lot of red felt around, and made the whole place look as if it were lighted by candles (it wasn't—the lighting was electrical).

"It's a charming place to have a party," said Mrs. Nathan Cummings, one of the models and one of the hostesses, "It's much nicer than being at the Hilton or the Americana and it gives you a feeling of our heritage."

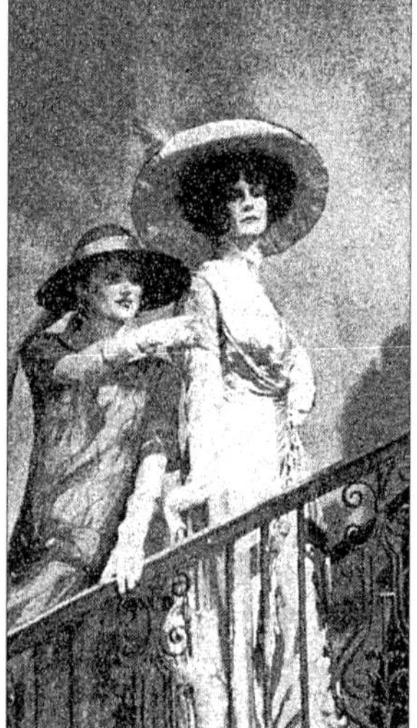

JANUARY 7, 1973

Art Notes

By GRACE GLUECK

NEW TURF

Emile de Antonio, the sprightly filmmaker who's brought you such partisan politico-documentaries as "Point of Order," "In the Year of the Pig," and "Millhouse" (about, respectively, the 1954 Army-McCarthy hearings; the Vietnam war and the rise of Richard Nixon) has shifted his lens to a slightly more neutral turf. His latest film (to be released next month by New Yorker Films) is "Painters Painting," a rambling, "highly personal" account of New York painters from 1940 to 1970. Its stellar, '60's-style cast includes Frank Stella, Willem de Kooning, Helen Frankenthaler, Jasper Johns, Robert Rauschenberg, Robert Motherwell, Barnett Newman, Clem Greenberg, Hilton Kramer, Andy Warhol, Henry Geldzahler, Leo Castelli and *(naturellement)*, the Sculls.

"D," a paunchy, wickedly cherubic (or is it cherubically wicked?)-looking fellow of 52, says his change in subject matter is simply an expression of his long-time interest in art, going back to the mid-1950's when he met John Cage, Rauschenberg and Johns. "My life has been political," notes "D," who, since Harvard in the 1930's, has been as flaming a radical as ever donned a dinner jacket. "Painting is apolitical. I wanted to make a personal film—my reaction to what I thought was the most interesting and important period in American art history. The film isn't democratic, but a matter of personal choice. I picked the painters I most admired, and left out some important people."

The film, with its spotty coverage, loose editing and deliberately structureless organization, is not the season's most rounded experience. But it has its moments: Frank Stella hinting at a Beckett influence on his early painting; Hilton Kramer putting down Ab Ex and Clem Greenberg doing ditto to Pop; Ethel Scull relating How Andy Did Her Portrait in the Photo Booth; Jasper Johns, recounting the famous story of his bronze beer cans ("I'd heard that de Kooning said Castelli could sell even two beer cans . . . so I did it, and he sold it"); Bob Scull recalling his desire to scoop up a whole Johns show ("No, no," protested dealer Castelli. "That's very vulgar.") And then there's Castelli himself, painstakingly examining the accusation that dealers are shaping the art market. "We're simply doing our job. And if critics and museums go along with us, then it's a consensus."

For de Antonio, who dismisses "conceptual art and earthworks," his movie is a monument to the end of three exciting decades. "It's fallen off now," he says. "The pushy urgency is gone, the fantastic hoofbeats, one after another. After Stella and Poons, who is there?"

OLD TURF

It's that pulse-feeling moment again for the good gray Whitney Museum, the time of its annual look at the state of American art. Only this time it's staging a biennial show, encompassing both sculpture and painting (the annuals, you remember, alternated between the two). Filling the entire museum with works by 221 artists, the Biennial will open in three floor-by-floor stages, starting Wednesday, then on Jan. 17 and Jan. 25.

By combining the media, points out Whitney director John I. H. Baur, a fuller survey is possible. What's more, since much art no longer lends itself to categorization, a work does not have to be labelled "painting" or "sculpture." One other advantage of a combiennial, points out Baur: "You only get clobbered every other year."

And the Whitney has been clobbered, you'll recall —not only esthetically, but from blacks and from women demanding equal time. The Whitney is cagey about revealing this year's numbers, but a fast rundown of exhibitors' names seems to indicate 55 women, a bit less than 25 per cent (last survey was 22 per cent; the times before that ran between 5½ and 10). Twenty-two of the women—nearly half — are first-time exhibitors.

No one has ever accused the Whitney of non-eclecticism. Exhibitors' names range from Louise Nevelson and Adolph Gottlieb to first-timers Andy Tavarelli and Arlene Slavin. And the work? That runs from—well, egg tempera on canvas to multi-media things that go bump in the night.

As of this writing, no demonstrations are planned.

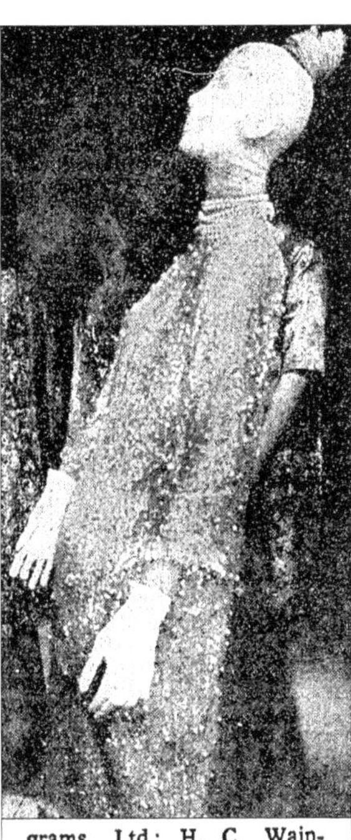

JANUARY 28, 1973

The Boom in Art for Corporate Use

Specialists In Choosing Works Are Multiplying

By MARYLIN BENDER

A partner in a law firm that recently moved to a new Wall Street skyscraper explained the appearance of colorful geometric and neo-realist lithographs on the office walls.

"We wanted to get away from decorating with portraits of other people's ancestors and pretentious reference to aristocratic blood sports that few lawyers ever practice," he said. The lawyer had served on a partners' committee that retained the Museum of Modern Art to make its art purchases.

He was alluding, of course, to those staples of American office art—the pompous portrait, the English hunting print and, though he omitted it, the soothing harbor scene.

They have been receding from view as business and its supportive professions move into the millions of square feet of new office space that cry for contemporary embellishment. This continuous corporate resettling is producing a new species of business activity. Enter the corporate art buyer.

Until recently, this undeveloped and unlicensed field had been staked out by free-lancing art critics and curators; housewives working out of their homes and reviving their college art history notes; a few dealers, and one conspicuous offshoot of a public relations firm, Ruder & Finn Fine Arts.

More formalized business entities are emerging on the landscape such as The Art Finder, which has handsome offices at 919 Third Avenue and a growing roster of clients such as Colt Industries, Inc.; Dun & Bradstreet, Inc., and the Wall Street law firm of Dewey, Ballantine, Bushby, Palmer & Wood.

Now the Museum of Modern Art is striding into the picture with its Art Advisory Service, geared to "the corporate environment." It has already enlisted clients like Distillers Corporation-Seagrams, Ltd.; H. C. Wainwright &. Co., and the New York law firm of Cleary, Gottlieb, Steen & Hamilton. The service will seek additional accounts through advertisements that are scheduled for March in business publications.

The proceeds of the service will be plowed back into support of the nonprofit museum, which has suffered balance-sheet blues despite the presence of such financial eminences on its board as William S. Paley, chairman of the Columbia Broadcasting System, Inc., and assorted Rockefellers, Whitneys and Burdens.

MOMA's service strikes some corporate art buyers as unfair competition because of its "noncommercial," public-service billing, which will undoubtedly attract businessmen who are uncertain about art ventures.

"It should help dispel the worries corporations have about buying art," said Mrs. John R. Jakobson, president of MOMA's Junior Council, which is the co-sponsor of the service.

Even if their public relations and industrial relations advisers have recommended it for image and employ morale, businessmen are nervous about buying art for their corporations in large measure because of their own inexpertise as well as their doubts about stockholder reaction.

Not all purchases have happy endings. The Security National Bank spent $29,000 on geometric and constructivist graphics by Vasarely, Gottlieb and Ives for its headquarters in Melville, L.I. As a result of adverse criticism "from inside and outside the bank," the pictures were taken down after their publicized display and dispersed where it is hoped they will not be noticed.

The matter of art as corporate investment is an edgy one for American businessmen. Unlike their Japanese counterparts, who justify their expensive foreign art purchases both as prestige and investment, Americans hesitate to talk of possible investment appreciation.

The Chase Manhattan Bank, whose decade-long program of buying art for its expanding worldwide facilities has been a seminal influence on other corporations here and abroad, values its collection "conservatively" at $2.9-million.

No effort is made to broadcast the fact that a little more than $1.5-million had been paid for the 2,200 works in the collection. The purchases are treated as a capital expense.

Pepsico, Inc., has one of the more ambitious, newer art programs in the modern sculpture park surrounding its headquarters in Purchase, N. Y. The company, which has opened the display to the public, does not disclose a value for its acquisitions. The company's holding includes such titans of modern art as Henry Moore, Alexander Calder and David Smith (a speculator's favorite among deceased, abstract expressionists).

Pepsico has just entered the elite circle of corporate commissioners of art by commissioning a work by Isamu Noguchi. Others in this group include Chase Manhattan, with its Dubuffet sculpture "Group of Four Trees" for its headquarters plaza in New York's financial district, and Philip Morris, Inc., which had Willi Gutmann, the Swiss sculptor, provide a work for its plant in Richmond.

Ruder & Finn Fine Arts, which has Philip Morris as a client, takes the emphatic position that art should not be bought as an investment.

Judith Horowitz and Ellen Schwarzman, who run The Art Finder, said, "Our clients won't just buy for investment." They added, however, "Everything we've sold has doubled or tripled."

"Red Lanikai," an etching by Gabor Peterdi, a Connecticut artist whose diversified abstract style makes him acceptable to businessmen with conservative art leanings, has been sold 25 times through The Art Finder. A year and a half ago, the price was $170; now it is $300.

MOMA's Art Advisory Service "won't base its advice on whether a work is a good investment," Mrs. Jakobson said. "But if asked, we'll say yes if we feel it is."

Unsigned posters in unlimited editions stretch a tight budget, but they are not likely to increase in value, Mrs. Jakobson said. With the "difficult" and "daring" art that the museum hopes to educate business to buy, "there is always a gap between purchase and appreciation until people come to understand it," she said.

Although an impressively limited number of American businessmen from the Chase's David Rockefeller to Robert Scull, the New York taxi fleet owner, have been patrons of avant-garde art, the more typical corporate executive runs true to tradition.

If the nation's new offices seem to be hung with abstractions, however, it's largely because they go much further on acres of blank wall space and limited funds than the more reassuring but costly older masters. The increasing popularity of tapestries can also be attributed to price as well as aesthetics.

Corporate art-buying consultants find themselves acting as educators of taste and economic reality so that the businessman who naively expects a representational oil, comes to accept an abstract lithograph or etching. He will not be permitted a reproduction, say of a comforting Rembrandt burgher, because reproductions are considered "wallpaper" lacking the intrinsic value of original work that graphics are held to be.

One of the best alternatives for traditionalist executives who can't afford what they like, said Renata Schurch of Ruder & Finn Fine Arts, is a "3,000-year-old primitive. They can associate with that though it may take a few weeks for them to get adjusted."

So it is that there are oases of pre-Columbian art in the 15 floors of offices of the J. C. Penney Company in New York. The dining room of the chairman, William M. Batten, is one of these oases.

When the Bristol-Myers Company requested traditional works, Ruder & Finn arranged for the rental of 19th-century American oils from the Brooklyn Museum of Art.

Under the Whitney Museum's corporate membership program, a company may borrow one work a year for every $1,000 it contributes.

There are two schools of thought about tying the subject matter of the art to the corporate product. Barbara Jakobson of MOMA disapproves. Richard L. Feigen, an art dealer, tries to foster such links.

Mr. Feigen sold a 17th-century still life by Il Maltese to the Venture Carpet Company of Atlanta for its boardroom. The painting depicts a rug draped over a table.

He also arranged for the Viviane Woodard Corporation, a cosmetics company that is now a division of the General Foods Corporation, to buy Renoir's "Woman Arranging Her Hair" for $400,000 in 1970. The company subsequently acquired a Bonnard, a Redon and a Bouguereau "to be used to enhance the appreciation of beauty in women, a goal that Viviane Woodard Cosmetics also seeks to achieve," the announcement said.

Corporate art buyers operate in different ways. The Art Finder receives a 40 per cent dealers' commission from art galleries. Their clients pay the retail price.

Framing is extra, which must be "made crystal clear," Miss Horowitz said, since some businessmen might be dismayed by a $100 charge for framing a $200 print.

The Art Finder also carries an inventory of works owned or held on consignment.

MOMA takes a 15 per cent commission from galleries and 25 per cent from independent artists. There is no charge for initial consultation or for time spent at the museum looking at slides. The time of a curator in the field evaluating a collection or supervising installation is charged at the rate of $50 an hour.

Ruder & Finn Fine Arts charges an hourly rate of $50 to $90 for various staff services and generally recommends a minimum purchase of $3,000 a floor.

Corporations approach art buying in various ways — from the convictions of the chief executive officer to the recommendations of architects or interior decorators.

The Chase Manhattan collection has been guided by the advice of a committee of museum curators and is administered by a curator, a director with vice presidential status, a part-time assistant curator and a registrar.

Some companies delegate art responsibility to a vice president in charge of real estate or to a committee of executives.

Corporate wives seldom interfere, noted Judith Horowitz "because if the president has a wife who wants to interfere, we wouldn't be brought in at all.

"But if you're in good with the executive secretary of the president, you've got it made."

FEBRUARY 4, 1973

Two Painful Years Later, a Hostess Returns to Her 'Real People'

By ENID NEMY

Robert Scull, who was wearing a purple and black cowboy-type shirt under his black and white tweed-mix beard, said he was a guest, just like everyone else.

"It's my wife's party," said the taxi mogul and art collector, standing beneath James Rosenquist's ceiling art of a house plan. "It's wonderful to see these rooms full of people again."

The event last Sunday, described as a party by Mr. Scull, a brunch by Mrs. Scull and a salon by some of the guests, marked the hostess's first venture in entertaining since she injured her back in a fall on a Barbados beach more than two years ago.

"I'm so desperate to come back to a life of usefulness," said Mrs. Scull, who was upright when the first guests arrived but retreated into a prone position on her bed at intervals throughout the afternoon.

"It's like Madame Recamier," she said, stretched out on the printed Porthault coverlet, extending a welcoming hand to the men and women who were ambling in and out of the room.

Mrs. Scull, who put on a black and white Adolfo caftan for the occasion, characterized her guests as "real," as opposed to "those other people."

"I'm so tired of that damn phony social scene with the same tired faces," she said. "I'm going to try to do this once a month or so, so there will be a place where artists, writers, actors, playwrights, poets and filmmakers can get together to exchange ideas and conversation. These are the kind of people I like . . . they have not been overexposed and they are highly intelligent."

Mr. Scull explained that his wife had little patience "for people who are famous for obscure reasons."

A lot of the people who accepted the turquoise and lime green invitation cards—a group that included Henry Geldzahler, curator of contemporary art at the Metropolitan Museum of Art; Dotson Rader, an author who is working on a new book on the end of the peace movement; Betty Friedan, the feminist; Lucas Samaras, who recently had a one-man show at the Whitney; George Segal, the sculptor, and Kevin McCarthy, the actor—were indeed famous, and for some very tangible reasons.

There was, for instance, Thomas P. F. Hoving, the embattled head of the Metropolitan Museum of Art, who managed to keep a smile on his face the whole time, despite the studied subtleties of both those who addressed him and those who didn't.

"You wonder whether he's going to survive," mused Robert Kenmore, the founder and former head of the Kenton Corporation, the conglomerate that owns Cartier, Valentino and Georg Jensen, to name but a few of its businesses.

Most everyone thought he would.

There was, too, Lucy Jarvis, the television producer, who was fuming, very politely, at a critic's comparison of her documentary on China with the one made by Antonioni.

•

Everyone around made soothing noises and Mrs. Jarvis was asked where she was off to next, now that she had filmed the Kremlin, the Louvre and the Forbidden City.

"I'm off to a new apartment," she said. "I'm moving because I need more room. I bought everything that wasn't nailed down in China. I'm loaded down with antiques."

Mrs. Scull said she was quite happy with her apartment because there was a lot of space in which to talk. The large white-walled rooms contain a minimum of furniture and a maximum of art.

"I really have to laugh now that all the decorators are saying get rid of everything, clean everything out," she said. "I've done that for years."

Joseph E. Levine, the movie producer, made his way past an Andrejevic painting of Mr. Scull as Father Time, a Jasper Johns sculpture of beer cans and an Andy Warhol painting of a Campbell soup can. He looked out the window at the main entrance of the Metropolitan Museum.

"There's a guy out there selling paintings," he announced. "Do you suppose he bought them from Hoving?"

Mr. Hoving was in another room so there was some laughter and more smiles.

Mrs. Levine, weighted down with Elsa Peretti's necklace, bracelet, ring and belt, chatted with Mrs. Scull. Mr. Levine said that, on occasion, he didn't care what his wife bought or what the prices were.

"When I've had a hit, I never look at the size of the checks I sign for my wife," he said.

Luis Estevez, the Los Angeles based designer, and Henry Callahan, a vice president of Saks Fifth Avenue, joined a group who had carried their buffet lunch of chicken and mushroom crepe, cold salmon mousse and salad into the den.

"I first met Ethel [Mrs. Scull] at the Museum of the City of New York and I was completely enchanted with her simplicity," Mr. Callahan recalled. "I'm fascinated with people in the commercial world who had the good sense to become patrons of art, who were among those who motivated this whole kind of art."

The Sculls were among the early admirers, supporters and collectors of such artists as Andy Warhol, Robert Rauschenberg, Larry Rivers, George Segal, Lucas Samaras, Larry Poons, Peter Young, Frank Stella and James Rosenquist.

Mrs. David Gibbs said that personally she was an admirer of Mrs. Scull's ramrod-like posture.

"I used to be as tall as she," said Mrs. Gibbs, who is known as Geraldine Stutz when she is at work as head of Henri Bendel. "Now she stands so erect, I'm several inches shorter."

She recalled that at one time she, too, had had marvelous posture.

"I went to convent schools and they made you wear those webbing braces. If you slouched, the sisters would make you tighten the belt . . . the minute I got out of school, I took off that brace and down went my shoulders."

Also among the guests were Rex Reed, the writer; Mrs. Isaac Stern, whose husband was in Paris; Mrs. William Cahan of the Metropolitan Museum's public affairs department, and Mrs. Drena Van Alen, who is currently working on a fund-raising project for the Bide-a-Wee Home Association.

•

The project involves Norman Rockwell-designed collectors plates, but Mrs. Van Alen still thinks fondly of an earlier money-raising idea she had that never got off the ground.

"I wanted to do an auction on television," she said. "I had a lot of nice gifts promised, including 1 per cent of the royalties of a Texas oil well. The man in Texas phoned me and said 'We'll surely be pleased to do it, ma'am, we're just looking around for the right oil well for you.' I wanted to do it for City Center, but it fell through."

The oil well is, apparently, still waiting.

FEBRUARY 7, 1973

Elegance on the Runway—and Off

By BERNADINE MORRIS

It was a throwback to a more gracious era. Pretty clothes on the runway (Arnold Scaasi's spring made-to-order collection). Pleasant lunch (chicken crepes and popovers, with blue, white and yellow chrysanthemums centered on the yellow table linen). And more than 400 casually but carefully dressed women to enjoy it all for $20 a ticket.

They all came together at the Hotel Plaza yesterday in a good cause—to support the thrift shop run by The Society of Memorial Sloan-Kettering Cancer Center. The luncheon wasn't all frivolity. There were hang tags on the table for the women to attach to their future contributions to the thrift shop and envelopes for checks or cash. And Mrs. Laurance Rockefeller made a plea for contributions of paintings to decorate the rooms and corridors of the center's new 15-floor hospital building, which is scheduled to open in May.

Even when they wore sweaters, the guests' clothes had pedigree. Mrs. Stanley Weintraub's black pullover was Ungaro's, Mrs. Robert Scull's chtcked and striped ones were by Adolfo and Mrs. Donald Chipman's peach twin set was by Bill Blass.

Favors Pants

Jo Copeland, the fashion designer, wore pants ("I fought this pants thing, but I've gotten to the point where I never wear a dress"), Mrs. Jane C. Murchison wore an understated red Norell, and Mrs. John A. Morris, who used to favor Mainbocher, said, "And now you see me done up in Scaasi."

At least 23 women wore something classic by Halston, including Mrs. Irving Koerner, who topped her black Halston pants outfit with one of the designer's ultra-suède coats.

Mrs. Koerner, one of the charity's patrons, didn't mind exchanging her pants for the striped sheer dress she wore on the runway. She was one of the volunteers who modeled some of the clothes to the applause of her friends.

Mrs. Walter B. Delafield, president of the society, was a big hit in her red sequin shirt dress and Mrs. Kerryn King scored with her navy skirt and ruffled white blouse. She was a little troubled before the show when she couldn't find the blouse.

Several women—Mrs. Martin Revson, Mrs. Locke McLean and Mrs. J. Frederic Byers 3d among them—modeled below-calf length outfits that Scaasi called "peasant length." They all said they felt fine.

Mr. Scaasi, who got his collection ready a month earlier than usual, was pleased with it because the clothes looked soft and cheerful. The women thought so, too. Mrs. King, who found her blouse, was so charmed with her outfit she bought it.

FEBRUARY 8, 1973

FASHION TALK

Givenchy: Classics Continued

By BERNADINE MORRIS

The classicists have the upper hand today in fashion. It's the time for pleated skirts, shirtdresses, sweaters and maybe a bit of frou-frou at night. Saint Laurent, Halston, Givenchy—the most influential designers—are all on the same wave length.

Yesterday it was Givenchy's turn to shine. A couple of hundred of the French designer's fans turned out to see his spring ready-to-wear collection introduced at Bergdorf Goodman. They overflowed the Nouvelle Boutique, which is devoted to Givenchy's clothes, spilled into the Halston room nearby and even filled the neighboring fur department.

Initials Everywhere

The rooms were dotted with Givenchy enthusiasts, including Mrs. John Barry Ryan, who described herself as "a terrific fan" and pointed out that her gray flannel dress with the pleated skirt was from an earlier Givenchy collection. Mrs. Edwin I. Hilson's black coat with the blue band near the hem was also a Givenchy—from Ohrbach's.

Tatiana Lieberman's black dress and jacket were by Saint Laurent, but then it isn't always easy to tell the classicists apart.

Givenchy tries to help by printing his initials all over things. The pattern on a short-sleeved white suit, for instance, is a series of little G's. And if you observe carefully the chain design on a long shirtdress, you can see that all the links are G's.

Fake Ivory

Nothing really escapes the visible identification. Even a swimsuit proclaims its creator in the trompe l'oeil belt knitted in at the waistline. The simulated buckle: two G's, hooked together.

In case your friends won't recognize the signals, there's a sure-fire way of making known your addiction. There's a fake ivory bracelet for $25 with the designer's name spelled out on it in fake gold letters. Now, Halston started the ivory bangle bit, though he didn't get around to putting his name on it.

Ethel Scull was a step ahead of the designers. The lettering on the navy sweater she wore over her white shirt spelled her own name. "Why should I wear somebody else's?" she asked.

Classic Necessities

The collection covers a woman's fashion needs from beach to ballroom, starting with a couple of swimsuits that are equipped with matching skirts, and ending with ruffled delicacies to wear at night after a hard day at the pool.

In between are all the classic necessities such as trench coats, pants suits and shirtwaist dresses. There isn't a bit of frou-frou on these, if you don't count the contrasting stitching.

Women apparently don't want the frou-frou. In the selling after the show, they aimed straight for the skinny red coat (narrow, but not fitted), the navy pants suit decorated only with a sea gull design and the navy swimsuit with the trompe l'oeil G's. For evening, a long pleated skirt with an off-the-shoulder sweater vied with a ruffled halter neck dress for best selling honors.

Close to Couture

Prices go from $45 for the swimsuits to $780 for the evening clothes.

"It's the closest the ready-to-wear has ever come to Givenchy's couture collection," said Elieth Roux, director of the Givenchy boutique at Bergdorf's. Which shows just how prevalent the classics are today.

The accessories, down to the stripping sandals, were all by Givenchy. Besides his name bracelets, there were necklaces of big, colorful beads (worn with the swimsuits as well as the dresses), a lot of clear, crystal-looking jewelry and of course signed scarves.

MARCH 20, 1973

'Painters Painting' Explores the Art Scene Here

PAINTERS PAINTING, a documentary feature produced and directed by Emile de Antonio; sound and editing, Mary Lampson; camera, Ed Emshwiller; distributed by New Yorker Films. Running time: 116 minutes. At the Fifth Avenue Cinema, Fifth Avenue at 12th Street.

With: Willem de Kooning, Helen Frankenthaler, Hans Hoffman, Jasper Johns, Robert Motherwell, Barnett Newman, Kenneth Noland, Jules Olitski, Philip Pavia, Larry Poons, Robert Rauschenberg, Frank Stella, Andy Warhol, Leo Castelli, Henry Geldzahler, Clement Greenberg, Tom Hess, Philip Johnson, Hilton Kramer, William Rubin, Robert Scull, among others.

By VINCENT CANBY

In the past, Emile de Antonio has made some fine documentaries, including "Point of Order" and "Millhouse," each a scathing, highly biased attack against someone or something. His newest film, "Painters Painting," represents a change of mood. It's a great big, cheerfully uncritical hug of a movie about a subject he adores, the contemporary New York art scene and the people who make it hustle.

Watching it is like being at a cocktail party. Robert Rauschenberg is there. Andy Warhol is there (with Brigit Berlin taking Polaroid snaps of him). Jasper Johns is there. As are Barnett Newman and Henry Geldzahler and Kenneth Noland and Frank Stella and Larry Poons. Robert Scull and Ethel are there, looking pleased and modest and just slightly uncomfortable, as if waiting for the next attack by the philistines who refer to him as the taxi tycoon when he is really the Lorenzo di Medici of pop.

•

The movie is mistitled. It should be called "Painters Talking." Although we do see Larry Poons ripping a large color-filled canvas off his studio floor, and although we see old still pictures of the late Jackson Pollock at work, most of the movie is devoted to the painters talking about themselves and their work.

A few make sense: Jasper Johns, Willem de Kooning, Andy Warhol (at least, he smiles a lot and looks genuinely modest). At one place or another, some basic points are made about the various trends in American art that followed abstract expressionism. Much of it, however, is cocktail party conversation. Says Barnett Newman: "Esthetics are for me what ornithology is for birds."

Mr. Rauschenberg says that to be an abstract expressionist one had to have time to feel sorry for oneself. He doesn't and didn't. Mr. Stella says that the kind of contemporary painting he represents is designed, among other things, to keep the viewer from "reading" the painting, and to make it difficult for critics to describe and thus difficult to carry out their function.

A lot of "Painters Painting" is funny (intentionally), some of it is boring (unintentionally) and a great deal of it is somewhat less informative than is absolutely necessary. Hilton Kramer, art editor of The New York Times, is given rather short shrift when he tries to trace the European roots of American abstract expressionism. In the festive context of the rest of the film, his attempt amounts to a social mistake.

I would assume that Mr. de Antonio has some opinions (not entirely favorable) about the parts played in the New York scene by various art dealers and curators. You wouldn't know it from "Painters Painting." It all looks like a warm, lovable rat race, even though one in which the stakes can be tremendous. Leo Castelli, the dealer, smiles benignly as he tells of the Jasper Johns that was bought for $2,000 and could be sold today for $200,000.

Mr. de Antonio has been an observer of the scene for years, and is obviously as fond of the artists as he is fascinated by their work, which has been beautifully photographed in color and black and white by Ed Emshwiller, who is a first-class film maker in his own right.

"Painters Painting," which opened yesterday at the Fifth Avenue Cinema, looks great. Like so much contemporary painting, however, it involves too much talk.

MARCH 23, 1973

The Era of Balenciaga: It Seems So Long Ago

By BERNADINE MORRIS

"It's so inspiring," said Halston. "It's the height of elegance. It's the most important statement of the century."

"It's like seeing old friends," said Mollie Parnis. "Everybody was influenced by him, but I'm not sure it's where we're going today."

"Most of it looks out of date," said Calvin Klein.

They were among the members of the fashion industry attending a preview of "The World of Balenciaga" at the Metropolitan Museum of Art Wednesday night. The exhibit, honoring the Spanish designer who brought the Paris couture to its apogee during the nineteen-fifties and the early nineteen-sixties, opens to the public today.

Everyone was awe-struck at the power, technique and taste of the designer whose clothes followed Dior's Edwardian "New Look" in worldwide influence. Not everyone was convinced the clothes were meaningful today.

Brown Lace Dress

The exhibit was assembled by Diana Vreeland, former fashion editor of Harper's Bazaar and for nine years editor in chief of Vogue magazine. She is now consultant to the museum's Costume Institute.

"Where have all the Balenciagas gone?" she lamented a few days before the show opened. She deplored the fact that such epochal designs as Balenciaga's brown lace dress of 1951 apparently exists today only in memories or in the bound volumes of old fashion magazines. The dress, which bypassed the waistline, marked the dramatic turn from Dior's hourglass designs to the angular chemise.

Though the brown lace dress has vanished, Mrs. Vreeland assembled hundreds of styles from the wardrobes of elegant women all over the world, including her own.

Contributors include the Baroness Philippe de Rothschild, the Marquesa de Villaverde, Mrs. Paul Mellon, Mrs. Charlton Henry and Mrs. Gilbert Miller. Mrs. Charles Wrightsman and Mrs. Loel Guinness sent clothes. So did museums in Paris, Chicago and Zurich.

The show begins with a few conventional evening dresses from Balenciaga's first collection in 1938 and ends with the wedding dress he came out of retirement to make in 1972, just before he died. It was for the Duchess of Cadiz, General Franco's granddaughter.

The dresses are displayed on mannequins of porcelain or steel, and the walls are hung with paintings by Goya, Picasso and Velasquez to suggest Balenciaga's Spanish heritage. (Mrs. Gilbert Miller threatened to take back her Goya because nobody could see it.)

Their Own Shapes

There are beaded velvet jackets, such as bullfighters' costumes, grand-entrance ballgowns with hemlines dipping like flamenco dancers' costumes, loose and floating lace "baby doll" dresses and austere chemises.

"They belong in a museum, like good paintings," said Stan Herman, respectfully. The designer added that today he thought women wanted to show their own shapes rather than have a shape imposed on them. Chester Weinberg didn't think the clothes could be worn today, but he pointed out that Balenciaga "made women look royal."

"Some are contemporary, some outdated, but it doesn't matter," said Kasper. "They are all beautiful."

"I'd like to have that back so I could wear it right now," said Mollie Parnis, standing before the short beige lace dress she had contributed to the show.

Among the women who were wearing Balenciaga dresses, there was the same difference of opinion as among the designers. Mrs. Robert C. Scull said she felt silly in her long green taffeta gown with a low flounce, but Mrs. Jack Saunders was perfectly happy in her two-piece pailletted dress.

"You felt he made them for you alone," said Beth Levine, the shoe designer, who contributed a black chemise and found another to wear.

"I keep shedding a little, like a chicken," said Mrs. Herbert Louis, whose 1948 Balenciaga dress was strewn with feathers.

Mrs. William McCormick Blair Jr. was wearing an eight-year-old white satin coat over a 10-year-old beaded top dress and said she had a lot of other Balenciagas in her closets that she uses all the time.

Fashion's Genesis

"People would tell me fashion started in the streets, and I would say I always saw it first at Balenciaga," said Mrs. Vreeland, looking at a raincoat of 1962 that was shown with boots and patterned stockings.

"They were made for pretty rooms, filled with flowers and lit by candles," she went on, moving toward the evening dresses in her jeweled black caftan by Valentino.

Attitudes have changed and so have life-styles. The architectural shapes Balenciaga devised have given way to soft clothes that take their shape from the body. Women today are more interested in comfort and convenience than grandeur.

"The World of Balenciaga" is a tribute to the haute couture at the time when it influenced the spirit as well as the shape of clothes made everywhere. Balenciaga closed his house in 1968, when fashion, like other institutions, was splintering. It's a shock to realize it was only five years ago.

MARCH 25, 1973

Scull Applies His Artistic Flair to Fleet of 135 Cabs

By FRANK J. PRIAL

A decade ago, Robert Scull was Mr. Big in the Pop art world. With his wife, Ethel, he was the discoverer, sponsor and friend of some of the famous names of the period, some of whom became permanent fixtures in the art world—Andy Warhol, Jasper Johns, Claes Oldenberg and Robert Morris were just a few of the artists who became famous under the Sculls' patronage.

Mr. Scull was able to indulge his whims in the art world because he had made a lot of money in the taxi business. Now he is applying his flair for the unusual to his first interest, his taxi fleet.

He has equipped all 135 of his cars with two-way radios, the first fleet taxi owner in the city to do so, and he has given his cabs a name: Scull's Angels. The Scull's Angels emblem is on each of his cabs. It is in violet and black, the same colors as a cowboy shirt Mr. Scull wears in a favorite portrait he had painted of himself. He also wore the shirt at a press conference recently to announce his taxi plans.

Suit Is Successful

Last year Mr. Scull successfully sued the city to get the right to equip his taxis with two-way radios. The Taxi Commission chairman, Michael J. Lazar, had hoped to limit the use of radios to nonmedallion taxis, which are banned by law from cruising for passengers and from using taximeters. They are limited to trips and fees arranged in advance by telephone and relayed to the driver by radio.

But in attempting to restrict the use of radios to the nonmedallion segment of the industry, Mr. Lazar had to accept the fact that a large part of the city-licensed, metered yellow cabs also had radios. These are the owner-driver operated cabs. There are about 12,000 yellow, medallion cabs in the city. About 5,000 are operated by their owners and about 25 per cent of these cars are equipped with radios.

Mr. Scull's fleet of 135 cars is a small part of the industry, but spokesmen say it is only a matter of time before other fleets get radios too.

"Bob Scull did the industry a favor in bringing that suit," said Arthur Gore, a spokesman for the Metropolitan Taxicab Board of Trade, which represents the fleet owners. "None of the others had the dough last year to bring a suit like that."

Mr. Scull's fleet is made up entirely of Checker cabs, the ones with the two jump seats and the high roofs. "They are all 1973's except eight, which are being replaced," Mr. Scull said.

The Taxi Commission expressed the fear last year that radio-dispatching would cut down the number of cabs cruising and available. "If a driver doesn't want to pick someone up," a commission aide said at the time, "he can always say he's on a radio call."

Mr. Scull insists this is not the case. "If a man is on call," he said, "and sees someone waiting on a corner, he can use the radio to send another cab to make the pickup."

Mr. Scull also argued that fleet radio taxis were preferable to the owner-operated cabs because the fleet cabs were always available. "The owner-driver doesn't stay out at night," he said "but our men do. Our cabs are available around the clock."

APRIL 11, 1973

To Get to Italy, They Had to Travel Only as Far as 59th Street

By CHARLOTTE CURTIS

Italian home furnishings designers have been the innovators in recent years, so it wasn't really much of a surprise last night to find an Italian theme to Bloomingdale's new model rooms.

The chic of Rome's steel, glass and glitter, along with Milan's imaginative design, is where decorating seems to be going these days. It was an obvious choice for Richard Knapple, the store's new room designer.

The message apparently wasn't lost on the Italian diplomats (whose Government gave the store money for the promotion) or the decorators invited to the opening night benefit. But whether it registered on the assembled Texans and New Yorkers was another matter.

Some were regular shoppers (also known as "Bloomingdale people"), those superconsumers whose tastes have been shaped by countless days spent searching for that special something, which, when acquired, further confirms their Bloomingdale image.

For the others, particularly the rich Texans, the primary interest was the Friends of Venice. The organization, with a heavy leavening of Texans and New Yorkers, is dedicated to the preservation of Venetian culture. They were there, courtesy of Bloomingdale's, to raise some $25,000—not just from tickets that cost $50 a couple but from an auction as well.

For starters, aides in Italian Renaissance costumes greeted the nearly 1,000 guests, escorted them to the fifth-floor designer rooms and left them to a tarot-card reader, a band of Neapolitan musicians, trays of Italian hors d'oeuvres (created by none other than Armando Orsini of Orsini's) and five bars. And the guests did study the new rooms.

"I wouldn't miss them for anything," Mrs. Harold Reed said. "The rooms are always slick—not your top, top quality but the best look and cleverly done."

Mrs. Reed, a benefit chairman, said she and her art dealer-husband nearly divorced over Bloomingdale's. She has always been transfixed by the displays. He has wanted to move on. The agreement was that he would never, never go to the store with her on Saturdays. Her interest, she said, was especially in the accessories.

"You go to Rome and you see these marvelous terra cotta basins and you don't have to lug them home," she said. "After a trip, I always go to Bloomingdale's and it's all there. You know, everything from those Italian espadrilles to the leather handbags."

Terra cotta basins were not really the order of the day. Instead, most of the rooms were more sophisticated, even intellectual, and involved that new modular furniture, those new geometric lamps, those ever-popular Sardinian folk pieces, that lounging platform, the raft furniture and walls electrostatically flocked with velvety nylon, paneled with mirrors or purposely plastered with bits of straw to give a special texture.

New, yes, and an aesthetic experience for many more than the decorators and "the Bloomingdale people," but hardly everybody's cup of Soave. Most people loved the rooms, or said they did, but even Bloomingdale's had its critics.

"Really too extreme," said Mrs. Gabriele Lagerwall, the perennial partygoer, after bouncing up and down on a side display of modular red cube chairs and sofas. "Not my taste at all."

To another woman, the handsome orange modular lounging platform was "too cubistic." A man likened the charm of a turquoise, white and vermillion country sitting room to an "attic." And Mrs. Robert Scull, the art collector, thought most of the furniture was "a bit too much."

"C'mon, Andy," she cried, grabbing a newly arrived but reluctant Andy Warhol by the sleeve. "I want you to see the really démodé things first."

After an hour of drinking, nibbling and browsing, Marvin Traub, the store president, attempted to announce a fashion show. People went right on talking.

An Auction Follows

"We're missing some models," he shouted into a microphone. "We can't start 'til they get here."

"It will be all right," Princess Egon zu und von Furstenberg told him off stage.

"I don't know," Mr. Traub answered her. "I'd sooner try to organize the whole store than this."

Eventually, the models (including John L. Fairchield, a new Bloomingdale's employe and son of the John B. Fairchild of Women's Wear Daily) arrived, and the show, mostly slinky things for lounging around your better palazzos, began. Wyatt Cooper, the writer, found the whole thing entirely too much.

"When I went to the rehearsal," he said, "I discovered they were going to do 'Love in Venice,' or some production number. It's not like marching up and down in a Bond's show. I'm too old for that. Sort of waltzing around is, well—too much, so I well—sort of left."

During the show, Mrs. Joseph Oliphant Lambert, widow of the Dallas landscape architect and a party chairman, slipped away. She was last seen in green chiffon, yellow stockings and a gold turban. She said she had to go to Venice.

What she missed, of course, was the auction. Despite a professional auctioneer, Princess zu und von Furstenberg, a minor celebrity since she and her huband discussed their sexual proclivities in New York magazine, did most of the auctioneering.

Newton A. Chanin of Somerset Associates got the Italian dinner for 12, which Stephen Birmingham, the author, promised to cook and serve in the winner's home. The price tag was $350.

"My wife's away," Mr. Birmingham confided. "She doesn't even know I've donated the dinner."

Princess zu und von Furstenberg asked to be invited, but neither Mr. Chanin nor Mr. Birmingham seemed to hear.

There were other donations, including paintings and sculpture, but the big prize was "Una Vacanza Dorata," or Golden Holiday, donated by Olympic Airways. The trip, which gets to Venice by way of Athens, naturally enough, included a weekend at Mrs. Lambert's Venetian villa and a dinner given by the Mayor of Venice.

A Texan, John Otis Cole, who'd come North with Mrs. Lambert and Mrs. Jane Murchison, another Texas chairman, bid the trip to $2,000 and won. He didn't say whom he was taking with him. But the Venetian expedition was cheap at the price. If he'd bought one of the model rooms, it would have cost him between $12,000 and $25,000.

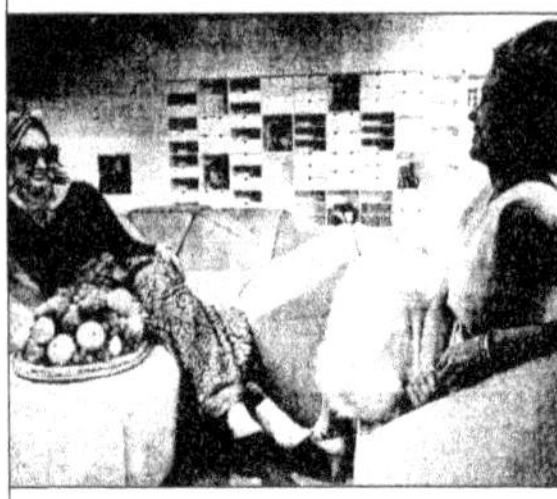

JUNE 5, 1973

COLLECTOR PLANS MAJOR ART SALE

Robert Scull Will Put Up 50 Items in the Fall

By DAVID L. SHIREY

Robert C. Scull, the art patron and taxi executive, will sell 50 paintings and sculptures next fall from his private collection in what might be one of the most important auctions of contemporary art this year, it was learned yesterday. The works, which are by leading American abstract expressionists and pop artists, are expected to bring between $2-million and $2.5-million. They will be sold by Sotheby Parke Bernet.

Mr. Scull, who is reported to be in a Nevada desert collaborating on a environmental art project, could not be reached for comment, but David Nash, a spokesman for Parke Bernet, said that the collector was selling many of his prize works because he felt that objects of such historical and esthetic importance belong in museums rather than storage. He said that Mr. Scull, who has amassed several hundred works since he started collecting 15 years ago, did not have sufficient room in his New York apartment to exhibit most of his acquisitions.

Moreover, Mr. Scull, said Mr. Nash, wants to devote his energies to collecting young, unrecognized artists. In recent years Mr. Scull has shown a preference for such environmental and conceptual artists as Michael Heizer and Joseph Kosuth. Mr. Nash said that it was not a matter of money. Mr. Scull is the owner of one of the leading New York taxi fleets.

He made his reputation as a collector in the nineteen-fifties and sixties by purchasing, among other things, the works of pop artists who were not well known. They have since become international figures in the art world.

The artists included in the sale are Claes Oldenburg, Morris Louis, Willem de Kooning, Mark di Suvero, Robert Indiana, Larry Rivers, George Segal, Tom Wesselman and Philip Guston. Such works as Franz Kline's well-known "Wotan" and Jasper John's renowned "Doube White Map" and "Target" will be offered for sale.

JUNE 29, 1973

FASHION TALK

Adolfo, Too, Shows the Longer Skirt

By BERNADINE MORRIS

Act II in the continuing saga of the longer skirt for fall, 1973.

Scene: opening of Adolfo fashion collection at St. Regis-Sheraton yesterday.

Action: first mannequin appears in fur jacket over brown knitted skirt with godets that level off about the middle of the calf. (Note: godets are triangular inserts of fabric, often set around a hemline to provide flare; Adolfo is crazy about godets.)

After interlude of soft Chanel-like suits, more mid-calf lengths, more godets.

Observation: two days after Halston lowers hemlines, Adolfo shows he's of the same mind. Difference: Adolfo only lowers some of his hems. That is, all the coats, trench or knitted, all the capes and a good many dresses. Some dresses still show the knees, some go all the way to the floor.

Positive Answers

Question: Will women get abusive, hysterical or suicidal at the Second Battle of the Hemline?

Answer: Not Adolfo fans. Examples: Ethel Scull, in three-year old Saint Laurent peasant dress, lower calf length: "I already have a closet full of long skirts." Glady Solomon: "Love the godet things—no short ones for me." Pat Buckley: "Looks lovely on other people—I will have to try them on me. When you're this tall [she's 5 feet 11 inches] you never know."

Through all this, Adolfo maintained a low profile. In a press release, he dwelled more on two women who inspired his collection than lengths. The women are Chanel, who supplied the prototype for his suits with boxy jackets, his boxy coats, chain-handle handbags and sling-back pumps, and Marilyn Monroe, who inspired his evening dresses.

The dresses, many of them calf-length, were beset with spangles and tended either to halter necklines that plunged to the waist or to strapless necklines, and bouffant skirts of pleated net. Really bouffant skirts. They truly embodied the spirit of the nineteen-fifties. But this is 1973.

Adolfo's skinny little black knitted dresses would upstage a woman in those spangled bouffants. So would his styles with handkerchief points, running the gamut of short and long hemlines in one dress.

The Chanel derivations, which give the effect of her tweeds in knitted materials, are often heaped with red fox or lynx. Not to mention chains and blouses with bows. The point is not exactly understated elegance.

But these are side issues. Are Adolfo and Halston going to make the world safe for longer skirts? Tune in next fall and find out.

JULY 29, 1973

Cause Party a Lasting Tradition in East Hampton

By ALDEN WHITMAN

Special to The New York Times

EAST HAMPTON, L.I.—"Hello, Leonard. You're looking good.'

"Hello, Alger. You look good, too; and I'm glad you could come.'

This snippet of talk took place here last weekend between Leonard Boudin, chief counsel for Dr. Daniel Ellsberg in his recent trial, and Alger Hiss, the central figure in an espionage case of 25 years ago. And it was only one of scores of such conversations, or starts of conversations, at the "cause party," a summer phenomenon in the Hamptons.

The cause party in this area is not new, but it is enduring; and it is based on the annual summer presence here of hundreds of vacationing liberal and wealthy New Yorkers, many of them in the arts. The cause party is also based on the prevalence of causes and the eagerness, or at least the willingness, of vacationers to attend parties.

Last year was a booming "cause" summer because of the Preidential campaign. There were at least 10 parties designed to raise funds for Senator George McGovern, the Democratic nominee. In addition, there were a few smaller parties where the cause was the Attica prisoners' defense or Angela Davis.

"I have the impression there are fewer parties this year," said Vivian Cadden, a McCall's editor, who attends many liberal events. "Why, Bella Abzug was out here a couple of weeks ago and there were three small parties for her, but no money raising. When she runs for re-election next year, of course, it will be different."

$2,000 Is Raised

Even without the dynamics of an election year, there have been (and will be) no dearth of cause parties. The party that brought Mr. Boudin and Mr. Hiss together was, for example, one of three last weekend. This party drew more than 100 people on a very rainy Saturday afternoon to the home of Robert Alan Aurthur, the writer who lives in The Springs, a section of East Hampton. It had been transferred indoors after the rain had washed out a planned lawn-gathering on a negihbor's grounds.

Besides honoring Mr. Boudin, the party benefited the National Emergency Civil Liberties Committee, a New York organization with which the lawyer is associated. As with many cause parties, the liquor and the buffet were donated by sponsors or their friends, so that the cause gets almost all the money raised.

Also a Social Event

The committee got about $2,000. According to Helen Rattray, an East Hampton woman who attends many cause parties and who keeps her eye on them, a party that takes in $3,000 does very well.

Money aside, the cause party is a social event. The Boudin party, for instance, offered an opportunity to meet a reigning celebrity and to hear him talk about Watergate. Moreover, there was a chance to chat with Robert Gwathmey, the painter; Tom Paxton, the entertainer; Edwin L. Smith, a former member of the National Labor Relations Board; Aaron Asher, the book editor; Joanne Grant, the writer; and Sheldon Harnick, the lyricist.

The presence of Mr. Hiss, a rare partygoer for a Hamptons resident, gave the gathering a special fillip. And he was the center of several conversational groups during the afternoon.

Last weekend's two other big parties also drew about 100 people each. One was a Sunday clambake, postponed from the week before because of rain, given at the East Hampton beachside home of Craig Claiborne, the food writer, for the Group for American's South Fork, Inc. Lobsters, clams and corn on the cob constituted the menu, along with a short speech on the ecological problems of the area.

The other party had myasthenia gravis, a muscular disorder, as its cause. This was laid on by George Plimpton, the author, and Evan Frankel, a local realty man. Held at Mr. Frankel's estate in East Hampton, the party drew scores of New Yorkers.

Nude Dip Recalled

For many partygoers, the cause is less important than the social occasion. For example, a fair proportion of those who ostensibly came to hear Mr. Boudin congregated at the kitchen bar while he was talking in the Aurthurs' living room.

And earlier this year, the center of Mr. Gwathmey's party for the Southern Conference Educational Fund was neither the artist nor Carl Braden, the guest of honor but Mr. Gwathmey's architecturally spectacular house in Amagansett. "It was worth $15 just to see the joint," said one departing guest to his wife, "but what did you say the cause was?"

None of this year's parties has so far reached the height of that given a couple of years ago by Ethel Scull, the wife of the taxi-fleet owner, in her East Hampton sculpture garden. There a guest's nude dip in her pool became more celebrated than the cause—the women's liberation movement.

The Democrats always seem to be a cause for liberal visitors and two brunches have been put on so far for the East Hampton Town Democratic Committee, one by Michael Tolson and the other by Edward Albee, the playwright.

However, the smash political party of the summer is expected to be that for Paul O'Dwyer on Aug. 11. Carter Burden will be the host at his home here, and the money will go for Mr. O'Dwyer's campaign for Council President in New York City.

A Cause for Everyone

For some, Aug. 11 will be an almost continuous party day. From mid-morning to mid-afternoon, the Springs Improvement Society will be holding its annual fair at Ashawagh Hall. It will be drawing such celebrities as Elaine deKooning, the artist; Jason Epstein, the editor; Jean Stafford, the writer; Arnold Hoffman, the artist; Dan Greenburg, the humorist, and Harold Rosenburg, the critic. Many of those will pass along later in the day to the O'Dwyer party.

In addition to these causes, there are dozens of others next month to engage the attention and the purse of the summer Hamptonite. There are house tours for Guild Hall, the region's cultural center; a gala for Southampton Hospital; church benefits everywhere and, probably at the end of August, a cause party for the Hampton Day School.

Last year Truman Capote was the star attraction. No. program has been worked out so far this year, but, according to Mrs. Rattray, "there will certainly be a party of some sort."

SEPTEMBER 20, 1973

Amy Vanderbilt's Lecture Tips Cabbies on Etiquette

By ISRAEL SHENKER

Amy Vanderbilt, arbiter of etiquette, yesterday lectured those who delight in being arbiters of just about everything else.

"Taxi drivers in New York have an unfortunate international image," Miss Vanderbilt said. "Some call them the rudest and toughest taxi drivers in the world."

Drivers beamed approvingly. There were about 100 of them in the east foyer of the Waldorf Astoria Hotel, drawn by an invitation from Robert Scull, president of Scull's Angels, a fleet of 135 taxis.

His beard neatly trimmed, his costume—slacks, jacket and shoes—modishly two-toned, Mr. Scull looked dapper enough to have stepped from a London taxi. Behind him stood one of his own cabs, unwontedly gleaming in the TV lights. Mr. Scull explained that this was the first lecture in a courtesy course to be given his drivers by Miss Vanderbilt.

In a beige pants suit that might have shocked Emily Post, Miss Vanderbilt began with first principles: "I feel that rude is bad, rude is very bad, rude is unnecessary."

Avoid Some Topics

What to call a passenger? Miss Vanderbilt wants to be called "Madam," she said, not "Madame" (flossy French"), and not "Sugar-plum" or "Hey you." Her husband wants to be called "Sir."

Drivers should watch their obscenities and wait to be invited before making conversation. "There are certain things you should avoid—religion and politics," she said.

"Lindsay!" a tax driver added, without waiting for an invitation.

"Mr. Lindsay is my distant fourth cousin," said Miss Vanderbilt, to a murmur of discontent from the ranks.

As though taxi drivers might run out of their own words, the public-relations outfit in charge of the lecture had distributed cards with questions to ask Miss Vanderbilt. Hasten K. Daniels actually asked his: "Businessmen, actors and professors wear beards. Doesn't a driver have the right to dress as he pleases?"

Miss Vanderbilt said she did not mind beards, within reason, or long hair, within limits.

What should the driver do when a woman passenger says she doesn't like to eat or drink alone? If you're married, Miss Vanderbilt suggested, say you'll phone your wife to make it a threesome.

"And if she says, 'Use the phone in my apartment?'" asked William F. Drew Jr., who is one of Scull's Angels.

Miss Vanderbilt did not reply.

Another taxi driver asked what the driver should do when passengers in the back seat make love. ("And now it's two guys," Mr. Drew added, in a stage whisper.)

"One of the rules of etiquette is to put yourself in the other person's place," Miss Vanderbilt replied.

Her book suggests that when the driver does not say thank you for his tip, the passenger can walk away and leave the door open. "That could spoil my whole day," Mr. Drew complained.

How to teach people to tip appropriately? "Be polite, no matter what happens," Miss Vanderbilt said, noting that when she forgets her wallet she takes the driver's name and sends him a check.

There were mutters of disapproval from the audience, and the merest suggestion of a snarl.

"Well, what can I do?" she pleaded.

"Leave a ring as security," Mr. Drew suggested.

By this time it was getting hard to know who was lecturing whom. One driver said he got good tips by entertaining passengers with ventriloquism. Others pass out candy or Kleenex.

Fred (Taxi) Mitchell sings to his passengers whenever he is stuck in traffic. When someone cuts ahead of him he sings, "Oh, when the saints go marching in." If the other fellow persists, he booms out, "I'll be glad when you're dead, you rascal you."

"You can feel human out there," he said, smiling. "People is just relative."

SEPTEMBER 24, 1973

Cowboy-Style Wedding Reception in an Old Bank

By **BERNADINE MORRIS**

Rosemary's wedding didn't take place in the safe deposit vault after all. This somewhat disappointed a few hundred friends and acquaintances who trooped to the old bank at 110 Hudson Street in the nighttime wasteland between Greenwich Village and Wall Street Saturday expecting to witness the ceremony.

It seems that Henry, Rosemary's fiancé, had trouble finding a judge who was free at the time. So Rosemary Arminia Kent and Henry Lewis Meltzer were hitched, as she put it, quietly Friday morning in the chambers of Judge Burton B. Roberts of the State Supreme Court. "I'm Episcopalian and he's Jewish, so we compromised on a judge," she said.

Then the couple and their parents, Mr. and Mrs. Lonnie Fox Kent of Houston and Baytown, Texas, and Mr. and Mrs. Samuel Meltzer of Great Neck and Santiago, Chile, slipped off to La Petite Ferme for the wedding luncheon.

In the afternoon, the bride, who is editor of Andy Warhol's brainchild, Interview magazine, which specializes in chronicling the thoughts and activities of rock heroes and movie stars, went to her office for a few hours.

But she was all done up in a white cowgirl outfit with a sweetheart neckline, gored skirt and red boots and spurs to greet her guests on Saturday night. She carried a white bouquet of lilies of the valley, mums and cactus that she said weighed a ton. Ever since she was a little girl she promised herself she would wear cowboy boots at her wedding, she said.

Her five bridesmaids, whom she called "cowgirlettes", were in pink and white pinafores and boots. So was her matron of honor, Pamela Sakowitz, whose husband, Robert, is executive vice president of his family's business, the Sakowitz stores in Houston. It was, you see, a Texas wedding.

Mr. Sakowitz looked quite comfortable in his beige suède cowboy suit, which he explained he wore a lot down home. He was also eager to elucidate the fine points of western dress. His boots, he said, were the stove pipe variety, built quite high so a rattlesnake can't climb in the top and so they won't rub when you are riding.

The boots the bride's mother was wearing with the white lace dress she made herself were called low quarters, he explained. Presumably for less strenuous activities, such a quare dancing to the Medicine Hat band, which played country and western music from its perch atop the teller's booths. Rosemary and her mother were the most vigorous participants.

His own costume was authentic, Mr. Sakowitz went on, except for one missing ingredient.

"There's a certain problem in bringing in a gun," he said.

Robert Scull, the taxi tycoon, whose black cowboy suit complemented his wife's white one, also said he was missing something: he wanted to bring a horse.

There was other livestock around, however. Elaine "Pinky" Wolman and Dianne Beaudry, the fashion designers who made both the bride's and the groom's cowboy suits, sent two live chickens. They were stowed in the bank's vault along with the other wedding presents.

Paulette Came as Herself

Peter Catalano, the jewelry designer, sent a monkey on roller skates.

Mr. Warhol carried his toy dachsund, called Archie Bunker, and Robin House brought a big, shaggy mutt called Sunshine with a bandana tied around his neck.

"Henry said, 'You've invited everybody you ever shook hands with,'" the bride murmured as she wove through the crowd asking everybody if they were enjoying the roundup.

Not everyone was in cowboy dress. Mrs. George Zauderer, the mother of Pamela Sakowitz, wore Saint Laurent's silver and black sweater with a black velvet skirt.

"The last time I was invited to a costume party was after Pamela's wedding, and I didn't have anything to wear then either," she said.

Pablo Manzoni, Elizabeth Arden's make-up director, wore semi-formal morning clothes with striped pants "because I was going to a bank" and Paulette Goddard wore a slinky long red Bill Blass dress with diamonds. The diamonds were around her neck and on her ears. "I came as Paulette Goddard," she said sweetly.

Chester Weinberg, the fashion designer, settled for an old blue denim workshirt but Calvin Klein pulled a pair of cowboy boots over his jeans. They belong to his partner, Barry Schwartz.

Cherry Vanilla, who does public relations for David Bowie, the British rock singer, was casual in black net tights under her denim shorts and a jacket with her name on the back.

"And to think I worried about what to wear," a conservatively dressed wedding guest remarked.

Signs outside the building identified it as the Meltzer National Bank. Actually, the site had been occupied by the First National City Bank and before that by the Bank of America, said Charles Low, who owns the building and manufactures nautical instruments on the upper floors.

"I invited Henry and Rosemary to use the place as a joke and they took me seriously," he said.

The Word From Warhol

The inside was banked with white mums and dahlias, by Parrish Woodworth, which planned the décor, and the teller's cages had signs proclaiming variously, "Champagne," "Big Macs," "Coca-Cola" and "Mousse."

The mousse was supplied by Bert Greene, who runs "The Store in Amagansett," and who said, "Everybody wants to do something for Rosemary." The hamburgers, each individually boxed, came from MacDonald's. They turned soggy as the evening wore on.

"I adore every minute of it," said Mrs. Meltzer, her mother-in-law. "It takes some of the stiffness out of weddings."

"It's so imaginative," said Mr. Warhol, who's been to his share of parties. "You think everything's been done and then someone comes along and does something new."

"It doesn't seem like a wedding and that's good," said Prince Egon von Furstenberg, who sells men's clothes.

But there was a wedding cake. As the bride was handed the knife she screamed, "I'm not domestic," but cut it anyway. Her bouquet was caught by Peter Catalano, who got his hand full of cactus spines as a result.

There was a wedding breakfast in Chinatown and after that the couple went to Nova Scotia for a week. They had planned a wedding trip to Santiago, but that didn't seem too good an idea at the moment.

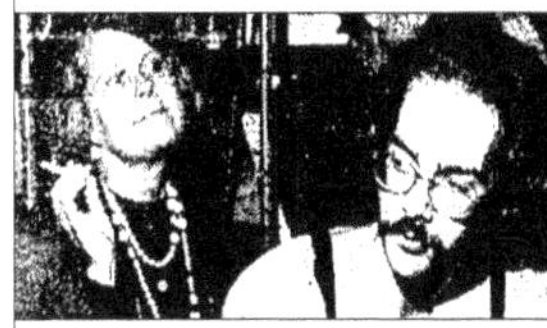

SEPTEMBER 25, 1973

FASHION TALK

Once the Saving Was Minimal—Now It Can Amount to Thousands

By **BERNADINE MORRIS**

Years ago, dowagers had their chauffeurs drive them down to 14th Street, where Ohrbach's was then located, so they could save a dollar on a pair of gloves or a handbag.

The stakes, or, if you will, the savings, are bigger now. Much bigger. What draws the haute monde today to Ohrbach's, now on 34th Street, and to Alexander's, on 58th Street, are copies of original Paris and Rome couture styles.

The savings can amount to thousands, according to the commentators at the showings both stores gave yesterday.

The jacket, pants and shirt by Yves Saint Laurent cost Ohrbach's $6,000, according to Irene Staz, a vice president.

The store's copies were priced at $135 in flannel, $175 in camel hair and $235 in the original fleece. A bargain any way you look at it, especially if it fits. Mrs. Robert Scull was so happy with it, she tried it on in the morning and wore it to the noon show.

Fox-Collar Sweaters

Alexander's paid $5,000 for a gray Lurex sweater coat by Valentino, according to Francine Farkas, also a vice-president. Its copies were $275 in midilength and $325 to the ankles. Both had fox collars.

Of course, the prices stores pay in Rome and Paris are often higher than the ones private clients pay, but the savings are considerable anyway.

Many of the shoppers could easily pay the prices of the originals, Doris Duke for example. She picked up a couple of Saint Laurent suits at Alexander's for $125 and $350.

Three Kennedy sisters did their shopping at Ohrbach's: Jean Smith picked up a couple of Saint Laurent evening outfits and a Dior suède ankle-length skirt, Eunice Shriver chose a Valentino and a Saint Laurent and Pat Lawford's order was for a Dior mohair coat that sold out almost immediately—the store was frantically wiring Paris for more fabric—and a Patou navy raincoat.

Outfit by Riva

Mrs. William S. Paley, a perennial member of best dressed lists, was the most economical-minded of all. She got a bloused jacket, pants and matching skirt by Heinz Riva at Ohrbach's all for $70.

After seeing the show, however, she asked to see three other styles: a Valentino sweater suit at $350, a Givenchy quilted jersey suit at $450 and the Dior mohair coat at $225.

Now, it isn't just fashion bargains that brings many women to these stores. There is also the charity angle. Alexander's charged $10 for tickets to its 11 A.M. show (for the benefit of the Metropolitan Opera Guild), and to its 3 P.M. show (for the Community Service Society). Naturally, women involved with both groups found it obligatory to attend, and to encourage their friends. (Shows at 1 P.M. and 7:30 P.M. were free.)

A Chance to Compare

Mrs. Schuyler G. Chapin, wife of the general manager of the Metropolitan Opera, came to a preview with Mrs. Georan Gentele, widow of Mr. Chapin's predecessor. Mrs. Chapin said she was enchanted with the clothes but would have to check with her husband before she bought any. Later, she returned for the Dior midriff cocktail dress with a pleated skirt. Mrs. Gentele opted for a Valentino suit and one from San Lorenzo.

Mrs. Andrew Heiskell, whose interest is the Community Service Society, brought Mrs. John V. Lindsay to the afternoon show. Mrs. Lindsay came willingly enough, so long as her husband didn't have to: She felt the Mayor has had his fill of fashion shows for a while.

Actually, it was quite possible for a woman to spend the day shuttling between the two stores, catching both shows, comparing the styles and the prices. Those who did could spot a couple of the same styles, such as the Valentino velvet short evening dress with the chiffon bodice, $99 at Alexander's, $85 at Ohrbach's, or the San Lorenzo wrap coat with epaulets, $135 at Alexander's, $140 and $165 (depending on the fabric) at Ohrbach's.

Enough people placed orders before the show to cause sellouts at both places.

"The Dior mohairs are all gone, the Venet cape coat is sold out in the original fabric and the copy fabric is almost gone, the Patou rain suit is going," Sydney Gittler repeated to customers at Ohrbach's who besieged him after the noon show. There were three more shows to go. "We'll be getting more in later," he went on. "Why don't you try on the sample?"

All in all, there was plenty of entertainment for a damp day for women who were interested in fashion.

SEPTEMBER 30, 1973

Late Listings for Today's TV

The following information about today's television programs was not available in time to appear in Section 2

"Sunday": Guests are Representative Edward I. Koch, Democrat of Manhattan, Robert and Ethel Scull, Channel 4, 9:30 A.M.

"Right Now": Jack M. Sable, the state's Human Rights Commissioner, is host; topic is Hellenic Greek society, Channel 9, 9:30 A.M.

"Point of View": The spirit of Yom Kippur, Channel 9, 10:30 A.M.

"Face the Nation": Representative Peter W. Rodino Jr., Democrat of New Jersey and chairman of the House Judiciary Committee, is guest, Channel 2, 11:30 A.M.

"Newsmakers": Representative Bella S. Abzug, Democrat of New York, Channel 2, noon.

Baseball: Mets vs. Chicago Cubs in double-header from Chicago, Channel 9, 12:30 P.M.

"Issues and Answers": John A. Love, director of the Energy Policy Office in the Executive Office of the President, Channel 7, 1:30 P.M.

"New York Report": Dr. Robert G. Newman of the city's methadone-maintenance program, Channel 9, 8 P.M.

"With Mayor Lindsay": Gordon Chase, the city's Health Services Administrator; Gerald Frug, Health Services Administrator-designate, and Dr. Robert G. Newman, assistant commissioner of the Addiction Services Agency, guests, Channel 11, 8:30 P.M.

"Black Pride": Ossie Davis, director - producer - actor; Joseph Hartfield, film producer; James P. Murray, film reviewer for The Amsterdam News, and William Maxwell of Wall Street, Channel 11, 9 P.M.

"The Puerto Rican New Yorker": David Smith, union apprenticeship coordinator, and Ana del Toro and Roberto Albertorio, recruitment and training officials, Channel 11, 9:30.

"Focus: New Jersey": Nina McCall, Ana Levine and Greta Kiernan of the New Jersey League of Women Voters, Channel 11, 10 P.M.

"Suburban Closeup": Raymond T. Schuler, the state's Commissioner of Transportation; Lee Koppelman of the Nassau - Suffolk Regional Planning Board, and Assemblyman Arthur Kremer of Nassau, Channel 11, 9:30 P.M.

SEPTEMBER 30, 1973

OCTOBER 7, 1973

America's Art Heritage—Going, Going, Gone?

By LEAH GORDON

A JACKSON POLLOCK canvas that was bought 20 years ago for $6,000 is now sold to Australia's National Gallery in Canberra for an incredible $2-million, the highest price ever paid for an American work of art. A European collector purchases a Jasper Johns for $150,000, thus setting a record for that artist and placing him along with Willem de Kooning as one of the most expensive living American artists. Not until 15 years ago could Jasper Johns even sell a painting.

The world-wide ascendency of American contemporary art is the great success story in the nation's art history, and to it may be added yet another chapter when 50 paintings and sculptures from the Robert Scull collection will be auctioned Oct. 18 at Sotheby Parke Bernet. The group, which spans the once-controversial years 1950 to 1968 and includes works by modern stars such as De Kooning, Johns, Barnett Newman, Robert Rauschenberg, Andy Warhol and Frank Stella, is expected, by auction estimates, to bring around $2.5-million.

"It's time for these paintings and sculptures to get out into the world," says Scull, a taxicab tycoon who has been collecting contemporary art for the past 13 years with the eagerness of a child gathering wild flowers. "I simply had no room to display them. They were sitting unseen in four warehouse rooms. Besides, I'm involved with more current things such as earthworks. These pieces are already part of art history."

Nevertheless, parting with his art is like breaking up the family. "It was my dream," says Scull, "that these things would have stayed together. Munich was interested in buying 40 of them for the Pinakothek. But they got involved with the Olympics and had also spent money for a Frans Hals. Munich will be most unhappy that they did not come through and buy my collection."

Among American museum directors, only Thomas Hoving of the Metropolitan Museum of Art showed any interest in the group. "When Hoving heard about the possibility of the pictures going to Munich," says Scull, "he called to see if there was anything we could do. But he had problems of his own — the $5.5-million Velazquez followed by the $1-million Greek vase." Scull confesses he would have been amenable to a deal that would have included giving some of the works as gifts just to see them remain as a group. It would have cost a museum only about $1-million. After Hoving's inquiry, he waited a year. There was not a single phone call. So he decided to sell through auction.

Ironically, museums, and especially the European institutions, are expected to be among the most active bidders at the auction, giving rise to concern in some quarters that perhaps the United States is allowing too much of its best modern art to be exported. The United States could find itself in the 21st century as the French did in the 20th when they awakened to find many of their best impressionist and post-impressionist canvases in foreign lands.

In a study made two years ago by dealer Leo Castelli, who handles some of the finest American artists, he found that 50 per cent of his sales were to Europeans. And the $2-million Pollock that was just sold to Canberra by dealer Ben Heller was once part of a collection of about 20 paintings that were ultimately destined for the Los Angeles County Museum of Art. But the individual who was to buy the group for $1-million didn't and the museum itself was in the midst of a building program with no available funds.

While most people are loathe to even suggest legislation limiting the sale of American Art abroad, the Association of Art Museum Directors has recently been discussing the need for some controls covering American works as well as art that has been in this country for a number of years.

"We need some kind of protection over the uncontrolled outflow of our creative artists, living and dead," says Richard Brown, director of the new Kimbell Art Museum in Fort Worth. "It would be shameful if Jackson Pollock's 'One,' which is now in the Museum of Modern Art, had been sold to a foreign collector. That painting is a definitive statement of an entire society's soul and being. It should be in its own climate for the same reasons that Botticelli's 'Primavera' should be in Florence."

On the other hand, J. Carter Brown, Director of Washington's National Gallery which has only recently become interested in contemporary art (see next item), says, "If our art is significant enough to be appreciated by the world, then it should be seen by the world. It is not as if these artists are prophets without honor in their own country. It would be tough to come up with a collection better than what we have at the Museum of Modern Art."

Robert Scull, who had hoped to have his collection remain intact is now resigned to seeing it scattered. "We're very happy to have things from all over the world in this country," he says. "So why not send our art abroad? We have plenty here. It is the greatest thing we can export."

GOING NATIONAL

While many eyes are focused on the Scull auction, another event of perhaps more lasting importance to American art is occurring in Washington later this month. For the first time in its 36-year history the National Gallery of Art is organizing its own exhibition devoted to modern American artists such as Louise Nevelson, Isamu Noguchi, Clyfford Still and Sam Francis. The show, titled "American Art at Mid-Century," is being shown in two installments, the first of which runs from Oct. 27 to Jan. 9. It should also put to rest the old accusation that the National Gallery is about as national as the National Biscuit Company.

That charge, although slightly exaggerated, implies some truth. While the National Gallery does contain many excellent examples of American art from Copley to the late abstractionist Ad Reinhardt, it has concentrated on assembling outstanding European masterpieces. For many years its policy had been to include only artists dead for more than 25 years. But that proviso was abolished in the mid-sixties to accommodate the Picassos in the Chester Dale collection which was being given to the museum.

After that the National Gallery paid more attention to the modern scene, assigning space to loan exhibitions of American as well as British and French contemporary works. But not until now has it initiated its own exhibition. The impetus is the distinctly modern, I.M. Pei-designed East building, scheduled to open in 1976, where the Gallery plans to display 20th - century works.

Yet no hand will be bidding for the National Gallery at the Scull auction. When it comes to buying, the institution still believes its mandate is time-tested, older art. The contemporaries will simply have to come as gifts.

OCTOBER 18, 1973

Works From Scull's Collection Of New York Art Go on Auction

By FRED FERRETTI

Fifty paintings, sculptures an constructions by the most notable artists of the New York School, all from the collection of Robert C. Scull, will be auctioned tonight at Sotheby Parke Bernet. theby Parke Bernet.

The sale, which represents a fifth of Mr. Scull's collection of works by modern Americans, has created widespread interest, not only because of the estimated prices the works could fetch — possibly 23 records could be set, the gallery said— but also because of the overseas interest in the sale.

Generally, European interest in art has traditionally remained with European artists, except for the German excursion into pop art several years ago. And Japanese buyers have been on a multiyear buying spree of French impressionists. There has been, art dealers and observers agree, only sporadic interest by foreign art buyers in American artists.

The Scull sale could see, these experts believe, a change in that attitude, reflected in the bidding tonight. One dealer pointed out that when Mr. Scull last sold several pieces from his collection, in 1970, there was "considerable German interest."

A random survey has disclosed that this sale has aroused interest among agents who buy for German, Japanese, Swiss and English customers, and among several Italian buyers who have apparently openly inquired of agents about pieces in the Scull sale.

Cab-Fleet Owner

For Mr. Scull, who owns a fleet of New York medallion taxis christened "Scull's Angels," the sale represents a way to get money to invest in the works of younger American artists.

The prices estimated by Sotheby Parke Bernet for many of the works are quite high. Among the paintings, de Kooning's "Police Gazette," for example, has an estimate of from $150,000 to $200,000, with the known record for any de Kooning only $45,000. Jasper Johns's "Target" has a top of $150,000 at least equal to the recorded record for a Johns sold privately. Kline's "Wotan," estimated at $90,000 to $120,000, is at least twice as high as the previous record for a Kline, $52,520.

Several observers noted that the high estimates could be indicative of extraordinarily high reserve prices set for the works, similar to the high reserves placed by Mr. Scull and other owners at previous sales, and that the estimates could be unreal. They note too that often with such high reserves, the owner will buy the piece back if the bidding does not approach the reserve. This possibility too will be watched by auction-goers this evening.

The scull sale will end two-days of sales of important works of the 19th and 20th centuries. Last night several notable sales were held at the gallery's 980 Madison Avenue selling rooms.

Two records were set. A 1905 rose-period Picasso, "Jeure Homme au Bouquet," was bought by Galerie Beyeler of Geneva for $720,000. The previous record had been $675,000, paid last July in London for a Picasso from the collection of the late actor Edward G. Robinson. A Matisse bronze, "Nu Couché I," was bought by a Zurich dealer for $360,000, exceeding by $100,000 the previous high for a 20th-century sculpture, paid last year for a Henry Moore.

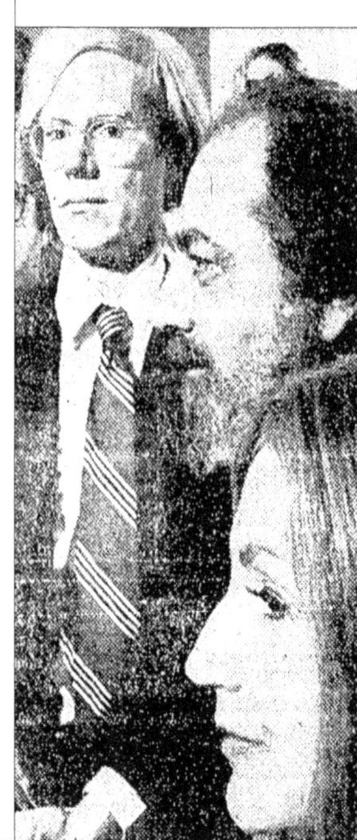

OCTOBER 19, 1973

Scull's U.S. Art Brings Record $2 Million

By FRED FERRETTI

Art collectors paid a total of $2,242,900—a record for contemporary American works for 50 paintings, sculptures and constructions by artists of the New York School, owned by taxi-fleet owner Robert C. Scull, at an auction last night that possessed as much decorum as post-game activities at Shea Stadium.

The sale, held simultaneously in Sotheby Parke Bernet's main selling gallery, at Madison Avenue and 76th Street, as well as in several television-equipped side galleries, was preceded by a brace of demonstrations attacking Mr. Scull, his taxicabs and his collecting habits. Despite the uproar a number of record sales were recorded.

Jasper Johns's works set five different auction records at the sale. His huge canvas, "Double White Map," executed in 1965, brought $240,000.

The price was $90,000 higher than the previous high recorded for a Johns painting, reportedly paid by a private European collector recently. It was double the auction record for a living American artist, which had been held by Georgia O'Keeffe, whose "Poppies" sold for $120,000 last March. It topped the auction record of $75,000 for a work of Pop Art held since 1970 by Roy Lichtenstein, as well as the auction record for any 20th-century American work of art. The previous holder was Yasuo Kuniyoshi with $200,000 for "Little Joe With Cow," sold in March.

Johns's sculpture, "Painted Bronze," consisting of bronze replicas of two Ballantine Beer cans on a platform was sold for $90,000, and established an auction record for sculpture by a living American artist. Claes Oldenburg's "Stove," at $45,000, had held the record since 1970.

Other record prices were established for works by deKooning, Kline, Rauschenberg, Poons and Rosenquist. In addition, the gallery said, the two extraordinarily high prices paid for two Barnett Newman paintings are expected to set the standard for that artist.

The paintings "L'Errance" and "White Fire II" drew prices of $140,000 and $155,000, respectively.

Aside from these spectaculars however, the sale was disappointing in several aspects. Most of the items put up for sale failed to reach the expected maximums estimated by Sotheby Parke Bernet, and many of them failed to reach expected minimums, and there were scattered "Ohs" and "Ahs" as many of these pieces went under the hammer.

The sale began late because of the crush of spectators who came to the gallery in such numbers that they had to be let through the front doors in groups of tens.

Their entry was not facilitated by a noisy, and well-televised, demonstration by the Taxi Rank and File Coalition, a group of cab drivers vying for recognition as an opposing bargaining group for cabbies. They carried signs suggesting that Mr. Scull was a "parasite" who "lived off the backs of cabbies" so he could "be with the beautiful people."

Not as noisy, but as persistent, were representatives of Women in the Arts who protested that only one woman, Lee Bontecou, was represented in the sale. Her canvas and steel construction brought $7,500, below its expected $8,000 minimum.

The Scull sale followed by one day the record sale at the auction gallery of 17 Picasso paintings and drawings, a vast collection of 19th- and 20th-century Impressionist and modern art. One rose-period Picasso established a world auction record for a Picasso, at $720,000. The Picassos all told sold for $2.57-million and the sale established a one-evening record of $7.8-million.

OCTOBER 30, 1973

Shows Open With Nostalgia, Not Revolution

By BERNADINE MORRIS

If it's revolution you're looking for, look elsewhere, New York fashion designers are saying as they draw the curtain on their spring collections.

Store buyers, some just back from viewing the offerings in Paris, and a sprinkling of personal friends who can't wait until the clothes get into the stores in a couple of months, had a nostalgic time yesterday.

The styles looked vaguely familiar, recalling Charles Dana Gibson's turn-of-the-century prints, evenings at The Late Show or last-year-at-Halston. Not even a hemline fracas to liven things up.

Nobody dozed and certainly nobody clamored for the midcalf lengths with which Paris designers entertained their audiences last week. The peace and quiet seemed eminently welcome.

Stark and Looser

Day clothes are stark and minimal, looser than they have been. Evening dresses tend to slink in a Jean Harlow sort of way. Ankle lengths provide the biggest excitement, but the week has just begun.

Prime advocate of the minimal look for day is Chester Weinberg, who indicated how the cooky crumbles by showing up for his opening in a double-breasted gray flannel suit with a shirt and a tie instead of his usual sweater or T-shirt.

His day clothes have that spare, casual look that in quieter times used to be associated with the best taste. Dresses have bloused tops, jackets are loose, with dropped shoulders, and there are lots of tents or overblouse styles.

The big news at this house is the men's clothes. Now it's Chester's turn to try his hand at men's wear. His things are in leather, including a lovely shade of blue pigskin, and the jackets also have dropped shoulders.

Everybody trooped out in the rain and up to the Hotel Pierre to see the Bill Blass recipe for spring, including the designer's personal friends. Mildred Hilson slipped into her apple green Courrèges raincoat, Ethel Scull into her long striped Saint Laurent sweater and Audrey Zauderer into her velvet Saint Laurent jacket with the fluffy fur collar and cuffs.

The Tailored Way

Mr. Blass's message was his own: neatly tailored clothes, some checked or dotted, an occasional one-shoulder neckline, a batch of hand-knitted sweaters (pretty enough to make you yearn for another even after this fall's avalanche).

There were a couple of mild surprises: a sequin-paved sport dress (Mr. Blass called it a sport dress himself) and a sequin-paved tailored suit (the designer called it a classic). The gallery went mad over them. They also wildly applauded the flouncy beige shirt with the long navy pleated skirt and the big floppy hat. Very Gibson Girl. Very romantic. Before The Late Show.

When it comes to tailoring, John Anthony goes all the way: square shoulders, pleated skirts and their accompaniments — a flower on the lapel, a bow at the neckline. The mannequins look trim, well put together, even when they wear pants. The designer sticks to a black, white or red color scheme: black and white shirt, red hat.

The hat's a shiny straw sailor with a straight brim and a veil. It has a rather quaint look. Nobody's gone around in anything like that much since the nineteen-fifties. Are we ready for another go-round?

The Japanese have been running around this country and Europe collecting fashion as avidly as they're buying up art. Now comes another step. Hanae Mori, the Tokyo designer, has set up a New York outpost on East 79th Street in what was the Feigen art gallery.

With its white marble floors and steel furnishings, it's far more impressive than your usual Seventh Avenue showroom. Mrs. Mori has been selling her clothes to such stores as Bergdorf Goodman, Neiman Marcus, Sakowitz and I. Magnin for a number of years. Obviously, she's ready for expansion.

Her prints are her specialty: butterflies, trees, peacocks, clouds—lots of clouds. They drift around in chiffon dresses for regal evenings and in simpler cotton styles that could manage in a country cottage. Floaty sleeves, sometimes longer than the dress itself, are a specialty.

It's all a long way from the kimono.

OCTOBER 31, 1973

Rockefellers Divided On the Mayoral Place

While Governor Nelson Rockefeller and a brother, David, president of the Chase Manhattan Bank, have contributed $5,000 each respectively to the mayoral campaigns of State Senator John J. Marchi the Republican candidate, and Controller Abraham D. Beame, the Democratic candidate. The Governor's former wife, Mary C. Rockefeller, has made a gift of $500 to Albert H. Blumenthal, the Democratic Assemblyman running on the Liberal line.

The Liberal party itself has given $10,000 to the Blumenthal campaign, which also has received a $2,000 contribution from the philanthropist Stewart Mott; $2,830 from the investment banker, Henri Doll; $2,000 from another investment banker, Paul LePercq, and $1,000 from a taxi-fleet owner, Robert C. Scull.

NOVEMBER 15, 1973

SHOP TALK

Status Symbol Couple Arrive to Show Styles

By BERNADINE MORRIS

Rosita and Ottavio (Tai) Missoni, whose knitted clothes have become international status symbols, like Vuitton bags and Gucci shoes, were in New York this week for a reason. For several reasons, in fact.

The couple, who live and work in Italy, appeared at a Saks Fifth Avenue show of their current collection. The show benefited Save Venice and the America-Italy Society.

Off to Dallas

They also introduced their spring and summer collection to store buyers who hadn't seen the clothes in Europe last month. And they were guests at a mammoth party given by Fieldcrest to herald the transference of their original patterns and colorings to bed clothes, towels and shower curtains.

Tomorrow they fly off to Dallas to appear in their boutique at Neiman-Marcus, but that's the way life is with status symbols these days.

"You put three outfits in a suitcase, and you're set for a whole season in Europe," said Mrs. Morton Seifter who, clad in a skirt, sweater, jacket and hat all in Missoni's related but not quite matching patterns, managed to snare a front seat at the Saks show.

"You can just reach into your closet and grab—everything goes with everything else," she explained.

Seek Smaller Sizes

"You can't tell how old anything is," said Mrs. George Goodman, another member of the audience. The striped mauve blouse she was wearing with a short black skirt was actually the top of a Missoni evening dress, she added. She couldn't remember how long ago she had bought it.

Instead of rushing off to lunch or to pay their telephone bills, the women flocked to the store's Potpourri room after the show to add to their collections.

Several complained that the smaller sizes were all gone by the time they were able to get into the room (Ethel Scull couldn't find a size 6 and Laura Maioglio, who owns Barbetta's restaurant, went looking for size 8). Store executives, looking harassed in a pleased sort of way, finally joined the sales people in soothing customers and assuring them that more things would be "coming up from the receiving department."

One of the usual characteristics of a status symbol is that it be limited in supply. Production of the clothes is limited because the Missonis want it that way. Then they know what's going on in every phase, explained Tai Missoni, who works out the fibers, knitting techniques, patterns and colorings while his wife takes care of the styling.

"It's very simple," said Rosita, speaking of the designs. "Everything's in the material."

Mrs. Missoni turned up at the Saks show in a floor-length checked skirt and a striped sweater set, observing that any length could be appropriate at any hour of the day.

Easy to Shorten

In her spring collection, skirts tend to stop a few inches below the knee.

"When the Americans complain, I tell them it's easy to shorten the skirts — it doesn't spoil the look," she said.

The innovation in the new collection is the addition of beach clothes, specifically bikinis that are almost always accompanied by skirts or jackets that can also be worn at night.

High price is another concommitant of status symbols. About the least expensive Missoni style is a long, skinny scarf that sells for $25 at Saks and Bloomingdale's. (As a kind of symbol of the complex patterns, the scarf has been passed out as a souvenir to store buyers viewing Missoni collections, and was sought after so avidly, it was recently put into production.) Bloomingdale's incidentally, also carries the clothes.

Limited Distribution

Only about 200 stores all over the world carry Missoni clothes, with half the production sold in the United States. But by spring, the Missonis will be broadening their scope.

The Fieldcrest home furnishings products reproducing the Missonis' special wiggles, stripes, dots and flowers will be available in April. A sheet will cost around $7.50, a towel about $5.

What the Fieldcrest people are proudest of is that the various patterns don't have to match. Like the clothes, they can be switched around in different ways. And besides being cheaper than the clothes, they're also washable.

NOVEMBER 17, 1973

Peter Max Party Recaptures 60's

By JUDY KLEMESRUD

Shades of the frivolous, freaky sixties. It was all there the other night—the far-out clothes, the frantic frugging (as they used to call it) to discothèque music, the mob of chic New Yorkers jam-packed together and sweating on each other.

The occasion for all of this see-and-be-seen gaiety, which was sort of tossed by the wayside by Vietnam and the other serious events of the last few years, was the opening Thursday night of Peter Max's new Artworks/New York gallery, at 325 East 75th Street.

"God, it's just like 1966," said a photographer who

stood outside the gallery, taking photographs of the guests as they arrived in limousines, taxis and at least one hansom cab from Central Park, driven by a cabbie who warbled, "Give my regards to Broadway."

The party had two official drawing cards: An exhibit by David Croland of his Art Deco paintings of some of the better known women of the fashion/society crowd, and a promise that Peter Beard would film a cinema vérité movie of the evening, à la Federico Fellini.

Some Show Up

Well, Mr. Croland's paintings were there, featuring the likes of Lee Radziwill, Gloria Vanderbilt Cooper, Marisa Berenson, Berry Berenson Perkins, Karen Bjornsen, Naomi Sims and Lou Lou de la Falaise, none of whom showed up to view themselves on display, as well as Pat Ast, Appolonia von Ravenstein and Cheyenne, who did.

But Peter Beard failed to show up ("He just didn't have the time," a party publicist explained), so instead, the cinema vérité movie à la Federico Fellini was shot by Anton Perich and a blond interviewer who called herself Tinkerbelle.

"This is hideous, absolutely hideous," said a pale and perspiring Mrs. Robert C. Scull, whose husband collects art and taxicabs, after she emerged from the crowded gallery after staying only 10 minutes.

"This isn't an art show, it's an Andy Warhol kind of thing, where they just bring all kinds of people into one room to look at each other."

A Flurry of Handouts

Perhaps one of the reasons that more than 400 persons jammed into the small, five-story graystone gallery was a high-powered publicity campaign in which a flurry of brown and white press releases had promised for weeks that the guest list would be "a primer of who's really who and what 1973 is all about."

If so, here is what 1973 is all about: Mrs. Scull and her son, Jonathan; Huntington Hartford, the A & P heir; Clay Felker, editor and publisher of New York magazine; Elaine Kaufman, owner of Elaine's restaurant; Mrs. Thomas L. Kempner, wife of the investment banker; Yoko Ono, the artist and wife of John Lennon; Caterine Milinaire and her 3-year-old daughter, Serafine; Mrs. William F. Buckley Jr.; Mr. and Mrs. Francis W. (Bunty) Lawrence; Francesco Scavullo, the photographer; Ruth Ford, the actress; Halston, Zandra Rhodes and Clovis Ruffin, the designers; and Cathryn ("Cherokee") Lacey, Penthouse magazine's 1973 pet of the year.

Fashion Show of Sorts

"I thought that's who you were," one blue-jeaned spectator said to Miss Lacey as she arrived at the red-and-white canopied gallery. "I have your nude picture from October hanging in my bathroom."

Besides glancing at the women's portraits, the guests also ate cheese and drank champagne; danced, not necessarily with the opposite sex, on the rooftop terrace; and ogled a greenhouse full of carnivorous plants.

There was at least one fight: A man dressed in black leather struck a woman repeatedly on the fourth floor landing, pausing long enough to politely inform another guest that the fourth floor was not open to the public. Then he resumed the pummeling, as other guests watched disinterestedly.

The clothes, like those of the sixties, were a mixed bag ranging from cowboy attire to one man's shocking pink satin jump suit to farmers' overalls to Japanese kimonos to this season's prescribed "elegance" for the older social types.

Mrs. Scull wore the $595 beige Chanel copy suit by Adolfo that all of the rich ladies seem to be wearing this season. The host, Mr. Max, wore a white suit over a red T-shirt that said, "Swing." A woman guest wore a black and white T-shirt that said "Ups and Downs."

Yoko Ono, when asked about her tight black lamé hot pants, commented airily: "This is the new feminist uniform."

Not all the guests were human. One who seemed to enjoy herself the most was Bo Peep, a black cocker spaniel, who came with her master, Peter Van Rensselaer, a writer who said proudly of his surname, "That's New York's oldest name."

And why did he bring Bo Peep? "She doesn't like to stay home alone," he explained as he left the party after staying about an hour.

DECEMBER 7, 1973

Advertisements For Themselves

By ENID NEMY

"You've got to be a little bit of an exhibitionist, but one who knows when to stop," said Mrs. Skitch Henderson, discussing the newest addition to her wardrobe.

The addition is a black cashmere floor-length dress, promoting the latest Henderson business venture, Daly's Daffodil, a restaurant-bar at 59th Street and First Avenue. The bodice of the turtle-neck dress is emblazoned with the restaurant name, and a daffodil, both outlined in yellow paillettes.

"I think it's kind of camp," said Mrs. Henderson, who is one of a small group of women who have become, on occasion, walking advertisements for the family business.

"I'd do this kind of thing only if it looked great and not goofy," said Mrs. Henderson, whose dress was designed by Jeanne Campbell of Sportwhirl. "It feels very nice and it's like an elegant sweatshirt."

The elegance, priced at about $170, was introduced earlier this month at the official opening (the actual opening took place in July) of the Daffodil.

"Everyone flipped for it," Mrs. Henderson reported.

To Mrs. Charles Wohlstetter whose two-piece outfit also came from Sportwhirl (Bernard Goodman, the president of the firm, had them especially made), the concept of advertising her husband's business is "fun."

"One has to have a sense of humor about the whole thing," said Mrs. Wohlstetter, whose blue cashmere skirt is topped with a brown jersey shirt (price: about $160). The shirt has an enormous C, outlined in white paillettes, a smaller T in silver paillettes, and a telephone in pale green paillettes, denoting Continental Telephone Corporation, of which her husband is chairman of the board.

Mrs. Howard Sloan's outfit (white double-knit skirt and navy mat jersey top) isn't quite what she had hoped for, but "I think it's amusing."

She had hoped for a reproduction of the Chateau Bouscaut wine label on the jersey top. Instead, she settled for the words "Chateau Bouscaut" outlined in red sequins.

"I'd rather have had something not so blandly advertising the business . . . the label would have been better but it didn't work out," said Mrs. Sloan, whose husband, a vice president of Frank B. Hall & Co., an insurance concern, is also president of the Chateau Bouscaut vineyard in the Bordeaux district of France.

Mrs. Robert Scull, the wife of the art collector and taxi mogul, and the woman who started the whole thing, said she wasn't at all self-conscious when she wore her "clinging and sexy" black mat jersey dress, adorned with the Scull's Angels logo.

"Instead of advertising some designer's name, I'm advertising myself and my husband's business," she said. "I think it's a much better idea."

Mrs. Scull, who has worn the $600 Halston design to a number of social gatherings, including the opening of the opera, said her only regret was that she forgot to list the telephone number.

"We just didn't think about it," she lamented.

DECEMBER 14, 1973

'This Show Will Have the Most Shattering Effect on Fashion'

By BERNADINE MORRIS

The new fashion show at the Metropolitan Museum of Art is a dazzler. You don't have to be a fashion buff to enjoy it. It spans 30 years before World War II, when the century was young, the arts were in ferment, and much of the excitement was reflected in clothes. It focuses on five designers who invented new ways to dress the modern woman who was struggling towards emancipation. Naturally, their work was Paris, the center of all culture. No upstart New York was yet calling itself the fashion capital of the world. Oriental opulence, the brilliant colors of the artists known as the Fauves and of Diaghilev's Ballet Russe are all influences on the clothes, but the marvels are the clothes themselves. They recall the time when it was not absurd to call fashion an art. The splendor of the fabrics is rivaled only by the imaginative designs.

"This show will have the most shattering effect on what's going to happen in fashion," said Bill Blass.

In addition to its being "the best show I've ever seen," Mr. Blass explained that it would have an inspirational effect on both designers and women who are interested in clothes.

He was one of the contemporary designers attending a preview Wednesday night that in itself turned out to be a fashion event of some magnitude. About 450 people, followers of fashion, art and occasionally both, paid $150 (two-thirds of it tax deductible) to sip cocktails in the museum's Medieval Sculpture Hall and dine on the balcony of the Great Hall, surrounded by the Chinese porcelains on permanent display.

Wearing His Dresses

The dinner of pâté, veal and oranges filled with ice was served on tablecloths in an Oriental pattern chosen by Oscar de la Renta to complement the porcelains.

Mr. de la Renta is president of the Council of Fashion Designers of America, which co-sponsored the benefit for the Metropolitan Costume Institute. He sent the fabric around to some of his members' workrooms to be stitched into tablecloth shape.

He also designed at least three of the guests' dresses: the mauve satin-back crepe dress worn by Mrs. C. Douglas Dillon, whose husband is president of the museum's board of trustees, and who served on the receiving line, the flowing aqua dress worn by Mrs. de la Renta and the flowing red chiffon worn by Mrs. Jacob Javits. Before the night was over, the last two dresses were sporting small holes in the cape sleeves from cigarettes or candles, pointing up the danger of flowing chiffon.

After dinner, the guests filed through the Egyptian hall and down to the Costume Institute where the exhibit was installed, and the best clothes of today were juxtaposed with the past.

'New York's Versailles'

Maxime de la Falaise was in a full skirted Zandra Rhodes ("My first ballgown since I was 17"). Mrs. Joseph Neff wore a brown moire taffeta by Ib Jrogensen that she bought in Dublin, and Denise Hale was in an old Halston caftan, spruced up with a diamond necklace. Simone Levitt wore a blue Givenchy tent and Glady Solomon had on an Adolfo with a handkerchief-pointed hem that she hoped made her look like a flapper.

Mollie Parnis glittered in a red bugle-beaded jacket that revived an old black dress, Ethel Scull thought her pleated yellow Halston made her look angelic and Marilyn Evans was ravishing in a black Galanos dress with Art Deco embroidery and a new short hairdo.

"This is New York's Versailles," said Danny Zarem, who works with Geoffrey Beene, referring to last month's fashion benefit in Paris.

Some people even managed to tear their eyes away from the other guests to look at the exhibits.

Estée Lauder, in a magnificent Dior, was stunned by the Vionnet dresses, which managed to impress everyone. Valentino, the star of the Rome couture, also was stunned by Vionnet dresses, the black ones. "So now, you can wear them today—the softness, the beauty, the simplicity," he said.

But the star of the show was Diana Vreeland, who selected the clothes which reconstruct couture's finest hour.

Resplendent in a red dress with Pierrot ruffles from Yves Saint Laurent, which miraculously arrived in time for the party, she gracefully accepted compliments and guided people around the rooms.

Anticipating complaints from those who will claim she left out their favorite designers, Mrs. Vreeland defended her choice.

"Many others did beautiful dresses, but these presented a new line for the first time."

The exhibit, officially titled, "The Tens, The Twenties, The Thirties: Inventive Clothes/1909-1939" attempts to prove her thesis that everything in fashion today originated during this period.

The show starts with Poiret, who helped sweep in the modern era with his corsetless, slender clothes. Though he freed woman's body, he shackled her ankles with the hobble skirt. Progress in fashion, as in anything else, doesn't always run in straight lines.

Next come the Callot Soeurs, three sisters whose work influenced Balenciaga but whose names are known only to specialists from the fashion history books. Their pale, fabulous chemise dresses epitomize the 1920's—but wouldn't have raised an eyebrow a decade ago when the chemise was in fashion.

Chanel's cardigan suits and sweaters are still the rage 50 years after she invented them and Vionnet's bias cut dresses are as significant a development to fashion as the arch is to architecture. Schiaparelli provides the fun and games with her circus-theme jackets, designs by Cocteau embroidered on her clothes and even with her revival of the bustle.

Clothes, if viewed properly, provide the best social commentary. These progress from the rather timid changes of the century's teen-age years, when skirts were shortened to the ankles because women began to drive cars, through the leg-show of the twenties to the sobriety of the thirties.

The exhibit is a tour de force. Disagree with Mrs. Vreeland's thesis, haggle over her choices, but see it.

DECEMBER 23, 1973

Photography

The Golden Age of Architectural Photography

By GENE THORNTON

THE collection of 19th century photographs of Italy on view at the Robert Schoelkopf Gallery through Jan. 17 is a fascinating reminder of a branch of art that is now entirely taken over by photography, but that was once the province of painters and engravers: the architectural view. Architectural views, or pictures of famous buildings, was once a specialty that supported many painters and engravers, especially in Italy.

A few of these artists, for example Canaletto and Piranesi, are still well known today, but there were many others in the 18th and early 19th centuries. The paintings and engravings they produced were the picture postcards and color slide transparencies of their day, bought by tourists as souvenirs of their travels. They were seldom very accurate representations.

Piranesi is notorious for the way he exaggerated the size and grandeur of his Roman ruins, and lesser artists played fast and loose with lighting, perspective and scale. The young American photographer, Fredrich Cantor, who recently spent several months photographing Roman monuments with a book of 18th century engravings as his guide, reports that he could seldom match with his camera the point of view, lighting and perspective of the old engravings. Nevertheless, these faulty views, so highly valued today for their stylish distortions, were greatly valued in their own day as the most accurate representations available.

*

The introduction of photography put an end to the handmade architectural view. As thoughtful observers predicted from the start, photography set a new standard of realism that few artists could achieve, and soon the public refused to buy views that were not photographic in origin. The early daguerreotypists produced photographic originals that were then engraved or lithographed for reproduction. By the 1850's, however, technical advances made possible the production of large numbers of original photographic prints from large, clear negatives, and a golden age of architectural photography then began.

The 73 photographs now at the Schoelkopf Gallery include many masterpieces by the great names of 19th century Italian architectural photography: Robert MacPherson and James Anderson of Rome, the Alinari brothers of Florence, Carlo Ponti and Ferdinand Ongania of Venice. There are also some striking views by a Roman photographer, Cuccioni, unknown to the standard historians of photography.

A few of the pictures are not architectural views. There are several genre scenes—a spaghetti factory, a Sicilian donkey driver with his cart—as well as a few landscapes. There is also a photograph of the twisted, rough surfaced plaster casts of victims caught in the lava at Pompeii, pictures that are likely to make the modern viewer think of a statute of Ethel Scull by George Segal, though that was certainly no part of the photographer's intention, or of the works of Frederick Sommer of Arizona, though in fact the photographer is Giorgio Sommer of Naples.

Most of the pictures, however, are architectural views of the principal tourist attractions of Rome, Florence, Venice and other Italian localities. They are, of course, more accurate than the views produced by any pre-photographic painters or draftsmen except Canaletto and his school, who used the camera obscura to achieve their accuracy. But they also have a sober drama that appealed to the serious-minded Victorian age. Where Piranesi and the Canali peopled their views with little prancing figures, the 19th century photographers emptied theirs of all except occasional transparent ghosts. They could hardly avoid this, since the photography of that era was still too slow to capture figures in motion, yet one feels they preferred it so for the monumental effect it gave to their scenes.

Wherever possible, they favored a frontal approach more characteristic of Ingres than of Piranesi, or if they had to photograph a building from an angle, they chose the simplest angle available. Partly their aim was show the building or site at its most characteristic, and often the aspect they chose had been consecrated by earlier generations of painters and engravers. They achieved, however, a grave and dignified effect that made it quite clear (in case anyone did not know) that these photographs were of classics, and therefore worthy of a place in the parlors of the most refined and discriminating tourists.

*

This combination of a slightly pompous presentation with a wealth of accurately rendered detail was the standard achievement of all such photographers. The best ones went on to achieve truly breathtaking combinations of minute detail and panoramic breadth that modern photographers seldom attempt.

To modern viewers these old photographs have the added charm of showing an Italy that is now half-destroyed by the march of progress and scientific archeology. I particularly liked two views of old Rome. One showed the Coliseum environed by hillocks and little unpaved paths instead of a madly whizzing traffic circle. The other showed the little Arch of the Pantini beside the ancient Temple of Mars Ultor before archeological excavation left the Arch hanging 20 odd feet in the air, a dead end instead of a neighborhood thoroughfare.

The Schoelkopf Gallery will be closed Dec. 23 through Jan. 1.

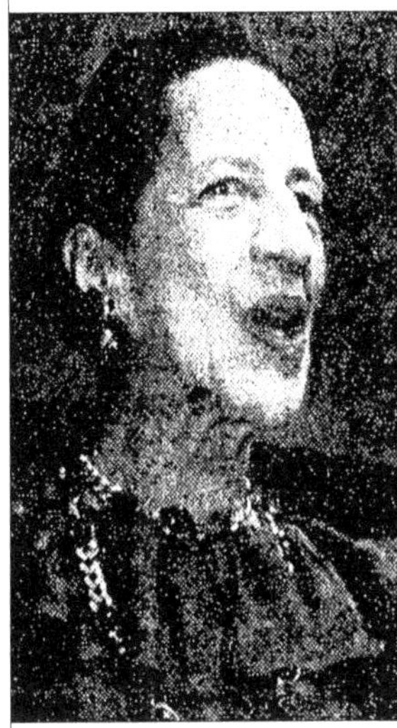

JANUARY 4, 1974

FASHION TALK

Chanel in Adolfo's Spring

By BERNADINE MORRIS

"The Scarlett O'Hara dress, now that's me," said Glady Solomon, a hint of Old Virginny still lingering in her accent.

"Not for me, the Scarlett O'Hara," said Ethel Scull, snuggling into her sable coat. "I'm not sixteen."

The dress in question was called Las Hadas, which refers to good fairies in Spanish and not Southern belles. The last number in the show of spring fashions by Adolfo, it had an off-the-shoulder neckline and a vast, billowing skirt of point d'esprit.

"Eight petticoats," the designer explained, as he was packing the clothes up after the formal presentation at the St. Regis Hotel yesterday at noon. "Plus ruffles, to make it stand out."

The dress epitomized the romantic flavor that ran through the show, but it wasn't Adolfo's special favorite. That would be the slinky ankle length dress in the Art Deco print with the godet-flare at the hem or maybe one of the two crepe georgette dresses inspired by Vionnet.

Chanel Is Evident

All of these were full of the artful seaming—godets at the ankle, triangular seams at the waistline—that shows up in the dresses from the nineteen-thirties in the current exhibit at the Costume Institute of the Metropolitan Museum of Art. Everybody said that it would prove influential on fashion.

But Adolfo didn't need the exhibit to remind him of Chanel. In his last collection, he paid tribute to her with a group of knitted versions of her cardigan suit, examples of which have been turning up all over New York. Now they're in lighter weights and bolder patterns—and there's even a version or two with pants. Romanticism or no, women are not about to give up their pants. You could tell by the applause.

Adolfo's Chanelisms, when they're skirts, stop just above the knee; Chanel's hems usually were an inch or two below. But don't feel that that settles anything. Adolfo shows a whole bevy of mid-calf length skirts, usually gabardine, often with a long tank top.

Pleats for Dressing Up

That's for casual wear. For dressing up—a garden party, for instance—there are pleated beige skirts that flare a lot and are worn with pale printed blouses in water color designs. You wear these with big-brimmed leghorn hats, in case you were wondering.

And for really dressing up, there are more pleats. Those tiny, fluid pleats made famous by Fortuny in the early part of this century. Adolfo intersperses a dress like this throughout his show, separating the Chanels from the long skirts, the ankle length dresses from the pants outfits. They're probably going to turn up at as many parties as caftans did last year.

The new ingredient is the fact that they're knitted. Adolfo says he's getting used to dealing with his knitting machines and learning to work out the effects he wants.

Plenty of women in his audience were wearing his knitted styles. Mrs. Scull wore one of the Chanels under her sable. Mrs. Solomon had on an ankle length brown knitted dress, one of five she owns. And Paulette Goddard's creamy white Adolfo dress was "from his first collection, when he stopped making just hats." That was back in 1968.

Miss Goddard also had a sable coat to throw over it. It was mid-calf length because "I always try to get as much fur as I can for my money."

Lynn Bohrer's new mink coat was down to her ankles. "It's supposed to be Saint Laurent length, but let's call it Adolfo's," said Mrs. Bohrer, who was at the show with her mother, Virginia Graham, and her 10-year-old daughter, Jan. Obviously, Adolfo fans are prepared for new hemlines, no matter where they fall.

Mrs. John Converse kept warm in heavy wool panty hose by Givenchy, which she buys every time she goes to Paris because she "can't find any here." Plenty of women wore pants, but hardly any wore boots. And a sable coat was the favored wrap to wear on a chilly day when you're thinking about your spring wardrobe.

JANUARY 27, 1974

MARCH 10, 1974

Charity Luncheons Thrive on Fashion

By BERNADINE MORRIS

The charity luncheon business is thriving these days, and it isn't even necessary to provide the lunch. Saks Fifth Avenue has discovered that all it has to do to pack its fifth floor is provide a digestible combination of good cause and popular fashion designer, with no more hearty comestibles than fresh strawberries and potatoes with caviar.

"We started with Kips Bay, and then we added Boys Club of New York, Just One Break and the Museum of the City of New York," a spokesman for the store observed. "Now everybody's after us."

Last Tuesday was the museum's turn, and the designer was Adolfo. Four hundred and fifty women turned up at 11:30 A.M., the usual hour. At $10 a ticket, all tax deductible, it was considerably less expensive for them than the usual dinner dance—and less fuss.

It wasn't necessary to get husbands involved ("If they don't have their own business dinners, they prefer to stay home," said one committee member), and the women didn't even have to have their hair done.

They could wear their new clothes if they had some, support one another's charity—and go on to lunch after.

The Next Day: Mme. Grès

The next day many of the same women turned up at the Plaza Hotel to support The Society of Memorial Sloan-Kettering Cancer Center and see the collection of Mme. Grès, one of the most durable designers of the French couture, paraded by her own models. For $20 ($12 of which was tax deductible), they also got to lunch on cream of mussels soup, chicken salad and fresh strawberries.

"Light enough for most dieters," said the reed-slim Mrs. Thomas L. Kempner, who was chairman of the committee that arranged the lunch. "If you're hungry like I am, you can snack off your neighbor's plate," she added.

Mrs. Kempner presided in one of Saint Laurent's new man-tailored glen plaid suits. It had a pleated skirt, not pants. The pants suits were just too man-tailored for her, she said.

Many of the guests carried out the couture theme in their clothes, even though Mrs. Thorburn Rand, president of the society, conceded that her tweed suit was "a Chanel type — not an original," and Mrs. Walter Nelson Pharr said her yellow, white and black coat was "last year's Givenchy."

Other Givenchy styles included the green snake-pattern suit worn by Mrs. Ezra Zilkha, which was from Ohrbach's, and the red snake coat worn by Mrs. William Levitt, which was from Givenchy. Mrs. Hansel Struve revived a 1958 Dior outfit, a three-quarter length loose coat over a narrow skirt.

The most-admired Grès styles were the draped evening things, and Mrs. Kempner couldn't wait to try on the white one with the bare midriff.

"They added half a dozen new evening styles for the show here," she said proudly. "They're what you keep for years and reach in your closet for when you don't know what to put on," she added.

At the Adolfo show, women who owned Adolfo styles— a goodly number —tended to wear them.

"I have more Adolfos than Carter has pills," said Mrs. Frederick Winship, chatting with Louis Auchincloss before the show. She was wearing a brown one. Mrs. Mortimer Solomon was in a blue one, Mrs. Robert Scull in a beige one.

Mrs. Henry Fownes, whose husband is a television producer, wore a black and white checked one, and Mrs. Irwin Stelzer, whose husband is an economist, wore the exact same style.

Mrs. Stelzer happened to win the door prize, an Adolfo style of her choice.

"I can't imagine which one I'll pick," she said. "I have most of the collection already."

The Adolfo's all these women had on were his versions of the Chanel style, so there was a bit of a French accent after all.

There was an occasional calf-length skirt in the audience.

"I couldn't believe they'd have the nerve to bring them out again," said Mrs. Kenneth Mann, whose long brown wool skirt matched her boots. "And then I found I liked it this time."

Eyes on Two Men

Mr. Auchincloss, president of the museum's board of trustees, demonstrated that besides being a lawyer and a novelist, he is becoming increasingly adept at fashion show commentary as the museum expands its fashion benefits.

He handled with aplomb the only non-Adolfo sequence, a group of wedding dresses from the museum's collection, modeled by volunteers.

He called attention to the wasp waist and leg o'mutton sleeves in Hilary Byers's 1895 dress, and pointed out that "Poiret eliminated the corset and brought on the boyish figure" when Fern Denny came out in her nineteen-twenties short dress.

The unexpected attraction at the Mme. Grès show was the appearance of Rudolf Nureyev to say goody to Lisa Sotilis, the sculptress who designed the jewelry shown with the Grès collection.

"He's going to dance in Canada tonight," Miss Sotilis explained. "He was supposed to have lunch with me, but he was too upset about Mr. Hurok's death to stay."

MARCH 12, 1974

Artists Seek Royalties in Painting Sales

By GRACE GLUECK

When a collector buys a contemporary work of art, then sells it at a profit, should the artist who created it get a royalty payment?

The question, increasingly pondered in the art world, has been given new impetus by escalating profits in the contemporary field, seen in such recent events as the $2-million sale of a Jackson Pollock painting to the Australian National Gallery by the collector Ben Heller (who paid $32,000 for it in 1956) and the $2.2-million brought by an auction of contemporary art from the collection of Robert Scull.

Spurred by such stimuli, and encouraged by lawyers and accountants, a rising number of artists are pushing for more control over the disposition of their works and a larger share of the financial pie than the fee-minus-dealer commission they get on first sales.

"Visual artists should have the same rights in their works as composers, authors and other creative people," asserted Rubin L. Gorewitz, a Manhattan accountant who has star artists such as Robert Rauschenberg among his clients. "At present, they receive no reproduction rights or exhibition fees, nor do they partake of profits made on the resale of their work."

To help remedy the situation, Mr. Gorewitz has recently drafted a proposal to provide a royalty system for visual artists that would work through Federal law. Backed by Mr. Rauschenberg, who has accompanied Mr. Gorewitz to Washington to help talk it up, the proposal is now under active consideration by Representative John Brademas, Democrat of Indiana, a frequent sponsor of arts legislation, and other Congressmen.

While supporting the idea of legislation, other artists have taken matters into their own hands, working with a form of voluntary contract they ask collectors to sign. They include Ed Kienholz, the California assemblagist currently working in Germany; Hans Haacke and Daniel Buren, conceptual artists; Jacqueline Winsor, a sculptor, and a New York-based group that calls itself the Artists Rights Association, headed by Judy Pendleton, a painter. Last fall the group held a show of works for sale only with a royalty contract.

"I'm not antagonistic to collectors," said Miss Winsor, who has sold work with a contract to Oberlin College and Charles Carpenter, a Connecticut collector, and is now negotiating for a contract sale to the Museum of Modern Art. "It's that the pieces are mine intellectually and I want to retain some kind of connection with them. The money is a way of making it a solid kind of agreement."

Mr. Kienholz drafted his own contract in 1969 and still uses it. A model for later ones, it provides for a 15 per cent royalty on the resale of his work for himself and his heirs, and a say in the way the work is exhibited. He has sold his art on that basis to a number of buyers in the United States and Europe, even withdrawing, in 1970, a work from sale to the University of California Art Museum at Berkeley after lawyers for the university had vetoed use of the contract.

Most of the other artists mentioned, including Miss Winsor, use a version of the Artists' Reserved Rights Transfer and Sale Agreement, devised in 1971 by Seth Siegelaub, then an art exhibition organizer, and Robert Projansky, a New York lawyer.

This agreement, bristling with clauses but generally employed in a simplified form, is designed to give the artist 15 per cent of appreciated resale price each time ownership of a work is transferred, the right to approve proposed exhibitions, all reproduction rights (by New York State law, artists retain reproduction rights to their work anyway) and half of any rental income from exhibitions. Benefits accrue to the artist for his lifetime and the life of a spouse, plus 21 years.

The collector, Mr. Siegelaub and Mr. Projansky maintain, gets such benefits as the formalized right to receive from the artist a certified provenance (history of ownership) of the work and the creation of "a nonexploitive one-to-one relationship between the artist and the owner."

While the Siegelaub-Projansky contract is voluntary, and hence not overly susceptible to policing and enforcement, Mr. Gorewitz's proposal would have Federal teeth. Basically, it also provides a 15 per cent royalty to the artist if work is resold at a profit, but for the initial and each subsequent resale, the seller would be required to apply to the artist for a certificate of authenticity (to be attached to his Federal income tax return for assurance of favorable capital gains treatment).

A copy would also go to the new buyer, who would be required to present the certificate to an insurance company if he wanted insurance on the work.

The certificate, Mr. Gorewitz holds, would attest to the authenticity of the work, as well as keep track of its provenance and provide a permanent record for the artist of its whereabouts.

French Law Cited

Another Federally applicable method of guaranteeing the artist a royalty on his work was suggested at the annual College Art Association meeting this January by Carl R. Baldwin, an art historian at Lehman College of the City University of New York. His proposal is based on the *"droit-de-suite"* (literally, "follow-up right") enacted into French law in 1920, allowing an artist to claim a percentage of the sale price each time his work is sold.

Mr. Baldwin urged the association to draft and support the text of an amendment incorporating a royalty system for visual artists in the United States copyright law. As things now stand, copyright law affords the visual artist *some* protection. As is the case with a writer or composer, he may prevent unsolicited reproduction or duplication of his work by registering it and applying the copyright symbol © in a conspicuous place. Few artists bother, however, disdaining the visibility of the symbol and the limited protection it affords.

But the key proviso of Mr. Baldwin's proposal, ongoing for 50 years after death, would state that each time a work of art is sold, exchanged or donated, a certain percentage of the sale price, or of the fair evaluation (in case of exchange or donation), would return to the artist or his heirs.

The Baldwin proposal would also give copyright protection on the first public exhibition of a work, entitling the artist to a flat commission or some percentage of the "gate" on each subsequent public exhibition.

"What got me into this was a reaction of frustration and outrage after reading about the Pollock sale," Mr. Baldwin explained. "As things stand now, the collector is the sole ruler of what the artist creates. There's no reason why a visual artist shouldn't have the same relation to his work as authors and musicians do."

Widespread Opposition

While some collectors, a number of dealers and most artists — but few museums — express enthusiasm for the idea of royalty contracts, there is opposition from all quarters on both philosophical and practical grounds.

For one, many art traffickers cite the difficulty and expense of administering Government regulation of royalty arrangements, and say further that such agreements would act as restrictions on the sale and "liquidity" of art.

And one dealer asked, "If the collector pays the artist when his work appreciates, shouldn't the artist turn around and pay the collector when his work goes down?"

Stephen E. Weil, administrator of the Whitney Museum of American Art and a lawyer well versed in art-world practices, maintains that it is difficult to judge when a work has made a "profit." Asserting that "95 per cent of all art sold decreases in value," he asked, "What about inflation and interest rates on investment? If a collector could have obtained interest on the money tied up in art, can you claim he's made a profit when he sells? What's needed are not restrictions but a broadening of the market, making it easier for people to buy."

March 24, 1974

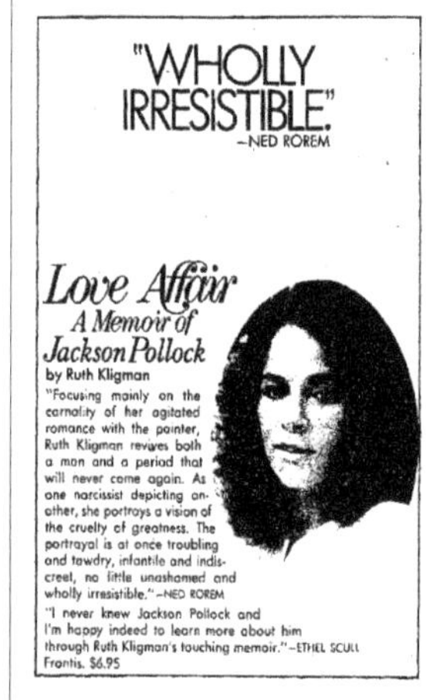

MARCH 26, 1974

The Shows Were Contemporary In More Ways Than One

By BERNADINE MORRIS

Streakers in sneakers. Mrs. Abraham Beame in Ultrasuède. Saint Laurent's man-tailored suits all over the place. Oh, it was a great day for fashion watchers yesterday.

The streakers, two women and a man, were part of the breakfast show at Alexander's. They were professional models, hired to give a contemporary tone, but the man didn't show up. So Bill Cronheim, an electrician for Entertainment Systems Consultants, who was setting up the lighting, volunteered to take off his clothes for $100. After the prologue, it was a little difficult to settle down to the clothes.

The Ohrbach's show was a far more serious business. There was Mrs. Beame in her green Ultrasuede coat ("not Halston — it's from Blassport," she said), checking off on her program a multitude of styles. They included the white Fabiani coat at

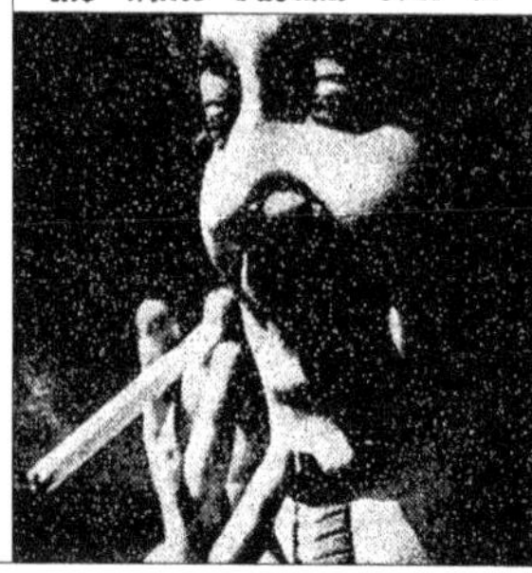

$135 ("so reasonable"), a red, white and blue plaid Givenchy suit, $450 and a striped Givenchy suit at the same price.

"I definitely know what looks good on me," Mrs. Beame said. "And I'm glad to see the suit is coming back."

Next to Mrs. Beame was Mrs. Kurt Waldheim, wife of the United Nations Secretary-General, and a few seats down was Mrs. John Connally, wife of the former Texas Governor.

"I came here last year and it was great fun," Mrs. Connally observed. Like many of the women, she was taken with the Saint Laurent pin-striped suit.

Mrs. Arthur Wirtz, whose husband owns the Black Hawks hockey team, left Chicago at 8 A.M. with her daughter, Betty Heuerman. Still shaky from the plane ride, she managed to nail down a couple of Givenchy styles and a Dior before the show went on.

The show, of course, was Ohrbach's semiannual classic roundup of Paris and Rome couture styles, translated in the original fabrics. It has, over the last 25 years, developed a loyal following of invited guests.

They packed the place an hour before show time, and Mrs. Hy Uchitel, wife of the restaurateur, swept off in a huff because nobody saved a seat for her.

The in-people turned up last Friday and Saturday to pick out their tailored Saint Laurent suits, which a number of them wore to the Alexander's show in the morning. There was some question whether the pants version was too mannish, but Ethel Scull didn't think so at all. Until a young man walked up to her and asked her where she got it.

"Do you think he wanted it for himself?" she asked.

It's not that Alexander's didn't have its own supply of Saint Laurent suits. But in line with its new policy this year, they were priced at $49.90 and $59.90. The fabrics were reasonable facsimiles, not the originals. One of the plaids came from Poland, the rest were American.

Everything in the Alexander's collection is under $100, which is fine for the pocketbook, but not so great if you're in the status-seeking race.

"Everybody likes the names on the labels, but not everyone wants to pay the price," said Francine Farkas reasonably. In addition to the Saint Laurents, the store's fashion coordinator collected a batch of Valentinos and a trio of Diors. Hermione Gingold was one of the women intrigued by the navy blue Valentino gown that spiraled around the body and cost $99.

The Ohrbach's collection started with a Valentino topper at $75 and stopped at those $450 Givenchy suits. But there were concessions. A shiny black ciré raincoat by Ungaro was $185 in the original fabric, $120 in a cotton and polyester copy. Similarly, a silk shantung duster by Dior, priced at $350, was $235 in cotton.

Which style do you pick? Which store do you go to? It depends, of course, on what you want to pay. But the true test is when you try on the garment. After all, nothing is a good buy if it doesn't fit properly.

And when you compare the copies with the prices at the couture houses in Paris, there are bargains at both stores. To mention two: the leather jacket with laced edges by Saint Laurent at Alexander's, $89; the pin-striped pleated skirt suit by the same designer at Ohrbach's, $220.

Both by Saint Laurent? Right, but he's the man of the hour. Look at his road record: pea jackets, trench coats, pants, sweaters— and now tailored suits.

"What's modern about that?" one woman said to her friend as one of the Saint Laurent suits came marching down the runway. "Marlene Dietrich wore them 35 years ago."

"Longer than that," her friend answered. Then they both headed for the fitting room to try them on. That's fashion for you.

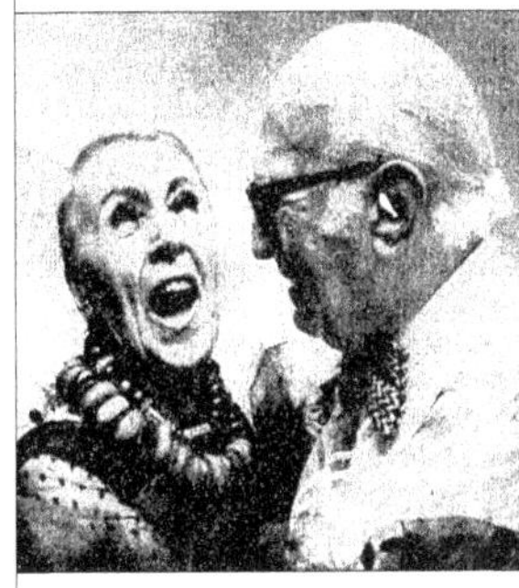

APRIL 19, 1974

Women Smokers: What Does Gender Have to Do With Problem?

By JUDY KLEMESRUD

Mrs. Kitty Panzer, a blonde, 65-year-old Queens housewife, strolled down Fifth Avenue the other day, cigarette in hand. In fact, she has spent much of the last 30 years of her life with a cigarette in her yellow-stained hand.

Mrs. Panzer is among the estimated 30 per cent of adult American women who are addicted to cigarettes. She started smoking, she remembers, when her husband bought her a Ronson lighter for no particular reason in 1944, about the time of a popular song that began:

"Smoke, smoke, smoke that cigarette, Don't stop puffing 'til you puff yourself to death . . ."

Those lyrics are perhaps even more relevant today as more and more people—especially women—are starting to smoke, smoke, smoke that cigarette. Last year, 52 million Americans consumed a record 583-billion cigarettes, up 59-billion from a decade ago.

At present, the estimated 30 per cent of adult American women who smoke is only about 10 per cent less than the number of adult males who smoke. Traditionally the gap has been much wider. But, while the number of male smokers has decreased steadily over the last few years, the number of women smokers has hovered around the 30 per cent mark.

Two recent developments, however, are causing health experts to tear at their hair: Women are smoking more cigarettes a day than ever before, and teen-age girls are starting to light up at an alarming rate. In 1972, the last year for which figures are available, cigarettes, and cigarette cases with time locks on them.

"I stopped smoking once," Mrs. Panzer said wistfully as she stood on sun-drenched Fifth Avenue. "It was in 1964, and I gave it up for eight years because my doctor told me I might get emphysema. I started again in Atlantic City two years ago, when my husband stopped to buy a pack of cigarettes. I said, 'I feel like having just one,' and ever since I've been smoking more than I ever did."

Several women said they started smoking either to lose weight or because they were afraid they might gain weight.

"I started because I wanted to lose weight and I did—25 pounds," Mrs. Carol Prager, an attractive, 32-year-old nurse from Holden, Mass., said as she stood in Rockefeller Center with her husband and two pre-school children.

She's Still Smoking

That was seven years ago, and Mrs. Prager is still smoking—and has no intention of quitting. "I enjoy it," she said firmly. "I find it relaxing, and I suppose to some degree it's a habit."

Unlike several other mothers interviewed, Mrs. Prager said she did not stop smoking during her pregnancies—even though studies have shown that mothers who smoke during pregnancy are more likely to experience miscarriage, stillbirth and the death of the newborn child. In addition, smokers' babies tend to weigh less at birth.

"Oh, the thought entered my mind [to stop smoking]," Mrs. Prager said, puffing on a cigarette. "But then my obstetrician told me the dangers were minimal, so I didn't quit."

Among the more prominent women smokers are Mrs. Henry Kissinger, the former Nancy Maginnes, who is said to be a chain smoker; Mrs. Aristotle Onassis; Princess Margaret; Lillian Hellman, the author; Dorothy Schiff, publisher of The New York Post; and Mrs. John V. Lindsay, wife of the former Mayor.

Women who refer to themselves as "occasional" smokers include Gloria Steinem, the feminist writer; Mrs. Richard M. Nixon, and Representative Bella Abzug. Well-known women who have kicked the habit include Barbara Walters, the television personality; Mrs. Ethel Scull, the socialite; and Mrs. Elinor Guggenheimer, the city's Commissioner of Consumer Affairs.

Lillian Wulff, 14, of Manhattan, is among the 11 per cent of teen-age girls who smoke. The other day she stood outside of Senator Robert F. Wagner Junior High School on East 76th Street during the lunch hour and tried to explain, in between drags on a cigarette, why, at the age of 12, she started smoking.

"I don't know, man, I just started," said the petite eighth grader, who claimed to have her parents' permission to smoke. "You see other people smoking and you want to, too. And I liked it—it's a beautiful feeling."

What isn't so beautiful is trying to quit.

"I felt like the Crimean Army was standing on my chest," said Caroline about 11 per cent of all girls aged 12 to 17 smoked, compared with 9 per cent in 1970 and 6 per cent in 1968.

Combined with the estimated 13 per cent of teen-age boys who smoked in 1972 (down 2 per cent from 1970), this translates into a staggering 3,000 new teen-age smokers every day.

And on top of it all, studies have shown that it is much harder for women to stop smoking once they are "hooked" than it is for men.

Why are women seemingly so attracted to cigarettes, also known as "coffin nails" and "cancer sticks" to some smoking foes? Are they unaware of the health hazards? Have they tried to quit? And if so, is it really harder for them to quit than it is for men?

These were some of the questions asked recently to women smokers chosen at random around Manhattan, as well as to health professionals and to prominent women smokers, "occasional" smokers and reformed smokers.

What emerged is this: Most of the women said they started smoking because it was the "smart" thing to do; almost all of the women said they were aware of the dangers outlined in the 1964 Surgeon General's report, which cited cigarette smoking as a major hazard to life and health; and almost all of the women smokers said they had tried at one time or another to quit, but had been unsuccessful.

Among the stop-smoking methods they used were: Hypnosis, medication, pacifiers, group therapy, stop-smoking clinics, "cold turkey" self-treatment, timers that a smoker can set to buzz at longer and longer intervals between Kirvin, a 28-year-old Manhattan research secretary, who has "quit" three times only to resume the habit.

She began smoking 13 years ago, she said, because her parents smoked and because she liked the "concept" of smoking—"It seemed a very relaxing habit, and I just liked the idea of sitting down and having a cigarette and a cup of coffee with friends."

Several women smokers said they had been the targets of the growing "nonsmokers lib" movement, in which nonsmokers are becoming bolder about complaining about cigarette smoke in public places.

Asked to Leave

Miss Kirvin said she had recently been asked by a fellow passenger on a train to Boston to smoke her cigarette in a restroom, which she did without complaining. Rose Marie Robinson, a Manhattan file clerk who vows she can quit smoking "anytime I want to," said her co-workers had recently become more vocal in their objections to her smoking.

Although all of the women interviewed seemed very aware of the health perils of smoking, many shared the feelings of Pamela Margoshes, 19, of Marblehead, Mass., a freshman at Barnard College, where she recently became known as "the Barnard streaker" for dashing nude across campus.

"Although I'm fully aware of the cancer business, somehow cancer's too unreal, too abstract," the curly-haired student said on campus the other day. "On the other hand, a cigarette in my hand is a more concrete thing to me."

Miss Margoshes and several other students said they thought more and more students were taking up smoking these days because they viewed it as something "adult," and also because of peer pressure and the tensions of college examinations.

One area where women were uncertain was whether it was more difficult for them to stop smoking than it is for men. However, Dr. Joyce Brothers, the psychologist and a nonsmoker, said there were several reasons why it's harder for women, among them:

¶Smoking helps a woman keep her weight down in a society where thin-is-in.

¶Smoking, because of such cigarette advertising campaigns as "You've Come a Long Way, Baby," helps a woman feel she's liberated.

¶Smoking helps a woman cope with her daily pressures.

"That's why I started to smoke—because it calms my nerves," said Mrs. Jennie Spath, a dark-haired 40-year-old school crossing guard from North Bergen, N. J., the other day as she stood in line outside Radio City Music Hall, waiting to see "Mame." By her side were her two daughters, Michele, 15, and Susan, 9, who refuse to buy their mother cigarettes because they are afraid she will get cancer.

"Sure it's harder for women to stop; it's because we have such an ordeal all day long," Mrs. Spath added authoritatively. "You know, the everyday drudge, the tensions, the children. Smoking just relaxes."

APRIL 28, 1974

Art Mailbag

TO THE EDITOR:

The Art Mailbag of March 31 carried a ludicrous letter from Ralph Colin of the Art Dealers Association on the very real problem of "royalties" to artists from the resale of original works of painting, sculpture, etc. Mr. Colin based his conclusion that everyone except the artist should benefit from an increase in the value of a work on a totally irrelevant "analogy" between an author's manuscript sold to a publisher with ensuing royalties from sales and the resale of a work of art by a dealer or collector.

What Mr. Colin fails to understand is that the book manuscript is not what is being bought and sold but *the publication rights.* The manuscript is *not* the work of art, the printed book is the product involved, and it can go into virtually unlimited printings and sales without loss of quality. The publication of the book is not a "re-use" of the manuscript; it is its primary, original use.

A painting or a piece of sculpture is a one-time thing and published reproductions are not the work of art. The original work cannot be experienced in reproduction, and certainly the Art Dealers Association knows this.

So when a Robert Scull buys at, let us say, $1,000 and sells at $10,000, the living artist who made the work gets a royal nothing from this accrual of value whereas an author's right to a continuing share in increased earnings through increases in sales is fully recognized. The sale of a fine painting is *it* — no income from thousands of copies or second or third editions from which the creator could draw a share follows.

Mr. Colin, there is a difference, and this difference calls for real solutions from which the creative visual artist could draw some sustenance.

BERNARD KASSOY
Painter

Member, Board of Directors,
Artists Equity Ass'n. of N.Y.

MAY 5, 1974

SUNDAY 7:30 P.M. **CITYSCOPE**
"THE BUSINESS OF ART"
DR. ROBERT S. HIRSCHFIELD
City University of New York
GUEST: ROBERT SCULL
Art collector/businessman
WNYC 31 TV

MAY 24, 1974

'Constructive Party' Pleases Louise Nevelson

By ENID NEMY

For a woman who has battled shyness most of her life, Louise Nevelson had a ball. Midway through the party on Spring Street, Wednesday night, she surreptiously kicked off her shoes and swept through the maze of rooms, that make up her home and studio, looking like what one fascinated spectator called "a Russian empress mingling with the peasants."

There were some pretty classy peasants around, and rich, too, and almost all of them were decked out in couturier outfits of black or white, or a combination of the two. It was the thing to do for an evening labeled "The Black and White Event." But most of the guests' eyes signaled defeat when they spied the hostess, her face as finely chiseled as one of her sculptures, her majestic figure in Scaasi's long and glittery black gown, framed by a ruffled tulle and jet coat, and her throat encircled by an enormous African necklace.

"I will always sacrifice comfort for beauty," said Mrs. Nevelson, sotto voce, her sooty curtain of false eyelashes sweeping over the scores of women who had bowed to the hot and humid weather with various degrees of décolletage.

Mrs. Nevelson, who prefers to be addressed as Louise Nevelson, but rarely is, said that she had always felt like a Russian empress, and no mind that she was born in Russia as something other than that.

Paid $100 Each

She also preferred that the evening be called "a constructive party," rather than the benefit that it was—for the Merce Cunningham Dance Foundation. It was indeed constructive. By the time it had ended, about 175 men and women had forked over $100 each for their silver dog tag admittance tokens, and the coffers of the Cunningham group were expected to swell by about $17,000.

"In my 74 years, I've never been more pleased than having this party for a great artist," said Mrs. Nevelson, smiling fondly at Mr. Cunningham, who said he had bought his black and white striped shirt at J. C. Penney in Seattle.

John Cage, the composer, hadn't gone anywhere for his outfit. He said he always wore his blue denim pants and jacket but, in honor of the occasion, he had added a black tie.

"I can wear these hunting wild mushrooms or giving a lecture or doing anything," he explained. "I used to waste a lot of time changing."

Mrs. Nevelson nodded understandingly and leaned over to whisper in his ear. Mr. Cage said, audibly, that he would be delighted.

"I asked him to get me a beer," Mrs. Nevelson confided. "I didn't want anyone to hear because beer doesn't go with my outfit."

Sculpture-Lined Walls

Nathan Cummings, the man who built the Consolidated Foods empire and a considerable art collection, and Mrs. Cummings, both in stark white, entered the sparsely furnished room and stood against one of the large black Nevelson sculptures. The sculptures line the walls of the five-story house, a former sanatorium, and the adjoining four-story building that has been cut through to it.

Mrs. Nevelson bussed the Cummingses on the cheeks and looked pleased with herself.

"Darlings, I know you now," she announced proudly.

"I used to be embarrassed at not remembering names," she said, in an aside. "Then I decided to forget it and not struggle. I say 'dear' if I like people and 'darling' if I like them very much." She did not add that she sometimes says nothing at all if she doesn't like them at all.

She liked Robert Monahan, president of the National Corporation well enough to try a little matchmaking. She reached for his arm and towed him along into a little room next to the bar.

"I've brought you a good looking bachelor," she said to Diana MacKown, her assistant. Miss MacKown and Mr. Monahan exchanged a few pleasantries and Miss MacKown moved off.

"She's playing an old-fashioned game," Mrs. Nevelson observed. "But the evening is young."

Before the evening got much older, the party was joined by Mrs. Samuel Newhouse, Mrs. Jacob K. Javits, Dr. Leonard Gordon and his wife, the actress Rita Moreno, Arnold Glimcher, the owner of the Pace Gallery, Calvin Tompkins, Mr. and Mrs. Frederick Winship, Mr. and Mrs. Charles Diker, Mr. and Mrs. Eugene Schwartz and Mary Moore, daughter of Henry Moore, the sculptor.

Mrs. Martin Ackerman, a committee member, inspected the buffet table, where Mrs. Noel Levine, the chairman of the event, was dishing out lamb and chicken curry, rice, flat round bread, mango chutney and coconut.

"It's not bad for $3 a head," Mrs. Ackerman commented. "But then the caterer [Bundo Kahan] was Louise's choice and if anyone has taste, she has."

Mrs. Robert Scull wasn't interested in food. She spread her white pleated dress on the floor and propped her head on a cushion she has carried since injuring her back several years ago.

Mrs. Nevelson looked disapproving. She gathered up two charcoal pillows and placed them on top of Mrs. Scull's own beige one.

"A black and white party is a black and white party," Mrs. Scull noted. "She didn't want to spoil the environment."

Even the city did its bit to cooperate with the theme. As guests left the studio, to pick up cars parked across from the shuttered Balkan Restaurant Delicatessen Fruit Market, they found the corner guarded by two police officers, a black woman and a white man.

AUGUST 19, 1974

Sotheby's Sales Rose 21% in Year

Sotheby Parke Bernet, with branches in London, New York, Los Angeles, Zurich and other cities, has announced that sales for the 1973-74 season totaled $216,762,480, an increase of 21 per cent over last season.

The main salesroom in New York had a record total of $69,394,156. Its subsidiary gallery here achieved an additional $3,730,869. Los Angeles emerged as the second art market center in the United States for sales. Its seasonal figure of $9,305,308 nearly doubled last year's total of $5,188,842.

Highlights of the season in New York were the dispersal of 50 American contemporary paintings from the collection of Mr. and Mrs. Robert C. Scull; 17 Picassos from the collection of Bernice McIlhenny Wintersteen, and a large group of 20th-century European and contemporary American paintings from the collection of Arnold H. Maremont of Chicago.

AUGUST 25, 1974

What I hate about clothes...

By Judy Klemesrud

Before the consumer revolution and the women's movement had made their marks, everything in the world of fashion was "lovely" or "terrific" or "fantabulous."

Nowadays, when women talk about clothes—and many are loath to admit that they do—the adjectives have soured to "shoddy" and "overpriced" and "impractical."

The complaints come not just from the frugal housewives who shop the 14th Street economy stores. They come also from some of the fashion world's Leading Ladies, those super consumers whose fashion chatter over lunch at La Grenouille often turns into gripe sessions.

But no matter whether the women are hovering near the poverty line or have made it to the loophole level, they all seem to have the same complaints about clothes. Here are just a few of them:

"My seams keep falling apart."

"Everything is so expensive."

"My pantyhose go to pieces after two wearings."

"Nothing fits anymore."

"Even expensive shoes have to have new heel lifts after a few weeks' wear."

"Skirts don't have hems anymore."

"Everything seems so sleazy these days."

These comments were obtained in interviews with two dozen New York women, representing a cross-section of ages, occupations and economic levels. Only one of the women interviewed, Susan Stein Shiva, the socialite, said she was satisfied with clothes just as they are.

Louise Escalera, on the other hand, is totally dissatisfied. "Clothes are very skimpy these days. Manufacturers are not making them true to size anymore," she said as she shopped at Klein's on Union Square.

"I'm a size 14, and yet I have to buy a 16 or larger to get something that fits," Mrs. Escalera, a supermarket cashier, said irately. "A large is just not a large anymore."

Gertrude Nelson, a silver-haired, 68-year-old retired city employe, thumbed through a Klein's rack of knit blouses. "Clothes don't wear as well as they used to," she said, "and prices are ridiculous. You bring a dress home from the store and the seams just fall apart. Everything in this country is falling apart!"

Well, maybe not *everything*, but according to William Seitz, executive director of the Neighborhood Cleaners Association, which represents 3,000 cleaners in the five-state metropolitan area more and more articles of clothing are having trouble holding together—at the cleaners, at least

"High on the hit parade of complaints," and that's the way he talks, "is the stiffening of vinyl plastic that is being used more and more in clothing. Vinyl plastic loses its plasticizer in the cleaning process and then it stiffens or peels."

"And then you get the knitwear from Hong Kong or Taiwan," he went on. "Generally, it is acrylic, and it sags and stretches. Once it stretches, there is no way you can shrink it back to its original form."

Other items that cleaners are having problems with these days:

Plastic buttons, which dissolve in the dry cleaning process.

Elastic waistbands, which lose their elasticity in dry cleaning.

Suède and leather garments that have been improperly handled or treated in the manufacturing process with the result that they shrink or lose their dye when cleaned.

Vivid prints that contain soluble dyes that fade. For example, red will fade to pink, and orange to yellow.

Some women, like Kathrin Seitz, a film consultant, swear by imported (especially French) clothes on the grounds that the American manufacturers don't know how to fit their slim figures. Others, like Mrs. Nelson, swear by American clothes, on the grounds that the imports are poorly made, and that their sizes cannot be translated accurately to American sizes.

"I think American-made clothes are much better," she said. "Besides, we've got to be loyal to our garment workers. If we keep buying these clothes from Europe, where the wages are much lower, we'll put our own union workers out of business."

Linda Stern, 32-year-old research director for WABC-Radio, had three clothing complaints: metal buttons that tarnish, pantyhose that fall apart, and pants that stretch. "And the expensive pantyhose—the sheer ones—are gone the second time you wear them," she said. "I find that the cheaper brands, even though they don't look as nice, wear much longer."

Pants, generally double-knits, often stretch when they're cleaned. "Then you have to pay to have them shortened," she lamented.

Do the rich have to put up with such things? Apparently. According to Ethel Scull, wife of the owner of the New York taxi company Scull's Angels, Inc., whenever she buys something off the rack in a department store, she can't wear it for more than one season. "It just falls apart," she said sadly.

And that is why, she said, she buys most of her things custom-made from Halston or Adolfo, where she generally gets quality for her money.

But not always.

"Last year, even Adolfo stopped lining things, and I complained about it bitterly," she said.

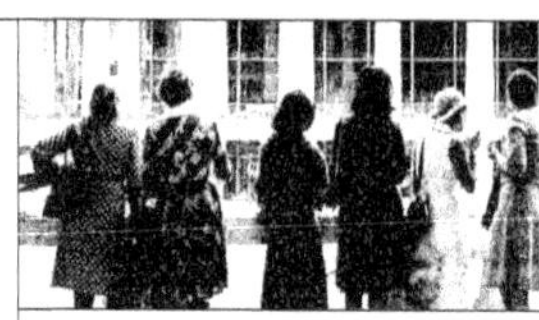

"Everybody tries to skip it if they think they can get away with it. I said, 'This skirt will bag if you don't line it,' so they lined it for me."

Judy Goldman, an East Sider and the mother of two grown children, questioned the validity of the various "washability" tags on clothes. "My daughter bought a cotton T-shirt that was supposed to be washable," she said, "but when she washed it, it went from large to smaller-than-small. Anyway, she took it back and they refunded her money."

Many clothing complaints are related to stores that do not give refunds in situations like that of the shrunken T-shirt. According to a spokesman for the New York City Department of Consumer Affairs, lack of uniform sizing and mail-order clothes that bear little resemblance to the way they were pictured in the catalogues are major complaints.

Marie Brenner, 24-year-old story editor for Paramount Pictures, spoke for many women who happen not to be built like New York's scrawny, boyish fashion models. "My main gripe about clothes is that they're all for flat-chested people." Miss Brenner's "chest" measures 39 inches.

Betsy Lubetkin is also a bit bigger than your average fashion model. "I'm 5-feet-10½ inches," and not a slim 5-feet-10½ inches, she said. She cannot find medium-priced "sophisticated" dresses that she can wear in her job as acting assistant administrator of the city's Human Resources Administration.

"Unless you get really expensive stuff, the medium-priced stuff is cheap—just too bright, garish and kinky. What happened to all those smartly cut, medium-priced, sophisticated clothes that were available during the Jackie Kennedy years?"

The "costume syndrome" was attacked by Mrs. John Mosler, New York State Deputy Commissioner of Commerce and wife of the millionaire safe manufacturer.

"The average woman simply cannot afford these fads, she cannot afford it when designers tell her she has to dress for the 40's and 50's," she said. "Only four years ago, they dropped those skirts to the floor, and nobody could afford more than two of them. Then came those bulky sweaters—they don't work for most women, and they're damn expensive."

Almost every woman had something to say about her favorite article of clothing—pants. Usually it was very flattering, but sometimes even these dearly beloved came in for criticism.

Sierra Bandit, a tall, slender, red-haired actress who appears in Robert Altman's upcoming movie, "California Split," said she wore only men's button-front Levi's because she finds women's pants are cut strangely—small in the waist, big in the hips. They make her look like "a ball walking down the street."

Linda Rosen, a freelance writer, said her pants are always falling apart, especially around the zipper.

"I had one rotten experience with pants—I wore them twice, washed them, and the entire pocket detached itself from the pants," said Mrs. David Newman. "I had to go to the tailor and pay $3 to have the pocket put back in."

"That really annoyed me," she added. "A big brand name, and they fall apart the minute you put them in the wash. I mean, if we're going to talk about women accomplishing things and doing something, then we've got to have clothes that will hold up while we're wielding a camera, or painting, or sitting in an office."

SEPTEMBER 10, 1974

They Attended Benefit Looking as If It Were Fall Already

By ENID NEMY

The calendar said "yes" and the weather said "no," but it wasn't really a contest. The calendar won, as it was bound to do with fashion involved. A lot of women were dying to show off their new fall outfits and they did. It was an ideal opportunity — the first of the seasonal round of fashionable fashion shows.

But if the audience at yesterday's Pauline Trigère show at the State Theater of Lincoln Center was a barometer of what one will be seeing around this fall, the forecast is for just about anything. The anything should, preferably, have a slightly longer skirt, but if it doesn't, no one will be shamed out of existence.

Not Clothes Horses

The 700 women — who forked out $25 each to benefit the New York City Opera Center of Music & Drama, to watch the Bergdorf Goodman-sponsored show and nibble on sandwiches and pastry boxed by Le Nôtre—were not dedicated clothes horses, with a few exceptions.

They liked fashion, most of them said, and they were aware of what was going on, but awareness did not necessarily mean agreement. A number of women wrote off the chemise with such comments as, "Unwearable," or "Why?" Still more said that although they would buy anything new with a slightly longer skirt, they would have no hesitation in continuing to wear their present knee and slightly above-the-knee lengths.

"Fashion isn't our business," said Elaine A. Flug, an arrangements co-chairman of the Opera Guild, who turned up in a classic shirtwaist-type dress. "Music is our business . . . and we are not accustomed to being such a social thing."

Mrs. Flug was, at that very moment, looking in the direction of two women who might very well be professionals in the fashion business, but aren't. They are, however, elegant amateurs and their costumes were the subject of almost as much admiration as their indomitable faces.

Merle Oberon, who was wearing a generous amount of gold jewelry with her forest green Ultrasuède outfit from Halston, said she was perfectly comfortable, despite the thermometer.

"Not too warm and not too cool," she said with a smile.

Kitty Carlisle agreed with the comments that her Bill Blass outfit was chic.

Trigère Outfits

"It is, isn't it, and it's so comfy," she said of the navy wool skirt worn with tweed pullover and cardigan sweater.

Both Mrs. Theodore Newhouse, chairman of the benefit, and Mrs. Irwin Davidson, a co-chairman, chose Pauline Trigère outfits. Mrs. Davidson was in a black wool pants suit, with David Webb diamond and jet jewelry; Mrs. Newhouse had on a chemise dress and cape.

"Pauline is so clever," she said enthusiastically. "She made this dress in the spring and it's a chemise!"

Trigère's wools, Blass's three-piece costumes and Adolfo's lightweight knits were among the popular fall choices of the women present, but lengths varied. Livia Weintraub and Ethel Scull had their black Adolfo knits well below the knee; Mrs. Irving Zakin wore her camel-colored knit at the knee. All three women said they felt perfectly comfortable.

In Many Colors

But then, the scores of women who completely ignored fall also apparently felt comfortable.

"These are the most wonderful dresses," said Mrs. Thayer Gilpatric of her pale blue Qiana shirtwaist. "I have them in every color and I traveled around the world in them."

"I'm not fashionable but I go by the weather, not the season," said Karin Megerle of Closter, N.J. Mrs. Megerle, a member of the benefit committee, wore a blue-banded white hat and a white pants suit.

"I can't put my mind to winter when it's so hot," said Elga Andersen, an actress who appears in the film, "Le Mans." Miss Andersen wore a red cotton pants suit, a red and white striped T-shirt and a straw hat. The outfit came from St. Tropez and "it feels like St. Tropez today," she said.

SEPTEMBER 10, 1974

'Cop Art': Artistic Brush With Police

By JOSEPH B. TREASTER

At first glance it looked like the most heavily guarded art show in the city. As it turned out, however, the men and women in uniform were the artists themselves.

They were standing proudly with their work yesterday morning as an exhibit called "Cop Art '74" opened at Police Plaza in lower Manhattan.

There were 42 artists showing 175 realistic and impressionistic paintings, line drawings, water colors and sculptures in marble, wood and metal.

Police Commissioner Michael J. Codd said the exhibit, which will run through Sunday from 10 A.M. to 6 P.M. with free admission, revealed another side of the force.

Roosevelt Dunning, the deputy commissioner for community affairs, said the exhibitors were "multidimensional people . . . they are truly true New Yorkers. . .not just law-enforcement machines focused only on crime."

Few of the artists chose police work as their subject matter, but the nature of their professional lives emerged distinctively in the bold, forceful treatment of landscapes and seascapes and in their straightforward portraits and stark sculptures.

Robert C. Scull, the millionaire taxicab owner and art collector who served as a judge, said he felt many of the artists had expressed "themselves in really lovely, gentle terms."

A tall, gray-haired officer was studying a canvas with thick red and white horizontal stripes and, in one corner, a patch of flaming colors with what seemed to be a nose protruding from it.

"That's my friend Nixon," said Officer Daniel Higgins, who had won a citation from the Brooklyn Museum for the work. "He's either behind bars or hiding behind the flag."

Inspector Samuel Fandel, the highest-ranking artist in the show, lingered next to his favorite piece, a mist-shrouded sloop that seemed to be dissolving into infinity. For him the painting suggested "the sort of feeling that nobody knows where they're going."

Officer Robert Philios, who led in the collection of citations, with seven, contended that police work offered a special vantage point for the artist. "You see things that other people don't see," he said.

Nearby, Detective Lucretia Belardo stood her ground as a woman pleaded with her to buy her darkly rich painting of a lone distant figure heading toward a village church. Sales were not permitted at the show, and besides, the detective said, "it's too near and dear to me."

The Police Plaza, which is in front of Police Headquarters, can be reached by walking east through the main arch of the Municipal Building at Centre and Chambers Streets.

SEPTEMBER 15, 1974

A Film Festival With No Stars Or Prizes, But Lots of Innovation

By GRACE LICHTENSTEIN

WHEN "Antonia: A Portrait of the Woman" opens the New American Filmmakers Series at the Whitney Museum this Wednesday, it will mark the fifth anniversary of a movie festival that, without much fanfare, has become the showcase for independent films in this country.

The eyes of the vast majority of movie buffs, of course, will be on another event that takes place each September — the New York Film Festival, which will run from Sept. 27 through Oct. 13 at Lincoln Center. But while its 21 feature films get the lion's share of attention, the Whitney fall series, which runs through Dec. 10, will undoubtedly attract its own faithful 16-millimeter fans, as it has since 1970.

The Whitney showing is not really a festival in the Cannes sense. No prizes are given, no starlets are likely to crowd their cleavage into the modest museum screening room, no raging disputes involving major studios will break out. Instead, the series will simply give New Yorkers who love documentaries, animation and experimental works a chance to see some of the freshest, most innovative movie work currently being produced.

"Antonia" is a case in point. Co-directed by two women, it tells the story of an indomitable woman musician now living in Denver who has never allowed her regret at failing to become a major orchestra conductor destroy her love of her art. It is a feminist documentary about the still overwhelmingly male chauvinist world of classical music, made by women working in the male chauvinist world of film. Yet it delivers its message with a kiss, not a punch in the nose.

"Warm" is the word most often used to describe "Antonia" by filmmakers and Whitney officials who have seen it, and indeed all the cliché synonyms — "sensitive," "touching," "affectionate" — apply. "It's a very accessible film," said Terry Kemper, coordinator of the Whitney Film Department, in explaining why "Antonia" was chosen to begin the fall season.

The movie had an interesting genesis, one which illustrates how independent filmmakers working on tiny budgets, but without studio pressures, can turn out films full of personal involvement.

Antonia Brico, now 73, had among her piano students back in the 1950's a girl named Judy Collins. Then an aspiring concert pianist, Miss Collins went on to stardom as a folksinger, but she remained in touch with her mentor throughout the years.

"There were only a couple of influences in my life that were female," Miss Collins said recently, chatting in her spacious upper West Side living room, "and Brico was the major one." While in Denver two years ago to work on some political campaigns, Judy Collins renewed her friendship with Miss Brico, and began thinking of making a movie about her. Finally, she called Jill Godmilow, a filmmaker acquaintance, to suggest they work together on the project. Miss Godmilow's reaction was, "Want to lose $1,000?" The folksinger said yes.

For the next six months, the two women, using a small camera crew, followed Miss Brico through her lessons, master classes and performances with her own Brico Symphony, a semi-professional orchestra.

The $1,000 eventually stretched into some $75,000, with the entire cost of the film borne by Miss Collins' company, Rocky Mountain Productions. The two women share directorial credit for the film, although Miss Collins freely acknowledges that Miss Godmilow, a 30-year-old Philadelphia native whose previous film was a 70-minute experimental documentary called "Tales," supplied the technical expertise.

According to both women, their collaboration was as satisfying as the end product itself, though it was not without shouting matches, soul-searching over which deeply personal material about Miss Brico should be left on film, and disappointment at not selling the film to a commercial television network.

At the start, Miss Collins recalled, "I was petrified. But Jill really taught me. I found it was very much like music. You have to phrase it, it has to flow, the themes have to be connected."

For her part, Miss Godmilow finished the film as enthralled by Miss Brico's personality as Miss Collins had always been. What the film shows, essentially, is a woman who was good enough to conduct the Berlin Philharmonic Orchestra at 28, good enough to make guest appearances at the Metropolitan Opera House, good enough to scare off the renowned baritone John Charles Thomas (he refused to sing under her direction because he was afraid of being upstaged), good enough to impress Arthur Rubinstein and Bruno Walter, yet somehow not acceptable enough to have been offered a permanent conductor's job she always wanted.

She is currently director of her own orchestra in Denver, but in one poignant scene, she throws off the cloak of sexless professionalism to pour out her "perpetual heartache." Talking to Judy Collins, who is off-camera, she demands, "How would you like to have just five concerts a year? I don't get a chance to play my instrument — the orchestra." At another point she describes her situation as being "like giving birth to a baby and then having it taken away from you."

Miss Collins admitted that she provoked the outburst, using her long-standing personal relationship with Miss Brico to "force out that pain." Afterward, Miss Godmilow wondered if they, as filmmakers, had the right to dig so deeply into any subject's feelings, but they justified their probing on the grounds that it illuminated a wholly human —and usually hidden—side of the woman.

Scenes like this make the film an extraordinarily moving document, the kind of personal statement that one sees too rarely in normal feature films. To critics and viewers, a prime value of the Whitney series is the rare opportunity to see such personal works, as well as the rest of the cream of the 16-millimeter crop usually available only though the Flaherty seminar (the annual filmmakers' gathering named after documentary pioneer Robert Flaherty), the Ann Arbor Festival and other specialized forums.

The difference between the New American Filmmakers Series and regular festivals is that each program—there are 10 in the fall collection—is shown in a theatrical setting several times a day for two weeks. The price of admission to the museum — $1 on weekdays, $1.50 on weekends—also includes a movie ticket on request. Film tickets go on sale each day five minutes after the start of the previous show and it's usually wise to line up early. Thus, for example, "Antonia" will be shown daily at noon, 1:30 P.M., 3 P.M. and 4:30 P.M., plus Tuesday evenings at 6, 7:30 and 9 PM. Tickets for the noon showing would be available when the museum opens at 11 A.M., for the 1:30 show at five minutes after noon, and so on. The screening room holds 120 people.

"It's a real run," said Terry Kemper, adding that the films are selected by the museum's film curator, rather than a panel of judges, but that anyone can submit a film to the museum for consideration.

The current curator, John G. Hanhardt, took over in July after a stint at the Walker Arts Center in Minneapolis. He chose the films in the fall series after seeing them at small festivals and open screenings. In addition to "Antonia," the series will include an 80-minute silent film by Andrew Noren, "Kodak Ghost Poems;" an ethnographic film about people in Southern Ethiopia by Robert Gardner, "Rivers of Sand;" a program of 11 new animated films; and a documentary by E. J. Vaughn about the auction of the Pop Art collection of Robert C. Scull that is already stirring controversy in art circles.

For independent filmmakers, the Whitney series is as important as a potential sales outlet as it is an artistic showcase. In the past, such films as Norman Mailer's "Maidstone" and Bob Dylan's and Howard Alk's "Eat the Document" have been bought for theatrical distribution after their premiere in the New American Filmmakers series. Other works have been rented for wider showings in regional museums, libraries and colleges, while a few filmmakers have been offered film jobs partly as a result of their Whitney showings.

John Hanhardt says that while the series "certainly gives a boost" to a film's chances for further distribution, there are still not enough outlets for such commercial showings. Critics who think highly of the Whitney series are disappointed that so few of the outstanding films in each year's series get commercial recognition afterward. "If they're lucky, they may get a shot at the Fifth Avenue Cinema," one critic commented.

Whether or not "Antonia" goes beyond its two-week Whitney appearance and future festival showings remains to be seen. Ironically, however, the movie may help its 73-year-old star to get a new lease on her conducting career. Miss Collins believes the city of Denver is suddenly beginning to realize that Miss Brico has been languishing in its own backyard. No one knows how much the publicity about the film has to do with it, but on Nov. 10, Antonia Brico will make her first guest appearance in over six years as conductor of the Denver Symphony Orchestra.

SEPTEMBER 15, 1974

OCTOBER 17, 1974

Movie Documents Auction of Scull's Art

AMERICA'S POP COLLECTOR: ROBERT C. SCULL. "Conceptualized and co-ordinated" by E. J. Vaughn and John Schott; edited by Leah Siegel and Mr. Schott; filmed by Susan and Alan Raymond and Ron Dorfman; originated and produced by Mr. Vaughn Running time: 72 minutes. EUPHORIA by Vincent Collins, 4 minutes. At the Whitney Museum of American Art, Madison Avenue and 75th Street. Through Tuesday.

By NORA SAYRE

Many people are going to enjoy "America's Pop Collector: Robert C. Scull—Contemporary Art at Auction," but I especially recommend it to publishers and movie makers—since this documentary makes the book or film industries look pure and pastoral in comparison to the art world. The movie, which was "conceptualized and coordinated" by E. J. Vaughn and John Schott, and filmed by Susan and Alan Raymond, opened yesterday at the Whitney Museum of American Art and will run until Tuesday.

●

Once you've witnessed the October, 1973, auction of 50 works of art from the collection of the taxi tycoon Robert Scull—the sale brought him $2,240,900—you may be glad that you don't paint, sculpture, own, sell, or buy contemporary art—which appears to addle many who come in contact with it. In fact, the movie makes the audience feel superior to those on screen—a sensation that's always pleasing, whether it's justified or not.

The sale included works by Willem de Kooning, Frank Stella, Robert Rauschenberg, Franz Kline, Barnett Newman, Larry Poons, Andy Warhol and James Rosenquist. When asked why he chose to sell his possessions, Mr. Scull answers repeatedly that the exhibition at Parke Bernet was the only way that he could see these paintings, sculptures and constructions together; he emphasizes the lack of space in his apartment, remarking that many pieces had been in storage. (Apparently, he had to part with these things in order to look at them.) He adds that owning art is "a different kind of high." Others criticize him for loving publicity, though he's also credited for his adventurousness in buying difficult works when they weren't popular, and Robert Rauschenberg stresses that the Sculls helped artists at a period "when there wasn't enough activity to support them."

Meanwhile, some are distressed at seeing these works leave the country. And although the question of artists' royalties isn't discussed in this film, it does raise the issue of a collector's making such gargantuan profits when the artists receive none. (Mr. Scull, who dodges queries about art as an investment, gets quite huffy about profits; he insists that he's raising the artists' price for their future work.) Throughout, he comes through as jovial and benign; though the film mocks him, he's allowed to appear likable.

In this documentary, the works of art are definitely treated as objects—they're filmed very casually, without perception or respect. It's hard to tell if this was totally intentional — if the film makers deliberately presented paintings and sculptures in the spirit of the market place, or if they were also somewhat insensitive. However, it's gripping to see the stuff handled about as tenderly as the airlines treat your luggage: a Larry Poons painting slips while it's being hung, and two Jasper Johns beer cans are shoved around as though they came straight from Ballantine's. All in all, there's a sense of no deposit, no return.

●

Some of the best parts of the film are the preparations for the auction; the ushers are instructed to "be forceful without being rude" and to make people sit in their assigned seats—which were "thoroughly researched" in light o most individuals' bidding records. The film is a very amusing putdown of an occasion that doesn't inspire reverence. Of course it's an easy target. But since the artists' talent or diligence are made to seem irrelevant, our laughter at those who were enriched by their work can refresh us in fierce economic times.

OCTOBER 17, 1974

'Women Observed' In Pictures, and at a Party

By BERNADINE MORRIS

Carolyn Wechsler, serenely elegant in her printed green velvet pants and chiffon blouse by Dior, marveled at the crowds.

"I've never seen so many people at Saks, at least not after the store was closed," she said. "We set up eight bars and that should be enough, but I don't know about the food."

As the wife of the store's president, she was concerned that everyone would have enough fresh strawberries, caviar-stuffed mushroom caps and endive leaves to nibble on.

Mildred Hilson, in a black velvet calf-length dress with a capelet top, reveled in the throng spread out over the store's men's department on the sixth floor.

1,000-Plus Tickets

"We've sold more than a thousand tickets at $25," she said, beaming as she moved among the guests. "That's a lot of money for cancer."

Mrs. Hilson, an ardent worker for the American Cancer Society, which benefited from Tuesday night's mammoth cocktail party, then grabbed Alexander Liberman's arm and gave it a loving squeeze.

"It's all because of the work he did for the cause," she explained.

Mr. Liberman demurred.

"When Mildred gets going, she moves the world," he said gallantly.

A Backward Look

Nevertheless, he had contributed to the party. As editorial director of Condé Nast, he had helped put together the main drawing card: the photographic exhibit called "Women Observed." It was taken from pictures run in Vogue over the last 50 years, thereby tying in neatly with Saks Fifth Avenue's fiftieth anniversary.

The exhibition will continue through Oct. 26 in the corner of the floor set up as an art gallery, and will be followed by one on the Ziegfeld girls.

"We tried to show women as personalities, as human beings, over the years," Mr. Liberman explained. "There's more to women than just fashion."

So there are women as mothers (Helen Hayes with her daughter, Mary, both on roller skates in 1937; Sophia Loren and her son, Carlo, in 1969), actresses from the past and present (Gloria Swanson, Ginger Rogers, Jane Fonda), dancers and artists as well as fashion models and designers.

Sees Her Portrait

"This is fantastic," said Jean Patchett, now Mrs. Louis Auer, as she spotted Irving Penn's photograph of 12 most popular models of 1947—and then his portrait of her dated 1950.

"This girl worked for me," said Vera Maxwell, the designer, picking out Meg Mundy in Mr. Penn's group photograph.

Caterine Milinaire dragged her friend, Christina Bellin, over to see the Penn photograph of herself and her daughter, Serafine, taken two years ago. "It's my favorite picture," said Miss Milinaire.

Ethel Scull and Pauline Trigère were both taken with the Steichen photograph of Garbo in 1928, while Polly Bergen admired the same photographer's portrait of Marlene Dietrich in 1932.

"I'm glad I'm not hanging here with a date on me," she said.

A young girl passing a photograph of Barbara Hutton taken by Horst in 1938 told her friend, "She was married to Cary Grant." Her friend retorted, "Lucky girl."

"It all looks so current," said Lee Evans, one of a sizable number of designers from Seventh Avenue, including Kasper, Bill Blass and Shannon Rodgers, who dropped by.

"Everybody looks so well-dressed," murmured Peter Brandon, Mr. John's associate. He was speaking of the guests, not the photographs.

The dress was eclectic, as might be expected at a 6:30 P.M. event, with everyone going on to dinner or the theater. Katharine Wilson, the wife of the Governor, wore a long blue covered-up dress as she stopped in before the Gil Hodges Memorial dinner. Muriel Shorenstein saw her and worried that her own green Chanel-type suit by Adolfo wasn't dressy enough, then brightened as she spotted another woman in the same suit, only in purple.

The closest thing to a uniform was the prevalence of black, looking newest when it was black velvet. Pat Mossbacher, Susan Newhouse and Muffin Wechsler were some of the women in black velvet suits with skirts or pants and soft blouses. It was the right way to look early in the evening for a picture show.

But the range was all the way from Christina Bellin's blazer-shirt-pants outfit to Irma Shorell's silver sequins.

Nan Kempner, who wore a pin-striped black suit by Dior, said she was hoping her escort, Bill Blass, would appear in pin stripes too. He didn't. He wore a solid color navy suit with a navy tie. For men, quiet classics are in.

OCTOBER 29, 1974

Panel Debates Artists' Rights, From Income Tax to Royalties

By GRACE GLUECK

Would paying artists royalties on the resale of their work adversely affect the market for their art?

Lawrence Fleischman, head of the Kennedy Galleries and a well-known dealer, said yes to that question last evening, and Robert Scull, the collector, said no. The two were among a vociferous group of panelists gathered at the Loeb Center of New York University for a three-part symposium to consider the question of artists' rights.

The symposium, sponsored by American Artist Publications, was prompted by increasing concern among artists throughout the country for improvement of their economic status. A similar symposium was held last month in Boston, for example, and a number of prominent state and Federal legislators have become interested in the issue.

Some 30 assembled artists, dealers, lawyers and one collector, Mr. Scull, conducted three consecutive panels with the general topic, "Residual Rights for Visual Artists," and discussed everything from the inequities of artists' income taxes to the possible revival of a long-running old show, the Depression.

As with panelists generally, they reached no hard-and-fast conclusions but, as Carl Zanger, a panelist and lawyer who heads the Committee on Art of the New York Bar Association, put it, one of the most encouraging things about the symposium was "the presence of dealers and others who accepted the principle that artists should get resale royalties on the sale of their work."

Mr. Fleischman argued that since more than 90 per cent of art depreciated rather than rose in value after it was sold, collectors would respond negatively to the idea of being tied to a royalty payment when they resold an artist's work.

Artists should be helped in other ways, he declared, by directing increased energy toward selling their work, by persuading the Government to allow them equal tax deductions with collectors when making charitable donations of their work, and by dissuading collectors from the "stock market" view of art.

Mr. Scull, recently the subject of a feature-length movie depicting a highly lucrative auction of works from his collection last year at Sotheby, Parke-Bernet, said he was for a royalty program and didn't believe it would make for slower art sales. "Art is too tough and powerful for that," he said, in suggesting that a "modest" royalty payment be imposed on resales, "one that is workable and manageable, that doesn't mortgage the buyer."

Among the artists expressing views were Nathaniel Kaz, who suggested that the 8 per cent sales tax collected by New York City on art purchases should be given to an artists' fund and Peter Max, who said that over the last few years a number of institutions and corporations had "profited greatly by ripping off" poster and other designs he had made. He suggested that American artists use the bicentennial as an occasion to take a stand about artists' rights throughout the world.

The binding of buyers to resale rights by contract was urged by Robert Projansky, a lawyer instrumental in drawing up the first version of a contract now in use by a number of artists. But Mr. Zanger argued that the artist needed a professional organization, perhaps one similar to the American Society of Composers, Authors and Publishers, to strengthen his bargaining position and influence Government legislation.

DECEMBER 1, 1974

Earth Artist Keeps Foot in the Gallery

By GRACE GLUECK

There were the Egyptians, creators of Sakkara, and the Mayans, erectors of Chichen Itza, and the Khmer, who built Angkor Wat. And now there is Michael Heizer, a sort of one-man civilization whose powerful monument, "Complex I of the City," has brought instant archaeology to the Nevada desert.

One of a breed of "earth artists" who surfaced in the 1960's, Heizer also keeps a reluctant foot in the gallery world. A show of his paintings is currently on view at the Fourcade Droll Gallery (36 East 75th Street). But mostly he operates in the desert where he has cut vast circles in a dry Nevada lake bed, carved "Double Negative" (1969), a pair of 1,500-foot trenches out of facing mesas, and this summer dragged three massive blocks of granite across Nevada to recreate "Displaced/Replaced Mass," a 1967 work done for the collector Robert Scull (and owned by him in situ). He has just finished "Complex I," a 140-foot-long mastaba of earth contained by steel-and-concrete sides and banded by a rectilinear motif of columns, the first component of a planned sculpture city that will spread over three square miles.

Heizer, a California boy who spent nine years in New York, returned this month from his desert haunts to drop in on his new show. "I'm tired of art," he announced, surrounded by his big, void-ful canvases in which blank, desert-like spaces are bounded by wide bands of earth color. "It's always been subservient to architecture in the West. Ever since Matisse, who finished off art as decoration, artists have had problems looking for other ways to react to the problems posed by art. Instead of sticking my hand in de Kooning's back pocket, I want to distill architecture."

The earth is, so to speak, in Heizer's genes. Sixty years ago, his grandfather ran the Nevada-Massachusetts mine, 100 miles from the current "City" site. His father, an archaeologist who took Heizer on digs in Mexico and Peru, is a research professor at the University of California. "I didn't go out there to be cute, I just went home," says Heizer, a pale, thin fellow of 30.

With his wife, Barbara, Heizer lives on a compound a mile up the road from his $200,000-plus project. Because of the liability factor in working with big equipment—drills and cement mixers and sandblasters and bulldozers—he's formed a company, Civa, with a foreman and general manager, that works on "City" with the know-how of a heavy construction gang. For backing, Heizer gives credit to Virginia Dwan, a collector and former New York dealer, who owns "Double Negative." "Without her, and Bob Scull, nothing," says Heizer.

Though he says he'll continue to paint from time to time—"It's my hobby, my public art"—he thinks he's into "City" for life. It doesn't disturb him that in the remote Nevada desert, "City" is on rather limited view. "It's not for this generation, but for the millennium," he explains, gently.

DECEMBER 2, 1974

GOING OUT Guide

MOVIES AND MAKERS

Two programs of interesting films, both including discussional appearances by contributors, start here today. The New York Public Library, which screens free short films at various branches throughout the year, tonight will open a series of eight features and programs titled "The Filmmaker Speaks: An Open Forum" at the Donnell Library Center, 20 West 53d Street.

Tonight's film at 6 o'clock, is "A Matter of Fat," a documentary on our contemporary obsession with losing weight, and with a central figure, a native of Quebec, whose poundage drops from 280 to 140 in the course of the film. Bill Weintraub will be present at the screening, as the producer for the National Film Board of Canada. Next Monday, T. C. McLuhan, the independent Canadian film maker, will show and discuss her biographical record of a famous American photographer, "Shadow Catcher: Edward S. Curtis and the North American Indian." On Dec. 16, Emile de Antonio will present his two-hour feature, "Painters Painting," in which leading American artists analyze their work. The commercial side of American painting is the subject of "America's Pop Collector: Robert C. Scull," set for Dec. 23. The documentary by John Schott and E. J. Vaughn records the auctioning of Mr. Scull's vast art collection last year at the Sotheby Parke-Bernet Galleries.

On Jan. 6, Jonas Mekas, the avant-garde spokesman, will screen his "Reminiscences of a Journey to Lithuania," describing his return to his homeland after 27 years. On Jan. 13, Amalie Rothschild's "Nana, Mom and Me" will examine three generations of women in the filmmaker's family. On Jan. 20, the Oscar-winning photographer, Boris Kaufman (for "On the Waterfront"), will discuss his association with the late French director, Jean Vigo, in the filming of "Zero for Conduct," after a screening of the 1933 classic. The final library feature, on Jan. 27, will be Martha Coolidge's "Old Fashioned Woman," an affectionate portrait of the film maker's 88-year-old grandmother, symbol of the Puritan New England tradition.

DECEMBER 5, 1974

Notes on People

Nixon Asks Private Road at Florida Home

A small storm is brewing in Key Biscayne, Fla., over attempts by Richard M. Nixon and two of his millionaire friends to have the street on which they have homes be made a private road. The former President, in a petition also signed by Charles G. Rebozo, the banker, and Robert Abplanalp, the industrialist, maintain that unless the county makes Bay Lane a private road it will become glutted with tourists and the curious.

Ray Goode, the county manager, has recommended that the Nixon group's request be granted, but some residents of Bay Lane said they intended to fight the petition at a hearing set for Dec. 18. According to the petition, security barriers at the Nixon bayfront compound will be removed soon. If Bay Lane is made a private road, only residents and their guests would be allowed access to it.

●

After 30 years of marriage, **Mr. and Mrs. Robert Scull,** the art patrons, are legally separating. "It's not a temporary thing, it's permanent," Mrs. Ethel Scull said yesterday. She said her lawyers were preparing the papers for her separation from the taxicab millionaire, with whom she has, over the years, assembled an impressive collection of contemporary American art.

●

Three hundred gold-decorated plates that were once part of the tableware collection of the royal Prussian court have been sold by a firm in Berne, Switzerland, for $120,000. The buyer was the **Shah of Iran.**

●

Reese Palley, an art dealer who two years ago flew 725 of his friends and customers to Paris for a four-day weekend celebration of his 50th birthday, is being forced to scale down his flamboyant ways.

Mr. Palley, who has galleries in New York, San Francisco and Atlantic City, styles himself "the merchant to the rich," but inflation has apparently hit the rich as well as the not-so-rich, and so his next two parties won't be so lavish as the one two years ago. They'll be given at Howard Johnson's Motor Lodge in Atlantic City, this weekend and next. About 20,000 invitations to the parties have been mailed by the National Association of the Friends of Reese Palley.

DECEMBER 12, 1974

You've read the books. Now see the movies.

One of New York's real delights is the Public Library's Donnell Library Center at 20 West 53rd Street. That's the bright and airy branch opposite the Museum of Modern Art.

The Donnell holds a nice surprise for you if you like good movies. It has a large, comfortable auditorium that occasionally is turned into a movie theatre for the enjoyment of outstanding films.

Screenings are free to the public, of course. But they cost the Donnell money, and we're glad to help with some of what's needed.

During the next few weeks you can enjoy these splendid films in the current Donnell series:

"Painters Painting," by Emile de Antonio. This is a two-hour feature with leading American artists discussing their work. The library says it is the most comprehensive film yet made on modern American painting. Showing: Monday, December 16th at 6:00 p.m.

"America's Pop Collector: Robert C. Scull," is the movie scheduled for Monday, December 23rd at 6:00 p.m. (Nice way to take a breather between Christmas shopping forays.) This is a documentary report on the auction in 1973 of a vast portion of the art owned by Robert Scull.

On January 6th at 6:00 p.m. the film will be "Reminiscences of a Journey to Lithuania"—a personal document by the avant garde film maker Jonas Mekas.

More fine movies are scheduled all through January, but we do not have the space here to list them. We suggest you stop in at the Donnell next time you're in the neighborhood, and pick up a film schedule.

Mobil

DECEMBER 13, 1974

The Skimp: Conspicuous by Its Absence

By BERNADINE MORRIS

The short and merry life of the skimp is just about over, at least chez Halston. Remember the skimp? It's Halston's revival of the minidress, which riveted store buyers when they first saw it at his spring ready-to-wear showings on Seventh Avenue a month ago.

Yesterday, at his couture show for private clients in his Madison Avenue salon, it had almost disappeared. At least, if you blinked you would have missed it.

There was one in blue silk shantung under a matching coat, another in beige silk under a white coat.

Lasting Imprint

The coats were just below the knee, most of the other dresses worn with them stopped just above it. But the skimp left its imprint.

"As we were fitting the collection, we made everything shorter than we had planned," Halston explained.

The skimp won't entirely vanish. Some of Halston's fans have already ordered them, he said — "important ones like Liza Minelli, Annette Reed, Elizabeth Weymouth."

Mrs. Weymouth was at the couture show in a calf-length black skirt and boots. Some Halston fans — Diana Vreeland, Ethel Scull and Pat Buckley, for example—were in pants. And a few, with a certain bravado, including Jean Tailer and Paulette Goddard, wore clothes by Adolfo. He's the only other major designer to make custom clothes as well as ready-to-wear.

Not that the private clients were dying to get into the skimp. Cathy Tankoos said her legs weren't up to it, and Lily Auchinloss said cautiously, "I'm waiting," and winked.

They were, however, enthusiastic about what they saw.

"The proportions were just perfect," murmured D. D. Ryan.

"The colors are fantastic," said Paulette Goddard.

Halston had succeeded in taking everebody's mind off skirt lengths.

Apparent Harmony

There are, after all, other dimensions to fashion.

Color, for one. To get the unusual effects the customers were sighing over, Halston mixed up different shades, layering one over another. In a rainbow dress, eight shades, including peach, mauve and pale green, were blended in apparent harmony.

Many dresses, including some of the chiffons, wrapped at the center and were tied with a scarf. Some had multiple strap arrangements, spraying across the back or over the shoulders.

The applause was enthusiastic—and electric. It exploded for the new wide-leg pants in peach cashmere, which appeared with a matching hooded coat, revved up again for a brown crepe dress that tied in front and erupted for a classic black siren dress with no back, closely fitted gores over the hips and a great sweep to the skirt.

"The point is, anything goes as long as it's becoming," Halston said with sincerity.

Some Short Dresses

Elsewhere in the fashion world, the skimp is not yet dormant.

Bergdorf Goodman received its first shipment of new Halston styles, all in Ultrasuède, and sold seven short dresses at $260. It wasn't displeased, but it doesn't feel this constitutes a run on miniskirts.

On Wednesday, Saks Fifth Avenue advertised a trio of skimps, each with a matching cardigan. It set up special displays and had models parading about in the clothes. By the end of the day, it had tallied 178 skimps and 120 cardigans. It was pleased, but it also recognized that another factor besides skirt lengths was involved. The dresses, in cotton knit, were priced at $11 and $13. The sweaters were $11.

Many of the shoppers were buying clothes for winter vacations.

Rare Prices

"The price is fantastic," said Carol Williams, who is heading for Jamaica. "The dresses will be great on the beach, and later I can wear them as tunics over pants."

How can I go wrong for $11?" asked Deidre McVey, who bought a red dress and matching sweater to wear on a cruise to Aruba. "I don't even have to take a travel iron," she said, pointing to the fabric.

The length did appeal to a man who said he was buying the dress for his wife and refused to give his name, and to Carol Strack, who was shopping with her husband, Sam. The couple both prefer short skirts.

But Candace Maluhy, a visitor from Brazil, turned away from the skimps and concentrated on some long chemises nearby.

"Short dresses are not pretty," she said. "Below the knee is best."

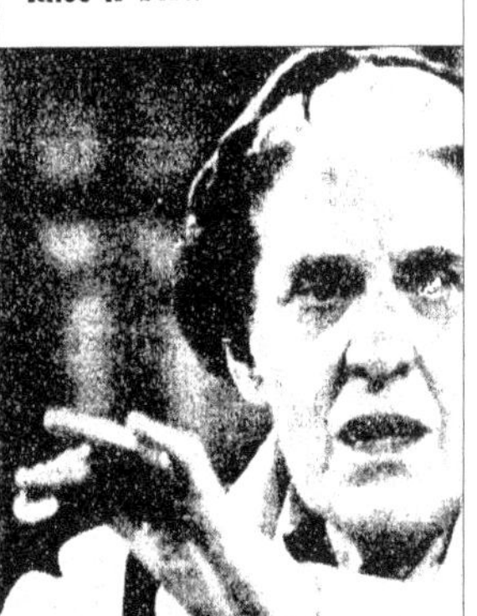

JANUARY 7, 1975

FASHION TALK

From Adolfo for Spring, Enter the 'Skivvy'

By BERNADINE MORRIS

Here comes Adolfo with his "skivvy," on the heels of Halston with his "skimp." Whatever you call it, it's a very short dress. Mini, you might say. Adolfo's friends and followers, who came to see his spring and summer fashion show at the St. Regis hotel yesterday as their first foray into fashion for the new year, managed to take it in their stride. Except for Livia Weintraub who murmured, "he must be joking," as the first "skivvy" came out on the runway. A white knitted dress, rather like a tennis dress, it had red bands at the neck and hem.

"I'm going to wear it on the boat, for Ping-Pong and such," said Glady Solomon, who's leaving Friday on the Queen Elizabeth II for a trip around the world. Anyway, she calls Adolfo's current collection "a creative symphony"—and has trunks full for her trip.

'For the South'

Obviously, she'd already seen the clothes.

Dorothy Sheckman didn't mind the short dresses. "They look very cute," she said. "You know, for the Hamptons or for the South." But the flat-heeled black patent pumps with which they were shown rather troubled her.

"I don't object to flats," she said. "But I've just gotten a whole batch of high heels for my long dresses."

Jan Chipman thought the short styles were "marvelous if you're under 30," and Joanne Winship lowered the age to "17-year-olds watching tennis matches in Palm Beach."

Some women just refused to get embroiled. Lyn Revson, who's going to Jamaica at the end of the month, is taking a bunch of "knee-length Adolfos—the kind I always wear" and Ethel Scull was feeling cozy in her Sonia Rykiels. "They're so soft and feminine," she said, cuddling into her mohair sweater. "I bought a whole batch."

'A Fun Look'

Among the professionals in the audience, Barrie Sommerfield of Saks Fifth Avenue said, "We bought them — they'll sell for $130," speaking of the tennis dress skivvies. And Robert Sakowitz of the Houston store said, "It's a fun sportswear look — last summer women went shopping in their tennis dresses."

Adolfo himself who said in his press release that he saluted Halston for his belief that short skirts belong in spring," reiterated that after the show. "It's a change," he remarked, adding that the skivvies were for "women who could wear them."

He provided plenty of alternatives, some knee-length, some longer. There are his trademarks, the Chanel-type suits in bouclé or nubby knitted tweeds, printed dresses with blazers, pants suits with loose tops and billowing sleeves.

The applause resounded for neat navy knitted dresses and jackets and pants suits with tailored vests and jackets.

But the real show-stoppers were at the end. They were white silk organdie pinafores worn over ascot-tie shirts. The pinafores were hand painted with bouquets of roses, jonquils, field flowers, violets or lilies of the valley.

Contemporary versions of what Marie Antoinette may have worn playing milkmaid at Le Petit Trianon, they had tiny waistlines, puffy skirts and floor-length hemlines. Even the over-30 crowd could look fragile and feminine in them at parties in Palm Beach this winter or Southampton next summer.

February 2, 1975

Writers, Composers and Actors Collect Royalties —Why Not Artists?

By ROY BONGARTZ

Seventeen years ago, when a young painter named Robert Rauschenberg was still struggling to pay his rent and feed his children, he sold a painting entitled "Thaw" for $900 to Robert Scull, the taxi tycoon and art collector. Over the succeeding years, Rauschenberg became famous for creating a new kind of abstract art which employed Pop Art materials, random objects, junk and so forth in order to make viewers ask what is real and what isn't. And so, when Scull got around to selling a number of the paintings in his collection at an auction at the Sotheby Parke Bernet gallery a couple of years ago, Rauschenberg's "Thaw" drew the tidy sum of $85,000. For Scull, not Rauschenberg, of course.

The figures in this case are dramatic but it was hardly the first time in history that a painter did not share in the profits earned by his work. Indeed, artists have long considered themselves uniquely discriminated against by the ways of the world. In every form of creative endeavor, with the exception of painting and sculpture, there are potential residual profits which the creator never loses. Every photograph, musical composition, film, design for costume jewelry, book, poem, bumper-sticker design, play or television show, if successful, is good for future money. If you're an actor and you snuffle once in an Alka-Seltzer commercial, that snuffle may still be paying you off at age 65. If you once sang for a recording the comprimario role of the maid in "La Traviata," you may have a tiny pension right there. If you once published a greeting card rhyme averring that roses are red and violets are blue, you could be in the chips for life. But if you are an artist you are supposed to stay home with your muse and not worry your ethereal head with such business matters as future royalties.

Nevertheless, these are times of protest against "the system," times of a raised consciousness for the rights of minorities and underdogs. And therefore, since Rauschenberg happened to be present at the aforementioned auction, he walked up to Scull afterwards and said:

"I've been working my tail off just for you to make that profit. The least you could do is send every artist in this auction free taxis for a week!" If Rauschenberg was in a kidding mood then, he wasn't once he got home and began to think the matter over. It occurred to him that the time might be ripe for artists to demand royalties—specifically, a 15 per cent cut of the profit from the results of their work. He found an especially enthusiastic listener when he mentioned the idea to his business manager, Rubin Gorewitz, a tall cheerful-looking native of Brooklyn who handles the affairs of many prominent artists. Since 1970, Gorewitz had been championing the so-called Projansky Agreement, a standard form drawn up by a New York art dealer named Seth Siegelaub and a lawyer named Robert Projansky which was intended to help artists get some benefit out of future profits on their work. Gorewitz had delivered speeches and written magazine articles on the subject and was recommending the use of the agreement on a voluntary, individual basis. But, said Rauschenberg, a voluntary agreement isn't enough; there ought to be a law. Gorewitz agreed and soon began making a series of trips to Washington in an effort to "educate" any members of Congress who would listen.

Meanwhile, Rauschenberg began talking up the idea among colleagues, and a number of them immediately lent him their support—the more notable including Carl Andre, a Conceptual sculptor; Sol Le Witt, another conceptualist; and Hans Haacke, a sometime earth artist who came to prominence a while ago when he started an artists' boycott of the Guggenheim Museum when it rejected his proposal for a show.

The idea has continued to pick up support among artists. For example, there is now something in existence called the Artists Rights Association whose members all insist on royalty contracts. Fourteen members of ARA, all professionals, recently held an exhibition at the Ward-Nasse gallery on Prince Street in SoHo. Judy Pendleton, an abstract painter who is an organizer of ARA, says: "The country is getting used to contracts. People accept them for anything they buy—a used car, an apartment—so why not a painting? Part of the job is trying to get the *artist* to accept the contract as part of the deal."

Neither Miss Pendleton nor Rauschenberg is trying to organize painters and sculptors into the kind of militant groups one associates with the advocates of rights for other minorities. There are no plans for paint-ins or even regular meetings.

•

But, as Rauschenberg and the others have continued to spread the idea among artists, Gorewitz has had some slight success persuading politicians as well as other artists. In December, Gorewitz addressed the attorneys general of the 50 states at their convention in Hot Springs, Arkansas, and he hopes to get a formal resolution supporting his cause at their next meeting this summer. He and Pop artist James Rosenquist proselytized some 300 artists in Chicago a few week ago, and there have been television interviews and visits to the National Endowment for the Arts and to Artists Equity to gain support. Specifically, Gorewitz is asking for a federal law requiring all resales of art works to include royalties.

New York Senator Jacob Javits, who last year introduced a bill to permit artists to enjoy the same tax deduction as art patrons when they donate works to non-profit institutions, now says he supports the royalty idea for at least the first resale. At present, Javits has his legislative aides studying the Copyright Act for the purpose of framing an amendment which would legalize a royalty. The advantage of an amendment to the Copyright Act as opposed to the making of private contracts is that the former would tend to make the artists' royalty universal and, also, should the buyer fail to pay, an artist could threaten to bring the owner of his work into federal court charged which a violation of federal law, and that is a more serious threat than the one of taking the offender into state court with a suit for breach of contract.

Another who favors the royalty is Representative John Brademas, the Indiana Democrat, who says: "Nearly all artists, musicians, authors, composers—generally receive some benefit from the future use of their artistic products. Painters and sculptors, however, do not, and that is why Congress should consider proposals to provide these visual artists similar benefit."

For all these strong words and noble sentiments, however, it would be wrong to say that a royalty for artists is an idea whose time has come. Most members of Congress, too preoccupied with the troubled economy to worry about artists' rights, are simply unaware that such a proposal even exists. Furthermore, when looked at closely the proposition has a number of hitches, and some Congressmen who are generally sympathetic to the cause of artists' rights, and many in the art world as well, oppose the royalty concept. For example, New York City's Congressman Edward Koch, whose district includes both the Whitney and the Museum of Modern Art, has serious misgivings. "While I'm anxious to give the artist full financial benefits for his art work," Koch says, "I am concerned that this proposal will inhibit art buying, particularly from young artists most in need of help. Many people seek out new artists from whom to buy work at modest prices because of potential gains in the future. We must be careful not to undermine art buying incentives, particularly in today's already depressed art market."

Gorewitz does not agree that that only rich, famous artists would benefit from royalty contracts. "This isn't true either in the future or present," he insists. "Today's well-known artists were yesterday's unknown artists. Likewise some of today's unknown artists will be tomorrow's well-known. So just because an artist's work doesn't command prices in the thousands now, doesn't mean that it won't in the future."

Another skeptic about a royalty for artists recently told New York Times art writer Grace Glueck, "If the collector pays the artist when a work appreciates, shouldn't the artist turn around and pay the collector when his work goes down?"

•

The royalty idea has also inspired some grumbling and not very amused scoffing from dealers and collectors. Like Congressman Koch, collector Scull thinks the 15 per cent royalty would simply kill the art market, but Scull would go along with, say, one per cent.

One New York dealer claims that a universally-accepted royalty contract would practically put him out of business because it is in the nature of works of art that they are *property* as well as things embodying aesthetic qualities. He says that to change that tradition would be disastrous. Most dealers have simply not taken the proposal very seriously, although there are those who handle a few artists who sell their works only with a royalty provision. The avant-garde SoHo gallery owner John Weber says, "If an artist wants to use it, it's all right with me." One artist in Weber's stable, Conceptual artist Sol Le Witt, requires the future royalty, and Weber says, "Not one sale was ever jeopardized by that contract. If the desire to buy a piece of work is in a person he will buy it anyway."

Gorewitz argues that the royalty idea really isn't as bad from a collectors' point of view as it might seem at first. To begin with, he says, his plan would apply to resales only when a profit of over $1000 is involved. He adds that the 15 per cent artist's cut isn't substantial for an art patron in the 70 per cent income-tax bracket who makes, say, $20,000 on an art sale since he would be paying only 4.5 per cent of his profit after taxes. The collector would also benefit from lower insurance costs and the royalty contract would provide him with a guarantee of authentic origin from the artist.

Another critic of the royalty plan is the New Yorker's art essayist Harold Rosenberg. "The artist has many serious problems," Rosenberg says, "but the question of royalties in not one of the main issues at all. It is not central. It is not a problem for most artists. The real issue is the scandalous problem of tax deductions denied to artists in donating their work, and in the inheritance situation where the IRS slaps a huge tax on the value of works left after death."

Gorwitz agrees on the importance of these tax problems and he is working for changes here, too, but he insists that the benefits of a royalty arrangement are meaningful indeed to artists. More than money is at stake, according to Gorewitz. His plan would always let an artist know where his painting is, and, Gorewitz says, "the artist will feel that a portion of the umbilical cord between his creation and himself will never be severed. A part of him will always reside in his works, and they will always, minimally at least, belong to him. Many artists do not now sell their works because of the strong personal attachment they feel."

Although the idea for a 15 per cent royalty appears to have originated with Rauschenberg and Gorewitz, the general notion that artists are being cheated and that something ought to be done about it goes back much further. Forty years ago in New York, Paul Chabas, who painted the romantic portrait of a young woman entitled "September Morn" that was sold in reproductions by the thousands around the country, was asked what he had made from that work, and he replied, "Not a sou. Although several fortunes have been made from my painting, nobody has been thoughtful enough to send me even a box of cigars." A more recent work by Robert Indiana, a design involving the word "love," was exploited by a jewelry firm in the form of charms selling at $23.99, but the artist was not rewarded.

Although it has been traditonal practice to leave artists out in the cold, there were a few early moves to come inside. In 1934, a group of American painters and sculptors demanded that museums pay them 10 per cent of the value of their works per month for the privilege of displaying them, and for a whole year the Whitney actually went along with this demand and paid the rental fees. In 1940, Grant Wood became an advocate of royalties when he found out that speculators had repurchased his painting "Daughter of Revolution" at four times the original price. His next sale had a contract calling for half the gain on any future sale.

•

If the idea never got anywhere in the past, it could be because the artists of earlier times did not have someone as effective as the artist *manqué* Rubin Gorewitz to do their talking for them. Besides royalties for his protégés he has other ideas: medical coverage for artists, credit cards, and the legal enforcement of a long-standing Congressional recommendation that one per cent of construction costs of government building be spent on art works to go into it or outside of it. (Already one state, Hawaii, as well as such cities as Baltimore, Philadelphia and Seattle are requiring that one per cent of all state money spent on public building be used for embellishment by artists and sculptors.)

He wants the USIA to take artists overseas on tours the way they used to do with Louis Armstrong. And he has one special tax proposal that is sure to set on edge the teeth of Congressmen who worked their way up through daddy's business by starting out as an office boy and who secretly hate daubers and chippers. The plan reads: "Allow an artist to depreciate the costs incurred in becoming an artist." ■

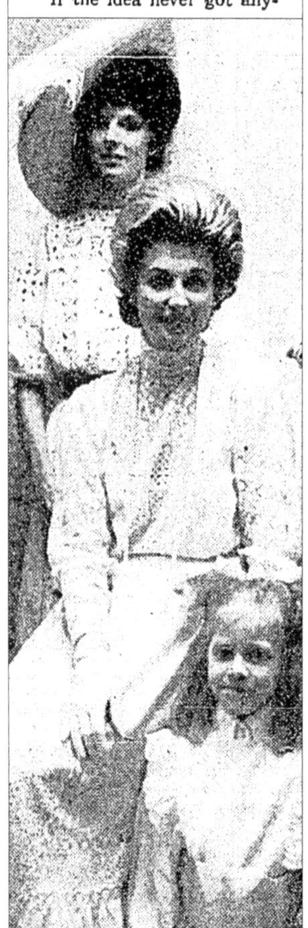

FEBRUARY 17, 1975

FASHION TALK

Givenchy: From Beach to Ballroom

By BERNADINE MORRIS

Hubert de Givenchy has a lot of fans. When Bergdorf Goodman showed off his spring collection the other day, Carol Channing, Anita Loos, Ethel Scull, Mildred Hilson, Denise Hale and Lyn Revson were among the hundreds of women who came to take a look.

Givenchy clothes have a way of looking better at Bergdorf's than they do in his own salon. That's because Elieth Roux, who selects them for the store, also takes great pains to decorate them with the right scarves, hats, jewelry and even shoes. Givenchy himself is much more casual about that. The shoes—high-heel T-strap sandals mostly—were particularly attractive this time.

The clothes run the gamut from beach to ballroom, and it would be quite possible to lead a rich, full life without wearing the styles of another designer.

Your swim suit can be one-piece or a bikini, and you can wrap it in a terrycloth skirt or cape. You go on to knitted pants with sweaters, including an ombré-striped set that carries out perfectly the Givenchy formula for understated chic.

Raincoats are wide as smocks but often belted and you can pair them with matching pants or skirts. Dresses are demure with puffed sleeves, square necklines and smock details, but they can get rather grand. Then they flutter and float in tiers of silk chiffon.

The grandest outfit of all is not one of the ballgowns, but a calf-length skirt and blouse in royal blue that received enormous applause. "It deserved it," said the model who wore it. "It's the prettiest thing in the show."

MARCH 6, 1975

FASHION TALK

Dressing for a 1900 Picnic

By BERNADINE MORRIS

Katie Tozer, 6 years old, loved her pinafore with the purple sash. Her mother put her in a taxi and sent her to Saks Fifth Avenue so she could model the Victorian child's costume at a benefit for the Museum of the City of New York. Later, Katie was told she could keep the sash. The grown-up models had almost as much fun decked out in their turn-of-the-century finery from the museum's costume collection, even though they couldn't keep any of it.

June Marston strutted down the runway in her handpainted silk dress as if she were, oh, Lilian Russell. "It's the ham in me," she said. "The dress does that to me."

Jordan Saunders loved her parasol so much she wanted to take it home and Beatrice Guthrie tried to imagine playing tennis in the checked taffeta skirt and tucked shirtwaist she was told was a tennis costume. And Joan Howard simply preened in her slanted ostrich-plumed hat.

Those Olden Days

Naturally, the models attracted wild applause as they came down the runway dressed for a fashionable picnic in New York circa 1900.

"Sugar cost 4 cents a pound then and eggs were 14 cents a dozen," Louis Auchincloss, the author, who is president of the museum, remarked as he introduced them.

The audience included 400 friends of the museum, some of whom also came to pay homage to Adolfo, whose somewhat more contemporary clothes were being shown.

"Actually, we came for both reasons," said Patricia Wood, who was there with her daughter, Hilary Geary. We're interested in the museum and we wear Adolfo's things."

Ethel Scull said she thought the designer's minidresses, which he calls "skivvies," would be "terrific for tennis — they'd distract the men."

Everyone went wild for the designer's handpainted silk organdie pinafores, which weren't too far in spirit from the Victorian picnic dresses. The price tags are more modern though—$695.

Romance must be in the air. At Arnold Scaasi's showing of his custom-made collection, a peach dotted Swiss dress with a high neck and Victorian ruffles created quite a stir among the audiences. He adapted it from a dress he made for the Metropolitan Museum of Art's current show of clothes from the movies, the designer explained. The original was in "Camille."

Just because he liked the look of it—he didn't think anyone would necessarily wear it that way—the designer added a big brimmed hat to the first dress he showed. The dress was a navy blue floor-length chiffon with a loose dotted jacket. There it goes — romantic again.

Scaasi reported that when he took the collection to his fans in Palm Beach two weeks ago, his dresses with handkerchief-pointed skirts attracted the most attention.

"Probably because, with the uneven hems, they could go to cocktails or dinner," he figured. The one-shoulder styles also had their following.

"I didn't really plan to do them, but the fabric just drapes so well that way," he said, pointing to a crinkled crepe dress with a satin stripe running through it.

The New York audience carried on about it, just as the women in Palm Beach did.

The high spot of Scaasi's collection, however, is his assortment of ombre chiffon dresses, shading from blue to green or beige to aqua as they flow gently and elegantly over the body.

"They're not jokes to amuse for a minute—they're real clothes you can wear forever," the designer said later, evaluating the chiffons. He, too, was pleased with them.

April 27, 1975

A lament for style

By Rosemary Kent

Men in New York may see themselves as peacocks, but most women in New York think men still dress for the birds.

Not that women are advocating fashion consumption in heavy doses for men. What they are advocating is a change in the quality of men's wardrobes, which they think are "dull," "unkempt," and "lacking in any kind of individual style."

"Most men are still carbon copies of each other," says Doreen McCurley, merchandise manager for Marboro Book Stores' retail catalogue division. "If something new is in, men recoil. It takes a lot of courage for most men to wear something different from what their friends are wearing," adds graduate student Merry Brooks. Dorothy Klein, an actress, says, "I can look at a man and read him by his clothes, and I haven't read any best sellers lately." And fashion reporter Phyllis Tweel says, "I think men are basically still insecure when it comes to dressing themselves."

The Big Gripes? Heading the list unanimously are poor fit and synthetics. Other complaints, not necessarily in this order, include knee-length raincoats, Hush Puppies, Gucci loafers with Gucci double "G" belts, madras jackets, mock turtlenecks, pinkie rings, maitre d' ruffled tuxedo shirts, tie clasps, religious medals, shirts unbuttoned to the navel, narrow ties, short-sleeve shirts worn with suits exposing bare wrists, white socks, white shoes, white shirts, lilac or pink shirts, boxer shorts, skin-tight underwear, I.D. bracelets, flannel pajamas, hip-huggers, ascots, see-through shirts, Hunting World safari hats, slipover sleeveless sweaters, studded Levi's, Bermuda shorts, Bermuda socks, Bloody Mary-colored linen slacks, zippered jumpsuits, hankies in breast pockets, thin belts, Dynel toupees and run-down heels.

Ill-fitting clothes, especially pants that are baggy or too short, drive women to complain the loudest. "Quite a few men look like they have dressed behind a Dutch door," says Merry Brooks. "From the waist up they may look great, but open the bottom half of the door and you see baggy, sack-like pants and pants legs that are inches too short."

Even Jim Brady, former publisher of Women's Wear Daily, used to be kidded unmercifully for wearing the pants of his bragged-about made-in-England suits three inches too short. Seen at Elaine's recently, Brady was still flashing his ankles. But then, a lot of men in New York are.

Bad-fitting clothes bother women a great deal more than men might suspect. "You have no idea what the man's body looks like under some of those clothes. He could have a paunch, or be bottomless for that matter. It's all hidden by excessive cloth," gripes magazine editor Laurie Jones. Dorothy Klein thinks well-fitting clothes say something about a man's body attitude. "It's funny how men tend to be so much more aware of a woman's appearance than their own."

Mention the words "double knit" or "drip-dry," and most women turn up their noses in distaste. "Men think polyesters are the greatest invention ever. Yet they never realize how the fabric looks when they stand up—there are actually knee imprints and other bulges. It snags; it balls up. Polyesters are like an insect on the street—I'd like to kill it walking," says Phyllis Tweel. Laurie Jones agrees. "Besides the fact that the material is so horrible, it's the way men boast about how easy it is to take care of and how they can just toss it in a washing machine. And yet these men are the ones who never go near a washing machine."

If there's one look selling well (selling safe) today, it's the riding crop/jodhpurs/sueded-patched-elbow hacking jacket, but a lot of women think the style smacks of "foppishness," "effetism" and is "too costumey" to be practical or "considered serious fashion."

Another big turnoff for women is men who wear their shirts unbuttoned at least three or four buttons, exposing their hairy or nonhairy chests and usually a couple of passé figas and shark's teeth dangling from a chain. A look that got started in warm Mediterranean countries by nubile beach boys, it was imported here by fortyish Madison Avenue boutique owners and hairdressers and taken up by aging suburbanites who drive the family into Manhattan for a Hunan dinner on Sunday nights. "It's a disgusting look," says Laurie Jones. "Why wear any shirt at all?"

Older men running around looking like a youthquake only get women's sympathies. "Everyone, women included, is afraid of growing old," says art patroness/socialite Ethel Scull. "But men who seem to think they can really prolong and recapture their youth and masculinity by wearing hip-hugger jeans and cowboy shirts are sad-looking."

To paraphrase Freud: "What then do women want" men to wear? Voted Most Popular Outfit: something old (a pair of scruffy, corduroy slacks), something new (a pair of L. L. Bean moccasins), something borrowed (an outsized crewneck Shetland sweater) and something blue (a button-down oxford cloth shirt with a few chewed-by-the-laundry buttons). Not exactly the kind of outfit to transfer stocks in, but it is The One women find "sexy," "irresistible," "cozy" and "super-masculine."

For the times when men can't wear the Most Popular Outfit, women would like to see them "risk and be daring occasionally," "break away from too much tradition in their wardrobes" and "look in the mirror, for God's sake, and make sure the clothes fit."

Will men change when they hear the complaints? No, says public-relations executive Peggy Siegal. "I think it's a rare man who knows who he is or could be fashion-wise. It's still going to take time to change some men." Merry Brooks says no, too. "I don't think men can take the dressing down about their lack of dressing up. It's too wrapped up with their male ego. They see themselves as a dominant force still and that includes their clothing styles. Men should be able to undergo the same amount of criticism that women get, but they don't, yet." □

MAY 1, 1975

From Paris to New York, the Timelessness of Chanel

By BERNADINE MORRIS

Betty Ford and some 750 other women, dressed to the nines, shared a rather unusual phenomenon yesterday at lunch at the Hotel Pierre: They watched time stand still.

The occasion was the presentation, for the first time in the United States, of the Chanel couture collection, exactly as it was shown in Paris in January.

Chanel collections don't travel around that much. Ten years ago, the late Gabrielle (Coco) Chanel herself took her clothes to the Soviet Union. After her death at the age of 87 four years ago, the clothes were shown in Spain at the behest of the Duchess of Alba. Later, they were presented in London at the request of the Duchess of Gloucester.

So it was for the fourth time only that they were seen outside Paris at the luncheon organized by Marion Feldman for the benefit of the American Cancer Society.

A Backward Trip

The President's wife watched the show in a severely tailored off-white suit by Kasper at the side of Mrs. Feldman, whose white suit was by Chanel. Besides Mrs. Feldman's husband, George, the former United States ambassador to Malta and Luxembourg, others at the table included Mary Lasker, the philanthropist, in a pale blue coat and dress by Halston, and Yanie Kosciusko-Morizet, whose husband is the French ambassador to the United States. Mrs. Kosciusko-Morizet's suit was a mauve Chanel, bound in green, which she saw on the runway.

For many in the audience, the showing was a backward trip through time. Mrs. Feldman remembered when her father took "my mother and me to Chanel when I was 18—daddy thought the clothes were economical because they were timeless."

For Ethel Scull, it was a chance to pull out a 12-year-old Chanel suit. Cecile Zilkha almost wore an 8-year-old one, but decided on a recent addition from Ohrbach's.

Jacqueline Citroen, the director of the Chanel salon, turned up in the identical red suit with navy wool edging, and, after examining Mrs. Zilkha's, declared "the copy is perfect."

There was a considerable difference in price. Chanel couture suits cost from $3,000 to $4,000 in Paris. Ohrbach's copies are around $500.

Arlene Dahl's navy blue Chanel suit was also a line-for-line copy from Ohrbach's, but there were Chanel-looking styles that had only the dimmest relation to the original. Pam Coleman, whose husband heads the New York City chapter of the American Cancer Society, bragged that her mauve-pink suit came "off the rack at Mr. Bergdorf's." It was "one of those Portuguese hand-crocheted things," she explained. And innumerable Chanel-type suits were the work of Adolfo.

'A Chanel Cult'

"There'll always be a Chanel cult," said Norman Wechsler, the president of Saks Fifth Avenue, surveying the audience.

Still, there were plenty of non-Chanel designer labels in the clothes women wore. Charlotte Ford Forstman's dress was by Courrèges—it had his initials all over it. Catherine (Deeda) Blair's printed dress was by Galanos, her white coat by Givenchy. And Mary Beame, the wife of New York's Mayor, stanchly insisted her white shirtdress with the green and red flowers on the shoulders and sleeves was a "Beame original."

"Everybody has always told me women dress for men, but it's quite obvious here that they dress for other women," said Lauren Peltz, whose blue and white printed shirtdress was by Ungaro.

"What a turnout," remarked her mother, Rae Stein, whose gray and white tailored suit was by Valentino. "It's a good charity," she went on.

Many women were enchanted with Mrs. Ford's radiant look after her own bout with cancer.

Exuberance and Serenity

"She looks a bit like Lady Bird Johnson," said Audrey Zauderer, who was wearing a striped jacket suit by Bill Blass. Her daughter, Cheray Duchin, was in an Oscar de la Renta print dress.

"They have the same exuberance," Arlene Dahl agreed.

"Serenity, I would say," corrected Mrs. Zauderer.

Professing she was happy to be at the luncheon, Mrs. Ford

paid rapt attention during the show. Before it started, she sent Ambassador Feldman to another table to ask Madeline Malraux, the pianist, to join her, and they watched the show together. Mrs. Malraux's Chanel-looking black suit was by Yves Saint Laurent.

"Mlle. Chanel always said after her it was him," Mrs. Malraux remarked.

After the show, Mrs. Ford said she'd "fallen in love" with a pink evening dress.

"And an aqua tweed suit too," Mrs. Feldman added.

While the audience responded enthusiastically to the suits they all recognized, as well as to the fine tucking, pleating and other dressmaker details that are no longer run-of-the-mill, there were some women who though it was all part of a departed era.

Even the show's commentator Betty Furness caught herself up when she described a floaty ruffled chiffon dress as a "garden party" style.

"Garden party?" she said. "Everybody I know is planting vegetables."

And Edna Levine, who was watching the show with a group of friends who were supporting the charity, said, "It was a beautiful show, but I don't think the average woman dresses like that anymore." She then amended her statement. "It's for the elegant woman," she said.

The show was presented by five mannequins from the Paris salon and was authentic down to the last gardenia and off-the-face roller hat. At the end, Jean Cazubon and Yvonne Dudel, who had worked with Chanel after she reopened her house in 1954, following a 15-year hiatus—to see her suits become world-famous, came down the runway to take a bow. They have been responsible for the last few collections, preserving a fashion that has lasted 50 years.

JUNE 24, 1975

Radio

9-9:30, WNYU: Soul of Reason. Dr. Roscoe C. Brown, Jr., host. Lee Archer, director, Equal Opportunity Affairs, General Foods, Inc.

9:15-10, WOR-AM: Jean Shepherd. Comedy.

9:15-9:30, WEVD: Postscripts. Katharine Balfour talks with Leslie Tonner, author of "Nothing But the Best," and with Barbara Seaman and Ethel Scull.

9:30-10:30, WNYC-AM: From the Renaissance On. Donald Furber of C.U.N.Y. discusses Moliere's "The Misanthrope."

9:30-10:30, WNYC-FM: Voices in the Wind. Oscar Brand, host. John Updike, Peter Seeger, Tom Rush, Peter Pears, Julian Bream.

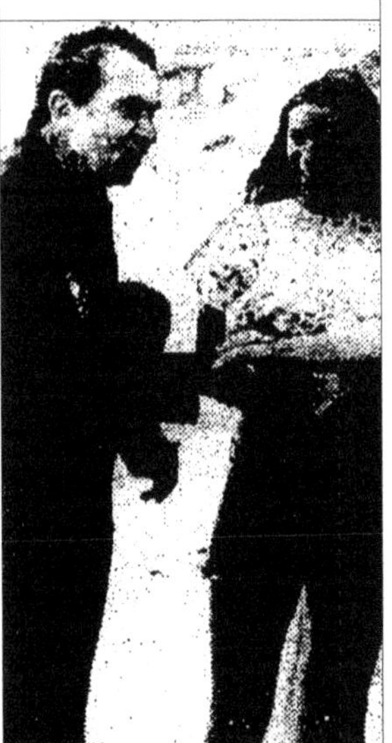

JULY 2, 1975

FASHION TALK

In Adolfo's New Salon, an Intimate Showing Brought Thoughts

By BERNADINE MORRIS

"If they want to truck them all over to my house, it would be all right," Glady Solomon sighed after seeing Adolfo's fall show yesterday.

She was one of the designer's many fans who climbed the carpeted stairs to his new salon at 538 Madison Avenue, near 54th Street and found the effort well spent.

Clothes Well Served

"It's just for friends," the designer murmured as he regarded the small rooms backed with Coromandel screens and filled with Adolfo-clad women such as Bess Myerson, Lyn Revson, Jean Tailer, Livia Weintraub and Audrey Zauderer. Ethel Scull was the maverick. She wore a Saint Laurent jumpsuit. Everyone else was in skirts or dresses.

The showing was more intimate than the ones Adolfo presented in hotels before moving to his new quarters, and it served the clothes well.

For women willing to think about fall before getting their bathing suits wet, it offered a lot of ideas to digest.

There is, for example, the continual preoccupation with la mode Chanel, which Adolfo is doing better than the Paris couture house these days. In case you miss the connection, and don't happen to recall that Chanel decorated her place with Coromandel screens, there are her quilted, chain-handled handbags and black-tipped beige pumps to remind you.

Colored Bands

The best Adolfo Chanel is a brown suit—knitted, as they all are—and banded in purple and pink edges instead of the heavy black braid associated with Chanel. Oh yes, there's also a brown vest, similarly banded.

The vest is the new note of the season. Knitted in tweedy patterns, it turns up with matching coats lavished with fox shawl collars.

Inexhaustible Ideas

There are vests with velvet skirts, cardigans and knitted shawls, and don't think that exhausts the designer. To tune into the Chinese fashion movement, Adolfo knits up the cheongsam, fitted within an inch of its life, and does jackets in magnificent brocade lined with marabou.

Of course he does separates. Who can avoid it? They're somewhat special, however: chenille jackets, velvet skirts or pants and stitched taffeta shirts. You run around in them at night when you're not wearing an ombre chiffon blouse and a velvet skirt or a skinny knitted black dress.

That doesn't exhaust the list. When you really want to get dressed up, Adolfo recommends pearl-embroidered flapper dresses in absinthe-colored chiffon. Chanel may have done things like that in the nineteen-twenties. Actually, she did.

Sophie Gimbel, who used to design custom dresses for Saks Fifth Avenue, said some beaded-bosom chiffons reminded her of dresses she had in her closet from years ago, though not as far back as the twenties.

His Happy Fans

Which only emphasizes the fact that Adolfo hardly left a stone unturned. As his fans pointed out happily enough, there is something for everybody. And for someone with a huge fashion appetite, there is a truckload. Everything, except for the black dresses trimmed with gold kid, is attractively done, and you'll be seeing a lot of the clothes around next winter.

JULY 15, 1975

Notes on People

Ford Has a Birthday, A Physical and Party

FRANK J. PRIAL

President Ford, who said he felt "about 40," celebrated his 62d birthday yesterday. He began the day with a 35-minute physical examination in his White House study and went on to a surprise party in the East Room.

The comedian **Flip Wilson,** who spent the morning visiting a community of the elderly poor with the President's wife, **Betty,** appeared at the surprise party in his role of Geraldine.

Dressed as a nurse, Mr. Wilson gave a humorous account of the President's physical and referred to Mr. Ford as "the main man." He called Mrs. Ford "first mama." And he announced that the Government had solved the problem of the President stumbling on the steps of his plane, Air Force One, by installing an elevator.

After the President's physical examination, his personal physician, **Dr. William Lukash,** said he had found Mr. Ford "physically fit" with the results of the laboratory test completely normal.

●

Marines at Camp Pendleton and elsewhere around the world were put on notice by their new commandant, **Gen. Louis H. Wilson,** yesterday that he would not tolerate overweight leathernecks. "If I see a fat marine," General Wilson said, "he's got a problem and so does his commanding officer." The commandant of the corps keeps himself fit by running two miles every day.

General Wilson, 55 years old, said he planned to toughen enlistment standards and to weed out marines unable to accept corps discipline. He acknowledged, too, continuing problems with crime in the barracks. "In the old days, a marine could leave his wallet on his bunk and expect to find it there when he got back," General Wilson said. "Such is not the case now."

●

In Munich, West Germany, **Col. Ernest R. Morgan,** who was held captive by Arab guerrillas in Lebanon for two weeks, was given a medical checkup and was questioned about his ordeal. The Army said Colonel Morgan had been taken to Germany "because it was considered more appropriate" than for him to remain in Ankara, Turkey, his regular assignment.

Colonel Morgan, 43, was kidnapped on June 29 when he stopped overnight in Beirut on his way back to Ankara from a meeting in Pakistan. He was taken from a taxicab during the street fighting between leftist Moslems and rightist Christians. He was released Saturday.

●

Former **President Richard M. Nixon,** barefoot and accompanied by three members of his family, signed autographs and posed for snapshots on a beach at Camp Pendleton, Calif., the huge Marine Corps installation near his San Clemente home. Clad in slacks and a dark jacket bearing the Presidential seal, Mr. Nixon strolled along the beach for an hour with his wife **Pat,** his daughter **Tricia** and her husband, **Edward F. Cox.**

●

In Washington, the conviction of a former Nixon aide, **Dwight L. Chapin,** for lying to a grand jury was upheld by the United States Court of Appeals. Mr. Chapin, the former President's appointments secretary, was sentenced to serve 10 to 30 months in prison in May, 1974. A jury had found him guilty of lying when he denied knowledge of some of the activities of **Donald H. Segretti,** another White House staff member. Mr. Segretti served time in prison for illegal campaign activities, including distributing faked campaign literature and leaflets on the sex lives of Democratic Presidential candidates.

Mr. Chapin's lawyer said no decision had been made on a possible appeal to the Supreme Court.

●

In Hollywood, a young couple came up with an unusual idea. Mari and Ed **Smith** threw a party to celebrate the end of their 15-month marriage. "The whole idea is to explain that Ed and I are still buddies," said Mrs. Smith, who is 24 years old. She said her husband, who is 44, "just wants to be single." She said she wants to travel.

At the unmarriage ceremony, Pete Kingsbury, the best man last year, removed the couple's wedding bands and placed them on the fourth fingers of their right hands.

The invitations to the April 14, 1974, wedding were engraved. The invitations to the unwedding were Xeroxed. They read: "You are cordially invited to join us in celebrating our divorce."

●

Ethel Scull, one-time doyenne of the pop art world, announced yesterday that her split-up with her husband, New York taxicab fleet owner **Robert Scull,** had resulted in $850 a week temporary alimony. Mrs. Scull said her lawyer, Julia Perles, was disappointed because she got **Martha Mitchell,** the former wife of former Attorney General **John N. Mitchell,** $1,000 a week temporary alimony.

An associate of Miss Perles said she had never represented Mrs. Mitchell.

SEPTEMBER 11, 1975

Avedon Show: The Place to Be Seen

By ENID NEMY

Not everyone in the world was at the Marlborough Gallery Tuesday night. It just looked that way.

There were approximately 3,000 men and women, and some that could have been either, milling around and lifting a glass or two at the opening of the first full-scale exhibition of Richard Avedon's photographs in New York.

Mr. Avedon himself, a slight man in a dark suit, was probably the most unobtrusive and retiring person in the throng that was described in terms from "glamorous" to "weirdo."

"This evening is a parody of itself," said one woman who was making a valiant, if unsuccessful, attempt to look at the faces hanging on the wall, rather than those in the crowd.

An elderly bearded man, escorting a young woman with a crimson kewpie-doll mouth and frizzy hair, lectured her on the importance of the occasion.

"This is THE place to be in New York tonight," he said, as her attention wandered. You'll see everyone."

She saw Warren Beatty, a highlight that was apparently enough to make her evening.

"Yeah," she said, with more enthusiasm than she had displayed previously.

It was, indeed, the place for anyone interested in a cross-section of the city's movers, climbers, doers, and faces familiar through constant exposure.

There were, of course, scores of photographers. Some of them were busy snapping and clicking, many concentrating on specific groups. One was interested only in well-known personalities, another said he was looking for "freaks" (he had no problem).

Busman's Holiday

Most of the photographers, however, were on a busman's holiday, Louise Dahl-Wolfe and Jack Mitchell among them. They were interested in the work of a colleague, and the breakthrough that put photography on a level with painting and sculpture in an art gallery. Mr. Avedon's photographs have appeared in Vogue and Harper's Bazaar magazines for 30 years.

Then there were such people as Lauren Hutton, in a cowboy hat from Calgary, and Halston in a turtleneck sweater from who knows where, both studiously ignoring the flash bulbs.

There were Nicky and Kenneth Lane, one in black chiffon and the other in black satin, hamming it up ("Can I put my finger in my mouth?" asked Nicky), Sylvia Miles looking for the ladies room, hordes of unknowns looking down Sylvia Miles's décolletage, and Ethel Scull looking for Sylvia Miles.

There was Christina Bellin, recovering from the "terrible things" that had happened to her after she had publicly announced that she had extramarital affairs, and Dr. Howard Bellin, her husband, telling her to ignore the whole thing.

"It's been awful — you wouldn't believe it," said the former Countess Paolozzi. "Everyone knows these things go on and it's all right if you don't talk about it."

William M. Kunstler, horn-rimmed glasses sitting atop his head, and a brown tie "out of the Attica trial" wound around his neck, was having more success than most looking at the photographs. For one thing, he was taller. Then, too, he refused, for the most part, to be deflected from the object of the evening.

Huntington Hartford was there, as well, ambling along in a brown and white striped suit and looking neither left nor right, nor up nor down.

At least two of the faces in the exhibition were also there in person. Andy Warhol was swallowed up by the crowd near his photograph; Polly Allen Mellen, a Vogue editor, was overcome by her photograph, which she had not previously seen.

"It was just taken a few weeks ago," she said. "These tears are of joy."

The tears shed by any designers viewing the crowd might well have been real. Other than Marilyn Evins in a black Galanos suit, Betsy Theodoracopulos in an apricot fleece outfit, Ethel Scull in a black Adolfo, Susan Shiva in a Chanel-inspired suit and Amy Greene and Kay Daly Leslie in black satin pants outfits, there were few sights to gladden the hearts of fashion purists.

Overwhelming Variety

Kimonos, Chinese-inspired tunics and coats, and fringed shawls were everywhere, but not in sufficient quantity to outnumber the attic clothes, the coveralls, the hip-hugging jeans and the karate outfits.

The men were equally diverse, black tie (although the evening was informal), dark suits, Yves Saint Laurent, American Indian, satin, velvet and everything in between.

Who else was there? Lots and lots and lots, from Gloria Vanderbilt Cooper, an early arrival with her two oldest sons, Stan and Christopher Stokowski, to D. D. and John Barry Ryan, Gil Shiva, Tom Hoving, Norman Mailer, Joanne Cummings, Mary and Tom Morgan, Nora Ephron, Emily and Bruce Davidson, Bruce Gelb, China Machado, Grace Mirabella Cahan and Dr. William Cahan, Sisi Cahan, Clay Felker, James Brady and Chauncey Howell.

And who was that somewhat largish woman, with the flowered dress, who greeted every second person and smiled at every tenth one? Well, if you didn't recognize Elaine, it probably wasn't your kind of party anyway.

OCTOBER 12, 1975

SoHo Grows Up And Grows Rich and Chic

By FRED FERRETTI

Only a few years ago, SoHo was a place where artists wandered, uninvited, into Larry Poons's loft for his weekly anybody-drop-in party. Nowadays, the social scene there is a great deal less casual. More characteristic, perhaps, is Robert Rauschenberg, wearing suits made entirely of sewn-together neckties, giving a chic by-invitation-only party for Princess Christina of Sweden—with salmon flown in fresh from the fjords—to the delight of such guests as Henry Geldzahler, August Heckscher, Robert Scull and other uptown culture mavens.

•

This change in party style is expressive of SoHo's transformation from a low-rent district for artists to a playground of uptown chic. Ten years ago, for $100 a month, artists could live and work in 2,500 square feet of high-ceilinged lofts in this area south of Houston Street. Today, SoHo is no longer cheap. Lofts are co-op apartments which sell for as much as $150,000 to doctors and psychoanalysts.

Some artists have stayed and accommodated themselves to the changes in their district—in fact, some say they like the diversity of the "new" SoHo—but others have fled, believing that SoHo is on its way to becoming another Greenwich Village, possessing a tradition of art but producing little worthwhile art, becoming a stage on which other aspects of culture ape the visual arts that inspired them.

SoHo's art history was short and mercurial. In 1965, artists looking for cheap working space began moving into the lofts, signing leases for what had been small factories. For years they lived illegally, because SoHo was zoned for light industry and manufacturing. In 1970, the zoning was changed to permit those who were certifiable artists to install the baths and kitchens that, under the law, they could not have put in previously. In the meantime, by 1968, the first galleries began setting up shop. In the next few years, the uptown galleries began descending to SoHo in force—Andre Emmerich, John Weber, Ileana Sonnabend, Leo Castelli, (all at 420 West Broadway). The Whitney came, too, opening a downtown branch. By 1973, when SoHo was certified as a landmark district by the city, those cheap $100 lofts were long gone.

Today, SoHo is inhabited mostly by the less than needy survivors of the last decade of the avant-garde—those artists, dancers and musicians who have made it, who are brought, watched and solicited by uptown money, who have been clever enough to crest with the trends and become part of them. A number of galleries—the smaller versions of the uptown transplants—exhibit poor but recognizable imitations in the styles of Rauschenberg and Rosenquist and Oldenburg and Stella.

Says artist Paul Harbut, "SoHo can't be isolated just for artists. It's sad. You just can't preserve it as an artists' neighborhood. . . . the artists have become cynically promoted. They've become technocrats, and the galleries lean to those painters who produce work done with a saleable technique."

Roy Lichtenstein's Guggenheim Museum poster sells for $15 in Poster Originals—another uptowner now downtown—but it's $500 signed. And dealer Ivan Karp, in his O.K. Harris Gallery across the street, offers a set of four photo-offset reproductions of artists in his stable for $275, framed, to the tourists awed by his Warhol Campbell Soup wall hanging.

Once Manhattan's red-light district, SoHo is now a neighborhood really on the make. It's hip, with it, Madison Avenue's replacement as the in place for a Saturday stroll in new Earth Shoes. The artists' collective restaurant at Prince and Wooster, called Food, now turns out crispy little salads and crepes instead of ladling out thickened okra broth and mashed eggplant. Few artists eat there because it is less affordable than when it opened three years ago. Kenn's Broome Street Bar is as pseudo-pubby as any Third Avenue singles joint, and the Spring Street Bar has joined the new Ballroom as one of those chrome-modern, ice cream and hamburger spots that busloads of suburban tourists like so much.

The strident leftness of The National Art Workers Community and the Art Workers Coalition has vanished, and SoHo is now decidely apolitical, more concerned with putting down efforts to rename West Broadway Jackson Pollock Place and blocking New York University's plan to raise a sports palace among the five-story, cast-iron facades than in political cause sharing.

True, Robert Indiana is still there, and so is John Chamberlain, and Jasper Johns still has his home-house-space in the bank he bought on Houston Street. But Larry Rivers is uptown on 14th Street, and Paul Jenkins and Elaine deKooning are up at 13th Street, away from it all. And the younger artists are looking in NoHo, SoCa and TriBeCa—north of Houston, south of Canal, and the triangle below Canal—for the cheap lofts they once went to SoHo for.

"It's a fancy St. Mark's Place now," complains painter Gerald Marcus. "At one time it was a neighborhood, a place to live and work. Now it's not. It's a singles and groupies scene. I lived there, but a couple of years ago I found there was nothing there for me. I moved.

And art critic Judy Beardsall, who abandoned SoHo for TriBeCa, says that SoHo "is changing too rapidly. It's so fluid you can watch it happening. Soon it will be Greenwich Village, a completely fake Bohemia, filled with dead ideas and dead art." Even SoHo's current art profile is somewhat of an illusion, she says. "The uptown galleries, Castelli and the others, they're not selling well. What they have are events—like a Rauschenberg opening and all the limousines come down. And so it looks like activity. The galleries making money are the supposedly avant-garde who deal in Old Masters on the side. They sell by mail to Wichita."

Sylvia Goldsmith, a filmmaker who works under the name of Sylviana and whose current project is documenting the life of a SoHo painter, says she is not disturbed by the changes of the last couple of years. "The community still exists for me. It goes on. It's vital. It's been good for me. When I moved in a few years ago it was pretty deserted, pretty daring. Well, to me the spirit of avant-garde persists despite the uptown influence. Having become more expensive has not killed that for me. I suppose it's true that the famous *are* harder to reach now, but that aspect of the SoHo scene was never mine."

Perhaps the soul of the new SoHo is The SoHo News, a cheeky sheet published out of an old tile-floored ice cream parlor on Spring Street on the western fringe of Little Italy. Its publisher, a former improvizational press agent named Mike Goldstein—who claims that he aims to out-circulate The Village Voice, so he has his delivery trucks surreptitiously follow Voice deliverers to the newsstands—says, "SoHo is not uptown or downtown. It's a town gone crazy. It's an artistic, creative hustle. SoHo is to the 1970's what Haight-Ashbury was to the 1960's. Only the location is new.

"The Sculls coming down in their black Checker is not new. What's new is that it's a hotbed of creative energy, 70 per cent of which is bull, 30 per cent fantastic. Ten years from now there'll be another place and they'll be saying, 'This is the *new* SoHo.'" ■

OCTOBER 19, 1975

Jumpsuit Proves Adept at Social Climbing

By BERNADINE MORRIS

Consider the jumpsuit.

First cousin to the farmer's overall, it's the work uniform of grease monkeys as they swarm over planes or cars; gas station attendants wear it as they ply the pumps.

Until recently, a one-piece protective covering—no pretensions to chic.

And now look!

Pauline Trigère wears one to lunch at La Grenouille—and to view the showing of Paris fashions by Alix Grès at the Pierre Hotel.

Audrey Smaltz wears one before more than 2,000 people attending the Ebony Fashion Fair at Avery Fisher Hall in Lincoln Center, where she was serving as commentator.

Lyn Revson wears one to the opening of the Music Fair in Westbury, L.I., and to dinner at Elaine's.

Jan Chipman turns up in one at Shea Stadium and at the showing of Ohrbach's European-copy fashion show.

Obviously, the jumpsuit is upwardly mobile. In fact, it may be the biggest social climbing fashion since the trench coat and the pea jacket slipped into everybody's wardrobe.

Its rise hasn't exactly been meteoric. Yves Saint Laurent, who doesn't believe in fashion but manages to start things periodically—he boosted the trench coat and the pea jacket, among other styles—showed jumpsuits about five years ago, but not everybody was ready.

They weren't ready when Kimberly, the American knitwear concern, showed them a little while later.

They're still hard to manipulate, but they have other qualities that make up for this difficulty.

"They're the easiest fashion to dress up or down," says one woman who acquired three Kimberley jumpsuits in the early offering and is still wearing them.

"You can wear them all day and

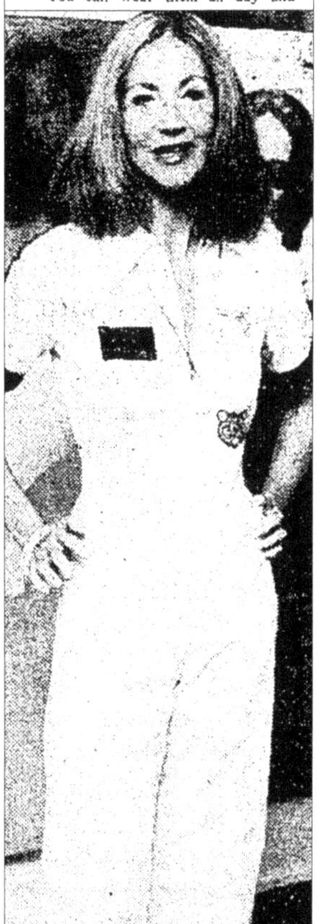

just change your belt and earrings and you're ready to wear them at night. But I wouldn't advise a woman who has weak kidneys to try them."

The resurgence in interest in jumpsuits this fall is due partly to the fact that women have been wearing pants for so long they're getting bored with them.

Miss Trigère reports that after her appearance at La Grenouille at least one woman called to order a jumpsuit for herself.

Like Saint Laurent, she says she's been making them for about five years "because they look slick under furs and they keep you warm." For a while, stores were mystified as to whether they should put them in dress departments or suit departments, but that difficulty seems to have cleared.

"I kept on making them because I feel if you have a good figure, they make you look better and if you don't, they slim you," Miss Trigère said. "They're the liberation of the body—you can move freely and you don't wear anything but pantyhose under them. Of course, they wouldn't be possible without the invention of pantyhose."

Saint Laurent has also revived his jumpsuits, and they're one of the "in" fashions at his Rive Gauche shop at 855 Madison Avenue, near 70th Street. At the moment, his jerseys (at $355) are practically all sold out, but a new shipment of the poplins (at $205) has arrived.

The women who enjoy wearing jumpsuits agree with Miss Trigère that there's nothing more flattering if you can get one to fit you.

Mrs. Chipman was so enchanted with her gray wool style by Bill Blass that she also bought one in beige wool.

"All I had to do was shorten them," she said.

Mrs. Revson has two styles, both by Giorgio di Sant'Angelo.

"He makes my bathing suits," she said. Her jumpsuits fit like bathing suits and are in stretch materials. The turquoise one has short sleeves, the black has long ones.

Mrs. Revson isn't too concerned about the bathroom problem.

"I just think of them as Dr. Dentons," she said. "The children always managed."

Ethel Scull has probably had the most fun with hers. She picked it up for $50 at a shop called Waterbags at 19th Street and Third Avenue, where she was taken by Sylvia Miles.

"So many people have asked me about it, I could have gone into business," she said.

Mrs. Scull's jumpsuit is in sturdy white cotton and it's the closest thing to what garage mechanics wear. In fact, it has a small appliqué on the chest saying "Esso."

When she wore it this fall to Bergdorf Goodman, Glady Solomon, who usually drives her own Rolls-Royce to town from her home in Purchase, N.Y., asked her sweetly if she would change her oil.

Mrs. Scull has a lot of jumpsuits. "A Halston in plain cashmere, very elegant; one by Saint Laurent, very old, and an Adolfo, very sexy," she enumerated.

But she has had the most fun in her mechanic's suit, she says.

"People stop me all day long."

October 26, 1975

Making the Buyer Beg —And Other Tricks of the Art Trade

By RICHARD BLODGETT

As the art market gathers momentum this fall with a round of gala gallery openings, champagne receptions and other rituals and razzmatazz calculated to fight off the recession blues and pep up sales, many of the truly big-time transactions will take place, as in the past, out of the limelight, behind closed doors. And one of the people certain to play a key role in these transactions is Leo Castelli, the urbane, witty, 68-year-old art dealer generally recognized as the greatest salesman the art market has known since Joseph Duveen, the master merchant of the twenties and thirties.

Castelli's current stable of artists includes many of the superstars of contemporary art — among them Jasper Johns, Robert Rauschenberg, Roy Lichtenstein, James Rosenquist, Andy Warhol, Claes Oldenburg, Ellsworth Kelly and Frank Stella. Few other dealers control such a powerhouse. As a result, during a year in which a number of lesser dealers have closed up shop, Castelli has continued to grow and prosper. In his most recent fiscal year, he sold about $2.5-million in paintings.

To be sure, Castelli's operation is not typical, and yet he has proved such a master of the techniques other dealers strive to perfect that a close look at his operation, headquartered in a small, elegant gallery at 4 East 77th Street, is revealing about the manner in which the more successful art dealers anticipate shifts in the cultural wind and then stimulate prices, attract customers and clinch sales.

Much of Castelli's success today stems from the fact that in 1957, when the diminutive Trieste-born businessman decided to move full-time into art dealing, he made a prophetic decision. That was the heyday of Abstract Expressionism, but Castelli sensed that important cultural changes were taking place and that soon a new form of art would come of age. The first two artists he signed up with exclusive contracts were Rauschenberg and Johns, now recognized as key figures in the transition from Abstract Expressionism to Pop Art, and from there he added to his stable other major Pop artists.

The ever-rising prices for works by Castelli's artists are not necessarily a result of free-market forces alone. Dealers in contemporary art are notorious for the little tricks they employ to give prices an extra boost; that, after all, is part of the game. And Castelli is a reputed master of at least two such tricks.

•

The first of these is based on the notion that if an exceptionally high price can somehow be achieved for one work by a given artist, all of that artist's works increase in value as soon as word gets around. This process can be started either by artificially bidding up prices at auction or by working out some sort of back-room deal in which a collector pays a huge price in a private purchase from a dealer. For example, it is said that throughout the late sixties Castelli had collectors bidding up works on his behalf at auction in order to call attention to high prices for works by "his" artists and that he offered special financial arrangements in return.

On private sales there was the classic case of the Rosenquist painting that Castelli sold out of his gallery in 1965 for a reported $60,000, a stunning new high at the time for a Rosenquist. Word of the transaction was quickly circulated to the press. Time magazine listed the $60,000 figure as fact. The Times said the price was "reported to be about $60,000" and quoted the buyer, Robert Scull, as asserting that the painting was "the most important statement made in art in the last 50 years." Castelli now concedes that the painting actually sold for less. "The *asking price* was $60,000, minus whatever discount I may have given," he says. He adds that he cannot recall how big the discount was. Another dealer believes it was at least $15,000.

As to bidding up prices at auction, Castelli states that it would be impossible for him to come up with the necessary cash to support current high price levels. "I can't do it any more," he comments, implying that he at least used to, when prices were lower.

Another important means of boosting prices in the art market—and in this area Castelli is frank to acknowledge his expertise—is that of selling to the right customer. Indeed, when Castelli gets an important painting from one of his artists, he does not simply "sell" it. He "places" it—and then spreads the word that the buyer, usually a well-known collector or museum, has just acquired a major piece by Lichtenstein, Robert Morris, Donald Judd or whomever at such and such a price. The objective is prestige which will ultimately drive up prices for the artist's work.

•

Price manipulation does little good, of course, unless there are *customers willing* to reach up to the sometimes stratospheric level established. Accordingly, another ingredient in Castelli's success is the skill with which he woos buyers. He does not rely on splashy openings and lavish press parties. Big openings, one collector notes, are for the publicity-conscious galleries like Marlborough. "Every once in a while," this collector adds, "Leo will have a special party for some charitable function. I was at one to 'save Venice.' But Leo is very anti-Marlborough. Whatever Marlborough does Leo does the other way around."

While not holding many parties of his own, Castelli has achieved the celebrity status that enables him to put in an appearance at everybody else's. "But he doesn't go around buttonholing you and saying you've got to own this, you've got to own that," the same collector says. "That's not his style at all. Instead he kind of puts himself in the position that people come to him and say, 'What should I do, Leo? What should I do?' And then he allows that you ought to buy a Rosenquist or a Rauschenberg. I saw him the other day and said, 'Gee, the art market seems pretty moribund.' And he said, 'Yes, for those who don't have Warhol, Lichtenstein, Rosenquist and Rauschenberg.' He's the consummate salesman."

Although the foremost buyers of the sixties were primarily from New York and California, contemporary American art is now being exported in increasing volume to Europe. Castelli says his two most active customers during the past few years have been Dr. Giuseppe Panze, an Italian industrialist, and Professor Peter Ludwig, an industrialist from Germany. "They have the most astounding collections in the world today of American art," he says, adding that he first met Panze when the latter "just dropped in" one day in 1959 and bought half a dozen Rauschenbergs. Ludwig dropped by eight years later, and also bought a number of paintings right away. These two leading European collectors now visit Castelli three or four times a year.

Castelli is more cryptic about his big American customers. He says he can count them on the fingers of his two hands, but declines to name names—to a reporter. However, other dealers say this group includes individuals such as Mr. and Mrs. S. I. Newhouse Jr. of the newspaper publishing family and Frederick and Marcia Weisman, long-time collectors of contemporary art. Weisman is a Los Angeles business executive. Trend-setting collectors of this high station generally are informed of major paintings in progress, are given first crack at these paintings as they come off the easel, and are offered somewhat better financial terms as a further inducement to buy. Sometimes the degree of favoritism is even greater. Castelli acknowledges that, before allowing the big U.S. collectors a look at major new works, he occasionally sends photographs of the paintings to Panze or Ludwig in Europe. "Then perhaps they pick one or two they like and ask me to please wait until they come next month before I sell them to somebody else."

The selling of high-priced paintings to rich collectors actually represents less than half of Castelli's overall sales volume. Other dealers are his biggest customers, particularly for the steady flow of more routine works. During the past 10 years Castelli has developed a highly efficient distribution network made up of leading galleries in such cities as Los Angeles, Houston, Minneapolis, Toronto and London. Dealers in this network have been assigned exclusive local rights to new works by specific Castelli artists. In the Los Angeles area, for instance, the Margo Leavin gallery holds local rights to new works by Warhol and Oldenburg. Complete exhibitions of works by these two are assembled by Castelli and shipped to Los Angeles for display at Leavin. Depending on the artist, Castelli himself generally takes a cut of anywhere from 33 per cent to 50 per cent of the retail price and he gives up roughly half of this commission on sales made through galleries within his distribution network.

•

Such distribution arrangements, while important and complex, lack the high drama of the way Castelli markets his very best works. Because he has so little trouble selling these major pieces, Castelli can afford to take his time about letting new collectors into the elite inner circle of individuals who are permitted to buy. Novice collectors sometimes are flattered, wheedled, maneuvered, cajoled and subtly pushed into buying certain lesser works by this or that artist. Only after their "education" is complete can these collectors move up to the really top pieces and choose as they see fit, perhaps with an occasional helpful hint from the master. Here is how one collector was initiated.

This collector, a wealthy businessman from the mid-West, began buying from Castelli in the late sixties. He was introduced to Castelli through a mutual friend, and he found that he never had much trouble acquiring "routine" paintings—those priced under $30,000 or $40,000. On the other hand, the major pieces were always unavailable to him, no matter how much he was willing to pay.

After steadily selling to him for nearly five years, Castelli finally held forth the hope that this collector might be able to acquire a major Lichtenstein—something the man had wanted right from the start. But Castelli told him that not just any Lichtenstein would do. It was important, Castelli said, to wait for the *right* Lichtenstein.

And wait the collector did. Another two years passed, with the collector's anticipation increasing almost daily. Finally Castelli invited the businessman to accompany him to Lichtenstein's studio in the Hamptons. It seemed the big moment was at hand. Or was it? Castelli mentioned casually that a number of paintings would be on display in Lichtenstein's studio and that one, in Castelli's opinion, was far superior to the others. He wouldn't say which one he had in mind. There was almost the feeling that if the collector didn't pick the right one he wouldn't be able to buy.

After arriving at the studio and studying the paintings for nearly an hour, the man nervously made his choice. There was a brief pause, and then a smile came over Castelli's face. Why, he said, that was just the one *he* had in mind. The collector quickly closed the deal. He won't say how much he paid, but based on prices for other recent Lichtenstein it probably was somewhere between $50,000 and $70,000.

•

Not every buyer goes through that kind of ordeal. Some buyers, especially those who already have achieved prominence within the collecting ranks, find entry to the Castelli inner circle much easier. But the point is that any collector is forced to play the game on Castelli's terms if he wants to get at the really "important" paintings.

Castelli admits that a great deal of price bargaining takes place. The "standard" discount from retail price, expected by all buyers, is 10 per cent. "Some do try to bargain for more," he says, "and depending on circumstances I'll go down more if necessary." Extended payment terms also are available in varying degrees, again depending in large part on the buyer's importance. Among old, established customers, it sometimes is customary simply to avoid paying for as long as one or two years. "Generally speaking, one expects them to pay within a reasonable delay," Castelli says with a nonchalant wave of the hand. "You'll never get paid, or hardly ever, before a month has gone by. But very often there are very great delays." What does he do if payment is not forthcoming at all? Not much, he replies, except encourage the buyer as gently as possible.

•

Castelli says the art business has made him a rich man by enabling him to accumulate a "small fortune" in paintings. His collection is made up mostly of pieces that, for various reasons, no one else wanted and he had the good fortune to buy from the artist.

He tells of one of his most famous and prized possessions—a painting left over from his first Jasper Johns exhibition in 1958. Alfred Barr of the Museum of Modern Art was extremely impressed by that show and helped arrange the sale of almost everything to benefactors of the museum. But then there was this one piece—a red, yellow and blue target with a row of small compartments across the top. Inside each compartment is a plaster model of a part of the human body, including a green penis. Barr loved that painting, but doubted whether the museum could display it without creating a scandal. Each compartment has a door, and Barr asked Johns whether it would be okay for the museum to exhibit the work with the door of the penis compartment closed. Johns replied that it would be perfectly acceptable to close the door occasionally, but not all the time. Barr decided not to buy.

Castelli was the one who got "stuck," keeping the work and paying Johns $1,200. A few years went by and, as Johns gained prominence, Castelli began to receive a stream of offers at ever-increasing prices. He says he has no intention of selling, but a smile does cross his face when he recounts the most recent bid: $400,000. ■

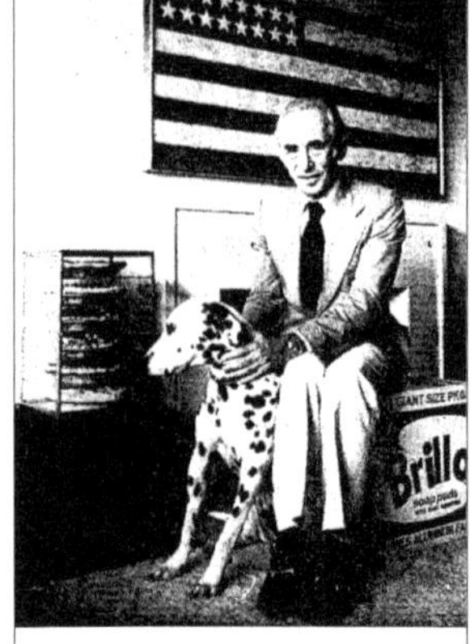

NOVEMBER 9, 1975

To the Editor:

The article by Richard Blodgett ["Making the Buyer Beg and Other Tricks of the Art Trade," Oct. 26], is so distorted throughout that it would be difficult to correct it in a statement shorter than the entire article itself. However, two stories as reported by Mr. Blodgett go beyond the area of distortion and are downright false.

First, the impression was given that, in connection with my sale of a Rosenquist painting to Robert Scull, I or my gallery was responsible for circulating to the press a reported purchase price of $60,000. The implication first made by Mr. Blodgett was strengthened by his statement that "Castelli now concedes that the painting actually sold for less." The fact is that neither I nor my gallery at any time circulated to the press or otherwise publicized any price for the painting and, accordingly, no later "concession" was necessary. Whatever publication of the alleged price took place must have been by the purchaser — for whose actions I am not responsible.

Second, I categorically deny that I have ever been party to an arrangement with any of my customers under which they have bid up prices at an auction beyond prices which otherwise would have been reached in exchange for which I have sold them other works at prices reduced by the amount of the excess they paid at auction. Such an arrangement would have been an immoral and possibly even illegal conspiracy to rig prices. I never have been and never will be party to such an arrangement. I myself have from time to time bid at auction on the works of artists whom I represent, have bid to prices which I thought those works were worth, and have paid the prices which I have bid as the best evidence of my conviction that the prices were justified. Such action is entirely proper, and in the course of my experience such actions have been proven justified in some cases and unjustified in others by subsequent market prices. However, the judgment, and the risks inherent in relying on such judgment, have been entirely mine, and I have involved no third persons in my bidding.

One final comment. As a dealer in contemporary works of art, it is my right and privilege to sell them at any prices I determine and to make different prices to different prospective purchasers as I may determine in my own interest or in the interest of the artist. Various factors influence my determination — the distinction of the purchaser and his collection, the frequency with which the purchaser makes purchases from me, my personal relations and friendship with the purchaser, etc. Anyone who does not understand this attitude by a dealer is indeed naive.

LEO CASTELLI
New York City

Richard Blodgett replies: I welcome the additional information Mr. Castelli has provided to enhance my article.

To the Editor:

If Richard Blodgett's article were nothing more than an exposure of unsavory practice in the art world, we would not object.

Professionals can report far worse and far better activities he fastens upon. We are particularly irked, though, by the impression he gives the readers that work by some of the most substantial American artists of our time has no more significance than to function as implausible objects fetching even more implausible prices, that they are the incomprehensible tokens of a financial rip-off and cultural con game. Under the guise of cautioning collectors, Blodgett's larger purpose is to titillate philistinism with which he is himself plentifully endowed.

JOHN COPLANS
Editor
MAX KOZLOFF
Executive Editor
NANCY FOOTE
Managing Editor
Artforum
New York City

To the Editor:

Rather than be characterized as a notorious moneymaker, Leo Castelli should be honored as an American who has no minuscule share in bringing to the fore what is great in America in the age of Vietnam and Watergate.

BERNARD BRODSKY, M.D.
New York City

NOVEMBER 13, 1975

Dressing Up for Charity and a Show

By BERNADINE MORRIS

"So many women," said Lauren Peltz, recoiling a little at the entrance to the dining room at the St. Regis Roof.

"I guess women really dress for women," observed Jean Van Waveren. "I'm glad clothes are getting attractive again," she added.

Despite the rain, 397 persons, mostly women, turned out yesterday for the 17th annual luncheon supporting Girls' Town of Italy. It was a tribute to the vocational training school near Rome, to Joanne Winship, the energetic chairman, and to Albert Capraro, the designer who won a modicum of fame and fortune by being invited to the White House to dress Betty Ford.

"Tatum O'Neal was up at his place yesterday trying on everything," said Polly Bergen, who introduced the Capraro fashion collection.

After modeling a jumpsuit with a quilted vest in a soft brushed indigo blue denim by Capraro, Miss Bergen went on to cite the designer's versatility.

"The nice thing is you can buy a beautiful ballgown for $200 and feel just as good as a woman who paid five times as much," she explained.

"That's for me," said a woman in an imitation Chanel suit, whose voice was heard over the applause.

There were real Chanels in the audience, too, besides the ones knitted by Adolfo, such as the black suit with the tweed cape flung over it worn by Marion Feldman. "It's not this year's," she confided. Mrs. Feldman has a closetful of Chanels of various vintages to draw upon.

Countess Jaquine de Rochambeau wore a muted print silk dress from Dior ("I just got it from Paris, it's the first time I'm wearing it") and Anne Oxenberg was in "half a Halston." That was the red silk blouse; the other half was a black wool suit.

The ratio has finally tilted from trousers to skirts, with the pants suit with matching jacket relegated to the same fashion oblivion as the dress with bust darts.

"Slacks, ugh," said Mrs. Van Waveren, who was in the imitation Chanel camp herself. "Tacky," she went on. "Five years ago everyone would have been wearing them."

Some Stylish Pants

Still, it was possible to wear pants with style. Ethel Scull managed in her cashmere Halston jumpsuit. Cornelia Sharpe did too in her wool culottes topped by a brown silk blouse by Karl Lagerfeld from Chloé. "It's all from Paris," the actress expained. "I never can find Lagerfelds here."

And Carolyn Wechsler looked casually at ease in her knitted pants outfit by Kimberly. Her jacket didn't match.

Mrs. Wechsler gets dressed up formally almost every night to attend one of the multitudinous farewell parties for her husband, Norman, the president of Saks Fifth Avenue, who is leaving at the end of the month to assume the same post at I. Magnin in San Francisco.

"I try to skip the daytime things," Mrs. Wechsler said. "It's too sad saying goodbye."

With all its diversity, the fashion show in the audience was almost worth the $30 admission.

"I came to see the people," said Glady Solomon, who wound a mink scarf around the neck of her brown Adolfo suit. "I got my money's worth."

An Italian Meal

For those who wanted more, there was the food, an Italian meal that left everyone comfortable, not sated. It started with antipasto, went on to a chicken crepe and ended with zabaglione and strawberries.

Because the room holds only 330 people when a runway is set up in the middle of it, the tables were placed so close together the waiters couldn't get around to serve.

"I guess everybody is so pleased to see it a success, nobody minds passing the plates," said Pyrma Pell, who served as anchorwoman for her table.

The show, which started with play clothes and ended with party dresses, made some new Capraro fans and pleased some old ones.

Mary Beame said she was always happy to see American fashions come off so well. Mary Capraro, the designer's mother, said she always thought Albert's clothes were pretty, and Connie Godin, whose daughter, Tawny, is the current Miss America, said her daughter was right.

"Three-quarters of her wardrobe is by Capraro—she adores him," said Mrs. Godin. "I'd like to have some of his styles for myself right now."

JANUARY 7, 1976

Lift Midwinter Spirits, a Note of Fun in New Designs

By BERNADINE MORRIS

Pleated culottes to stroll down the street in.

Satin basketball suits to lounge about in, wear under clothes (maybe the culottes), substitute for nightgowns or pajamas—and even to wear when you're taking a shot at the basket.

Sleek, slinky one-piece bathing suits to divert attention from all those bikini-clad show-offs at the beach.

These are just a few of the notions thrown out in the last few days by fashion designers—and the year is barely a week old. It all presages an upturn in imagination and certainly in attitudes toward clothes. Fashion may even turn into fun again. Who knows?

●

The culottes are the contribution of Adolfo, who does his best for a certain kind of upper-crust woman who returns the devotion such women reserve for their dressmakers and hairdressers.

His culottes are white and pleated. A knitted pair is shown with a navy and lavender striped cardigan, which carries out the Chanel genre that Adolfo has made his own. In addition to the traditional cardigan jacket, he also shows a number of knitted coats that descend a few inches below their matching skirts. No reason they couldn't be worn with the culottes, except why cover them up?

The other culottes are in white gabardine, accompanied by cinnamon, navy or red gabardine blazers and white silk shirts. Quite possibly next spring's uniform among upper-crust women, if they can tear themselves away from the standard knitted Chanel.

Now the culottes do not begin to exhaust Adolfo's bag of tricks. Remember hot pants of exactly five years ago? They're back again, now in printed linen, and accompanied by ciré belted jackets Fine for resorts.

Jumpers seem headed for an even richer, fuller fashion life. They're accompanied by the obligatory white silk blouse, they're crocheted, and they are street or floor length.

The apotheosis of the jumper is the series in cream colored crepe de chine with flowers, butterflies or birds hand painted on them. These are for evening. Adolfo's clients go out a lot at night.

Not every Adolfo style is to die over. Some of his most devoted fans had reservations about his tendency to cut a swath of shirring over the hips, or to tie a scarf there instead of over the shoulders.

"You have to have a flat fanny for that and I don't," said Barbara Walters, with feeling.

"Carmen Miranda, revived the wrong way," muttered Ethel Scull.

"I should lose ten pounds," said Livia Weintraub wistfully.

●

The basketball suits are the contribution of — who else? — Rudi Gernreich. They're short jumpsuits, actually, with tank tops and elasticized waistlines, and they could pass for boxing suits if that happens to be your sport.

They're from a collection of contemporary—you might even call it advanced—undergarments that he has constructed for Lily of France and that also include boxer shorts and jockey shorts.

"There's no confusion about unisex, because if a girl is a girl . . ." the designer said at his show, letting his voice trail off.

"All you have to do is go raiding your husband's closet," a viewer said, helping him out.

The shorts were shown with matching shirts, ties, half-high socks and garters. Men's garters. If a girl is a girl . . .

The basketball suits are divided into two colors, each vibrant, such as yellow top with orange bottom the whole thing outlined in fuchsia. Should be visible from the upper tier of Madison Square Garden.

Enough for the underwear - loungewear - basketball clothes. Gernreich has also designed some swimsuits. Before he was inspired to create the topless suit 12 years ago, Mr. Gernreich was known for his one-piece styles without bones or padding.

The one-piece numbers are back now in stretch nylon with coated metal springs for straps. Two-piece styles are, of course, around too. They have dog-leash clasps for fastening. A one-shoulder toga that covers them is also fastened with a dog-leash clasp. Inventive, that Gernreich.

Most of the loungewear styles will sell for $8 to $20. The two-piece swimsuits, some mere strings, are $20, the maillots, $25. You'll have to wait for March for these.

●

Donald Brooks is a man in a quandary.

"The more body you expose to sun and water, the better it is," he says. "On the other hand, the one-piece styles look more fashionable."

Quite right. But then Donald Brooks is no novice when it comes to swimsuits. Though this is his first collection for Maidenform, he designed them for five years for Sinclair, and when he made sportsclothes, he would toss a few into his own collections.

These days, he's big on film and theater clothes and two of the stars of his current Broadway show, "A Musical Jubilee," woke up early enough yesterday to catch his breakfast fashion show at the Four Seasons.

"I love the one-piece styles," said Patrice Munsel, huddled in a white mink suit. "They're low in the back and high on the legs and sexy."

"I love the skirts that go over them, so you can have lunch," contributed Tammy Grimes.

The skirts are cut like a square, with a waistband, so the hem dips in handkerchief points. Shirts are made the same way.

Everything is in purple, peach or black, and there are bikinis as well as one-piece suits with such elaborate cutouts they might as well be bikinis.

But the suit to watch out for is a body-covering strapless style with some gathers at the sides. It has a little skirt in front. These days, that counts as a breakthrough. At any rate, it made the bare ones look a bit vulgar.

It has a secret too. It stretches so much it can fit anyone from a size 6 to a size 12. The wave of the future.

All the suits are one-size-fits-all. The prices are $22 to $38 and the delivery date tothe stores is March.

JANUARY 18, 1976

Arts and Leisure Guide

Lectures

ART—The last in a series based on the film "America's Pop Collector: Robert C. Scull," followed by speaker Ivan C. Karp. Metropolitan Museum, Fifth Ave. at 82d St. Today, 1:30. Free.

MARCH 23, 1976

Ballroom on a Ballroom Wall Is Unveiled in SoHo

By GRACE GLUECK

A SoHo dream scene with an ideal SoHo cast takes place in The Ballroom Restaurant.

The shy sculptor Marisol shares a table with Robert Scull, the collector and man-about-Soho. Two dealers, Max Hutchinson and Paula Cooper, disport with the artist Alex Katz. At the bar are the video artist Rudi Stern and the painter Larry Rivers, while John Perreault, the art critic, gabs with the painters Deborah Remington and the late Adolph Gottlieb at a well-placed table in the center.

The fantasy scene in The Ballroom is actually a big new mural, unveiled last evening at The Ballroom itself, a real SoHo restaurant-cabaret at 458 West Broadway. Painted by Marion Pinto in the photorealist mode, the mural was commissioned by Gregory Dawson, a co-owner of The Ballroom, in an attempt to portray significant SoHo-ites who have figured in the area's development as "in an international art center."

Most of the "cast" had been posed at The Ballroom by ones and twos, then photographed by Miss Pinto before she did the painting.

Last evening, a number of them dropped in in the flesh to see how they looked on canvas.

"We had to leave out a lot of people," Miss Pinto said, explaining that the 19 figures who actually made it (including Miss Pinto herself, a back view) were "the most I could handle."

The idea for the mural, measuring 14 feet by eight feet, was hatched more than a year ago when Mr. Dawson met Miss Pinto, a SoHo resident who recently had her first solo show there, at a cocktail party.

"We thought, what fun to have a painting of SoHo people," Mr. Dawson said. "From its beginning three years ago, The Ballroom has shown art for sale, and I've always felt that the same sensibility that responds to food is receptive to art."

Mr. Dawson, who sees the new work as a worthy companion to such prominent restaurant art in the city as the Howard Chandler Christy murals at the Cafe des Artistes on West 67th Street, the Ludwig Bemelmans frieze at The Carlyle, and the Maxfield Parrish mural at the St. Regis, added: "I'm ecstatic that it works so well."

At 6:30 last evening, when the shimmering white curtain that covered the mural was drawn, there was a moment's silence, then a burst of applause. By and large, the eight or nine cast members who showed up had kind remarks for what Miss Pinto had wrought.

"I love it," said Miss Remington. "We're all so idealized, none of us has a wrinkle." Mr. Rivers said, "I feel slightly flattered. She took something of me and enveloped it in a kind of glow."

Robert Indiana, the painter, noted coolly: "It comes off well. Of course, I wouldn't want to be having dinner here with everyone in the picture." And Alex Katz mused: "I think I look kind of distinguished, and it's looks that count. I'm glad she didn't try for inner truths."

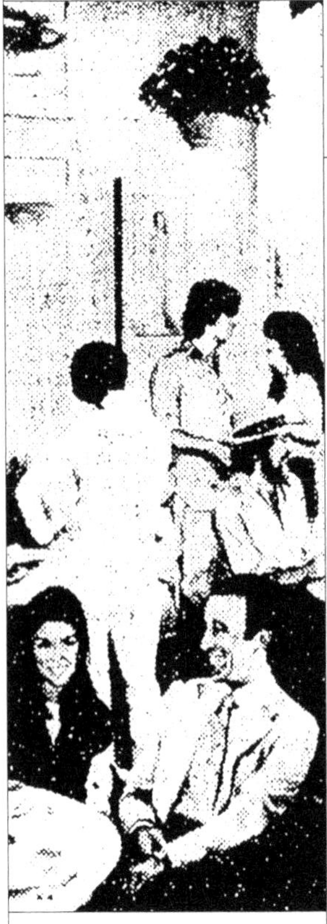

MAY 14, 1976

Art People

Grace Glueck

The latest artist to limn the features of Robert Scull, the Pop-art collector who unloaded some of his holdings for $2 million at auction several years ago, is William Crozier, a sculptor whose work is on the traditional side. "Why not? I want all kinds of art," notes the collector, who sat to Mr. Crozier for six hours every weekend for 14 months. The bronze bust, he reports, is "a very realistic head and part of the chest, and I'm beginning to like it."

So far, Mr. Scull has had his portrait done by the painters Alfred Leslie, Milet Andrejevic, the earthworks artist Michael Heizer (a print), and George Segal (twice in plaster). The new likeness should make Mr. Scull's physiognomy almost as well documented as that of another art worldling, the Metropolitan Museum's curator of 20th-century art, Henry Geldzahler.

JUNE 18, 1976

High Society Hails Taxis At Museum

Taxi! All those folks who usually purr along in limousines with interesting license plates switched to cabs the other night at the Museum of Modern Art. They didn't have any trouble catching them, but then the taxis weren't going anywhere. The museum's annual spring benefit party centered on two American and three European-designed cabs that form the newest exhibit, called "Taxi."

The cars certainly proved that a taxi needn't fit a rider like an iron lung.

Although the museum hadn't meant the exhibit to be a "please touch" affair, there was no stopping the 1,500 merrymakers from climbing in and out of the cabs, bouncing on the seats and doing some just-for-fun smooching in the back seats.

They looked like an especially well-dressed cast for a Marx Brothers movie: Rockefellers, Phippses and Paleys in chiffons and jewels or black tie tried out not only the cabs, but also some of the wheel chairs they were equipped with. Halston escorted his newest "sweeticake," Elizabeth Taylor, who naturally wore one of his popular tunic-and-pants numbers. Hers was blue chiffon, Babe Paley wore a similar one in white.

Francis Kellogg opened a cab door and caught his wife necking with Tiffany's president, Harry Platt. Mr. Kellogg wasn't upset—after all, that's what cabs are for. Jane Cunningham wore the perfect taxi dress: a white jersey Sant'Angelo with a skirt slit to the waist, and got appreciative whistles as she climbed in and out.

There wasn't a genuine, tough-talking New York cabbie at the party, but the fleet owners were represented: Ethel Scull wore her "Scull's Angels" dress and emphatically did not ride a cab with her estranged husband, Robert.

JULY 9, 1976

New York Notables List Their Favorite Haunts

By JUDY KLEMESRUD

When the delegates to the Democratic National Convention flock into the city, Mayor Beame recommends that they take time out to go boating at City Island in the Bronx. The restaurateur Pearl Wong thinks they should make a trip to Monmouth Park racetrack in New Jersey, and Betty Friedan wishes they would "just get out and walk in the streets."

They, like many other notable New Yorkers, feel that the essence of their hometown can be captured in many other places besides the same popular tourist attractions they are sure to see.

"There are so many fun, out-of-the-way places to visit," said Dr. Joyce Brothers, the psychologist. "I'd recommend the Good Housekeeping Institute at 959 Eighth Avenue at 56th Street, where they give free tours and let you see all the various tests they do on products. And a visit to the Cloisters [the art museum in Fort Tryon Park] is fascinating, because you feel like you're back in the days of King Arthur."

When it comes to dining, Dr. Brothers recommended the Parkway Restaurant, at 163 Allen Street, on the lower East Side. "It's very unusual," she said. "It's the only place I know of where they give you a bottle of seltzer and chicken fat at your table. You can also get unborn eggs there."

Tom Seaver, the pitcher for the New York Mets, and his wife, Nancy, both urged the delegates to go to a Broadway show during the convention. Two that they recommend highly are "The Magic Show" and "The Wiz."

"We're both from California," Mrs. Seaver said, "and even on the West Coast you have to go all the way to San Francisco to see theater of any consequence. One of my big fears is that the theater may not survive, and that's why I wish that everyone could go as often as possible."

Billy Wilson, who choreographed one hit show on Broadway, "Bubbling Brown Sugar," and directed another musical that begins previews tomorrow, a black version of "Guys and Dolls," suggested that the delegates take a trip to 125th Street in Harlem.

"There is a marvelous market all across 125th Street, from one end to another," he said. "You can buy a lot of African jewelry, and a lot of soul food. And the wigs—they go on for days. It's very colorful and I always enjoy it."

Besides the boating trip at City Island, Mayor Beame also recommended fishing in Sheepshead Bay and a visit to the Aquarium, both in Brooklyn, a "trip into history" at the Richmondtown restoration in Staten Island, and a visit to the Hall of Science museum in Flushing Meadow, Queens.

Donna Shalala, who is treasurer of the Municipal Assistance Corporation, advised delegates to eat at the Oyster Bar in Grand Central Station "because it's like eating in a castle. The food's good, and it's very noisy, and you can see all of New York in it, because there are all kinds of people there."

Donald J. Trump, one of the city's biggest realtors, suggested that the visitors "sit back and look at the skyline of New York, because it's really the most magnificent skyline in the world. It's fantastic!"

He said he thought that the best views of the skyline could be seen from Brooklyn near the Brooklyn Bridge, or from a cruise around Manhattan Island on a Circle Line boat.

Harry Reams, the pornographic film star who was recently convicted in Memphis of conspiracy to transport interstate obscene materials, recommended a visit to the China Fair, an arcade at 6 Mott Street in Chinatown that features The Dancing Chicken and The Imperial Dragon.

"You put a quarter in a machine and a real live chicken comes out and dances," he said. "Then he pulls a string and releases some food and eats it, and then goes back in his box. You put a quarter in another machine and a papier-mâché dragon begins to rear his head up, and his red eyes light up, and smoke comes out of his nostrils."

Representative Bella Abzug suggested that the delegates visit Ellis Island, "the gateway for millions of people to this country. And I think they should visit the Lower East Side, where many famous people grew up, and where they still have some great eating places."

Three of the city's best-known women—Bess Myerson, Betty Friedan and Marion Javits—all recommended that the delegates take walks around New York as the best way of getting to know the city and its people.

"I think they should go to Times Square, where you can still see the circus of life, the human acrobatics," Miss Myerson said. "And where else can you see a sign that's a block long?"

To Miss Friedan, "the nicest thing about New York is simply its streets. I'd tell the delegates to walk in the streets, walk in Greenwich Village, walk on the West Side. The whole life of New York is the streets, the people and the music."

Marion Javits, wife of the senior Senator from New York, suggested "lovely long walks along Fifth Avenue from 58th to 34th Streets, and then back up along Madison Avenue to see all the lovely shops and people and restaurants.

"Then I'd tell them to walk along Sutton Place and Beekman Place to see the East River. It's a part of New York City that's unscathed, where people just sit on benches and enjoy the city."

As Robert F. Wagner Jr., a Manhattan City Councilman-at-Large sees it, the delegates should visit "some of the more desolate parts of New York, such as the South Bronx."

"The South Bronx made a tremendous impression on Jerry Brown when he was here," Mr. Wagner said. "Maybe it would help the visitors get a sense of some of the problems we have, and vote for aid to New York City."

Joan Hackett, the actress, who was born at 120th Street and First Avenue, recommended a visit to the Egyptian Gardens, a belly dancing establishment at 301 West 29th Street, and bowling at the bowling alley in Madison Square Garden, "which is a hoot," she said, "if you bring some of those intellectually oriented people along. They're so incompetent."

Halston, the fashion designer, suggested the delegates munch on a hot dog ("They're the best ever") in Paley Park, the tranquil vest pocket park, complete with waterfall, just off bustling Fifth Avenue at 3 East 53rd Street.

"I would also advise the delegates to see the fabulous show at the Costume Institute at the Metropolitan Museum of Art," Halston added. "It's called 'Great American Ladies,' by Diana Vreeland. And at the Museum of Modern Art there is the taxi show, all about taxis of the future. It's a great show for civic minded people."

To Bobby Short, the entertainer, the "No. 1 place in New York" is the Windows on the World restaurant, on the 107th floor of the World Trade Center.

"I've just come from eating there," he said, "and the view is spectacular! For a large restaurant, it's run extremely well, and the food is marvelous, and the people are nice, and it's all extremely spic and span. The only thing that comes close to it anywhere in the world is the Eiffel Tower."

Ethel Scull, the socialite and Pop art collector, suggested the delegates visit SoHo, the artists' community south of Houston Street in lower Manhattan.

"I'd wish they'd wander along West Broadway, and stop in at the galleries and see the younger artists who are appearing there. They should also go into the Spring Street bar and have lunch. There are always a lot of artists around there."

Pearl Wong, hostess at the popular Pearl's Restaurant, at 38 West 48th Street, recommended that the visitors go to the racetrack ("My favorite is Monmouth Park") or to Yankee Stadium to see her beloved New York Yankees play.

"I'm a rabid Yankee fan," she said, "and I think they're doing well since they got Catfish Hunter last year. The players are finally pulling themselves together."

JULY 20, 1976

Taxis and Dignity

To the Editor:

The attack on the Modern Museum of Art's taxi exhibit by Robert Scull in his letter (July 12) proves that your writer Ada Louise Huxtable was a true prophet when she wrote that the fleet owners would fight the idea of new taxi design "to the last drop of their wretched meters."

His letter seems a deliberate attempt to mislead. It implies that vast amounts of public and MOMA funds were involved and states that the money spent on the taxi project would have been better spent encouraging new art talents. He surely knows that the exhibit was funded by the Urban Mass Transportation Administration, an unlikely source for launching painters and sculptors but a logical one for the development of industrial design, an art form in which MOMA has always shown interest.

The Times has reported that two companies, American Machine & Foundry and Steam Power Systems, received U.M.T.A. grants of $1 million each ("huge sums handed to giant corporations," according to Mr. Scull) and that the museum was funded with $60,000, a figure matched by Mobil Oil—hardly the "tremendous amount of money" and the "windfall" described by Mr. Scull. I understand from The Times reports that Volkswagen and Volvo undertook the project with their own money.

Is it "foolish design" that provides a modicum of human dignity to taxi passengers? Or that allows thousands of would-be active New Yorkers who need their wheelchairs for mobility to travel at nondiscriminatory cost? The new cabs which allow easy access for wheelchairs could deprive Mr. Scull, I suppose, of his income from the New York State Department of Vocational Rehabilition, which pays him $3 over the meter every time his taxis are used by the department's clients.

It's not the new taxi designs that are "an affront to our intelligence" as he charges. It is Mr. Scull's taxis and his attempt to confuse the issue.

FRANCES BARISH
Dir., New York Metropolitan Chapter
National Paraplegia Foundation
New York, July 13, 1976

JANUARY 5, 1977

Adolfo and His Batwings: 'Perfect'

By BERNADINE MORRIS

You know what you do the week after New Year's Day, when winter has settled in and the snow lies graying at the curb? You slip into your furs and go see Adolfo so you can plan what you're going to wear when you go south, when you come back and spring looms, and, later on, when the summer sun is high. It's a tradition.

The furs were diverse at his morning show at the St. Regis yesterday, which broke in time for everyone to go to lunch and discuss the clothes. All the regulars were there—Marion Feldman in her sable ("not new, but I love it—as it ages, it gets cozier"), Jan Chipman in her red fox,) Glady Solomon in her lynx, Gisèle Masson her sea otter, Laura Johnson in her black and white spotted calf pants suit with the legs thrust into boots. That's Laura Johnson for you.

•

The clothes were pretty diverse, too. Miniskirts—yes, miniskirts—for those who want them. Peasant outfits for those who've found Adolfo's taffeta skirts such fun to wear at parties this fall. Great big batwing blouses floating over snug shirred elastic hipbands and worn over silk pants or shorts.

Neat Chanel-inspired knitted suits and coats, which Adolfo has done for years, parade cheek by jowl with flamboyant Merry Widow black velvet laced tops, which Yves Saint Laurent revived six months ago. Something for everyone, you might say.

Take the minis first. They're for Palm Beach or Palm Springs, the designer says, and for young people who can wear them. He's not dictating—that's out of fashion—and he's not joking either.

Wht did the fans think?

"I wish I could," said Mitzi Newhouse, wistfully.

"No way," said Ethel Scull, definitively.

"Never," responded Mrs. Feldman. Then she relented, "Except on a boat without shoes."

•

"Not right this season," said Mrs. Chipman. "I have to wear the clothes I've already got."

"I'm not ready," said Mrs. Masson. And Carolyn Amory. And Kay Meehan.

Next question.

What about the batwing blouses?

"Perfect." "Imaginative." "A fresh idea to wear at home." Batwing blouses passed. You could tell from the applause anyway. Maybe when the women tried them on, there might be some reservations, but en masse, big approval.

And the peasant look, in its infinite variations, from tiered and pleated flowered skirts to embroidered voile overskirts with white organdy peeping out the bottom?

"Sensational." "Feminine." "Great fun," came the responses.

Peasants passed too. And the Chanel suits are legion. And the knitted styles are beyond reproach—half the audience was wearing one version or another, sometimes the same one.

Culottes? No problem.

Wrapped tops? Ditto.

Silk raincoats, in colors such as teal blue, apricot or apple green? The applause made it clear how the audience reacted to that idea—con brio.

So don't worry about the minis, Adolfo. You've plenty of other things going for you. It was a great show. And who knows? By the time you get your next show together, everybody may be sitting in the front row with knees sticking out. That's fashion for you.

JANUARY 20, 1977

Standing Room At a Benefit For Dancers

By ENID NEMY

At the last minute, quite a few people (47, said those who should know but are inclined to exaggerate) decided that the Merce Cunningham benefit at the Minskoff Theater was the place to be Tuesday night. They were, according to the same source, turned down because it looked as though there wouldn't be another inch of space.

Then the telephone jingled again and a caller offered $1,000. Who could turn it down—certainly not a committee that thought it was doing well to get $125 a person for the Cunningham dancers' introductory performance on Broadway, the champagne party on stage and the black-tie supper following it. Another couple of inches of legroom were found, but the big spender wasn't identified. Benefit committees know from whence they collect the butter on their bread.

Mind you, another big spender was identified, primarily because she had paid the going price for about 25 tickets, and given most of them to dancers, many of whom equate $125 with the United States budget. Christophe de Menil, the fairy godmother who waved the checkbook, comes from a family involved in oil equipment and other little goodies, which puts $125 in a somewhat different perspective.

"We had to stop Christophe from buying tickets," said Harriette Levine, the benefit chairman. "She wanted to get them for a lot of dancers and associates of Merce who couldn't afford them . . . but we wanted a variety of people at the benefit."

Dale and Patricia Keller were part of the variety. The Kellers, who list Hong Kong as their official residence, flew in from Saudi Arabia (Dale) and London (Patricia) within hours of the event, barely on time for Mrs. Keller to don some gewgaws that were either emeralds or the next best thing.

Mr. Keller, who is in the international interior design business, said he was busy with the construction of three "contemporary" palaces in Saudi Arabia but that he wouldn't have missed the benefit for anything.

"Merce and 30 of his associates were guests at our house in Hydra, Greece, last summer," he said.

A number of guests didn't think that mentioning Hydra was quite cricket. They weren't shivering, but they weren't any too warm, either.

Thibaut de Saint Phalle, seated near a window at the supper party, looked across Broadway at the Winston man blowing smoke rings.

"I wish he'd blow some of that smoke this way," said Mr. de Saint Phalle, a lawyer and lecturer in international finance at the University of Geneva, who wore his coat most of the evening.

Louise Nevelson didn't wear her coat but had it draped on her chair as a security blanket. Every so often she'd pat it fondly.

"All this and heaven too," she said. "All this" was a floor-length ermine.

Although a number of the announced table hosts didn't show up—Edward Albee, George Balanchine, Buckminster Fuller, Anne Jackson and Philip Johnson among them—there were few complaints. What with Carly Simon, James Taylor, John and Yoko Ono Lennon, Jasper Johns, Robert Rauschenberg and Jacques D'Amboise mingling with such as Lily and Douglas Auchincloss, Alice Kaplan, Joan Davidson, Joanne Cummings, Gerald Abrahams of Aquascutum in London, Geoffrey Holder, Marion Javits, Jo Carole Lauder, Ethel Scull and some 325 others, there was more than enough of the variety Mrs. Levine had set her heart on.

Thomas Hoving, who had a lecture date at the Metropolitan Museum of Art and saw part of the performance, couldn't stay for the party but he didn't go hungry. Mrs. Levine had sent him on his way in her car, with a box lunch and a split of red wine. She was asked why she hadn't made it a bottle.

"I'm chintzy," she said.

But not too chintzy to allocate a $300 contribution (there was still an estimated $40,000 headed for the dance foundation) to commemorating the evening with a revolving message spelled out in lights on Broadway.

"Broadway salutes Merce Cunningham and Dance Company," it said.

MARCH 6, 1977

The auction crowd

By Stephen Birmingham

Rush right out now and reserve a seat at Sotheby Parke Bernet for 2 o'clock Saturday afternoon, May 7. And, while you're at it, book a table at Les Pleiades in the Surrey Hotel, across the street, for lunch beforehand. Are you back? Then we'll tell you why the date is so important. That is when the glittery collection of Mr. and Mrs. Alfonso Landa will go under the gavel at the famous auction house. Mr. Landa is the wealthy Washington lawyer and chairman of the Fairbanks Whitney Corporation, among other things. The collection, including porcelains, French furniture, chandeliers and other decorations, is from the Landas' Palm Beach house on El Vedado Way, which is also up for sale. A lot of the Palm Beach crowd will turn up at the Landa sale. All seven of the Annenberg sisters may be there. Rose Kennedy might show up. And so on. Very definitely, Sotheby Parke Bernet will be an important place to see and be seen on the 7th of May.

Not that the Landa sale will be one of Sotheby Parke Bernet's "great" sales—on the scale of such recent sales as those of the collections of Norton Simon, Robert C. Scull and the late Geraldine Rockefeller Dodge. (People sell their collections for such reasons as stock-market losses, divorce, or out of sheer boredom and an urge to collect something else. The Landas now plan to live mostly abroad, and will keep only a small *pied-à-terre* in Palm Beach.) The Landa sale might be categorized as a small, "fun" sale where, among the 128 items that will go on the block, you might pick up a pair of Edward Marshall Boehm birds for as little as $200, or an Italian carved gilt mirror for around $700. The most costly item in the sale, a Louis XV ormolu-mounted tulipwood table, will probably not fetch more than $50,000. There will probably not be excitement of the sort that was generated recently when the auction house sold—for a record-breaking $200,000—a 125-year-old Heriz Oriental rug which had been used to cover the pool table in Emily Stifel's house in Wheeling, W. Va. But, the Landas being who they are it will be fun. And the Landa sale will more or less kick off the fashionable auction "season," of which there are two, in May and in October, in case you didn't know. In May, too, Christie's, the renowned London auction house, opens its doors in New York for the first time in newly decorated quarters in the Delmonico Hotel.

The fact is that collecting —not just collecting paintings but also silver, rugs, antiques, Chinese export porcelains, Dorothy Doughty birds (now bringing as much as $15,000 a bird since Dorothy died), in fact, collecting anything — has become one of the major routes, if not the major route, for today's social climber. A collection of any kind conveys instant status. And at the heart—indeed at the very backbone, since "heart" seems too generous a word—stand the auction houses. The collecting rage accounts for the fact that a house like Sotheby Parke Bernet, which did a modest business of $10 million in 1964, had topped $90 million 10 years later. Last year, Sotheby's international sales were over $175 million, with $70 million coming from its New York salesrooms alone. The sale of Mrs. Dodge's collection brought in $7 million, even though a Sotheby representative cheerfully admits that a great deal of the Dodge sale amounted to "junk." (At the auction, buyers bid furiously for her old fur coats, bought Louis Vuitton trunks for $1,000 and more—simply because Mrs. Dodge and her spookily shuttered and empty Fifth Avenue house had been objects of so much local mystery and speculation for so many years.)

And of course auction houses like Sotheby Parke Bernet—or "P.B." as it is called by aficionados — have happily helped to account for the collecting rage. P.B. has rubbed its corporate hands with glee at the epidemic spread of auction fever, which is the art world's euphemism for simple human greed.

Anyone who has ever haggled over a used toaster at a garage sale knows that an auction can be exciting. But the urge to collect on an important scale is fed by other forces. On May 4, 1970, for example, the Dow Jones industrial average dropped 19.07 points, to its lowest level since November 1963. The Stock Exchange had barely closed on that gloomy note when that same evening a 72-by-54-inch painting titled "Campbell Soup Can With Peeling Label," done by Andy Warhol in 1962, was sold at P.B. for $60,000—which at the time was the highest price ever paid at auction for a work by a living American artist. Clearly, though the tables at La Cote Basque and the aisles at Cartier might have been empty that day, the rich were still spending money on art—as an investment. "Good art holds up even in a bad market," said Peregrine Pollen, then P.B.'s president, at the time.

But there are other reasons for the art-and-antiques boom. While a good painting hung on one's wall is undoubtedly more esthethically pleasing than a framed I.B.M. stock certificate, there is also the feeling that good art is somehow immortal, and that owning good art places the owner among the immortals. Owning good art, furthermore, creates the impression that the owner is a person of taste, breeding, cultivation and refinement—qualities rated high among social assets. "A good art collection can do wonders for you socially," says Mrs. Frederick M. Winship of New York. "The most boring people can give the most boring parties, but people will go to them if their houses are filled with beautiful things." Owning art makes you more than chic. It makes you a Patron of Fine Things, and what could be finer than that?

A good art collection can also be a passport to membership on the boards of one of the great art museums—the Metropolitan, for example, or the Museum of Modern Art. And nothing these days carries more social cachet.

It also makes a certain amount of sense these days. Jewels and furs used to be status symbols. Today, the feeling is that mink is for football games and that diamonds, emeralds, rubies, sapphires, and pearls are for "older" women. "Diamonds make you look old," says one woman (Elizabeth Taylor has apparently not heard of this rule). Art, on the other hand, is with-it and trendy and makes you look young. More than that, it is much more difficult for a burglar to remove a coromandel screen or a Louis XV commode from an apartment than it is to snatch a handful of earrings from a drawer or a fur from a closet. And a well-known painting is harder to dispose of than an emerald necklace, which can be broken up and fenced in a matter of hours. There are practical reasons for collecting art.

Into the art-buying boom and urging it along have stepped, suavely, such auction houses as Sotheby Parke Bernet, which now calls itself the largest firm of art auctioneers in the world. The auctions have become enormously important. Auctions provide open, public bidding on a particular piece of art or furniture. Though pricing a painting by a particular artist in terms of the comparative price brought by another painting by the same artist is a tricky business with many variables (size, quality, period, and so on), this remains the only way to determine the value of art. Museums make their insurance evaluations from auction catalogues. Dealers move prices up and down according to auction sale figures, and collectors learn the value of their works from auction sales. Auctions establish prices. When P. B. sold van Gogh's "Le Cyprès et l'Arbre en Fleurs" to a "mystery bidder" on the evening of February 25, 1970 for $1,300,000 (a record for a van Gogh), anyone owning a van Gogh painting learned that his possession was worth something in seven figures.

Obviously, when sums like these are involved, art auctions are not for the unwary or naive. There is, for example, the matter of the secret "reserve" price. This is simply the price which the seller of the piece of art may place *on it as the lowest he will accept.* If the bidding does not reach this level, the auctioneer is obliged to "buy in" at the seller's price, and return the item to the seller. The commission charged on a buy-in is a mere 5 percent. (Standard commissions for selling art at auction slide from 25 percent on the first $1,000 of the sale price to 12½ percent on that portion of the price over $15,000.) In other words, many works of art that appear to have been sold have not, in fact, been sold at all, many "mystery bidders" are often the sellers themselves, and many of the prices achieved are not real prices at all.

There is nothing illegal about buying in, and the system is explained in each P.B. catalogue. However, to some people it is a distasteful practice. In May 1970, for example, a collection of Impressionist and Post-Impressionist paintings and sculpture belonging to Mr. and Mrs. William H. Weintraub went under the gavel, and was sold for a stunning $1,074,000. Later, it turned out that "almost half" the Weintraub collection had not been sold at all but had been bought-in for the Weintraubs. A tall Giacometti bronze was bought-in for $230,000, which was more than any Giacometti had ever brought at auction and which exceeded the highest price—$160,000 for a Henry Moore piece—paid until then at auction for a piece of sculpture.

There had been a previous bid for the Giacometti of $225,000 and, at the time, the Weintraubs were considered foolish to have placed so high a reserve price on the piece, since they could have sold it for a mere $5,000 less than they were asking. "I told him," said William Rubin, curator of the Paintings and Sculpture Collection at the Museum of Modern Art. "That night when I saw him, I said, 'You made a mistake.'" But Mr. Weintraub may not have made such a mistake after all. There is no way of telling whether or not the previous bid of $225,000 was legitimate, or whether the bid was the auctioneer's attempt to bring the price up to the seller's reserve. In any case, now that the fact that the Giacometti was bought-in by the Weintraubs has been leaked to the press and the art-buying public, one wonders whether the $230,000 price is really "established." One will have to wait until the Giacometti goes under the gavel again to see.

Auctioneers themselves may bid prices right up to the reserve, as Liz Robbins, of P. B.'s public relations firm, Clark, Nelson Ltd., admits. "Oh, I can tell," she has said, "I've stood at the front of the room, and I can tell when the auctioneer's drawing bids out of the air. He may make two or three bids in hopes of drawing someone fresh into the bidding."

For years, the secrecy surrounding buy-ins had been impregnable. But after the Weintraub sale, the system came more and more under question. Suppose, for example, having "established" a price for his piece of art by buying it in, the owner might decide to donate it to a university or a museum. He could then, presumably, claim a charitable deduction in the amount of the work's "established market value," on his tax return. Furthermore, the public was losing faith in the veracity of auctions. Finally, in January 1971, a reluctant P. B. was persuaded by the Art Dealers' Association to drop buy-ins from its list of "Final Bids Received." On the price lists issued following sales, instead of listing buy-ins as though they had actually been sold, P. B. now merely omits them from the record, which some people find almost as objectionable. During the bidding, it is still impossible to tell whether an item is being bought-in or not. One can merely guess.

Auctioneering at a place like Sotheby Parke Bernet, meanwhile, is done in such a rapid-fire fashion—with bid-spotters moving about the room and suave, boyish-looking John Marion, P. B.'s president and chief auctioneer, briskly calling out bids that climb by $50, $1,000, or even $10,000 leaps—that it is almost impossible for the neophyte auction-goer to tell who is doing the bidding. It took less than two minutes for the Heriz rug from West Virginia to peak at the $200,000 level. Bids are placed by prearranged secret signals. One bidder may uncap a pen to indicate a bid, another may tug an ear, and another may wink an eye. One collector, John Marion knows, always keeps one earpiece of his glasses dangling outside his breast pocket to indicate that he is in the bidding; when the earpiece goes inside, he is out of it. When Richard Burton's agent was bidding for a 70-carat diamond for Burton's wife, Elizabeth Taylor, he did it simply by folding his arms. At the $1,000,000 level, the agent dropped his arms and the stone went to Cartier for $1,050,000. (Burton later bought it from Cartier at an undisclosed price.)

And at the same time bidding is going on in the Madison Avenue auction room, bids also may be coming in from Paris drawing rooms and Dallas hotel rooms by telephone. In 1968, an Italian dealer was instructed by Carlo Ponti to purchase a flawless 34.3-carat emerald ring which P. B. was selling, and which Ponti wanted as a gift for his wife, Sophia Loren. While Ponti's agent was bidding in New York, Enid Annenberg Haupt was bidding from a pay phone booth in Washington. In a photo finish, Mrs. Haupt won the gem for $265,000. At the time, Ponti's agent protested that her higher bid was not according to the rules, but John Marion disagreed. (Four years later, at another P. B. auction, Mrs. Haupt sold her stone for $385,000, explaining nonchalantly, "My jewels no longer fit my lifestyle." But to friends she explained that the ring—which cost $50,000 in insurance premiums each time she took it out of the vault—had just become too costly to wear.)

Just as it bemuses the average auction-goer, the system of secret and long-distance bidding often infuriates the seasoned professional art dealer. Not long ago, a Midwestern dealer, convinced that a P. B. auctioneer was "drawing bids out of the air" on a Queen Anne lowboy that had quickly reached the $1,500 level, jumped to his feet and demanded angrily, "Please tell me who has bid $1,500 for this piece!" In the stunned silence that followed this breach of auction etiquette, it turned out that, sure enough, no one had. Of course it could have been that there was a legitimate aid from the floor, and that the bidder was simply cagily refusing to show his hand. The Midwestern art dealer thinks not—"There were fake bids," he insists. In any case, wearing a pained look, the auctioneer returned to the highest bid which anyone in the audience would acknowledge having made, which was $250.

Dealers also inveigh against the secret reserve and buy-in system. "It's completely phony," says one dealer. "They aren't real prices. Someone puts on a high reserve. It's bid up to the reserve—and bingo! You've established a new record for your work." But dealers admit that the reserve is a useful mechanism for protecting the market. In the long run it lifts prices and brings new buyers to the market, which is good for dealer profits. And sellers like it because it protects their sales and lets them avoid the often humiliating experience of trying to sell art to a dealer. (Anyone who has bought a $2,000 painting from a dealer, and then tried to sell it back to the same dealer a few years later, knows that he will seldom be offered even half of what he paid. In fact, if a dealer sees a customer come into his gallery carrying a painting to be sold, the dealer may lock himself in his office. A dealer's business philosophy is simple—buy as low as possible, sell as high as possible. This is why, though selling at auctions involves risk as well as excitement, it is often a way to realize better prices.)

At Sotheby Parke Bernet, with offices and auction rooms now in Buenos Aires, Brussels, Toronto, Paris, Munich, Amsterdam, Hong Kong, Teheran, Florence, Milan, Monte Carlo, Stockholm, Johannesburg, Madrid, Zurich and London, as well as in New York and Los Angeles, there is no set auction-going crowd. Rather, there is a variety of different crowds which turn up depending on what is being sold. The jewelry sales, for example, seem to attract mostly white-haired widows. The major, black-tie "by ticket only" invitational sales held in the spring and fall, are evening affairs, attended by prominent collectors or their representatives, and are usually preceded by cocktail-and-canapé soirees held several evenings before the sales themselves. For these events, Rolls-Royces line Madison Avenue and the perfumed smell of money is so thick you could cut it with a knife as art connoisseurs, museum directors, celebrities and the usual sprinkling of society folk—most of whom know each other—rub elbows and finger costly objects. The Norton Simon sale was one of these, though for some reason it lacked the excitement that was expected of it. The total take was $6,500,000, but the bidding was labored and sluggish, raised in painful $500 denominations while the crowd rustled restlessly and riffled the pages of the catalogue—"A boring evening," according to one guest. The Scull sale of Pop Art, on the other hand, though it netted less was more exciting, and bidders showed up in French-cut jeans, leather midi skirts, and cartridge belts.

On Saturday afternoons, as many as 5,000 people may wander in and out of P.B.'s New York rooms — dealers, decorators, housewives and just plain auction buffs. (The Landa sale, though a Saturday afternoon affair, is expected to draw more chic people than Saturdays usually do because of who the Landas are). But look carefully on a Saturday, and you might spot Jacqueline Onassis and her daughter Caroline (who took an art appreciation course at Sotheby's in London last year) among the Saturday throng, or lunching beforehand at Les Pleiades, the fashionable auction-goer's eating place, or at the Carlyle across the street. There has been, according to publicist Liz Robbins, no noticeable influx of Arabs of late at the New York auctions—"no burnooses, no camels in the salesroom," she says. But there was, she says, a sudden "invasion" of Japanese buyers a couple of years ago. They show up at P.B., as they customarily travel, in tightly-packed groups.

On weekday mornings and afternoons, P.B. sales run the gamut from objects priced at a few hundred dollars to those selling for several hundred thousand dollars, from very expensive items to what some people might think of as junk. Filtered through the firm of Clark, Nelson, Ltd., most of P.B.'s publicity stresses record-breaking prices and elegance. ("Elegant" is Clark, Nelson's favorite word.) As a result, many ordinary mortals are actually frightened to pass through the splendid portals of 980 Madison, lest they be entering an emporium that is quite out of their league. They need have no such fears, says Miss Robbins. She points out that the cheaper stuff is the bread and butter of P.B.'s business, and that more than 60 percent of the items P.B. sells go under the hammer for less than $1,000, 25 percent under $300.

Among the many criticisms that have been levelled at the worldwide conglomerate that is Sotheby Parke Bernet—at the reserves, the sealed bids, the auctioneers' bids and at the amount of "junk"—perhaps the most serious one that comes from the most high-minded in the art world is that P.B. has succeeded in "vulgarizing" the art market. It is certainly true that P.B. has resorted to tactics more commonly associated with the ad game, further down on Madison Avenue. There are, for example, Sotheby Parke Bernet shopping bags—"Very status-y," says Liz Robbins. The gallery also sells Sotheby Parke Bernet T-shirts, also presumably status-y. Such gimmickry highly offends the purists in the world of art, but P.B. president John Marion suavely defends it all, saying, "Shouldn't art be for everybody?' The purists are hoping for a measure of relief in May when Christie's opens. Christie's, though not as old as Sotheby's—1766, as opposed to Sotheby's birthdate in 1744—calls itself "the world leader of fine art auctioneering," with emphasis on the "fine." Christie's is expected to deal purely in quality, as it has traditionally done, and let P.B. handle the quantity. "It will be interesting to see what happens vis-à-vis Christie's," is Liz Robbins's only comment at the moment.

The purists in the art world also shuddered when, not long ago, P.B. announced that it was going into the international real estate business, and had hired Charles Seilheimer—formerly of Previews, Inc.—to head this operation of marketing and selling luxury homes and apartments. To mix real estate and art seemed—well, rather crass, as inappropriate as serving caviar with bagels. P.B.'s logic, of course, was that it had for years been selling the *contents* of stately homes. Why not also sell the homes themselves? Among the more spectacular of P.B.'s current offerings is the triplex apartment at 450 East 52nd Street belonging to Mr. and Mrs. Henry J. Heinz II. A 21-room affair decorated in palazzo style, with seven bathrooms, a two-story ballroom, balcony and wine cellar, it is priced at $500,000, with maintenance running at $3,915 a month. An additional $500,000 is being asked for the apartment's Italianate contents. (For further information, please apply to exclusive agent.) It is not that the 57-brands Heinzes need the money, incidentally. It is just that they have found another apartment they like better. P.B. is also offering a 45-acre farm in Norfolk, Conn. ($380,000), and is handling the sale of the Landas' Palladian Palm Beach villa (three bedrooms, three baths) for which the Landas are asking $1,100,000. And so on.

And now you might like to know who bought, say, Andy Warhol's "Soup Can" at auction for a record-breaking $60,000 (it was expected to go for around $40,000) and achieved, thereby, a sharp jump in social status. The answer is that nobody knows for sure. It was said at first that the bidder was a German dealer. Then it was said that the picture had been bought by a German museum. Then a third version appeared in a German magazine, Capital, which suggested that the buyer was a dealer with a large Warhol collection who drove the price up to the point where, for an investment of a mere extra $20,000, he had enormously enhanced the value of his entire collection. The original owner was a young businessman named Peter Brandt, and the buyer was a Swiss art dealer named Bruno Bischofberger, who was a friend of Brandt's. Both Brandt and Bischofberger denied the allegation that they had driven up the price to establish a new value for Warhols. But there was no denying that a new value for Warhols had indeed been established. "Soup Can" did later go on sale in Mr. Bischofberger's Zurich gallery—for $75,000.

Moral: If you have an Andy Warhol painting, you have an investment that is going up. Up with it will climb your social standing. ■

August 14, 1977

Royalties for Artists: California Becomes The Testing Ground

By WILLIAM BATES

SAN FRANCISCO

Robert Rauschenberg is trying, without much success, to squirm unnoticed out of his chair at center stage during a heated public debate over California's law that provides royalties to artists.

Rauschenberg, who was in town for the opening of his retrospective exhibit at the San Francisco Museum of Modern Art here, no doubt was seeking to flee the jammed University of California auditorium for nothing any more controversial than a dinner engagement. But the artist had been on the defensive all evening—and surprisingly, under attack not only from art collectors, who oppose bitterly the royalties they must now pay artists under the California law, but from younger artists, who see the royalties due established artists as a threat to their own careers. At one point in the debate, Rauschenberg, his back pinned figuratively to the wall on this last issue, was forced to save himself with a quip. "Any one of these people," he said angrily, waving his hand toward the younger artists in the audience, "could be in the same position."

"I didn't," he added with an air of finality, "used to be a Rauschenberg."

Rauschenberg, however, cannot really escape his position as a central figure in the dispute over royalties for artists in California, which began last year with the passage of the California Resale Royalties Act. The Resale Royalties Act, which took effect Jan. 1, 1977, is the first law of its kind in the United States: Under the California law, art collectors must now pay artists a 5 percent "royalty" when they resell their work for a profit and above a threshold price of $1,000.

The idea that artists should receive royalties—or payments of some sort, by whatever name—when their early work goes up in value has been around for years, and indeed is an increasingly frequent feature of the contracts drawn up by artists when they sell their work to collectors. But with the passage of its Resale Royalties Act, California has become the first state to require such payments by law.

This experiment with legally mandated royalties is being watched closely in other quarters—and, not least important, by the Carter Administration. At least a half-dozen other states, including New York, have artists' royalties legislation pending, although the groups favoring these measures see quick national legislation, rather than a state-by-state approach, as the most desirable outcome of their efforts. Two months ago, representatives of the various groups that backed the California legislation—and a few of their opponents—met in San Francisco with Mrs. Joan Mondale to explain the royalties law while her husband was here on a speaking tour. A Beverly Hills Congressman, Representative Henry Waxman, has announced that he plans to introduce a royalties measure to Congress this year, and other national efforts are under way.

•

Yet, despite the momentum that the royalties idea seems to have gained, the results of California's six-month-old experiment with its new act are far from reassuring. The Royalties Act is the object of intense dislike by many art dealers, some of whom openly defy its provisions. Meanwhile, the law, which requires artists to sue art collectors if they are not paid the royalty, has gone unenforced, and may well, for reasons both financial and emotional, be unenforceable. "Nobody's paid, nobody's sued, everybody's avoiding it," is how Ben Horowitz, president of the Los Angeles Art Dealers Association, summarizes the situation. "It's like the Prohibition thing. A bill that's not acceptable to anybody is just not going to work."

What the bill has done, however, has been to prompt a verbal bloodbath as a result of the infighting among artists, art dealers, art collectors and museums. For art dealers, to judge by their inflammatory rhetoric, the Resale Royalties Act has the same symbolic quality that the Stamp Tax had under King George. "It's largely a symbolic statute," says Monroe Price, an arts law specialist at the UCLA School of Law. "But people have been known to go to war over symbols, and that seems to be what's happening." A group of dealers in southern California have formed an organization with the ominous and somewhat paramilitary acronym CADRE (which in fact stands for a benign Concerned Artists and Dealers for Responsible Equity) to take their fight to the courts, and have received contributions in support of their cause from as far away as New York and Chicago.

But the immediate result of the opposition of art dealers to the Royalties Act has been to drive at least part of the art market underground. No one is quite sure how many works of art are resold under the conditions that, in California, require payment of the royalty. Horowitz asserts that there have been "hundreds" in the first six months the law has been in effect, but other official observers are skeptical of such estimates. "I've had one member of the Los Angeles Art Dealers Association tell me the law is going to affect approximately 3,000 sales a year," says Julia Connor, deputy director of the California Arts Council, the state agency in some ways responsible for enforcement of the royalty provisions, "and another member of the same organization tells me it won't affect as many as 50."

In the only known case of an art dealer defying the royalties law, Howard Morseburg, a Los Angeles art dealer, refused to pay two artists, Andre Balyon and Antoine Blanchard, royalties on different works sold at $1,400 and $1,200 respectively. Morseburg, supported by CADRE, has gone to court, hoping that the Royalties Act will be thrown out as unconstitutional. California's major art collectors—as well as most museums—seem to be sitting on the sidelines while the dispute is raging. "We're holding our position," says Harry W. ("Hunk") Anderson, owner of one of the most important collections of modern art in northern California, "until we get the bill changed or provisions of it declared unconstitutional. This law doesn't have to affect us one single bit. A collector has a number of options open to him. He doesn't have to sell. He doesn't have to sell work by living artists. And he doesn't have to buy work by living artists."

It is precisely this possibility—that the royalties law, which affects only resales of art, or the so-called secondary market, will somehow damage the primary market, in which art is sold for the first time—that has younger artists nervous about the royalties scheme. "If the law turns off the collectors," says Bruce Beasley, an Oakland sculptor who opposes the law and who was one of the group that met with Mrs. Mondale, "and has a negative effect on selling art in the first place, then all we've done is lost something."

Some collectors and dealers, however, disagree that the royalties paid to artists will drain funds from the art market. "Put yourself in the shoes of the average person who goes in to buy something," says Stanley Crinstein, a southern California collector and owner of the Gemini G.E.L. Gallery, which specializes in limited edition prints. "Do you think you're going to buy or not buy just because there's a law that says that if you resell, and if you make a profit, then you have to pay somebody 5 percent? You're probably thinking you'll be glad if it goes up, and you make a profit, and you have to pay the 5 percent. The opposite would be like turning down a gift of a million dollars because you didn't want to pay the taxes."

A number of artists and art dealers who oppose the law, however, do so because they feel it is based precisely on this sort of speculative misconception—one might even say fantasy—of the actual art market. "Everybody thinks paintings go up," argues Horowitz. "Picassos have gone down. There are many, many artists whose paintings go up and down. If you're playing the art market like the stock market, stocks go up and down, too. If we have a depression, the art market will be flooded with paintings."

The fact that many collectors sell work when they are—relatively speaking—in financial difficulty has led to emotional entanglements in the enforcement of the royalties law that were clearly unanticipated in the original legislation. "Take an artist like Sam Francis," says Henry Hopkins of the San Francisco Museum of Modern Art, citing a hypothetical example. "He's selling now in the $30,000 to $40,000 range for a major canvas. Let's say a collector who bought one of his works 15 years ago for $3,000 decides, for the benefit of his family, to sell now for $40,000. I'd think it would put Sam in a terrible moral position. Does he press the 5 percent claim or not? After all, the person who bought his work for $3,000 back in the old days did more for Sam than $2,000 now will ever do."

Critics of the Resale Royalties Act have harped on the fact that primarily established artists with international reputatons—like Rauschenberg or Sam Francis—will benefit substantially from its provisions. "This is a Robert Rauschenberg benefit statute," says Professor John Merryman of the Stanford Law School, himself an art collector and one of the outspoken critics of the law. "The only artists it helps are those who have the most and need the least."

The defenders of the bill concede that most artists who receive royalties in the $1,000 to $2,000 range will have new work selling for prices that will dwarf whatever contribution to their income the royalties might make. They argue, however, that the royalty is a question of right, not economics. "It was no accident that a painting that was bought for $600 then later costs $70,000," says Rauschenberg, speaking of a situation similar to that of his collage "Thaw," which he sold to collector Robert Scull in the 1950's for $800 and which was later auctioned by Scull for $85,000. "Suppose I'd just stopped working, or started being really lazy or indulgent. Then that painting wouldn't be worth $70,000 today."

Rauschenberg has announced that he intends to put his California royalties into a fund, similar to Change Inc., to help indigent artists. The Federal royalties legislation proposed by Waxman makes use of a sliding scale, by which part of the royalty amount would go to the artist and part to a fund to purchase works by lesser-known artists for public buildings.

From the California experience, however, royalties appear to be a thin bootstrap on which the arts can pull themselves up. "This isn't social welfare legislation for artists," says Hamish Sandison, whose group, called Bay Area Lawyers for the Arts, was instrumental in designing the California law. "There is not a huge bonanza out there.

"It's ironic that the royalties law has been criticized for not doing enough for starving artists. It's not intended to do anything for starving artists. The Resale Royalties Law, like copyright law, works on the capitalist principle that the one who's making the most money gets the largest royalty."

Some cynical observers feel that royalties legislation allows politicians an easy out—"pro-art" legislation that costs the taxpayers nothing. Others, however, see the politicians as victims of their good intentions. "They have a kind of 'La Bohème' image in their mind," says Beasley. "At the same time they have no conception of the actual business aspects of the art world. Instead they assume we're so childlike and naïve we can't manage our own affairs, so the state has to step in and manage them for us."

Whatever its results might be, California's experiment with resale royalties has nonetheless provided one minor pleasure: that of hearing artists discuss politicians while the latter are in the act of legislative creation. "I'm glad they're doing something," observes Sam Francis. "But I'm not so happy about what they're doing. Anyway, I think something will eventually work out of this chaos." He then adds a final bit of advice from his experience as a painter: "But it can turn out badly, you know." ■

SEPTEMBER 10, 1977

Fashion Shows Pop Up All Over As Fall Puts Summer Behind It

By BERNADINE MORRIS

Fashion, as most everybody knows, is not simply silk and a seam. It's also a state of mind. A little hoopla doesn't hurt in establishing the proper mental climate. The drum beating for fall began almost the instant Labor Day signaled the end of summer. Fashion shows, big and small, covered a variety of clothes, conservative and advanced. Often they were sparked by the designer's presence. Often the designer was from Europe, taking a close look at American fashion preferences, before finishing up his next collection.

The past week brought numerous opportunities for New Yorkers to view new clothes while contributing to good causes at shows sponsored by leading fashion stores, to scrutinize two new Madison Avenue shops specializing in French fashions, and to see the work of two new young women designers.

Tinka is one of them. That's what everybody calls Katina Arts Meyer, a 30-year-old woman who has modeled for Dior in London, studied art since the age of six, and created a hand-painted hat three years ago that had a certain vogue. She soon moved on to dresses—soft, fluid crepe de chine things—that she sold to stores such as Bendel's and Bloomingdale's.

"She's always dressed beautifully—she's the kind of girl you see at a party and you go shopping for two days, but you still don't end up looking as good as she did," said Lois Rounick.

Mrs. Rounick was one of the friends and acquaintances Tinka invited to her first fashion show, held in the Park Avenue apartment of Richard and Lis Wasserman. He's the realtor who is interested in art. Mrs. Wasserman was among the special friends who were invited to model. So was Margaret Trudeau, whose plane arrived from Canada just in time for her to slip on a strapless tunic and green pants.

"She told me it was her modeling debut and she worried about going out in it because it was too see-through," Tinka said.

Cristina Ferrari was six months pregnant, but she didn't worry about swirling around in a big, fuzzy cape, which is Tinka's favorite outdoor wrap.

Some of her friends bought clothes after the show, but mostly Tinka sells to stores from her studio at 25 Tudor City Place, where her prices sweep from $30 to $600.

France Andrevie, also 30, has had success with the shop she opened a year ago on the Place des Victoires in Paris.

This week, she showed her voluminous, easy clothes to some 250 friends of The Lighthouse for the Blind who spent $15 for the chance to meet the designer. She turned out o be a determined young woman who does the same shapes for evening that she does in sports clothes.

They run to double skirts, in printed taffeta as well as wide wale corduroy, tunic tops with sleeveless jackets superimposed on them and oversize blazer jackets. The proportions are so generous that she needs only two sizes to fit everyone in her skirts and vests—skirts and pants come in a more traditional size range.

Miss Andrevie designed flat-heel sandals, which she wears with ankle socks, to go with the day clothes, and suggests ballet slippers at night. She likes the juxtaposition of a bulky sweater over a thin printed wool skirt or a leather jacket with zippered pockets with other soft clothes.

She designs her own fabrics and calls everything sportswear, even when it's lace. Next season, she'll keep the same oversize shapes, but she'll do everything in synthetic fabrics, she says.

•

Miss Andrevie is among the new wave of French ready-to-wear designers. Daniel Hechter is part of the old guard. He was still in his teens some 20 years ago when, along with Emmanuelle Khanh, Gerard Pipart and Christiane Bailley, he started bringing zesty styling to the then-dull ready-to-wear field in Paris.

He has established his hold in Europe; now he is embarking on a 15-day trip through the United States, including Cincinnati, Pittsburgh, San Francisco and Boston, to size up this country's needs. He's planning to open his own company on Seventh Avenue, with one of his assistants installed to direct the operation here, and will himself visit four or five times a year.

"I want to be as powerful here as I am in Europe," he told the room full of store people he invited to lunch at The Grand Cafe.

Mr. Hechter said he wants to open a boutique in New York, where whole families could shop together. He designs clothes for men and children as well as women.

•

Rodier, a renowned French company with roots in the 19th century, has brought its classic breed of knitted clothes to a new shop at 715 Madison Avenue, near 63d Street and naturally there was a party to celebrate. The shop is owned by Phyllis Mailman, who usually wears Galanos styles, and her niece, Ellen Langner.

"Isn't it nice not to see gypsies?" said Dorothy Rodgers, wife of the composer, as she inspected the stock of turtlenecks and cardigans.

"It's the nicest knitwear the French have to offer," commented Cecile Zilkka, who usually wears couture styles and this time chose a braided flowered dress by Saint Laurent.

"Everything is washable, except the flannel skirts," Mrs. Mailman told her friends. "You won't make a dent in your budget," she added.

With $34 price tags on the pullovers and $61 on the cardigans, she wasn't being unrealistic.

The Missoni cult is enthusiastic. They began lining up two hours early for the showing of the Italian knitted styles at Bonwit Teller, applauded with unusual vigor during the presentation, and afterwards told Rosta and Ottavio (Tai) Missoni how much they loved the clothes.

"I've had this almost 10 years and it travels beautifully," said Eileen Rush, who works for David Garth, a public relations firm. She was referring to her striped pullover and cardigan in the varied colors and zigzag patterns the Missonis specialize in.

"I've got an entire wardrobe," said Margaret Berkery, supervisor of employment for an engineering company, whose striped sweaters were of more recent vintage.

The Missonis stopped in to supervise the show at Bonwit Teller before moving on to Washington, Los Angeles and Detroit as part of their week-long tour of the country.

One of the biggest crushes of the past week took place at Emanuel Ungaro's new shop at 803 Madison Avenue, near 68th Street.

Marjorie Reed in a one-shoulder linen dress by Grès, Ethel Scull in a crinkly cotton by "a lady in Southampton," Rita Lachman in the biggest bouffant hairdo of two continents and Lee Radziwill all stopped in to inspect the new premises, where the workmen had not finished their labors.

The fashion show took place at one end of the narrow rectangular store and few people could get to see it, but that didn't bother anyone. Livia Weintraub talked about her new perfume, "Livia," that Bloomingdale's will launch. Audrey Smaltz talked about her new shop for European ready-to-wear that will open next month, and Eunice Gardiner was a little upset by the heavy wool sweaters and tall boots the mannequins wore. She and her husband, Robert D. L. Gardiner, the owner of Gardiners Island, which nestles between the two eastern forks of Long Island, were among the few to see the show.

"We live in Palm Beach in the winter," she explained. "The boots are too much."

Zandra Rhodes, her green bangs contrasting nicely with her pink dress, introduced her first collection of lingerie at Bloomingdale's yesterday morning. The English designer's usual sense of fantasy—green hair has been a personal trademark—was evidenced in her underwear designs, and her nightgowns.

First, there were her delicate, fantasy prints, like her own hieroglyphics. Then there were the triangles of lace, usually écru, that formed borders and insets. And finally, there were her topless styles. These were bosom-baring camisoles and nightgowns to be worn under clothes or in the privacy of one's own home. They were accepted with unanimity. The world has moved onward since Rudi Gernreich's topless swimsuit of 1964.

SEPTEMBER 20, 1977

A Party for Warhol's 'Folk and Funk'

By JUDY KLEMESRUD

A throng of ceatively dressed New Yorkers turned out last night to view Andy Warhol's latest artistic achievement. A collection of Pop Art? No. An underground movie? No. Well, what then?

An exhibition of Mr. Warhol's personal collection of, of all things, American folk art, which the silver-haired Pop artist insisted on calling "Folk and Funk."

What does that mean? "Well, funk means junk," Mr. Warhol said, shortly after he arrived at the Museum of American Folk Art, at 49 West 53d Street, where the collection will be on display through Nov. 20.

The museum's two small exhibit rooms were so hot and crowded that many of the guests, after a minute or two of viewing the cigar store Indians, weather vanes, carousel figures, ships' figureheads and other items of Americana, walked out of the museum and sipped their champagne on West 53d Street instead.

Mr. Warhol, wearing his customary black corduroy jacket and blue jeans, joined them for about 10 minutes, chatting and signing his name on exhibit programs and even on female hands.

A Steam Bath

Among the guests who braved the steam bath inside the museum were Louise Nevelson, Merce Cunningham, Diana Vreeland, Ethel Scull and Geoffrey Holder.

Louise Nevelson's huge and elaborate silver necklace, which she sculpted herself, seemed to draw as much attention as any item in Mr. Warhol's collection.

When asked what she called her necklace, Miss Nevelson smiled and replied: "All This and Heaven, Too."

Geoffrey Holder, dressed in a black satin tuxedo and a black bowler, said he was especially impressed with the German carousel figures in the collection.

"I'm a folk art collector, too," he said, in his basso profundo voice. "In fact, I'm having a new house built near Gramercy Park to house my collection."

And what was Mr. Warhol's own favorite piece in his show? "I like the door best," he said, referring to a pale blue, late-Georgian-style door, circa 1780. "You can go in and out of it and still go nowhere."

After viewing the folk art and chatting for a while on the sidewalk, the guests, who paid $100 each, trooped over to Park Avenue and East 52d Street, where they had cocktails in the Seagram Building lobby. They then moved around the corner for a veal scaloppine dinner at The Four Seasons, where the centerpieces were "Folk and Funk," too—19th-century wooden duck decoys.

Ethel Scull, as usual, was one of the most fashionably attired guests. She was wearing a black velvet corselet that laced up the front and a flowered challis skirt, both by Yves Saint Laurent.

"That Yves, he makes you feel like you have a bust," she said. "The only time I ever feel like Sophia Loren is when I wear this corselet."

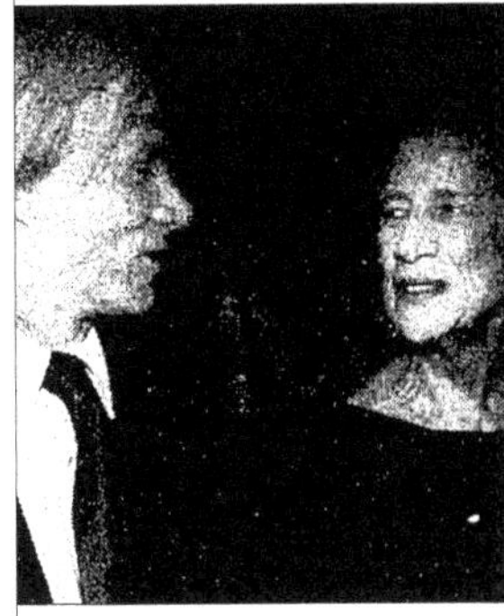

SEPTEMBER 25, 1977

'Serious' Filmgoers Drawn To Party for 15th Festival

By JUDY KLEMESRUD

"Woody! Woody! Woody!"

Agnes Varda's film about two women friends "One Sings, the Other Doesn't," may have been screened at the opening of the 15th New York Film Festival, giving it strong feminist overtones, but it was a male director—Woody Allen—who drew the most screams and attention.

Mr. Allen, looking as tense as he does in his movie, "Annie Hall," slipped through a side door of Avery Fisher Hall on Friday night, a gray wool fedora pulled low over his forehead.

But the disguise did not work. The film fans recognized both him and his companion, Michael Murphy, the actor, and more or less chased the two men to their seats.

Relatively Subdued Dress

Aside from the mobbing of Mr. Allen, the festival's opening-party night was relatively tame. There were only a handful of celebrities present, and the audience's costumes, in the past often flamboyant and far out, were relatively subdued this year. Aside from a few starlet types, who dress up for anything, no one really glittered.

But then, it was raining outside.

"I like it that no one's dressed up," said Judy Pfeiffer, the author and editor, who was wearing what she called "a beige cashmere sweatshirt" over black pants. "It's more real this way. This is a serious audience that wants to see a film rather than be seen. It reminds me of the crowd that used to go to the Y.M.H.A. to hear a concert, or an Alice Tully crowd."

15 Was the Special Number

There was something special about the number 15 at the opening. Fisher Hall, then known as Philharmonic Hall, had opened exactly 15 years earlier. And the film festival was observing its 15th year. And, naturally, the official opening-night film started 15 minutes late.

Before it began, Richard Roud, the festival's director, introduced Miss Varda, who was wearing a medieval-style silk gown in shocking pink and lavendar. Tripping slightly as she walked out on stage, Miss Varda recovered to tell the audience that what they were about to see was "a film about women who are also people."

The heavily female audience cheered.

"There are good vibrations here," Miss Varda observed, her short, jet-black hair glistening like patent leather under the spotlights.

Miss Varda Was Happy

Miss Varda, who was accompanied by her longtime friend, Jacques Demy, the director, had said earlier upon arriving at the theater that she felt "really good" about being the first woman director, had said earlier upon arriving a New York Film Festival.

"We will soon have so many, many, many women's films," she predicted, as she swept through the crowd.

The guests included Richard Rodgers, the composer, his wife, Dorothy, and their daughter, Mary; Kurt Vonnegut Jr., the author, with Jill Krementz, the photographer; Robert Benton and David Newman, the former screenwriting partners who have branched out into directing; Ethel Scull, the socialite; Bill Boggs, the television personality, with Francine Lefrak, the real estate heiress; Eleanor Perry, the screenwriter; Dina Merrill, the actress; Lester Persky, the film producer; Judy Collins, the singer, and Louis Malle, the director.

Afterward, many trooped across the plaza to the New York State Theater, for a party, where the fare was drinks and tiny goldfish crackers. "The festival doesn't have much money," one of its planners explained, when asked why there was no food.

A More Select Group

"Terrific, superterrific, dynamite!" Miss Perry said, when asked what she thought about Miss Varda's film opening the festival. "What's great about it is that it's about two women who are friends. All I get are requests to write films about two lesbians."

Mr. Allen was joined at the party by his long-time friend Diane Keaton. And because the partygoers were a more select group than those who had attended the film, neither Mr. Allen nor Miss Keaton were mobbed.

One of the most colorful guests at the party was Annie Hickman, a young woman who was dressed like a clown, carried a puppet named Pouff on her hand, and wore a sign that said "Freckles for Sale."

"I go around pasting freckles on people," she said, pasting a pink sequin on a passer-by's cheek. "They just love it."

As Robert Benton saw it, the evening was "the beginning of the year." He glanced around at the hundreds of film buffs, smiled and added, "It's just like the freshman social."

OCTOBER 3, 1977

'Valentino' and 'Julia' Bring Stars Out in the Rain

By JENNIFER DUNNING

As if the New York Film Festival and all its attendant rites were not enough, two additional screening parties drew crowds of dancers, the literati and stargazers of high and low birth out into the rain this weekend.

On Friday night, 100 guests turned up at the Fifth Avenue townhouse of the Iranian Ambassador to the United Nations and Mrs. Fereydoun Hoveyda for a buffet supper after a private screening at Lincoln Center of Ken Russell's "Valentino," which opens in the city on Wednesday.

Rudolf Nureyev, the guest of honor and star of the film, never did get to the caviar flown in from Iran for the occasion. The competition was too intense in the jammed upstairs rooms where the party took place. As the crowd thinned, Ethel Scull was visible, clothed in purple from her left shoulder down to her feet. Andy Warhol stood languidly under one of his silkscreen prints (a portrait of the Empress Farah of Iran), bending occasionally to talk with Diana Vreeland, who looked like a Warhol poppy in her red pants suit.

Young dancers clustered in corners murmuring of the ballet companies they planned to leave or join. Erik Bruhn spent the evening chatting quietly with Maria Tallchief, who had flown in from Chicago for the party. Natalia Makarova disclosed she'd like to make a film or two herself. The ballerina, who is expecting a baby in February, had found a black velvet gown that was, as she put it, "happily fashioned for maternity."

Congratulations for the Star

In another room, guests stopped to congratulate Mr. Nureyev, who looked sleek in a close-fitting black shirt and pants, and black boots. The peripatetic Russian had flown in that morning with Charles Kirby and Vanessa Harwood of the National Ballet of Canada, with whom he had performed "The Sleeping Beauty" just the night before. Having crammed in a television taping and rehearsal before the screening, he planned to leave yesterday for London.

How had it felt to see himself on screen? "It's eerie," he said with a grin. Would there be other films? "Well, sure," he said. "As long as I can go on dancing."

Jamie Wyeth, whose drawings of the dancer will be on view at the Coe Kerr Gallery next month, bubbled with enthusiasm over Mr. Nureyev's acting. "Rudolf can walk through walls," Halston added. "He has all the magic of the theater in a film, on a stage, in a room. Very few people do. Elizabeth Taylor has it. Martha has it," he said, referring to Martha Graham, who was seated nearby looking regal in a black and gold caftan he had designed for her. Miss Graham had already seen the film twice.

A Party for 'Julia'

On Saturday night, nearly 700 people surged into Cinema I for a screening of "Julia," which opened here yesterday. The film is adapted from Lillian Hellman's "Pentimento" and stars Jane Fonda as Miss Hellman. On his way in to the screening, producer-director Sydney Pollack looked happy after passing the lines waiting next door to see his film, "Bobby Deerfield." But many in the audience left the theater visibly shaken by "Julia."

Next on the agenda was a buffet dinner at the Oyster Bar in Grand Central Station for those who had paid $100 to benefit the Committee for Public Justice, a group Miss Hellman formed seven years ago to act as a citizens' early-warning system against threats to constitutional rights.

Leonard Bernstein was one of the first to arrive, clutching a set of Greek worry beads his wife had given him. "It's not a rosary," he said. Wet-eyed, he talked of the film: "I haven't stopped crying since. It's bigger than all of us—so modest and strong." Woody Allen passed, a fugitive vision in tweed, only to be spotted by Claudette Colbert. "I'm mad about your film," she called to him.

One of the younger guests was 15-year-old Susan Jones, a New York schoolgirl, who plays Miss Hellman as a child in the film. Dressed in a velvet blazer and long plaid skirt, her hair streaked blonde from an inadvertent overdose of lemon juice, Miss Jones smiled when complimented on her acting debut. "It was a product of everyone being kind," she said.

Miss Hellman was reluctant to talk about the film, as friends pressed in around her. But Marcel Ophuls, sitting at another table, was eager to discuss "Julia." "This is a very scrupulously made, classic film," he said. "And I'm so fascinated by seeing the woman I've always loved playing one of my best friends." Nearby, investigative reporter Carl Bernstein had decided to turn his talents to other fields. "I'm trying to learn about the paparazzi business," he said, twisting around from a discussion with two young photographers.

December 11, 1977

At the Sovereign There's Distress Amid Splendor

By DEE WEDEMEYER

Alice Baker recently had a friend call and assure her that anytime she was afraid to stay in her apartment she could sleep at the friend's house. A retired executive who lives in the same building says his daughter asks him, "How's your building getting along?" Joseph Braswell, an interior designer, says that whenever people find out where he lives they declare, "Oh, you live in *that* building."

"That" building is the Sovereign at 425 East 58th Street, which since it opened in June, 1974, has attracted an unusual amount of attention as a kind of less-than-perfect paragon of luxury apartment construction.

From the beginning the building was celebrated for its rents, the highest of any new building of its time—$765 to $2,130 a month—and it soon came to symbolize some sort of ultimate in the rental market (excepting, always, certain apartments of the very rich on Fifth Avenue, Sutton Place and the like.)

But as this image was forming, the building was having problems. It took much longer than anyone expected, for example, to fill up. Only 60 of its 360 apartments were rented when it opened, and a year later only 125.

There have been several managers (the most recent change was last week) and several rental agents. There was a rent strike in 1976 by a dozen tenants and six are still withholding two months' rent.

And there has been what all luxury tenants have nightmares about: crime. According to the Police Department, there were 19 burglaries and one robbery reported in 1976 and seven burglaries and two robberies so far this year, including a spectacular one in which the thief swung onto a terrace on the 30th floor and one in which a man on the third floor was killed. Most recently, there was a knifing incident on Thanksgiving Day in a service hallway.

No apartment building is entirely free of crime, of course, but the idea of such goings-on at the Sovereign—where people might assume, enough funds and staff would be available to keep the peace—has created a first-class to-do.

This takes the form, on the inside, of considerable tenant unrest—tenants in two apartments protested by placing their garbage in the lobby and one tenant said she threatened to throw a pie in the face of the owner, Sigmund Sommer—and, on the outside, of considerable publicity. Indeed, telephone calls from reporters are almost commonplace.

But through it all the affection of many tenants for the building seems to have held firm. Even in the midst of the most recent furor, the rental agent said, five new leases were signed.

Now in the latest development, Mr. Sommer has submitted to the New York State Attorney General's office a proposed prospectus to convert the building into a cooperative.

In an interview in his office on the 14th floor of the Bankers Trust West building, Mr. Sommer defended the Sovereign as the "finest building ever developed." He said the staff was two to three times the size of most luxury buildings and that the security was better than that in "99 and 9/10s" of other buildings in New York City and good enough to keep out all but the professional criminal. "Nobody will ever stop the professional," said Mr. Sommer.

He said the building has only two or three vacant apartments and a waiting list. He said he believed there are a few "bad apples" and "cry babies" among his tenants and he had said he believed that the building had received adverse publicity because "the Sovereign is the finest building in the world."

"I love the building," he said. "I think once the building has a good manager and the 'creeps' get out, this thing will run like a little clock."

Mr. Sommer said he was selling the building because "we are trying to become very, very liquid." According to the prospectus, he proposed selling shares of the apartment corporation that owns the Sovereign and a secondary building, at 405 East 58th Street, for $41,280,000. Tenants in the building who purchase their apartments would get a 20 percent discount, however, so the final figure would probably be less.

The 8.6 percent mortgage, which would stand at $24,317,774 as of next July, the proposed date of the sale, would be assumed by the new shareholders; Mr. Sommer would pay off a $2.8 million note.

Prices range from $61,600 for apartment 3F (four rooms, one bath and a powder room, monthly maintenance of $641.67) to $220,000 for 45H (eight rooms, five baths and a powder room, maintenance of $2,291.67).

One recent day, there were several Cadillacs and chauffeur-driven automobiles entering the driveway. Three cars with diplomatic plates were parked in a no-standing, trucks-only zone. Laura Tulloch, a full-time housekeeper walking her employer's lhasa apso, stopped to chat briefly and said she was afraid to take out the garbage. "I wait until my boss is back to take it out," she said.

Inside the office of J.R.D. Sales, a plastics distributor on the ground floor, a salesman, Jerry Prior, said, "My car was stolen out of the building's garage Wednesday night. It was just unbelievable. It's a darn shame in such a beautiful building . . . I'm not scared to come to work but I'm a little bit more careful."

The building is the home of Calvin Klein, the designer, Vera Brodsky Lawrence, the music historian, William T. Seawell, chairman of the board of Pan Am, a prince, and several diplomats, among others.

If there is one area in which Mr. Sommer and many of his tenants agree it is on the spaciousness of the apartments and their spectacular views. The rooms are nine feet high, about a foot higher than those of most new buildings. Bathrooms are of marble, except maids' rooms, which get white ceramic tile. Each apartment has a washer and dryer and climate-control units. Several apartments on each floor have a floor-through living area that gives both a northern and southern exposure.

There is an intra-building telephone and moiré style wallpaper in the small hall that every two apartments share with one elevator. The doormen and others wear black uniforms with buttons decorated with an "S."

Not everyone feels insecure in the building. Barbara Bishop, who moved from Valley Forge, Pa., about a year ago, said she had been stopped by building employees who did not recognize her when she changed her hairdo. She said she had three locks and a burglar alarm.

"I love the building," she said. "The employees are very nice. As far as I know the security is very good. I feel very safe here. There was only one murder and that can happen anywhere."

"We like the place," said a retired business executive, who said he moved from the Imperial House in June. "We like the service. We think it is the best apartment house in New York. I think the controversy may be just a few people. I think a lot of people tend to exaggerate a lot of problems."

"I want to stay here as long as I live in New York," said Alice Baker, a widow and past president of the United Nations Hospitality Committee. Mrs. Baker said, nevertheless, she believed Mr. Sommer had not protected his investment by making it as pleasant as possible for the tenants and allowing the building to acquire a bad reputation.

Ethel Redner-Scull (the way she spells her name since separating from her husband Robert, with whom she became well-known as a collector of Pop art), said she wanted to stress that not every one who lives in the building is rich and that the building is certainly not her idea of posh.

"It's a very ordinary building," said Mrs. Redner-Scull one morning recently as she drank Sunsweet prune juice in her sunny apartment, which has a sweeping view of the Queensboro Bridge. "I've lived in a posh building. I've lived in a posh house. They might ask high rents—that doesn't mean it's posh. Go over to 600 Park Avenue and you find the posh people. Go to the River House. Posh people."

On Thanksgiving Day, after hearing reports of the knifing incident, she and a friend, Carole Baer, decided to protest. Mrs. Baer, her husband Alan, two guests and Mrs. Redner-Scull carried their garbage in the front elevator to the lobby pointing out to the staff that they were too afraid to use the service hallway.

"It was very elegant garbage," said Mrs. Redner-Scull. "I wore a long, white Adolfo and the garbage was in a Dumas bag."

"We had Dag bags," said Carole Baer, who joined Mrs. Redner-Scull for the interview.

Mrs. Baer said she moved from the Bristol on East 56th Street, breaking her lease and losing her security deposit, because she did not want to miss the opportunity to move into the Sovereign. "I'm not an L-shaped-living-room person," she explained.

The first drawback for her became apparent one day, she said, when she was walking through her apartment undressed and the police knocked on her door and asked if she had seen anyone go by her windows. "I said, 'Who, Superman?' " she recalled.

The second bad sign was when her husband, with whom she is in the art security business, left a Degas pastel, a Delacroix oil, and a Rodin bronze in the trunk of his car because the office burglar alarm was being worked on and he thought the apartment was unsafe. The art work, which he said belonged to a client, was stolen, he said, while the car was parked in the building's garage.

Mrs. Baer has the plans for the decoration of her apartment taped to the living room wall but she has postponed the work until they decide if they will stay in the building. Right now in the living room she has about three dozen paintings leaning against the wall on the floor and only a red lip-shaped couch and a few other pieces of furniture moved in.

She said she loves the building and its location near the East River Drive and Bloomingdale's. She has discovered several childhood friends living in the building.

"When I was a kid I grew up in the Bronx," she said. "I used to go up on the roof. I used to look at the city and I'd say when I grow up, that's where I want to be. The ironic thing is now when I'm in my apartment and I look out, I see the Bronx. Well, my life has come full circle."

APRIL 22, 1978

They Ate, Drank And Were Charitable

By ANGELA TAYLOR

Robert Joffrey had a good time at Bergdorf Goodman the other night when the store officially opened its handsome new second floor, coincidentally raising money for the Joffrey Ballet. "I love fashion shows," he said. "I used to choreograph the shows for the April in Paris Ball years ago; it was lots of fun."

Mr. Joffrey, a cheerful man with a pepper-and-salt beard that matched his loose, pepper-and-salt sweater, made good-natured comments as Muriel Grateau's designs went by his chair: "Wonderful coat . . . funny shoes . . . those look like vamp dresses, can you imagine going down subway stairs in them?" The last referred to the French designer's hobble-hemmed skirts that required the mannequins to mince along in baby steps, and were hardly meant for the BMT.

Department stores' mutually benefitting romances with good causes continue — the store gets a chance to display its wares to affluent customers, the charity gets cash. Bergdorf's, wanting to show off its new imports, played host to 200 people, supplying drink, food and the fashion show early in the evening. Then everybody trooped off in limousines to the City Center for a performance of the Joffrey company, including the world premiere of its "Suite Saint-Saens." A $50 ticket covered both functions.

A Tour, Too

The benefit attracted such culture buffs as Anthony Bliss, the Samuel Peabodys, Nancy Zeckendorf of the real estate clan, Joan Ward, who was co-chairman of the event, Ronay Menschel, one of Mayor Koch's deputy mayors, and Ethel Redner-Scull, the art collector. Mrs. Scull, attired in candy-pink satin, kept complaining that she couldn't get a glass of water before the fashion show — "I could die of thirst, it's like being in the desert."

The fashion mannequins were caught in rainy day traffic, but the delay worked out nicely. It gave Ira Neimark, Bergdorf's president, a chance to give guests a tour of the floor devoted to individual boutiques for European fashion houses: Saint Laurent Rive Gauche, Givenchy, Fendi, Chanel, Ripa furs, Mila Schoen and Muriel Grateau in her American debut. (Giorgio Armani's furs are also first-timers.) A harmonious beige and black decor pulls the shops together, but in every case, Larry Laslo, Bergdorf's decorator, has reproduced touches from the designers' European establishments.

In the middle of all the French and Italian houses, Geoffrey Beene stands out as the only American in the group. "Geoffrey's international now," Mr. Neimark said, referring to the Beene collections that were shown recently in Milan and Paris.

Geoffrey Beene himself was more modest. If he was rewarded by inclusion, he said, it was because he had been especially diligent about overseeing his former location in the store. "I would stop by on Saturdays and change the flowers and see that everything looked all right."

But it was Miss Grateau's night. The fashion show combined her summer things with the fall collection she showed in Paris this month. A young woman with dark hair streaming down her back, Miss Grateau had the good sense to wear one of her black-tie pants suits. She could hardly have moved through the crush in her kite-shaped dress with the tight hem.

JUNE 1, 1978

In the City, a 'Night on the Nile'

By ANGELA TAYLOR

TUTANKHAMEN did his bit for charity last night. The Egyptian boy king's treasures, currently touring the country and expected at the Metropolitan Museum of Art in December, inspired a "Night on the Nile" party to benefit the American Cancer Society.

And despite the downpour, charity-minded New Yorkers got into their floating dresses and black ties and pretended they were in sunny Egypt. As a matter of fact, two of the women got into the same drifty Adolfo number, an off-the-shoulder affair wreathed in flowers and with wide, wing-like sleeves. Carolyn Amory, chairman of the event, had found her peach-colored dress at the designer's just hours before the party. Glady Solomon said she'd had her white one for a couple of weeks. The women laughed, agreed it was the prettiest balldress in the city and worth repeating.

Chiffons pretty well took over the evening. Gisele Masson, of La Grenouille restaurant, got her violet and white flowered one at Dior. Her friend, Marie Alleman wore a cream-colored, somewhat Victorian dress with a high neck. "It's from that woman who dyes her hair green," she said. "Oh yes, Zandra Rhodes. Charlotte Ford's full-skirted dress was black, scattered with small flowers, while Dolly Raisler made a dramatic entrance in a gold-threaded, striped chiffon from Venet, with a sort of bejeweled peasant scarf wrapped on her head. Kimberley Farkas, of the Alexander's clan, added a feather boa to match her Nile green, slender dress. The tall and willowy chose long tunics over narrow trousers: bright red, plus a collar of etched gold for Cheray Duchin, white with a simple bar pin for Diane von Furstenburg.

•

The charity, explained Carolyn Amory, tries to do something more for its bashes than the usual dinner dance. Last year, it chartered a cruise ship and sailed the merrymakers up the Hudson. This year's Nile sail was stationary, anchored in the Grand Ballroom of the Waldorf Astoria. But the décor, done by Jim Patterson with his own Egyptian-like prints, helped transport the guests to a romantic evening on the fabled river. And without mosquitoes to plague them.

The star turn was taken by Thomas Hoving, former director of the Metropolitan, who showed slides of the Tutankhamen artifacts and explained their significance to an audience of 450 who had paid $150 each for their tickets.

Thanks to the excitement generated by the King Tut show, Egypt seems to have become this year's chic country. "The Egyptian show is the most important and exciting event of the year," Mrs. Amory said. "Only about 10 percent of the people who want to see it will be able to get into the Metropolitan. This way, they will be able to see blown-up pictures of the treasures and be aware of small details they wouldn't spot even if they got into the exhibit."

Mrs. Amory, a blonde with gold-green eyes, is married to Thomas Carhart Amory, president of an executive-placement company. She is a great believer in getting the details straight. She flew to Los Angeles to see the Tutankhamen show for herself before discussing décor with Mr. Patterson, who is a veteran of several exhibits at the Metropolitan. Assisted by Lauren Peltz of the decorations committee, he transformed the ballroom with Egyptian-like printed fabrics, centerpieces of papyrus sheaves, and votive candles flickering among bowls of dried fruits and nuts. Rented palm trees also helped.

•

The diners feasted on cold cucumber soup, chicken breasts with champagne sauce, asparagus, pilaf of cracked wheat with apricots, pine nuts and raisins, and ended with various sherbets. Peter Duchin's orchestra pretty well stayed with local tunes, but except for the Egyptian diplomatic contingent, it was unlikely that the guests were adept at the hip-wiggling dances of Cleopatra's country.

Mrs. Nelson Rockefeller was billed as honorary chairman and the Gerald Fords were listed on the honorary committee. But the Rockefellers and the Fords were traveling elsewhere, so the partygoers would have to settle for Andrew Young, Ambassador to the United Nations, to hold the local diplomatic fort.

It would take very pressing diplomatic business to keep the Egyptians away: Ambassador to the United States Ashraf Ghorbal, A. Esmat Abdel Meguid, permanent representative to the United Nations, Abdul Halim Badawi, deputy representative, and Consul General Yousef Sharara, and their wives. Zeinab Sharara, who has astonishing blue eyes under her cap of black hair, had been active in the plans from the beginning. Mrs. Sharara loves New York — "Everything is happening here" — and even has kind words for the traffic jams and the dirt. (Mohammed Ibrahim Kamel, Egypt's foreign minister, had wanted to attend, but was advised against it for security reasons.)

No charity party is complete without raffle prizes. The ones for last night's event were enticing enough for the crowd to buy raffle tickets at $50 a chance (three for $100), hoping to win the grand prize of a trip to Egypt, including a real cruise on the Nile.

In addition, there was a porcelain copy of King Tut's mask and other objets d'art donated by Helen Boehm, a copy of a gold signet ring inscribed with the name of Cheops, the builder of the great pyramid of Giza (the original ring is in the Brooklyn Museum), plus dresses and jewelry donated by local designers such as Mary McFadden, Adolfo and Bill Blass. And there were free favors for the women: handsome boxes decorated in Egyptian motifs, full of Helena Rubinstein goodies.

Carolyn Amory, who didn't have time to get to the hairdresser's and had washed and rolled up her own hair, thought it was all worth while. When the bookkeeping is done, Mrs. Amory hopes the American Cancer Society will be at least $75,000 richer.

Philanthropic New Yorkers who bought tickets for the party included the George Abbotts, the Emil Mosbachers, Sheila Mosler, the George Zauderers, Mary Lasker, Mrs. Boehm, widow of Edward Marshall Boehm, the sculptor, the Claude Arpelses, Marie Jose Paglai, Betsy von Furstenberg, Samuel Lefrak, the Henry T. Mortimers, the David Musses, the Ira Neimarks, the Howard Oxenbergs, Bo Polk, the Martin Revsons, Ethel Scull, Mildred Hilson, the Stanley Weintraubs and Jerome Zerbe.

And the patrons and committee members: Shirley Anderson, Mrs. Edgar Bronfman, Noreen Drexel, Pat Dunnington, Dorothea Darlington, Sandra Gilman, Liz Groves and Nannette Kreizel.

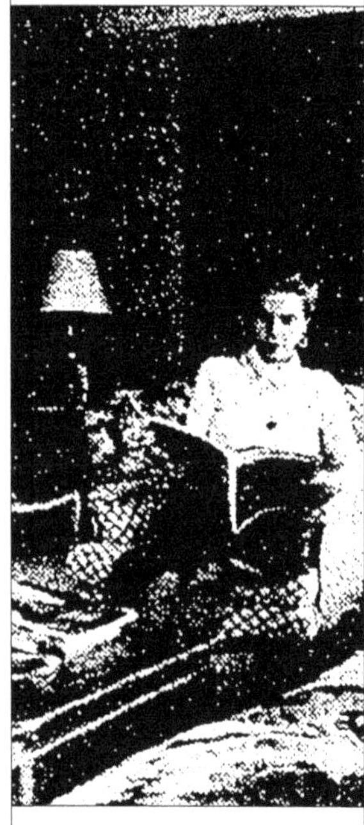

JANUARY 5, 1979

Adolfo's Spring Comes in Zinging With Color

By BERNADINE MORRIS

It's more than a fashion show — it's a social event.

The opening of any new Adolfo collection always serves to kick off the new fashion season. Everybody comes, swathed in furs in January, wrapped in sun tans in July.

The dates are chosen for the customers' convenience, the designer explained at yesterday's presentation of spring clothes at the St. Regis hotel.

"They're set for the time the women begin to think about new clothes," Adolfo said.

The women are, of course, mostly private clients rather than store executives, because Adolfo is one of the few American designers who do made to order clothes.

"He's nice to everybody and everybody adores him," said Glady Solomon, one of his ardent fans.

Mrs. Solomon had a hint of what was to be a highlight of the show when her friend, Alice Sumergrad, phoned and asked her not to wear a brown suit they both had bought.

"I wore it instead in purple and wine," said Mrs. Solomon, "and look what my husband bought me to go with it." She held out a hand with a big ruby ring rimmed in diamonds. "I think rubies go with everything."

Mrs. Sumergrad wore the brown tweed suit with the silk shirt in matching plaid. So did Isabelle Leeds, a special assistant to Governor Carey; Mary Lou Block, who runs a chain of beauty shops; Dorothy Hess, whose husband is a dentist, and Dr. Joanne Stroud, who teaches psychology in Dallas.

In fact, counting brown suits was a major divertissement before the show started. They weren't all identical, but they clearly came from the same designing hand.

Enjoyed the Commotion

"I think everybody ought to come in the same style as a tribute," observed Mrs. Solomon. "I'd even buy it for them if they'd do it." She thought it was silly to worry about what other people were wearing. So did most of the people in the brown suits as they seemed to enjoy the commotion.

What will be the next big success?

"It will probably be this one," Adolfo said, pointing to a black and white style with a narrow skirt and a loose bolero-like jacket. He also liked a rose colored and a mauve suit.

All of them were in the Chanel mood, a genre Adolfo has made his own. The fabrics are knitted and supple and the blouses always silk. He usually adds a matching handbag with a gold chain — and so do many of his clients.

"The suits are expensive, but they last a long time and people order another jacket or another skirt to make them go further," he said. Prices start at $695, where they've been for five years.

Adolfo started his show this time with a couple of short, fitted-jacket suits that had flaring skirts and belted waistlines. He then moved into his Chanel series, followed by suits in zinging colors: green blazer with orange skirt, purple jacket with yellow skirt. Some jackets curved at the bottom to follow the arc of the skirt hemline and narrow skirts were eased with slits.

But suits are only part of the Adolfo story, which ranges over almost everything a woman of a certain affluence would care to put on her back. There are sailor styles for day and night — the nighttime ones with middy tops and bouffant taffeta skirts. They're the only long dresses in the collection. And bare tube tops sheltered by little shrug jackets and accompanied by red, green or blue skirts. And sweaters pulled over printed silk skirts, with a matching print scarf to drape over the shoulders.

The suits were followed by the main event: the clothes women will wear this spring to cocktail parties, dinners and dances, where practicality is not the first consideration.

Here the choice is particularly wide. Knitted dresses with appliqués at the shoulder or hip. Loose tops in coin-size dotted silk over narrow pants. Trousers made in two parts that wrap around the leg — and open at the bottom to show a good portion of the limb.

Some soft print dresses with drawstrings at the waist and small straps over the shoulders are lovely in a conventional way. Hemlines are either top-of-the-calf or dipping to the ankle.

The dresses that Adolfo is particularly pleased with, however, have strapless necklines, flaring skirts and are made in stiff silks gleaming with embroidery. The embroidery is from Bucol in France, the silk organdy and tulle fabrics by Abraham of Switzerland. In colors such as peach, pink and pale blue, gleaming with rhinestones, gold embroidery or multicolor flowers, they represent Adolfo's concept of the contemporary short dancing dresses. The hemlines end just below the knee.

The audience, which included Caroline Amory, Livia Weintraub, Ethel Scull, Mildred Hilson, Gisele Masson and Rae Stein, in addition to the women in the brown suits, seemed to approve, as they do with most styles the maestro proposes. They really do adore him.

MAY 13, 1979

Big Auction To Measure Art Market

By RITA REIF

The strongest test of the contemporary art market in five years will take place in an auction Friday night at Christie's, Manson & Woods, Park Avenue at 59th Street. The sale of 67 selections of post-World War II art works is expected to bring up to $2.4 million and may well upstage the Robert C. Scull sale of October 1973 that totaled $2.1 million, the world record for contemporary art.

Ivan Karp, who heads O.K. Harris, the SoHo gallery, and a top dealer in contemporary art, describes the auction as "pretty juicy." He said that the art market in all areas "has been very, very active in recent months" and contemporary art has rebounded dramatically.

Allan Stone agrees. "The market today for A-quality art is even stronger than in 1973 and 1974," he said. The East 86th Street art dealer added, "I think that the sale at Christie's looks terrific."

Although most top-quality contemporary works never dropped in price when the market softened in 1974, secondary examples of Abstract Expressionist, color field, Pop and Op Art did. "Today you don't seem to have as many middle-quality players," Mr. Stone said. "Most seem to be out to lunch."

The paintings that are stirring the most advance interest in the sale are the abstract oil on canvas Franz Kline completed in 1952, which, Mr. Stone said, "is probably one of the finest Kline ever painted," and the Morris Louis, which Mr. Stone described as "probably the best of its kind." The presale estimates on those paintings are, respectively, up to $250,000 and $150,000. Notable too, are Robert Rauschenberg's "Cartoon," painted in 1962 (the presale estimate is up to $140,000), an Arshile Gorky untitled abstract (up to $125,000), and a Willem de Kooning (up to $125,000).

The sale appears to be strong too in artists who command lower prices, including Ellsworth Kelly (there are two, and each may go to as much as $50,000), Roy Lichtenstein (there are four, one of which, "Art," may sell for up to $75,000) and David Smith (up to $35,000).

The resurgence of interest in and buying of contemporary art is due, in part, to "a new generation of collectors," according to Martha Baer, a Christie's vice president who assembled the sale. Miss Baer said that these **younger buyers were replacing not only** older American collectors, but also many of the Japanese and West German buyers who pulled out after the oil crisis and fluctuating currencies had thrown the contemporary art market into turmoil in 1974.

OCTOBER 24, 1979

Benefit Evening Salutes Dior's Marc Bohan

By ANNE-MARIE SCHIRO

MARC BOHAN says he was bowled over. Although the French designer is a regular visitor to New York and has shown his Christian Dior collection in stores here before, he admits he was dumbfounded when he saw a retrospective of his clothes in Altman's windows and aisles.

"I couldn't believe it," he said, his gaunt face breaking into a broad smile. "All the past was brought back in front of my eyes."

The designer was here this time for Altman's two-week salute to Dior, focusing on the last two decades — the Marc Bohan years — with storewide displays of Dior merchandise for women, men, children and the home.

But the highlight of the salute was a charity party last night to benefit St. Luke's Hospital Center for Hospice, which is a care and counseling program for terminal cancer patients and their families.

Carolyn Amory, chairman of the benefit committee, had Mr. Bohan design a dress especially for her to wear. It was red silk shot with gold threads and had a tulip-shaped skirt.

"I feel so good in red," Mrs. Amory said. The color — combined with her pale blond hair — certainly helped her to stand out in the crowd, especially since the knee-length skirt showed off her red stockings and shoes.

"The short evening dress is very important now," Mr. Bohan said. "Women are tired of long dresses. They want a different look — a less formal look."

Maybe that's why Altman's scheduled the party to run from 6:30 to 9 P.M. — so women wouldn't have to get decked out in ballgowns to go to a department store.

Short Dresses or Black Suits

Most of them didn't. They chose short party dresses or black suits. But Barbara de Portago went all out in a real ballgown with a bouffant black taffeta skirt and a brocade top. Audrey Zauderer and Evelyn Hall, who arrived together escorted by Alfred Olmer, both chose long black dresses. Jan Chipman's long dress was white.

Nan Kempner combined white wool with black velvet in a dramatic bicolor suit from Yves Saint Laurent's fall couture collection. Gloria Schiff and her twin sister, Consuelo Crespi, both wore red. Bonnie Swearingen, who flew in from Chicago for the party ("My husband had to stay home to run our oil business," she said), wore a vintage Dior dress with appliques of peach flowers that she'd found in London.

Ethel Scull, who was in a new black velvet suit, said, "I'm sorry I gave my old clothes away. I feel like calling the Met and asking for them back."

Mr. Bohan, who was wearing a double-breasted gray suit, said he had to fly to Paris right after the party to attend a dinner for Queen Elizabeth. He never had a chance to sample the buffet of coulibiac of bass, brie en brioche, baked ham and chicken liver terrine. Nor did he get to taste the rich chocolate cake baked from his own recipe. But he did get to admire the ceiling-high columns on the main floor that had been draped in gray and topped with gigantic bows for the festivities. "They look very Dior," he remarked. He also approved of the gray-painted fountains banked with white mums.

More Than 600 Guests

Actually, with the crush of more than 600 guests at the party, the decor wasn't easy to admire, but Mr. Bohan had seen it Monday when he was in the store fitting models for the fashion show that preceded the buffet and meeting with customers. He also found a few moments to talk — in fluent English — about fashion, past and present.

"It's very important for a designer to mix with people, to be involved with life," he said, lighting a Gauloise. "You can't design in an ivory tower. You have to feel what people want and what they don't want anymore. Timing is very important when you come out with a new design. It must not be too early or too late."

"When Christian Dior came out with the New Look in 1947," he went on, "everything was changing. The war was over and people were looking for a change."

He does not feel that this is the right time to go back to miniskirts and other styles of the 1960's. "It's too close," he said. "I don't think people are ready for that. Knee length is the length now."

Most of the women at the party seemed to agree with him. Perhaps Mrs. Amory, had alerted many of them. She knew most of the guests at the party, of course, because she's been involved in raising money for cancer causes for 12 years and is the first woman to become chairman of the board of the American Cancer Society. As charity parties go, last night's was a bargain for some of the guests. Since Altman's underwrote all the expenses, the guests were offered a choice of contributing $35 or $100.

"More people paid $100, I'm happy to say," Mrs. Amory reported. "That means more money for Hospice."

MARCH 7, 1980

Celebrating Roseland Romances

By RON ALEXANDER

Sylvia Miles wasn't there, and neither was Diana Vreeland or Bill Blass or Ethel Scull or Andy Warhol or any of your usual run-of-the-mill partygoers. In fact, they weren't even invited. But Adele and Albert Goldfarb and John and Bunny Viola were, and the guest list also included Englebert and Sherle Bick, Honey and Harold Tamarin and Frank Vaccara, among others.

The party, which gently shook the rafters at Roseland on Wednesday evening, was given by Nancy Brecker Leeds, daughter of the ballroom's founder, and her husband, Richard. The couple met 35 years ago at the original Roseland on Broadway and 51st Street (it opened in 1919 and moved to its present site on 52d Street in 1956) and their invitations announced that the occasion was to "romantically commemorate the happily wed couples who originally met at Roseland." (Mrs. Leeds has their names on file. "Merely living together doesn't count," she says.)

Adele and Albert Goldman, who arrived from Flushing at 5:30 on the dot, were the first guests to receive a big "Hello, it's so good to see you again" from Mrs. Leeds, plus a pair of big buttons that proclaimed: "I Met My Mate at Roseland."

While the Goldmans couldn't agree whether they had met in 1922 or 1923, they were in accord, as they pinned on their buttons and peppily chachaed toward the bandstand, that "Roseland has the best dance floor in the world, bar none."

Jack and Sally Hillman ("Everyone calls us The Dancing Hillmans," they said in unison) arrived from their home in Mount Vernon a few beats later. Mrs. Hillman, who wore pink pants, a pink blouse and small pink roses in her hair, pointed out the diamond-centered gold rose tie tac she had given to her husband.

"Roseland is our home away from home," Mr. Hillman said.

"We've been coming here every Sunday since we got married on Aug. 10, 1959," Sally Hillman added. "We found each other dancing and we never dance with anybody else." Then, as the band began a bluesy rendition of "Deep Night," she reached for her husband's arm and they headed to the dance floor.

By 7 o'clock close to 200 of the invited guests, joined by several hundred patrons who paid $10 each to dance and dine on Roseland's Wednesday night buffet, were happily swaying to such crowd pleasers as "I Hear a Rhapsody" and "On the Sunny Side of the Street."

The couple who had come the farthest for the party — they had flown in from Miami Wednesday afternoon — requested that their names not be used. "Why should our relatives know we have the money to take a plane to a party?" the gray-haired husband asked as he nibbled on a piece of Chicken à la Roseland.

Not everyone came in couples. Estelle Allison took the subway from the Bronx by herself. Her husband, whom she married in 1953, died some time ago. "He was 20 years younger than me," she said, "so who would have thought he'd go first? I come back here for old time's sake." Suddenly, her face brightened into a sly smile. "I only wish they'd start the disco sessions earlier than 11 o'clock," she said as she smoothed out her black satin disco pants.

Frank Vaccara also arrived alone, although he said he didn't expect to leave alone. The 67-year-old Mr. Vaccara, who is in the scrap metal business in Passaic, N.J., has been married four times. His first wife died and his last three marriages — all with mates he met at Roseland — ended in divorce.

"There was one Ruthie and two

Jeans," he recalled. "I taught them all how to dance." Was he looking for wife No. 5? "Certainly. If Mickey Rooney can do it, so can I."

And so can Harry J. Blatz, who at 83, was dancing up a storm to "Lady of Spain" with his third wife, Betty. "Roseland has been good to me," Mr. Blatz reported. "I met all my wives here."

A few minutes before 11 o'clock the couple took one final dip and headed for the check room.

"It's been a wonderful party but the disco session is about to start," Betty Blatz said with a sigh. "That, I think, is not for us."

MAY 18, 1980

Week's Art Auctions Rewrite the Record Books

By RITA REIF

Auction history was rewritten last week when five days of sales of Impressionist, modern and contemporary art totaled an astounding $55.8 million at New York's two largest houses, almost double the $29.6 million record for a week of art auctions in New York in November.

It was, of course, the sales of the spectacular collections formed by the automotive fortunes of Henry Ford 2d, Edgar William and Bernice Chrysler Garbisch that registered more than half that total, and most of the week's stunning prices. The Ford sale at Christie's, Park Avenue at East 59th Street, totaled $18.3 million and was part of a larger sale that reached $25.5 million, the highest total for a single auction session of art in the world. "I think it will take a little while to beat that," David Bathurst, Christie's president in New York, said.

The Garbisch dispersal at Sotheby Parke Bernet, Madison Avenue at East 76th Street, was $14.8 million.

In each of the major sales, there were stunning prices paid for major art works, notably the $5.2 million paid in the Ford auction for Van Gogh's "Le Jardin du Poète Arles" ("The Garden of a Poet in Arles"), making that oil the second most expensive art work ever sold at auction, exceeded only by an old-master painting. It was also a record for a post-Impressionist work, for 19th-century art and for the artist. At the Garbisch sale, the $3 million paid for Picasso's "Saltibanque (Acrobat) Seated With Arms Crossed" was the highest price at auction for 20th-century art and for the artist.

6 Records for Artists

Six of the 10 paintings in the Ford collection established records for artists. In addition to the Van Gogh, the others were Cèzanne at $3.9 million for "Paysan en Blouse Bleue," a portrait of a peasant in a blue shirt; Gauguin at $2.9 million for "La Plage au Pouldu," a painting of a Breton landscape; Degas at $900,000 for "Etude de Nu" ("Study of a Nude"); Modigliani at $600,000 for "Nudo Seduto" ("Seated Nude") and Boudin at $480,000 for "La Plage" ("The Beach"). In the second part of the evening, there was a new high for Redon of $600,000 for "Plantes: Cinque Panneaux Decoratifs" ("Plants: Five Decorative Panels.")

In the sale of the 40 selections of Garbisch art, there were other artist records. But only one, the $1.8 paid for Gauguin's "Tahitian Women Under the Palms," was still standing when the gaveling had finished at the Ford sale the following night. So spirited was the bidding and so high were the prices at Sotheby's on the first night of the sales that John L. Marion, who wielded the hammer, took a moment out to send a message to Norton Simon, who was on the telephone bidding through David Nash, Sotheby's director of fine art:

"Tell Norton Simon that the Depression is late in coming," Mr. Marion said. At Sotheby's and at Christie's, the West Germans and Japanese figured prominently in the bidding and went away with many of the prizes.

Post-World War II Records

Artist records were also registered at the sales of post-World War II art in each of the houses. At Sotheby's on Thursday night, seven highs were accomplished, including Roy Lichtenstein at $210,000, the price paid for "Oh Jeff . . . I Love You, too . . . but . . ." and Francis Bacon at $180,000.

Other highs for artists in that sale included $57,500 for Ellsworth Kelly; $55,000 for Robert Motherwell; $47,000 for George Segal; $16,000 for Robewrt Natkin, and $29,000 for Karel Appel. The week's total for Sotheby's was $25.8 million.

And at Christie's on Friday night, the sale totaled $2.6 million, the highest figure ever reached for a sale of post-World War II art, eclipsing the $2.1 million set with the sale of Robert Scull's collection at Sotheby's in 1973. The star lot in Christie's sale was Jackson Pollock's "Four Opposites," which sold for $550,000, a record for the artist.

De Kooning Ties Record

Other artist records were $250,000 for Barnett Newman's "Primordial Light" and $180,000 for Morris Louis's "Beta Khi." Willem de Kooning's study for "Marshes" sold for $180,000, tying his record.

The six other artist records were for Frank Stella at $85,000; Adolph Gottlieb at $70,000; Milton Avery at $41,000; Carle Andre at $29,000; Joan Mitchell at $18,000, and Jules Olitski at $18,000. By week's end Christie's had chalked up sales of $30 million.

In all sales, it was agreed, the selections of lesser quality did not sell. In some cases, expectations were too high. The post-World War II art sale at Sotheby's carried estimates that were unrealistically high. In both houses, sculpture prices were unusually strong and there was brisk bidding on School of Paris paintings, including Utrillos and Kislings. At Sotheby's, it was apparent that the Surrealist market was still sluggish, with buyers being very selective.

AUGUST 22, 1980

Auctions

Record art sales and hint of dip.

Rita Reif

It will come as no surprise to auctiongoers who watched the sales of the Garbisch collection and of 10 paintings from the Henry Ford 2d collection last May that the season's top prices at both major houses were paid for Impressionist and modern-art works. This put them far ahead of jewelry, traditionally their liveliest competitor.

The figures for paintings, drawings and sculptures advanced so dramatically during the season that began last September and ends this month that these art sales now seem to be in a totally different sphere. Last month, however, sales in London showed that the boom had faltered, with a large proportion of offerings either selling for less than expected or not finding buyers. At Sotheby's sale of Impressionist and modern art, for example, 40 lots of 99 offered did not sell. At Christie's, 31 art works out of 93 did not find buyers.

At Christie's in New York, the figure for Impressionist and modern-art sales skyrocketed from $9.7 million to $33 million — with the Ford pictures responsible for $18.3 million. (Jewelry sales, which surpassed this art category a year ago with a total of $9.9 million, reached $20.3 million this year.) At Sotheby Parke Bernet in New York, the sales of late-19th- and 20th-century art works totaled $48.6 million, compared with $23.8 million a year ago and $16.9 million two years ago. What accounted for the decisive difference this season was the Edgar William and Bernice Chrysler Garbisch collection of 40 pictures, which brought $14.8 million. Sotheby's jewelry sales also increased, but not nearly so impressively — going from $18.2 million to $23.1 million.

The climax of the season came in Christie's sale of the Ford paintings. The $18.3 million figure was a world record for a sale of Impressionist and modern art, and a new high for an American auction. When the bidding had ended on Mr. Ford's paintings and on the 88 other works offered that night, the total for the auction was $25.5 million, a world record for a single session art sale and a figure that was second only to the $34 million registered at the Robert von Hirsch multisession auction in London in 1978.

Records fell faster than tenpins that night, and the new highs for individual works by artists included $5.2 million for a van Gogh ("The Garden of a Poet in Arles"), a record also for any post-Impressionist work. Other records in the Ford sale were $3.9 million for a Cézanne (his portrait of a peasant in a blue shirt), $2.9 million for a Gauguin (a painting of a Breton landscape), $900,000 for a Degas (a study of a nude), $600,000 for a Modigliani (a seated nude) and $480,000 for a Boudin (a beach scene).

Post-World War II paintings and sculpture enjoyed brisk bidding later that week, when Christie's reported a record of $2.6 million for a sale of such art works, eclipsing the $2.1 million registered in the sale of the Robert Scull collection at Sotheby's in 1973. New highs for artists included $550,000 for a Jackson Pollack ("Four Opposites"), $250,000 for a Barnett Newman ("Primordial Light"), $180,000 for a Morris Louis, $85,000 for a Frank Stella, $70,000 for an Adolph Gottlieb, $41,000 for a Milton Avery and $29,000 for a Carl Andre.

Last November, Christie's sales were quieter, although several major records in post-World War II art and other modest records in modern art were set, including $170,000 for a Robert Rauschenberg, $130,000 for an Ad Reinhardt and $30,000 for a Reuven Rubin.

Sotheby's enjoyed a lively autumn as one major collection after another appeared, with prices reaching new heights in several categories and for many artists. The collections of William N. Copley, the artist, and Paulette Goddard, the actress and widow of Erich Maria Remarque, the author, were the major attractions last November. The sale of the Copley group, which Sotheby's called the finest collection of Surrealist art ever offered at public sale, confirmed renewed interest in the style after a five-year lapse.

In the Copley sale the record for Surrealist art was set with the sale for $750,000 of Man Ray's "Observatory Time: The Lovers," showing giant red lips over a landscape. The figure was a record for the artist as well. New price levels also were reached for Max Ernst, $620,000, paid for "Surrealism and the Painter"; Joan Miró, $330,000, for "Bird Pursuing a Bee and Kissing It"; Rene Magritte, $270,000, for "Listening Room"; Yves Tanguy, $270,000, for "There It Is," and Giorgio de Chirico, $170,000, for "War." Other artist records were $165,000 for a Jean Balthus, $130,000 for a Victor Brauner, $110,000 for a Jean Arp, $57,500 for a Joseph Cornell; $50,000 for a Marcel Duchamp; $40,000 for a Theo van Doesberg, and $27,500 for a Hans Bellmer.

Four additional records were established soon after with the sale of the Remarque collection and works from other owners. The most important of these was the $250,000 paid for a Pierre Bonnard, a painting of two women feeding cats. Other new highs were $130,000 for a Johan Barthold Jongkind and $87,500 for a Moise Kisling. The Matta record of $55,000 was tied at this sale.

The high point of the Garbisch auction was the sale for $3 million of Picasso's "Acrobat Seated With Arms Crossed," setting a new high for the artist and for a 20th-century painting. Another record was the $490,000 paid for Paul Signac's "The Port of St.-Tropez." Later that week, other records were established, including $400,000 for a Miro, his "Young Girl Sliding."

Post-World War II art sales at Sotheby's produced records for Roy Lichtenstein, $210,000; Francis Bacon, $180,000; David Smith, $135,000; Helen Frankenthaler, $62,500; Duane Hansonat, $60,000; Adolph Gottlieb, $35,000; Ronald B. Kitaj, $34,000, and Isamu Noguchi, $28,000.

The only records registered in London in the above categories this season were two at Christie's: $120,000 for Mario Marini's "Rider (The Town's Guardian Angel)," a new high for a sculpture by a living artist, and the $80,660 paid for David Hockney's "Blue Interior and Two Still Lifes"; and two at Sotheby's: $506,000 for a watercolor by Cézanne (a still life showing a creamer, sugar bowl and seven apples) and $318,600 for a painting by Juan Gris ("Guitar on a Table").

Sales of modern Latin American art held in October and May at Sotheby's in New York totaled $3.1 million, and a spokesman called them a resounding success. Now the auction house has set up a separate department to organize more such sales. Major records established for Latin American art were the $130,000 paid for a Diego Rivera (a portrait of a girl), a new high for the artist as well as for Latin American and Mexican art; $125,000 for a Rufino Tamayo ("The Watermelon Eater"), and $125,000 for a Jose Maria Velasco ("The Town of Guelatao"). Lesser records: $95,000 for a Wilfredo Lam, $51,000 for a Frida Kahlo, $49,000 for a Fernando Botero and $27,000 for a Jean Charlot.

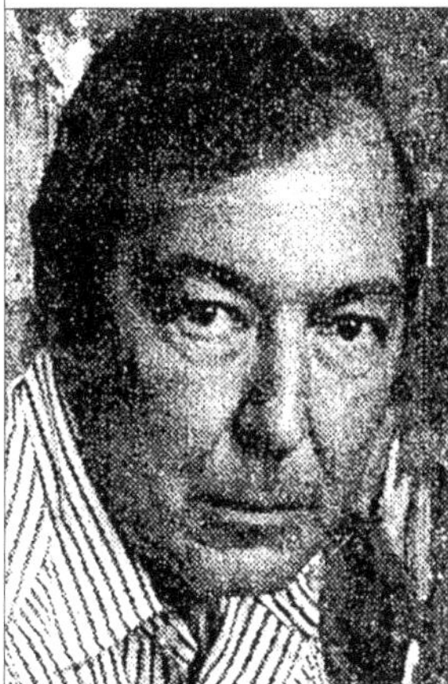

SEPTEMBER 27, 1980

Painting by Jasper Johns Sold for Million, a Record

By GRACE GLUECK

The Whitney Museum of American Art has paid $1 million for a painting by Jasper Johns, believed to be the highest price ever for the work of a living artist. The 1958 painting, a famous precursor of the Pop Art movement, is "Three Flags." It was sold by the Pace Gallery of New York, acting as agent for Mr. and Mrs. Burton Tremaine of Meriden, Conn., who bought the painting in 1959 from the Leo Castelli Gallery for $900 plus a $15 delivery charge. The artist will not share in the proceeds from the sale.

The painting, which measures roughly 30 by 45 inches, is a triple image of the American flag, painted on three successively smaller canvases, one superimposed on another.

It was hailed yesterday by Tom Armstrong, director of the Whitney, as "without doubt a monument of 20th-century art, a unique statement emerging from the dominance of Abstract Expressionism. Through it and subsequent work the artist has had an influence on the course of art history."

The Whitney had been trying to acquire the work, which appeared in the Jasper Johns retrospective mounted by the museum in 1977-78, for five years, he added, and had made "a very special effort" to get it in conjunction with its current 50th anniversary celebration. Without confirming the price, Mr. Armstrong said that money to buy "Three Flags" had come from four donors — Mr. and Mrs. Leonard A. Lauder, Mr. and Mrs. Charles Gilman Jr., A. Alfred Taubman, a Detroit businessman and member of the Whitney's National Committee, and another National Committee member who asked to remain anonymous.

Mr. Lauder is president of Estée Lauder Inc. and vice president of the museum. Mr. Gilman is president of the Gilman Paper Company. Mrs. Gilman is a Whitney trustee and head of its committee on painting and sculpture.

As far as can be determined, the price surpasses that paid for the work of any artist during his lifetime, a record that Mr. Johns appears to have sustained for some time. In 1977, another Johns painting, "According to What" (1966) was sold to a collector for a reported $600,000. In 1972, Mr. Johns's "Double White Map" set an auction record for the work of a living American artist — $240,000 at a sale of works belonging to Ethel and Robert Scull.

The record price for a work by a 20th-century American artist, living or dead, is believed to be the $2 million paid in 1973 by the Australian National Gallery of Canberra for Jackson Pollock's "Blue Poles."

Reached by telephone at his house in Stony Point, N.Y., Mr. Johns said he felt "nothing other than amusement" at the price of the painting, for which the Castelli Gallery had paid him $600 in 1959. "I was brought up in the Depression," the 50-year-old artist said, "and $1 million is a very important figure to one who grew up at that time. It has a rather neat sound, but it has nothing to do with painting."

Related to Morton's Salt Girl

The work, one of a series of flag images that Mr. Johns made early in his career, was related to "the picture of the little girl on the Morton's salt box," he said. "She carries a salt box, and her image is on that, and that image carries a salt box, and so on. You see the picture of the picture, if you know what I mean."

The Tremaine collection, from which the work was sold, is known as one of the outstanding holdings of contemporary art in the United States. Its range is from Cubism through Abstract Expressionism to the works of Pop and Minimal artists, including such names as Picasso, Léger, Mondrian, Rothko, Pollock, Frank Stella and Lucas Samaras. The Tremaines also own several other works by Mr. Johns. Mrs. Tremaine is a member of the Spreckels family of California. Mr. Tremaine is chairman of the Miller Company of Meriden, producer of sheet metal and lighting fixtures.

Until recently, the couple had indicated that their collection of Pop Art plus pre-Pop works by Mr. Johns and Robert Rauschenberg would go to a museum. The National Gallery of Art in Washington, to which they had over the years given a significant number of works, had seemed the most likely candidate.

But they have sold works from the group over the last few years, and last year, 10 paintings, most of them for sale, were shown at the Pace Gallery. From the Pace exhibition, held in conjunction with Leo Castelli, Andy Warhol's diptych "Marilyn" was bought by the Tate Gallery of London for $300,000. The Tremaines were not available for comment.

The artist has been represented by Leo Castelli since 1957, the year Mr. Castelli opened his gallery in New York. Mr. Johns's first one-man show was held at the gallery in 1958, and Mr. Castelli recalls that he received "Three Flags" from Mr. Johns shortly after that. "In 1959, the Tremaines saw it, and bought it, as they'd bought other Johnses from me," he said. "The price was $1,000, less 10 percent, plus a $15 delivery charge. I must have been poor — I wouldn't make such a charge today."

Recently, he had heard rumors of "Three Flags" being for sale at $1 million, Mr. Castelli said, and in calling Mrs. Tremaine on another matter, told her he had a client for the painting:

"She said she would let me know. This week, she called to ask me for Jasper's number, and I again inquired about the painting. She said it had been sold. My lifeblood has been my relationship with Jasper and his paintings — and it has been a faithful, loyal relationship. My selling the work was a matter of principle, not a commercial thing."

Arnold Glimcher, president of the Pace Gallery, said yesterday that he had sold "many paintings to and for the Tremaines over the years," and that the sale of "Three Flags" was his idea. "The Johns work was one of the most important paintings they owned, and this summer, in discussing the sale of other works, I urged that it be placed during their lifetime, so they'd know where it was. I suggested the Whitney because it's the quintessential American painting — a masterpiece that speaks of Johns, American painting and the Pop movement. Then I went to the Whitney. Tom Armstrong was excited by the idea, and made its acquisition a priority."

Mr. Armstrong said "Three Flags" would be exhibited temporarily in the museum's lobby gallery Oct. 14-19 and would go on permanent view in a new installation of the permanent collection next year.

SEPTEMBER 25, 1981

MAY 22, 1982

Three-Ring Benefit Show

By RON ALEXANDER

It was, as it most certainly should have been, a Happy Ending topped by a Truly Spectacular Production Number. In fact, the only thing lacking on Thursday night was, to everyone's relief, a cliffhanging climax.

The fortunate finale had been assured two weeks ago when Thomas Armstrong 3d, the director of the Whitney Museum of American Art, stood in the museum's lobby and announced, "The Calder Circus has been saved and will remain in the United States at the Whitney!"

The Robert Wood Johnson Jr. Charitable Trust (Mr. Johnson was a grandson of one of the founders of Johnson & Johnson, the health care products company) had come up with a big Band-Aid indeed: a gift of $625,000, which was one half of the sum required to keep Alexander Calder's troupe of wire and cloth miniature sculptures from being sold to settle taxes owed by the artist's estate. With that amount in hand, it wasn't difficult to match it with other donations.

So what the Whitney had originally scheduled to be a benefit performance at Madison Square Garden — the Ringling Brothers and Barnum & Bailey Circus, the Garden's current tenant, donated free seats — turned into a three-ring celebration. Not only did those benefit patrons who contributed $250 or more get to see the Greatest Show on Earth, they were also invited to a preperformance cocktail party at the Garden's Penn Plaza Club and, the biggest draw of all, to a backstage tour after the show.

Dressed as Clowns

Joan Washburn was one of the 90 or so benefactors who, good deeds aside, showed up because, she said, "How can you resist seeing your friends dressed as clowns?"

She was referring to Flora Miller Biddle, president of the Whitney, and to Mr. Armstrong, the museum's director, both of whom submitted to clown's costumes for the occasion.

"They decided I was the street tramp type," Mr. Armstrong said with an uncertain smile as he greeted guests wearing his grayish makeup, pink cheeks, a plastic red nose and a patched clown jacket, which only partly covered his preppy bow tie.

For her part, Mrs. Biddle, in white face, manic red hair and tablecloth-checked overalls, said she hoped that this was one occasion when people wouldn't tell her how alike she and her daughter look. By now Mrs. Biddle is an old hand at such things. Some weeks ago, to get the fund-raising off the ground, she rode up Madison Avenue tucked in the trunk of Targa, an elephant. During Thursday night's performance she and Mr. Armstrong appeared, center ring, in the clowns' wash-the-dog act.

"Such lovely people, circus people," Mrs. Biddle said, adjusting her clown's nose.

"I've never been to the circus before," Ethel Scull said. "My children always went with their Nana."

"You've got to be kidding," said Shirley Polykoff.

Visitors From Venice

Rosella Zorzi, who with Alida Cagidenetrio was visiting from Venice, Italy, said, "It's so New York the way people respond to something like this." Tammy and Tommy Parish, both graduates of Clown College in Venice, Fla., nodded their funny-hatted heads in agreement.

During the performance, some of the guests' well-manicured fingers were on occasion used to dim the sound of the circus music, but mostly they applauded all the "legendary," "extremely difficult and rarely performed" "death-defying" and "unparalleled in circus history" feats that the rest of the audience cheered.

"I liked the elephants best," said Mrs. Scull, whose dress had a polo horse designer insignia, after the last performer had shot out of the last rocket launcher. "When it's done so perfectly, it's a joy to see once," she added, emphasizing the "once."

Betty Wold Johnson, the widow of Robert Wood Johnson Jr., stared politely at the towering rhinestone-and-plumed headpiece atop the head of Karen Laverack, a circus dancer.

"My dear, how do you keep it on?" Mrs. Johnson inquired.

"With a nude-colored chin strap," the performer told her.

"Oh," Mrs. Johnson said.

After the tour of dressing rooms, time machines, clown cars and stables, one of the clowns announced, "It's time to go, folks. The elephants are packing their trunks."

The folks gave a groan and departed. Siam the elephant and her pals headed for the hay and carrots.

AUGUST 13, 1982

EDWARD ALBEE · ROGER ANGELL
PHILIP JOHNSON · CAROL BELLAMY
BRENDAN **YOU'LL BE** ROBERT
GILL **IN GOOD COMPANY** BLY
MAX **AT THE NEW SCHOOL** MIKE
LERNER **THIS FALL** WALLACE
DAVID SCHOENBRUN · LARRY RIVERS
NORMAN COUSINS · JULES FEIFFER

Course #A0046.
Inside Today's Art World

Ever wonder what artists choose for their own collections? Find out in this revealing exhibition/lecture series conducted by noted collector **Ethel Redner Scull.** Guests include **Larry Rivers, George Segal, Audrey Flack, Colette, Carlo Cariccio, Julian Schnabel, Jean-Michel Basquet, Ben Heller, Gloria Ross, John Perrault, Lowry Simms, Paul Jenkins** and **Tom Meser.**

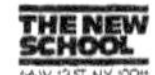

66 W 12 ST, NY 10011

Just one of more than 2000 courses for adults listed in our Fall 1982 catalog. To receive your free copy, just call **(212) 582-5555** 24 hours a day, 7 days a week.

NOVEMBER 12, 1982

Auctions

Top price for sculpture.

Rita Reif

DAVID SMITH'S "Two Doors" brought the highest price ever paid for a post-World War II American sculpture at auction Wednesday night, when it was sold at Christie's for $572,000 to an American buyer who was not identified. The Smith sculpture, fabricated of polished steel in 1964, was one of 10 post-1945 art works that established records in the sale.

The others were the $385,000 paid for Robert Rauschenberg's 1960-61 "Studio Painting"; $220,000 for a Richard Lindner, his 1961 oil on canvas "The Walk"; $198,000 for a Richard Diebenkorn, his 1961 oil on canvas "Seated Nude — Black Background"; $88,000 for a Helen Frankenthaler, her 1964 acrylic on canvas "Red Support"; $70,400 for a Joseph Cornell, his 1950's construction "Celestial Navigation"; $66,000 for a James Dine, his 1979 oil on canvas "Our Dreams Still Point North"; $41,800 for a Mark di Suvero, his 1960's steel and wood "Queen's Rook"; $33,000 for a Jules Olitski, his 1964 acrylic on canvas "Inside Voyage," and $9,900 for a Sol LeWitt, his 1974 painted aluminum "Incomplete Open Cube."

The sale, all works in the collection of Dr. Joseph and Mildred Gosman, brought $3.14 million, including the 10 percent buyer's fee. This was the highest total for a single-owner sale of post-World War II art, exceeding the Robert C. Scull auction in 1972, which brought $2.2 million in a period before the buyer's fee was introduced.

June 5, 1983

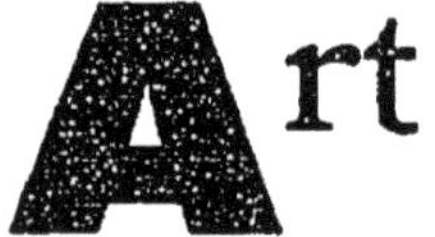

GALLERIES SOHO

Group Shows

PLEIADES, 164 Mercer St. — "Collector's Choice — Selections by Ethel Scull." Opens Thur. Through June 28. Closed Mons.

JUNE 10, 1983

NEW YORK

Day by Day

A Decision for Mrs. Scull

In the 60's and early 70's, Ethel and Robert Scull, the art collectors, were known as "the mom and pop of Pop," she in her Halstons and Adolfos, he the man behind the fleet of Sculls' Angels taxis.

By the time they separated in 1974, four years before ending the 30-year marriage, they auctioned off millions in Pop and Abstract Expressionist art. A State Supreme Court justice in Manhattan awarded Mrs. Scull alimony of $1,300 a week and six artworks but found the rest of the collection — sold and unsold — to have been Mr. Scull's, bought with his income.

Now an Appellate Division court has accepted Mrs. Scull's claim that the taxi business — a gift from her father — was a joint asset. It also found the collection "a joint effort" ("Curiously enough, defendant admitted he was color-blind," the ruling said.)

Mr. Scull lives on Warren, Conn. property that the court also held to be joint. Raoul L. Felder, Mrs. Scull's lawyer, put its value at $2 million and her share in the collection, present and past, at $10 million.

Mr. Scull's lawyer, Bernard Furman, said yesterday he disagreed with the figures and would take the decision to the Court of Appeals.

June 12, 1983

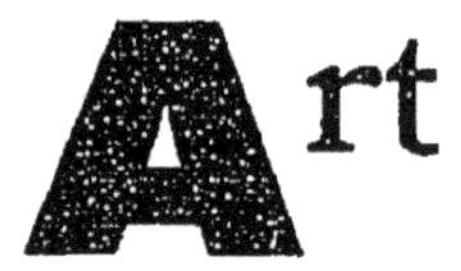

GALLERIES SOHO

Group Shows

PLEIADES, 164 Mercer St. — "Collector's Choice — Selections by Ethel Scull." Through June 28. Closed Mons.

June 19, 1983

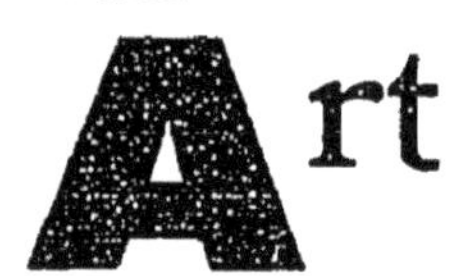

GALLERIES SOHO

Group Shows

PLEIADES, 164 Mercer St. — "Collector's Choice — Selections by Ethel Scull." Through June 28. Closed Mons.

MARCH 7, 1984

At the Whitney, Flowers, Flowers

By RON ALEXANDER

"GIVE them something lovely and they'll turn out," Cynthia Phipps was saying happily on Monday evening as the well-dressed crowd of 250 began arriving for the $1,000-a-plate dinner-dance given by the Whitney Museum of American Art. Indeed, some of the patrons of the Whitney arrived from as far as Lincoln, Neb.

Miss Phipps, the evening's chairman, was wearing a rose-colored Stavropoulous dress — only appropriate since the occasion was a black-tie affair in honor of the museum's recently opened exhibition, "Reflections of Nature: Flowers in American Art." Perhaps the first major museum exhibition devoted to a survey of American flower painting, it will run through May 20.

"Flowers have been considered a rather frivolous subject for art, the lowest of the low," Ella M. Foshay, the exhibition's guest curator, told the guests as they dined on roast loin of veal in the museum's fourth-floor gallery, transformed for the evening into a flower-filled ballroom washed in pastel lights. One purpose of the show, Miss Foshay said, was to rectify "three centuries of cultural bias against flowers."

It was also an opportunity — on Monday night, at least — for women to plant, as Bunty Armstrong, wife of Tom Armstrong, the museum's director, chose to do, geraniums in hairdos or wear, as Lily Auchincloss did, floral-printed gowns. ("I thought it would be too kitchy for me to wear anything with flowers," said Miss Foshay, who settled on an opal butterfly necklace.)

And there was the chance, as the guests sipped wine, nibbled hors d'oeuvres and viewed the 100 or so works of art, for them to vent feelings, pro and con, on the subject of flowers. These ranged from Mary Rockefeller's "I love armfuls of them" to Ethel Scull's "Quick, get me a chair! I think I'm going to faint with all these flowers around. I prefer de Kooning."

In the opinion of Cornelius Vanderbilt Whitney, whose mother, Gertrude Vanderbilt, founded the museum, "Part of having an attractive house is having a lovely garden."

Jerry Zipkin said, "I don't know one from the other but I like it when anyone sends them to me."

"I know absolutely nothing about flowers," Philip Johnson said. "I'm here because I love the museum."

Mario Buatta, the designer-decorator, commented: "For years I was laughed at with all my floral chintz, but now botany has become the trend."

Ann Hudson and Diane Young, both from Fort Worth, were extolling their state flower, the bluebonnet. "We have only corn in Nebraska," complained their companion, June Schorr.

In an informal favorite-flower poll it was the orchid that proved to be the easy winner. "So beautiful, so sinister," Kitty Hawks said.

"So divine!" said Baroness Vittorio de Nora, adjusting the head of her red-on-one-side, black-on-the-other fox fur.

"Women do things in front of orchids that they would do nowhere else," Marjorie Reed said in a voice that turned several heads and spilled at least one glass of champagne.

For Peter Duchin and his orchestra the celebration was a chance to play the likes of "Violets for Your Fur" and "Red Roses for a Blue Lady," although, he confided, "It's really the old show tunes that get them out on the dance floor."

This, after all, was a crowd whose members, young and old alike, shunned red bow ties and trendy wing-collared formal shirts. Nor would they ever have dreamed of exiting with Robert Isabell's dramatic floral centerpieces (a different species on each table).

What it was, said Ruda Dauphin around midnight, was "an enchanting crowd." "At my table there was even a man," she said, referring to John Dobkin, director of the National Academy of Design, "who reads 'The Letters of Madame de Sevigné' on the subway. You just don't meet people like that at an ordinary soiree."

JANUARY 3, 1986

Robert Scull, Prominent Collector of Pop Art

By GRACE GLUECK

Robert C. Scull, the taxi tycoon who assembled a world-famous collection of Pop and Minimal art in the 1960's, died Wednesday night at his home in Warren, Conn., of complications from diabetes. He was 70 years old.

Mr. Scull rose quickly to art-world prominence in the 60's by virtue of the well-publicized zeal with which he and his first wife, the former Ethel Redner, bought works by such upcoming artists as Jasper Johns, Robert Rauschenberg, Andy Warhol and James Rosenquist. They were encouraged by the dealer Leo Castelli and by Richard Bellamy, whose innovative Green Gallery Mr. Scull backed for the five years of its existence.

In 1973, the couple was castigated by some artists and critics for the sale — in an auction that drew $2.2 million — of 50 of those works, which had been acquired at comparatively little cost. The auction broke records for contemporary American art in several categories. At a news conference afterward, the artist Robert Rauschenberg accused Mr. Scull of "infidelity" and the auction house of encouraging "profiteering."

The Sculls' collecting activities began in the field of Abstract Expressionism, and by 1965 they had acquired some 30 works by Willem de Kooning, Barnett Newman, Mark Rothko, Franz Kline and others. Their first auction sale, of a dozen works, was held in 1965. Its purpose was to raise money to encourage unknown artists, and the proceeds went to establish the Robert and Ethel Scull Foundation.

Liked 'Being Involved'

With the foundation's money, Mr. Scull commissioned environmental works from such then-unknown artists as Michael Heizer and Walter de Maria, and also gave artists stipends, bought them food and clothes and paid for their materials. He did it, he said, for the thrill of "being involved." When an interviewer asked about accusations that he bought art for investment and for social climbing, Mr. Scull responded, "It's all true. I'd rather use art to climb than anything else."

Born on Manhattan's Lower East Side to Russian immigrant parents whose name was shortened from Sokolnikoff, Mr. Scull was encouraged in his art interests by his paternal grandfather. A high school dropout during the Depression, he worked at a number of jobs to help support his family, and also took art courses. His up-and-down career as a freelance illustrator and industrial designer came to an end when his wife's father left him a share of a lucrative taxi business. Mr. Scull parlayed his share into the Super Operating Corporation, a fleet of 130 cabs operated by 400 drivers (later known as Scull's Angels). With the same flair for attention-getting that distinguished his art-collecting, at the height of the fleet's prosperity he hired the etiquette expert Amy Vanderbilt to give his drivers lessons in courtesy.

Mr. Scull, who divorced in 1975, sold his taxi business several years ago and moved to a farm in Connecticut. A legal tangle over the artworks the couple collected has still not been settled. Over the years he continued buying art by young contemporaries, and in 1978 he set up the Robert C. Scull Foundation, which gives money to younger artists and to institutions devoted to contemporary art.

Mr. Scull is survived by his second wife, Stephanie, and by three sons, Jonathan, Stephen and Adam. A funeral service will be held today at 1 P.M. at Frank E. Campbell's, 1076 Madison Avenue, at 80th Street.

MAY 2, 1986

Auctions

Key Pop Art Up for Sale.

Rita Reif

JASPER JOHNS'S "Target," a 1961 version in red, yellow and blue of one of the artist's favorite early icons, is the most important of a number of major Pop Art and Abstract Expressionist works going on view today before their sale next week at Christie's and Sotheby's. Mr. Johns's painting of a bull's-eye, from the period when he was also executing images of flags, numbers and alphabets, is expected to sell for $2 million, which would be the highest price ever paid at auction for a work by a living artist.

The painting, which has hung since 1978 at the Art Institute of Chicago, on loan from its owner, who has not been identified, will be auctioned Tuesday at 7 P.M. at Christie's, Park Avenue at 59th Street. The sale of 64 artworks valued at $6.6 million to $7.7 million also includes 21 sculptures — one of the largest of such artworks ever offered at auction. Outstanding among them is David Smith's 1963 welded-steel "Voltri-Bolton XXIII," one of 25 works from this series, which was given by the artist to its owner — Sarah Dora Greenberg, daughter of the art critic Clement Greenberg — when she was 1 year old. Christie's expects the rod-and-disk work, suggesting a person half sitting, half standing, to sell for $1 million.

Commenting on the presale estimate for Mr. Johns's "Target," the art dealer André Emmerich said: "It is a quintessential picture of the period — but $2 million is high. For the time being at least, inflation is over in the art market. Two, three years ago, one expected automatically new records to be set for spectacular artworks. Now I think that this time is largely over."

But Martha Baer, Christie's specialist in post-World War II art, defended the estimate. "It's not difficult to offer and sell an expensive work of art if it's worth it," she said. A commanding work with an Expressionist treatment of its surface in hot wax, oil paint and newsprint, the Johns painting is one of the few targets that the artist did in this large square, 66 inches by 66 inches. In 1973, this target was sold at Sotheby's in a landmark contemporary art auction of the Robert C. Scull collection, and brought $125,000.

•

In 1980, another painting by Mr. Johns, "Three Flags," was sold to the Whitney Museum of American Art for $1 million, a figure then believed to be the highest price ever paid for a work by a living American artist. Since then, that figure has been surpassed a number of times at private and public sales. The auction record for a painting by a living artist is $1.98 million, the price paid for de Kooning's "Two Women" in a 1984 sale at Christie's.

This offering of the Johns "Target" follows Sotheby's sale last November of Mr. Johns's "Painting With Ruler and Gray" for $687,000, the highest price paid at auction for a work by the artist and for a Pop Art work. The painting was a major success in a week of aggressively ambitious contemporary art sales at Christie's and Sotheby's. Buyers were found for only two of eight major works that were expected to sell for $500,000 to $2.5 million apiece. The sales that week raised many questions among collectors and dealers about the heady prices sought for post-World War II art.

Leo Castelli, the dealer who has represented Mr. Johns since the 1950's, said this week that he could not predict what would happen at the Christie's sale with the 1961 target painting, which he said was commissioned by Mr. Scull and completed about five years after Mr. Johns's first major targets.

"There are so many collectors who do not have an important Jasper Johns and they would pay any price for the earlier targets, but I do not know what they would pay for this one," Mr. Castelli said. He reported that the most important of Mr. Johns's current paintings were selling for $600,000 each.

•

Roy Lichtenstein's paintings were chosen for the covers of both Christie's and Sotheby's catalogues and each house is also offering a major sculpture by the artist. At Christie's, Mr. Lichtenstein's "Red Painting," a 1965 work of bold brush strokes in scarlet on a blue-dotted screened background, is expected to sell for up to $700,000. The artist's "Modern Sculpture With Velvet Rope" — brass poles linked by red velvet rope inspired by the barriers in Art Deco movie houses — is expected to sell for up to $250,000.

The auction at Sotheby's, York Avenue at 72d Street, next Monday night at 7 is a smaller sale with 57 works valued at from $4 million to $5 million. Lucy Mitchell-Innes, Sotheby's specialist in contemporary art, said the subdued quality of the sale, both in the type of works offered and the estimates of the prices expected, was intentional. "There are no very high-risk works in this sale as there were last November," she said. The auction includes eight Calders, four Lichtensteins, four Hofmanns and three Rothkos.

Sotheby's catalogue cover shows Mr. Lichtenstein's "TZING," a comic strip war painting depicting a soldier with a gun in bright yellow, with black, white and red accents. This large work, 68 inches high and 56 inches wide, is one of five panels from the "Live Ammo" set, which has been broken up. This one, from the collection of the late Carl Stroher, a West German collector who made a fortune in pharmaceuticals, is expected to bring $400,000 to $500,000.

"Lichtenstein's early comic strip images have achieved $1 million and even higher prices in private sales," said Mr. Castelli, who represents the artist. "The comic strip paintings most in demand are those where a girl appears. Some war pictures also are incredibly high in price."

The artist's 1978 painted-bronze sculpture "Glass V" is a man-sized vessel 70 inches tall, one of only three casts completed of this image. It is expected to sell for up to $300,000.

Miss Mitchell-Innes explained that the inclusion of so many Calders was not arbitrary. "The Calders are all different," she said. Of the four consigned by the Solomon R. Guggenheim Foundation, three are differently shaped hanging mobiles, and one is a standing mobile. An extremely wide shallow mobile, measuring 106 inches by 24 inches, comes from the estate of the actress Anne Baxter, and there is a rare painted-wood mobile from the holdings of the late Henrique E. Mindlin, a Brazilian architect. These range in estimates from $40,000 to $130,000.

SEPTEMBER 9, 1986

Sculls' Art To Be Sold At Auction

By RITA REIF

Pop and Minimal art collected in the 1960's by Ethel Redner Scull and Robert C. Scull, the taxi tycoon, will be auctioned in separate sessions on Nov. 10 and 11, Sotheby's said yesterday. The Sculls were flamboyant in their collecting, buying art in a public way and entertaining lavishly. They amassed one of the first major collections of 1960's art.

The Sculls divorced in 1974 and were in court on and off over the next 11 years over the division of the art they had collected during their 30-year marriage. In March 1985, Mrs. Scull was awarded 35 percent of the Scull artworks by a decision in the Appellate Division of the New York State Supreme Court. The actual division of the art did not take place until after Mr. Scull's death at the age of 70, last Jan. 1. Mrs. Scull has appealed the court's award to her and is asking for 50 percent. Her appeal is to be heard next month. All parties to the auction say they have agreed that these legal moves will not affect the sale.

The nine works Mrs. Scull is selling have been estimated to be worth between $1.9 million and $2.7 million, and the 140 works from the estate of Mr. Scull have been valued at about $4 million.

"We had a meeting in May at the warehouse with Sotheby's, and I won the Johns with a flip of the coin," Ethel Scull said yesterday, referring to the most important of the nine works she was awarded. It is also thought to be the finest work remaining from the Scull collection — Jasper Johns's "Out the Window," from 1959.

Loose, Gestural Style

The highly expressive work painted overall in bold reds, yellows and blues is described by Sotheby's as one of the earliest in which Johns adopted a loose, gestural painting style and extravagant color. It consists of three horizontal panels on which the words "red," "yellow" and "blue" in block letters are partially obscured by the layers of paint. Sotheby's expects the Johns to sell for from $1.25 million to $1.75 million.

The Johns and several other works carry estimates by Sotheby's that, if realized, would establish records for the artists. Of the eight other works consigned by Mrs. Scull, four are by Johns, and the others are by Cy Twombly, Bruce Nauman, Walter de Maria and Robert Morris. Of these, the most historically interesting is Johns's "Construction With a Toy Piano," from 1954, one of the earliest Pop works by the artist. This work, a newspaper collage on canvas applied to the toy piano, is expected to sell for up to $100,000. Johns's "Alphabet," a tightly textured work from 1960-61, is a study of letters in black and grays in oil on paper, mounted on canvas. Sotheby's expects it may bring up to $450,000.

The 40 most important works from Mr. Scull's estate will be sold in a separate evening sale, with the remainder dispersed the following day.

Lucy Mitchell-Innes, Sotheby's spe-

cialist in post World War II art, described Mr. Scull's segment as "as a key group of Pop and Minimalist artworks, most of which were bought straight from the artist in the late 1950's and 1960's and are a direct reflection of his collecting taste."

Outstanding are Johns's "Double Flag," a large work from 1962 that is expected to sell for "in excess of $1.5 million"; James Rosenquist's "F-111" from 1965, the largest art work ever to be offered by Sotheby's — it measures 10 feet high and 85 feet long and is expected to sell for more than $600,000; Andy Warhol's "200 One Dollar Bills," from 1962, which may bring $200,000, and George Segal's 1965 "Portrait of Bob and Ethel Scull," a plaster, wood and cloth work, which may bring up to $120,000.

Henry Geldzahler, former Commissioner of the city's Department of Cultural Affairs and former curator of 20th-century art at the Metropolitan Museum of Art, said yesterday that Robert Scull had been well in advance of others in recognizing the importance of the Pop and Minimal art movements while he was still collecting Abstract Expressionist works. He said that he thought he had developed an eye through his work as the head of an industrial concern.

"I think it was astonishing that Bob Scull, in 1960 and 1961, understood that something new was happening in Pop and Minimal art, with Walter de Maria and Donald Judd and that he was seriously looking at these pieces while also buying works by Rothko and de Kooning," he said. "I was with him, going to studios and sitting in the back of galleries, and saw how he selected these artworks."

Richard Bellamy, who heads the Oil and Steel gallery in Long Island City and was director of the innovative Green Gallery, which Mr. Scull backed in the years it operated from 1960 to 1965, said yesterday that the Scull collection was "certainly not a compendium of contemporary art as many of the bigger collections aimed to be."

"We are seeing a fragment — a very good fragment — that represents a little less than half of a collection that, when seen as a whole, contained a number of masterpieces," Mr. Bellamy said. He said Mr. Scull's early understanding of Walter de Maria and Mark di Suvero before others discovered these artists showed Mr. Scull's "grand sense of adventure."

Ivan Karp, the dealer who heads the O.K. Harris gallery, described Mr. Scull as a collector who "was fierce and resourceful with instinctual judgment." He added: "Mr. Scull bought his first significant contemporary object from me — a John Chamberlain crushed-metal sculpture, when I was at Martha Jackson's gallery in 1958."

Raoul Felder, Mrs. Scull's attorney, said yesterday that the claims his client has made that are pending in court against Mr. Scull's estate would not interfere with the sale or the transfer of the paintings as a result of the auction. He said an agreement was drawn between Mrs. Scull, the estate of Robert Scull and Sotheby's stating that Sotheby's would hold $2 million in escrow to settle any claims that might be in her favor.

Thomas Epstein, attorney for the estate of Mr. Scull, confirmed the agreement yesterday. "It is agreed among all concerned that there will be no interference with the auction," he said. "We have agreed that Sotheby's would withhold a certain amount of money in case she is successful."

The sale promises to establish almost as many records for artists as were achieved at the landmark sale of 50 paintings from the collection of Robert C. Scull held at Sotheby Parke Bernet in Oct. 1973. That sale totaled $2,242,900, an auction record for post-World War II art and new highs were established for Johns, Rosenquist, de Kooning, Kline, Poons and Rauschenberg. Jasper Johns's 1965 "Double White Map" sold for $240,000.

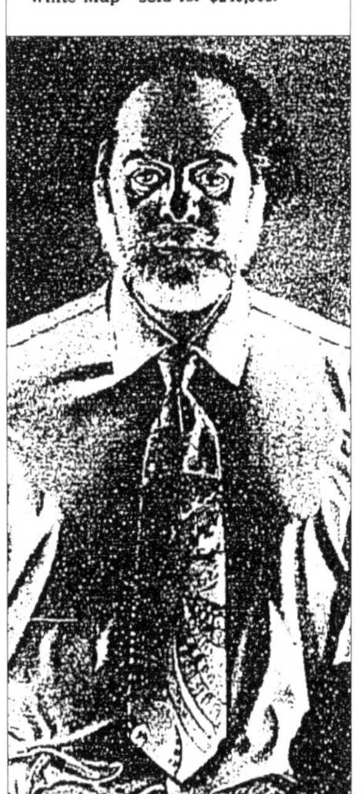

SEPTEMBER 13, 1986

Saturday News Quiz

Linda Amster

Questions are based on news reports in The Times this week.

1. Nipper has a new master. Explain.
2. "I think it is now time to send the Ambassador," said a participant after a meeting that was salvaged by an agreement on Taba. What meeting was it, who made the remark and what is Taba?
3. The race for the United States Senate seat in Maryland is only the second in American history with a distinguishing characteristic. Explain.
4. "Had he brought those charges to me, you can be sure it would not have been an Inspector Clouseau operation." Who made this remark and to what was he referring?
5. Bracelets, hats and a dollar bill with an unsigned note — "I've owed you this for years" — are among the mementos that the Park Service is collecting. What mementos are they?
6. One foreign government released an opposition leader who had been imprisoned for three and a half weeks, and another foreign government said it would free all 225 prisoners being held for their political views and activities. What governments are they?
7. When Ivan Lendl, the men's singles tennis champion, appeared in the United States Open final, it was his (second/fifth/seventh) consecutive appearance in the championship.
8. "This is an incentive for public school students from the inner city to go to college and stay in it," said a business executive. To what city and what incentive was he referring?
9. In the busiest session in New York Stock Exchange history, the Dow Jones industrial average dropped a record 86.61 points, or 4.61 percent. To have equaled the worst plunge in percentage terms, that of Oct. 28, 1929, the average would have had to have fallen about (120/180/240/360) points.
10. "The message beat money," said the winner of a New York State primary race. Who made the remark, to what was he referring, and how did Mayor Koch respond to his victory?
11. What is happening here?
12. On a visit to a foreign country, a prominent American attended a ceremony as scheduled but canceled a meeting. Identify the American, the ceremony and the meeting.
13. "Her mother carried her for nine months, and I am honored to give her part of me." Who made this remark and what were the circumstances?
14. The realignment of top executives at CBS Inc. was also a realignment of allegiances among those involved. Explain.
15. Works from one of the first major collections of Pop and Minimal art, acquired by a taxi tycoon and his wife in the 1960's, are expected to bring record prices at two auctions next month. Identify the collectors.
16. Pritham Singh, a 33-year-old real estate developer, said $17.25 million was a "fair price" for 100 acres of historic property in Florida. What did he buy?
17. Time Inc. seems committed to turning one of its magazines into a profitable late bloomer, as it did with Sports Illustrated, which lost money for 11 years before going into the black. Identify the magazine.
18. Four volumes of what is to be a 12-volume Great Dictionary of the Yiddish Language are devoted to a single letter, aleph, the first letter of the 22-letter Hebrew-based alphabet. Why is it given so much space?

Answers to Quiz

1. The General Electric Company plans to sell 75 percent of its stake in the RCA Corporation's RCA/Ariola record unit to Bertelsmann A. G., a West German concern that owns the remaining 25 percent. The dog has been a symbol on phonograph records since 1901 when the Victor Talking Machine Company was founded.
2. After the first Egyptian-Israeli summit meeting in five years, President Hosni Mubarak announced that Egypt would return its Ambassador to Israel. Taba is a 700-yard stretch of beach on the border between Egypt and Israel
3. It is the second race between two women for a seat in the Senate.
4. Mayor Koch referred of any one of three informers who brought allegations of corruption at the Parking Violations Bureau to the City Department of Investigation in 1982 and 1983, which botched the investigations.
5. Mementos left at the Vietnam Memorial in Washington.
6. Pakistan. Poland.
7. Fifth.
8. Boston. Leading businesses have organized a $6 million program that will guarantee financial aid to all graduates of the city's public high schools who get into college and then provide them with jobs when they finish their education.
9. 240.
10. Mark Green, a consumer advocate and writer, was referring to his victory over John S. Dyson, who spent $6 million on the campaign for the Democratic nomination for the United States Senate. The Mayor said he would not endorse Mr. Green.
11. The statue of Hadrian is being vacuumed for the opening of an upcoming exhibition at the Metropolitan Museum of Art.
12. Coretta Scott King, the civil rights leader, attended the installation of Archbishop Desmond M. Tutu as the first black to lead the Anglican Church in southern Africa and canceled a meeting with President P. W. Botha of South Africa.
13. Senator Jake Garn, a Utah Republican, donated a kidney to his 27-year-old daughter, Susan Horne, a diabetic who had suffered kidney failure.
14. In his tenure as CBS Inc.'s chairman and chief executive officer, Thomas H. Wyman squeezed out William S. Paley, who in 1980 chose him to run the company, and welcomed Lawrence A. Tisch to sit on the board. In the realignment, Mr. Wyman was forced out by Mr. Paley and Mr. Tisch, the respective acting chairman and acting chief executive.
15. Ethel Redner Scull and Robert C. Scull.
16. The 100-acre Truman Annex in Key West, with 19 historic structures, including President Truman's "Little White House."
17. Discover
18. Aleph accounts for almost all the vowel sounds in Yiddish.

NOVEMBER 2, 1986

SOTHEBY'S
FOUNDED 1744

1334 York Avenue at 72nd Street, New York, N.Y. 10021 • (212) 606-7000

EXHIBITIONS TODAY 1-5 pm

Fine English, Continental and Australian Silver
Auction: Wednesday, November 5 at 10:15 am
Exhibition: Today from 1 to 5 pm; November 3 by appointment only; November 4 from 10 am to 3 pm.
Illustrated catalogue $21, sale code SLIGO-5493.
Inquiries: Kevin Tierney and Ian Irving, (212) 606-7160

Fine Old Master Paintings
Auction: Wednesday, November 5 at 2 pm.
Exhibition: Today from 1 to 5 pm; November 3 by appointment only; November 4 from 10 am to 3 pm
Illustrated catalogue $21, sale code MANTUA-5509
Inquiries: George Wachter and Heidi Chin, (212) 606-7230

Important Paperweights
Auction: Thursday, November 6 at 10:15 am.
Exhibition: Today from 1 to 5 pm; November 3 by appointment only; November 4 from 10 am to 5 pm; November 5 from 10 am to 3 pm
Illustrated catalogue $17, sale code MAGNUM-5496.
Inquiries: Debe Cuevas, (212) 606-7180

UPCOMING AUCTIONS

Photographs
Auction: Monday, November 10 at 10:15 am and 2 pm.
Exhibition: Opens November 6 at 10 am.
Illustrated catalogue $20, sale code PARALLAX-5510
Inquiries: Beth Gates-Warren, (212) 606-7240

Contemporary Art, Part I including Property of Mrs. Ethel Redner Scull
Auction: Monday, November 10 at 7 pm
Exhibition: Opens November 6 at 10 am
Illustrated catalogue $25, sale code TARGET-5507
Inquiries: Lucy Mitchell-Innes, (212) 606-7254

Contemporary Art, Part II
Auction: Tuesday, November 11 at 10:15 am
Exhibition: Opens November 6 at 10 am.
Illustrated catalogue $22, sale code OCEAN-5542.
Inquiries: Lucy Mitchell-Innes, (212) 606-7254

Contemporary Art from the Estate of the late Robert C. Scull
Auction: Tuesday, November 11 at 7 pm and Wednesday, November 12 at 10:15 am.
Exhibition: Opens November 6 at 10 am.
Illustrated catalogue $25, sale code SCULL-5540
Inquiries: Lucy Mitchell-Innes, (212) 606-7254

GENERAL INFORMATION

Catalogues: 1-800-255-9898 with credit card. (In Massachusetts, call 1-617-229-2282.)

24-hour auction and exhibition information: (212) 606-7245

NOVEMBER 7, 1986

Auctions

Rita Reif

POSTWAR art acquired in an extremely public way by Ethel Redner Scull and Robert C. Scull, the taxi tycoon, and in a private way by Ted Ashley, vice chairman of Warner Communications, will be auctioned next week at Sotheby's and Christie's.

The sales will present the largest number of major works by Jasper Johns, Roy Lichtenstein, James Rosenquist, Robert Rauschenberg, Andy Warhol, George Segal and Francis Bacon ever offered at auction. The combined value of the Pop, Minimalist and Abstract Expressionist works up for sale at Sotheby's is between $15 million and $19 million for 410 offerings. Christie's will offer 254 works valued at between $5.6 million and $7.4 million.

Virtually all that remains of the Pop and Minimalist art collected by the Sculls will be auctioned in separate sales Monday and Tuesday night at Sotheby's, York Avenue at 72d Street. The nine works Mrs. Scull is selling are expected to bring between $2.25 million and $2.9 million, and the 135 works from the estate of Mr. Scull have been valued at $4.3 million to $5.7 million.

Ethel Scull recently recalled when she and Robert Scull visited the lofts of artists in the early 1960's to acquire their works. She also described the arranging of the paintings and sculptures in their Fifth Avenue apartment, where they gave lavish parties, and the discomfort it caused her to pose for George Segal's white plaster portrait of the couple.

The Sculls were divorced in 1974, and were in court on and off over the next 11 years over the division of the art they had collected during their 30-year marriage. In court testimony, William S. Lieberman, chairman of the department of 20th-century art at the Metropolitan Museum, said: "Bob and Ethel were really a brilliant adornment in the New York art world. They were wealthy. They were also an extremely attractive couple."

The Appellate Division of New York State Supreme Court decided in September 1984 that Mrs. Scull was entitled to some part of the art holdings, an amount later set at 35 percent. Mrs. Scull chose Johns's "Out the Window," the most valuable of this artist's works in the sale, a painting expected to bring as much as $2 million.

She said that although most of the artworks in their home were changed every year or two, "Out the Window" was "never removed." The 1959 painting — a highly expressive work painted overall in bold reds, yellows and blues — is one of the earliest works in which Johns adopted a loose gestural painting style and extravagant color.

"I asked Jasper to do me a favor and paint me a flag and a target," she recalled. The two works that resulted are the target that was sold by Sotheby's in the first Scull sale in 1973 for $125,000, and "Double Flag," which is in the sale of Mr. Scull's estate. The double-flag painting is expected to bring up to $2 million.

"I'm losing the Jasper Johns because I need money to live on," Ethel Scull said. "My devastation comes from the fact that I have to sell these objects."

Segal's portrait of the Sculls, she said, "was done against my own fear of it," because she did not realize that the process required that she be covered head to toe with gauze and plaster. "You can't move your mouth and you can't swallow," she said. "I could breathe but it was panic time for me." Recalling that sitting this week, Mr. Segal said that if he had known of her fear ahead of time, he would never have asked her to pose. "I ended up making the face by hand," he added.

NOVEMBER 7, 1986

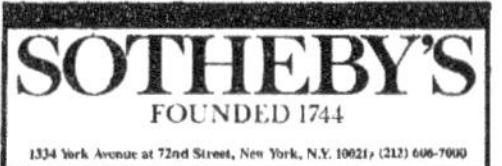

FOUNDED 1744

1334 York Avenue at 72nd Street, New York, N.Y. 10021 • (212) 606-7000

WEEKEND EXHIBITIONS

Photographs
Auction: Monday, November 10 at 10:15 am and 2 pm.
Exhibition: Today and Saturday from 10 am to 5 pm, Sunday from 1 to 5 pm.

Contemporary Art, Part I including Property of Mrs. Ethel Redner Scull
Auction: Monday, November 10 at 7 pm.*
Exhibition: Today and Saturday from 10 am to 5 pm, Sunday from 1 to 5 pm

Contemporary Art, Part II
Auction: Tuesday, November 11 at 10:15 am.
Exhibition: Today and Saturday from 10 am to 5 pm; Sunday from 1 to 5 pm

Contemporary Art from the Estate of the late Robert C. Scull
Auction: Tuesday, November 11 at 7 pm* and Wednesday, November 12 at 10:15 am.
Exhibition: Today and Saturday from 10 am to 5 pm; Sunday from 1 to 5 pm.

*Admission to Evening Sales by ticket only, call (212) 606-7303

Auctioneers: [illegible]

NOVEMBER 9, 1986

SOTHEBY'S
FOUNDED 1744

1334 York Avenue at 72nd Street, New York, N.Y. 10021 • (212) 606-7000

EXHIBITIONS TODAY 1-5 pm

Photographs
Auction: Monday, November 10 at 10:15 am and 2 pm.
Exhibition: Today from 1 to 5 pm.
Inquiries: (212) 606-7240

Contemporary Art, Part I including Property of Mrs. Ethel Redner Scull
Auction: Monday, November 10 at 7 pm*
Exhibition: Today from 1 to 5 pm; November 10 from 10 am to noon
Inquiries: (212) 606-7254

Contemporary Art, Part II
Auction: Tuesday, November 11 at 10:15 am.
Exhibition: Today from 1 to 5 pm; November 10 from 10 am to noon.
Inquiries: (212) 606-7254.

Contemporary Art from the Estate of the late Robert C. Scull
Auction: Tuesday, November 11 at 7 pm* and Wednesday, November 12 at 10:15 am.
Exhibition: Today from 1 to 5 pm; November 10 from 10 am to 5 pm; November 11 from 10 am to noon.
Inquiries: (212) 606-7254.

EXHIBITIONS OPENING AT 10 AM NOVEMBER 13

The John R. Gaines Collection Old Master and Modern Drawings
Auction: Monday, November 17 at 7 pm.*
Inquiries: (212) 606-7154.

Important Tribal Art
Auction: Tuesday, November 18 at 10:15 am and 2 pm.
Inquiries: (212) 606-7325.

Property from the Estate of the late James Johnson Sweeney
Auction: Tuesday, November 18 at 7 pm*
Inquiries: (212) 606-7360

Impressionist and Modern Paintings, Drawings and Sculpture, Part I
Auction: Tuesday, November 18 at 7 pm* following the Sweeney Collection.
Inquiries: (212) 606-7360.

Expressionist Watercolors from the Collection of Charles Tabachnick, Toronto
Auction: Wednesday, November 19 at 10:15 am.
Inquiries: (212) 606-7154

Impressionist and Modern Drawings and Watercolors
Auction: Wednesday, November 19 at 10:15 am, following the sale of Expressionist Watercolors.
Inquiries: (212) 606-7154

Impressionist and Modern Paintings, Drawings and Sculpture, Part II
Auction: Wednesday, November 19 at 2 pm.
Inquiries: (212) 606-7360

GENERAL INFORMATION

*Admission to Evening Sales by ticket only, call (212) 606-7303.

24-hour auction and exhibition information: (212) 606-7245.

Catalogues: 1-800-255-9898 with credit card. (In Massachusetts call 1-617-229-2282.)

NOVEMBER 10, 1986

Agenda Nov. 10, 1986

Arts and Entertainment

Pop Art on the Auction Block Pop and minimal art collected by Ethel Render Scull and Robert C. Scull, the late taxi tycoon, will be auctioned at Sotheby's today and tomorrow. Up for sale are more than 140 works expected to fetch in excess of $7 million, among them Jasper Johns's "Out the Window" and "Double Flag." The Sculls, who amassed one of the first major collections of 60's art, were divorced in 1974 and in and out of court in the next decade dividing their holdings. Mrs. Scull, who is selling nine of her pieces, said, "I need money to live on." *7 P.M., York Avenue at 72d Street, Manhattan*

NOVEMBER 11, 1986

Jasper Johns Painting Brings Record Price

By RITA REIF

Jasper Johns's boldly colored and Expressionistic "Out the Window," from 1959, was sold last night for the highest price ever paid at auction for a work by a living artist and for a *post-World War II painting.*

The spirited bidding on the exuberant work, which combines encaustic (melted wax and pigment) with newspaper collage, sparked applause throughout Sotheby's gallery when the chairman, John L. Marion, brought down his hammer. It was sold for $3.63 million to an unidentified buyer who bid over the telephone.

"I'm exhausted. Emotionally exhausted," Ethel Redner Scull said after the sale of her painting — the favorite, she said, of the nine works she had consigned to the sale. "It is wonderful that it brought a record price, but I am devastated at losing it."

Lucy Mitchell-Innes, Sotheby's specialist in postwar art, said she was not surprised by the price. "There is an awareness amongst collectors of contemporary art that the great masterpieces in this field are few and far between," she said.

The previous record for a living artist and for postwar art was $1.98 million paid in November 1984 for Willem de Kooning's "Two Women."

Artist Was Unexcited

Leo Castelli, the dealer who sold the painting to Mrs. Scull and Robert C. Scull in February 1960, spoke to Mr. Johns after the sale. "He was not terribly excited about the extraordinary price," Mr. Castelli reported later. "He was, however, very happy that Christian Gelhaar, director of the Basel Kunst Museum. had acquired his 'Toy Piano.' " The construction was sold for $176,000, well above the $100,000 that Sotheby's had expected.

When the gaveling was finished, the sale also had set a record for a single session of postwar art, with the total of *$13.2 million eclipsing the $12 million* total at a Sotheby's auction in May 1985.

The evening seemed as spirited and spiced with controversy as was the 1973 Scull sale, a landmark event that set several records for artists. Last night, also, the artist Robert Rauschenberg was a controversial figure. In a news conference after the first sale, he had accused Mr. Scull of disloyalty and the auction house of encouraging "profiteering"; this time Mr. Rauschenberg was not present, but Theodore Kheel, his lawyer, repeated his protest against the wording used to describe four of the five Rauschenberg paintings that were consigned by Frederick R. Weisman, a *Los Angeles* businessman and collector.

No Floor Prices

These paintings were part of a two-year-old dispute between Mr. Weisman and the artist that flared anew last week when it was discovered that Mr. Weisman had consigned the works without the protection of floor prices, known as reserves. All four paintings were sold, at prices between $49,500 and $88,000.

Mr. Marion announced before the bidding that there was a dispute between the two parties about the purchase price, and said that the auction house would take no position.

An untitled Rauschenberg painting from 1963 was sold for $137,500, despite an announcement by Mr. Marion that its ownership was being argued. The painting, Miss Mitchell-Inness reported later, had been owned by the J. B. Speed Museum in Louisville, Ky., in the early 1960's, and was lost while on a tour. The painting, recently recovered, was consigned by the Aetna Insurance Company, which had paid the insurance claim after its disappearance.

Other Records Set

Works by several other artists set records last night. Ellsworth Kelly's "Block Island," from 1959, was bought for $242,000, almost double the artist's previous record at auction, by a Canadian collector whose name was not disclosed. Larry Rivers' "Dying and Dead Veteran," from 1961, also doubled the artist's previous record, when it went for $126,500 to an American collector who also was not identified.

"Whew," Mr. Rivers said about the price in a telephone conversation after the sale. "I had done a lot of these veterans' paintings, and this was the last of the series."

An untitled Bruce Nauman rope-and-beeswax construction depicting folded arms was bought by Thomas Ammann, a Zurich dealer, for $220,000 — 10 times the house's expectations — in one of the most exciting contests of the evening. It, too, was a record for the artist.

NOVEMBER 12, 1986

Rosenquist Painting Sells for Record Price

By RITA REIF

James Rosenquist's "F-111" painting — the largest artwork ever auctioned — was sold last night for almost 100 times the price paid to the artist when it was acquired in 1965 by the Robert C. Sculls. The painting, one of 44 artworks auctioned from the Scull collection, was among nine that established records at auction for artists in a sale that brought the highest total for a single-owner collection of post-World War II art.

Mr. Rosenquist was in the room last night for the sale of his painting, which was sold for $2,090,000, and recalled later that he had been paid $22,500 for the work. Jeffrey Deitsch of Citibank, who made the winning bid on the enormous painting — it measures 10 feet high and 85 feet long — would not reveal for whom he was bidding. Thomas Armstrong, director of the Whitney Museum of American Art, a disappointed underbidder, lowered his paddle after his bid of $1.1 million was exceeded.

The auction dispersed all that remains of the Pop and Minimalist art collected by the Sculls in the 1960's and 1970's before they were divorced in 1974. Mr. Scull died at the age of 70 last January. The first sale of their collection in 1973 dispersed 50 paintings from their collection for a total of $2.2 million, then a record sale for post-World War II art. Last night, the 42 works out of 44 that sold brought a total of $7.9 million, double the figure of any other single-owner auction of Contemporary art.

Drawing Brings High Price

For the second night in a row, a single painting from the Scull collection sold for almost as much as the entire collection did in 1973. On Monday night, Jasper Johns's "Out the Window," from Ethel Redner Scull's collection, sold for $3.63 million, a record for postwar art and for a work by a living artist.

"It's not the age of Aquarius — it's the age of Jasper Johns," said Allan Stone after Jasper Johns's drawing of "O through 9" from 1961 was sold for $880,000, the highest price for a drawing by the artist or any postwar drawing. The buyer was not identified. Mr. Johns's "Double Flag," from 1962, sold for $1,760,000 to an American collector who was not identified.

The buyers' names were not disclosed on the other major purchases, all of which were auction records for works by the artists: George Segal's "Portrait of Ethel and Bob," from 1965, was sold for $154,000 to a Japanese buyer; Walter de Maria's "Candle Piece" went for $49,500; Mark di Suvero's 1959 construction of weathered timber rope and nails "I Have Lost My Eurydice," brought $319,000, and Neil Jenney's "Row and Row," an acrylic on canvas from 1968, was sold for $143,000.

"I think we are going to tell our grandchildren about the night that 'F-111' was sold," said Richard Feigen, the dealer, who was sitting with Mr. Rosenquist at the sale. "It's a major icon of the postwar period. It's the one political painting he has done — this ill-destined plane that hadn't even flown at that point. It has had a tremendous effect on many artists."

Mixed Emotions

Mr. Rosenquist said he had mixed emotions about the sale. "I'm very, very excited," he said. "I'm very, very happy." He was nostalgic, too, he said. "I remember the Scull apartment at 1010 Fifth Avenue. I remember their house in Great Neck, with all the Klines, Rothkos, Poons, Segals there." He said that when he visited Mrs. Scull recently, her walls were empty. "I really felt a sense of loss of place. It was fun and an exciting time when all my friends were hanging in one place," he said.

Ben Heller, the art dealer, who had purchased Mr. Johns's "Double White Map" from 1965 at the first Scull sale for $240,000, then the record for the artist or any work by a living American artist, said last night, "This is not as much of a show — it is more of an event."

John L. Marion, Sotheby's chairman, who was the auctioneer at all three sales of the Scull collection said: "There was the same electricity as in 1973," he said. "This is really the supreme coming of age of contemporary art at auction. It confirms everything that happened in that first Scull sale."

NOVEMBER 13, 1986

'78 Work By Bacon Is Sold

By RITA REIF

Francis Bacon's "Seated Figure," a 1978 painting showing two men — one crouching, one in profile in suit and tie against a gloriously colored background — was sold last night at Christie's for the highest price at auction ever achieved for a work by the British artist.

The painting, one of the artist's favorites, was the most important of 10 works from the 20th-century art collection of Ted Ashley, the 64-year-old Warner Communications executive. It was purchased by a collector who was not identified for $935,000, almost double the previous record at auction for the artist, which was $517,000, the price paid in 1985 at Sotheby's for "Landscape Near Malabata, Tangiers."

Pop Art Works

Bidding was brisk on the Bacon and on two record-breaking Pop Art works consigned by Mr. Ashley, who is selling, according to Martha Baer, Christie's specialist in postwar art, because he "is going on to a different phase in his personal life." Roy Lichtenstein's "Blang" from 1962 was sold for $792,000 to Thomas Ammann, a Zurich dealer, eclipsing the previous record of $522,500 paid for "Reclining Nude," in May 1985 at Sotheby's. And Claes Oldenburg's "Girls' Dresses Blowing in the Wind," from 1961, was purchased by a New York dealer who was not identified for $203,500, blotting out the previous high of $181,500 paid for the artist's "Typewriter Eraser," in 1984 at Sotheby's.

The sale was the third of postwar art this week that established more than a score of records for artists, and all of the sales featured major Pop Art works. The two paintings by Andy Warhol that were auctioned last night, for example, brought extremely high prices. "Campbell's Soup Can With Can Opener" was purchased for $264,000 by James Mayor, the London dealer, and the "Triple Elvis" was sold for $203,500. Neither rewrote the record at auction for this artist, which was established Tuesday night at the Robert C. Scull sale at Sotheby's when "200 One Dollar Bills," sold for $385,000. But both prices exceeded the artist's previous record of $165,000, which was paid for "S & H Green Stamps" at Sotheby's in 1985.

Seller Is 'Thrilled'

The bidding was brisk but less spirited throughout than at Sotheby's on Monday and Tuesday, when what remained of the Pop and Minimalist works collected by Ethel Redner Scull and Robert C. Scull were auctioned. Nevertheless, Christie's auction of 60 works, in which 8 did not find buyers, totaled $8.6 million — the highest total for a sale of contemporary art at this gallery. Mr. Ashley's 10 paintings totaled $4.4 million.

Mr. Ashley, who assembled his art collection quietly over 20 years and had not granted interviews before the sale, attended the auction unnoticed.

"He was at the sale, slid away quietly and sent word back that he was thrilled," said Christopher Burge, Christie's president. Mr. Burge said the evening was a success on several levels.

"We had this steady succession of pictures — selling for prices of $300,000 to $900,000 — that two or three years ago would have shocked the world if they had brought $200,000.

Abstract Expressionist works also registered new highs. Sam Francis's "Summer No. 1" from 1957 sold for a record $825,000 to a Chicago dealer who also bought Mark Rothko's "Light Earth and Blue" from 1954 for $660,000 and Franz Kline's "Wax Wing," from 1961, for $352,000. The same Chicago buyer purchased Julian Schnabel's "Tower of Babel (for A. A.)" from 1976-78 for $121,000, a record for the artist.

For the second time in two days the record for Pierre Soulages was rewritten. On Tuesday his "27 August 61," was sold for $58,300, and last night "13 August 1959" was sold for $90,200 to a European collector who was bidding over the telephone and was not identified.

Sotheby's sales over the two and a half days totaled $24.6 million and included a record single session auction of postwar art (the Monday night session, which totaled $13.2 million), and a record single-owner sale of such art (the $8.6 million from the Robert C. Scull sale Tuesday night). In these dispersals there were 18 records for artists, including the $3.6 million paid for Jasper Johns's "Out the Window," the highest price ever paid for a postwar work of art or for a work by a living artist.

NOVEMBER 16, 1986

Sellers and Buyers Prepare for a Bonanza of Artworks in Week's Auctions

By RITA REIF

ARTWORKS valued at more than $110 million — the largest offering of art ever staged anywhere — will be auctioned this week. Buyers and sellers — spurred by changes in the tax laws that take effect Jan. 1 and lured by opportunities in a booming art market — are expected to help set new records in a series of sales at Sotheby's and Christie's, starting tomorrow night.

The works to be auctioned — which are on view today — range from Old-Master drawings and tribal works to Impressionist and modern paintings and sculpture. Much of the art comes from well-known estates and collections, including those of the art historian and museum director James Johnson Sweeney, the film director Otto Preminger, the Kentucky horse-breeder John Ryan Gaines, and the Texas oilman Jack Frost.

Leonardo da Vinci's drawing "Child With a Lamb" — one of the very few drawings by the artist in private hands — will be auctioned at Sotheby's tomorrow night in the opening sale of a week-long marathon of bidding. Sotheby's expects the pen-and-brown-ink sketch to bring as much as $3 million out of the $12 million to $16 million expected from the sale of the Gaines collection. Mr. Gaines is a director of the National Gallery of Art in Washington and owner of Gainesway Farm in Lexington, Ky.

The forthcoming auctions follow a week of record-breaking sales at Sotheby's and Christie's that included the dispersals of the postwar art collections of Ethel Redner Scull and Robert C. Scull and of Ted Ashley, vice chairman of Warner Communications. These sales totaled an unprecedented $35 million and established 29 records at auction for the works of Pop, Minimalist and Abstract Expressionist artists. The most important work was Jasper Johns's "Out the Window," which was sold at Sotheby's last Monday for $3.6 million.

'Capital Gains'

Richard Feigen, an art dealer, gave his analysis of the current art market after the Robert C. Scull sale Tuesday night at Sotheby's — a sale that realized more than $8 million.

"A lot of it is capital gains," he said. "There wasn't one player in this postwar art field who wasn't in the room. You've got mega-billions running loose in the streets. The money is out there. They are throwing money at art. You had fellows in that room who have made vast fortunes. These fortunes are not going to be gone tomorrow. And next week it's a whole different cast of characters — all of whom will be just as determined to buy art."

The increase in the capital gains tax, which rises to 28 percent from 20 percent on Jan. 1, has prompted a number of collectors to sell their art now. Others are selling because of the soaring art market and an economy that has greatly increased the financial assets of many art collectors, according to investment bankers, stockbrokers and art dealers.

Sotheby's expects this week's sales to total as much as $76.5 million, and Christie's, up to $34.7 million.

John L. Marion, Sotheby's chairman and president in the United States, attributed the booming art sales to the strong art market, consignments of major estates, and changes in the tax law.

"The new tax law has encouraged owners to sell somewhat earlier than they might have," Mr. Marion said. "On the other side of the ledger, people think they are going to have more money because of the lower tax rates, and they are spending it more freely."

Christopher Burge, Christie's president, agrees. "People are keen to sell before the new tax laws come into effect," he said. "On the other hand, they recognize the importance of taking advantage of a booming art market. What we are seeing is the incredible buoyancy of the art market. It is not the larger number of lots and its not the highest quality of all time."

For Jeffrey Deitsch, a Citicorp vice president who is the bank's specialist in 20th-century art, the economy is not the only factor. "The supply of great works of art is really diminishing. Now, just as we see in the securities market and the currency markets, we see the globalization of the art market — everyone going after the rarities wherever they appear."

Richard Jenrette, chairman of Donaldson Lufkin Jenrette, stock brokers, said, "There really have been a tremendous number of people who have crossed the million-dollar threshold in the last few years. Maybe they think its a good investment — it's the one pleasurable thing you can do that you think is a good investment."

Robert S. Salomon Jr., managing director of Salomon Brothers, said, "It's not so much a booming economy as a boom in financial assets. We have added over a trillion dollars to the value of stocks. That enormous increase in wealth finds its way into various forms. Collecting represents a form of conspicuous consumption, and I think that's what is influencing the high-quality art market."

Two major sales at Sotheby's will offer modern and tribal works collected by James Johnson Sweeney, the art historian and museum director who headed the Solomon R. Guggenheim Museum in the 1950's and earlier was a major figure at the Museum of Modern Art. Mr. Sweeney died in April. The seven works up for bidding Tuesday night, which are expected to total between $5.4 million and $7.6 million, include paintings by Miró, Léger, Mondrian and Gris.

The most important is Mondrian's "Composition in a Square with a Red Corner" — one of 16 known diamond-shaped works by the artist and one of two in private hands. It was purchased by Mr. Sweeney from Mondrian at his studio in 1936. The black, white and red oil on canvas is expected to bring up to $3 million. Other major paintings from Mr. Sweeney's collection include Gris's "Hot Water Jug and Bowl," a cubist still life from 1916; Miró's surrealist "Woman in the Night" from 1945; and Léger's "Composition No. 1" from 1925, a large oil-on-canvas study of everyday objects, painted with great precision.

Mr. Sweeney's tribal works include a robustly carved Fang squatting figure from Southern Cameroon and a New Guinea turtleshell mask, the face in a triangular shape with a hooked nose and pierced ears.

The prize of the tribal art sale is a Hawaiian Islands sculpture consigned by the Roger Williams Park Museum of Providence, R.I. It is a powerful crouching figure, its head blackened, with red lips and large unseeing eyes of mother-of-pearl. The carving is expected to bring $250,000 to $300,000.

Mr. Gaines, whose father, Clarence, founded the Gaines dog food company, regards as one of his favorite drawings Rembrandt's "Landscape With Inn" from 1650, one of four by the artist in the collection. The pen-and-ink study shows the same house from two angles on two sides of the sheet. Van Gogh's "Head of a Peasant Woman," from 1884-85, is a compelling work that seems many times its 3-by-5-inch size. The collection includes drawings by Dürer, Turner, Degas, Van Gogh, Matisse and Picasso.

The sales at Christie's feature major works from the estate of Otto Preminger, who died in April, that are expected to sell for between $1.3 million and $1.65 million. The two most important works are Miró's "Composition" from 1953, a powerful painting 8 feet long by 5½ feet wide of fuzzy squares and circles — his root celestial images — that may sell for up to $900,000, and Henry Moore's 5-foot-tall bronze "Woman" from 1957. Christie's thinks the Moore may sell for up to $600,000.

Ted Ashley's collection includes modern paintings by Léger, Gris and Miró and sculpture by Brancusi, Matisse and Degas. Brancusi's "Muse," one of two plasters of this subject that Walt Kuhn purchased from the artist, is being sold with documentation stating that it was in the landmark 1913 Armory show in New York. It may sell for up to $900,000. There are impressive pedigrees on other works in this collection. Matisse's "Seated Woman Against Black Background," a bronze from 1907, once belonged to Nelson Rockefeller, and Juan Gris's "Book and Glasses," from 1914, was in the collection of Gertrude Stein.

Also up for bidding at Christie's will be Picasso's "Head of a Jester," from the Hirshhorn Museum and Sculpture Garden. This is a duplicate cast, originally thought to be from the 1950's, that has been re-examined since it was withdrawn in May from a Christie's auction; it is now identified as a cast completed prior to 1939 and is expected to sell for twice the original estimate, up to $150,000.

Artworks are not the only things that have been registering record prices. In the past month, buyers have paid more than $1 million at auction for several antiques and for jewelry. A Louis XVI secretary was sold for $2 million; an 18th-century gold box brought $1.1 million, and a Philadelphia wing chair was purchased for $1.1 million.

The rush to sell and buy is not confined to New York. Rembrandt's "Portrait of a Young Girl Wearing a Gold-Trimmed Cloak," from 1632, will be sold in London on Dec. 10. Its American owners were notified in September by the Rembrandt Research Project that its authenticity had been reaffirmed, "It's being sold now for tax reasons — we wanted to have a 1986 transaction," said Jonathan Phillips of the Fiduciary Trust Company of Boston, who represents the owners, who are the heirs of Robert Treat Paine 2d and Richard Cushing Paine of Boston.

And, at Robert W. Skinner in Bolton, Mass., on Nov. 1, a rooster-embellished stoneware butter churn — without its stick and missing its top — sold for an unprecedented $31,900, a record for a butter churn.

Will all the art purchased now retain its value? Michel David-Weill, senior partner of the investment banking firm Lazard Freres, is not sure. "Whether we like it or not," he said, "the phenomenon of fashion is phenomenally great."

The sales of major Impressionist and modern art will take place at Sotheby's on Tuesday at 7 P.M. and at Christie's on Wednesday, also at 7. Lesser works will be auctioned at Sotheby's on Wednesday at 10:15 A.M. and 2 P.M. and at Christie's on Thursday at 10:30 A.M. and 2 P.M. Tribal works will be sold at Sotheby's on Tuesday at 10:15 A.M. and 2 P.M.

NOVEMBER 18, 1986

Leonardo's 'Child With a Lamb' Sells for Record

By RITA REIF

Leonardo da Vinci's "Child With a Lamb," one of very few works by the artist in private hands, was sold last night for a record at auction for an artwork by the artist, and the highest auction price in America for an Old Master drawing.

Leonardo's pen and brown-ink drawing — three sketches of a child hugging a lamb fill one side of the 5-by-8-inch piece of paper, with the head of an old man, some machinery and mirror writing on the other side — dates from 1500-1506. It brought $3.6 million and was the most important work in the record-breaking sale of Rembrandt-through-Redon drawings at Sotheby's from the collection of John Ryan Gaines, a director of the National Gallery of Art in Washington.

Adrian Ward Jackson, the London dealer, was the buyer, bidding for the J. Paul Getty Museum in Malibu, Calif.

The sale of 46 drawings totaled $21.28 million, well above Sotheby's most optimistic expectations of $16 million, and also established new highs for the drawings of 25 other artists.

"I feel very appreciative, I feel very joyful and I feel very humble," Mr. Gaines said after John L. Marion, Sotheby's chairman, brought down the hammer on Matisse's "Dance," from 1939, which sold for $935,000, a record price for a drawing by the artist. "I am really so thrilled that my approach to collecting has been affirmed in this way."

Coincidentally, the Leonardo brought the same price as Jasper Johns's "Out the Window," a 1959 painting owned by Ethel Redner Scull that measured 54 by 40 inches and had sold exactly a week ago in the same room.

"I don't think you can compare them," Mr. Marion said. "What this sale means is that Mr. Gaines bought great quality drawings very recently and their values held tonight."

Mr. Gaines, a horse breeder, owns Gainesway Farms in Lexington, Ky., and is the son of Clarence Gaines, who founded the Gaines dog-food company. He collected these drawings since 1972. The sale attracted buyers, dealers and collectors from Europe, Japan and throughout the United States.

Outstanding among the other Old Master drawings were Rembrandt's "View of Houtewaal," a two-sided drawing from 1650 that was sold for $957,000 to Stanley Moss, a New york dealer who was bidding for the Ian Woodner Family Collection. It was a record for a drawing by the artist. Watteau's "Three Studies of the Head of a Young Girl," from about 1716, was sold for the record $852,500 to Andrea de Socebran, an art agent.

"The Redon I bought was a bargain, but the Rembrandt was full price," Ian Woodner, the 83-year-old New York architect, builder and art collector, said after he had acquired these two works. He paid $82,500 for Redon's drawing of a man's skull and also bought two red-chalk drawings from 1515 by Raphael for $605,000.

Armand Hammer was seated directly in front of Mr. Marion and bid successfully for Dürer's "Satyr's Family," from 1505, which sold for $440,000, and Veronese's "Studies for a Judith and Holfernes," from 1582, which he purchased for $440,000.

"I was the underbidder on several other drawings, but some of the prices in this sale were too high for me," said Mr. Hammer, the California oil industrialist. He added that he had purchased the Dürer and the Veronese to present to the National Gallery.

Frederick D. Hill of Berry-Hill Galleries purchased Mr. Gaines favorite drawing, Rembrandt's "An Inn Beside a Road," from 1653, for $506,000. "It's a very special piece," Mr. Hill said of the landscape study.

NOVEMBER 23, 1986

Can Artists Control the Work They've Sold?

THE art collectors Ethel Redner Scull and Robert C. Scull bought Jasper Johns's painting "Out the Window" in 1960 for $2,250. Two weeks ago, Mrs. Scull sold it at auction for $3.63 million, the highest amount ever paid for a work by a living artist.

In Lower Manhattan, no one knows what to do with "Tilted Arc," the 120-foot-long steel sculpture in Federal Plaza that was ordered removed after thousands of people signed a petition against it. The sculptor, Richard Serra, has said that relocating the work would destroy its integrity.

The cases are different, but some artists would argue that they point to the same principle: a right to control and benefit from one's artistic creation after it has become the property of someone else.

Last week, Senator Edward M. Kennedy, Democrat of Massachusetts, held a hearing in Manhattan on a bill he is sponsoring that would establish such a right. The legislation calls for artists to share in the proceeds when a work is sold for more than $500 and for more than 140 percent of the price paid by the seller. The bill would also give artists the right to sue the owners of artwork that was destroyed or altered in any way. Following are excerpts from the hearing and other comments on the proposed law.

Art Is Not Just Property

Recently, I was at a social gathering talking to a group of lawyers from a distinguished New York law firm. The topic of art and the law came up, and I told of a case concerning a painting that had won a prize in an exhibition. The owner, as well as the painter, claimed the prize money.

I then asked who should have received it. The lawyers unanimously opted for the owner. After all, the picture was his property. Even after I pointed out that the prize was being awarded for the creation of the work, not its purchase, a few of the lawyers held out for the collector.

It is high time Federal law acknowledged that a work of art is not just a piece of property like a chair or a table to do with as its owner would. At least it ought to possess the status of a dog or a cat. We have laws prohibiting cruelty to animals. We ought to have laws prohibiting cruelty to works of art.

An artist has a residual interest, a residual right, in his or her work of art.

Irving Sandler, professor of art history, State University of New York at Purchase.

Protecting Artists — And Owners

Although artists should participate in the appreciation of their work, the same as rock stars, writers and inventors, the implementation of this bill is totally different from those situations. Most of the other creative "products" are mass-marketed, whereas in the case of art we are dealing with a specific seller and buyer.

If I wish to have a collection of pornography in my home, I can buy this without registering my purchases with the Government for tax or royalty purposes. It remains my private affair.

If the law requires registration of a work with a Government agency, then in fact it is a very different situation than royalties paid on mass market selling.

It is one thing to require a recording of a sale of an artwork to the I.R.S. for tax purposes, and quite another to make public the name of sellers of artworks through procedures established to monitor artists' royalties. We have to protect both the artist and the owner of the artwork.

Title should not be unduly encumbered. If a proper balance between a fair profit participation for artists, and privacy and simplicity of ownership and enjoyment of collectors is not struck, then the sale of art of living artists, particularly unknown artists, will suffer.

Ronald Feldman, art dealer.

In Duplication, Degradation

This bill recognizes that the issue of moral rights is a national concern, not one to be addressed state by state, as it is now.

When artists' rights in this regard have been ignored, very often it has been due to naïveté and ignorance. After the unethical aspect is pointed out, understanding and acceptance follows. This amendment will help to educate the naïve.

I did a major commission for the Xerox Corporation headquarters in Rochester. A few years later my daughter who was going to school at the Rochester Institute of Technology discovered a student copying the sculpture in small scale. When questioned about it, he said he was asked to make an award for the Xerox Corporation.

She referred this to me and I referred it to my dealer . . . who wrote a letter to the president of Xerox. In two days the president called the gallery and said that he was sorry, that he was not aware that it was unethical and he would cease and desist . . . .

In this day of great technical development, almost anything can be duplicated, enlarged, diminished in any quantity in almost any material and thereby degraded.

I know of sculpture that has been repainted, revised, relocated, rebuilt and reproduced without permission from nor consultation with the artists concerned.

These, along with neglect, come under the category of mutilation: physical, aesthetic and moral.

Roy Gussow, sculptor and president of New York Artists Association.

For the Creative, Minimalist Wages

The 1965 legislation creating the National Endowment for the Arts stated that ". . . It is necessary and appropriate for the Federal Government to help create and sustain not only a climate encouraging freedom of thought, imagination and inquiry, but also the material conditions facilitating the release of this creative talent."

Despite this statement of intent, the N.E.A. has reported that the real earnings of artists declined by 37 percent during the 1970's and that the median annual earnings in 1979 of visual artists who are painters, sculptors, craft artists and printmakers was $8,576. All signs indicate that these dire circumstances persist in the 1980's.

The United States cannot tolerate a situation where some of its most creative members live on the fringes of society, in poverty or near poverty, with little acceptance or recognition. . . .

The visual rights amendment says to our visual artists that our society recognizes their value and importance, appreciates and wants to protect their unique relationship to their work and acknowledges that they should participate in the increasing value of their creations.

Jack Golodner, Director, Department for Professional Employees, A.F.L.-C.I.O.

A Chilling Effect On the Buyer

Very few paintings, if you take all paintings done in America, are ever again sold the second time for as much as they are sold the first time. Young artists by definition are experimental — it's always a gamble.

If you go back to The New York Times or to the art magazines of the 1950's and early 1960's and see who are the artists who are written about, that the famous galleries showed and embraced, how many of them are still remembered? Some, of course, but many, many are forgotten, including mine.

Normally, when an artist does become famous and his prices go up, his new work, too, becomes very expensive. Once in a blue moon, you get an artist whose early work is valued and his new work not at all. But it's very rare.

On the other hand, to make such a law, as they did in California, and set up the machinery to enforce it is so expensive and so cumbersome. And to whom are you going to give the money? To the rich artist? That's somewhat silly. At the price of discouraging the buying of art? After all, if you buy a young, unknown artist's work for very little money, you're taking a gamble, too. It's the artists who set the price.

I think it's a good thing to encourage the buying of art, especially American art by young artists. This kind of law would be a serious discouragement.

André Emmerich, art dealer.

DECEMBER 7, 1986

Home Design

The Celebrity Cult

BY CAROL VOGEL

THE ADAGE THAT THERE IS NO place like home is truer today than ever. Your home, along with everyone else's. Indeed, the subject of home design is no longer simply a casual topic of conversation; now, it has become something of a spectator sport. As the number of books and magazines devoted to interiors, architecture, gardening and the decorative arts has increased in recent years, people are transfixed by page after page of luscious photographs, enjoying the fun of seeing how others live.

Voyeurism to be sure, but voyeurism of a harmless sort. And one that has resulted in the meteoric rise of the architect and designer. Mark Hampton and his wife, Duane, are regularly featured in society columns. The flower designer Marlo Phillips has been the subject of magazine articles. The decorator Mario Buatta thinks nothing of being asked for his autograph by admireres who have bought the chintz he designed, seen him on television or heard his lectures.

All of this is quite a change from the old days, when decorators were mere tradesmen who visited clients' houses through the back door and architects were considered discreet members of a "gentleman's profession." Now, personalities bordering on stardom, their fame is often earned for something other than their designs. The architect Robert A.M. Stern, for instance, is better known for his performance as the narrator of an eight-part television series that aired on PBS stations across the country last spring than he is for his houses. And, after public appearances, the architect Michael Graves has recieved marriage proposals in the mail, complete with pictures from the hopeful candidates. In fact, when controversy struck over Graves's proposed addition for the Whitney Museum of American Art, it only helped to sell the teakettle that he had designed. While local groups were meeting to ponder the new plan, across the street from the museum, D.F. Sanders, the housewares store, was selling the $80 teakettle faster than it could keep it in stock. So was Bloomingdale's, which reports that people were so eager to get a piece of the action that they began stealing the little red bird from the spout. Alessi, the manufactuer, has sold over 80,000 so far.

Design labels, as in fashion, now seem to mean everything. Not simply the label attached to objects such as teakettles, dishes or sheets, but the one that comes with an architect's or designer's special look. Label mania is penetrating auctions as well. Just last month, French furniture and decorative objects from the estate of the late tin magnate Antenor Patino sold for over $8 million. The cachet of owning an object with a famous provenance helped to escalate prices well beyond the estimates. The same was true of the contemporary art belonging to Ethel Redner Scull, which was sold at another Sotheby's auction. This one made record prices for works by Jasper Johns and Larry Rivers.

Paying high prices for furniture and art is surely a reflection of an increasingly materialistic age. But, thankfully, people aren't just interested in buying. They are also interested in learning. After all, becoming knowledgeable means investing wisely. As a result, each week, museums, auction houses and cultural centers offer lectures to standing-room-only crowds. The number of people visiting auction rooms — as they would museums — has grown, too. Last year, for example, over 200,000 people went to view exhibits at Sotheby's. Museums are also feeling the enthusiasm for design and the decorative arts. The Metropolitan Museum of Art, for example, has held several major design shows in the last two years, something it had not done since the 1930's. Moreover, the museum's expansion plans include more space for the decorative arts. Under construction are two new galleries devoted to Louis XIV, and at the Lila Acheson Wallace Wing for 20th century art, which is scheduled to open to the public in February, there will be a full-time curator concentrating only on decorative objects.

For both museums and collectors, design fever is very much a function of necessity, although for different reasons. In the museum world, the decorative arts are still a growth area, at a time when the availability of fine art is diminishing. On the home front, while Americans have traditionally been a people who believe in moving on — the rocking chair was the symbol of Western expansion — real-estate prices are such that, for many people, staying put and channeling money into fixing up existing houses or apartments is an economic reality. In the process, homeowners are becoming far more educated, recognizing for the first time the value of pieces stashed in attics or basements and assessing purchases they have already made.

The result is that people are just beginning to learn to live with less, realizing the value of saving up for quality pieces rather than buying objects just to fill a room. In turn, the home-furnishings market will steadily sell name items to customers who begin to understand that the architect's or designer's teakettle of today will surely become tomorrow's collectible. And as their recognition grows, these talented design personalities will be pressured to produce exceptional goods for a much tougher and more savvy clientele. ■

DECEMBER 19, 1986

The **Evening** Hours

By NADINE BROZAN

WHAT does it feel like to wear a gown of foam rubber? Or one of metallic plastic overlaid with polyethylene? Wonderful, said the guests at the New York Art Theatre Institute's "Gods and Goddesses Ball" at the organization's loft.

As Ethel Scull, dressed in pristine white foam rubber to represent Mnemosyne, the goddess of memory, put it, "It makes me feel just like a cloud." Christophe de Menil was in green foam as Tethys, wife of the sea god Oceanus, and Karen Crumley was in black, red and floral plastic symbolizing Persephone, goddess of fertility and queen of the underworld. The fact that Ms. Crumley's ensemble resembled a shepherdess's dress was readily explained by Vanessa James, the company's costume and scenic designer, who created the gowns: "It is an 18th-century interpretation of a Greek goddess."

And what was the connection with mythology of the Pucci bow ties that the men all wore? "Pucci is my God," the designer said. ■

MAY 5, 1987

De Kooning Painting Ties Auction Record

By RITA REIF

Willem de Kooning's "Pink Lady" from 1944 tied the record at auction for a contemporary painting and for a work by a living artist when it was sold last night for $3.63 million at Sotheby's. The large and glowing Abstract Expressionist oil and charcoal on panel in pinks, red, bright green and yellow, was sold to an unidentified buyer who bid over the telephone through Lucy Mitchell-Innes, Sotheby's contemporary-art specialist.

"It's very sad — it's tough," said Betty Warner Sheinbaum, a Los Angeles artist who sat with her husband, Stanley K. Sheinbaum, an economist, in the front row to watch the sale. "We've owned that painting for 30 years." It was the first time they had sold a work from their collection at auction, Mr. Sheinbaum said, adding that they were happy with the price and were thinking of buying the works of younger artists.

Hugh M. Hefner, who did not appear at the sale to watch two of his paintings go under the hammer, was represented by Richard S. Rosenzweig, executive vice president of Playboy Enterprises.

"He was very pleased," Mr. Rosenzweig said after he delivered the news to Mr. Hefner that his two artworks had brought more than $5 million — well above expectations. "He said that these prices confirmed the reason we were correct in our assessment of the market, making the paintings available for sale. It was an exciting sale."

A Joyous Shout

Mr. Hefner had consigned de Kooning's "Woman," which was sold for a remarkable price — $2.53 million — to Morimasa Ohkawa, a 46-year-old real estate developer from Tokyo who was bidding at the back of the room. Mr. Ohkawa shouted joyously when the hammer came down. Mr. Ohkawa also was the underbidder on Mr. Hefner's Jackson Pollock, "November 26, 1950," which went for $2.57 million, a record at auction for the artist. The buyer of the Pollock was not identified.

"Mr. Ohkawa is buying art for his own pleasure," said Ikkan Sanada, an art consultant who accompanied Mr. Ohkawa to the sale. "He has been buying Impressionist paintings and School of Paris until now. Today he bought his first contemporary paintings — the de Kooning and a Lichtenstein." The Lichtenstein was "Girl in Mirror," for $165,000.

"The Japanese are buying with 50-cent dollars and the Europeans with 60-cent dollars," Allan Stone, an art dealer, commented.

Surpassed November Auction

The evening auction offered 84 works, 15 of which did not find buyers, in a sale that totaled $18.9 million, a record for a single session in an auction of contemporary art. The sale eclipsed the $13.2 million total achieved last November in a Sotheby's offering of 93 works, of which 86 were sold. That auction was dominated by 10 works from the collection of Ethel Redner Scull, including Jasper Johns's "Out the Window," which brought the same price as de Kooning's "Pink Lady" last night.

Arshile Gorky's 1945 "Portrait of Y. D." (the initials stand for Yvonne Duchamp, the sister of Marcel Duchamp) was sold for $572,000 to a European dealer in the room who would not disclose his name. The buyers of other works that sold for record prices also remained unidentified.

JUNE 5, 1987

Artists Rally to Fight AIDS

By ANNE-MARIE SCHIRO

Never underestimate the power of a movie star. Especially a superstar like Elizabeth Taylor. Once she attached her name to the American Foundation for AIDS Research, it became not only acceptable but desirable for other celebrities to become involved in the cause.

Her presence at a benefit party brings in both the crowds and the donations. And so it was last night when an event called Art Against AIDS opened with a cocktail reception for nearly 1,000 people at Sotheby's. Mayor Koch showed up briefly, but the highlight of the evening was the appearance of the actress, sparkling in beaded green silk and diamonds, to accept a check for $400,000 from Leo Castelli, the art dealer. "It's just a modest beginning," he said.

"I just love men with checks," she said.

Art Against AIDS involves 72 dealers, who are selling works by 600 artists and giving a percentage of the expected multimillions to the foundation. The goal is $5 million, and nearly $1 million has already been raised. That included more than $100,000 from a Robert Rauschenberg painting donated by the artist, and $200,000 from a drawing given by Jasper Johns, plus $120,000 from tickets for the reception, dinners that followed, and a midnight show at the Tunnel.

Among the guests mingling at Sotheby's were Roy Lichtenstein, Robert Mapplethorpe, Bianca Jagger, Matt Dillon, Tina Chow, Dick Cavett, Holly Solomon, Richard Gere, Peter Max, Ethel Scull, Mary McFadden and Dr. Mathilde Krim, head of the foundation. Plans called for them to go on to mingle with other stars of the art, literary and entertainment worlds at dinners scattered among 10 restaurants around town.

Celebrity Hosts at Dinners

The restaurateurs picked up the tabs for the dinners, which had celebrity hosts for added glamour. Louise Nevelson and Edward Albee were asked to do the honors at L'Acajou, while Debbie Harry, Matt Dillon and Tony Shafrazi were assigned to Barocco. Richard Gere was asked to share the duties of host at Raoul's with Alba and Francesco Clemente. Da Silvano got Mr. Castelli, while Nell's drew Mr. Mapplethorpe and Susan Sarandon. Christo and his wife, Jeanne-Claude Christo, were to be cohosts at Georgine Carmella, while Cafe Luxembourg got Yoko Ono and André Gregory.

Pity the unsuspecting diners who might have called for reservations at those restaurants, or at Odeon, Indochine and Mr. Chow, where the other dinners were held. ■

JANUARY 20, 1988

Metropolitan Diary

Ron Alexander

Letter from our friend the frequent partygoer:

Back in the 60's, Ethel Redner Scull was well known on the New York art scene as a collector of abstract art. Her name was synonymous with salon-type parties honoring such artists, then just making names for themselves, as Jasper Johns, George Segal, Robert Rauschenberg, Claes Oldenburg and Andy Warhol.

Then, in 1971, Mrs. Scull broke her back; in 1978, she and her husband, Robert Scull, were involved in a nasty divorce, and she all but disappeared from the social scene.

Well, the other night Mrs. Scull gave her first party in 11 years. "Because I was broke," she said in response to those who asked her why so much time between parties.

"Because I wanted people to see that I've begun collecting on my own," she told those who asked, "What made you decide to make a comeback?" She added that, after much legal wrangling, the sale of property and paintings had put her in the chips again.

The guest of honor at the black-tie affair was Sally Kirkland, the actress, and the 71 other guests included Norman Mailer, Norris Church, Isaac and Vera Stern, Frank Perry, Barbara Goldsmith and Morton Gottlieb. Artists included Jeff Koons, David Salle, Peter Halley, Meyer Vaisman and Eric Fischl, all of whom Mrs. Scull now collects.

"Art on my walls again!" said a delighted Mrs. Scull, who looked great in a short black Galanos. "My walls are positively smiling."

"This is like an elegant almuni reunion," Sylvia Miles told her.

After cocktails at Mrs. Scull's Upper East Side apartment, everyone dashed into taxis and headed for l'Orangerie at Le Cirque, where they ate fettuccine, veal and lemon soufflé.

"After 11 years I'd forgotten the angst of giving parties," Mrs. Scull said with a sigh at the end of the evening.

"You still give the greatest parties," George Segal assured her. "Just don't wait another 11 years."

"It feels great to be back in the swim again," Mrs. Scull said, with a smile as wide as her walls. Positively.

APRIL 22, 1988

The Blasé Are Awed by 10,000 Items of Warhol

By PATRICIA LEIGH BROWN

"Where did he *put* all this stuff?"

That was the question the dropjawed crowd of collectors, dealers, society people and others who've seen everything were asking last night as they descended upon Andy's half-acre: the three floors of Bakelite bracelets, cookie jars, watches, Art Deco cigarette holders and the rest of the 10,000 items in the tag sale of the century, the Andy Warhol Collection, to be auctioned off in a 10-day sale beginning Saturday.

"It's like walking inside Imelda Marcos's shoe closet," said one of the awed, Larry Williams, an investment banker.

The guests, mostly an uptown crowd, paid $200 to $350 a ticket to attend the reception and special preview at Sotheby's, a benefit for the Whitney Museum and the New York Academy of Art. But mostly, they came to mull over the mystery of the man with the platinum hair and white skin whose death a few blocks away at New York Hospital last year unleashed a tidal wave of Warholmania.

The hype, as neatly packaged as Mr. Warhol's famous Brillo pads, didn't seem to bother them. "They all want a piece of Andy," said Ethel Redner Scull, one of the first collectors of Pop art. "He's a hero, like Elvis Presley." Of the hoopla, she said: "I think Andy would have loved it. He was a voyeur."

Since the collection opened to public view last weekend, over 10,000 people have passed through Sotheby's doors at 72d Street and York Avenue to ponder the juxtaposition of Kermit the Frog ties with the Art Deco masterpieces of Emile-Jacques Ruhlmann. Among last night's voyeurs were Leo Castelli, chairman of the New York Academy of Art; Frederick Hughes, executor of the Warhol estate; Stuart Pivar, a longtime friend; Cornelia Guest; "Dynasty" producer Douglas Kramer, Roger and Suzanne Schlaiffer (who will be licensing Warhol products); Mr. and Mrs. François de Menil; the director of the Whitney, Tom Armstrong; the chairman of Sotheby's, A. Alfred Taubman, and the writers Joan Didion and John Gregory Dunne.

"It looks like a grandmother's house," Ms. Didion said. "It's mesmerizing how much one can accumulate."

"Maybe Andy should have had a dumpster," muttered Mr. Dunne.

"If anyone asks me the meaning of the word 'eclectic,' now I know what to tell them," said Fred Gerard, a New York attorney.

"I saw plastic chairs that we used to have in my college dormitory," said Garrick Utley, the broadcast journalist, who was viewing the cookie jars with his wife, Gertje. (Like all the objects in the collection, the cookie jars bore paper tags with auction lot numbers and Mr. Warhol's face.) "But the collection changes your idea of him. His art was part of his larger passion."

Some said the bizarre bazaar put their own obsessions in perspective. "Compared to Andy, what I collect is nothing," said Betsy Post-Miller, a collector.

For others, the evening had more melancholy meaning. "I miss him so much I can't stand it," said Jane (Baby Jane) Holzer. "I wish he was here living in that house, and we were all going to parties together."

Later, half the guests moved on to the Whitney, where, surrounded by the museum's collection of Mr. Warhol's Maos, Marilyn Monroes and electric chairs, they ate a dinner of fruit-stuffed Cornish hens. They talked of art, horse racing and other money matters, seated around black-cloaked tables (Andy loved black) and chairs wrapped with tin foil (he loved that, too).

At the close, the guests toted home favor bags containing a can of Campbell's tomato soup, a box of Brillo, miniature Absolut vodka (Mr. Warhol did an ad for it) and a copy of Interview, the magazine he founded.

Not all the Warhol gang was there. Jean Stein, the biographer of Edie Sedgewick, a Pop-era personality, decided not to go at the last minute. "All the publicity," she said. "And his death was so stunning. The whole thing is slightly necrophiliac, don't you think so?"

Alan Midgette, the Warhol impersonator ("I do paintings like Andy's but I do them by hand") wasn't there either. The night before, he had tried to infiltrate the press preview at Sotheby's and was politely escorted out by the auction house staff.

Viva, the former Warhol movie queen, was also nowhere to be found. She does not approve. In an interview before the party, she said, "I would sooner blow the $300 on a personal trainer than dinner at the Whitney."

JUNE 19, 1988

THE UNFLAGGING ARTISTRY OF JASPER JOHNS

By Deborah Solomon

IN 1959, WHEN JASPER JOHNS was 29 years old, a photograph appeared in Time magazine that shows him standing beside one of his paintings. A slim, brooding young man dressed in a coat and tie, Johns radiates the sort of demonic intensity the public no doubt expected of him. He was, after all, "the brand-new darling of the art world's bright, brittle avant-garde," as the accompanying article explained. "A year ago he was practically unknown; since then he has had a sellout show in Manhattan, has exhibited in Paris and Milan. . . ."

No artist was ever catapulted into fame more suddenly than Johns. His 1958 exhibition at the Castelli Gallery in New York, which brought together paintings of targets, numbers and the American flag, was seen as a brilliant assault on the high-minded strivings of the Abstract Expressionists who then dominated the art scene. What could a picture of a target, even if it *was* nicely painted in lush green strokes, reveal about the agony of existence? Absolutely nothing, and that was the point. As Johns himself later stated, "I don't want my work to be an exposure of my feelings."

In the 30 years since his shining debut, Johns has never been out of the limelight. When the Venice Biennale opens next Sunday, it will be Johns whose work is represented in the United States pavilion. It's a distinction of the highest order, and one that confirms Johns's reputation as the venerated father of the Pop Art movement of the 60's.

In some ways, it's hard to imagine a less likely star than this allegedly hermetic artist who rarely gives interviews or appears in public, and whose work, though based on the most commonplace of images, is difficult, clandestine, and at times vexingly self-involved. But that hasn't kept Johns from winning either an avid audience or commercial success. Last month, his 1962 painting "Diver" sold for $4.2 million, the highest price ever paid at auction for the work of a living artist. (The previous record, held jointly by Johns and Willem de Kooning, was $3.63 million.)

Yet the one development in the artist's career nowadays generating the most interest has nothing to do with money or fame. At 58, Johns has found himself preoccupied by his own vulnerability in the face of age and loss, and eager to surrender his famous detachment to the imperatives of his discontent. His recent work pursues the autobiographical as diligently as his early targets and flags renounced it.

Johns, who lives and works in a handsome white stucco town house on the Upper East Side, speaks of the dramatic change in his work elliptically: "One wants one's work to be the world, but of course it's never the world. The work is *in* the world; it never contains the whole thing."

The artist, a large, gracious, soft-spoken man who characteristically speaks of himself in the third person, is sitting on a hardwood chair in his studio. The room overlooks a stone courtyard and seems surprisingly bare for a workplace. There are no easels displaying works-in-progress, no paint splatters staining the pale marble floor. About the only sign of life is a row of flowerpots filled with rare orchids on a window ledge. "Someone gave me a subscription to an orchid club," he explains.

Johns answers questions with short, careful, literal replies, like a witness testifying in court. The information that he chooses to disclose merely underscores his reserve. In 1959, he recalls, he was befriended by Marcel Duchamp, the Dada artist whose "ready-made" sculptures — bottle racks, snow shovels and other manufactured objects proclaimed by the artist to be high art — have had such a large influence on Johns's own work.

Were the two artists close? "I wasn't inclined to approach him," Johns says. "I found it difficult to be with him in a graceful way because there were things I would have liked to ask him, but I couldn't imagine that he would be interested in giving me the information I wanted. Much of it dealt with the past, and who wants to sit around talking about the past?"

The moral of the story is clear: To ask an artist to reflect on the past is to demonstrate bad manners. Johns is particularly touchy on the subject of his childhood. But then it wasn't a happy time for him.

THE ONLY SON OF A FAILED FARMer, Johns spent his earliest years in Allendale, S.C., a small town not far from Charleston. He was raised by his paternal grandfather, a Baptist farmer who took Johns in after his parents were divorced. When Johns was still in grade school, his grandfather died. The young boy was shuttled around to various relatives, and eventually ended up in a town called The Corner, living with an aunt who taught in a one-room schoolhouse. Asked why he lived with his father's sister as opposed to his father, Johns sits quietly before replying. "He didn't invite me," he finally says, erupting into loud laughter.

Johns recalls his years in The Corner as a time of intense isolation. "It was very rural — no telephone, no electricity at first. I had no sense of the world, and still have very little of it."

Early on, Johns retreated into the world of art. From the time he was 5, he drew all the time. "Making drawings was something I liked to do," he says, "and probably it attracted attention. People said, 'Oh, *he* does that!'" He knew for sure he was going to be an artist someday, even though the only artist he had ever heard of was a grandmother he never met, a Sunday painter whose landscapes he saw in the homes of his relatives. He still remembers what her work looked like: "Swans on a stream, cows in a meadow. A heron. I remember a tall painting with a tall heron on it."

At the age of 19, after studying briefly at the University of South Carolina, Johns came to New York to pursue a career in art. Before long he was working as a messenger boy and hazily wondering how best to proceed with his nonexistent career in art. The question was deferred in 1950, when he was drafted into the United States Army for two years of service during the Korean War.

After his discharge, Johns returned to New York and found a job as a sales clerk at a Marlboro bookstore on West 57th Street, next door to The Russian Tea Room. "I had no focus," he recalls. "I was vague and rootless. This image of wanting to be an artist — that I *would* in some way become an artist — was very strong. I knew for a long, long time that that's what I would be. But nothing I ever did seemed to bring me any nearer to the condition of being an artist. And I didn't know how to do it."

A turning point came in 1954, when Johns became friendly with Robert Rauschenberg. He, too, was a transplanted Southerner (he came from Texas). Far more accomplished than Johns, he had already had several one-man shows, and his iconoclastic "black paintings" and "white paintings" had won him considerable attention. As extroverted as Johns was introverted, Rauschenberg knew most of the leading avant-garde figures of the day. Johns has described him as the first serious artist he ever met.

By the mid-1950's, Rauschenberg was living in a loft building on Pearl Street, one flight above Johns. Over the next few years, the two painters traded ideas on a daily basis, criticized each other's work, and "nourished each other," as Rauschenberg puts it, "by being such contradictory personalities."

They offered each other practical assistance, too. In those days, Rauschenberg was supporting himself designing windows for Bonwit Teller on a freelance basis; one day he asked Johns for some help. "I saw that what Bob did was do something, have some money, run out of money, find something to do, get some money." Johns quit his job at the bookstore and began working with Rauschenberg.

Now that he had time to paint, Johns decided to start over, and in 1954 destroyed every work in his studio. "I think I must have recognized some aspect of self-hatred in my aimlessness," he says. "I hoped to instigate a new state of affairs, to change the form of my thought and the content of my work."

Johns wasn't sure exactly what form his new work would take, but he knew what form it would actively resist. By the mid-50's, Abstract Expressionism was the dominant style of the day, and many young artists were eagerly adopting the thrusting brushstrokes, free-wheeling lines and heroic scale of artists like Jackson Pollock and de Kooning. Johns, however, was never one for hero-worship. "I didn't want to do what they did," he says of the Abstract Expressionists. "I decided that if my work contained what I could identify as a likeness to other work, I would remove it."

One day in 1954, Johns casually mentioned to Rauschenberg that he'd had a crazy dream the previous night. "How crazy was it?" Rauschenberg asked. "Well," Johns replied, "in this dream I was painting the American flag." *The American flag?* Rauschenberg didn't think it was crazy at all. "That's a really great idea," he said.

And so Johns returned to his studio and, over the course of several months, painted his first star-spangled flag. Based on the image of an American flag unfurled and stretched tautly across a canvas, Johns's "Flag" was a complicated painting. Is it a flag, or does it just *look* like a flag? Should we stand up before it and recite "The Pledge of Allegiance" — or approach it instead as a pure abstraction, a rectangle divided into bands of color? Like much of the work that Johns did after it, "Flag" blurred the distinction between a painting and the object it depicts, raising basic questions about reality and perception.

After completing several variations on his first "Flag," Johns went on to paint the alphabet, archery targets and the numbers 0 through 9 — "things that are seen but not looked at," he explains. He lavished great care on their execution; most of his work was done in encaustic, a wax-based medium that gave his surfaces a dense, sensuous look. It never occurred to Johns that his paintings of flags or the alphabet might cause an uproar; when he exhibited his "Green Target" in a group show at the Jewish Museum in 1957, no reviewers made note of it.

But Johns's obscurity didn't last long. One day in 1957, Leo Castelli, who had just opened a gallery devoted to avant-garde art, climbed the three flights to Rauschenberg's loft to look at his work and discuss the possibility of giving him a show. When Rauschenberg mentioned that he was going downstairs to get some ice for drinks from Johns's loft (they shared a refrigerator), Castelli's ears perked up. "Jasper Johns?" he asked. "The one who painted the green picture in the Jewish Museum show?" Castelli headed downstairs to look at Johns's work. "It was an astounding experience," he recalls. Forgetting about Rauschenberg for the moment, Castelli scheduled Johns's first show for January 1958.

When Johns's show opened at the gallery, the public was astonished. Here were paintings with names like "Flag," "White Flag," "Target with Four Faces" — and the willful banality of their subject matter seemed to mock the high seriousness of art. Unlike the Abstract Expressionists, Johns had no interest in lofty strivings or romantic ideals or heroic quests for the sublime. The only emotion suggested by his work was a cool, astringent irony. The art historian Leo Steinberg, one of the artist's early champions, has described the reaction of a well-known painter who visited the gallery: "If this is painting," he said, "I might as well give up."

Johns's work was instantly recognized as an ingenious negation of Abstract Expressionism. His flags, targets and stenciled numbers were emptied of all illusion or grandeur, and they made viewers wonder whether a painting, like a cup or a chair, wasn't just an ordinary material object. "At one stroke," the late critic Harold Rosenberg has written, "Johns extinguished speculation about the meaning of individual paintings and directed attention to them as objects among other objects."

Some critics dismissed Johns's work as a reheated version of Duchampian irony ("Dada's the Disease," grumbled Emily Genauer in The New York Herald Tribune); in more influential quarters the reaction was overwhelmingly favorable. The Museum of Modern Art, which was notorious for its wait-and-see approach toward acquiring the work of younger artists, promptly purchased three of Johns's paintings.

Johns's variations on flags and targets, though layered with ambiguity, were relatively accessible compared to earlier avant-garde art, and collectors didn't hesitate to snap them up. Taxi-fleet tycoons Robert and Ethel Scull, delighted by Johns's "number" paintings, commissioned him to paint a picture of a big number five — "our good luck number since three children and the two of us made five," Mrs. Scull explains.

No one was more surprised by Johns's success than the Abstract Expressionists, who had come of age when artists still lived in cold-water flats, rarely made a sale, and prided themselves on their outsider status. One day news got back to Johns that de Kooning had bitterly joked about Castelli, "You could give that son of a bitch two beer cans and he could sell them." The comment inspired Johns's best-known sculpture, "Painted Bronze," in which a couple of cans of Ballantine Ale stand side by side with a dignity befitting Egyptian tomb figures.

BY THE EARLY 1960'S, JOHNS had become a highly influential figure. When Frank Stella painted the austere black-striped canvases that heralded the beginning of Minimalism, he was improvising on the "you see what you see" literalness of Johns's flags and targets. When Andy Warhol painted a picture of a Campbell's soup can, when Claes Oldenburg made a sculpture of a giant hamburger, when Roy Lichtenstein elevated comic-book blondes to the realm of high art, they were all exploring the ideas set forth in Johns's (and Rauschenberg's) paintings of commonplace subjects.

Yet the Pop Art movement, which embraced the whole range of vernacular culture and sought to demystify high art, had little in common with the intellectual riddles inscribed in Johns's flags and targets. As Pop gained ascendancy, Johns left New York for Edisto Beach, S.C., and his flags and targets gave way to a more personal and despairing iconography. "Periscope (Hart Crane)," done in 1963, includes an image of a grasping arm, a reference to the poet's suicidal death by drowning. "Souvenir," in which an actual flashlight is affixed to the canvas, along with a dinner plate bearing a photograph of the artist, is a bitter meditation on the limitations of art, which can no more shed light on human suffering than can the flashlight in the photograph.

As the years passed, Johns's work became more hermetic. Throughout most of the 1970's, while dividing his time between the wooded seclusion of Stony Point, N.Y., and a former bank building in downtown Manhattan, he devoted himself to a group of abstractions known as the "crosshatchings" — little clusters of parallel lines arranged in all-over rhythms. Critics had a field day interpreting the "hatches," and everything from human fingers to "a prolonged cry" to a secret code known only to Johns and his closest friends was said to be embedded in their imagery.

In the early 1980's, Johns found himself increasingly dissatisfied with the smooth, seamless surfaces of his crosshatchings, and anxious to express himself more directly. The result was some of his most forceful paintings ever. "Racing Thoughts" of 1983, a big, horizontal canvas rendered in a *trompe l'oeil* style, depicts a view of a bathroom cluttered with personal mementoes — a photograph of Leo Castelli, some pots by the American ceramicist George Ohr (whose work Johns collects), a Swiss poster bearing a skull. It's an elegiac painting that shows the artist racing to recapture a whole lifetime of experience, but able to retrieve little more than faded old photographs and other fragments of his past.

Why would Johns, who is in good health, be moved to confront his own mortality with such directness and urgency? "I suppose I've become increasingly aware of the ways things can be cut off," he says. "I don't know whether it's the loss of friends. . . ." He stops, and retreats to safer ground. "I think my early work exposed me just as much as any other bit of my work."

Last year, Johns generated enormous publicity with the unveiling at the Castelli Gallery of four big paintings collectively entitled "The Seasons." The result of nearly two years' work, "The Seasons" delineate the familiar theme of man's passage through time, from the bloom of spring to the cold, gray deprivation of winter. They're dominated by the image of the artist's own shadow cast life-size onto the canvas — the first full figure Johns ever painted, his first true self-portrait.

In each of "The Seasons," the shadow is shown inside a studio, surrounded by cryptic images from the artist's past: an American flag, a decoy duck, the Hart Crane hand. These various motifs lend themselves to endless interpretation, but one doesn't have to be a detective to recognize "The Seasons" as a personal lament in the face of old age and death. The shadow lurking in the four paintings isn't a figure of mystery or romance. He's simply a sad, faceless spook, a gray silhouette helplessly watching as his world decays around him.

Despite Johns's reputation for being "the sacred cow" of the art world, as the writer Calvin Tomkins once called him, the reaction to "The Seasons" wasn't unanimously reverent. Some critics found the works contrived; their reviews were laced with stinging phrases like "mere illustration" and "Currier and Ives cartoons." Even the artist's most fervid admirers concede that "The Seasons" have none of the daring originality of Johns's early flags and targets. The skull, pots and other objects gathered together in the four paintings link them to the old European tradition of "melancholia" still-life, in which a person is shown surrounded by an arrangement of possessions that evoke life's transience and uncertainty.

"When an artist makes a great contribution to the course of art early in life, people tend to be disappointed later on," says Mark Rosenthal, a curator of 20th-century art at the Philadelphia Museum of Art who organized the current Johns exhibition in Venice. (The show, a survey of the artist's work since 1974, will be seen in Philadelphia in the fall.) "People look at Johns and want to know: Is he still contributing to the flow of art history the way the flags contributed? There is definitely a problem that way for the artist; people don't look at what he's trying to do."

One of the more common complaints about Johns's work is that it's indulgently self-referential, featuring a narrow range of imagery and ideas. Like a kid with only one box of toys, Johns is always playing (and Johns does play) with the same old motifs: a flag, a flashlight, a Savarin coffee can stuffed full of paint brushes. Usually after he finishes a painting, he reworks the image in drawings and prints, cannibalizing his own imagery. "It would be wonderful to leap over certain obstacles and be in a superior position to the one one is in," Johns says. "One sees that one is, in a sense, helplessly concerned with one's concerns. One has to have the thoughts one has, one can't just have the thoughts one would like to have."

Johns tends to work exceedingly slowly. It is not unusual for him to spend two years on a single canvas, and his total output over 30-plus years numbers fewer than 300 paintings. But even when his work is going smoothly, Johns is cautious, critical, painstaking; he manipulates brushstrokes "like cards in a patience game," the critic and painter Fairfield Porter once wrote. Johns doesn't paint so much as he repaints, building up his canvases layer by layer in a process of continuous self-revision.

Johns's slowness as a painter, his careful application of pigment, his endless reworking of the surface, his difficulty finishing paintings — it all hints at the sense of doubt so pervasive in his work. His flags and targets, as much as the quivering shadow in "The Seasons," are emblematic of the incomplete, fragmented nature of existence — and of art's inability to make us whole. "It seems to me," Johns says, "one can never make a comprehensive statement. One just continues to do things — this, that and the other — and then it stops."

JOHNS'S FRIENDS INvariably describe him as a private, guarded man. How private is he? "I don't think I should answer that," replies the author Susan Sontag. "It's a violation of his privacy."

"Knowing him is a great pleasure because you're constantly in the state of a tourist when you're with him," says John Cage, the avant-garde composer. "Every moment is new." Cage's affection for the artist is abundantly evident in the several poems he's published in his honor, one of which ends: "the difficulties/you and your work have given/i cherish more than any others."

Anyone who has ever spent a few hours in Johns's presence would have no trouble understanding "the difficulties" alluded to in Cage's poem. "He's hard to get along with," says the collector Ethel Scull. "If he's in a mellow mood you're on easy street, but he can be icy cold." Rauschenberg, who has known Johns as long as just about anyone, says ruefully, "I'm not certain that he has any close friends. He's cautious and terrified of extending himself and I don't know how he survives."

For all his efforts to protect his privacy, Johns is by no means a loner. Evenings when he's not home watching television ("mostly I just switch the channels") or indulging his omnivorous taste for literature (he reads everything from *Wittgenstein* to *dime-store mysteries*), he can often be found at dinner parties. He is said to be an excellent cook who enjoys entertaining at his Manhattan town house and at his island retreat on St. Martin. "He's very sociable," says Leo Castelli, his art dealer. "You can't imagine how many people he knows. I don't think he would go anywhere not having somebody around who he could see right away, if he wanted to."

Even when he's working, Johns isn't completely alone. He is kept constant company by his dog Whisky, a golden-colored mutt. Johns is obviously fond of the dog, and the only real story he volunteers during my visit is the saga of how he came to own her. A decade ago, this story begins, Johns was visited in St. Martin by Teeny Duchamp, the widow of Marcel. "We went to the house of these friends and the hostess was saying she had gotten these pups and she was taking them the following day to the vet to be put to sleep. Teeny said, 'You're not taking them to have them killed! I'm taking them to Paris!' So we put the dogs in a champagne carton, put Teeny on an airplane, and sent her to Paris . . . One of the dogs mated with a King Charles spaniel and gave birth to Whisky and her blond sister, Champagne. I was visiting Paris when Whisky was a tiny little pup and I said, 'Well, I would like her.' But she was too young then to travel. Later, she was put on the Concorde, and I met the airplane."

When I noted that it seemed peculiar to bring a mongrel all the way from France, Johns protested. "Well, not with Whisky's background! Her long hair is from her father, the King Charles spaniel. Teeny always called those dogs her Gauguin dogs because they look like the dogs in his paintings of Tahiti."

It was getting late, and I still needed to ask Johns about the shadow that had figured so prominently in "The Seasons." Why had he decided after so many years to paint his first explicit self-portrait? And why had he depicted himself as a quivering spook?

Once again, Johns paused. "It was an easy solution to filling a large part of the canvas," he finally said, letting loose one of his raucous laughs.

But then the laughter stopped, and his long face assumed its usual inscrutable expression. "I wanted something that would be literal," he said. "It is less literal than I intended it to be, but nevertheless it started out as a literal tracing. I stood in the sunlight and there was a piece of paper on the ground and someone drew my shadow. I used that in the painting."

And so it turns out that Johns didn't draw the shadow after all. A friend drew it for him. No one but Johns could have thought to create his first and only genuine self-portrait in someone else's hand. ■

JULY 8, 1988

Auctions

Rita Reif

■ **A Japanese dealer is in the forefront of a shift to contemporary art.**

Kazuo Fujii, one of the first Japanese dealers to stock Impressionist art in the 1960's, is in the vanguard again, buying major contemporary artworks.

He has paid record prices for Jackson Pollock paintings at recent New York auctions, acquiring canvases not only for clients, but for himself as well. During a 10-day trip to New York, Mr. Fujii spent $20 million, purchasing works by George Segal, Jean Arp and others at auctions and from dealers for his two Tokyo galleries. He stocks postwar art by Pollock, Mr. Segal, Willem de Kooning, Helen Frankenthaler, Franz Kline and Andy Warhol at the spacious white-walled Fujii Gallery Modern, and he exhibits Impressionist paintings and early-20th-century modern masters in the more intimate setting of the Fujii Gallery, which he calls "the head office."

"The taste now in Japan is very much for Impressionists and Post-Impressionists," Mr. Fujii said. "But more people are shifting toward the contemporary market. I am sure in 10 years the Japanese art scene will be drastically changed."

Mr. Fujii, who is one of the top five art dealers in Japan, said that Japanese collectors were responsible for much of the switch to contemporary art. "Japanese collectors are really getting more knowledgeable, and dealers are pushed by those collectors," he said, adding that some of the collectors were buying both prewar and postwar art.

•

Mr. Fujii attended his first contemporary-art auction in May, at Sotheby's in New York, where he paid a record $4.8 million for Pollock's "Search," the highest price paid at auction for postwar art and the most important work sold that night. The 1955 oil-and-enamel canvas — vibrantly spattered with red, black, green, yellow and white — is one of the artist's last paintings.

At Christie's that month, Mr. Fujii raised his auction paddle again and bought another Pollock, "No. 31, 1949." The $3.5 million he paid was the second highest price at that sale and for any Pollock purchased at auction. Mr. Fujii said this abstract painting — a fine web of black, white, blue, red and yellow splashed with dribbles of brilliant colors — was acquired for a client.

The Pollocks were the costliest works Mr. Fujii bought during his trip here. The Pollock he bought at Christie's was selected by a Japanese collector who told Mr. Fujii that his mother wanted to "change her savings into an investment." When the son chose the Pollock for his mother, Mr. Fujii said, he decided that if clients were buying contemporary art, he should also.

Mr. Fujii was not the only Japanese dealer bidding at the contemporary-art auctions in May. According to Ikkan Sanada, a Japanese art consultant based here, the popularity of American postwar artists in Japan can be attributed to increased travel to the West by the Japanese and the many contemporary-art exhibitions held over the last decade in Japan. "It does make a difference when artists are exhibited there," he said.

•

George Segal's work created a sensation when it was first exhibited at Tokyo's Seibu department store in the early 1980's, Mr. Sanada said. Ever since, Japanese collectors and dealers have bought his work at auctions and from galleries. Mr. Segal's portrait of Robert and Ethel Scull was purchased at Sotheby's in 1986 by a Japanese. At least two works in the Segal exhibition at the Sidney Janis gallery in May went to Japan — one of them to Mr. Fujii.

Until now, Mr. Sanada said, Mr. Fujii and other Japanese dealers have concentrated mostly on less costly contemporary works by Western artists — drawings, multiples, prints and less important paintings by major and minor postwar artists. In 1986, Mr. Fujii asked Mr. Sanada to organize a contemporary print show of 35 major works by Jasper Johns, Robert Rauschenberg, Roy Lichtenstein, James Rosenquist, Kenneth Noland, Christo, Warhol, Frank Stella, Richard Estes and Robert Longo. The exhibition was well received, and brought many new clients to the Fujii gallery, Mr. Sanada said. Three months later, Mr. Fujii bought his first contemporary painting, a Frankenthaler, for which he paid less than $100,000.

The amount Mr. Fujii spent in May in New York did not surprise Mr. Sanada. "Twenty million may seem enormous," Mr. Sanada said. "But for a gallery of Mr. Fujii's standard, it is not such a huge amount. To give you an idea how big the Japanese art market is — some dealers make more than $100 million and many are making between $50 million and $100 million."

Mr. Fujii, the son of an antiques dealer based in Toyama, studied art and after he completed university in 1948, went to work for a Tokyo dealer. Two years later, he went into business for himself, opening his own gallery in 1960. He was among the first Japanese dealers to buy Western art after the war, when he acquired a Monet in 1965 from William Acquavella, a New York dealer.

Lucy Mitchell-Innes, who heads Sotheby's contemporary-art sales in New York, said she was convinced the Japanese buying of postwar art was not a passing fancy. "I think it is a real commitment," she said. "Several of the Japanese people — dealers and collectors — are now seriously buying contemporary American art."

NOVEMBER 6, 1988

Friends Recall Young Artist With Music and Verse

By CONSTANCE L. HAYS

It was all very downtown, except that it was uptown, as about 220 of Jean Michel Basquiat's friends and admirers packed a Manhattan church yesterday to pay tribute to the artist who died in August at the age of 27.

With monologues, music and poetry, a handful shared their memories of a man who had no formal art training, grossed millions of dollars in his brief career and fought endlessly for recognition.

Many in the standing-room-only crowd at St. Peter's Lutheran Church on East 54th Street were dressed in black and leather, the current choice of the contemporary art world. A few wore high-top sneakers and colorful hats, and one woman drew tissues silently from a green "Land of the Lost" lunchbox.

On the altar was a color photograph of Mr. Basquiat, who was born in Brooklyn, in front of a painting he created showing two angular human figures with the words, "Nothing to be gained here."

Regarded as a Genius

For most, the afternoon service was the only formal expression of grief they had shared. Mr. Basquiat was found dead Aug. 12 in the East Village apartment he rented from Andy Warhol's estate.

His funeral last summer was a mostly private affair, said Jeffrey Deutsch, a collector, critic and dealer of art."The family wasn't comfortable with this whole world," Mr. Deutsch said, his eyes sweeping across the people at yesterday's service. He added that no one from Mr. Basquiat's immediate family was there.

Regarded by many contemporary art experts as a genius, Jean Michel Basquiat was remembered as a man who pursued every aspect of his life with drive and devotion, including those that were destructive.

"He could be a jerk," Nancy Brooks Brody, who said she had known Mr. Basquiat since they were teen-agers, told the crowd. "But he was a jerk with such incredible energy." She added: "He put that same energy into taking drugs. He went out to the edge."

'He Would Make the Rules'

The artist Keith Haring noted Mr. Basquiat's desire to control the art world, not be controlled by it. "He disrupted the politics," Mr. Haring said. "He said if he had to play their game, he would make the rules."

Ingrid Sischy, a critic who is a former editor in chief of Art Forum magazine, called Mr. Basquiat "a rearranger of language and images — a discoverer, and a recoverer." His paintings often included words or phrases, and he once said he used words like brushstrokes.

Ethel Redner Scull, the collector, was among the mourners. "The world doesn't realize it has lost a great artist," she said after the service. "Everybody keeps saying he was Andy Warhol's friend. But Andy needed Jean Michel. He was drained of his ideas. Jean Michel was filled with brilliant ideas."

A band called Gray performed songs dedicated to Mr. Basquiat, a former member. John Lurie played a haunting composition on his soprano saxophone. People wept at times, laughed at times, applauded and embraced each other.

Jennifer Goode, another friend, drew laughter when she described Mr. Basquiat as someone "who knew every White Castle hamburger joint in the five boroughs." She also said he was a man who, because he was black, "couldn't get picked up by a cab to get to his own show."

She read a poem by Robert Frost, "Acquainted With the Night," which concludes:

And further still at an unearthly
height
One luminary clock against the sky
Proclaimed the time was neither
wrong nor right.
I have been one acquainted with the
night.

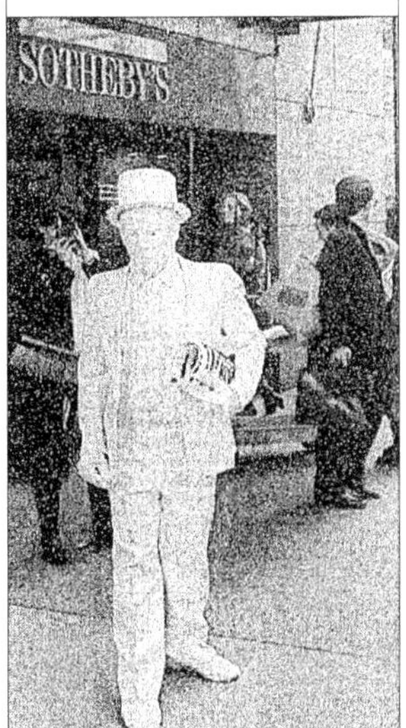

NOVEMBER 15, 1988

Traffic Is Heavy on the Art Auction Route

By RITA REIF

Art buyers have shuttled between Christie's and Sotheby's for more than a week, viewing and bidding on more postwar, modern and Impressionist art valued at more money than has ever been presented at auction. The numbers are staggering. Sotheby's presented 792 artworks estimated at between $166.6 million and $220.2 million and by Saturday night had sold $231.2 million — the highest total in history for such sales. Christie's offered 722 works valued at a total of $113.8 million to $155 million. By Saturday, Christie's sales of contemporary art totaled $42.9 million.

There was gridlock in front of Christie's Sunday night as art enthusiasts and socialites arrived in dark suits, silks and sables to look at works by Picasso, Renoir, Cézanne and Degas that William and Edith Mayer Goetz, pioneer Hollywood collectors of Impressionist and modern art, acquired 40 years ago. Hundreds who arrived by stretch limousine and taxi found there was gridlock upstairs too, as art enthusiasts crowded into the viewing of the Goetzes' and other owners' art, valued at from $100 million to $134 million, that were to be offered last night, tonight and tomorrow.

•

Christo, the artist, and his wife, Jeanne-Claude, swept through the crowd Sunday night, heading for the corner of a Christie's gallery where a Giacometti bronze from the Burton and Emily Hall Tremaine collection was being shown along with other Giacometti works.

Mary Lasker never removed her sable-edged mink coat, so eager was she, she said, to see her favorite Goetz painting — Picasso's portrait of his son Paulo dressed as a clown. The philanthropist and collector said she had admired it often in the Goetzes' living room — "It's so happy" — which she visited for the last time a year ago. Mrs. Goetz, who was widowed in 1969, died in June at the age of 82.

The Goetzes' two daughters, Barbara Windom and Judith Goetz Shepherd, were greeted by Christopher Burge, Christie's president, and then went to look at a Degas ballet dancer. Mrs. Windom said she was surprised that people looked at art in the Christie's previews as if it were in a museum. She and her sister did not, she said. She touched the Degas and jokingly said to Mr. Burge: "We want to pull her hair ribbon one more time."

•

At noon Friday, as hundreds were filing in and out of Sotheby's to view works by Renoir and Degas being sold that night and Saturday, a man resembling a George Segal plaster sculpture showed up, covered from head to toe in white silicone, wearing a white silicone top hat and carrying a white silicone newspaper.

The man identified himself as Harold Olejarz, a sculptor and performance artist from Tenafly, N.J., and said he made a living driving a limousine. He keeps his "sculpture suits" in the trunk of his car, he said.

When asked if he came to Sotheby's because George Segal's "Self-Portrait" had sold there the night before for a record price of $242,000, he said: "No. Most artists have a gallery show. I decided to go directly to art buyers and demonstrate my own art."

•

Ezra and Cecile Zilkha carefully inspected the Impressionists and modern paintings at the Christie's preview. When asked what he thought of the prices paid last week — including $17 million for a Jasper Johns painting — Mr. Zilkha, an art collector, investor and former banker, said: "I think it is crazy. When things get too excessive, something not-so-good will happen."

•

Mystery buyers show up every season or so at art auctions and pay huge sums. This season's unknown buyer did not remain so for long — and by choice. Hans Thulin, a 40-year-old Swedish real-estate investor, flew in from Stockholm to be in New York on Wednesday night. He bought Jasper Johns's "White Flag" at Christie's, for a record $7 million. He bid for the ghostlike "Flag" over the telephone through Lillemor Malmstrom, the director of Christie's Stockholm office, who was present at the sale.

On Thursday Mr. Thulin flew to Miami, and that night was on the telephone again from Boca Raton. This time he bid through Lucy Mitchell-Inness, Sotheby's head of contemporary-art sales, to buy Robert Rauschenberg's "Rebus" for a record $6.3 million, the highest price ever paid at auction for a work by this artist.

"I'm very happy; I got two good cornerstones on which I will build my collection," he said. "My goal is to pick 2 works of the 10 best American artists."

Mr. Thulin said he was a self-made man. After his university education, "I started out with empty hands," he said. "You can do anything in Sweden today but you can't die, because they take everything away from you in taxes when you do."

•

Leo Castelli checked his files after the Johns "False Start" was auctioned Thursday night for $17 million at Sotheby's. He found that he had sold the painting to Robert C. Scull in February 1960 for $3,150 — of which Johns was paid $1,575.

Yesterday, the man collecting the $17 million, François de Menil — an architect and a member of the Texas art-collecting family — who bought "False Start" and Andy Warhol's "Marilyn Monroe (Twenty Times)" from Mr. Scull, said he was "still recovering." Not only did the Johns bring a record price, but the Warhol did also, going for $3.96 million. "The Jasper was purchased in 1981 and the Marilyns in 1980," Mr. de Menil said. "I'd rather not say what I paid, but it was considerably less than what I received."

•

Michael Findlay, who is in charge of Impressionist and modern-art sales at Christie's, said yesterday that he had been delighted by the arrival of three different groups of people on Saturday morning who — after selling art at good prices on Friday night — wanted to see what was still to be auctioned at Sotheby's.

"The money is not staying very long in their pockets," he said.

•

Bidding these days is done by art buyers who for the most part are far away from the public eye: in darkened rooms overlooking the salesrooms, from limousines parked outside the auction house, from telephone booths in the lobby and from corporate board rooms all over the world.

Last week, Susan Rolfe of Christie's took bids from one man who was attending a funeral at Frank E. Campbell's on Madison Avenue. Another bidder at Christie's contemporary sale was due at a dinner at an East Side restaurant. "We got him on the phone — and he bought the work," said Mr. Findlay.

FEBRUARY 3, 1989

Looking Back at Warhol, Stars, Super-Heroes and All

By MICHAEL BRENSON

FOR years now, Andy Warhol has been almost everywhere. His pale priestly face frets or blesses from newsstands. Images he appropriated from popular sources are studied like sacred scrolls. Just about every scrap he breathed upon is coveted like a religious relic. Moving through the spectacle of the Warhol retrospective that opens Monday at the Museum of Modern Art, it is clear just how many artistic disciples he now has.

At a moment in American art over which he all but presides, this show probably had to be a blockbuster. With more than 300 works spread over two floors, with an accompanying program of Warhol films, it is the most ambitious solo show at the Modern since the Picasso retrospective in 1980. The scale is not so much a canonization as a recognition that the canonization has already taken place.

Marilyn is abundantly present. So are Jackie and Liz and Elvis, all glamorous enigmas now enshrined, with Warhol himself — partly because they *are* glamorous enigmas — in the American cultural hall of fame. The simulated Brillo boxes are here. So are Superman and Popeye, they too his artistic alter egos, one of them a mild-mannered reporter, the other a common sailor until spinach begins blasting through his veins.

Here also are the electric chairs, with the sign in the background asking for silence, acknowledging the presence of an avid public at this deathly ritual, calling attention as well to the silence that even Warhol's dairy cow — impassive and anonymous, staring without guile or judgment, churning out its product day after day — seems to need.

The exhibition underlines Warhol's enormous importance and gift. The Warhol effect derives from the casual inevitability of his images and the way raw, upstart ambition scratches soundlessly at the quiet, self-effacing surface. The effect is also the result of timing and humor. And it has to do with his ability to grasp basic changes in American culture and suggest new ways of making art as museums began to resemble department stores and an increasing number of educated Americans decided they needed art to consume.

With his Roman Catholic and Eastern European upbringing and their tradition of icons, Warhol understood the power of images and the mass media. He was one of the first to recognize that art was being usurped or threatened by television, fashion and film, and that it had to begin to deal with them on their terms. Every source, including tabloids and mug shots, was legitimate. So was the language of commercial art and design. If the mass media and popular culture were going to use art, then art had to use them in return.

Warhol also understood the double effect of film and television. On the one hand, they make everything seem immediate, desirable, larger than life, and they assemble a bank of images from which everyone can draw. On the other hand, they turn everyone on the screen and in front of it into an abstraction. Warhol helps clarify the dilemma of a culture in which desire is shamelessly stoked and manipulated, and increasingly insatiable.

As much as anything, the Warhol effect derives from the extreme two-sidedness of his work. On the one hand, it is quiet, passive, tolerant to the point of being all-accepting, a blank slate on which American popular culture seems to have written itself. On the other hand, it is tremendously violent, bewitched by loss and doom, determined to wipe out everything alien to it as his grisly car wrecks wipe out the people in them.

•

In the introduction to the almost 500-page catalogue, Kynaston McShine, a senior curator at the Modern and the organizer of the show, underlines the vulnerability of the artist and his "celestially cool and catholic art." In his catalogue essay, "Andy Warhol's One-Dimensional Art: 1956-1966," the art critic Benjamin H. D. Buchloh uses words like "liquidate" and "annihilate" to describe what he believes to be the effects of Warhol's radical artistic program.

This is not a revisionist show. Perhaps 75 percent is devoted to the early and mid-1960's, which has been generally understood as Warhol's great period. All of his media are represented, including ID photos and a hand-made monochromatic painting of a before and after advertisement promising that a simple nose job can miraculously transform homeliness into glamour and youth. Most works are the photo-silk-screens for which Warhol is best known.

The installation is partly chronological and partly thematic, and there are nice touches. The portraits, icons and lips inspired by Monroe's death are among the best works Warhol did, and they put an exclamation point to the first half of the show. The charged paintings of electric chairs open the second half with a jolt. Placing the 1963 "Portrait of Ethel Scull" so it faces the 1976 painting "Skulls," with the variety of poses and color in both, is an effective curatorial pun.

But the installation also creates problems. It is easy to forget that the disaster paintings and the paintings of Monroe and other film stars were done during the same period. And because many of the disaster paintings in the second half of the show are essentially monochromatic, it is almost possible to lose sight of Warhol's sense of color. In the context of the show, the chromatic eruption in the late work makes little sense.

•

The work also has limits. Warhol was not comfortable expressing feeling, and his art has a restricted emotional range. Because he moved quickly and did not want an art of contemplation, his works cannot be inexhaustible containers, like the recent paintings of Jasper Johns. When his work is successful, banal images seem to be profound riddles; when it fails, banality is banality. And any artist who gives himself so totally to the moment will not have an easy time evolving.

In the last years of his life, Warhol seems to have been obsessed with the kind of gestural expressionism he had been fighting against. His abstract oxidation paintings — made by urinating on canvas covered with bronze or copper paint — could be seen as an irreverent tribute to Jackson Pollock. He was interested in an Expressionist like Edvard Munch, who, like Warhol, was fascinated with femme fatales, self-portraiture and death. Warhol made paintings inspired by Rorschach tests, which define pent-up feelings and fears and get beyond the camouflage of the self. If Warhol had not died in 1987, at the age of 59, he might have surprised everyone.

One of the keys to Warhol is his esthetic of self-effacement. His desire to be a machine is well known. So is naming his studio the Factory. So are his films in which nothing happens. He loved the camera, and in some way functioned like one, preferring to appear a neutral force that simply presented what it saw. Many of his images just seem to be there. The more monochromatic his photo-silk-screens are, the more the images seem to be in the process of disappearing.

•

Self-effacement and transformation went together. Mr. McShine underlines Warhol's "history of dissatisfaction with his appearance" and his yearning to be someone else. He was Andrew Warhola, who became Andy Warhol. Although he was born in Forest City, Pa., the son of working-class Czechoslovak immigrants, he encouraged various people to believe that he was born in Cleveland, Philadelphia or Pittsburgh.

Everything he did, no matter what the subject, was a portrait. But a portrait of a particular kind. With everyone, from Liza Minnelli to Mick Jagger to Philip Johnson, he served the person. He was not critical, allowing people to be as they wanted.

Change was a Warhol theme. He liked transvestites. He loved Marilyn Monroe, the former Norma Jean Baker, with her exaggerated and self-conscious femininity and her superstardom that seemed to reduce her self to a tiny yet inextinguishable song. He was drawn to artists like Leonardo and Botticelli, who painted figures whose sexuality does not seem fixed. He loved taking nobodies and making them stars or turning a Campbell's soup can into a cultural icon.

His art has a great deal to do with the possibilities of erasure. The paintings of electric chairs and car wrecks involve actual obliteration. In his Most Wanted Men series, Warhol showed men who obliterated others. In his painting "Atomic Bomb," he presented an object that has threatened to obliterate the human race. Throughout his career, Warhol was fascinated with the ultimate erasure, death.

•

The need for self-effacement and change is essential to his achievement. Warhol was someone for whom accepted values that might hinder change had to be wiped out. To the end, he challenged good taste and believed that anything in art was possible. Using images appropriated from sources available to everyone and rejecting the mystique of the artist's touch, he helped define an alternative to the personal emphasis and metaphysical longing of Abstract Expressionism.

Warhol is a very American artist. His flat images, painted in a flat tone, existing in a non-space from which past and future have been banished, are locked into the present. They are rootless, homeless works. Because of the artist's refusal to judge, they also seem remarkably pure. This body of work makes the present seem absolute and eternal — in other words, transcendent.

Part of Warhol's achievement was to legitimize his love of secular, profane subjects by attaching to them traditional religious values. For those who love popular culture, love stars, need the American mainstream, his purity, self-effacement and belief in a transcendent present hold out the promise of salvation. Warhol argues that self-effacement and sensual excess, purity and trash, the moment and eternity can exist together.

This helps explain why Warhol is so important to so many people. His work speaks for a large and important group, almost a class, that has been rising out of the great blank spaces of American culture since World War II. Many are rootless, or determined to deny their roots. Many are new to money. They want to believe they can change at will and invent themselves from scratch. Warhol reassures them that the present can be home, as fixed and permanent as whatever it is they are trying to escape or erase. One of the large questions unanswered by this show is whether, at the end of his life, Warhol still believed this himself.

FEBRUARY 5, 1989

Yoko Ono's New Bronze Age At the Whitney

By PAUL TAYLOR

AS WELL AS BEING ONE OF THE world's most fabled widows, Yoko Ono is one of its wealthiest artists. Yet even stranger for one so famous is that her art is actually little known. A participant in New York's underground scene of the early 1960's and one of the very first members of the international Fluxus art movement — a loosely knit group of musicians, artists, poets and film makers who tried to blur the boundaries between art and life, and in some ways were the first hippies — Yoko Ono became the personification of way out, experimental art after she met John Lennon in 1966.

As an artist, Ms. Ono was a curiosity, and a bit of a shock. She was also an occasional whipping boy for the press through the late 1960's and the 1970's — blamed for splitting up the Beatles and denounced as an artistic opportunist. Once she published a sales list of her art's prices as a work of art. On another occasion, in 1965, she offered 200 shares in herself for sale at $250 each. As a joke on the newly invented label of Conceptual Artist, she proudly dubbed herself a "con artist."

The Whitney Museum of American Art begs to differ, and beginning Wednesday (through April 16) will present "Yoko Ono: Objects, Films," an exhibition of her art from the early 60's on.

■

"Yoko Ono was an artist who was part of a movement involved in exploring conceptual issues. Younger artists are again interested in these themes, so it seems a good time to bring them back into view," said Barbara Haskell, curator of painting and sculpture at the Whitney and co-curator of the exhibition. This show, comprising two dozen of the artist's sculptures and films — some of which are nominally familiar to avant-gardists and Beatles fans alike — will be held in the museum's lobby gallery and film and video theater. Financially and spatially, it is a modest project for the museum. But in terms of attendance, the Whitney expects a blockbuster.

Clearly, the life and work of Yoko Ono, who turns 56 this month, continues to inspire debate. The jury is still out on her art. Recollections of her work in the early 1960's vary wildly. Richard Bellamy, who directed the influential Green Gallery in New York, says, "I thought of her as a particularly severe case of 'suffering artist,' and was sympathetic. But there was little I could do about it practically except, for example, to ask Bob Scull to buy her 'Sky Piece,' and later to send her $50 when she appealed from London. I wanted to help on a personal level, but I couldn't get behind her art."

To David Bourdon, however, former art critic at The Village Voice and Vogue, "Grapefruit," Ms. Ono's book of instructions for musical and artistic pieces, is "one of the monuments of conceptual art of the early 1960's.

"Yoko has a lyrical, poetic dimension that sets her apart from the other conceptual artists," he says. "Her approach to art was only made acceptable when white men like Joseph Kosuth and Lawrence Weiner came in and did virtually the same things as Yoko, but made them respectable and collectible."

And the performance artist Charlotte Moorman, a friend of Ms. Ono's from the early 1960's, adds: "The Beatles were fantastic. They left their mark. But a hundred years from now, it's Yoko Ono the world's going to remember, and not John Lennon or the Beatles."

Ms. Ono started sowing the seeds of her return to the art scene two years ago, after an absence of almost 20 years. In 1987 she accepted an invitation from the Carl Solway Gallery in Cincinnati to participate in its tribute to John Cage on the occasion of his 75th birthday, and minted an edition of eight all-white enameled bronze chess sets, priced at $7,500 each. Soon afterwards, with the help of Arthur Solway, the son of the gallery owner, she quietly got to work on finding an outlet for the pieces in New York. She says that she started wandering into art galleries to "check them out."

■

Arthur Solway suggested Nature Morte, an important, small East Village storefront gallery (it closed last fall). Peter Nagy, director of the gallery, was keen to exhibit Ms. Ono's works in one of the gallery's last shows. "I think her early stuff was some of the best Fluxus stuff done," he says. But when they met and he showed her the work of other artists represented by the gallery, she remained silent. "She said almost nothing," he says. "She was stone-faced, just smoked cigarettes and didn't even take her sunglasses off. Six months later I got word that she wasn't interested. The bottom line I got was that she wasn't interested in being shown as an old 60's artist. She wanted to come back into the art world as a functioning, contemporary artist. She also wanted a big, splashy reentry."

A show was pitched to the New Museum of Contemporary Art in SoHo. But the museum was preparing its Malcolm McLaren show and was slow to respond to a proposal involving another crossover figure from the art and music scenes. Unaware of her efforts to secure an exhibition, John G. Hanhardt, curator of film and video at the Whitney, and co-curator of the exhibition that opens this week, approached Yoko Ono through a common friend. Mr. Hanhardt says that he has long wanted to screen Ms. Ono's films, and when the artist made her sculptures available too, Barbara Haskell, curator of painting and sculpture, and the rest of the museum swung behind him. Within weeks the dates were set, but the final selection of objects was made only last month.

For the Whitney retrospective, Ms. Ono decided to exhibit some of the surviving art works from her early days alongside new versions of the same pieces. Her crystal ball from 1964, "Pointedness," which is displayed with the caption "This sphere will be a sharp point when it gets to the far side of the room in your mind," will stand beside a bronze cast of the same ball, made in 1988. There is also the white chessboard, as well as new casts of some of the artist's earlier objects. These new works, which have been cast in editions of nine, are being offered for sale by the Carl Solway Gallery for between $7,500 and $12,000.

Simultaneously, the museum's film and video department is exhibiting her films, many of which were made in collaboration with John Lennon. They include "Rape" and "Up Your Legs Forever" — which features the legs of, among others, John Cage, Jasper Johns, Robert Rauschenberg, Rolling Stone magazine publisher Jann Wenner and the film maker Jonas Mekas — as well as "Bottoms" and "Fly," the latter starring a representative of the insect kingdom who washes and struts across the landscape of a naked human body. It is accompanied by Yoko Ono's shrill vocal soundtrack — sounds that were typical of the music she recorded with Lennon and the band they formed after the demise of the Beatles, the Plastic Ono Band.

■

Ms. Ono lives surrounded by art in the apartments she shared with the former Beatle in New York's grand Dakota building. Her plush environment is the antithesis of the downtown loft where she took some of her first steps as an artist in New York's experimental scene. For a six-month period in 1960 and 1961, her home on Chambers Street was an important meeting place and concert venue for composers, performance artists, poets and others. This sparsely furnished loft in an industrial area of Lower Manhattan — housing nothing but a knocked-about grand piano and chairs made from old orange crates, which the artist would rearrange into a bed at nighttime — was a lonely outpost in the art world of the time.

Thanks to these concerts, says the composer John Cage, "Yoko became an important person in the New York avant-garde. People came from long distances to attend the performances. They were the most interesting things going on." Among the audiences were Mr. Cage, who was the group's spiritual leader; George Maciunas, who soon became its impresario; Max Ernst and Peggy Guggenheim, and Marcel and Teeny Duchamp.

"I was definitely part of that fringe scene," Ms. Ono says, "but I don't think that anybody was doing work like mine. My sources were in everything."

In 1961 Maciunas opened the AG Gallery on Madison Avenue and offered Yoko Ono a show, her first. She exhibited paintings with little burnholes and a piece of canvas on the floor titled "Painting To Be Stepped On." The "painting" was an irregular piece of canvas. "I didn't have the money to buy a canvas," she says, "so I was given a piece from the Army disposal store downstairs, and just used that."

■

Yoko Ono virtually dropped out of the art scene in 1972, after a retrospective at the Everson Museum in Syracuse. Last summer, when the Whitney provided her with a means of re-entry, the only problem was what to exhibit.

Then one day, over spaghetti at Da Silvano restaurant in Greenwich Village, Ms. Ono's live-in companion, Sam Havadtoy, an interior decorator, suggested to the artist that she recast her old pieces in bronze. "I got very upset," she says, "because I thought that this person just didn't understand anything about my work. My work was about a representation of ideas, and ideas are just like water or air. The work had an ethereal quality."

■

Soon, however, she came to appreciate the suggestion. "I realized that for something to move me so much that I would cry, there's something there. There seemed like a shimmering air in the 60's when I made these pieces, and now the air is bronzified. Now it's the 80's, and bronze is very 80's in a way — solidity, commodity, all of that. For someone who went through the 60's revolution, there has of course been an incredible change. . . . I call the pieces petrified bronze. That freedom, all the hope and wishes are in some ways petrified."

What were once slight, papery and translucent glass sculptures and see-through mesh paintings are now being presented in cold, impenetrable, permanent versions. A reflection, perhaps, of Yoko Ono's own story over the last 30 years, ever since she first appeared in New York as an eccentric and ambitious new arrival? □

MAY 5, 1991

In Stamford, Whitney Offers Diversity of Faces and Figures

By VIVIEN RAYNOR

THE show at the Whitney Museum's Fairfield County branch in Stamford comes from the museum's gallery at Federal Reserve Plaza in lower Manhattan, where it was organized by Kathleen Monaghan, director of the Whitney at the Equitable Center, in midtown. Its title is "Image and Likeness," and its contents are 22 figural paintings and sculptures drawn from the permanent collection at the Whitney's home in uptown Manhattan.

God made man in His own image, but since then, the meaning of the word "image" has changed. No longer a likeness, it is something constructed by an artist (or a public relations firm). As Ms. Monaghan proposes in her brochure essay, the change was brought about by the introduction of photography. Freed by the new medium from the "dictates of objective realism," artists, she says, "turned to issues of formal interpretation, a shift that reflected the rise of Modernism." Or was one of its causes.

Painters were hardly rebelling against the constraints of realism before the camera arrived, but many were happy to use it as a shortcut to representation. Still, art aided by photography was looked down upon until the mid-20th century, when, quite suddenly, it became acceptable, and the term "photographic" was no longer a slur.

While there are more images than likenesses in the show, the most imposing of the works is a likeness in all respects save size. It is the 9-by-7-foot photograph of the composer Philip Glass, airbrushed on canvas by Chuck Close. Until recently, the giant portrait in Western art was the perquisite of despots, but now, the power it bespeaks is that of advertising. This 1969 example, in black and white, looks like a billboard awaiting the addition of a brand name. Mr. Close has been regarded as a Minimalist for his dispassionate way of mapping faces, yet he seems very much out of Photo-Realism and, hence, out of Pop.

There is only one picture of Mr. Glass, but there are 36 (count 'em) of Ethel Scull, the wife of Robert Scull, the late collector of Pop Art. As silkscreened in decorator's colors by Andy Warhol (in 1963), Mrs. Scull plays to the camera with and without sunglasses, looking every inch the fashion model. The 12-foot-wide canvas is another reminder of Warhol's genius for persuasion, for it is not as though the images he appropriated were extraordinary in themselves or that he did much to transform them.

By the way, the Pop wizard himself is present in the form of a portrait painted by Alice Neel in 1970, after his attempted assassination. He sits, eyes closed, shirt off, displaying the stigmata on the milky skin of his midriff. Like most of Ms. Neel's portraits, this is a straightforward likeness except for cartoon-style feet and hands.

Alex Katz offers two small painted wood cutouts of his wife, Ada, and a 9-by-12-foot canvas filled with slickly-painted male and female faces. Philip Pearlstein is represented by one of his pallid nudes, recumbent on a pink Oriental carpet and reflected in a mirror. George Segal's white plaster figures stand at a traffic light, doomed never to "walk." These are all images, as is William Bailey's rubbery nude, posed seemingly in a vacuum. The "Great American Nude No. 57" of Tom Wesselmann, however, is more an icon, for, despite its Matissean associations, it is a symbol of the national consensus on nubile glamour, as dictated by commercial photography. Figure painting was not Fairfield Porter's forte, and "Screen Porch" is surely one of his more pedestrian efforts. Still, Ms. Monaghan makes the picture a conversation piece by reporting that, of the figures occupying the foreground, the young man reading is the artist's lover. Mrs. Porter is the white-haired woman "exiled" to the garden outside the porch.

Duane Hanson's effigy of a gone-to-seed housewife slumped in a chair, reading her mail with only her curled-up poodle for company, is a likeness for sure. Yet, the pitiless way the artist itemizes details like grubby toenails makes the subject more specimen than woman.

Apropos decay, Robert Arneson had his own in mind when modeling his oversize self-portrait with quizzical expression; he was ill at the time (1976). Even so, the only clues to this are the dark gray color of the clay and the title, "Whistling in the Dark," which is inscribed around a glazed yellow base.

The remaining works are images, the most noteworthy being de Kooning's semi-abstraction, "Woman and Bicycle" (1952 to '53), "Girl Looking at Landscape" by Richard Diebenkorn (1957) and the painted steel sculpture that is David Smith's ideogram for his daughter running (1956). "Image and Likeness" strays from its theme with the inclusion of some works, particularly "The Entry of Christ into Chicago, in 1976," an amusing homage by Roger Brown to James Ensor's vision of Jesus entering Brussels. But it does illustrate how insidious the effect of photography on art and life has been.

SEPTEMBER 22, 1991

LONG ISLAND GUIDE

BARBARA DELATINER

ART FROM THE 60'S and 90'S

Two exhibitions opening today at the Parrish Art Museum in Southampton explore art from the 60's to the present.

The 60's are covered in "Minimalism and Postminimalism: Drawing Distinctions," drawings by Carl Andre, Sol LeWitt, John Newman and Richard Serra.

In the second show, "Selections From the Elaine and Werner Dannheisser Collection: Painting and Sculpture from the 80's and 90's," works by artists like Georg Baselitz, Jeff Koon, Bruce Nauman, David Salle and Cindy Sherman show collectors' interests and the art scene today.

Accompanied by programming like "America's Pop Collector," a film about Robert Scull, at 6:30 P.M. on Friday, the exhibitions run through Nov. 17 at the Parrish on Job's Lane. Information: 283-2118.

OCTOBER 10, 1996

Modern Acquires 2 Icons Of Pop Art

By CAROL VOGEL

The Museum of Modern Art acquired two icons of American Pop Art yesterday, Andy Warhol's "Campbell's Soup Cans" and James Rosenquist's "F-111," along with an early and important painting by Ellsworth Kelly from the 1950's.

"These are critical works we felt must be here," said Glenn D. Lowry, the Modern's director, in announcing the acquisitions.

The Warhol and the Rosenquist, he said, fortify the museum's holdings from the 1960's and put them more on a par with its collections of American works from the 1950's and of European prewar art.

"Campbell's Soup Cans" has 32 panels, 20 by 16 inches each, with different kinds of soup. The work is partly a gift, partly a purchase from the New York art dealer and collector Irving Blum. Mr. Blum was a young dealer in 1962 when he bought it from Warhol, paying him $1,000 in 10 installments. It has been on loan to the National Gallery in Washington for eight years.

Neither museum officials nor Mr. Blum would discuss the price, but people close to the negotiations put the total figure at $15 million, among the highest prices ever paid for a work of contemporary art and far surpassing the $4 million auction record for Warhol's "Red Shot Marilyn" in 1989.

"F-111" is thought by some to be Mr. Rosenquist's seminal work, a reaction against American military power and consumer culture. Influenced by advertising billboards, which the artist once painted for a living, the work is 10 feet high, 86 feet long, a mélange of images from advertisements, newspaper photographs and other sources that include depictions of an F-111 bomber. The painting was on the cover of the catalogue for the famous Robert Scull sale at Sotheby's in 1986, when it was bought by Richard Jacobs, the Cleveland-based real-estate developer, for more than $2 million. Mr. Jacobs is thought to be the seller today, working through Jeffrey Deitch, the New York dealer.

The Warhol and the Rosenquist were in the Modern's 1990 show "High and Low: Modern Art and Popular Culture." "I've dreamed of having them in the museum ever since," said Kirk Varnedoe, chief curator of painting and sculpture.

Mr. Varnedoe has also had his eye on Kelly's "White Plaque: Bridge Arch and Reflection" (1951-55), which has two white panels separated by a wood strip. "It's a crucial addition to our permanent collection," he said. "Kelly gave us the great masterpiece, 'Colors for a Large Wall,' and this is a very different work. It speaks to the whole history of Minimalist abstraction."

Mr. Varnedoe noted that the acquisition virtually coincides with the opening of the Kelly retrospective next week at the Solomon R. Guggenheim Museum. The painting was acquired through a London dealer, Leslie Waddington, from a collector there, Mr. Varnedoe said. He declined to give the price but said a trustee, Emily Raugh Pulitzer, paid half the price as a gift.

Mr. Lowry said the large-scale acquisitions anticipated the museum's expansion. The Modern now owns the Dorset Hotel on West 54th Street and three brownstones on West 53d Street, which will eventually allow the museum to double its size. As it grows physically it is also increasing its holdings.

JANUARY 30, 1998

INSIDE ART

Perhaps Shot, Perhaps Not

Carol Vogel

As familiar as Andy Warhol's image of Marilyn Monroe has become in the visual vocabulary of popular culture, the actual paintings the artist executed in the early 1960's rarely appear on the market. When they do, they generate a good deal of excitement among Pop Art collectors, which is the case with "Orange Marilyn."

"Orange Marilyn," which will be sold at Sotheby's in New York on May 14, is from the famous Ströher collection, a German collection of 20th-century art that was one of the first in Europe to include American Pop Art.

This isn't the first time works from the Ströher collection have turned up for sale. In 1989, Sotheby's in New York sold several of them, including Warhol's "Red Jackie" from 1963 and a 1961 Claes Oldenburg, "Bacon and Egg."

"Orange Marilyn," which the auction house estimates will bring $4 million to $6 million, was last for sale 30 years ago, when Karl Ströher bought it from Leon Kraushar, a Long Island collector. With Robert and Ethel Scull, he was among the pre-eminent Pop Art collectors of the 1960's. The painting has moved from Mr. Ströher, who put the collection together in the 1950's and 60's, to one of his descendants, who is now the seller.

For years, the painting has been on loan to museums, first the Hessisches Landes Museum near Frankfurt and most recently the Museum of Modern Art in Frankfurt. It was last exhibited in the United States in the 1970's.

"It is the sexiest image on earth," said Tobias Meyer, who heads Sotheby's contemporary art worldwide. "Not only is this a classic Warhol image but the orange used for the background is his most classic color."

The painting is listed in the catalogue raisonné of Warhol's work as "Shot Orange Marilyn." In 1964, Warhol painted five colored Marilyns, all in a 40-inch-square format but with different colored backgrounds: red, orange, light blue, sage blue and turquoise. The paintings were stored at the Factory, Warhol's studio on East 47th Street in Manhattan.

Like "Shot Red Marilyn," the image of Marilyn with a red background, which sold at Christie's in

APRIL 3, 1998

Richard Bellamy, Art Dealer, Is Dead at 70

By ROBERTA SMITH

Richard Bellamy, a New York art dealer whose Green Gallery was one of the most important showcases of avant-garde art during the American art explosion of the early 1960's, died on Sunday at his home in Long Island City, Queens. He was 70.

He died in his sleep, said his son, Miles.

A boyish, usually stylishly disheveled man with a charming, somewhat nervous manner, Mr. Bellamy was known for his brilliant eye, his skill at installing exhibitions, his love of tennis, his "towering modesty" (as his shyness was sometimes called) and his devotion to new art and its creators. The names and locations of his galleries varied, as did their efficiency and public hours, but for more than four decades he was rarely without one, or at least an office for private dealing.

Richard Hu Bellamy was born in Cincinnati in 1927, the only child of parents who had met at medical school. His father was a doctor. His mother, who was from a Chinese missionary family that sent its daughters to the United States to be educated, never practiced medicine. Mr. Bellamy credited her with his lifelong passion for music and literature and said that the small jade sculptures she brought with her from China triggered his first understanding of beauty.

He enrolled in the University of

Ohio in Cincinnati, quitting after one semester. In 1949, at the suggestion of a friend who was also interested in art, he visited Provincetown, Mass., known for its summer art colony, and stayed, discovering that he enjoyed the company of artists. He supported himself with odd jobs and worked briefly as a radio announcer on WCNX in Middletown, Conn., until he was caught reading "The Waste Land" over the air, and dismissed.

Mr. Bellamy settled in New York in the early 1950's, and soon began working as director of the Hansa Gallery, a new cooperative on East 10th Street whose members included Allan Kaprow, Alfred Leslie, George Segal, Richard Stankiewicz, Jean Follett, Robert Whitman and Jan Müller.

Hansa closed in 1959, and Mr. Bellamy opened the Green Gallery in 1960 with backing from the collector Robert Scull. The gallery's meteoric five-year life spanned an unusually fertile period in New York art: in the wake of Abstract Expressionism, a new generation of artists, diverse in talent, was giving shape to esthetic tendencies that would soon be labeled Color Field painting, Pop Art and Minimalism.

Mr. Bellamy gave first or second shows to a remarkable number of these emerging artists, building an exhibition record that speaks for itself. The Green Gallery had the first exhibitions of Claes Oldenburg's soft sculptures, the first exhibition of Donald Judd's cadmium red light sculptures and the first three shows of Robert Morris's work. Others on the list included Mr. Segal, Mark di Suvero, Tom Wesselman, Yayoi Kusama, Larry Poons, Jo Baer, Lee Bontecou and Lucas Samaras. But, disconcerted by lack of sales, Mr. Scull withdrew his support and the gallery closed in 1965. Mr. Bellamy placed many of the artists with Leo Castelli, another leading gallery.

After Green, Mr. Bellamy continued to show young artists and always kept up with developments on the art scene, but he also turned to artists he considered unjustly neglected or whose work was unwieldy, like the large-scale sculpture of Mr. di Suvero, whom Mr. Bellamy continued to represent until his own death.

In the late 1960's and early 70's, Mr. Bellamy rented an office in the gallery of Noah Goldowsky on Madison Avenue, where he organized exhibitions of the work of Richard Artschwager, Peter Young, Keith Sonnier and Richard Serra. He also became a trusted adviser to collectors, museums and younger art dealers; and in the late 1980's and early 90's was partner to the dealer Barbara Flynn in her gallery at 113 Crosby Street in SoHo.

In 1980, he opened one of the first galleries in TriBeCa, on an upper floor of a building on Chambers Street that had sweeping views of the Hudson. Here he often worked with artists who showed infrequently, or were known for a certain reclusiveness. These included Mr. Leslie, Ms. Baer, Michael Heizer, Neil Jenney, Richard Nonas and Mr. di Suvero, for whom he organized retrospectives at the Storm King Art Center, Mountainville, N.Y., in 1985 and 1995.

By 1985, Mr. Bellamy had moved to a pier on the East River in Long Island City, where Mr. di Suvero already had a large studio. Devoting most of his time to Mr. di Suvero's career, he ceased to have regular hours, but oversaw a changing display that could be seen by appointment of works by the artists whose work he loved most.

A memorial service is to be held on May 13 at 3 P.M. at the P.S. 1 Center for Contemporary Art, 22-25 Jackson Avenue at 46th Avenue, Long Island City.

In addition to his son, Mr. Bellamy is survived by his companion, Sally Gross, and her children, Rachel and Sedonia, all of New York City.

MAY 15, 1998

$17.3 Million 'Marilyn' Sets Warhol Record

By CAROL VOGEL

"Orange Marilyn," Andy Warhol's iconic 1964 image of Marilyn Monroe, broke all records for the artist and became the highest-priced painting of the spring auction season last night when it was sold at Sotheby's for $17.3 million, more than four times the previous record for a Warhol. Two unidentified telephone bidders fought a tense battle, and when it ended, the packed salesroom burst into thunderous applause.

The price set the tone for the evening. The sale totaled $35.6 million, far above Sotheby's high estimate of $25.5 million. Of the 56 works offered, 45 found buyers.

Before the sale, contemporary-art experts said the Museum of Modern Art was trying to buy the Warhol. So, it was thought, were the Andy Warhol Museum in Pittsburgh and the Tate Gallery in London. Among the collectors said to have been contenders were Stephen A. Wynn, the Las Vegas casino owner, and the publishing magnate S.I. Newhouse Jr. All Sotheby's would say was that a collector had bought it.

The previous record for a Warhol was set in 1989, at the height of the art market, when Christie's sold "Shot Red Marilyn" — named for a bullet hole it sustained in 1964 when a woman entered Warhol's Manhattan studio, aimed a gun at his forehead, missed and hit several paintings stacked on the floor instead — for $4.01 million. In 1994, after the market fell, it was sold again for just $3.6 million. Sotheby's estimated "Orange Marilyn" would bring $4 million to $6 million last night.

Warhol based his iconic images on a still photo from the movie "Niagara." He painted five Marilyns in 1964, all in a 40-inch-square format, but with backgrounds in different colors: red, orange, light blue, sage blue and turquoise. The paintings were stored at the Factory, Warhol's studio in Manhattan.

Part of the reason for the painting's success was its provenance. It was being sold by a descendant of Karl Ströher of Darmstadt, Germany, whose collection of 20th-century works was one of the first in Europe to include American Pop Art. Mr. Stroher bought it from Leon Kraushar, a Long Island collector who, with Robert and Ethel Scull, was among the pre-eminent Pop Art collectors in the 1960's.

"It was a wise buy at this price," said Tobias Meyer, director of contemporary art for Sotheby's worldwide, who was the evening's auctioneer. "It will soon be worth as much as a Picasso or any landmark work of this century."

The sale also broke a record for Lucian Freud with "Large Interior WII (After Watteau)." With an estimate of $2.5 million to $3.5 million, it was bought by Lucy Mitchell-Innes, a Manhattan dealer, for $5.8 million. Painted from 1981 to 1983, and inspired by Watteau's 1712 "Pierrot Content," now in the Thyssen-Bornemisza Museum in Madrid, it depicts two of the artist's children and three friends in a rundown London interior.

There has been an outcry in London that the painting is a national treasure and never should have left the country. Ms. Mitchell-Innes said the painting has now indeed left England, but she declined to identify the buyer. It was being sold by was James Kirkman, who was Mr. Freud's dealer from 1972 to 1992.

(Final prices include the auction house's commission, 15 percent of the first $50,000 an 10 percent of the rest. Estimates do not reflect commissions.)

A far less important Warhol, "Untitled (Flowers)," from 1964, had four serious bidders. It ended up selling to an unidentified telephone bidder for $910,000, far above its $650,000 high estimate.

From there the sale's quality and price levels dropped drastically. But because of an influx of new, moneyed American buyers whose budgets range from $500,000 to $1 million, there were a few surprisingly strong results.

Take Robert Motherwell's "Elegy to the Spanish Republic No. 134," from 1974. Two buyers were determined to have the black-and-white abstract painting, one of the best examples of Motherwell's most important series. It finally sold for $860,500 to an unidentified telephone buyer bidding through Diana D. Brooks, Sotheby's chief executive worldwide. The price high estimate had been $500,000.

The sale was strong in Minimalist art. "It's the the new esthetic," Mr. Meyer said. "Like Pop Art, people can understand it visually."

Carl Andre's "Zinc-Copper Plain," a 36-unit square floor piece from 1969, was expected to sell for $150,000 to $200,000; it went to Jim Cohan, who works for Anthony d'Offay, the London dealer from New York, for $310,500. Brice Marden's "2 Part Study," a 1966 painting on two canvases, was expected to bring $250,00 to $350,000 and sold to an unidentified bidder for $475,500. Another choice work, Robert Ryman's "Untitled," a 12-inch-square painting of different white brush strokes estimated at $120,000 to $150,000, was choice not only for its size but also for its date, 1961. It sold to a telephone bidder right at its high estimate, bringing $156,500.

Another artist whose work fared particularly well was Alexander Calder, perhaps because of the high quality of the material or because he is the subject of a major current retrospective at the National Gallery of Art in Washington. But when his delicate early wire sculpture, "Acrobats" (1929) came on the turntable, four paddles began waving furiously in the air, and three of Sotheby's crew taking telephone bids started waving their hands. "Acrobats" finally sold to one of the telephone bidders for $794,500, more than five times its $150,000 high estimate.

The sale did have its casualties. "Criss Cross," a mostly black 1958 painting by Frank Stella with an estimate of $1.4 million to $1.8 million, failed to spark one bid and was stalled at $850,000.

Two out of three works by Cy Twombly failed to sell at Christie's on Tuesday night, and last night, "Untitled (Rome)," from 1962, one of the artist's graffitilike images of blackboard scribbles, also went unsold. No one was willing to pay even the $700,000 low estimate.

The work of Roy Lichtenstein, who died in September at 73, has been tested this week. At Christie's on Tuesday night, two of his paintings brought strong prices. Last night, his cartoonlike "Still Life With Stretcher, Mirror, Bowl of Fruit" (1972), estimated at $600,000 to $800,000, just squeaked by, selling for $640,500 to a telephone bidder.

But it was "Orange Marilyn" that staggered even the most seasoned experts. "We saw something tonight that we haven't seen for nine years: two people willing to pay any price for a painting," said Richard Gray, a dealer who has galleries in Chicago and New York. "Recently the market has been so strong and so sensible. It makes me a little nervous."

JULY 3, 1998

Julia Perles, Groundbreaker In Divorce Law, Is Dead at 84

By ERIC PACE

Julia Perles, a longtime Manhattan lawyer who played an important part in bringing about a significant change in New York State's divorce legislation, died early Wednesday at Sarasota Memorial Hospital in Sarasota, Fla. She was 84 and had lived in Sarasota for about four years.

The cause was not immediately clear, but she had had a fall at her home, said Janet Post, a friend.

Ms. Perles is widely considered to have played the leading role in bringing about the passage of what is popularly known as New York State's equitable distribution law, which went into effect in 1980. The law brought about what its admirers have called a revolutionary change in the practice of matrimonial law and in the rights of marital partners.

At her death, Ms. Perles was still affiliated with the law firm of Phillips, Nizer, Benjamin, Krim & Ballon, based in Manhattan, where she became a partner in 1970, having been invited by Louis Nizer to head the firm's matrimonial practice.

She went on to become a senior partner until about eight years ago, and remained head of her department until she moved to Florida. After that, she continued to be affiliated with the firm and its matrimonial department.

While she was practicing matrimonial law, she became chairwoman of a special committee of the New York County Lawyers Association. The panel's members were respected specialists in marital law who favored getting the equitable-distribution change made in the state law. Committee members communicated with the State Legislature in Albany repeatedly, former colleagues of Ms. Perles recalled, and it took much attention and perseverance to persuade the Legislature to make the change.

Under the law as it was passed in 1980, both spouses, in the event of a divorce, are enabled to share equitably in the assets that either or both of them have accumulated during the marriage, even if title to the property — a house for instance, or a business — is in the name of only one spouse. Parties to a marriage did not have that legal right in New York State before the law was passed.

The underlying assumption behind the law is that both parties to a marriage contribute to the acquisition, maintenance and growth of the marital assets.

Ms. Perles's clients over the years included Woody Allen; Nancy Allen, the actress-wife of Brian De Palma, the movie director; the former Eve Ella Sherpick Green, the first wife of Harry B. Helmsley, the New York real estate titan; David Merrick, the producer; and Ethel Scull, who once was called the doyenne of the pop art world.

Ms. Perles was a former president of the New York Women's Bar Association, a fellow of the American Academy of Matrimonial Lawyers and a member of the Dirty Thirty, an organization of American lawyers prominent in the field of matrimonial law.

She was born and raised in Brooklyn, and she wanted to be a lawyer from the time she was 12 years old. Rona J. Shays, a close friend, recalled that Ms. Perles used to say that her own mother had not wanted her to go to law school and had said to her, "No one will want to marry you if they think you're smarter than they are."

Nevertheless, Ms. Perles went on to attend Brooklyn College, and she received her law degree in 1937 from Brooklyn Law School.

She was an associate in the Manhattan law firm of Schwartz & Frohlich from 1942 to 1952 and then a partner at the Manhattan law firm of Greenbaum Wolff & Ernst before going to Phillips, Nizer.

In 1951 she married Howard Singer. He died in 1989.

Her survivors include a brother, David Perles, who lives in Boca Raton, Fla.

AUGUST 15, 1999

ART

Museums/Institutions

P.S. 1 CONTEMPORARY ART CENTER — "David Reed Paintings: Motion Pictures." "Animal.anima.animus." Works by 125 artists, including Marina Abramovic, Hubert Duprat and Dennis Oppenheim. "Philippe Starck: Furniture and Objects." "0044: Contemporary Irish Art in Britain." Works by 20 artists. "Anna Oppermann: Being Different (Why Is She So Different?) 1970-1986." A multimedia installation. "John Tweddle: Paintings From the Robert C. Scull Collection." Outdoor Gallery: "Robert Ressler: Public Space, Private Thoughts, Private Space, Public Thoughts." Wood Sculpture. All through Aug. 29. 22-25 Jackson Ave., at 46th Ave., Long Island City (718-784-2084) Sun., Wed.-Sat., noon-6.

AUGUST 22, 1999

ART

Museums/Institutions

P.S. 1 CONTEMPORARY ART CENTER — "David Reed Paintings: Motion Pictures." "Animal.anima.animus." Works by 125 artists, including Marina Abramovic, Hubert Duprat and Dennis Oppenheim. "Philippe Starck: Furniture and Objects." "0044: Contemporary Irish Art in Britain." Works by 20 artists. "Anna Oppermann: Being Different (Why Is She So Different?) 1970-1986." A multimedia installation. "John Tweddle: Paintings From the Robert C. Scull Collection." Outdoor Gallery: "Robert Ressler: Public Space, Private Thoughts, Private Space, Public Thoughts." Wood Sculpture. All through next Sunday. 22-25 Jackson Ave., at 46th Ave., Long Island City (718-784-2084) Sun., Wed.-Sat., noon-6.

AUGUST 29, 1999

ART

Museums/Institutions

P.S. 1 CONTEMPORARY ART CENTER — "David Reed Paintings: Motion Pictures." "Animal.anima.animus." Works by 125 artists, including Marina Abramovic, Hubert Duprat and Dennis Oppenheim. "Philippe Starck: Furniture and Objects." "0044: Contemporary Irish Art in Britain." Works by 20 artists. "Anna Oppermann: Being Different (Why Is She So Different?) 1970-1986." A multimedia installation. "John Tweddle: Paintings From the Robert C. Scull Collection." Outdoor Gallery: "Robert Ressler: Public Space, Private Thoughts, Private Space, Public Thoughts." Wood Sculpture. All through today. 22-25 Jackson Ave., at 46th Ave., Long Island City (718-784-2084) Sun., Wed.-Sat., noon-6.

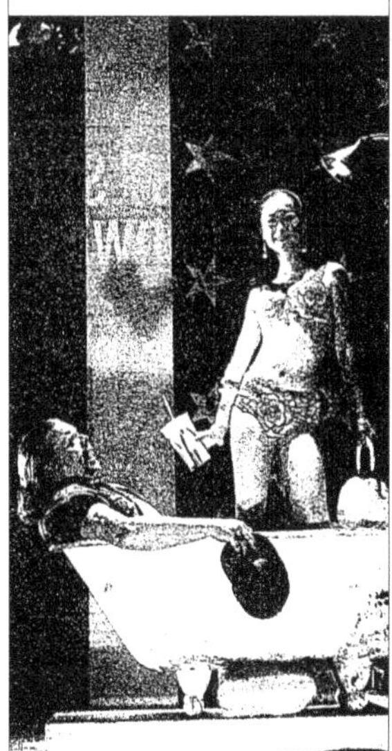

JANUARY 16, 2000

MICHAEL HEIZER

Just the Facts

To the Editor

Suzaan Boettger may not like the way Michael Heizer talked about his art [Letters to the Editor, Jan 2], but the facts support Mr Heizer's statements, as Michael Kimmelman reported them in his article "A Sculptor's Colossus of the Desert" [Dec 12]

Robert Smithson did accompany Mr Heizer to the Nevada desert when Mr Heizer was executing a nine-piece series commissioned by Robert C Scull This series was photographed by and written up in Newsweek during the summer of 1968

Later that same summer, Smithson was a guest at Mr Heizer's cabin at Lake Tahoe

It was Walter De Maria who encouraged Mr Heizer to document the date on which he executed his first pieces on the land, which Mr Heizer did in 1967, thus substantiating that they were the first done in the genre that the critics at first named "earth art" and then, later on, "land art"

You may not like the words Mr Heizer chooses, but you cannot deny the fact that he was the first The facts exist.

S E KEAYS
Lake Worth, Fla.

JANUARY 12, 2001

Clicking: Warhol With Camera

By HOLLAND COTTER

"ANDY WARHOL DEAD AT 58," boomed a New York Post headline in 1987, and nobody could believe it. But there he was in a grainy front-page photograph, standing in front of one of his signature images, a silk-screened head shot of Marilyn Monroe that he had lifted from a Hollywood publicity still.

Warhol left a lot of himself behind when he died of complications from surgery. Most important was a far-reaching artistic influence, which is still in good working order. But there were also physical things — cartons, closets, entire buildings crammed full of them — including nearly 100,000 photographs.

Some of these were family snapshots and vintage fine-art items. But most of the pictures, in the form of prints, contact sheets and negatives, were by Warhol himself. Starting in the 1960's, after he had transformed himself from a Wally Cox nerd to a silver-haired E. T., he carried a camera with him wherever he went and shot whatever he saw: dinner parties, sex acts, shop signs. Some people tend to daydream or hum a tune when they walk down a New York street. Warhol went click, click, click.

Some 300 pictures in various formats are included in "Andy Warhol: Photography" at the International Center of Photography, the first major exhibition devoted to this aspect of his career. Originally organized by Christoph Heinrich for the Hamburg Kunsthalle and seen at the Andy Warhol Museum in Pittsburgh, this is an entertaining and sometimes enlightening show, cleanly installed in a design by Julie Ault and Martin Beck. But taken strictly as a display of photography, it feels awfully thin, mostly because Warhol's output in the medium was almost willfully insubstantial.

The presence of several of his paintings helps to bulk things up, and the center has done some creative editing to give the show a clearer shape than is evident in its hefty but episodic catalog. The work has been arranged thematically rather than chronologically. The selection has been tailored both to highlight Warhol's innovative early output and to focus attention less on his photographs as aesthetic objects than as sources for his work in other mediums.

Virtually everything Warhol did was photo-based; that's apparent at a glance, and it makes sense given his history. He was born in 1928 to a working-class family in Pittsburgh. His earliest view of the world came from the tabloids, his fantasy life from movie magazines and films. A sickly, effeminate child with a disastrous self-image, he understood right away that photographs were emotionally powerful records of fact, but also magical things that could, in the right hands, make the ugliest duckling look like a presentable swan.

His personal investment in the medium is suggested in the show's opening section, "Warhol as Icon," in which he appears in front of the camera more often than behind it. The assembled photographs, spanning decades, clearly demonstrate how an ambitious and audacious artist shaped a public image. But they also document how a morbidly self-conscious man searched for a look he could comfortably live with without ever really finding it.

In pictures taken by a college friend, Leila Davies Singeles, in the early 1950's, Warhol is exuberant and sweet, a natural clown. In a series of 1958 portraits by Duane Michals, he tries on Garbo and Truman Capote poses, then hides his face behind his hands. The Factory years of the 1960's brought wigs and shades and a deadpan inscrutability, evident in Timm Rautert's 1970 studio portrait, in which Warhol faces the camera with eyes closed.

His self-portraits, by contrast, could be surprisingly open-eyed. While recovering from the near-fatal attempt on his life in 1968, he snapped Polaroids of himself in a mirror, as if to get an objective image of his bullet-scarred torso. In the 1980's he took a series of pictures of himself in drag. In some he vamps it up; in others he looks worried, even scared. These contrasting attitudes more or less sum up his conflicted self-presentation.

When his gaze turns to other subjects, however, it tends to be either blankly adoring or unflinchingly voyeuristic. His films are far more important than his still pictures, and a few of them run continuously in the show. They are essentially prolonged staring sessions, usually focused on people who can't or don't stare back, as in the case of a six-hour film of a man sleeping and a series of films of couples kissing.

Warhol also tapped into the erotic thrill of American tabloid culture as expressed through images of violence and death. His candy-colored silk-screens of car wrecks, derived from newspaper clippings, have an orgiastic look, with their splayed and ruined bodies. The monumentally scaled faces in the 1964 "Most Wanted Men" series are based on police mug shots, though Warhol has chosen only young, good-looking felons who project a kind of rough-trade allure.

The original 1962 New York police department handout in which these mug shots appeared is included in the exhibition, as are the sources of many of Warhol's celebrity portraits and, in several cases, the finished works derived from them. The promotional photo used for "Marilyn" is here, as are the magazine clippings on which his various "Jackie" series were based, some of the images pasted up in a beautiful little study for the multipanel paintings to come.

A section of the show is devoted to the photo booth strips that Warhol used for his first big commissioned likenesses, including those of the art collector Ethel Scull and the art dealer Holly Solomon. Elsewhere there is a selection of the Polaroids he routinely took for the V.I.P. portraits of the 1970's and 80's that made him rich but eroded his critical reputation. Farrah, Liza and Bianca all sat for Warhol's camera, their faces coated with makeup the artist insisted they wear to hide even the smallest blemish.

Warhol admired, even emulated beautiful women but he loved beautiful men. The show — overseen at the center by Brian Wallace, its chief curator, and Christopher Phillips, curator — devotes a section to homoeroticism in Warhol's work, and that's a good idea. Sure, it's obvious, but sometimes the obvious needs to be spelled out, just for the record. Warhol's sexuality is central to his work and was formative in his career in complex ways, not least because it was a red flag to some of his most vociferous detractors.

In any event, the exhibition's take on it is pretty tame. At one point he routinely asked men visiting the Factory, his Union Square loft, to drop their pants for a quick photo session. None of the results are here. The closest thing to them, apart from a few "Nude Model" snapshots, is his Michelangelesque full-length portrait of a jock-strap-clad Jean-Michel Basquiat from 1984, his body photographed in a series of Polaroid close-ups, which are joined to make the silk-screen.

Basically, Warhol's entire aesthetic is one of fragments: images clipped and cropped, moments arrested in time, look-alike things pulled at random out of the flow. He seems to acknowledge this directly in his late photographs of cluttered tabletops and shelves of candy bars and a series of pictures stitched together with silver thread. And it's fitting that the show ends as it does with one of his "time capsules," cardboard boxes that he periodically filled with the clutter around him, then sealed and dated and stored away.

Some 600 boxes have been traced, though only about 100 have been opened. The one in the exhibition is particularly rich in photographs, and its contents are like Warhol's photographic output as a whole, at once trivial and revealing. Certain items have much to say about the artist himself. (A little ink drawing of an angel by his mother seems to hold a key to his early illustrational style.) Others are valuable for giving a sense of his own time in American culture and history.

Whatever history will finally say about Warhol himself, "Andy Warhol: Photography" isn't an occasion for summings-up or re-evaluations. Mostly it tells us what we already know, which is that many of the things we take for granted in contemporary art — its high-low culture mix, its cross-breeding of mediums, its inflection by what is sometimes called a gay and lesbian sensibility — were set in motion by him some 40 years ago.

His photography and his use of it was also part of that innovative package. His cut-and-paste use of found photographic sources makes him a prophet of art's present digital age. And his spirit lives on in the work of many high-profile younger photographers: in Wolfgang Tillmans's lifestyle scenes, in Jessica Craig-Martin's party pictures, in Andreas Gursky's panoramas of material proliferation. Even if Warhol gradually moves out of the immediate foreground of contemporary art and into its deep background, there's no question of his continuing presence from here on.

AUGUST 28, 2001

Deaths

SCULL—Ethel Redner. Wife of the late Robert C. Scull. Devoted mother of Jonathan, Stephen Paul and Adam. Loving grandmother of Jamie Ryan and Riley Cooper. Dear sister of Lillian Koplan. Services private.

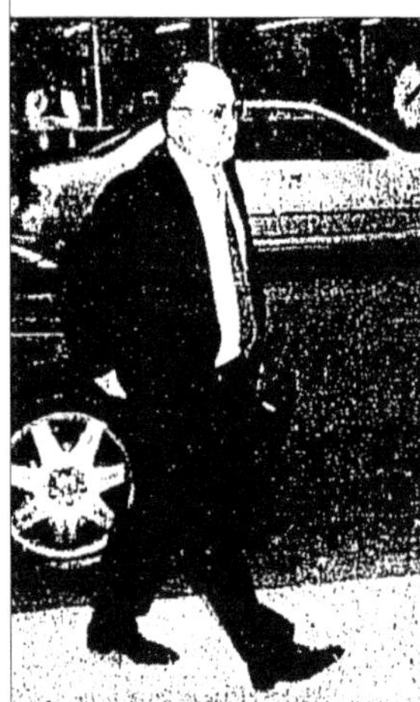

SEPTEMBER 1, 2001

OBITUARIES

Ethel Redner Scull

A socialite who with her husband, Robert, built one of the first major collections of Pop and Minimal art and became the subject of an Andy Warhol portrait, she was 79.

SEPTEMBER 1, 2001

Ethel Scull, a Patron of Pop and Minimal Art, Dies at 79

By GRACE GLUECK

Ethel Redner Scull, who with her husband, Robert, achieved fame and social status in the 1960's by building one of the first major collections of Pop and Minimal art and becoming the subject of an Andy Warhol portrait, died on Monday at a retirement home in Manhattan. She was 79.

The cause was a heart attack followed by a stroke, her son Jonathan said.

Once an ardent partygoer and a devoted fashion buff, Mrs. Scull lived with her husband in an art-filled apartment on upper Fifth Avenue and wore creations by designers like Halston, Adolfo and Yves St. Laurent. But after the Skulls divorced in 1975, she had to curtail her way of life, eventually moving to a small one-bedroom East Side apartment.

Her parting with Scull, a taxi tycoon, after a 30-year marriage, involved her in more than a decade of litigation with him and with his estate; he died in 1986 at 70. One of her major grievances, she said, was that although she had fully participated in their art purchases, her husband tried to take sole credit for them.

After they parted in 1974, she told an interviewer in 1986, she could not get access to 35 paintings he had earlier put in storage when their apartment was being redecorated. And she had "not enough for a sea urchin to live on," she said.

In the litigation she went after what she said was rightly hers: half the paintings, property and money that the couple had acquired. In 1985 a State Supreme Court justice finally awarded her a 35 percent share in Scull's art holdings, including $2.5 million worth of paintings and more than $1 million in cash from paintings sold since 1973.

Both sides met at a warehouse to divide the works in 1986. By the flip of a coin, Mrs. Scull won one of the most important, Jasper Johns's 1959 "Out the Window." Later that year she sold it at auction for $3.63 million, then the highest amount paid for a work by a living artist. Calling its departure devastating, Ms. Scull said, "I'm losing the Johns because I need money to live on."

But prolonged physical therapy for a back injury and a penchant for spending, her son said, gradually ate up the money and her alimony. Meanwhile her active social life ground to a halt. "When you're not giving parties and not having the big shots of the world over, you're not invited," she said. "And if your name is not in the columns, you fade away from the scene."

Besides Jonathan, of Manhattan, Mrs. Scull is survived by two other sons, Adam, of Miami Beach, and Stephen Paul, of Los Angeles; a sister, Lillian Kaplan of New York and Florida; and two grandchildren.

Ethel Redner was born in the Bronx in 1921. Her father, Ben Redner, owned a taxicab company, and she led a privileged life. A tall, striking woman with a mane of tawny hair, she met her future husband, when she was 23.

At the time she was studying advertising art at the Parsons School of Design, which she described as "more of a finishing school then." In 1944, after a five-month courtship, she married Scull, who had dropped out of high school during the Depression and had an up-and-down career as a freelance illustrator and industrial designer.

At first the couple lived in a small apartment near the Museum of Modern Art, and Mrs. Scull studied at the Art Students League, where she painted realist canvases.

When her father retired, he gave shares in the business to his three sons-in-law. Within a few years Scull had built up his share into a fleet of 130 cabs with 400 drivers. By that time the couple lived in a house in Great Neck, N.Y., bought for them by Mrs. Scull's father. But the couple were culturally and socially ambitious and soon began looking for a larger theater than suburbia.

At Mrs. Scull's prompting, they found it in Manhattan, where, with the rise of Abstract Expressionism, the art world was beginning to generate glamor and profits. At first the Sculls collected Abstract Expressionists but in the early 1960's discovered a world of newer, younger artists like Warhol, Robert Morris, Mark di Suvero and Larry Poons.

In 1965 they auctioned off part of their Abstract Expressionist collection and used the money to start the Robert and Ethel Scull Foundation for the encouragement of unknown artists. It commissioned environmental works from aspirants like Walter de Maria and Michael Heizer and gave artists stipends, bought them food and clothes and paid for their materials.

Mr. Scull also backed the Green Gallery, a showplace for innovative art founded by Richard Bellamy, for the five years of its existence.

Their patronage established the Sculls, at first considered upstarts in the art world, as big-time players. Giving lavish parties themselves, they soon were celebrities.

Gossip and art writers sought them out, and Mrs. Scull regularly made the fashion pages. In 1963 Warhol did her portrait, "Ethel Scull 36 Times," comprising 36 silk-screen images made from snapshots taken in a Times Square photo booth. The couple was cast in plaster by the sculptor George Segal, with Mrs. Scull wearing a Courrèges dress. They established a base in East Hampton, N.Y., then the art world's summer summit.

But in 1973, when they auctioned 50 works by up-and-coming artists for $2.2 million, at the time a record for contemporary American art, they were castigated by some artists and critics, among them Robert Rauschenberg, because they had acquired the art so cheaply. Mr. Rauschenberg accused the Sculls of infidelity and the auction house of encouraging profiteering.

Later, asked by an interviewer about accusations that he and his wife bought art for investment and for social climbing, Mr. Scull replied: "It's all true. I'd rather use art to climb than anything else."

SEPTEMBER 19, 2003

INSIDE ART

A Private Collection From the First Days

Carol Vogel

Some auctions get attention for the staggering sums of money that change hands, others for their historical importance. One collection for sale this fall at Christie's is already creating a buzz: a group of more than 130 works, including paintings, drawings, sculptures, prints, furniture and folk art put together by Dorothy C. Miller.

Miller, who died in July at 99, was one of the first curators hired by the Museum of Modern Art in 1934. Over the years she championed painters like Jackson Pollock, Mark Rothko, Frank Stella and Jasper Johns. The contents of her Greenwich Village apartment are to be sold in a series of auctions at Christie's beginning Nov. 11 and are expected to bring $9 million to $12.6 million. They chronicle the 35-year career of a woman who helped shape modern art.

Among the highlights is "Gray Numbers," a 1957 painting by Mr. Johns. The first of three in a series by him, it is the only one with hand-painted instead of stenciled numbers.

"Gray Numbers" was exhibited at the artist's first big show, at the Leo Castelli Gallery in Manhattan in 1958. At that show the Museum of Modern Art bought three works for its collection: "Target With Four Faces" and "Green Target," both from 1955, and "White Numbers" from 1957.

Mr. Johns, speaking of the Modern's founding director, Alfred H. Barr Jr., said, "If my memory is correct, when Alfred saw the show he telephoned Dorothy, who came to see it."

Barr and Miller made purchases for the Modern, but Miller bought "Gray Numbers" for herself. Castelli was asking $350 but because Miller was in the business, she received a 10 percent discount, Christie's said. With tax she paid $325.45. Christie's estimates the painting will fetch $5 million to $7 million.

"It has never been publicly exhibited," said Brett Gorvy, international co-head of Christie's department of postwar and contemporary art. "She was extremely private and felt that these were things she bought for herself." They were also works she lived with, and when she was bedridden later in life, curators hesitated to ask her to lend them for exhibition, Mr. Gorvy added.

The sale will also include a 1961 Johns drawing, "The Litanies of the Chariot," which features a series of phrases taken from Duchamp's "Green Box" (1934). Mr. Johns remembers making the drawing for Robert Scull, a pre-eminent Pop Art collector from the 1960's, to give to Miller. Christie's expects it to bring $120,000 to $180,000.

Another important work on paper in the sale is a 1953 abstract pen-and-ink drawing by Philip Guston, estimated at $80,000 to $120,000.

Calder was a close friend of Miller, and over the years he gave her some of his work, including "Red Ghost," a 1949 mobile of a ghostlike form cut into painted red metal that is estimated at $500,000 to $700,000. Also for sale is Calder's "Black Rocker" (circa 1940), a stabile estimated at $350,000 to $450,000.

Another work in the auction is a black-and-white painting by Franz Kline, "Four Square" from 1953, estimated at $1.5 million to $2 million.

Along with financial incentives, marketing always plays a role in being chosen for these coveted sales. Christie's executives said a catalog of Miller's collection for the sale would include her gifts to museums and archival photographs. The auction house plans to display her collection, including original catalogs, manuscripts and letters that are not for sale, in roomlike settings that will be open for public viewing from early October until the sale.

OCTOBER 12, 2003

Rauschenberg's American Beauties

A Life in Theatrical Collage

By PETER PLAGENS

NOW 77, Robert Rauschenberg has been — to employ the understatement of the year — a working artist for well over a half-century. His encyclopedic oeuvre ranges from newspaper photographs splashed with lighter fluid and rubbed onto drawing paper, to electronically squawking junk sculpture and huge but delicate works made from exotic textiles wafting in the breeze. Playfully embracing automobile tires and images of astronauts, J.F.K. and Roger Maris, taxidermicized animals and the architecture of brick-and-fire escape New York, Rauschenberg's work is about nothing if not America itself. And Rauschenberg's America is primarily the freewheeling, optimistic and inclusive (well, compared to other countries) U.S. of A. we knew back in the 1940's, 50's and 60's. Compared to Jack Kerouac's Beat wilderness or Tennessee Williams's Gothic humidor or Arthur Miller's dark moral tribunal, it's a relatively happy place.

Rauschenberg has also led a long and full life. Hailing (like Janis Joplin) from Port Arthur, Tex., he was in the service during World War II, and made himself a conspicuous rebel even at the legendarily progressive Black Mountain College in North Carolina. He had an early marriage and a son with the painter Susan Weil, and then an intense relationship with Jasper Johns while the two were struggling artists in Lower Manhattan. He became famous, drunkenly blew up at the collector Robert Scull (that was caught on film), but also founded the globetrotting and generous Rauschenberg Overseas Cultural Exchange.

His life, his work and the fact that he is probably the most pervasively and directly influential artist around (without him there would simply be no Matthew Barney, Kiki Smith, Ann Hamilton or half the Generation Z installation artists in Williamsburg, Brooklyn) make him an obvious candidate for — what shall we call it? — theatricalization.

But Rauschenberg is a deceptively difficult case. While he's not one of those quiet classicists like, say, Poussin, Ingres, Mondrian or Agnes Martin, who will most likely never wind up fodder for dramaturges and screenwriters, he's not one of those tortured scenery-chewing figures like Michelangelo, Caravaggio, Vincent van Gogh, Stanley Spencer or Jackson Pollock that dramatization seems to demand.

If you want to "do" him, an indirect approach is probably best.

That's the tack that the experimental director Anne Bogart, with her SITI company, and the playwright Charles L. Mee have taken in their collagist "bobrauschenbergamerica," to be presented beginning Tuesday at the Harvey Theater as part of the Brooklyn Academy of Music's Next Wave Festival. (The work had its premiere at the 2001 Humana Festival in Louisville, Ky., a video of which I recently watched.)

On a set that is one big Old Glory serving as a clapboard Texas house, the surface of the moon and other locales, a serpentining group of characters, both particular (Rauschenberg's aproned Mom) and generic (a bikini babe, a biker, a curator, an engineer and a homeless guy, among others), hook up, separate and recombine for an hour and 45 minutes like fragments in a Rauschenberg assemblage.

They argue, fall in love, order pizza, iron, play checkers, have cheerfully metaphorical sex (sliding around on a piece of plastic sheeting greased with gin, vermouth and olives) and dance to — this being current American theater — soundtracky snippets of very period-specific music. It's a kind of "Our Town" for the 21st century.

Rauschenberg himself doesn't appear as a speaking character, as if Mom's recollection to the audience that "art was not part of our lives" is still the way things are. But, of course, all of this is indeed art, and we may well be watching from inside Rauschenberg's head.

Rauschenberg's art, albeit jauntily designed in the extreme, always arrives with intimations of deep meaning, or at least hints that behind his juxtapositions matters are a little David Lynchian. Sure enough, in "bobrauschenbergamerica," the homeless guy crawls out of his cardboard box to direct a conspiracy-theory movie. The fellow who delivers pizza also delivers a soliloquy on human self-forgiveness that comes with the anchovy-like revelation that he committed a triple murder — of his sister, her husband and their kid — while carrying a Bible in his pocket.

But in the finale, Mom returns to reminisce about the local Church of Christ and linoleum on the kitchen floor, and to tell us that her son "can see the beauty in almost anything." The implied lesson here is that we, like the multicultural cast, which ends up dancing joyously together to Cuban music, should, too.

I'm down with that, at least part way. Rauschenberg once said that he wanted to operate not entirely within art, but in the "gap between art and life." That gap is a funny place, somehow devoid of a lot of the sentiment peculiar to both art and life. Theater, however, often uses sentimentality to establish an essential emotional connection with the audience, and, in effect, repair the gap. Which, like Rauschenberg's art, is a very generous thing. □

NOVEMBER 12, 2003

$62 Million in a 'Fast and Furious' Sale

By CAROL VOGEL

The hungry horde of art dealers and collectors who overflowed Christie's salesroom last night couldn't stop shopping. They fought and fought over works from the 1940's right through to the 90's.

"It was fast and furious the whole night," said Christopher Burge, Christie's honorary chairman in America and the evening's auctioneer, after the nearly two-hour sale. "This is a rip-roaring market."

Of the 68 lots, only 11 failed to sell. The auction totaled $62 million, right in the middle of its estimate of $50.3 million to $68.4 million. Records were set for 11 artists.

Among the evening's most desired pieces were the paintings, drawings and sculptures collected by Dorothy C. Miller, who died in July at 99. Miller was one of the first curators hired by the Museum of Modern Art in 1934, and over the years she championed painters including Jackson Pollock, Mark Rothko, Frank Stella and Jasper Johns. That provenance was hard to beat. And Miller's holdings were sold early in the evening, adding to the frenzy.

All eyes were on Mr. Johns's "Gray Numbers" (1957), the cover image of the sale catalog. The first in a series of three paintings, it is the only one with the numerals hand-painted instead of stenciled. Three bidders went for the painting, which sold to Andrew Fabricant, director of the Richard Gray Gallery in Manhattan, for $5.2 million, just above it $5 million low estimate.

(Final prices include Christie's commission: 19.5 percent of the first $100,000 and 12 percent of the rest. Estimates do not reflect commissions.)

Some of the smaller works, many of which Miller received as gifts from artists or friends, inspired wild bidding. Seven bidders went for an untitled wall relief by Lee Bontecou that was in the artist's first exhibition in 1960, the year it was made. It, too, sold to an unidentified telephone bidder, for $298,700, a record for the artist and more than four times its $70,000 high estimate.

Works on paper that Miller owned were in demand. An unidentified bidder bought "Litanies of the Chariot," a drawing Mr. Johns made in 1961 for the collector Robert Scull to give Miller, which was influenced by Duchamp in its subject matter. The price was $298,700, far above the $180,000 high estimate.

Philip Guston's "Drawing" (1953), reminiscent of an abstract landscape, was estimated at $80,000 to $120,000. Four bidders went for the brush-and-ink work, but an unidentified telephone bidder paid $242,700. The price may have been influenced by the artist's current retrospective at the Metropolitan Museum.

"Number 14," a 1949 painting by Bradley Walker Tomlin, a lesser-known Abstract Expressionist, sold for $242,700, more than twice its $90,000 high estimate. The dark gray canvas with the artist's calligraphy-style patterns is the type of work that doesn't often come on the market.

Another abstract painting brought the evening's top price. An untitled Rothko from 1963 sold for $7.1 million, far above its $6 million high estimate. Mr. Fabricant was the buyer, beating out four other bidders.

He was also willing to pay a hefty price for a 1964 Warhol self-portrait. Three people wanted the image, which has become famous since it was made into a postage stamp in 2001, and it brought $1.4 million, far above its $900,000 high estimate.

The Cleveland Museum of Art bought Lee Krasner's "Celebration," a brightly colored canvas from 1960. Diane Upright, a private dealer in Manhattan representing the museum, was one of four bidders. The price was $1.9 million, a record for the artist and nearly five times its $400,000 high estimate.

A Calder sculpture set another record. A bidding war broke out over an untitled bright red stabile from 1968 that was being sold by the Camino Real Hotel in Mexico City. A telephone bidder identified by Christie's only as a "private institution" paid $5.8 million, above the $5 million high estimate.

De Kooning's "Untitled XVII," a large 1984 canvas (80 by 70 inches) of abstract ribbons of orange, blue and yellow was estimated at $1.5 million to $2 million, but five bidders wanted the painting, which sold to an unidentified bidder for $3.7 million.

After the sale, collectors and dealers milled around trying to make sense of the strong prices. "There's a lot of pent-up desire," said Mr. Fabricant, one of the evening's biggest buyers. He said he was bidding for collectors from all over the country, "West Coast, Midwest and East Coast."

Philippe Ségalot, a Manhattan dealer, said he thought everybody in the room was surprised at the market's strength. "There's a lot of money to be spent," he said. "And a lot of confidence in the future."

FEBRUARY 15, 2004

AN APPRECIATION

Recalling the Life of an Instigator of Fun

By HELEN A. HARRISON

FOR nearly 40 years, it seemed that whenever a group of artists, writers, theater people and other creative types gathered to socialize in the Hamptons in the summer, the painter Syd Solomon, who died on Jan. 28 at age 86, would be there. Often he was the host or the instigator of events that hindsight would raise to legendary status.

"I think he always had a gregarious nature," said his son, Mike, who is also an artist and lives in East Hampton. "But when he and my mother came out here and settled, it just flowered."

Beginning in the mid 1950's, the Solomons divided their time between summers in East Hampton and winters in Sarasota, Fla. They continued that schedule until the early 1990's, when illness forced them to move permanently to Florida.

Mr. Solomon, known for his multilayered abstract paintings, which are in many museums and private collections, found that both locales provided him with the maritime environment that became his primary subject matter; his works capture the essence of reflected light, humid atmosphere and shoreline scenery natural to both the East End and Sarasota.

But Mr. Solomon did not come to East Hampton just for the scenery. He was equally attracted to the company.

In 1959, Mr. and Mrs. Solomon rented the gatehouse at the Creeks, Alfonso Ossorio's remarkable Georgica estate — where Clyfford Still, Grace Hartigan and other artists had also been tenants — while they looked for property of their own. When the Solomons found the land they wanted, on nearby Baiting Hollow Road, Mr. Solomon built a house and studio that became the scene of many a memorable happening.

The artists Jim Dine and Conrad Marca-Relli were neighbors, as were the collectors Robert and Ethel Scull and the songwriter Jerry Lieber and his wife, Gaby Rodgers, an actress and Off Broadway producer. Their daytime hangout was Georgica Beach, where they and their wide circle of friends would meet to plan the evening's festivities.

Bored by cocktail parties, Mr. Solomon and Ms. Rodgers began to organize performances, using the Solomons' decks as outdoor stages. Hundreds of people might turn up to feast on hot dogs catered by the local beach wagon or whatever potluck was available, fortify themselves with Mr. Solomon's lethal "artillery punch," and take in the show.

One of the more notorious occasions, complete with fireworks, live rock music and go-go dancers, celebrated Neil Armstrong's moonwalk in the summer of 1969. Dressed in a silver Mylar space suit made by the sculptor Bill King, Mr. Solomon descended a ladder from the roof onto the second-floor deck and sprayed the startled audience with water from a hose mounted between his legs, declaring his act to be "a giant leak for mankind."

In 1966, the Solomons' lawn was the site of the first officially organized artist-writers softball game, precursor of the star-studded charity match that is now a staple of summers in the Hamptons. The first pitch was fouled through an upstairs window, and the batter, an artist who had never before played the game, ran triumphantly from home plate to third base. When a home run was hit into the Sculls' yard, they refused to return the ball, which then entered their renowned collection of Pop art.

In the 1970's, the Solomons moved to Sagaponack, where their house boasted a croquet court on which Mr. Solomon was famous for his cutthroat tactics and shameless cheating. One dispute became so heated that his neighbor, the writer and Zen master Peter Matthiessen, stormed over to complain that the noise was disturbing his mediation.

Another Sagaponack neighbor, Kurt Vonnegut, enjoyed Mr. Solomon's colorful stories of his service in a camouflage unit during World War II. Several of these anecdotes are incorporated in the résumé of Rabo Karabekian, the protagonist of Mr. Vonnegut's 1987 novel, "Bluebeard," which is set in the area and features a cameo performance by Mr. Solomon.

Mr. Vonnegut places him at a generic Hamptons soiree, where he is charming an attractive young woman. "How can you tell a good painting from a bad one?" she asks him. "All you have to do, my dear," Mr. Solomon replies, "is look at a million paintings, and then you can never be mistaken." ■

OCTOBER 12, 2006

Works by Johns and de Kooning Sell for $143.5 Million

By CAROL VOGEL

Feeding art-world anticipation of one of the biggest auction seasons in history, the entertainment mogul David Geffen has sold in private transactions two postwar paintings by Jasper Johns and Willem de Kooning for a total of $143.5 million.

The buyers, Kenneth C. Griffin and Steven A. Cohen, are among today's most successful hedge fund billionaires and are both building high-profile art collections.

Mr. Griffin, managing director and chief executive of the Chicago-based Citadel Investment Group, and his wife, Anne, bought "False Start," a seminal 1959 work by Mr. Johns, for $80 million. Mr. Cohen, the founder and manager of SAC Capital Advisors in Stamford, Conn., purchased de Kooning's "Police Gazette," an abstract 1955 landscape, for $63.5 million.

The wave of private sales comes just a month before the New York auction houses' November sales, among the largest ever. Christie's Impressionist and Modern art sale alone, scheduled for Nov. 8, carries a low estimate of some $300 million.

Paul Gray and Andrew Fabricant, consultants to the Griffins and directors of the Richard Gray Gallery in New York and Chicago, confirmed that the couple had privately bought "False Start," their first acquisition of a work by Mr. Johns. "Their goal as collectors is to find works of singular quality that moves them," Mr. Gray said. "It was clear they had a real passion for 'False Start.' "

The Griffins have emerged as prominent art world benefactors, having just given $19 million to the Art Institute of Chicago to help finance a 264,000-square-foot modern art wing scheduled to open in 2009.

Several months ago, Mr. Gray said, he took the Griffins to view Mr. Geffen's collection in Los Angeles. Among the many masterpieces there, they were particularly struck by the Johns painting, Mr. Gray recalled, though there was no talk of a sale then. Discussions began a few months later, when Mr. Geffen expressed an interest in selling the painting.

The bright 1959 canvas, in blues, reds, oranges and yellows, is stenciled with letters spelling out the names of colors, arbitrarily placed on a tapestry of Impressionist brushwork. Considered an immediate forerunner of Pop art, it is one of Mr. John's best-known images and comes with a long, distinguished history. It belonged first to Robert Scull, the New York taxi-fleet owner, and his wife, Ethel; the Sculls sold it privately in the 1960's to the architect François de Menil.

Mr. de Menil sold the painting at Sotheby's in 1988 to the publishing magnate S. I. Newhouse for $17 million, at the time a record price for a work by a living artist. Mr. Newhouse sold it to Mr. Geffen in the early 1990's along with other works, including a Barnett Newman canvas, "Who's Afraid of Red, Yellow and Blue I" and a later painting by Mr. Johns, "Weeping Women," for a price that was not disclosed.

Sandy Heller, Mr. Cohen's adviser, confirmed that Mr. Cohen had bought de Kooning's "Police Gazette." "It's one of the most important landscapes by the artist left in private hands," Mr. Heller said. One of the de Kooning's more abstract canvases, primarily yellow, red and green, it was painted while he was living in New York City before moving to East Hampton, N.Y.

Like "False Start," "Police Gazette" has had a succession of distinguished owners, including the dealer Sidney Janis, who bought it from de Kooning; the dealer and collector Eugene Thaw; and Mr. and Mrs. Scull. The Sculls sold it at Sotheby's in 1973 for $180,000, a record price at the time. The buyer was said to be the Basel dealer Ernst Beyeler.

About 10 years ago Mr. Geffen bought the de Kooning, along with works including Roy Lichtenstein's "Torpedo ... LOS" (1963), from Stephen A. Wynn, the Las Vegas resort and casino owner.

The sales are feeding speculation that Mr. Geffen is trying to raise money to buy The Los Angeles Times. Mr. Geffen, whose art collection is one of the finest in the country and includes seminal works by Mr. Johns, de Kooning and Pollock, declined to comment on the sales or on his intentions regarding The Los Angeles Times.

But it is clear that like many other seasoned collectors, including Mr. Wynn, the actor Steve Martin and Mr. Newhouse, he is taking advantage of a red-hot market infused with money made by today's crop of hedge-fund billionaires.

Among the most highly anticipated offerings at next month's Impressionist and modern sale at Christie's are four paintings by Klimt, a Tahitian-period Gauguin and a Blue Period Picasso.

January 14, 2007

Art of the Deal

THE GIRL WITH THE GALLERY
Edith Gregor Halpert and the Making of the Modern Art Market.
By Lindsay Pollock.
Illustrated. 483 pp.
PublicAffairs. $30.

By RICHARD B. WOODWARD

DE KOONING once grudgingly praised the art dealer Leo Castelli by declaring, "That son of a bitch, you could give him two beer cans and he could sell them." Sure enough, after the impish Jasper Johns responded to this taunt by making a pair of Ballantine Ale empties, Castelli sold the 1960 work to the collectors Robert and Ethel Scull. This classic of Pop art is now in a German museum.

Art dealers prefer the term "gallerists" these days, a euphemism meant to put some distance between themselves and dealers in cars and junk. The profession can certainly be an honorable one, serving to link artists and the public. Just don't be fooled by the intimidating air of their white-walled emporiums. Art dealers are essentially shopkeepers in the business of selling you something you don't need.

The chief virtue of "The Girl With the Gallery," Lindsay Pollock's biography of Edith Gregor Halpert, is that the author, a journalist, has not unduly glamorized Halpert or her livelihood. This largely unheralded figure from the midcentury New York art scene, with an impressive roster of artists that included Arthur Dove, Stuart Davis, Yasuo Kuniyoshi, Charles Sheeler and Jacob Lawrence, is presented here as a superior saleswoman who had to fight for everything she earned.

There was almost no market for American art, abstract or realist, when Halpert opened Our Gallery (soon renamed the Downtown Gallery) in Greenwich Village in 1926. She spent her adult life tirelessly promoting her artists to a clientele not easily persuaded to appreciate — or pay decent money for — contemporary work by non-Europeans. From records Halpert left to the Archives of American Art at the Smithsonian, Pollock has traced gallery sales to influential collectors, notably Abby Aldrich Rockefeller, and followed the trail of money and donations into museums. Many biographies of art dealers fail to mention crucial facts of their economic lives — for example, how much was needed to pay the rent. This book has the goods, offering a refreshingly candid view of the mundane realities and strategies behind the art business at a time when New York was becoming the world's art capital.

Halpert had plenty of moxie. A Russian-Jewish émigré who started her career in a department store selling fur coats and Persian rugs to upper-crust New Yorkers, she married the artist Samuel Halpert and readily adapted to his bohemian milieu. Before they divorced in 1930, the "little girl from Odessa," as she called herself, used her connections to entice artists with an offer to take only a 33 percent commission rather than the usual 50 percent. Culling the phone directory, she sent fliers to the best addresses in the Village, alerting residents to the new gallery. It became a welcome refuge for struggling artists — Halpert lived alone in an apartment above — during the Depression and World War II.

If only Pollock were as skilled at recapturing the electricity of these years as she has been scrupulous in notating Halpert's financial transactions, this biography would be an absorbing read. As it is, the focus is largely on the dealer's relationships with her clients. Interesting as these could be — Henry Ford's son, Edsel, was another buyer — one searches in vain for pungent anecdotes revealing what the dealer thought of her artists, or they of her. Five pages about Halpert's affair with Sheeler in 1934-35 tantalize: "Edith didn't have time for Sheeler's infatuation. Her favorite companion was Adam ... a small brown dachshund, who remained defiantly un-house-trained." But Halpert was in many respects all business.

Many of Halpert's artists have for years been excised from histories of the period because curators and critics, led by Alfred Barr and Clement Greenberg, denigrated the figurative and socially oriented work she favored. Ben Shahn's 1947 retrospective at the Museum of Modern Art, for instance, was trashed by Greenberg as "not important." But Pollock makes little of this decisive factor in Halpert's present obscurity. Nor are the ardent voices that supported (or denounced) abstraction and political art in the 1910s, '20s and '30s heard in these pages. I'm not sure how one writes about 20th-century art in New York without once mentioning Picasso. But Pollock has done it.

The best chapter recounts Halpert's mad attempts in the early '50s to coax a show from Georgia O'Keeffe, who had moved to New Mexico to paint and remove herself from the bother of a career. Being an art dealer often requires as much bargaining with artists as with collectors, and Pollock recreates in painful detail the wooing of the reclusive diva, who makes one demand after another, each of which Halpert agrees to only to be double-crossed in the end. It is a relief when she finally explodes at O'Keeffe: "I am not accustomed ... to being treated as an underling, being scolded and railed at. Frankly, I do not like it." The artist was unfazed: "I hope you recovered from your grouch," she wrote back with blithe unconcern.

Pollock, who draws heavily on an 800-page oral history Halpert completed five years before her death in 1970, is perhaps too enamored of her subject's plucky spirit. But Halpert was indeed a remarkable figure. Historians of the American folk art market, created in part by her salesmanship, will find plenty of details to chew on. The rest of us can wonder about the book that another year or two of work might have produced. □

NOVEMBER 2, 2009

Traditional Offerings, Bargain Prices

By CAROL VOGEL

The images splashed across the pages of this fall's auction catalogs are as familiar as they are telling: Degas dancers and Pissarro landscapes; Picasso portraits and Warhol dollar bills. All are well-known paintings and drawings by tried-and-true artists carrying estimates as low as sellers are willing to go.

In the year since the worldwide recession devastated the art market, prices have tumbled, collectors have retreated and auction houses have instituted layoffs. And now Sotheby's, Christie's and Phillips de Pury are tiptoeing carefully. When the two weeks of big fall auctions start Tuesday evening, buyers will find traditional paintings, sculptures and drawings intended to appeal to today's more conservative tastes. Gone are the lucrative financial incentives like guarantees (a minimum sum offered to a seller regardless of the outcome of a sale) that were regularly doled out when times were good. Gone too are extravagant parties and lavish catalogs the size of telephone books.

Prices are also a lot lower. Last season many paintings carried estimates in the tens of millions of dollars, though the majority didn't sell. Sticker shock is no longer an issue. The most expensive works carry a high estimate of $12 million. "It's a more considered market," said Tobias Meyer, who is in charge of Sotheby's contemporary art department worldwide. "People now think carefully about what they buy and how much they are willing spend."

Prices are also lower because there aren't many blockbuster artworks on the market. There were none in the few estate properties that were up for grabs recently, and collectors who don't have to sell are, for the most part, holding on to their art as they gauge price levels.

This season's offerings reflect what have jokingly been called the three D's: death, divorce and debt. Sellers include the Merce Cunningham Trust, which administers the rights to the work of the choreographer and dancer who died in July; the newsprint magnate Peter Brant, whose divorce has been tabloid fodder; and Matthias Rickenbach, a Swiss lawyer indicted in a tax evasion case in August.

Putting together the sales has been tough, auction house executives admit. "Without guarantees it's been all about relationships and creativity," Mr. Meyer said.

As often happens, the work of an artist who has recently been the subject of a museum exhibition suddenly surfaces at auction. It is no coincidence that a Kandinsky is being offered on the heels of a career retrospective, seen at the Pompidou Center in Paris in the summer and now at the Solomon R. Guggenheim Museum in New York. In this case the heirs of Arthur M. Sackler, the American art collector who died in 1987, decided it was the right time to part with a 1932 Kandinsky filled with his abstract geometric forms. It is expected to bring $6 million to $8 million at Sotheby's on Wednesday.

Perhaps the buzz around "Pop Life, Art in a Material World," a show that opened last month at the Tate Modern in London, has something to do with the number of Warhols and other Pop artists up for sale. The undisputed star at Sotheby's postwar sale on Nov. 11 — and what may well be the hottest work of the season — is Warhol's "200 One Dollar Bills," a 1962 painting from his seminal first series of silk-screens. A private European collector is selling the work, which was once part of the celebrated collection of Robert C. Scull, the taxi tycoon and Pop and Minimalist collector who died in 1986. That year the seller bought the painting from a Sotheby's auction of Scull's estate for $385,000, at the time a record price for Warhol at auction. Now it is expected to fetch $8 million to $12 million.

Mr. Brant is also selling a Warhol. "Tunafish Disaster," a 1963 painting from the "Death and Disaster Series," is being offered at Christie's on Nov. 10 with an estimate of $6 million to $8 million. In addition Mr. Brant is selling a 1983 six-panel painting by Jean-Michel Basquiat, "Brother Sausage." Christie's experts believe it could bring $9 million to $12 million.

Tuesday night's sale of Impressionist and modern art at Christie's is perhaps the weakest of the season. "It's been a struggle," said Conor Jordan, head of Christie's Impressionist and modern art department in New York. Among the highlights are traditional Impressionist works like an 1896 Degas pastel of a dancer rubbing her feet, which comes from an unidentified Japanese collector and is expected to sell for $7 million to $9 million. An 1873 panoramic landscape by Pissarro is estimated at $3.5 million to $4.5 million. It is being sold by the London collector Lord Harris of Peckham, chairman of Carpetright, a floor covering company.

There is dealer property too, like Mondrian's "Composition II, With Red, 1926" that other dealers say is from the Nahmads, a family that runs galleries in London and New York. They bought the abstract canvas at Christie's in London five years ago for $2.9 million and are now hoping to get $4.5 million to $6.5 million.

Sotheby's sale on Wednesday night is bigger and the material is stronger. One of the most important sellers that night is offering works described in the catalog as property from "an important European collection." That collection, experts familiar with the lots say, is Mr. Rickenbach's and includes canvases by Bonnard and Modigliani, Degas and Corot. There is also a Kees van Dongen image of a half-nude Arab boy, inspired by a trip he took to North Africa in 1910. It is estimated at $7 million to $10 million, one of the most expensive works of the evening.

Another big-ticket item at Sotheby's is a Giacometti sculpture, "L'Homme Qui Chavire," conceived in 1950 and cast a year later. It is being sold by S. I. Newhouse Jr., the publishing magnate who owns Condé Nast, another business that has recently undergone layoffs. The $8 million to $12 million estimate may seem high, but the Giacometti has been unsuccessfully offered for sale privately by both Christie's and the Gagosian Gallery for nearly twice that estimate. Experts say that the auction process will help sort out prices for Giacomettis.

Christie's has made some estimates in its postwar and contemporary art sale on Nov. 10 purposely low. It is selling several gems that once belonged to Cunningham and John Cage, his partner in life and work who died in 1992. They include "Dancers on a Plane," a cross-hatch canvas by Jasper Johns that is estimated at $1.5 million to $2 million. Paintings by Mr. Johns have sold privately for as much as $80 million.

Brett Gorvy, a head of Christie's postwar and contemporary art department, explained his firm's approach this season: "We have consciously stayed away from young artists who either have not yet been tested or whose prices have already got way too high."

NOVEMBER 12, 2009

Hot Warhols Help Sotheby's Top $134 Million at Auction

By CAROL VOGEL

It was the sale of the season. When a seminal Warhol — one of the artist's first silk-screen paintings — came on the block at Sotheby's auction of contemporary art on Wednesday night, the auctioneer, Tobias Meyer, opened bidding at $6 million and was stunned when a bidder instantly doubled it.

The price rose at breakneck speed as five collectors vied for the classic image, "200 One Dollar Bills." It ended up selling for $43.7 million (including fees to Sotheby's), more than three times its high estimate of $12 million. The buyer, whom Sotheby's refused to identify, bid by telephone through Bruno Vinciguerra, the company's chief operating officer. Sotheby's would also not identify the seller, although people familiar with the collection said it was Pauline Karpidas, a London-based collector.

Buyers with deep pockets snap up all but two of the works on offer.

Just a year after the art market was in the doldrums with the world's financial markets, buyers with deep pockets were not shy about stepping up for tried-and-true artists. The sale topped Sotheby's expectations, totaling $134.4 million, well above its $67.9 million high estimate. Of the 54 works on offer, only two went unsold. The evening also eclipsed Christie's auction of postwar and contemporary art on Tuesday night, which brought in $74.1 million. While both sales featured big-name artists, Sotheby's had just enough blockbusters to make for a successful evening.

In pristine condition, "200 One Dollar Bills" was enticing to any Pop Art collector. Add to that the provenance — it had once been part of the celebrated collection of Robert C. Scull, the taxi tycoon — and it was irresistible.

(Final prices include the commission paid to Sotheby's: 25 percent of the first $50,000 of the hammer price, 20 percent of the next $50,000 to $1 million and 12 percent of the rest. Estimates do not reflect commissions.)

Warhols of all ages and subjects brought strong prices. A 1965 self-portrait with a top estimate of $1.5 million sold to Laurence Graff, the London jeweler, for $5.4 million ($6.1 million with Sotheby's commission). Warhol himself gave the work to Cathy Naso, who as a teenager in the mid-1960s worked after school in his legendary Factory.

Scared that it might get stolen, she had stashed it in the closet of her Connecticut home. As a result, its purple and red background colors were as brilliant as they were when it was painted, and collectors knew that. Mr. Graff, who sat in the first row of Sotheby's salesroom on York Avenue, was not intimidated by five competing bidders.

"It's a gem," he said after the sale. "I came to New York for it and for the little Dora Maar," he added referring to a Picasso painting at Sotheby's last week. "And I am talking both home."

Even Warhol drawings fetched solid prices: A 1962 sketch of a roll of cash topped expectations when Larry Gagosian, the Manhattan dealer, bought the work for $4.2 million, above its high $3.5 million estimate.

And one of Warhol's "Tunafish Disaster" silk-screen paintings, this one from 1963 and being sold by Mr. Gagosian, was snapped up, too. It had been estimated at $1.5 million to $2 million, and Jose Mugrabi, a Manhattan dealer, bought it for $1 million ($1.2 million with fees). At Christie's on Tuesday night, a more compelling composition of the same subject was up for sale by Peter Brant, the newsprint magnate. It had been estimated at $6 million to $8 million, but there were no takers.

By contrast, on Wednesday, a 1957 Jasper Johns painting, "Gray Numbers," drew a lot of interest. In 2003 Richard Hedreen, a Seattle collector, bought it for $5.2 million. On Wednesday it was estimated at as much as $7 million, and brought $8.7 million.

Philippe Ségalot, a Manhattan dealer who was one of the unsuccessful bidders for "200 One Dollar Bills," said: "I think the painting was worth it. It was rare and great. And the appealing estimate helped encourage bidding. It was really Warhol's night."

NOVEMBER 16, 2009

Art Prices (And Mood) Inch Back Up

By CAROL VOGEL

Oh the drama of auctions: the salesrooms packed with smartly dressed collectors; the tension of having to decide in seconds whether to drop another million dollars on an artwork or let it go; the steely smile of the auctioneer trying gently to squeeze another hundred thousand from bidders. And the final results of the last two weeks of Impressionist, modern and contemporary art auctions in New York, which saw the return of a surprising number of collectors, their wallets open, but only if the price was right.

"The numbers may not be the same as they were two years ago," said Guy Bennett, a former co-head of Impressionist and modern art at Christie's who is now a private dealer, "but confidence is back."

And when it comes to auctions, confidence is everything. As soon as one person in the audience senses hesitancy, others sense it too. But when a collector is sure enough about an artwork to keep bidding, that kind of conviction becomes contagious.

The feel-good factor is one thing, the reality quite another. While prices for the best works seemed high and bidding was often deep, the volume of sales — nearly $600 million between the two companies — was vastly diminished from a year ago, when Sotheby's and Christie's sold a combined $729 million or two years ago when the market peaked at $1.6 billion. But the relief that prices are crawling back up was palpable.

"A year ago people were distracted and primarily assessing their own net worth," said Marc Porter, president of Christie's in the Americas. "Now that the worst of the financial crisis seems to be over, people are once again focusing on collecting."

Last fall there was a sense of panic because nobody knew if prices had hit bottom, not just for art but for any asset, and even the richest collectors froze. This season was all about the estimates. "Ultimately that's what provided buyers with the confidence to bid," said Tobias Meyer, worldwide head of Sotheby's contemporary art department, who added that for some artists, prices have dropped more than 40 percent from their high two years ago.

The deliberately low estimates became catnip for bidders. Or so it seemed when Warhol's 1962 silkscreen painting "200 One Dollar Bills" incited a bidding war among five collectors and ultimately sold for a staggering $43.7 million (including Sotheby's fees), more than three times its $12 million high estimate.

Would what proved to be the star of the last two weeks have made more at the peak of the market? No, said both Mr. Meyer and Mr. Porter. Mr. Meyer pointed out that during the boom, big money went for highly colorful images like a 1976 triptych by Francis Bacon ($86.3 million in May 2008) and a Rothko canvas, the 1950 "White Center (Yellow, Pink and Lavender on Rose)," from the collection of the retired banker David Rockefeller ($72.8 million in 2007).

"Because this Warhol is black and white, it could have very well been overlooked at the height of the market," Mr. Meyer said. "Although it is art-historically important, it takes a little knowledge to appreciate."

It also took a sophisticated collector to realize that the 1962 image was rare and few like it come up for sale. Or to appreciate the luster of its provenance: it had once belonged to Robert C. Scull, the taxi tycoon who amassed a world-class collection of Pop and Minimalist art. When it was offered for sale at Sotheby's in 1986, the year Mr. Scull died, Pauline Karpidas, a London collector, bought it for $385,000, then a record price for a Warhol at auction. Yet when she decided to sell it 23 years later, the high estimate of $12 million seemed cheap. And that enticed buyers.

Another perceived bargain was a Giacometti bronze, "L'Homme Qui Chavire" (or "Falling Man," conceived in 1950) at Sotheby's. A similar sculpture brought $18.5 million at Christie's in 2007. The seller of this season's work, S. I. Newhouse Jr., the publishing magnate who owns Condé Nast, bought it from a London gallery for more than $20 million. He spent a year trying to sell it privately through Gagosian and then Christie's. Its price went from $22 million to $18 million, and Mr. Newhouse ended up consigning it to Sotheby's, where it was estimated at $12 million tops. Six collectors, thinking it seemed cheap, bid it up and the sculpture wound up selling for $17.2 million, or $19.3 million, including Sotheby's fees.

At Christie's a group of paintings and drawings that were presents to the dancer and choreographer Merce Cunningham, who died in July, and his partner in life and work, John Cage, who died in 1992, were also priced low despite their celebrated past. Jasper Johns's "Dancers on a Plane" (1980-81) brought $4.3 million (including fees), more than $2 million above its high estimate, and a drawing of clocks by Robert Rauschenberg made more than six times its high estimate, selling for $780,000 ($938,500 with fees).

"We had 10 to 15 active bidders on it," Mr. Porter said. "I hadn't seen that since the boom. It may have been lower priced, but nearly $1 million for a drawing is still real money for anybody."

With art prices readily available at Artnet.com, collectors can easily do their homework. So if something appears too expensive, it often fails to sell without a bid. That was the case with "Brother Sausage," a six-panel painting by Jean-Michel Basquiat at Christie's that was estimated at $9 million to $12 million.

Of the two auction giants, Sotheby's came out the winner this season in total sales because it had secured several prized properties and was able to price them conservatively. Its Impressionist and modern art sale featured a group of paintings that had belonged to the fabled Paris dealer Paul Durand-Ruel as well as works from Arthur M. Sackler, a leading collector who died in 1987.

But if any one artist dominated the auctions it was Warhol. Besides "200 One Dollar Bills," several of his drawings made strong prices. And a 1965 self-portrait by the artist that was expected to bring a high of $1.5 million at Sotheby's sold for $5.4 million ($6.1 million with fees) to Laurence Graff, the London jeweler.

Who bought "200 One Dollar Bills" remains a mystery. That element, guessing who is actually paying, is part of the magic of auctions. Officials at Sotheby's and Christie's said there were buyers from Russia and Asia — parts of the world that were barely represented six months ago — as well as the United States.

But only the auction house knows for sure who took home the $43.7 million Warhol. Some dealers said it might have been Steven A. Cohen, the hedge fund manager who collects contemporary art like Damien Hirst's famous shark, or Philip Niarchos, the contemporary-art collector who is a member of the Greek shipping family. Others said it was a Russian oligarch like Roman Abramovich, who is said to have bought the $86.3 million Bacon triptych. Or maybe even Victor Pinchuk, the Ukrainian billionaire and contemporary art collector. And if it was Mr. Pinchuk, will "200 One Dollar Bills" be on view at his art foundation in Kiev?

Mr. Meyer's lips were sealed.

PARASITIC VENTURES PRESS, 2015
ISBN 978-0-9813263-6-8

www.ingramcontent.com/pod-product-compliance
Ingram Content Group UK Ltd.
Pitfield, Milton Keynes, MK11 3LW, UK
UKHW050615260726
13967UKWH00009B/2882